Windows and Linux Integration:

Hands-on Solutions for a Mixed Environment

Windows® and Linux® Integration:

Hands-on Solutions for a Mixed Environment

Jeremy Moskowitz
Thomas Boutell

Wiley Publishing, Inc.

Wiley Publishing, Inc.

Credits

Acquisitions and Developmental Editor
Tom Cirtin
Technical Editor
Bill Boswell
Production Editor
Elizabeth Campbell
Copy Editor
Sally Engelfried
Production Manager
Tim Tate
Vice President & Executive Group Publisher
Richard Swadley
Vice President and Publisher
Neil Edde
Vice President and Publisher
Joseph B. Wikert
Book Designer
Judy Fung
Compositor
Craig Woods, Happenstance Type-O-Rama
Illustrator
Jeffrey Wilson, Happenstance Type-O-Rama
Proofreader
Nancy Riddiough
Indexer
Nancy Guenther
Cover Designer and Illustrator
John Nedwidek, Emdesign

For all the women in my life who taught me that it's best to play nicely with others.

—*Jeremy Moskowitz*

For Eleanor, my daughter

—*Tom Boutell*

Acknowledgements

I wish to thank Ernie Coats, Rocco Caputo, Corprew Reed, and Ronan Waide for their technical insight as well as their friendship. Thanks also to the Immortal Legion of the Divine Order of Good Eggs: Lindsay, Jill, Brian, Mark, Katie, Mary, Lindsay, Jon, and honorary members Alisa, Amanda and Shelle. Thanks to Eleanor for patience above and beyond the call of a six-year-old, and to Michele for flexible parenting schedules. Thanks always to my brother, my sister and my mother for going the journey with me, and to my late father for a lifetime of love and support. And, of course, many thanks to Jeremy for his friendship and for focusing my energies in a challenging year.
—Tom Boutell

I want to first thank my assistant Jon, for tirelessly taking on tasks (book related, business related and personal related) that mere-mortals simply couldn't do. Jon, you're a prince, and I'm glad to have you aboard. I'd like to thank the people who were simply "there for me" during this huge undertaking: Alisa, Jill, Beccah, and Mom & Dad. I particularly want to thank Tom for his tireless contributions, amazing ego-free abilities to watch his material get modified, re-written or cut, and simply taking the quality time each example needed to make it as best as it could possibly be. You did an amazing job -- both at writing the book, and eating more of my wheat thins than should humanly be possible during a weekend. In all, you're a wonderful friend, and I'm honored to have worked alongside you and called you my co-author and continually call you my friend.
—Jeremy Moskowitz

This book owes its existence to the tireless efforts of thousands of open source innovators and also to the dedicated folks at Microsoft. We particularly wish to thank Gerald Carter and Jeremy Allison of the Samba project and Alan DeKok of the FreeRADIUS project. Additional thanks to the folks within Microsoft for genuinely taking an interest in our book and helping us make it our best: Patrick O'Rourke, Jason Zions, Rik Wright, Jackson Shaw (now at Vintela), Jon Reese, Jay Paulus, Gaurav Daga, Dan Boldo, and more.

Bill Boswell's contributions as technical editor improved this book to an enormous degree. You are a super-brain with super-style and super-powers. Thank you, Bill. Thank you to Tom Cirtin, Elizabeth Campbell, and Sally Engelfried within Sybex for once again helping take our book's vision and making it a tangible reality. Thank you to everyone inside Sybex and Wiley for being behind us, working with us and championing our cause in such a huge effort.
—Jeremy and Tom

Contents at a Glance

Contents

Introduction

This book isn't about holy wars. It's about harmony.

There are plenty of books you can get which describe how to walk away from your Windows investment and, blink! ... go 100% Linux. But there are two problems with the "walk away from Windows" idea:

- *First, it's often not possible.* That is, there is a good chance you will always have Windows applications which run your business. And they might never be able to run natively on Linux.

- *Second, it's simply not realistic.* Assuming every application could be re-coded for Linux, you've already got a lot invested in Windows desktops, applications, architecture, training, manpower and more.

And yet, Linux offers undeniable advantages of its own. Compelling open-source applications, like the Apache web server and the MySQL database engine, are available today and will continue to appear. And the option of running these applications on an open-source operating system presents undeniable cost advantages. Yes, Linux has its own costs, such as re-training users and administrators who are familiar with Windows. But the presence of Linux in your business can save money and solve problems today.

In short, neither Windows nor Linux are leaving this planet (or the datacenter) anytime soon. And for that reason, it's more important to be able to cooperatively utilize what "the other guy" has to offer. Instead of trying to punch his lights out.

The good news is that it isn't too difficult to get along—if you have a roadmap for how to safely travel into each other's foreign territory. If you're suddenly asked to make your Linux machines work in a Windows environment, or the other way around, this is the book for you.

I (Jeremy) am not an "insider" Linux geek. And Tom isn't an "insider" Windows geek. And yet, between us, there is proof that there can be harmony in the world.

In college, many years ago, Tom and I were dorm-mates at the University of Delaware—living under the same roof. Tom was a Unix guy, soon to become a Linux enthusiast. I was an Amiga and Windows guy. When we were in college, Tom and I were some of the first people on campus to get Ethernet in the rooms, and 24/7 Internet access to the world. And, even back then, we made it our solemn geeky duty to get our disparate machines to talk to each other and utilize each other's resources to the fullest. He had a printer, while I had a scanner and audio digitizer (ye olde name for "Sound Card")—and we made it all work, between all of our systems.

Times are different now. Things are arguably more complex than ever. Tom has specialized as a Linux guy, with a mastery of C, Perl and system administration. I've got a Windows pedigree with large enterprise systems, with Active Directory and Group Policy as my fortés. Nice skills to have, but no one is an island. If you *can* do more by working together, then you should.

Tom and I were able to peacefully co-exist under the same roof. And we made the most of what the other guy had to offer. It's interesting that that same model would be a metaphor for the same basic idea that drives this book, some eleven years later. That is, Windows and Linux can peacefully coexist under the same roof and take advantage of what "the other guy" has to offer.

Are we expecting you to be both a Windows and a Linux expert? No. If you're like most administrators, you are likely stronger in one technology than the other. The best part is that you won't need to know the ins and outs of the other guy's operating system for this book to be effective. This is because we'll show you, specifically, how to set up the features in direct step-by-step style so your time can be immediately practical.

The Practical Philosophy

Whenever possible, we will initially emphasize the functions and tools "in the box" for either Windows or Linux where applicable. However, a big part of system administration is simply getting the job done. To that end, we will additionally be highlighting some key open source and 3rd-party tools which might be necessary (or the most straightforward path) to get the job done.

We know Linux administration can be very command-line intensive. So, whenever possible, we'll try to avoid the command-line and go GUI. But when that's impossible or impractical, we'll just dive in and perform the necessary command line functions. Even in the Windows world, there are times when we need to go to the command line. In other words, our #1 goal is to get the job done.

You're not going to know it all by the time you finish this book. For our purposes, we'll set up the most usual case of the sharing or resources. We'll refer you to Sybex, other publisher's texts, and web resources for more intense studying on any particular subject. A concept like Windows RAS or Linux SAMBA is simply too big to explore into every nook and cranny. We can only delve so far into each subtopic in a book of this size. However, by the end of this book you'll have a good foundation to understand how you can get disparate systems to talk together... and the resources to discover the intimate details of tweaking as you need to.

If you're ready to bring piece and symbiosis to your environment, then this is the book for you.

Integration at Many Levels

Integration of your Windows and Linux systems can happen at one, or many levels. Right away, in Chapter 1, you'll start out with very loose integration at the DNS level. By Chapters 2 and 3 you'll learn how to integrate directory services. By Chapter 4, file services.

You'll continue onward to integrate printers, desktops, remote computing solutions, DNS, VPN solutions and finally web development.

In short, integration of Windows and Linux is where it's at. Why?

Because Windows is here to stay....

And Linux is here to stay.

And the organization that can take advantage of the best of both worlds will reap benefits unavailable to those who insist on discarding one operating system or the other.

We all have to play nicely together and get along. While it's not a cakewalk, hopefully this book will give you the fundamentals required to make that happen.

Thanks from the Authors

Thank you for reading this book.

As you progress through your journey, we hope to see you on our website, www .WinLinAnswers.com. We hope to get your feedback, hear how this book helped you, or accept any error reports. Additionally, we're looking forward to hearing you share your knowledge and stories of integration to additionally help the community at large.

Thanks, and enjoy the journey. We certainly have!

Jeremy Moskowitz

and

Tom Boutell

www.WinLinAnswers.com

 NOTE   Don't forget to check out the downloadable resources on www.WinLinAnswers .com, including example code, updated information, and a whole additional chapter on Windows 2003 / R2's built-in Unix/Linux support!

1

Installation and Getting Around

The thing about Windows networks is they're so easy to set up. Or so they seem. And poor Linux, it gets the bad rap of being harder to set up. (Well, maybe that used to be true. Or if it's still true, it's getting easier.)

It's quite likely that you picked up this book because you already have a Windows network and you're looking to augment it with the free stuff Linux has to offer. Or maybe you want to try some of the experiments we present to see for yourself what the hubbub is all about.

Even if you already have a Windows Network set up, it's recommended that you utilize this chapter to help set up your test lab. That way, you'll be working with our specifications. The idea is that eventually you'll transfer the knowledge you gain here to the real world. But getting started first in the test lab, not the real world, is highly recommended. Why? Because in the real world you might not be using the exact same configurations we are, and we'd hate for you to curse out loud, have someone from Human Resources walk by at just that moment, and have you hate us forever.

In short, please: test lab first, real world second.

In this chapter, we'll set the stage for the rest of the experiments in this book. To properly prepare for the road ahead, you'll be loading:

- Windows 2003 Server (Standard or Enterprise)
- Windows XP with Service Pack 2
- Fedora Core 3 as a server
- Fedora Core 3 as a client

In Chapter 2, you'll be creating another Fedora client to specifically test interactions with Active Directory. But more on that later.

Once the installation of these systems is performed, you'll be ready to rock.

So let's roll.

Yikes, I Don't Have That Much Hardware

Yes, it's a lot of hardware to have on hand. But you don't have to have it all. Instead, consider using a virtualization tool to load multiple "guest" operating systems onto your real (host) machine.

The two major players here are VMware Workstation (from VMware) or Virtual PC (from Microsoft). The purpose of this type of software is simple: it allows you to pretend to have more machines than you really have.

You'll need one really huge box to act as the host to all these guests. But once you have it, you can perform all your work on one machine without a ton of messy cables. If this sounds like a good idea to you, I suggest you read two articles I (Jeremy) wrote for *Redmond* magazine about virtualization software, either at http://mcpmag.com/features/print.asp?EditorialsID=428 or at http://mcpmag.com/features/article.asp?editorialsid=429. For an alternative opinion, check out www.win2000mag.com/Windows/Article/ArticleID/42269/42269.html.

We'll talk more about using virtualization software to solve some real Windows/Linux integration issues in Chapter 7, so stay tuned.

The Story and the Roadmap

When we began writing this book, we had a lot of ways we could have designed our test bed. But in the end, we decided we wanted our test environment to be something that shows up time and time again in the real world.

In many companies, the Windows guys and the Unix/Linux folks never really fraternized. Because these two factions historically never really talked, two whole universes grew up quasi-separately. The Unix/Linux guys did their thing, and the Windows guys did their thing.

Only when Windows Active Directory was born did the two sides really *need* to sit down and really talk. And why did they need to talk then, when they never needed to talk before?

The Domain Name Service, or DNS.

DNS is fundamental to both Linux and Active Directory, whereas Windows NT and earlier didn't depend on DNS.

So the two sides started talking. They had to work together, or they'd blow something up.

In this chapter, which sets the stage for the rest of the book, we wanted to make sure we captured the most common scenario we've seen in medium and larger environments. That is, when it comes to who "owns" the DNS, nine times out of ten, it's the Unix/Linux guys. However, since Active Directory also needs DNS, the Active Directory guys need a way to play too, which (a) doesn't interfere with the Unix/Linux guys' DNS and (b) allows the Windows guys maximum flexibility.

That way is called a *delegated subdomain*. To explain this without getting knee-deep in DNS theory, this allows the Linux guys to be the king of the castle and own the internal DNS name—say, `corp.com`. However, it also permits the Active Directory guys to have their own sandbox to build their own Active Directory sandcastles in—say, a DNS domain named `ad.corp.com`.

To squeeze the maximum out of this book, we'll spend a little extra time in this first chapter setting up this common (and not all that complex) scenario. At the end of the chapter, you'll have one Windows 2003 Server running DNS, one Linux server running DNS, one Windows XP client (talking to the Windows server for DNS lookups), and one Linux client (talking to the Linux Server for DNS lookups). This is representative of the usual story we described: two factions that historically didn't talk much.

We'll also have one little bridge between the two DNS domains: the delegated subdomain from `corp.com` to `ad.corp.com`.

Figure 1.1 shows what our test network will look like by the end of the chapter.

FIGURE 1.1   This is what your test network will look like at the end of the chapter.

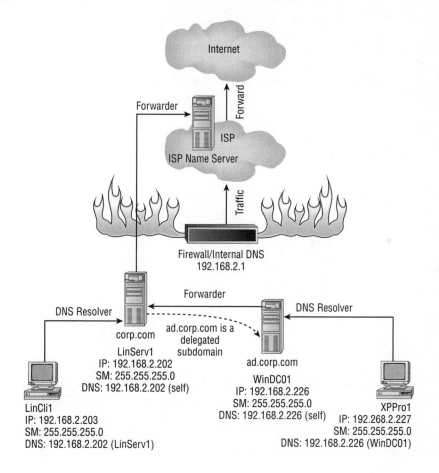

You'll install Windows in two parts and Linux in two parts. Here's how the rest of the chapter will go:

- You'll install the basic operating systems on your Windows 2003 and Windows XP machines.

- You'll install the basic operating systems on your Linux server and Linux client machines.

- You'll configure your Linux server as the primary master DNS server for corp.com. You'll then enable your Linux Server to delegate authority for a subdomain named ad.corp.com to your Windows DNS server.

- You'll configure Active Directory to reside in the ad.corp.com subdomain—just as many corporations do in the real world.

The Benefits of Subdomain Delegation

A delegated subdomain allows you to retain the benefits of a robust Linux-based DNS server for the corp.com domain, while still allowing the Active Directory server to be authoritative for DNS queries within ad.corp.com. By delegating authority for ad.corp.com to the Active Directory server, the primary DNS server for corp.com enables all machines in the corp.com domain to resolve names in the ad.corp.com subdomain. For example, you can be working on a workstation in the corp.com domain and still resolve hostnames such as xppro1.ad.corp.com.

Here, you see the delegation relationship between the corp.com domain and the ad.corp.com domain.

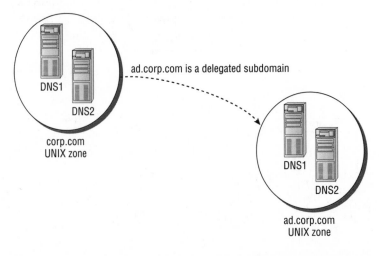

Don't worry if your real-world Active Directory doesn't live in a delegated subdomain. There's a huge number of Active Directories out there that are completely unrelated to what the Unix/Linux guys have done. In the following example, an Active Directory resides in a domain that is completely unrelated to the original corp.com. It's called ad.corp.com, but no relationship has ever been established.

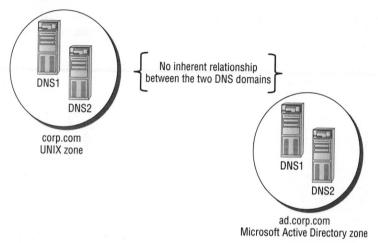

There's nothing wrong with that, per se. It just means that you won't be able to look up hostnames within the Active Directory domain from elsewhere in the corp.com domain.

There are alternative ways around this problem if subdomain delegation doesn't work for your needs, and we'll explore them right at the top of Chapter 9, "Windows/Linux Network Interoperability." In that chapter, we'll discuss some alternative designs that we've seen out there, as well as how to tweak your DNS settings to make everyone see everyone else.

Again, for the purposes of this book, we suggest that you follow along and create the machines and such exactly as we describe. Okay, these examples might not 100 percent perfectly match your precise environment. However, by first working through the examples with our baseline setup, you'll later be in a much better position to put the skills you learn here into practice into your real world.

Installing Windows

The whole reason that Windows has taken over 95 percent of the desktop (and is all over the server room) is because of its swell GUI, or graphical user interface. Users like it, admins like it. Heck, my grandma likes it. And this swell interface gives the appearance that Windows networking is easy. It's not. It just looks easy. Ask anyone who's left a career as a plumber, a tennis pro, or a cab driver to become a Windows networking expert and make the fabled bajillion dollars a year. Turns out, it's not easy…it's deceptively hard.

Windows Server 2003 + SP1 and Windows XP + SP2: The Right Windows (at Least for This Book)

There are lots of Windows flavors in use in the world, from Small Business Server to Windows Embedded. Most organizations are walking away from Windows NT 4 and looking onward and upward. Most corporate and educational installations are now Windows 2000 or Windows 2003.

To that end, we had to pick which Windows will most likely get the most use in the upcoming years, and the winner is Windows Server 2003 + SP1 for the server and Windows XP + SP2 on the client. As of now these are the most up-to-date versions. Additionally, there's not *that* much difference between Windows 2000 Server (the next most popular version of Windows' server OS) and Windows 2003, so even if your organization is using Windows 2000, you'll be in good shape. However, where things are different between Windows 2003 and Windows 2000, we'll try to bring them to your attention. Specifically, file sharing can react differently between the two, and we bring you this information in Chapter 4. And, additionally, we'll demonstrate how Windows Server 2003 / R2 shakes things up. Check out the Web Appendix for that information.

In this first part of the book, we'll zip through installing Windows 2003. We'll install Windows XP a little later.

Windows 2003 Editions and Capabilities

As we said, Windows 2003 has multiple varieties. By my count, there are nine varieties, as listed next. Don't panic or feel inferior if you haven't had a chance to play with all of these. In my travels, I've only actually seen four (and I get around a lot).

Windows 2003 Server Edition	Where Used	Number of Processors Supported	Amount of RAM Supported
Small Business Server	Small businesses with 75 client systems or fewer. This setup takes an "everything in the box" approach to networking.	2	4GB
Web Edition	Web server only. Not meant to be used as a file server or Active Directory server	2	2GB

Windows 2003 Server Edition	Where Used	Number of Processors Supported	Amount of RAM Supported
Standard Edition	General purpose. A perfect choice for this book. Makes a great Active Directory Domain Controller or file, print, or VPN server.	4	4GB
Enterprise Edition	General purpose (see the list after this table for the enhanced feature set beyond Standard Edition). Has increased fault tolerant clustering capabilities.	8	32GB
Datacenter Server Edition	Huge high-availability environments.	32	64GB
Windows Server 2003 Standard for 64-bit Itanium-based Systems	If you can afford an Itanium, this is for you.	4	4GB
Windows Server 2003 Enterprise for 64-bit Itanium-based Systems	Adds the Enterprise features listed after this table.	8	64GB
Windows Server 2003 Datacenter Edition for 64-bit Itanium-based Systems	Massively scalable.	32 (64 in some OEM versions)	512GB
Windows Server 2003 Standard x64 Edition (for 64/32-bit processors like the AMD Opteron and Intel Xeon EM64T)	If you get an Opteron or Xeon EM64T, this is for you.	4	4GB
Windows Server 2003 Enterprise x64 Edition (for 64/32-bit processors like the AMD Opteron and Intel Xeon EM64T)	If you get an Opteron or Xeon EM64T and need the Enterprise features listed after this table, this is for you.	8	32GB

The two realistic choices are Windows 2003 Standard Edition and Windows 2003 Enterprise Edition. Either is an acceptable choice for use in the lab and for most of the exercises in this book, though there are some reasons you might want to get your hands on a Windows 2003 Enterprise Edition copy (or an evaluation edition).

To help you decide what to use in production and for this book, here's a handful of ways where the two are different (note not all differences are listed here.)

- Enterprise Edition supports shared-disk clustering of up to eight nodes; Standard Edition does not support shared-disk clustering

- Microsoft Identity Integration Server (MIIS) 2003 is an add-on that helps you synchronize passwords (and more) between disparate directories. It runs only on Enterprise Edition. We touch upon MIIS 2003 in Chapter 3.

- If your hardware supports it, you can *hot-add memory* to Enterprise Edition. That is, you can add memory to a server while it's running and allocate that memory to the rest of the server. Sexxxxy.

You can locate more of the differences between the server editions at Microsoft's website: www.microsoft.com/windowsserver2003/default.mspx. Specifically, there's a super-duper chart you can spy at www.microsoft.com/windowsserver2003/evaluation/features/ compareeditions.mspx.

Lastly, if you cannot get your hands on a production copy of Windows 2003, you can order a free evaluation kit. It costs only a couple of bucks to have it shipped. The evaluation lasts 180 days for each server you build, and you can build as many test machines as you like, knock 'em down, and start your 180 countdown all over again. Order it at www.microsoft.com/ windowsserver2003/evaluation/trial/evalkit.mspx.

Windows 2003 Requirements

Before you get crackin' with installation, make sure the hardware you're using fits the bill. Here are Microsoft's published minimums, and our suggested realistic use recommendations:

	Minimum Standard	Minimum Enterprise	Recommended Standard	Recommended Enterprise	Will Work for This Book
CPU Type	Pentium II	Pentium II	Pentium III, 4, or M	Pentium III, 4, or M	Pentium III, 4, or M
Speed	133Mhz	133Mhz	1Ghz–4Ghz	1Ghz–4Ghz	800Mhz
RAM	128MB	128MB	196MB–1GB	256–1GB	256MB
Disk	1.5GB	1.5GB	4GB–6GB for C; more for applications, data, etc.	4GB–6GB for C; more for applications, data, etc.	4GB–6GB for C; more for applications, data, etc.

Windows XP Editions

Like its bigger, badder Windows 2003 brother, Windows XP also has several editions. At last count, there were five editions:

Windows XP Edition	Where Used	Number of Processors Supported	Amount of RAM Supported
Home Edition	Home and networks without domains	1	4GB
Professional Edition	Anywhere you want to authenticate to an Active Directory domain	2	4GB
Media Center Edition	Bundled with specially enhanced media PCs (think TiVO-esque)	1	4GB
Tablet Edition	Bundled with tablet-style laptops	1	4GB

There's a great overview of all the editions from Microsoft at www.microsoft.com/windowsxp/evaluation/compare.mspx.

For our purposes, there's really only one choice: Windows XP Professional. Windows XP Home cannot be a member of an Active Directory domain, nor get domain-based Group Policy—the essential nutrients of a Windows 2003 domain.

Automatically Installing the Service Packs with the OS

A Windows service pack is a several-hundred-megabyte file full of fixes and updates. As of this writing, Windows XP Service Pack 2 is current, as is Windows 2003 Service Pack 1. To that end, make sure you've got each of those on your test machines as you work through the exercises.

Sure you can, if you want, just load the service pack on after the operating system is already loaded. Or you can be super-cool and "embed" the service pack right onto the installation media! This is called *slipstreaming*.

To create your own slipstreamed installation CD, take a look at www.winsupersite.com/showcase/windowsxp_sp2_slipstream.asp.

You'll want to repeat similar steps for Windows 2003 with its Service Pack 1. Another great resource on slipstreaming and burning your own CD-ROMs can be found at www.petri.co.il/windows_2000_xp_sp_slipstreaming.htm.

Windows XP Professional Requirements

Before we get crackin' with installation, let's make sure the hardware you're about to use fits the bill. Here are Microsoft's published minimums, and our suggested realistic use recommendations:

	Minimum	Recommended	Will Work for this Book
CPU Type	Pentium II	Pentium III, 4, or M	Pentium III, 4, or M
Speed	133Mhz–233Mhz	500Mhz+	800Mhz
RAM	128MB	1GB+	256MB
Disk	1.5GB	4GB+	4GB–20GB for C; more for applications, data, etc.

Beginning the Windows 2003 Installation

We'll assume you have a blank hard drive to start. That is, you have no other OSes previously installed. To start, you'll need to make sure your computer's BIOS is set to boot from the CD-ROM drive. At this point, you'll be able to step through each installation screen. Note that while we'll briefly describe each installation screen you should encounter, we won't show them all.

Once the computer's BIOS is set to boot from the CD-ROM, insert your Windows 2003 CD-ROM into the CD-ROM drive and turn the computer on.

Text-based Setup Screens

For all the GUI power that Windows 2003 wields, it still has to be kick-started with some text-based setup screens. You'll start your journey in what looks like DOS. It isn't DOS, though. It's just enough Windows Server to get Windows GUI mode bootstrapped.

Welcome to Setup Screen

The Welcome to Setup screen appears as shown in Figure 1.2. Since we're assuming you have an empty machine, you can get started by pressing Enter.

Windows Licensing Agreement Screen

On this screen, you'll ever-so-quickly read the licensing agreement. (Yeah, right.) When ready, press F8 to continue. Why F8? Because after this screen, you're sealing your *F8* (Fate, get it? Who says I'm not a conspiracy theorist?).

Partitioning Screen

In Figure 1.3, you can see where you can choose to utilize the entire first disk or partition it. Do what you will here; at the end of your dicing and slicing, though, be sure to have at least an 8GB partition for the C: drive.

For the purposes of this book, we won't concern ourselves with RAID, SAN, iSCSI, or other add-on hardware disk technologies. The point of this book is to demonstrate integration techniques, so we'll keep it simple with a simple disk configuration on a simple disk, like an IDE disk.

FIGURE 1.2   The Windows 2003 initial setup screen

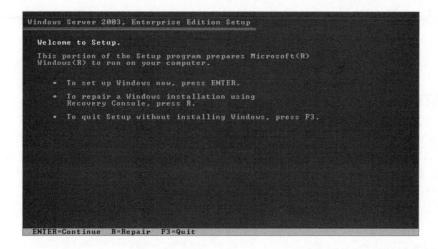

FIGURE 1.3   You can partition your hard drive here if desired.

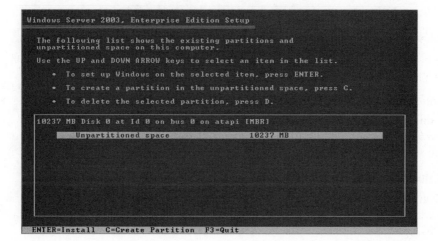

Formatting Screen

Next, you'll see Windows 2003 format the partition. This can take several minutes to more than several minutes, depending on how large the disk is and how slow the hardware is.

Copying Screen

As you can see in Figure 1.4, Windows will start copying files to the hard drive to get enough Windows loaded to load "go GUI." This will be the last text-based setup screen you will see.

Graphical-based Setup Screens

At this point, you'll be presented with the remainder of the installation within a GUI, replete with mouse control.

Personalize Your Software Screen

On this screen you'll be able to type the "owner" of the software and the organization name. This has very little bearing on the operation of the OS. It's only displayed when you run a winver command to get some general statistics about the machine. These names don't have to match the name of your domain, or anything else for that matter. The name cannot be "Administrator," but everything else is fair game.

Your Product Key Screen

Ah...the dreaded product key. For Microsoft, this is a necessary evil to prevent people from rampantly copying their software. Your key should be on the CD jacket that came with the software. Later in the process (once the server is fully installed), you'll have to activate your copy of Windows 2003. Indeed, you must even activate 180-day evaluation copies.

FIGURE 1.4   This is the last text-based setup screen.

```
Windows Server 2003, Enterprise Edition Setup


              Please wait while Setup formats the partition
     C:  Partition1 [New (Raw)]             10229 MB ( 10228 MB free)
          on 10237 MB Disk 0 at Id 0 on bus 0 on atapi [MBR].




        Setup is formatting...
                                  25%

        [                        ]
```

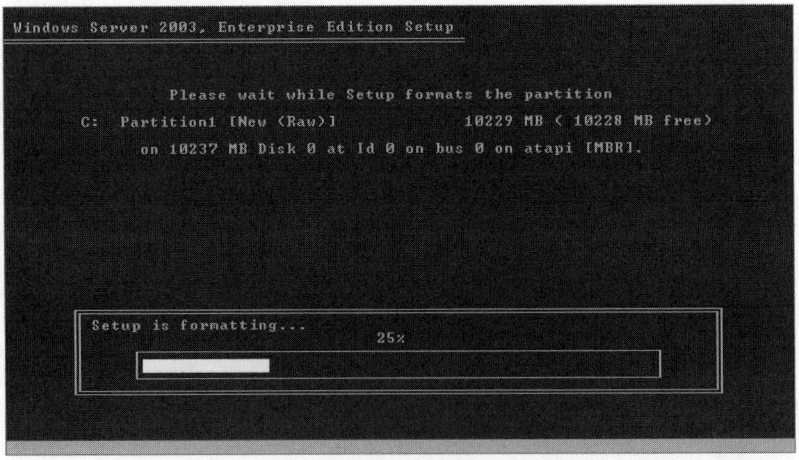

Licensing Mode

Depending on how you licensed Windows 2003, you can make your choice between "Per server" or "Per Device or Per User."

Per server mode   In this mode, each inbound connection must have its own license (called a CAL, or Client Access License).

Per Device or Per User   Each device or user that could possibly connect to the server must have its own license. Most organizations choose this mode because they have licensed Windows XP or Windows 2000 machines. If you're guessing which to use, use this mode.

Computer Name and Administrator Password

On this screen, shown in Figure 1.5, you'll be able to enter the computer name and a password. That password is for the explicitly named account of Administrator. In Windows, usernames aren't case sensitive. (In Linux, names are case sensitive.)

For the experiments presented in this book, call your Windows 2003 machine WINDC1 (though for readability, we'll type it as WinDC1). We also suggest that you set the password to p@ssw0rd. (That's an "at sign" as the second character and a zero for the letter O.) This password is strong enough for the default strength requirements for both Windows and Linux. When ready, click "Next."

Date and Time Settings

Make sure Windows sees the right time. Sometimes it doesn't pick up the computer's BIOS time correctly, or the BIOS clock is just plain wrong, so be sure the time zone settings are correct. You'll run some experiments later in the book which might not work if the time zone isn't correct. Additionally, a little later (when you perform some post-configuration settings), you'll ensure that the date and time stay in sync with some authoritative time source. Click "Next" when ready.

FIGURE 1.5   Enter the computer name and the Administrator password.

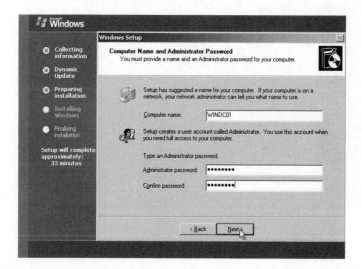

Networking Settings and TCP/IP Properties Page

At this point you'll be able to specify Typical Settings or Custom Settings. Typical settings mean that your server will try to request an IP address via DHCP. This isn't generally advised. Therefore, in this case, select Custom Settings, then proceed to change the TCP/IP settings to a static IP address. In our examples, you'll set WinDC1's IP address information as follows (as shown in Figure 1.6):

IP address: 192.168.2.226
Subnet Mask: 255.255.255.0
Default Gateway: 192.168.2.1
Preferred DNS Server: 192.168.2.226 (itself)

Yes, in this case, you're telling the Windows 2003 server to use itself as the "go to" place for DNS lookups. A little later, you'll set up the DNS service and tell that component to go out to the Internet for any queries that are outside your private DNS domains. But for now, this is fine.

When ready, click "OK", then click "Next" when back on the "Network Settings" page.

Workgroup or Computer Domain Screen

You'll next have the opportunity to join a domain or plunk yourself in a workgroup. For now, keep the machine in a workgroup. A little later (after the machine is fully up and running), you'll make this machine a domain controller. If you add subsequent workstations or servers to the domain later, you'll use this screen to join them to the domain you'll be creating.

FIGURE 1.6   Enter the static IP information.

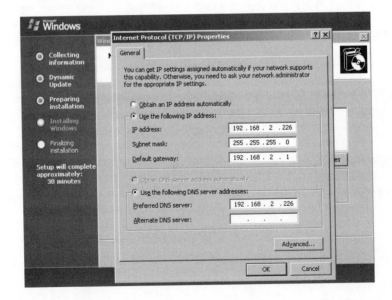

Final Installation Screens

At this point, go get a cup of coffee. You've done the hard work and answered the barrage of questions Windows has pummeled you with. Windows takes a while to finish loading, and when it does, it prompts you to do what Windows does best: reboot!

Once rebooted, you'll be ready for post-installation tasks.

Post-Installation Tasks

At this point, you should be able to log on with the one account you created—the Administrator. Again, case doesn't matter for the username, but it does for the password. Once entered and you're all logged in, you'll be able to complete several steps to set you on the right path for the rest of the book:

- Install additional operating system components
- Set up a DNS server
- Form your Active Directory
- Product activation

> Once you log on for the first time, you might be presented with the Manage Your Server Roles Wizard. By and large, you won't use this wizard and will instead opt for the more traditional way of configuring our server. It's up to you if you want to check the check box that permanently tucks it away.

Installing Additional Operating System Components

One of the first things you should do after your test server is up and running is set up the additional components. Heck, you may never use them, but they're good to have ready to go should you ever choose to partake. You'll do this via Window's Control Panel. Just go to Start ➤ Control Panel ➤ Add/Remove Programs. Once there, select "Add/Remove Windows Components." When you do, you'll see a list of available goodies as shown in Figure 1.7.

You are looking at the list of top-level options to select. In most of these top-level options, there are suboptions, too. Just double-click the words of the option (not the check box area)—and you'll be able to dive in and see more stuff.

Here's what we recommend you select. You'll be using some, but not all, of the options in this book.

Top-level Option	Default	Stuff to Choose within the Level	Why You Need It
Accessories and Utilities	Some on	As you wish.	Has calculator, Paint, other odds and ends.

Top-level Option	Default	Stuff to Choose within the Level	Why You Need It
Application Server	Off	Double-click inside and select Internet Information Services (IIS). Other options will automatically be selected once IIS is selected.	You'll use IIS in Chapter 10.
Certificate Services	Off	You'll install this in Chapter 3. Stay tuned.	You'll use this in Chapter 3 to secure your traffic to Active Directory.
E-mail Services	Off	None for this book.	Windows 2003 has a basic POP3 server. We'll talk about Exchange in Chapter 6.
Fax Services	Off	None for this book.	You can set Windows 2003 as a fax gateway.
Indexing Services	Off	None for this book.	Enables fast-find searches within Windows.
Internet Explorer Enhanced Security Configuration	On	De-select this. Yes, turn this off.	If left on, this component warns you each and every time you visit a new site. Might be useful in production environments, but not necessary for our purposes.
Management and Monitoring Tools	Off	None for this book.	Contains some networking services including a packet sniffer (Network Monitor).

Top-level Option	Default	Stuff to Choose within the Level	Why You Need It
Networking Services	Some on	Double-click inside and select the following services: Domain Name System (DNS) (this should have already been selected while creating your Active Directory), Dynamic Host Configuration Protocol (DHCP) (we'll talk about this in Chapter 10), Windows Internet Name Service.	Provides the basic services you need to provide plumbing on your Windows network.
Other File and Print Services	Off	Double-click inside and select Print Services for Unix. We'll talk about it in Chapter 4.	Will allow Unix printers to print via Windows.
Remote Installation Services	Off	None for this book.	Allows you to build a machine from bare metal via PxE boot.
Remote Storage	Off	None for this book.	Provides a mechanism to offload older files to, say, tapes or rewritable optical disks.
Security Configuration Wizard	Off	None for this book.	If you installed 2003 + SP1, this wizard helps secure your system.
Terminal Server (and Terminal Server Licensing)	Off (for now)	Don't select this now.	We'll talk about Terminal Services in Chapter 8.
UDDI Services	Off	None for this book.	An additional component for distributed web services

Top-level Option	Default	Stuff to Choose within the Level	Why You Need It
Update Root Certificates	On	None for this book.	Automatically downloads certificates for well-known certificate vendors (Verisign, etc.).
Windows Media Services	Off	None for this book.	Allows you to host streaming media using Windows 2003.

Installing Windows 2003 + SP1

If you didn't perform a slipstreamed installation of Windows 2003 + SP1, now is an excellent time to load SP1. It provides a bajillion little bug fixes, plus it adds some security.

You can download the several-hundred-megabyte patch from www.microsoft.com. At last check it was at www.microsoft.com/windowsserver2003/downloads/servicepacks/sp1/default.mspx. If it changes, just search the Microsoft website for "Windows 2000 Service Pack 1." Installation is easy; just double-click the file to open it and follow the wizard along. It will force you to create an "uninstall" directory, which by itself will also create several hundred megabytes. In short, be sure your C drive has at least 2GB free space before you get started.

Once finished, you'll be forced to reboot. Do so and log back in.

FIGURE 1.7   Here you can select the optional Windows components to use.

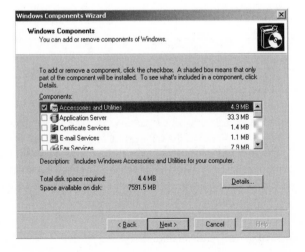

When Good Windows Goes Bad

In my experience, installing Windows XP and Windows 2003 works pretty darn well, but I have seen Windows installations fail. Less often than going full belly-up, I've seen a certain portion of the computer not work properly. Here's how to start to troubleshoot Windows installations:

BIOS Upgrades   Most modern computers have the ability to have the BIOS flash upgraded. That is, you simply download it from the manufacturer, pop it on a floppy, reboot, and voilá—updated BIOS. If you have a failed Windows installation, go ahead and give it another shot.

ACPI Enabled or Disabled   ACPI is the specification for how power management should be handled. Many computers' BIOSes have the option to turn ACPI on or off. If Windows fails to install, try flipping it: On to Off or Off to On.

Drivers   Windows might load, but the wired or wireless network won't start. Or Windows will load, but the video drivers are all whacked out. The usual reason for Windows failing to load is almost always some driver incompatibility. Sometimes Windows will make a best guess at what the driver is and try it as the closest match. Better still, before you start, determine the specific brands of hardware you use—network, video, wireless, sound, etc.—and have all the drivers ready to go on floppies so you can tell Windows what to use when the time comes or after Windows is fully installed.

System Tools   Additionally, many computer manufacturers, such as Dell and HP, have add-on system tools specifically for Windows. Even motherboard manufacturers—the kinds that white-box system builders use—make chipset downloads available specifically for the operating system you are using. With the use of these system tools or chipset downloads, I've seen Windows go from dog s-l-o-w to downright awesome!

We hope you won't need any of these tips—Windows will just install, and you'll be ready to roll!

Installing Linux

Linux installation is a process that causes anxiety for many. Negative experiences installing earlier versions of Linux have led to a conventional belief that Linux installation is always difficult. But it doesn't have to be. Installing a well-known Linux distribution on common hardware can be nearly as smooth as a typical Windows installation. Of course, it does pay to select compatible hardware. There are several websites that provide hardware compatibility information for Linux. These include:

- Linuxquestions.org, which offers a non-distribution-specific Linux hardware compatibility list at `www.linuxquestions.org/hcl/index.php`.

- The Linux Hardware Compatibility HOWTO, which is slightly dated but offers a good overview with links to sites about specific types of hardware at `www.tldp.org/HOWTO/Hardware-HOWTO/`.

- The Red Hat Enterprise Linux Hardware Compatibility List. Because of the close relationship between Fedora and Red Hat, most information here is also relevant for Fedora. See `http://bugzilla.redhat.com/hwcert/`.

Ease of installation is not the only criteria for selecting the flavor of Linux to use, but it is an important one. Fedora Linux offers a reasonable balance between installation convenience and the feature set we're looking to demonstrate in this book.

Fedora Core 3: The Distribution We're Suggesting for This Book

There are many fine Linux distributions. For purposes of this book, we needed to draw a line somewhere and simply make a choice, so we chose to use Fedora Linux. The Fedora distribution of Linux is the freely downloadable successor to the original Red Hat Linux system. The good news is that it remains closely related to the commercial version (read: pay version) of Red Hat Linux, now known as Red Hat Enterprise Linux. Indeed, many Red Hat employees are involved in the ongoing development, care, and feeding of Fedora.

In fact, new features in Red Hat Enterprise Linux often get their sea legs in Fedora first. Of course, the best part of the deal is that Fedora is 100 percent *freely downloadable*, with an active, independent support community.

Fedora Linux makes the best choice for this book because the skills you learn on this free distribution can be easily transferred to just about any Linux distribution. Fedora's features are generally well tested, and an active user community exists to support it.

Other Linux Distributions

Of course, Fedora is not the only Linux distribution available. As an open-source system released under a free software license, Linux invites the creation of different distributions specialized for different needs.

Walking down the aisles of your local computer store or surfing online, you'll locate distributions of Linux such as Red Hat Enterprise, SuSE, Slackware, Debian, Gentoo, and more. Some distributions are more popular and more distinctive than others. For instance, Slackware was one of the first Linux distributions. Debian is noteworthy because of its lack of a single parent company involved in its origin; the Debian project is and always has been run on a strictly non-profit basis. Several commercial distributions, such as Xandros, were based on Debian. Red Hat Enterprise is a commercially supported relative of Fedora.

One of my favorite distributions is called Knoppix. Not just because it has a Katchy, er, catchy name, but because it requires no installation whatsoever. It's simply a CD-ROM ISO image which, once burned as a CD-ROM, can just be booted and off you go! Nothing to install and nothing to commit to. While not an ideal choice for the production environments described in book, it does provide a nice demonstration to those who have never seen Linux before. The official Knoppix website is `www.knopper.net/knoppix/index-en.html`.

Installing Fedora Linux

The installation process can be broken down into several steps. First, you must determine that your system meets the requirements to run Fedora Linux in a practical fashion. Second, you must obtain the Fedora Linux distribution CDs. Third, you carry out the "official" installation process provided by the Fedora Linux installer. Fourth, you take care of the post-installation steps, especially updating the system with the latest critical security fixes and other upgrades to the packages you have installed.

To take full advantage of this book, you will want to carry out the last two steps twice. First, to create a typical Linux server system with Windows interoperability features. Second, to create a typical client or workstation system. We'll refer to the server system as *LinServ1* and to the client system as *LinCli1*. In later chapters, you'll create additional client and server systems specifically configured to participate in a Windows Active Directory domain in various ways.

System Requirements

First, you must ensure that the system meets the minimum installation requirements. For our purposes, assume that Linux is the only operating system to be installed on each computer. Dual-boot setups are not usual in a practical business computing environment, though you may find them useful for personal testing.

If you do decide on a dual-boot environment, be sure to take the disk space requirements of the other operating system into account. In general there must already be free, unpartitioned disk space if you wish Linux to share a single hard drive with another operating system. Tools such as Symantec's Partition Magic can be used to adjust the size of existing partitions, creating free space for a Linux installation. Again, in general, however, we don't recommend a dual-boot configuration. If testing without purchasing new hardware is your goal, consider using VMware or a similar virtualization product, as described in Chapter 7.

Resource	Minimum	Recommended for Production Use	Will Work for This Book
Disk Space	8GB	8GB (client), 20GB (server)	5GB (client or server)
Memory	128MB	512MB or more	256MB
CPU	Pentium III	1Ghz Pentium 4, Athlon, or equivalent	600Mhz Pentium III, Athlon, or equivalent
Network	10/100Base-T Ethernet	10/100Base-T Ethernet	10/100Base-T Ethernet
Video	800×600 or better display	1024×768 or better display	800×600 or better display

NOTE   While nothing prevents a Linux server system from running most of the exercises in this book with 5GB or less of disk space, allotting 20GB provides more room for real work in a production environment.

Maximum Capabilities

In a previous section we presented the maximum memory size, number of physical CPUs, and so forth for various versions of Windows. Fedora Linux is available free of charge, with complete source code, so the maximum capabilities of Fedora Linux are the current limitations of Linux in general. But it's fair to say that the capabilities built into the currently shipping Linux operating system kernel in Fedora Core 3 are worth mentioning specifically. We'll also mention the maximum capabilities for those who are willing to consider recompiling the Linux kernel (which we will not be doing in this book). For simplicity, we assume a 32-bit architecture. However, note that 64-bit versions of Fedora Linux also exist for various hardware platforms.

Resource	Maximum, as shipped	Maximum, with a Custom Kernel Build
Memory	8GB	64GB
Physical CPUs	4	64
File System Size	2TB (terabytes)	2PB (petabytes), if hardware permits
Single File Size	1TB	2PB

Obtaining Fedora Linux

You can get Fedora Core 3 in a number of ways. If your friends have it, they can legally burn you a copy on CD or DVD. Or if no one has it handy, it's available for download from `fedora.linux.com` as ISO files which you can burn to the appropriate media.

You can also buy a copy from various sources. One of my faves is `www.cheapbytes.com`, where you can pick up the DVD for $8.99.

Beginning the Installation Process

To start, you'll need to make sure your computer's BIOS is set to boot from the CD-ROM drive. Once you do, insert Fedora CD #1 (or the Fedora DVD) into the CD-ROM drive and turn the computer on.

WARNING   Is there already an operating system on this computer that you want to keep? Are there files on this computer that you want to keep? Back up any important files before installing an additional operating system! You should also have unpartitioned free disk space on your hard drive or a second drive with unpartitioned space in order to install a second operating system in a dual-boot configuration. As noted earlier, however, we recommend using VMware or a similar virtualization product instead. See Chapter 7 for more information.

The Welcome Screen

The "Welcome" screen with the giant Fedora Core should appear, as shown in Figure 1.8.

Press "Enter" to begin the installation process with a user-friendly interface. Experienced users may prefer to choose the text-based installation option, but there is no particular benefit to doing so, unless the video driver for your hardware is not included on the boot CD or DVD. We recommend simply pressing "Enter" to follow the same steps that are shown in this chapter.

The Media Test Screen

After a few moments, you will be asked whether you wish to test the CD-ROM media before continuing with installation. All sorts of nastiness could happen when you download ISO files of several hundred megabytes, so press Enter to be safe and allow the CD or DVD to be tested. Better to know *now* than halfway through the installation that you've got a bad disk. It's time well spent.

Depending on your system's configuration, the mouse may or may not be available at this early stage of the installation process. That should change when the graphical user interface takes over.

The Graphical Portion of Setup

At this point you should be able to see graphics and use your mouse. If you're having trouble doing that, you might want to restart your computer and select text-based setup. It's a little clunkier, but it gets the job done. If, however, you're in good shape with the graphical part, continue onward.

Welcome Screen

The screen shown in Figure 1.8 will welcome you to the Fedora installation process with a fully graphical interface and complete mouse support. The installation process uses a wizard-style interface with "Back" and "Next" buttons allowing you to freely move backward and forward if you make a mistake or change your mind during the process. As expected, click "Next" to move to the next page of the installation wizard.

The Language Selection and Keyboard Configuration Screens

The next screen, entitled "Language Selection," offers the opportunity to select the language of your choice for the remainder of the installation process. Select your preferred language and click "Next."

The following screen, entitled "Keyboard Configuration" allows you to select your computer's keyboard type. Click "Next" after making your selection.

The Installation Type Screen

The next screen is entitled "Installation Type," as shown in Figure 1.9.

FIGURE 1.8   Initial Fedora installation screen

FIGURE 1.9   Installation Type screen

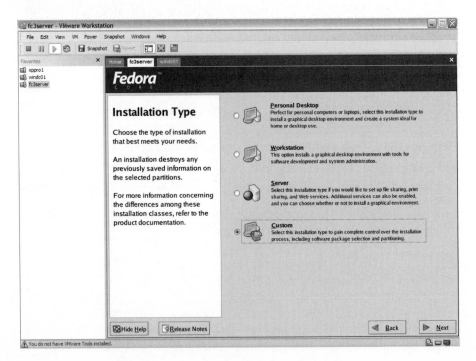

Fedora Linux is suitable for many purposes, from personal desktop systems to development workstations to web servers. To simplify installation, save disk space, and improve performance, Fedora installs only the options that make sense for the computer's intended purpose. For purposes of this book, we strongly recommend that you select the "Custom" option as shown in Figure 1.9 and then click "Next." This will allow you to select the package groups you'll need to follow the examples in this book. If, however, you're in a rush, you can get away with selecting Server for the server and Workstation for the workstation.

Disk Partitioning

Installing a Unix-like operating system usually requires that the hard drive be partitioned in order to assign disk space to various portions of the Linux file system. Linux and Unix do not use drive-letters to reference partitions. Instead, each partition is represented by a *mount point* within the file system. The picture is made somewhat more complex by Fedora's use of the Logical Volume Manager (LVM), which allows partition-like chunks of space to be managed in a more flexible way. See the sidebar for a more detailed discussion of partitions and logical volumes.

Disk partitioning, multibooting, RAID drives, and other disk stuff on Linux can take up a whole book in and of itself. None of that stuff is the goal of this book, so we'll work with the easiest case and have you leverage the Fedora installer's automatic partitioning. Once you've made your selection, click "Next," as shown in Figure 1.10.

FIGURE 1.10   Disk Partitioning Setup screen

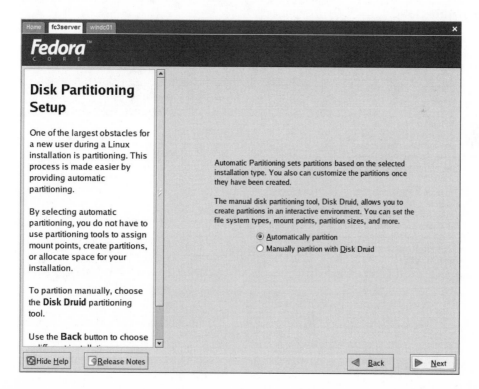

If your hard drive is new or the partition table has been erased, you will be prompted with a final "Warning" dialog. Click "Yes" to proceed with the creation of a new partition table.

You will next be presented with the "Automatic Partitioning" screen, as shown in Figure 1.11. Here you will be asked whether you want to remove all existing partitions on the hard drive, remove all existing Linux partitions on the hard drive, or use only free, unpartitioned space in the partition table. Again, assuming that Linux is to be the only operating system on the computer and you have no files on the hard drive that you wish to keep, select "Remove all Linux partitions on this system." If you wish to install Linux only on a single hard drive in a multiple-drive system, clear the check boxes for any hard drives you do not wish to use, then click "Next."

Since this operation can remove existing information from the hard drive, you will be prompted (one last time) to confirm your choice. Take a deep breath, then when you are ready, click "Yes."

A final disk partitioning-related screen, the "Disk Setup" screen, appears next and is used to adjust the automatically selected partitions. In this case, there is no need to change them, so click "Next" to move on.

FIGURE 1.11   Automatic Partitioning screen

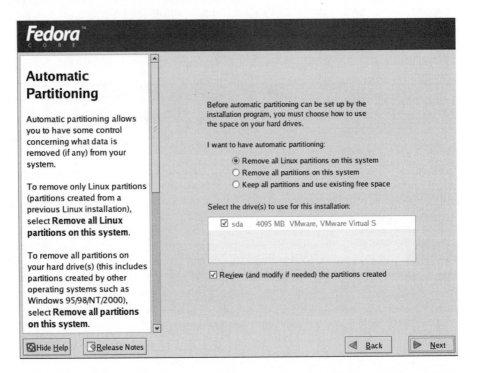

Understanding Linux Hard Drive Devices and Partitions

We recommend that you go with the automatic partitioning scheme offered by Fedora Linux. But what if you want to understand matters a bit more deeply? In this sidebar, we'll explain how Linux labels drives and partitions within drives. We'll also talk about the Logical Volume Manager (LVM) and common partitioning choices for Linux systems.

As in Windows, there are two key types of hard drives on Linux systems: IDE and SCSI.

Hard drives in Linux always have corresponding device names. These device names appear as special "files" in the /dev directory, or in a subdirectory of /dev. IDE hard drives appear as /dev/hda (think "**h**ard **d**rive **A**"), /dev/hdb, /dev/hdc, and so on. Note that the two connectors on the first IDE interface are always /dev/hda and /dev/hdb, even if one of the connectors is unused. /dev/hdc and /dev/hdd are the two connectors on the second IDE interface, and so on.

SCSI hard drives appear as /dev/sda (think "**S**CSI **d**evice **A**"), /dev/sdb, /dev/sdc, and so forth.

What about partitions within a single drive? The partitions within /dev/sda have the device names /dev/sda1, /dev/sda2, /dev/sda3, and so on. However, Fedora Linux complicates the picture a bit through the use of the Logical Volume Manager (LVM), which manages space in a higher-level way. In the past, you might have created /dev/sda1 for bootstrap booting purposes. You might also have made /dev/sda2 for the root file system, that is, everything beneath that isn't explicitly part of a separate file system. And /dev/sda3 could have been the /home file system, to keep Joe Smith's personal MP3 downloads from filling up the root file system, with /dev/sda4 assigned to virtual memory, known in Unix as "swap space."

But partitions can't be easily resized, and the preceding arrangement would forever fix the size of each of these file systems. Traditional solutions to this problem typically involved moving half the user accounts in /home to another partition. LVM improves on this situation by allowing the operating system to see virtual partitions that can actually be enlarged later if the system administrator chooses. These *logical volumes* can also span multiple physical hard drives. In Linux, logical volumes are named /dev/VolGroup00/LogVol00, /dev/VolGroup00/LogVol01, and so on.

On an automatically partitioned Fedora Linux system with a single drive, two physical partitions are created: /dev/sda1 is a bootstrap partition at the start of the drive for booting purposes, and /dev/sda2 is given over to LVM. LVM then subdivides it into /dev/VolGroup00/LogVol00, which is the root file system, and /dev/VolGroup00/LogVol01, which is used for virtual memory. Since no separate file system is explicitly created for /home, home directories are kept in the root file system in this design.

Boot Loader Configuration

What follows is the "Boot Loader Configuration" screen, shown in Figure 1.12, which allows you to decide how the booting process should be handled. When your computer starts up, the *grub* bootloader program is used to launch Linux and any other operating system you may have chosen to install. By default, grub will launch Linux after a very brief delay designed to give you an opportunity to interrupt the boot process and specify any special boot options. Since you aren't creating a dual-boot system, we recommend that you accept the default configuration of the boot loader by clicking "Next." If you want to create a dual-boot system with multiple operating systems, you will need to carefully inspect this screen to ensure that your second operating system was recognized and included in the boot list.

Network Configuration

You will now see the "Network Configuration" screen, as shown in Figure 1.13. Here is where you will be invited to select your networking options. When configuring a server, it is appropriate to give it a static IP address, especially if it will be a DNS and/or DHCP server.

While most client systems in the wild use DHCP to automatically obtain an IP address, you'll assign static IPs for the purposes of this chapter. To assign a static IP address, make sure eth0 is highlighted in the list box at the top of the screen, then click the "Edit" button to open the static IP address configuration dialog.

Clear the DHCP check box. Here's what to enter for your LinServ1 server:

IP address: 192.168.2.202

Subnet Mask: 255.255.255.0

Default Gateway: 192.168.2.1

FIGURE 1.12   Boot Loader Configuration screen

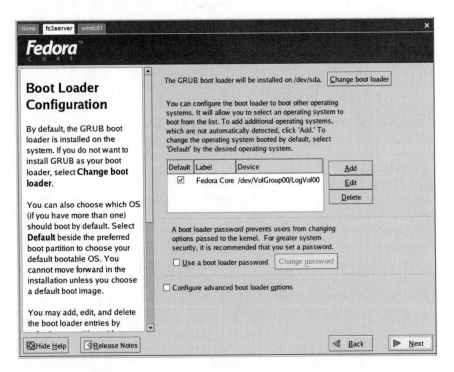

Here's what to enter for your LinCli1 client:

IP address: 192.168.2.203

Subnet Mask: 255.255.255.0

Default Gateway: 192.168.2.1

Be sure to keep the "Activate at Boot" check box checked for each machine.
Figure 1.13 shows the correct settings for LinCli1.

Since you are not relying on DHCP for this example, in addition to configuring IP addresses, you must also configure the hostname and DNS server settings for the client and server systems. After completing the Edit Interface dialog, enter the hostname of the new system, the IP address of the gateway to the Internet, and the IP address of the primary DNS server.

The settings for LinServ1 and LinCli1 are similar. The main difference comes in the DNS server setting, which should be the router's IP address (192.168.2.1) for the server and the server's IP address (192.168.2.202) for the client.

Here's what to enter for your LinServ1 server:

Hostname: `linserv1.corp.com`

DNS server: 192.168.2.1

Gateway: 192.168.2.1

Here's what to enter for your LinCli1 client:

Hostname: `lincli1.corp.com`

DNS server: 192.168.2.202

Gateway: 192.168.2.1

FIGURE 1.13   Network Configuration screen: Edit Interface eth0

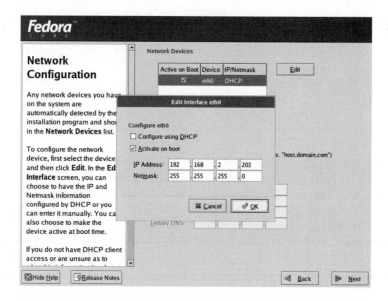

FIGURE 1.14   Network Configuration screen: Hostname and Miscellaneous Settings

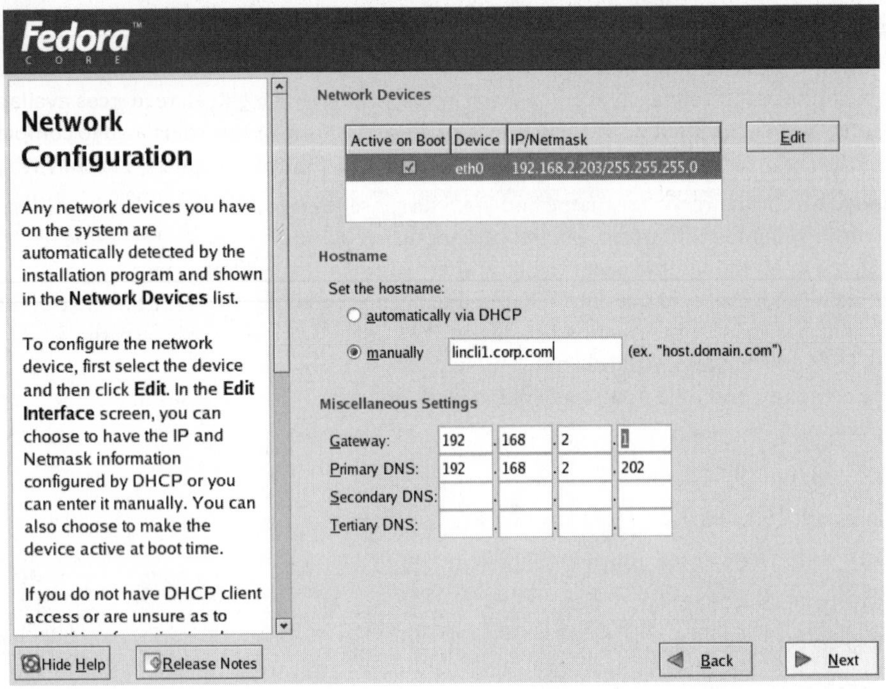

Firewall Configuration

Any administrator who connects a computer to a network should be concerned with security—doubly so if the computer is connected to the Internet. Like Microsoft Windows XP and Windows 2003, Fedora Linux offers a firewall as a standard part of the operating system. In Figure 1.15, you are provided the option to enable the firewall.

By default, the firewall will prevent access to a variety of services that we intend to make accessible to other users on the same network, since it is our goal to demonstrate ways that Linux and Windows systems can interoperate. A tough security policy is a good default for an operating system, but it does not suit our purposes to block the services we'll discuss in this book.

When configuring a server system, be sure to check the Remote Login, Web Server, File Server, and Mail Server boxes on the firewall screen before clicking "Next" to continue.

If you're configuring a client system, leave all the boxes unchecked.

You will make additional adjustments to the firewall configuration in later chapters.

Whether you're building your Fedora client or server, check the SELinux option. SELinux provides fine-grained security checks that further reduce the risk that a misbehaving process will be able to subvert your system.

About SELinux

SELinux is a recent innovation, originally generated under the auspices of the National Security Agency (NSA). Traditionally, Linux processes run under an all-or-nothing security model in which a process such as the web server process had access to any and all resources available to the user ID under which it was run. In the case of the root user ID, this translated to complete control of the system. SELinux introduces a means of fine-grained control over exactly which features of the Linux kernel are available to a given process. The goal is to limit the harm that can be done by a single program in the event of a security compromise. For more information, see the Fedora Linux SELinux FAQ at `http://fedora.redhat.com/docs/selinux-faq-fc3/`.

Additional Options and Root Password

The next screen you'll see is entitled "Additional Language Support." This allows for multiple languages to be displayed in the user interface once the operating system has been successfully installed. Select any preferred language(s) and click "Next" to move on.

FIGURE 1.15   Firewall Configuration screen with choices appropriate for linserv1

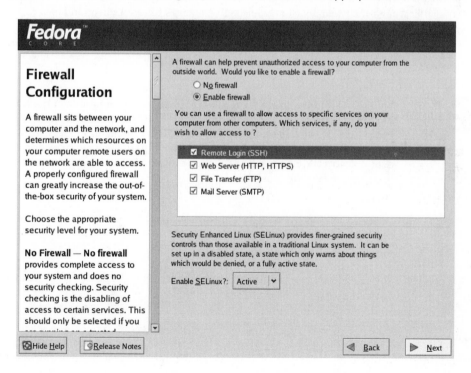

The next screen you'll see is entitled "Time Zone Selection." Select your desired time zone and click "Next" to proceed. Later, we'll address the issue of keeping the system time accurate through the use of a Network Time Protocol (NTP) server.

The next screen is called "Set Root Password." Linux, like other Unix operating systems, always has a "root" account with full administrative access to the system. This is not unlike the "administrator" account on many Windows systems, although the administrative account of a Windows system could be renamed to just about anything.

In a real-world installation, a sound choice of root password involving letters, numbers, and no recognizable words is essential. Strictly for purposes of the examples in this book, however, use the password p@ssw0rd. (That's an "at sign" as the second character and a zero for the letter O.) This password is strong enough for the default strength requirements for both Windows and Linux.

Package Selection

The "Package Group Selection" screen, shown in Figure 1.16, allows you to customize just how much of Fedora Linux you want to install. Since you chose a custom installation rather than one of the prearranged types such as "Personal Desktop" or "Server," you have the opportunity to select all of the packages to meet the needs addressed in this book.

Only the first page of the "Package Group Selection" screen is shown in the figure. You will need to scroll through the package list and select all packages for your client and also for your server configuration, as listed below. Certain packages, such as the development packages and, in the case of a server, the graphical desktop packages, may be unnecessary in your environment, but all are useful for at least one purpose in this book.

 You'll note that we chose the GNOME desktop environment over the K Desktop Environment (KDE). We did so because GNOME is the default desktop in Fedora Linux. We have nothing against KDE but wanted to be consistent throughout the book in our choice of a single graphical user interface wherever possible. When specific KDE applications are useful, you can still run them on the GNOME desktop.

Selected Option	Fedora Server	Fedora Client	Purpose	Chapter
Desktops: X Window System	Y	Y	Foundation of all GUI operations in Linux	All
Desktops: GNOME Desktop	Y	Y	Standard Fedora desktop	All
Applications: Editors	Y	Y	Editing Text	All

Selected Option	Fedora Server	Fedora Client	Purpose	Chapter
Applications: Graphical Internet	Y	Y	Web browser (Firefox)	All, especially 10
Applications: Text-based Internet	Y	Y	wget, other Internet utilities	All ("under the hood" in other tools)
Applications: Office / Productivity	N	Y	Microsoft Office–compatible document handling	9
Servers: Server Configuration Tools	Y	N	Configuring printing, DHCP, other services	All
Servers: Web Server	Y	N	Serving HTTP content	10
Servers: Mail Server (Postfix/IMAP)	Y	N	Delivering e-mail	6
Servers: Windows File Server	Y	N	Windows-compatible file and printer sharing	2, 4, 5
Servers: DNS Name Server	Y	N	DNS resolution for the corp.com domain	All, especially 1
Servers: MySQL Database	Y	N	Data storage and retrieval for websites and collaboration	6, 10
Development: Development Tools	Y	Y	Compiling software from source, developing new software	All ("under the hood" when installing Perl modules and similar), especially 10

Selected Option	Fedora Server	Fedora Client	Purpose	Chapter
Development: X Software Development	N	Y	Compiling software with a GUI	4 (for optional sidebars), 10
Development: GNOME Software Development	N	Y	Compiling software with a GNOME GUI	10
System: Administration Tools	Y	Y	Control Panel–like features of the System Settings menu such as Network Settings, Authentication Settings, etc.	All, especially 2, 3, 4
System: System Tools	Y	Y		
System: Printing Support	Y	Y	Printing, both local and remote	5, 9

FIGURE 1.16 Package Group Selection screen

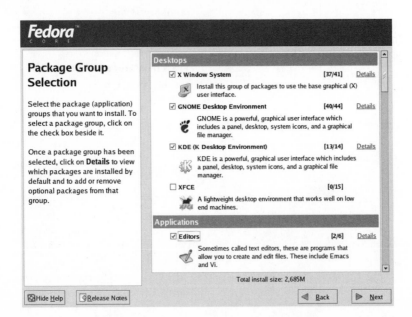

From the appropriate column in the preceding table, select each of the necessary packages in the "Package Selection" screen, then click "Next" to continue.

The "About to Install" screen follows. This screen informs you that the installation process is about to begin copying files to your hard drive. Click "Next" to proceed.

The "Required Install Media" dialog lists the CDs that are required to successfully install your Fedora Linux installation. If you followed the preceding steps exactly and you are using Fedora Core 3 CDs burned to CD-R, you will only require the first three CDs. The first CD should already be in the drive at this point. You may require additional CDs if you chose to install packages not listed above. At the "Required Install Media" dialog, click "Continue" to begin the copying.

The installation process is finally under way! The Fedora installation system will first format the various Linux file systems, then copy packages to disk from CD, and finally configure those packages and bring the system up for your use. This process will take some time, and you will be prompted to insert the second and third CDs at appropriate points.

When all packages have been copied to disk, the "Congratulations" screen as seen in Figure 1.17 will appear, confirming that the basic installation process has succeeded. Remove the last CD from the CD-ROM drive and click "Reboot" to continue.

FIGURE 1.17   The Congratulations screen

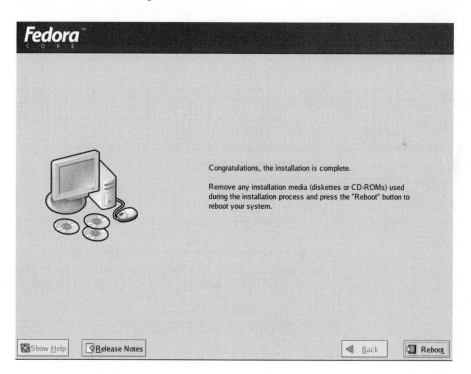

If You Have Linux Installation Problems

If you are installing Fedora on typical hardware that meets the requirements given in this chapter, it is reasonable to assume that you will reach this point without incident. However, it is always possible that something will go wrong.

The most common cause of Fedora Linux installation failure is a lack of Linux drivers for critical hardware. Perhaps you have a wireless Ethernet port or SATA (Serial ATA, where ATA stands for "AT Attachment," dating back to the IBM AT days) hard drive interface that is not properly recognized by Linux. At this point, the cleanest way to work around these problems is to avoid the hardware in question, at least until your system is fully installed and you are able to run the update agent and obtain a newer kernel which supports your hardware. In the case of Wi-Fi, you can most easily work around this by using a wired Ethernet connection. Wired Ethernet ports not supported by Linux are very rare at this point.

In the case of SATA, there is typically a first hard drive in the system that is not on a SATA interface. Consult the hardware compatibility lists mentioned earlier in this chapter before buying, especially with regard to SATA chipsets. And, of course, if Fedora Core 4 has been released by the time you read this, start with that version. You are much more likely to find that drivers for your newer hardware are included.

If your graphics card is partially recognized but you do not find the graphics resolution displayed to be satisfactory, it may be simpler to continue with the installation process and experiment with the system configuration tools after fetching updated packages. If a serious problem that causes your system to lock up or fail to recognize your network card persists, consider simplifying your system by removing hardware that you do not actually require, such as nonstandard audio cards.

Most of the remaining cases of installation failure are caused by overly creative option selections from screens such as the Disk Partitioning screen. If you have deviated from the steps suggested in this chapter, we recommend that you begin the installation process from scratch and follow the text precisely.

In rare cases, installation failure may be caused by defective hardware. The installation of a new operating system does occasionally reveal a damaged processor or damaged RAM; failing parts that manage not to reveal their problems while carrying out one well-worn series of tasks may suddenly reveal their defects when new tasks are attempted. We recommend installing Linux on relatively new hardware when possible, especially if your goal is to build a production server.

Post-Installation Configuration

Upon a successful reboot, Fedora will display the "Welcome" screen seen in Figure 1.18, explaining that a few post-installation questions must be answered to complete configuration of the system.

Specifically, you'll have to buzz through the following screens:

- License Agreement
- Date and Time
- Display
- System User
- Sound Card
- Additional CDs
- Finish Setup

Click "Next" to proceed.

FIGURE 1.18 The Welcome screen

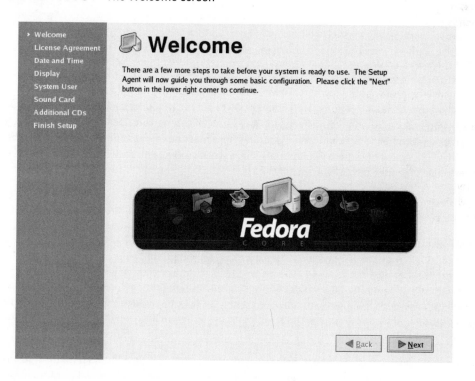

License Agreement

The next screen, entitled "License Agreement," will display the Fedora Linux license agreement. When you have finished reading the license agreement, click "Yes, I agree to the License Agreement" and then click "Next" to continue.

Date and Time

The next screen is "Date and Time." These may already be correct if your system clock is set properly. The default is 24-hour military style time (13:00 for 1:00pm). Correct the date and time if necessary, then click "Next" to go on.

Linux, Open Source, the GPL, and Other Open Source Licenses

Every component of Fedora Linux can be freely copied and redistributed. This is in sharp contrast to traditional closed-source software. This is also in contrast to other Linux distributions that contain commercial software along with open source software (OSS). For example, SuSE and Mandrake have license agreements that state they cannot be freely copied and redistributed.

The Linux operating system "kernel" at the heart of Fedora is distributed under the terms of the GPL (GNU General Public License), one of many open source licenses. GNU is a recursive acronym for "GNU's Not UNIX" and is found at www.gnu.org.

This license expressly permits you to make as many copies of the kernel as you wish, grants you full access to the source code, and requires you to share the source code to any changes you make if you choose to share your changes in any form. Of course, this does *not* mean that every document or program you create on a Fedora system must be released under the terms of the GPL. The GPL does not require you to freely share work products made with the licensed software, only changes to the software itself.

Many parts of Fedora are released under licenses more permissive than the GPL with regard to keeping your changes private. For instance, applications linked with the GNOME libraries can be sold commercially as closed-source software without violating the terms of the LGPL (Lesser General Public License), which allows such activities provided that any changes *to the libraries themselves* are shared freely with the public in accordance with the GLPL.

Although the software that makes up Fedora is open source, there are trademarked graphics present in the system. With those images removed, though, the entire Fedora system could be redistributed under a new name without violating the software licenses involved. We mention this to illustrate just how thoroughly open the licensing of Fedora Linux is.

Open source licensing ensures that the hard work of free software developers remains free and continues to grow and improve to the benefit of the entire Linux community. For more information about the GPL and open source licensing, visit www.fsf.org.

Display

The next screen, titled "Display," asks you to select your monitor type, indicate how many colors should be simultaneously displayed, and select a screen resolution. If your video card was properly recognized, you should be able to select 1024×768 or a higher resolution and millions of colors. It is not uncommon or cause for concern to see "Unknown Monitor" listed as the monitor type. If your video card was not immediately recognized, you should still be able to select a lower resolution such as 640×480. In some cases, the Fedora hardware detection system may be overly optimistic about the maximum resolution of your graphics card. Compare the claimed resolution to what you actually know about your hardware's capabilities. If possible, pick a resolution that is already known to work with the same video hardware in Windows. Then click "Next" to continue.

If your display does not appear normally after a few seconds, it may be that the Fedora hardware detection system did not correctly sense the limits of your graphics card. Unfortunately, you will probably have to reboot at this point and repeat the installation to this stage. When you reach this point again, we recommend selecting a lower screen resolution, which often avoids the problem.

WARNING   If you're performing your tests with VMware, you'll need to load the VMware tools for optimal viewing. See Chapter 7 for more on VMware and a sidebar on how to install the VMware tools within Linux.

Using the System User Screen to Create an Unprivileged User Account

While it is possible to operate a Linux system exclusively while logged in as the root user, this is usually not a wise choice. The use of the root account for all activities means that an accidental misstep while deleting files can lead to the loss of crucial system files, like the contents of the /bin or /etc directories. Linux uses file permissions and ownership to ensure that the root password must be presented in order to perform various hazardous activities. Similarly, Windows 2003 and Windows XP enforce security permissions for a variety of crucial files in C:\Windows, certain critical registry keys, and so on.

Fedora Linux user account names should be 32 characters or less and must not contain uppercase letters or spaces. Use the Full Name field to enter the proper name of the user, such as **Thomas Boutell**.

In a production environment, you should select a password made up of both letters and numbers and containing no recognizable words. Your password must be at least six characters long. Strictly for purposes of this book, however, we have used the user account name homestar and the password p@ssw0rd. (That's an "at sign" as the second character and a zero for the letter O.)

As shown in Figure 1.19, enter the user account name, full user name, and password that you prefer, and click "Next" to move on.

FIGURE 1.19   System User screen

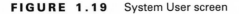

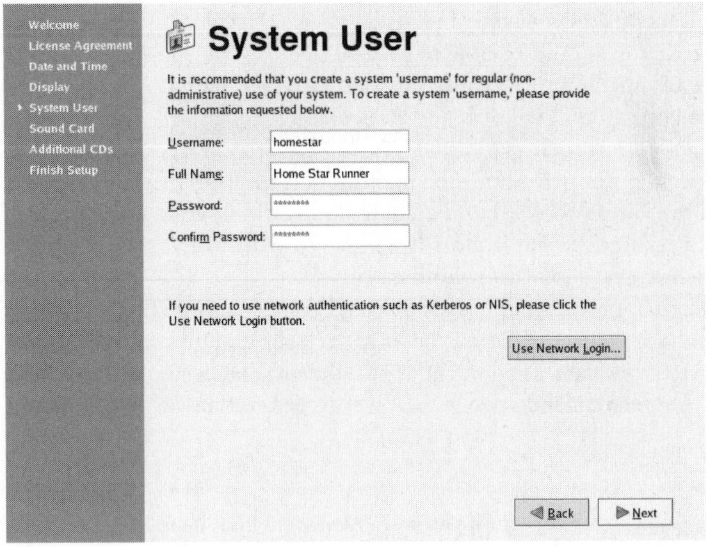

Sound Card

At the "Sound Card" screen, you will be prompted to test your sound hardware by listening to a test sound. (Older versions of Linux were very hit-or-miss when it came to sound production, so we think the Linux installation guys just want to prove now that they "do" sound by giving it its very own screen.)

If you wish to have sound capabilities, click "Play test sound," then click "Yes" when asked to confirm that you were able to hear the sound. If sound does not play, you may have better luck later after updating the kernel. However, sound is not used in any of the examples in this book, so there's no immediate cause for concern. Now click "Next" to continue.

You will be prompted at this time to supply any additional CDs of third-party Red Hat Linux-compatible software installation programs that you wish to use. For purposes of this book, and for most users in general, this will not be necessary; additional software is usually installed later via the up2date and rpm package managers discussed later in this chapter. Click "Next" to proceed.

First Login

You've finally make it to the "Finish Setup" screen. You can now use your Fedora Linux system. However, before your system is ready for serious use, you still need to fetch software updates via the Internet in order to address any security problems discovered after the release of the current version of Fedora Linux. The updates you'll receive also include bug fixes in general; not all fixes available are for security holes. Click "Next" to move on.

The Fedora Linux login prompt will now appear. In the "Fedora Core" logon screen, as shown in Figure 1.20, enter the name of your user account (yes, your nonroot account).

FIGURE 1.20   Username screen

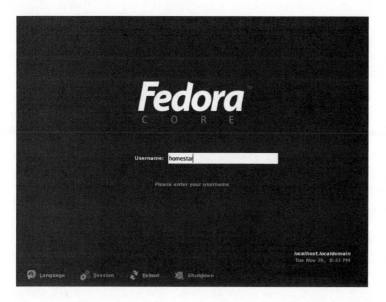

Log into the homestar account you created in Figure 1.19. After entering the username, press Enter to move on to the Password screen. Again, the password for the example is p@ssw0rd. Fedora Linux will now launch the GNOME desktop.

The Linux Desktop: GNOME and KDE

The Microsoft Windows platform has a single user interface standard; every user knows what a dialog box will look like, or should look like, on any given version of Windows.

The Linux platform does not currently have a single dominant user interface. At present, there are two competing standards, GNOME (GNU Network Object Model Environment) and KDE (the K Desktop Environment). Both are open source projects, although there are significant licensing differences between the two:

- GNOME licensing

    As mentioned earlier, software linked with the GNOME libraries can be sold commercially as closed-source software without violating the terms of the LGPL (Lesser General Public License). The LGPL allows such activities provided that any changes *to the libraries themselves* are shared freely with the public in accordance with the GLPL.

> ▪ KDE licensing
>
>> Those developing software for KDE must choose between license fees for the underlying Qt user interface toolkit and releasing their own product as open source under the GPL. Before you ask, the name Qt was chosen because it didn't conflict with existing toolkits, and the Q looked good in the developer's favorite terminal window font!
>
> This dual licensing is not unreasonable, but it does make the GNOME desktop more attractive to some developers. Still, the general excellence of each system continues to drive healthy competition between them.
>
> For purposes of this book, we will use the GNOME desktop; most Linux–Windows interoperability concerns are not significantly affected by the choice of GNOME or KDE, and applications written for GNOME can operate correctly under the KDE desktop, and vice versa.

Fetching Updates

At this point, it may appear that you are done; the operating system and the desktop user interface are up and running. If you click the Applications menu next to the Fedora icon in the upper-left corner, which is analogous to the Microsoft Windows Start menu, you will discover that a variety of applications are available. However, just as with Microsoft Windows, it is crucial to obtain updated versions of system software via the Internet to avoid security and stability problems.

While unpatched Fedora Linux systems are not typically compromised immediately once introduced onto the Internet, it is still crucial to take security seriously, and the automatic updating of other applications that are part of the system is a cool additional benefit.

As seen in Figure 1.21, you will note the appearance of a white exclamation point in a red circle in the upper-right corner of the display.

This is an invitation to use the built-in **up2date** tool to fetch operating system updates. Much like Microsoft Windows Update (which you'll use later), the Fedora **up2date** tool makes it possible to painlessly apply important security and bug fixes to software on your system, as well as offering the opportunity to install new software. When the exclamation point is animated, this is an indication that new updates are available. Click the exclamation point to begin the update process for the first time and install fixes for flaws discovered after Fedora Core 3 was originally released.

FIGURE 1.21   Desktop with up2date icon

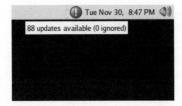

When you click the exclamation point, the Red Hat Network Alert Notification Tool will appear, listing the packages that have been updated. To actually install these updates, you will need to click the "launch up2date" button. Do so to continue.

You'll be prompted to provide the root password. This is required because up2date can be used to add or remove any software package from the system, a privilege reserved for the root user. Enter the root password, which is p@ssw0rd in the examples, and click "OK."

The next dialog box gives you an opportunity to select the Red Hat Network Server you wish to fetch updates from. We recommend clicking OK to select the default, which should be reasonable for all typical installations. This will be followed by a message explaining, somewhat obscurely, that all Fedora packages are cryptographically "signed" with a secure key to verify their identity. Click "Yes" to accept this key as your indication that packages have not been modified by third parties.

The Red Hat Update Agent will now launch. Click "Forward" to move past the initial welcome screen. On the "Channels" screen that follows, you will note that files from the fedora-core-3 and updates-released-fc3 channels are available; you want both of these and they are selected by default, so click "Forward" again to move on.

The next screen, "Packages Flagged to be Skipped," does require some action on your part. By default, Fedora is configured not to fetch new operating system kernels, but there have in fact been significant security flaws found in Linux kernels in the past few years, so we strongly recommend that you check the box next to the kernel package before clicking "Forward," as shown in Figure 1.22. Yes indeed, you *do* need to check the check box, though it might appear that you should do the opposite. It's a badly formed dialog box, to say the least. In any event, ensure it is checked as seen in Figure 1.22 and continue.

FIGURE 1.22   Packages flagged to be skipped

Similarly, on the "Available Package Updates" screen that follows, you should update every package you have installed. Be sure to check the "Select all packages" box before clicking "Forward."

Once you have completed these steps, the actual process of retrieving updated packages from the Internet can begin. Your system may take some time to download all of the updates, especially if you choose to do so during business hours or right after a hot patch comes out. The downloading and installation steps are presented separately, with all downloads taking place before any packages are installed. Just click "Forward" when each step completes; when both stages are finished you will be rewarded an up2date Finish page.

Unfortunately, up2date will occasionally stall for long periods and fail to complete the update. Since the up2date servers for Fedora are free, they do sometimes become overwhelmed. If up2date stalls for an extended period of time, it may be necessary to use the "Cancel" button and start the process again at an off-peak time.

Congratulations! Your system is now protected against any security exploits currently known to the Fedora package maintainers.

Leveraging Webmin

For Linux administration, the command line is king. However, a GUI interface can be added to do a huge percentage of the administration duties. One such tool is called Webmin. Webmin provides a web browser–based interface to administer most aspects of a Unix/Linux server. Webmin provides useful capabilities that in some cases go beyond what is supported by Fedora's GUI-based configuration tools. Since Webmin is browser-based, it can also offer the additional advantages of convenient remote administration.

Generally speaking, Webmin excels at configuring the features that most Unix systems include, such as printer administration, file sharing, and so on. To that end, we will use it for such tasks in subsequent chapters. An additional bonus of using Webmin is that if you decide to use another Linux distribution—say, SuSE or Mandrake—the skills you learn in Webmin are portable across nearly all Linux platforms. This makes it especially attractive.

There are times when you won't be able to use Webmin to perform a task. For instance, some cutting-edge features such as Linux to Active Directory authentication (discussed in Chapter 3) and less frequently used features are less likely to be thoroughly supported by Webmin. We have chosen not to install Webmin on client systems where Fedora's graphical administration tools are sufficient to do most jobs.

Accordingly, we rely on the built-in Fedora GUI or command line when required and appropriate.

Installing Webmin

We have already discussed the up2date package manager. Programs that are a standard part of Fedora can be easily installed via up2date. Unfortunately, Webmin is not yet among these.

However, the authors of Webmin have made an RPM package available.

About RPMs

RPM (Red Hat Package Manager) is a system that goes back to the very first days of the Red Hat Linux distribution. RPM files provide not just a way to store application files, but also the scripts to correctly install and initially configure them. RPMs also contain version control and dependency information that the system can use to determine whether required prerequisites are also installed; if not, the rpm command refrains from installing the software until the administrator installs the prerequisites.

The friendly up2date interface is layered on top of the yum package manager, which is layered on top of rpm. yum provides ways of locating the RPMs you need to achieve a particular goal automatically. However, not every program that is available in RPM format is part of the official Fedora Core 3 repository or an alternative repository that provides similar services, so it is not uncommon to manually download RPM files and install them with the rpm command.

To download the Webmin software to LinServ1, visit the Webmin website with the Firefox browser, easily launched via the Applications menu or by clicking the web browser icon to the right of the Applications and Actions menus. The URL of the site is www.webmin.com.

Click "Downloading and Installing" to reach the download page. Finally, click the "RPM suitable for Redhat" link. Or perhaps by the time you read this, the website may be updated to offer a download specifically for Fedora. Note that you do *not* want to download the source RPM. You will save time and effort by using already-compiled software. Select a nearby download mirror server on the page that follows.

Firefox will display a dialog box offering to open the RPM file with the "Install Packages" tool. In our experience, this approach was not successful and did not provide meaningful feedback, so we recommend that you check the "Save to Disk" box instead and click OK as shown in Figure 1.23.

FIGURE 1.23   Downloading Webmin

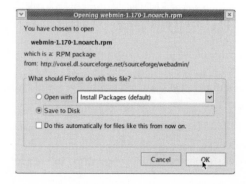

Once the download operation is complete, you're ready to install the rpm package. To do so, you will need to make your first use of the command-line shell prompt, otherwise known as the Bash shell. To access the command line, click the Fedora icon in the upper-left corner, select System Tools, and finally, select Terminal.

Terminals and Shells

The Linux terminal window and Windows' cmd.exe command prompt are analogous. Unlike the Windows command prompt, however, the Bash shell is still very much an integral and respectable part of the operating system. While the design of Windows allows essentially all operations to be performed without the use of the command shell even at the lowest level, many operations in Linux are still performed via Bash shell scripts analogous to batch files in the DOS and Windows environments. Of course, it is perfectly possible to wrap a graphical interface around these scripts, and this is how user-friendly administration tools for Linux often work under the hood.

Basic Bash shell commands include ls, which lists the contents of the current or another directory; rm, which removes files; mv, which renames files; nano, a simple text file editor; and man, which can be used to read documentation of any command available on the system. Another noteworthy shell command is apropos, which fetches a list of manpages (documents that can be read with the man command) that relate to a particular topic. For instance, apropos nano lists all manual pages that are relevant to the nano text editor. To learn more about any of these commands, just type man *command* to read the relevant documentation. Press q to close the man page and return to the shell.

As it stands, you're currently logged in as homestar, your mere mortal user. But you want to update your system, and mere mortals cannot do this on their own. Therefore, elevate your privileges and temporarily log on as root. Do this with the su - command, which stands for Super User. The dash following su specifies that you should log in fully as root, which gives you the benefit of root's settings for things such as the PATH environment variable. That means that commands like service and chkconfig that root uses can often be found automatically in /sbin or /usr/sbin.

Once you type su - at the command prompt, you'll be prompted for the root password, which you set to p@ssw0rd.

Once you log in as root, the terminal prompt changes to the # symbol, a useful indication that you are acting with root's full authority.

WARNING   If you receive "command not found" errors when running some commands as root, make sure you used su - and not just su to switch to the root account.

You're ready to install the RPM package. At the terminal prompt, enter the following command, changing the name of the RPM file to match its current version as shown on the Webmin site.

Note that the following command assumes that you accepted the default download location when downloading the file with the Firefox browser. By default, Firefox saves downloaded files to the home directory of the user running Firefox, `homestar` in this case. When you gave the `su -` command, you assumed root's identity, but the current working directory remained set to `/home/homestar`. If you saved the file in an alternate location, you'll need to substitute the path where you saved the file.

```
rpm -i webmin-1.170-1.noarch.rpm
```

The word noarch, in this case, means "no architecture." In other words, this RPM is not specific to a particular binary platform such as the Intel architecture. Be sure not to pick the source RPM, which won't do what you expect when you use the simple installation command given.

The `-i` (install) option instructs the `rpm` package manager to install the specified package on your system.

The preceding command should produce output similar to the following:

```
warning: webmin-1.170-1.noarch.rpm: V3 DSA signature: NOKEY, key ID 11f63c51
Operating system is Redhat Linux Fedora 3
Webmin install complete. You can now login to http://linserv1.corp.com:10000/
as root with your root password.
```

Accessing Webmin for the First Time

Return to the Firefox browser and access this URL:

```
http://localhost:10000/
```

Complete the login prompt shown in Figure 1.24 with `root` as the username and `p@ssw0rd` (in our example) as the password. Then click the "Login" button to continue.

Note that you are entering your root password into a web form. What's more—that form *does not* use SSL encryption for security. Does this sound like a safe thing to do? Turns out, yes!—but only if you enabled Fedora's firewall at installation time. By default, port 10000 is not open to connections from other machines in Fedora's firewall configuration, so Webmin can so far only be accessed from the server itself. A bit later, you'll enable secure remote access to Webmin.

Once you complete the login prompt, Webmin will display its web-based interface, as shown in Figure 1.25.

FIGURE 1.24   Logging in to Webmin

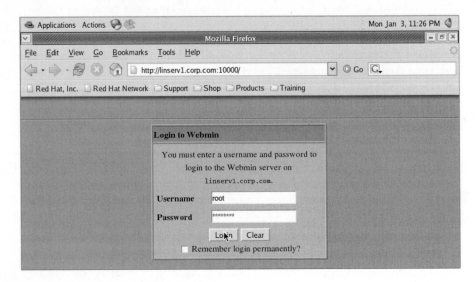

FIGURE 1.25   Webmin user interface

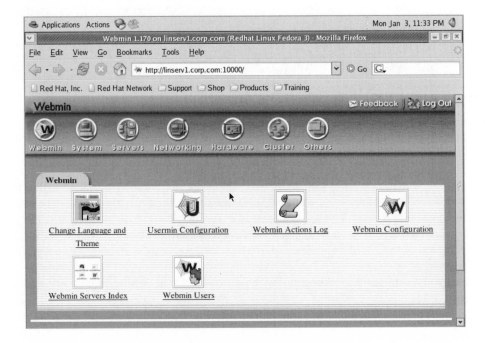

Securing Webmin for Remote Access

One of Webmin's greatest features is remote administration, but how do you make that operation safe? By enabling SSL encryption, the technology used by all secure websites, that's how.

First, click "Webmin Configuration." On the page that follows, click "SSL encryption."

The next page will display bad news: Webmin is written in the Perl programming language, and Fedora Core 3 does not ship support for SSL with Perl, so you'll need to install that support. But this is where you get your first taste of Webmin's system administration power: Webmin offers to install the required modules for Perl by itself!

Click the "download and install the required Net::SSLeay module for you" link to begin the process.

The progress display page will keep you updated as the required files are downloaded, then present you with a list of "Perl module install options." The key word here is *options*! You don't want to pass any additional parameters to Perl's module configuration process. Just click "Continue With Install" to move ahead.

As Webmin must configure, compile, and install Perl modules behind the scenes using your system's development tools, the next page will take longer to complete. Don't interrupt your browser; just be patient. When the process completes, scroll down to the end of the page, and you should see a display similar to Figure 1.26.

FIGURE 1.26   Webmin after successful `Net_SSLeay.pm` installation

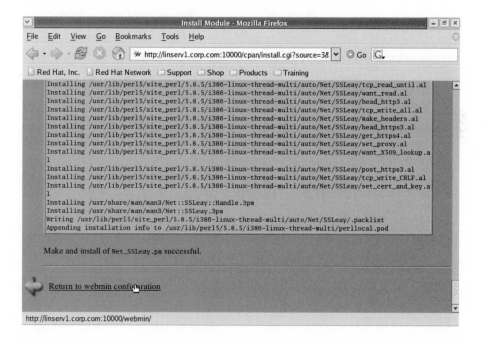

To finish the job, click "Return to Webmin configuration." On the page that follows, click SSL Encryption again. This time, you will see a different screen, one which announces that your system *does* have support for SSL in Perl programs. As part of configuring Webmin itself, you have completed your first successful system administration task via Webmin.

Just one step to go! Scroll part way down the page to reveal the form shown in Figure 1.27 and complete it as shown, then click the "Save" button. You are instructing Webmin to accept only secure logins.

When you click Save, Webmin will redirect you to a secure URL, and Firefox will display a dialog box warning you that the identity of the website cannot be verified. This is not cause for great concern. The encryption key provided with Webmin is simply not signed by one of the major certificate authorities (like Verisign), because this would involve needless expense for each and every Webmin installation. But you already know that you are talking to the system you intended to talk to. You simply want the conversation to be secured using a certificate you trust (even if it doesn't come from a company like Verisign). We suggest clicking either "accept this certificate for this session" or "accept this certificate permanently."

If you are not immediately redirected, you may receive a warning message instead suggesting that you change http:// to https:// in the URL you are accessing. Edit the URL shown in the address bar at the top of the Firefox window and press Enter to load the secure version of the page.

FIGURE 1.27   Webmin SSL support form

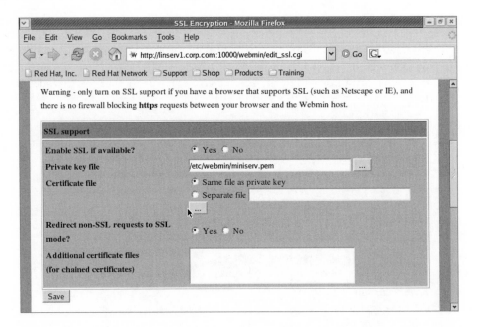

There *is* one real security concern here—if you are concerned about IP address and DNS spoofing attacks. While difficult, these attacks are possible if you are accessing Webmin remotely from outside your company's network *and* your routers are in some way compromised. If you're concerned, you may prefer to generate your own secure key for Webmin. This ensures that you can tell the difference if a completely bogus `linserv1.corp.com` is substituted by an extremely clever hacker in a man-in-the-middle attack. If you are keen to pursue this issue, simply scroll further down the SSL Encryption page and explore the possibilities of the key generation form.

After a moment, Firefox will be redirected to a slightly different URL:
`https://linserv1.corp.com:10000/`

That extra `s` in `https` makes all the difference! Now that your copy of Webmin requires a secure connection, you can allow system administration from remote desktops. And when your server is a box in a rack, that's a good thing.

Allowing Webmin through the Firewall

In order to remotely administer your system via Webmin, you'll need to relax Fedora's firewall rules to allow connections on port 10000. Click Applications ➢ System Settings ➢ Security Level. Enter the root password when prompted.

In the Security Level application shown in Figure 1.28, add the port `10000:tcp` to the comma-separated list of ports to be allowed through the firewall, as shown in the figure. Then click "OK."

Finally, try accessing `https://192.168.2.202:10000/` from `linclil.corp.com` or another desktop on the network. Congratulations! You can now perform many system administration tasks remotely and in many cases with considerably greater flexibility than that provided by the Fedora tools.

FIGURE 1.28   Security level configuration

Active Directory under One Roof

As we stated at the beginning of the chapter, it is common to find the Unix/Linux staff "owning" the internal DNS. However, the Active Directory folks need their own DNS sandbox. Hence, they need what's called a *delegated subdomain* to allow them near autonomy in their own world without disturbing the existing DNS.

Using Linux to Create a DNS Server and a Delegated Subdomain

To create a DNS domain, `corp.com`, you need a DNS server to answer queries about that domain. It needs to hand out all sorts of information about computers in `corp.com`, such as the IP address of its client systems or the IP address of the mail server. And your Linux server can do this job beautifully.

However, some of your systems will be part of a DNS subdomain, `ad.corp.com`. That allows you to have a separate namespace for machines that are part of your Active Directory domain. And you can configure the DNS server to expressly delegate queries regarding the `ad.corp.com` subdomain to the server you're creating for Active Directory. The first Domain Controller in `ad.corp.com` will be WinDC1 with a fully qualified domain name of `windc1.ad.corp.com`.

Previously, we elected to install DNS while bringing the first Linux server online. Here, you'll turn on that DNS service and configure it to respond directly to queries about hosts in the `corp.com` domain, such as `linserv1.corp.com` itself. You'll also configure it to tell clients that they should send queries regarding the `ad.corp.com` subdomain to the Windows Domain Controller. That means that the Linux server doesn't have to be explicitly aware of each and every Active Directory domain member. Nor does the Windows Active Directory server have to be aware of every system in the `corp.com` domain that is not a domain member.

By the time you're done, all of your Linux clients in `corp.com` should be able to "see" any Windows client that's registered in the `ad.corp.com` Windows DNS.

Configuring the DNS Server with Webmin

Now that you have Webmin installed, you can take advantage of it to set up DNS in a relatively painless way. First, log in to Webmin. Then select Networking ➢ BIND DNS Server. This page provides tools to configure the BIND (Berkeley Internet Name Daemon) DNS server.

Here you can configure general settings that affect the server as a whole. You'll want to:

- Configure forwarding for queries about domains other than `corp.com` itself.
- Add "A" (address records) to resolve the names of your host systems in the `corp.com` domain to IP addresses.
- Set up subdomain delegation, instructing clients to send queries regarding the `ad.corp.com` subdomain to `windc1.ad.corp.com`.

Forwarding for Queries Outside the *corp.com* Domain

Other systems within the corp.com domain will be looking to linserv1.corp.com to answer *all* of their DNS queries. But naturally linserv1 is not authoritative for other domains beyond corp.com, such as winlinanswers.com. When a client asks linserv1 for the IP address of www.WinLinAnswers.com, the BIND DNS server software can ferret out the answer directly. Depending on your networking equipment, you might have a router that also acts as a DNS server (that's what we have on our network). Forward queries for which you are not authoritative to your router, 192.168.2.1, in this example. As a fallback, you'll also configure the server to look things up directly if the forwarder you send the query to doesn't respond.

To configure forwarding options for the DNS server, follow these steps:

1. Log into Webmin as described above.
2. Click on "Servers."
3. Click on "BIND DNS Server."
4. Click on "Forwarding and Transfers."
5. In the "IP address" column of the "Servers to forward queries to" table, enter **192.168.2.1**, as shown in Figure 1.29.
6. Select "Yes" for "Lookup directly if no response from forwarder."
7. For "Maximum zone transfer time", select "Default."
8. For "Zone transfer format", select "Default."
9. For "Maximum concurrent zone transfers," select "Default."
10. Click "Save." You will be returned to the "BIND DNS Server" page.

FIGURE 1.29 Forwarding configuration for DNS

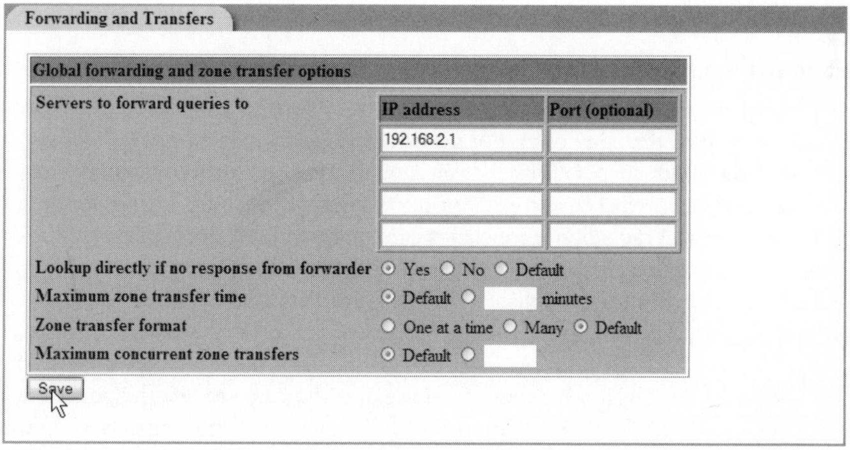

Creating the *corp.com* DNS Zone

Linserv1 is ultimately responsible, or authoritative, for all queries about hosts in the `corp.com` domain. With the exception of hosts in the `ad.corp.com` subdomain, it should answer those queries directly. You're almost ready to add address records, known as "A" records, for each host in the `corp.com` domain that is not in the `ad.corp.com` subdomain.

But first, you need to create a DNS zone for the `corp.com` domain. In BIND, a zone is a particular domain or other entity for which the server is configured to respond to queries. You'll do this using the "Create Master Zone" link on the "BIND DNS Server" page, which is counter-intuitively hidden away in the "Existing DNS Zones" section. A master zone is one for which the server holds the records directly, rather than fetching them from another master. Master-slave DNS configuration is beyond the scope of this book. Your zone will be a forward lookup zone, meaning that it resolves names to IP addresses. You'll designate `linserv1` as the master server—the first and only DNS server for `corp.com` in this simple configuration. You'll also specify a contact e-mail address for DNS-related questions from other administrators.

To create the `corp.com` DNS zone, follow these steps, continuing from where you left off:

1. Immediately beneath "Existing DNS Zones," click "Create Master Zone."
2. The "Create Master Zone" page appears.
3. For "Zone Type," choose "Forward (Names to Addresses)."
4. For "Domain name / Network," enter **corp.com**.
5. For "Records file," choose "Automatic."
6. For "Master server," enter **linserv1.corp.com**.
7. For "Email address," enter **root@corp.com**.
8. Accept the defaults for the remaining settings, which are beyond the scope of this book.
9. Click "Create" to create the zone.
10. The "Edit Master Zone" page appears.

Adding Address Records for Hosts in the *corp.com* Domain

Now you can add the "A" records for the two hosts in `corp.com`, `linserv1.corp.com` and `linclil.corp.com`, that are not part of the `ad.corp.com` subdomain. You will also add an "A" record for `windc1.ad.corp.com` itself, even though it *is* a part of the `ad.corp.com` subdomain. You do this to avoid a "chicken and egg" problem. When you delegate queries for the `ad.corp.com` subdomain to `windc1.ad.corp.com`, clients can't ask `windc1.ad.corp.com` to look up its own address! You escape this problem by adding an "A" record for this one host on the Linux server.

Adding "A" records is accomplished very easily with Webmin. When you complete the "Create Master Zone" page, you are automatically taken to the "Edit Master Zone" page. Here you can click "Address" to add your "A" records. On the Add Address Record page, enter hostnames and IP addresses. Here you can choose to abbreviate the name to just the portion without the domain (for example, `linclil`) or specify the full name with a trailing period (`.`) to signify that the domain should not be appended (for example, `windc1.ad.corp.com.`). You'll use the first form for `linclil` and `linserv1` and the second form for `windc1.ad.corp.com` because the shorter version, `windc1.ad`, is more than a bit confusing!

To add "A" records for the hosts in the `corp.com` domain, just continue with these steps:

1. Click "Address" (the giant "A" icon, hard to miss!) The "Add Address Record" page appears.

2. In the "Name" field, enter `linserv1`.

3. In the "Address" field, enter `192.168.2.202`.

4. Accept the defaults for the remaining options, which are beyond the scope of this book.

5. Click "Create" to add the address record. The "Add Address Record" page reappears, ready to accept another address record.

6. Repeat steps 2–5 with the name `lincli1` and the address `192.168.2.203`.

7. Repeat steps 2–5 with the name `windcl.ad.corp.com.` (note the trailing `.`, which is required) and the address `192.168.2.226`.

8. Click "Module Index" to return to the "BIND DNS Server" page.

Delegating the *ad.corp.com* Subdomain to the Active Directory Server

You've come to the final stage of DNS configuration. You're ready to delegate queries regarding the `ad.corp.com` subdomain to `windcl.ad.corp.com`, the Active Directory server. To do that, you'll need to add an additional name server or NS record to the `corp.com` zone.

To delegate queries for the `ad.corp.com` subdomain to `windcl.ad.corp.com`, follow these steps:

1. Scroll down if necessary and click `corp.com` near the bottom of the "BIND DNS Server" page, under the "Existing DNS Zones" heading. The "Edit Master Zone" page appears.

2. Click the "Name Server" icon.

3. In the "Zone Name" field, enter `ad.corp.com`.

4. In the "Name Server" field, enter `windcl.ad.corp.com.` (note the trailing period (`.`), which is required).

5. Accept the default for the "Time-To-Live" field.

6. Click "Create" to add the NS record.

Starting the DNS Server, Now and on Every Reboot

That's it—your Linux DNS configuration is complete! To start the DNS server, simply use the "Start DNS Server" link on the "BIND DNS Server" page. Then, since this feature is absent from Webmin, you'll need to take care of a few command-line steps to ensure that BIND is restarted every time the system reboots.

Starting the DNS server is the easiest part. Follow these steps:

1. Click "Module Index" if the "BIND DNS Server" page is not already displayed.

2. Scroll to the bottom of the page.

3. Click "Start Name Server." That's it!

Configuring the DNS server to restart every time you reboot linserv1 is just a little bit harder. When you selected packages to install on your Linux server (linserv1), you included the DNS server package. The necessary software is already present on the server but has not yet been configured to start running each time the server is rebooted. Fortunately, there's a simple command-line utility the root user can use to configure Fedora to start various services at boot time. That utility is called chkconfig.

Every service in Fedora Linux is controlled by a script in the directory /etc/init.d. One of these is /etc/init.d/named, which controls the naming daemon (the BIND DNS server). Fedora decides which of these scripts should actually be run at startup time. The chkconfig command configures Fedora to include or exclude various scripts from the list to actually be started at boot time and stopped at system halt time.

A thoroughly optional note for experts: the "list" of scripts to be started at boot time is actually implemented as a subdirectory containing cleverly named symbolic links to the scripts. These symbolic links are given numeric names that lead them to sort in the correct order so that the services start in the right order. You can see some of these symbolic links in the directory /etc/rc3.d. However, a full discussion of the rcN.d directories is beyond the scope of this book, since chkconfig does the job very well.

To ensure the DNS server is always activated upon reboot:

1. To access the command line, click the Fedora icon in the upper-left corner and select System Tools ➢ Terminal.

2. When the terminal window appears, type **su -** and press Enter to switch to the root user account. Enter the root password when prompted (**p@ssw0rd** in our examples).

3. At the prompt, instruct the server to activate the DNS server on future reboots by entering the command **chkconfig named on**.

Yes, the word really is named, and it is pronounced *name dee*. This is the naming daemon.

If the chkconfig utility complains that the named service is not installed (possibly because you did not select that package when installing Fedora), it's not too late to solve the problem. You can install it now via the up2date package manager utility, accessible by selecting Applications ➢ System Settings ➢ Add / Remove Applications. If the chkconfig command is not found, double-check your su command. If you didn't include the -, type **exit** to go back to your non-root account, then do su - again to ensure you have your PATH environment variable set up correctly to find chkconfig and similar utilities.

Allowing DNS Queries through the Firewall

You configured your Linux server with a strong firewall that doesn't allow most traffic through. In order to accept DNS queries from other systems, you must relax Fedora's firewall rules to allow connections on port 53. You'll need to allow both UDP and TCP traffic. The DNS standard allows both types, and Windows systems in particular sometimes take advantage of the TCP option in addition to the more common UDP method.

Select Applications ➤ System Settings ➤ Security Level. Enter the root password when prompted.

In the Security Level application shown previously in Figure 1.28, add the ports `53:tcp` and `53:udp` to the comma-separated list of ports to be allowed through the firewall. Then click "OK."

Testing the DNS Server

You now have a DNS server that can answer simple queries about two hosts in the `corp.com` domain. You can verify your success by using the host command to look up the address of `linclil.corp.com`:

```
host linclil.corp.com
```

This will produce the following output:

```
linclil.corp.com has address 192.168.2.203
```

You are also ready to forward all queries regarding hosts in the `ad.corp.com` subdomain to the Active Directory server. Now it's time to actually set up Active Directory on your Windows server. *Once your Active Directory server is up and running*, you can test the delegation easily using the following command:

```
host myhost.ad.corp.com
```

Where *myhost* is, of course, the name of a host that exists in the Active Directory. Again, in our little world, Active Directory doesn't yet exist. That's what you'll do next.

Setting an Authoritative Time Source for Linux

How can you keep the clocks of your Linux and Windows systems synchronized? The best way is to configure them to use the same authoritative time source. You'll configure `linserv1.corp.com` to use the master time servers at the United States Naval Observatory, and you'll configure `linclil.corp.com` and other Linux systems to use `linserv1.corp.com` as a time source. You can accomplish these things thanks to Fedora's support for the Network Time Protocol, or NTP.

To configure `linserv1.corp.com` as an authoritative time source:

1. Select Applications ➤ System Settings ➤ Date & Time. The "Date/Time Properties" tool appears.

2. Click the "Network Time Protocol" tab.

3. Check the "Enable Network Time Protocol" box.

4. Select the first server listed in the list box and click "Delete" to remove it.

5. Repeat step 4 for all of the remaining servers.

6. In the "Server:" field, enter **192.5.41.40**.

7. Click "Add."

8. Repeat steps 8 and 9, this time entering the server **192.5.41.41**.

9. Click "OK" to save your work.

That completes NTP configuration for linserv1. For lincli1, follow the same steps, except that you should add linserv1.corp.com as the only NTP server.

Installing Your Active Directory

Now that the Linux folks have delegated ad.corp.com to the Windows folks, you'll be ready to proceed. To have an Active Directory, you need a Domain Controller, and you're almost there with WinDC1. You just need to tell it it's a Domain Controller. You do so by clicking Start ➤ Run and typing **dcpromo**.

When you do this, you'll be prompted to install Active Directory. It takes several screens to do the deed. After you see the "Welcome to the Active Directory Installation Wizard" screen, click "Next" to continue.

Operating System Compatibility

At this screen, you'll be informed that older Windows clients and Samba clients (such as what you'll use in Chapter 4) might have trouble making contact to a Windows 2003 server. This is because Windows 2003 uses SMB Signing, a way of ensuring the data isn't being modified as it goes across the wire. For now, click "OK."

Domain Controller Type

At this screen, you'll choose "Domain controller for a new domain" because this is the first Domain Controller you've created. If you decide to add additional Domain Controllers for testing, you'll choose the other option "Additional domain controller for an existing domain."

Create New Domain

Here, you are presented with three options.

Domain in a new forest   This is what you want. This creates a brand spankin' new domain.

Child domain in an existing domain tree   If you already had a domain, you could add other domains as a child. You're not going to do this.

Domain tree in an existing forest   This will create a new, noncontiguous namespace in the forest. If you had company.com and you wanted to create subsidiary.com, you'd choose this option. Both company.com and subsidiary.com would be in the same forest.

New Domain Name

This is where you'll specify the Fully Qualified Domain Name of your new domain. For the purposes of this book, call it `ad.corp.com`, as seen in Figure 1.30, but in the real world you can call it anything you like.

 Again, in this book, this domain will be a delegated subdomain of your Linux-owned DNS domain called `corp.com`.

Once you've entered the domain name, click "Next."

NetBIOS Domain Name

This screen presents you with the name "older clients" (such as Windows 9X and Windows NT) use when talking to the domain. Choose whatever you like, but it's customary to pick a name that's darn close to the name you chose one screen earlier. The dcpromo wizard will choose the leftmost element of the name you've entered, so for this book, go with the recommended name of AD.

Database and Log Folders

Active Directory needs to store its database stuff somewhere. It's suggesting some defaults. For testing, the defaults will be fine.

Shared System Volume

This is the location of the Windows SYSVOL directory. It holds logon scripts and the file-based components of Group Policy Objects. Like the previous setting, it will recommend a default, which is fine.

FIGURE 1.30   Remember, your Active Directory is to be self-contained in its own domain entitled `ad.corp.com`.

DNS Registration Diagnostics

On this screen, as seen in Figure 1.30, you'll be prompted about how to handle DNS. You already set up the DNS server components; they're just waiting for you. When you were bringing up this server, you told the server to look to itself for DNS information.

With that in mind, choose the second option, "Install and configure the DNS server on this computer, and set this computer to use this DNS Server as its preferred DNS server." This is shown selected in Figure 1.31.

FIGURE 1.31   Select the second option and make sure your Windows 2003 CD-ROM is in the drive.

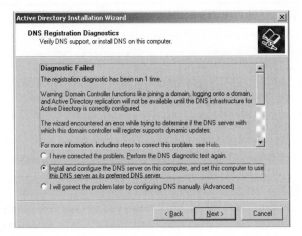

Permissions

This screen helps prevent anonymous users from enumerating all the users in the domain. You'll have two choices here: "Permissions compatible with pre-Windows 2000 server operating systems" and "Permissions compatible only with Windows 2000 or Windows Server 2003 operating systems." Best practices dictate to choose the latter, so that's what you should choose here.

Directory Services Restore Mode Administrator Password

In this book, you don't need to worry about what happens if the Active Directory requires repair. However, when bringing up a new Domain Controller, a special password is required for Active Directory emergencies.

For now, you can enter the same password you've been using all along, p@ssw0rd. (That's an at sign as the second character and a zero for the letter O.)

Summary Screen

At this screen, as shown in Figure 1.32, you'll get one last chance to verify your settings and make sure you're happy. When ready, click "Next."

FIGURE 1.32   Make sure your settings are correct and select "Next" to install Active Directory.

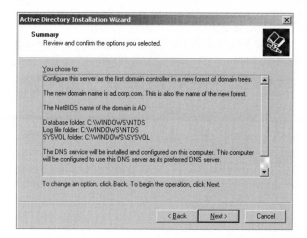

At this point you'll be off and running, and your first Domain Controller (WinDC1) will be born into your domain (ad.corp.com). Your Domain Controller's Fully Qualified Domain Name (FQDN) will be WinDC1.ad.corp.com.

Completing the Active Directory Installation Wizard

Eventually, you'll get to the "Completing the Active Directory Installation Wizard screen." Here, you'll be prompted to click Finish, then Active Directory will install. At the end, you'll reboot the machine.

Once completed, go ahead and log in. The Administrator account (and associated password) you created when you installed the server has been migrated to Active Directory, so you can use the same password, p@ssw0rd.

Installation of Windows XP

Loading Windows XP from the ground up is similar to loading Windows 2003 from the ground up. As with Windows 2003 and SP1, it's highly recommended that you also create an installation of Windows XP with Service Pack 2 already slipstreamed into it. References for how to create slipstreamed CD-ROMs were provided earlier.

In this section, we're not going to describe every detail of a Windows XP setup. However, you'll likely want to have the same settings we did while writing this book. That way, your test lab will match ours. Here are the specific screens you'll need to pay attention to:

Computer Name and Administrator Password   This screen will appear similar to the one previously shown in Figure 1.5. Here, you'll be able to enter the computer name and password for the local machine's Administrator account. Again, in Windows, usernames aren't case sensitive. (In Linux, login names are case sensitive.)

For the experiments presented in this book, call your Windows XP machine xppro1 (though for readability, we'll usually type it out as XPPro1.) I'm also suggesting that you set the local Administrator password to p@ssw0rd. (That's an at sign as the second character and a zero for the letter O.) This password is strong enough for the default strength requirements for both Windows and Linux.

Networking Settings and TCP/IP Properties Page   At this point you'll be able to specify "Typical settings" or "Custom Settings." Typical settings means that the machine will try to request an IP address via DHCP. You haven't yet set up DHCP, so for now, select Custom Settings, then proceed to change the TCP/IP settings to a static IP address. In the examples, you'll set XPPro1's IP address information as follows:

> IP address: 192.168.2.227

> Subnet Mask: 255.255.255.0

> Default Gateway: 192.168.2.1

> Preferred DNS Server: 192.168.2.226 (which is the IP address of WinDC1.ad.corp.com— the Domain Controller and DNS server you just created)

Workgroup or Computer Domain Screen   You'll have the opportunity to join a domain or plunk yourself in a workgroup. You can add yourself to the domain at this point. You'll need to provide credentials as anyone in the domain; you needn't have administrative credentials to add a computer account.

Sometimes, for seemingly no reason at all, you cannot join the domain from this screen. Typically, it's because there is some kind of DNS name resolution problem. If you are unable to join the domain at this point, for now, leave this machine in a workgroup. After the Windows XP machine is fully up and running, try to fix the name resolution problem, and once again try to join the domain. Do this by right-clicking over My Computer and selecting Properties. Then, on the Computer Name tab click the Change button. At that point, you should be able to enter the name of the domain to join, provide credentials, and join!

Managing Windows DNS

Windows DNS is essential to the proper care and feeding of Active Directory. To that end, we'll briefly explore two areas to make sure you're properly caring for Active Directory and its oh-so-important DNS.

To do this, you'll run the DNS Server manager on your Windows 2003. Do this by launching the DNS manager via Start ➢ Programs ➢ Administrative Tools ➢ DNS. When you do, the DNS manager console will launch as seen in Figure 1.33.

FIGURE 1.33   Use the Forwarders tab to forward to the LinServ1 domain controller that owns `corp.com`.

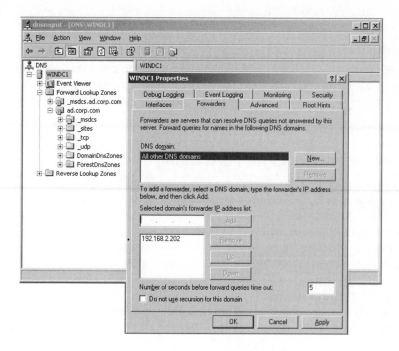

Ensuring Windows DNS Is Working Correctly

First things first you need to make sure that after you installed Active Directory the DNS is working properly. After the DNS manager is up and running, drill down into WINDC1 ➢ Forward Lookup Zones ➢ `ad.corp.com`. You'll see several key entries as shown in the background window in Figure 1.33. Specifically, you want to make sure the following entries are automatically generated before continuing:

- _msdcs
- _sites
- _tcp
- _udp
- DomainDNSZones
- ForestDNSZones

This isn't the place to delve into each Active Directory DNS entry. However, if these are not present, don't immediately panic. First, go get a cup of coffee, wait 30 minutes, close then reopen the DNS manager, and see if they magically appear. These entries could just be being built in Active Directory's first several minutes of life.

If after 30 minutes they're still not present, you may have to do some Active Directory troubleshooting.

Here is a list of the key MSKB articles that can help you if you're having trouble making the key records appear:

- MSKB 260371: Troubleshooting Common Active Directory Setup Issues in Windows 2000
- MSKB 241505: SRV Records Missing After Implementing Active Directory and DNS
- MSKB 241515: How to Verify the Creation of SRV Records for a Domain Controller
- MSKB 237675: Setting Up the Domain Name System for Active Directory

You can simply Google for MSKB and the number to find the articles you need.

Setting up Windows DNS for Forwarding

On the Windows side of the house, you're missing one last piece of the puzzle. That is, you need to instruct your Windows Active Directory DNS server where to go if it doesn't have the answer to where things are in `corp.com`. This is called *forwarding*. The idea is that if the DNS servers in `ad.corp.com` don't know where to go, they'll forward the request to a DNS server that does. In this case, you want your `ad.corp.com` DNS server (`windc1.ad.corp.com`) to forward to `linserv1.corp.com` when it doesn't know the answer.

To finish setting up, there's not a lot you need to configure right now. The only thing you need to change is where this machine forwards to. That is, when a DNS client such as a Windows XP machine, a Linux machine, or this machine itself needs to look up an address that your DNS server doesn't have, where is it going to look? That's where the *forwarding address* comes in. To set the forwarding address, right-click over the server name (highlighted in Figure 1.33) and select "Properties," then select the "Forwarders" tab, as shown in Figure 1.33.

Enter the IP address of your `corp.com` Linux server, click "Add," and select "OK." The idea is that if this server doesn't know where to look, well, your `linserv1.corp.com` Linux server that owns `corp.com` should know the answer. And, if LinServ1 doesn't know the answer, it will ask your ISP.

At this point, you should be able to open Internet Explorer and get to, say, `www.google.com` or anywhere else. This is because your Windows 2003 machine's DNS client (set in the network card's properties) now sends its queries to the Windows DNS server, and it can forward to the Linux DNS server when it needs to.

Post Active Directory Installation Tasks

Once Active Directory is loaded and ready to go, there are a few housekeeping items you need to do before continuing. Then, you'll need to set your Windows 2003 machine so that it knows about an authoritative time source. Additionally, you'll activate your Windows 2003 installation. Finally, you'll run Windows Update on your Windows 2003 machine to ensure you're up to date with the latest security patches.

Let's do these things now.

Setting an Authoritative Time Source

Sure, your computer has an internal BIOS clock, but Windows needs something authoritative to hang its hat on. So to keep Windows happy (and to keep a gaggle of events out of the event log), you really should set an authoritative time source. Contrary to popular and misunderstood beliefs, for Active Directory networks you only need to perform this procedure one time— here—on the first Active Directory Domain Controller. This first Domain Controller has a special role as the master timekeeper. All other machines will hierarchically request the time from this machine. All you need to do is tell it what your authoritative time source is. To that end, the command is

```
net time /setsntp:servername
```

The best server to request is one of the master time servers at the United States Naval Observatory. To request it, simply run either the command

```
net time /setsntp:192.5.41.41
```

or

```
net time /setsntp:192.5.41.209
```

Find out more about the SNTP service in MSKB 314054.

Product Activation

Depending on the version of Windows 2003 your company is licensed for, you may or may not have to *activate* your copy of Windows. If activation is required, you'll see a balloon pop-up at some point after initial setup, similar to what is seen in Figure 1.34. By clicking the balloon (or the little keys icon in the system notification area by the clock if the balloon isn't present), you'll be able to activate Windows via the Activation Wizard (not shown).

In our examples, we've ensured our Windows 2003 computer can see the Internet. Because of this, the Activation Wizard will use our Internet connection, do what it has to do, and close. If your Windows 2003 cannot see the Microsoft mothership, you will have to use the dial-up activation service that is assisted by the wizard.

Windows Update

Once you can see the Internet and Windows has been activated, you should take a moment to surf on over to `windowsupdate.microsoft.com`. You might be asked to install the latest version of the update software. After that, zip through the Express Install, which will get you up to date on any security fixes. You may have to reboot your Windows 2003 server when finished.

FIGURE 1.34   You must activate most editions of Windows Server 2003.

Running Windows Update on your Windows 2003 server doesn't magically protect all your other Windows clients and servers. However, Microsoft does have some magic that will do this. It's called Software Update Services, or SUS, and it has a follow-up Windows Server Update Services (with the doofy acronym WSUS).

 Space limits us from delving into either SUS or WUS technology; however, you can check out two articles that I wrote about SUS to help you protect all your Windows clients and servers on an ongoing basis: `http://mcpmag.com/Features/article.asp?EditorialsID=336` and `http://mcpmag.com/Features/article.asp?EditorialsID=342`. Also check out an article my pal Don Jones wrote about WSUS: `www.redmondmag.com/columns/article.asp?editorialsid=905`

Getting Around

Once Windows and Linux are installed and talking to each other, it's still a big, big world in there. To that end, here are some guidelines for getting around if you want to explore on your own.

Getting Around in Windows

There are four main tools with which you can modify settings, make configuration changes, and perform other functions that change the system.

Basic Functions

Getting around Windows doesn't have to be hard. Indeed, it's likely that you've already spent some time with these tools.

Invoking Help

Windows help is only getting better. In fact, I'm consistently impressed with how much better it's gotten over the years. With that in mind, the Windows 2003 and Windows XP Help can really help you out of a jam if you need it. In most cases, simply press F1, or select Help and Support Center from the Start Menu.

Control Panel

The Control Panel is the main way to change various "look and feel" settings, as well as printers, network cards, and a lot of other stuff. You can locate the Control Panel right from the Start menu. Select Switch to Classic View if you want to see even more categories right away.

My Computer ➢ Properties

When you select Start and see the My Computer icon, you can simply right-click over it and select Properties. Here's where you can, among other things, change the name of the computer (don't do this), change how potentially unsafe hardware drivers are handled, set up a way to perform remote computing (explored in Chapter 8), manage startup and recovery functions, and handle updates.

Advanced Functions

There may be times when you need a little more oomph to get something done inside Windows. Here are some additional places to try to make it happen.

My Computer ≻ Manage

When you select Start and see the My Computer icon, you can simply right-click over it and select Manage. Here you'll be able to do lots of stuff, including play around with the server's hardware and disk configurations, check out the system Event Logs, defragment the hard disk, use start and stop services, and manage local users and groups.

Command Prompt (aka the DOS Box)

Opening up a command prompt is easy. Either select the Command Prompt icon from the Start Menu, or select Start ≻ Run, type **cmd**, and press "Enter."

Local Group Policy Editor: *GPedit.msc*

Group Policy is a mechanism to help you control lots of settings very easily. You can do so on individual computers, or from "up on high" using Active Directory. If you have a single computer you want to manage, you can select Start ≻ Run and type **GPedit.msc**, and you'll be presented with the Group Policy Object Editor. Inside, you find a bajillion things to play with, but be very careful. One false step, and you could be in for a world of hurt. In this book, we won't be going too deep into Group Policy with Active Directory other than to discuss a third-party tool that helps extend it to Linux. Group Policy is a really big deal, and to that end, I (Jeremy) have a really big book and website dedicated on the subject which you can check out at www.GPanswers.com.

Note that GPedit.msc is only valid for machines that aren't Domain Controllers.

Print and Online Resources

Although there are simply too many to mention them all, if you're looking for more information on general Windows administration, we suggest first going to Microsoft's website, which has a specific section for IT Pros. Start at www.microsoft.com/windowsserver2003/default.mspx.

As for print books to help you get around, Sybex has an armload of books you should check out. One our favorites is Mark Minasi's tome *Mastering Windows Server 2003* (Sybex 2003).

Also valuable is Bill Boswell's *Inside Server 2003* (Addison Wesley.)

Additionally, you can locate a myriad of community forums, such as GPanswers.com, for Group Policy–specific information or ScriptingAnswers.com for scripting solutions.

Getting Around in Linux

Navigating a Linux server or desktop is not as difficult as historical accounts of Unix unfriendliness might lead you to believe. On a Fedora Linux system, friendly tools comparable to most Microsoft Windows Control Panel and management functions are available.

Help

General help is available, to an extent, via the Help option on the Applications menu. Unfortunately the GNOME Help browser does not cover all of the Fedora-specific utilities on the System Settings menu. Luckily, those utilities do offer their own Help buttons and are fairly self-explanatory to begin with.

System Settings

Most configuration options can be changed via the System Settings submenu of the Applications menu. Here you can adjust the date and time, change authentication settings, set IP addresses for network cards, and so forth. Printers can be administered via the Printing option, and most locally connected printers are automatically configured and installed when first connected to a Fedora system. Help is available via the Help button in most of the System Settings utilities.

System Tools

Certain tasks that don't fit neatly within the aforementioned System Settings are handled via the System Tools submenu of the Applications menu. The Internet Configuration Wizard is particularly helpful for dial-up clients, and the Terminal option needed to access the command line is also here. However, most system administration activities only require the System Settings menu.

Application Software

Desktop applications, such as graphics editing tools and the free OpenOffice Microsoft Office–compatible suite, are accessible via the Graphics and Office submenus of the Applications menu. OpenOffice provides a fairly compatible way to read and write Microsoft Office file formats, including Word documents and Excel spreadsheets.

Computer

The Computer desktop icon allows easy browsing of the entire file system, including removable devices and any configured network file systems. The GNOME file browsing interface, known as Nautilus, provides capabilities similar to the Microsoft Windows desktop environment. Floppies and CD-ROMs can be easily accessed from here.

You may also wish to check out an introduction to the GNOME user interface:

```
http://www.gnome.org/learn/users-guide/latest/
```

Powering Down

Does anyone still turn off their computer? If you find yourself shouting "*Jane! Stop this crazy thing!*" it might be the right time.

First, select "Log Out" from the Actions menu, which is to the right of the Applications menu. When asked to confirm, you may wish to check the "save current setup" box if you like your current arrangement of browser windows, terminal windows, and the like. After confirming and returning to the login screen, click the "Shut Down" button at the bottom of the screen.

Print and Online Resources

As with Windows, there are too many to list here. But for information on Fedora Linux, begin with the official `http://fedora.redhat.com/` site and the independently run community site `www.fedorafaq.org/`. For general Linux information, be sure to check out `www.kernel.org/`.

In print, Sybex offers a series of excellent Linux books, notably *Linux System Administration* by Vicki Stanfield and Roderick W. Smith (Sybex, 2002).

Final Thoughts

You've set up your two universes the way most companies have developed over time. That is, the Linux folks are initially only talking Linux, and the Windows folks are only talking Windows. Except there is that one little delegated subdomain thing, where the Windows folks have their own sandbox to play in.

This lack of communication between the two camps isn't wonderful —it's just the way it is. But from this point forward, together we'll try to bridge the gap.

Your initial systems are now ready. However, in future examples in this book, prepare to install additional systems for testing. For instance, in Chapter 3 you'll need a Linux client machine specifically for authenticating to Active Directory via LDAP. And in Chapter 6 we suggest you install a Windows 2003 server just for Exchange email. We'll cross these bridges as we come to them.

2

Linux Authentication Services

Authentication is the point at which some server provides your clients the "keys" to get on the network and do stuff. Without authentication, you can't really get around or do too much. Sure, you can authenticate to your local box, but that's not that exciting. It only really gets exciting when you have some kind of centralized authentication authority for your network. (Okay, perhaps our definition of exciting is different than yours, but we digress.)

Older Windows authentication (NT 4 and earlier) used NT authentication (LM, NTLM, and NTLMv2 protocols). Modern Windows authentication uses Kerberos (or, if necessary, it can drop down to NTLMv2) with user information stored in Active Directory for centralized authentication. Though some shops certainly still use Novell's eDirectory or possibly even other services, Active Directory is pretty much the industry standard way Windows clients get on the network.

Unix and Linux traditionally store accounts and passwords locally in a file called /etc/passwd (or possibly a combination of /etc/passwd and /etc/shadow.) Inside an /etc/passwd file, you'll find a simple list of lines, one line for each user, laid out like this:

accountname:password:uid:gid:GECOS:directory:shell

Here's a breakdown of what all this stuff means:

accountname   What the user is called on this specific Linux machine. A user might have a totally different accountname on another system.

password   Unix systems never store passwords directly. Instead, they store the result of *hashing* the password using a cryptographic function. When the user attempts to log in, the password entered is also hashed and then compared to the password hash. Originally, this was considered good security because having the password hash doesn't tell you what the user's password is. However, it *does* allow you to make password-guessing attempts as fast as you like using an automated process, so most modern Unix systems don't store the password hash in /etc/passwd. Instead, it is stored in an additional file called /etc/shadow as part of a scheme called *shadow passwords*. Since only the root user can read /etc/shadow, this is an effective way to limit the speed of password guessing attempts. On a typical Fedora Core 3 system, the password field in /etc/passwd just contains an "X"

uid   This is the *user identifier*. Each user must have a unique uid on any particular Linux machine.

gid   This is the default *group identifier*. A user can be a member of more than one group, and the /etc/group file records additional group membership information. However, every user is always a member of a *default* or *primary* group. The group ID number (gid) of the user's default group is given here. Group IDs and group names are defined in the /etc/group file.

GECOS   No, this isn't the company that can save you 15 percent or more on car insurance. This is the General Electric Comprehensive Operating System field. It typically contains only the full name of the user, but it can also contain the user's full name, office location, office telephone extension, and home phone number as comma-separated subfields.

Directory   This is where the home directory of the user is.

Shell   This is set to the path of the shell the user uses when they log in; for instance, /bin/sh or /bin/bash.

As noted, a second file called /etc/shadow actually contains the hashed password, plus information about when the password will expire. We won't go into detail about the password expiration fields; try the command man 5 shadow if you are curious. The /etc/shadow file is only readable by the root account, so it's got more protection on it than the /etc/passwd file, which is readable by applications and mere-mortal users.

If you're only trying to authenticate users to this local box, this little system works great. But you might need to provide access to thousands of users across 30, 300, or 3000 Linux boxes. You could set up a synchronization job to share a single /etc/passwd file between many Linux machines, but it's cumbersome at the very least. In short, you need a way to get centralized.

Linux has a myriad of centralized authentication and directory services options. These provide a shared, networked alternative to /etc/passwd files on individual unrelated systems. Here's a quick breakdown of the possibilities you could find on your Linux (or pre-Linux) network:

NIS   This system, originally designed by Sun Microsystems, helps centralize accounts. The point is to help get away from only being able to look at locally contained /etc/passwd files. Instead of looking up passwords stored on the local machine, this scheme allows administrators to put all passwords on *master* and *secondary* servers. In the Precambrian era, this was formerly called "Yellow Pages" until the phone company got all uppity and hired some lawyers and made Sun change the name from Yellow Pages to something else (NIS). NIS is not hierarchical. That means there is no efficient way to examine, for instance, only the users in the marketing department. NIS also has major difficulties working through a firewall.

NIS+   NIS is riddled with security problems. A quick Google search for "NIS security issues" yields dozens of pages explaining all the possible attacks. A nice article that explains the problem and has some solutions can be found at www.securityfocus.net/infocus/1387. NIS+ attempts to solve some of these problems by adding in "security levels" (and other added protections), some support for a hierarchical structure, and other fixes for the problems of traditional NIS. NIS+ is a Sun Microsystems-centric solution that isn't generally available for Linux systems and is not included with Fedora.

OpenLDAP   This is an up-and-comer in the Unix world. It's meant to provide directory services to Unix clients. Some critics have described its scalability as needing a bit of work. It's hierarchical, which means it is potentially a better choice than NIS when a large number of accounts is involved. And, since it was designed with the expectations of modern firewalls in mind, it is also much easier to pass through a firewall than NIS.

Samba 3.*x* Samba allows a Linux machine to pretend to be a Windows file server, print server, or NT 4 Primary Domain Controller, or PDC for short. Samba can also act as a Backup Domain Controller (BDC), provided that the PDC also runs on Samba. Samba 4.*x* (forthcoming as of this writing) will additionally provide the ability to pretend to be an Active Directory Domain Controller (yikes!). This means Samba can store accounts centrally in its own database or in an LDAP database, and then Windows users can authenticate to Samba. It is also possible, in theory, for Linux users to authenticate to Samba, but since Windows domain authentication has no concept of uids or gids, this approach can lead to aggravation. As we'll explore later in this chapter, we chose instead to layer Samba on top of LDAP. That way, Linux users can authenticate directly to LDAP, and Windows users can authenticate to Samba. One OpenLDAP server can serve as the back end for both.

> There's another option on the horizon (but not explored in this book): Netscape Directory Server. This is, arguably, a more robust LDAP implementation than OpenLDAP, but it had one major drawback: it was expensive. Recently, Red Hat bought this Netscape asset and announced it will be open-sourcing the product. So, in theory, it will be free to use. We'll all stay tuned to see how this pans out.

Kerberos Kerberos is a highly robust network authentication protocol, and both Linux and Windows clients and servers can use Kerberos to authenticate logons. However, Kerberos is *not* a directory service. Its task is to authenticate user identities, not to store information such as user and group IDs. "Kerberized" Linux systems use Kerberos in addition to, not in place of, directory services such as NIS or LDAP, which store the rest of the information traditionally found in /etc/passwd.

Table 2.1 shows a quick comparison of the more popular authentication and directory information systems.

In this chapter and the next chapter, we'll discuss and demonstrate how you can leverage existing Active Directory or Linux authentication services. In other words, we're going to show you how to have Linux clients use Active Directory as their authentication point and how to have Windows clients use Linux as their authentication point.

Again, this book is about harmony, not about building walls, so there might be legitimate times where you want one camp to "own" the authentication services. With that in mind, we'll present the most common cases of sharing— and also of keeping—all the marbles.

In this chapter, we'll survey the various Linux authentication mechanisms and show how you can get your Windows machines to utilize them.

Hold on to your hats, folks, making peace can be a bumpy ride.

TABLE 2.1   A Comparison of the Various Authentication Methods Available

	NIS	NIS+	OpenLDAP	Kerberos	Active Directory
Namespace	Flat	Semi-hierarchical	Hierarchical	Flat (but not meant to store all user details)	Hierarchical
Server Types	Master/slave	Root domain master/ Subdomain master/ Replica	Master/slave	Master/slave	Multi-master (in full native mode), master/slave in mixed mode
Security	Wide open	DES public/ private key	SSL and/or Kerberos and SASL	Kerberos	Kerberos

Authentication to NIS

NIS was one of the first solutions to the shared authentication problem, and it is one of the simplest. A client asks the NIS server for the equivalent of the desired line of /etc/passwd or /etc/group or, in more recent years, /etc/shadow, and the NIS server coughs it up. Not much to it. And there's a lot to be said for simplicity.

Unfortunately, NIS is built on RPC (Remote Procedure Call), an older system of communication between programs on different computers. RPC is old enough that it predates modern firewalls, and it is not compatible with firewalls that rely on simple port filtering.

In general, NIS is designed with an older "trusted host" security model in mind. The trusted host way of thinking goes like this: all the workstations on the local network have been locked down and can be trusted. In this philosophy, no one would *ever* put a rogue machine on the LAN. And you certainly would never want NIS access over that newfangled Internet, so why worry about solutions for less trustworthy clients? These were reasonable assumptions when NIS was born. They are less so today.

As stated, NIS is old, crusty, and insecure but still in heavy use around the world. With that in mind, you might very well have to get both your Linux and Windows to authenticate to an existing NIS structure. It's likely not a good choice to bring up a new NIS structure from scratch when there are so many better options. But you can if you want to.

Historically, NIS was known as "Sun Yellow Pages." So, many of the commands and services were created with 'yp' as an obvious prefix. While the metaphor was effective, it eventually ran afoul of Sun's legal department and was renamed NIS, but most of the NIS-related programs are still named with the yp prefix.

In this next section, we'll show you how to set up a Linux-based NIS server—but you'll be doing it only so you can test other components later (such as having Windows authenticate to NIS). Figure 2.1 shows a typical NIS setup. That is, there must be a master NIS server (which you'll be setting up on your Linux server) and, optionally, one or more read-only slave NIS servers. Slave servers are usually spread across the environment (but you won't be setting them up for the examples in this book). You will, of course, have clients that will authenticate to your NIS structure: Linux and Windows clients.

FIGURE 2.1   Here's what a typical enterprise NIS structure might look like.

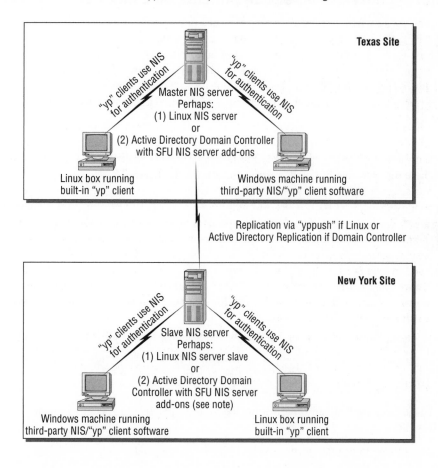

Yes, as you can see in Figure 2.1, it's possible to have an Active Directory Domain Controller pretend to be a NIS server. We'll talk about that in the next chapter.

Outside of the lab environment, if you already have a NIS infrastructure in place (on Linux, Sun, or something else), you'll likely want to skip the creation of a NIS server and proceed to making your clients talk with your existing NIS server.

Creating a Linux-Based NIS Server

Creating a Linux-based NIS server is straightforward. You'll start out by disabling the Linux firewall (NIS doesn't play well with it), then you'll install the NIS server components.

Installing the NIS Server Components on Linux

First, you must disable the firewall software on the Linux server. This is necessary because NIS relies on the RPC (Remote Procedure Call) standard, a system that involves unpredictable TCP/IP port numbers. Rather than listening for connections at a well-known port, an RPC service registers for a port number when the service starts. While some types of firewalls can indeed cope with this by directly understanding RPC messages, the simple firewall provided with Fedora Core 3 doesn't cut it. Systems relying on NIS should definitely use it only *behind* a firewall, trusting only systems on the same network.

To disable the firewall for NIS:

1. From the Applications menu, select System Settings ➢ Security Level.

2. Click the "Disable Firewall" button to turn off the firewall.

 If you install an NIS server purely as an experiment, we suggest you reenable your firewall later when you have finished your exploration of NIS.

Next, you will need to install the NIS server software itself. You did not do this in Chapter 1 because we don't really want to implement NIS as part of a Linux server environment when better alternatives are available. However, for this set of experiments, here's how to install the NIS server software on a Linux server:

1. From the Applications menu, select System Settings ➢ Add/Remove Applications.

2. In the "Package Management" dialog, scroll to "Network Servers" and click the "Details" button to the right. Select "ypServ" (the NIS server software) from the package list. You may need to scroll down.

3. Click "Update." When the "Completed System Preparation" window opens, click "Continue."

4. When installation is complete, close the Add/Remove Applications tool.

Configuring the Server

Webmin, the web-based configuration program you installed in Chapter 1, comes in quite handy for NIS configuration. First, you'll need to install the NIS configuration module, a standard Webmin module available from the Webmin website. Webmin itself offers an interface to fetch such modules automatically, so you don't need to browse the Webmin web site manually.

Begin by logging into Webmin in the usual fashion by opening a browser and pointing it toward `https://linserv1.corp.com:10000` (don't forget the `s` in `https`). In the "Webmin interface," click "Webmin Configuration," then "Webmin Modules." Then select the "Install Standard Module" radio box and click the "..." browse button next to it. From the list of modules that appears, select "NIS Client and Server." Then click "Install Module" to carry out the installation. A progress display will appear.

When installation has completed, click "NIS Client and Server" at the bottom of the progress display page. Or, the next time you want to configure the NIS server, select the "Networking" button at the top of Webmin, then click "NIS Client and Server."

To configure the NIS server software:

1. Click the "NIS Client and Server" button in the Networking page.

2. Click the "NIS Server" button.

3. Select the radio box labeled "Enable NIS Server."

4. In the "Serve NIS domain" field, select the radio button near the empty field, then enter the name you want to give the NIS domain. For the examples, enter **nis.corp.com**, but even a "short" name is acceptable. We chose the NIS "domain name" `nis.corp.com` for consistency with the way we name domains in other authentication systems discussed in this book. However, a NIS domain name need not resemble a fully qualified DNS name. Simply **corp** or **nis** would have worked as well. In this respect, NIS domain names are not unlike traditional NT NetBIOS names.

5. Select the "Master NIS Server" radio box.

6. At this point, you'll edit the NIS Tables list box. Specifically, you want to specify that only certain tables are to be selected. Hold down the Ctrl key and click to select these three tables:

   passwd
   group
   shadow

Historically, NIS was also used to share the IP addresses of various hostnames. It was a sort of "poor-man's DNS" solution that is no longer necessary—in fact, it only creates confusion and lost time for administrators trying to configure an NIS server.

You're almost there! Click "Save and Apply" to move on.

Can You Harden NIS?

NIS is insecure because of a fundamental design flaw: the server does not validate the user's login attempt. Instead, the NIS server just publishes the data in the passwd and shadow tables. Clients request the user information, including the password hash, for the user who wishes to log in. Then the client, not the server, hashes the user's password attempt to see if it matches the password hash the server returns.

This is more secure than sending passwords to the server in cleartext for verification, of course. And, at the time NIS was designed, this may have seemed like the only viable alternative because SSL (Secure Sockets Layer) was not yet available. However, it is a bad design for a modern network where client computers cannot always be trusted. A misbehaving client machine can choose to *hold on* to the password hash and keep throwing variations on dictionary words at it locally, with no restriction on speed, until an account is successfully cracked.

You can lock things down by IP address, which does prevent this behavior from outside the local network. But within the local network, bear in mind that anyone with a network sniffer can still grab the password hashes as they fly by.

NIS servers do offer one feature that may appear to solve this problem, but truthfully it doesn't. The feature is this: you can lock things down so that when queries are not made from a "privileged" port number on the client, bogus information is returned for the password field of the shadow table. This may appear to solve the problem, but actually you are *still trusting the client computer to use a privileged port number for legitimate login attempts only.* Read that again: you are trusting the client computer to be the good guy.

Sure, only the root account can open a connection from a privileged port on most Unix operating systems. But this does you no good if the user has obtained root access to just one workstation. A user could just bring their own Linux laptop in, and, bam! They're root!

All you've done here is prevent non-root users on workstations *that have not been physically compromised or otherwise subverted* from using commands like ypcat to list the password hashes. But all it takes is one physically compromised or hacked *client* system, and the password hashes can be readily mirrored.

There are only two solutions that provide some real protection against rogue client systems: enforcing very strict password selection policies so that dictionary attacks will consistently fail, or not using NIS.

Still, we'll do the best we can to help you slow hackers down. First, you'll limit the range of IP addresses that can access the NIS server, and you'll implement the restriction to privileged ports only. This is no help at all with compromised clients or rogue PCs on the LAN or with network sniffers, but it does raise the bar a bit higher by requiring that someone add a PC, use a sniffer, or obtain root access to a workstation. And, of course, it does keep external Internet traffic out entirely.

To restrict usage of the NIS server to clients from the private (trusted) network:

1. Use Webmin, then select Networking ➤ NIS Client and Server ➤ Server Security.

2. Select the radio button next to "Netmask" and enter the network number and netmask for your internal network. For example, if you use a private IP network such as 192.168.0.0, you would enter a netmask of `255.255.0.0` and a network/host address of `192.168.0.0`.

Or you could enter each client IP addresses, one at a time. This will get frustrating fast, but that's the breaks. To do so, in the Netmask section, select the "Single Host" radio button and in the "Network/host address" field, enter the IP address of the system you want to allow. Then click "Save and Apply." When you do, you'll be sent back one full screen and you must re-select "Server Security." (Frustrating, I know.) Repeat.

3. Now you'll limit access to the password hash field to connections from privileged ports. As stated, this is only a measure to keep well-behaved client operating systems in line, and it provides no protection from rogue or compromised clients. This is referred to as *mangling* the password field and only affects non-root users on well-behaved clients who are attempting to use the ypcat command to dump the shadow table. To do this, you leverage a different Webmin module. It's called NIS Server Security and is located in Networking ➤ NIS Client and Server ➤ Server Security, as shown here.

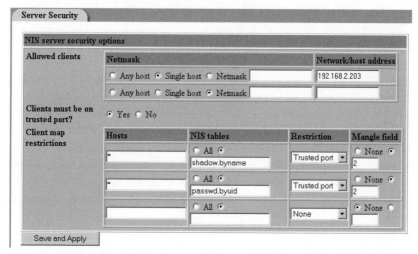

4. Select "Yes" for the "Clients must be on trusted port?" option and ensure "Mangle field" is set to 2. Column 2 of the shadow file contains the password hash, so you're blocking that field from being displayed. In essence, non-root users on well-behaved Unix clients cannot see the shadow file; hence, they cannot hack at it. There's no penalty for selecting "All" in the NIS Tables column; you're just hiding, er, *mangling* column 2 from all tables that NIS is using. Since column 2 is the password field in all of the standard /etc/passwd-like files that NIS is modeled upon, there's no harm in doing so.

Launching the NIS Server

The NIS server is ready to run. At the terminal prompt, as root, enter the following commands. The first command ensures that the NIS server software will be launched at boot time; the second launches it now so that rebooting is not immediately necessary:

```
chkconfig --add ypserv
service ypserv start
```

Creating Unix Users and Groups with Webmin

Naturally, you'll want to test our NIS server. While Webmin provides a separate interface to add new accounts from within the NIS "Servers and Clients" module, NIS operates simply by publishing the server's /etc/passwd file, converting its contents into a simple database format at regular intervals. Therefore, we recommend that you add new accounts via the Webmin's standard "Users and Groups" module, already installed and accessible by clicking the "System" button.

Since this is the first time you've created users and groups with Webmin, it's worth touching on two oddities. First, although the "Users and Groups" page contains the phrases "Local Users" and "Local Groups," you *are* exporting these via NIS, so they are more than just "local" in reality. Second, there's a potentially confusing distinction made between "normal passwords" and "pre-encrypted passwords." When you select "Normal Password," you are really asking the system to hash the password for you. That's the easiest way to set up a password.

To create users and groups with Webmin:

1. Open Webmin. Select "System" and locate "Users and Groups." Click the "Create a New Group" link. For the group name, enter **eastsales**, then click "Create." Repeat this process to create **westsales**.

2. Next, you'll add actual user accounts, two for each group. Click the "Create a new user" link, then enter the username **eastman1**. In the password field next to the "Normal Password" radio button, which should already be selected, enter **p@ssw0rd**. Enter the real name **East Man One**. You may accept the defaults for the remaining fields.

3. Under "Group Membership/Primary group," select "Existing group" and use the provided "…" browsing button to locate and select the **eastsales** group.

Finally, click "Create." Then repeat the process for eastman2, westman1, and westman2, placing westman1 and westman2 in the westsales group.

Authenticating Linux Clients to the NIS Server

Your NIS server is ready to go; time to test it by convincing your client system to allow logons via the accounts you just created. First, as with the NIS server system, you must unfortunately disable the Fedora firewall. You can do this by selecting Applications ➤ System Settings ➤ Security Level and then selecting the "Disable Firewall" option in the dialog box that follows. If you are not committed to actually using NIS, we recommend reenabling the firewall when you are through experimenting with NIS.

To configure your Linux client to authenticate to NIS:

1. From the "Applications" menu, select System Settings ➢ Authentication.

2. In the "Authentication Configuration" dialog box (seen in Figure 2.2), the "User Information" tab should be automatically selected. On this tab, select "Enable NIS," then "Configure NIS." In the NIS Domain field, enter **nis.corp.com**. In the NIS Server field, enter **linserv1.corp.com**. Or leaving the NIS Server field blank will tell the client to broadcast for the server.

> Under the hood, these steps add NIS to the list of authentication services to be consulted for password file information via the /etc/nsswitch.conf configuration file. They also enable NIS as an authentication mechanism in /etc/pam.d/system-auth, which controls the mechanisms that are allowed to authenticate logins.

Next, you must enable and launch the ypbind service, which takes care of communication with the NIS server. To do so, enter the following two commands as root at the terminal prompt:

```
chkconfig --add ypbind
service ypbind start
```

You're almost ready to go. If you tried a login now, it would succeed, but the user would have no home directory to log into. This can be addressed by enabling the pam_mkhomedir.so module, which automatically creates a home directory when it does not already exist for users whose login credentials are valid.

FIGURE 2.2 In the "NIS Settings" dialog, enter the NIS Domain and NIS Server names.

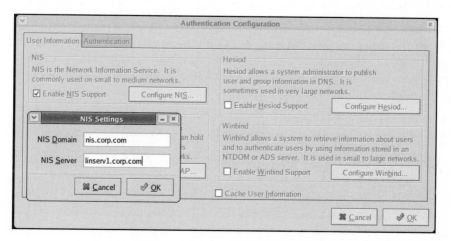

Remember, earlier we described three typical ways users log on and interact with the system:

- The shell, logging in at the console without a GUI

- Remote encrypted shell (via SSH)

- The GNOME interface (the usual gdm login manager)

Therefore, you need to tell each of these authentication mechanisms how to create home directories. The line you'll add is

```
session      required      pam_mkhomedir.so skel=/etc/skel umask=0077
```

About *skel* and *umask*

Here's the skinny on `skel`. Sometimes administrators want a newly created user directory to be prepopulated with files. By setting the `skel` option to a directory that contains such files, the administrator can arrange for those files to be automatically copied to the home directory of a new user. On a freshly configured Fedora client, /etc/skel is an empty directory, so the new home directory starts out empty. That's fine for our purposes.

The umask option determines the initial permissions of the newly created home directory. Unfortunately, it doesn't accept the relatively friendly "symbolic" syntax we've been using to assign permissions with the `chmod` command. For instance, in other parts of the book, we've suggested you use the syntax `chmod a+rx` *filename*. This sets "All" users' "Read" and "Execute" permissions on the filename. This is very clear and shows "who" gets permission and "how" much permission they get.

However, there's an alternate way of expressing the "who" and the "how." It's called the octal format, and it is mandatory for the umask option. Most Linux administrators who choose to use this syntax with the chmod command just have a bunch of the umasks memorized.

For instance, it's enough to know that a umask of 0077 means that the file or directory will be readable, writable, and executable (for a directory, this means the directory can be descended into) by the owner and by users who are members of the owner's default Unix group but not by "others." In other words, a umask of 0077 is like specifying three separate chmod commands: `a-rwx,g+rwx,u+rwx` in the symbolic syntax.

Another useful value for the umask argument is 0007, which means that only the owner can read, write, or descend into the directory and is equivalent to `a-rwx,u+rwx`.

For the geek in all of us, here's how the umask is calculated in octal (where a digit cannot be larger than 7).

- 1 represents "executable"

- 2 represents "writable"

- 4 represents "readable"

- These three can be added together in any combination.

- The rightmost digit represents permissions for the owner. The second digit counting from the right represents permissions for members of the group that owns the file. The third digit from the right represents permissions for everyone else. Zero is the only practical value for the leftmost digit in this context.

- For more information about setting permissions in this "old school" numerical way, try reading the online documentation for the chmod command. The man chmod command will show it to you.

Simply append the preceding line to the following three files:

- /etc/pam.d/login
- /etc/pam.d/sshd
- /etc/pam.d/gdm

Each file controls policies for how clients log on to the Linux machine. The /etc/pam.d/login is for plain-text console and serial logins, /etc/pam.d/sshd is for SSH encrypted shell logins, and /etc/pam.d/gdm is how most users graphically log on via the Fedora Gnome desktop.

Now you're ready to log on via NIS. To test the system, log out of your Linux client system via the "Actions" menu, then log in again using the username eastman1 and the password p@ssw0rd. You will be notified that a home directory has been created, and logon will then proceed as normal.

If It Doesn't Work

Here are some things to check if you cannot authenticate a Linux client to NIS:

- The most common cause of failure is the firewall, so ensure port filtering is off. For good measure, if you can, turn off SELinux. Double-check that you have followed the preceding instructions with regard to disabling the Fedora firewall and the SELinux subsystem on both the client system and the server.

- Be sure that you have actually started the ypserv service on the server. You can use the command ps -A | grep yp | grep -v grep (as one line) to show whether the ypserv process is running. The ps command lists currently running programs. The -A option makes sure that all programs are included. The grep command searches its input for a particular string, and grep with the -v option searches for lines that *don't* contain a string. You do this to avoid confusion by not including the grep commands themselves in the final output.

- Be sure that you have started the ypbind service on the client. You can use the ps command in the previous point to check.

Authenticating Windows Clients to the NIS Server

Out of the box, there isn't a way for Windows XP machines to authenticate to a NIS server. There are, however, multiple add-ons that can do the job.

One option is a freebie called pGina. The other option is to leverage commercial software. One package we'll demonstrate is WRQ's Reflection 12 Client for NFS. There are other options available, but we'll only discuss these here.

Windows to NIS Authentication via pGina and the NIS Plug-in

Windows has a way to inject additional (or alternate) methods of authentication via the pluggable "GINA" module. GINA is the code you see when you are asked to press Ctrl+Alt+Del upon startup. Out of the box, GINA is coded to talk to NT Domain Controllers, Active Directory Domain Controllers, and other things which talk "Windows." If you could just replace that code with something that could natively talk to NIS, you'd be in business.

Indeed, you are in business: that "something" is called pGina, and it's downloadable via http://pgina.xpasystems.com/. pGina is a framework that allows for multiple GINA plug-ins allowing nonnative authentications, including NIS (which you'll use now), LDAP (which you'll use in a little bit), and some other optional authentication possibilities.

The Windows download of pGina and installation is very straightforward: just download it, run it while logged in as a local administrator to install it, and take all the defaults. Once installed, you'll also need to download and install the required plug-in(s).

This particular plug-in will install a Windows service called *ypbind* that is needed to run the NIS client piece for pGina. The service provides a way for this Windows client to broadcast and find your NIS server.

Once the plug-in is downloaded and installed, you're ready to configure pGina for NIS authentication.

To configure a Windows client using pGina for NIS authentication:

1. Select Start ➤ Programs ➤ pGina ➤ Configuration Tool to run the pGina configuration tool.

2. Once launched, locate the "Plugin" tab and click "Browse." Enter the path to the .dll that you just installed that performs the NIS function. The default location is c:\pGina\ plugins\NISplugin.dll, as shown in Figure 2.3.

3. On the "Plugin" tab, click the "Configure" button. In the dialog box named, appropriately, "Dialog," enter the name of your NIS domain (**nis.corp.com** in the example). You'll also see a text box in which to enter the "Password Map" file. Enter **passwd.byname**, as shown in Figure 2.3. This is the table in NIS that is used when you pass in a username at logon time. Once you pass in a valid username and password, NIS will return a password hash (not the password itself). If the password hashes match, you're in!

4. At the "Dialog" dialog box, click "Save." At the "pGina Configuration" window, click "OK."

Now reboot your Windows machine to ensure the settings stick (logging off isn't enough). When you next press Ctrl+Alt+Del to log on, you'll be presented with a very different picture than usual, as shown in Figure 2.4.

FIGURE 2.3   Set up pGina's NIS plug-in for your NIS domain.

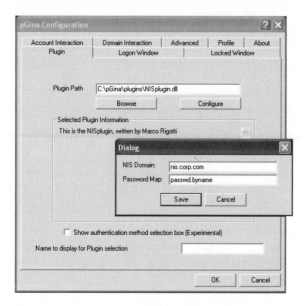

FIGURE 2.4   You can now use NIS to authenticate Windows clients.

pGina can be used as either the only authentication mechanism (as presented here), or in *addition* to a regular Active Directory domain login. The pGina documentation is pretty thin, but it does describe how to do this. Don't forget to actually join your XP client workstation to the Active Directory domain, however, or Active Directory authentication won't work.

Troubleshooting pGina

pGina is great in concept, but working with it and troubleshooting it can be a challenge. In our opinion, pGina and the plug-ins have that "not quite ready for prime-time" feel. With that said, there are lots of installations (universities, mostly) currently running pGina the way it was intended.

When it comes to troubleshooting pGina, here are our top three tips:

- There is a new Windows Event log available for pGina events, but in our testing all events had the same ID and had little useful information. Nonetheless, you may discover why pGina isn't functioning by digging into the Windows Event Log and finding a gem.

- The "Plugin Tester" tool (located in the pGina group in the start menu) can help you bang against an authentication source (such as LDAP or NIS) without having to log out and use the Ctrl+Alt+Del screen over and over again after you make a simple configuration change.

- An ongoing support message board is located at http://forums.xpasystems.com. Here you can post your questions about pGina as well as the available plug-ins. This is your best bet. It's heavily trafficked by the guys who wrote pGina, and they're pretty willing to help.

Windows to NIS Authentication via WRQ Reflection 12 Client for NFS

There are several commercial packages which additionally assist Windows machines to authenticate to NIS servers.

One package is by the WRQ company and is called the Reflection NFS Client. Yes, it's called the NFS client, but it does both NFS *and* NIS. You can learn more about it at www.wrq.com/products/reflection/nfs_client. There's a free trial available if you want to give it a test drive.

To configure the WRQ Reflection 12 Client for NIS authentication, enter the WRQ Reflection NFS utility (as seen in Figure 2.5) from the Start ➢ Programs menu. Once launched, Select View ➢ Settings. Select the "NFS General" tab and select "Use NIS for authentication" (not shown). Then, on the "NIS" tab, enter the name of the NIS domain, as well as how you want to locate the NIS server (by Hosts name or by Broadcast). Then click "OK" and reboot your machine.

Once you reboot, first log on to the local machine (or Windows domain) normally, then you'll be presented with the "NFS Logon: Primary" window asking you for your NIS credentials, as shown in Figure 2.6.

Of course, as commercial software, this utility has a bajillion features and has lots of support options. It's available from WRQ at www.wrq.com.

Checkout: Using NIS for Authentication

In this section, you've set up your Linux machine to be an NIS server. You've already authenticated both Linux Clients and Windows Clients to NIS.

Here's a quick rundown of how you did it.

To configure your NIS Server:

- NIS Server doesn't like firewalls, so you turned off both the regular port-filtering firewall and the SELinux subsystem.

- You used the Add/Remove Applications utility to add the NIS software, *ypServ*.

- You used Webmin to configure the NIS server. You made the Linux server a Master NIS server, and called it `nis.corp.com` (but you could have called it anything, including a short name, such as NIS).

- You added NIS to start at boot time with the command `chkconfig --add ypserv` and started it with `service ypserv start`.

- Optionally, you hardened NIS with Webmin by specifying which client computers can connect. Additionally, you hardened NIS by specifying that two NIS tables (`shadow.byname` and `passwd.byuid`) are not readable by anyone other than programs or users who act as root.

- You used Webmin to add some test users and groups via the Users and Groups interface.

FIGURE 2.5   Use the WRQ Reflection NFS client utility to configure your NIS settings.

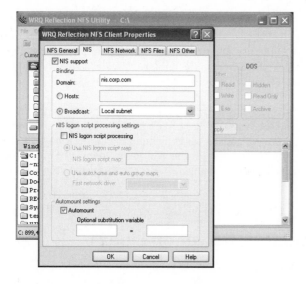

FIGURE 2.6   Enter your NIS username and password credentials.

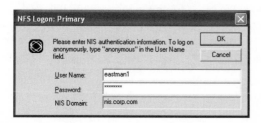

To get a Linux client to authenticate to your NIS server, you:

- Used the "Authentication Configuration" dialog box and pointed it to the NIS domain (and optionally the NIS server).

- You instructed the NIS client to start at boot time with the command `chkconfig --add ypbind` and started it with `service ypbind start`.

- You changed the three usual login methods, the shell, the encrypted SSH shell, and the graphical GNOME interface to authenticate to your NIS repository.

To get a Windows client to authenticate to your NIS server, you:

- Downloaded and installed the pGina tool.

- Loaded the pGina NIS plug-in and specified the NIS domain name and password map file.

- Alternatively, you used a commercial third-party tool, such as WRQ Reflection 12, and specified the NIS domain name.

Authentication to OpenLDAP

OpenLDAP is the open-source answer to the call for rich directory services. LDAP is the basis of both this product and Active Directory. Hence, there will be some similarities. OpenLDAP is still a work in progress and needs a little help in the "ability to scale" category, but it's getting better all the time.

 Turns out OpenLDAP doesn't just run on Linux boxes. If you wanted to, you could also run it on various other Unix-style machines too—and also Windows boxes! The home page for the Windows OpenLDAP project is http://lucas.bergmans.us/hacks/openLDAP/. If it has "hacks" in the URL, you know it's going to be fun!

Setting up an OpenLDAP Server on Linux

Setting up your first OpenLDAP server on Linux takes only a handful of steps. One thing that's not immediately obvious, however, is that an OpenLDAP server doesn't have any inherent security during the transmission of data. To shore that up, we'll show you how to use Secure Sockets Layer (SSL) to encrypt the LDAP traffic. Buuuut...it's not quite as easy as flicking a switch somewhere labeled "Enable Encryption." In order to do the job right, you'll need set up your server to encrypt its traffic, and to identify itself with an SSL "certificate." That certificate will be signed by an authority that the clients recognize and trust. We'll show you how to set up such an authority and teach clients to trust it.

Here are the steps you'll need to take to make a secure OpenLDAP server:

1. First, you'll adjust the firewall and install the OpenLDAP server software itself if it is not already installed.

2. Next, you'll create your own Certification Authority (CA). Not only might this process come in handy later, but right now you'll need it to pump out an SSL certificate for your OpenLDAP server.

3. Finally, you'll be ready to move your attention to the configuration of the OpenLDAP server itself.

Firewall Passthrough

Using LDAP does not require that you disable you Linux server's firewall. However, you do need to allow traffic from two additional ports. Specifically, you need to open up traffic on ports 389 and 636 for both TCP and UDP traffic. To open your firewall to allow traffic on ports 389 and 636 for both TCP and UDP traffic:

1. From the Applications menu, select System Settings ➤ Security Level. When you do, the "Security Level Configuration" dialog appears.

2. If you disabled your firewall for NIS and are no longer using NIS, you may safely reenable it now for OpenLDAP. In the "Firewall Options" tab, ensure the "Enable firewall" selection is active. Then, in the "Other ports:" dialog box, add the following entries, separated by spaces:

```
389:tcp 389:udp 636:tcp 636:udp
```

3. Click "OK" to finish.

Verifying Installation of the LDAP Server

It's easy to miss the installation of the LDAP server, even though we covered it in Chapter 1. That's because it is necessary to use the "Details" button and specifically select it from the "Network Servers" list during the package selection process. To verify that the server software is installed and, if necessary, install it, follow these steps:

1. Select Applications ➤ System Settings ➤ Add/Remove Applications.

2. At the "Package Management" dialog box, scroll down to the "Servers" section, locate the "Network Servers" entry and click the "Details" button. When you do, the "Network Servers Package Details" appears, as shown in Figure 2.7. Check the "openldap-servers" box, if it is not already checked, and select "Close." Then click "Update," accept the disk space requirements, and you're golden.

3. Select "Quit" to leave the Add/Remove Applications tool when the installation is complete.

Don't go running off and starting the OpenLDAP services quite yet; you're not secure enough for prime time. In the next section, we'll show you how to shore up OpenLDAP so you can have decent security as you go.

FIGURE 2.7   Ensure that "openldap-servers" is selected.

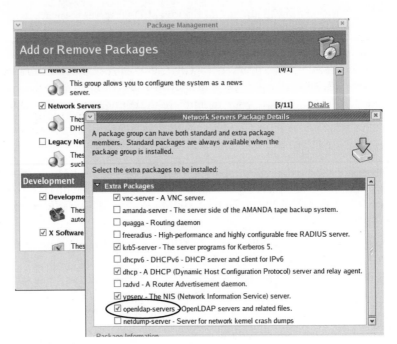

Creating a Signed SSL Certificate without Paying for It

Out of the box, OpenLDAP traffic isn't encrypted. But it can be.

Specifically, your goal is to encrypt logon attempts via SSL, the same protocol that underlies secure websites. You may be familiar with SSL certificates and the need to purchase them from a well-known Certification Authority (CA), such as Verisign. Using SSL certificates establishes secure communications, so sensitive information can flow between two points. In web browsers, the "lock" icon appears to alert users to this secure nature.

SSL certificates are also used to secure OpenLDAP transactions. These SSL certificates must also be signed by a Certification Authority. Fortunately, however, it is not necessary to rely on an expensive third-party Certification Authority, because you have control over the client systems and the power to decide which certificate authorities they *trust*. A client trusts a Certification Authority by storing a copy of the public key certificate for that CA in its local certificate store. Using this certificate, it can decrypt the digital signature applied by the CA to the certificates it issues.

This means that you can create your own Certification Authority and use it to sign your own certificates.

You can also, of course, choose to obtain each LDAP server's certificate commercially from Verisign or a similar company. By doing so, you'll avoid the need to make each LDAP client aware of your own newly created Certification Authority (as you'll have to do a little later). Windows and Fedora Core 3 ship with the Root CA certifications from Verisign and other companies. Some Linux distributions do not.

About Public-Key Encryption

To understand certificate authorities and certificates, it is necessary to understand a few simple things about public-key encryption. Let's compare it to regular symmetric-key encryption. This is where both parties agree on a password in advance and they use that password to encrypt and decrypt their messages. This is the encryption method used by Winzip to protect zipped files.

The problem with symmetric key encryption is that the person who encrypts the file (the sender) has to phone or e-mail the person who needs to decrypt the file (the receiver) and tell them the password. And that could be the time when the bad guy is listening.

If the sender and receiver don't have a confidential way to agree on a symmetric-key password, how do they communicate something privately *over a public channel*? Indeed, how can you use something ludicrously insecure, such as the Internet, *without* first exchanging a password privately in advance?

Public key encryption, despite the name, actually solves this problem by using *two* keys. The sender generates a key pair, two very large numbers that are mathematically related, so that anything encrypted with one key can only be decrypted by the other.

One key is designated as a private key, which the sender keeps confidential. The other key is called the public key and the sender shares this key freely. *There is no practical way to deduce the private key from the encrypted message.*

So how does this allow us, the sender and receiver to talk privately? Simplifying somewhat, it works like this:

1. We send you our public key.

2. You send us your public key.

3. You encode a message for us with our public key.

4. We decipher your message with our private key.

5. If we wish to respond, we encode a reply with your public key, which you decipher with your private key.

All well and good, but how do we know we're really talking to you and that your public key wasn't tampered with in transmission? If the bad guy taps into the line and replaces your public key with his own, we'll wind up sending our private message encrypted in a way that the bad guy can read!

One solution would be to exchange public keys in advance over a channel we know to be secure. But this is no better than symmetric key encryption. And what if we want to talk to thousands of people? A more practical solution is needed. This is where Certification Authorities come into the picture.

A Certification Authority (CA) is a server with two jobs: it validates the identity of entities who generate key pairs, and it puts its stamp of approval on the public key of the key pair by placing that key in a digitally signed certificate.

Other entities that trust the CA can use their copy of the CA's public key to validate the authenticity of the CA's digital signature, and then they can trust the public key found in the signed certificate. The Certification Authority signs the certificate like this:

1. An entity such as a web server or LDAP server sends a "certificate request" to the Certification Authority along with acceptable proofs of its identity. A "certificate request" contains a newly generated public key and a short description of the entity.

2. The CA validates the entity's identity then places the public key in a certificate that has information about the entity and the CA. It then calculates a hash of the certificate and encrypts the hash using its private key. The algorithm used to calculate the hash is so sensitive that if one little bit within a byte of the certificate is modified, the resulting hash will be wildly different than the original. The CA includes the signature inside the certificate.

If you want to send a secure message to the entity holding the certificate, you obtain a copy of the entity's certificate and use the public key inside to encrypt the message. You can be assured of the authenticity of the public key if you trust the CA that issued it. Here's a typical transaction:

1. An entity in `corp.com` transmits a copy of its signed certificate to an entity in `boutell.com`.

2. The entity in `boutell.com` uses the public key of the CA that issued the certificate to decrypt the signature on the certificate.

3. The entity in `boutell.com` now hashes the certificate using the same algorithm used by the CA that issued the certificate. If the result matches the hash in the decrypted signature, then the entity in `boutell.com` accepts that the entity in `corp.com` is the genuine article.

4. The entity in `corp.com` now sends a message encrypted with its private key.

5. The entity in `boutell.com` decrypts the message with the public key extracted from the certificate.

Creating Your Certification Authority

Installing a Certification Authority of your own gives you the power to issue certificates to entities in your own organization as long as you have the ability to distribute the CA's public key certificate to each of the systems that will participate in secure transactions.

Creating a Certification Authority is a bit of a chore, but the `openssl` library already installed on the server does include a script that simplifies the process.

To create a Certification Authority:

1. Open a terminal prompt and ensure you're logged in as root.

2. Enter the following command:

```
cd /usr/share/ssl
```

3. Now enter this command:

```
misc/CA -newca
```

You will see the following prompt in response:

```
CA certificate filename (or enter to create)
```

4. Press Enter to create the CA certificate. At this point, you're creating the private and public keys for your Certification Authority. The private key will be stored in a file with restricted permissions and a special password. That's because the private key can be used to sign new certificates. The public key will be copied to each client and server on the network.

5. Next, you'll encounter a prompt that says `Enter PEM pass phrase`. Enter a strong password and keep it in a secure place. It will only be possible to sign certificates for additional servers using this password. Enter the password again when prompted.

6. You will next be prompted for additional information about your organization. Most of your answers here are not crucial, but answer sensibly to reassure nosy users who decide to check the certificates installed on their client systems. Our example responses are shown in bold in the reproduced interaction below:

```
Country Name (2 letter code) [GB]:US
State or Province Name (full name) [Berkshire]:Pennsylvania
Locality Name (eg, city) [Newbury]:Philadelphia
Organization Name (eg, company) [My Company Ltd]:corp.com
Organizational Unit Name (eg, section) []:
Common Name (eg, your name or your server's hostname) []:linserv1.corp.com
Email Address []:
```

So far, so good! You have created your own Certification Authority. The CA certificate, consisting of the public key and identifying information, is now in the file:

```
/usr/share/ssl/demoCA/cacert.pem
```

Later, you'll copy this file to each of the systems involved so that they can use it to verify the certificates you sign.

The CA private key, which needs to remain confidential, is now in the file:

```
/usr/share/ssl/demoCA/private/cakey.pem
```

The CA utility doesn't do a good job of securing this file, so fix that using the chmod command:

```
chmod a-rwx,o+r /usr/share/ssl/demoCA/private/cakey.pem
```

This ensures that only the root user can read the Certification Authority's private key file. Read the sidebar "About chmod and chown" to learn more about the meaning of this syntax.

Next, you'll create an SSL certificate for your LDAP server. The LDAP server will use this certificate to identify itself at the beginning of every conversation with an LDAP client (SSL handshake) and to encrypt traffic to and from the client (SSL encryption). LDAP clients will then verify the server's certificate using the CA certificate installed on each client.

Creating Your LDAP Server Certificate

Now you'll create a *certificate request*, a file that contains a potential public key for a new server-identifying certificate, and you'll ask the Certification Authority to sign that certificate request.

 WARNING We recommend that you not change the filenames involved at this stage because the signing command that follows expects newreq.pem. We will rename things later.

To generate a certificate request:

1. At the terminal prompt, enter the command:

   pwd

   It should inform you that you are in the /usr/share/ssl directory. If not, type **cd /usr/share/ssl** first.

2. Next, enter

   openssl req -new -nodes -keyout newkey.pem -out newreq.pem

3. A series of prompts will appear in the terminal window. Your exchange should look similar to the following. As with the creation of the Certification Authority, your answers are not too critical, but answer reasonably to avoid disturbing nosy users who check certificates:

   ```
   Country Name (2 letter code) [GB]:US
   State or Province Name (full name) [Berkshire]:Pennsylvania
   Locality Name (eg, city) [Newbury]:Philadelphia
   Organization Name (eg, company) [My Company Ltd]:corp.com
   Organizational Unit Name (eg, section) []:
   Common Name (eg, your name or your server's hostname) []:linserv1.corp.com
   Email Address []:

   Please enter the following 'extra' attributes
   to be sent with your certificate request
   A challenge password []:
   An optional company name []:corp.com
   ```

Once again, your answers can vary from the preceding example, but it is *absolutely crucial that the "common name" field match your LDAP server's DNS name.* Clients will verify that they match! This may seem like an annoyance, but bear in mind that avoiding man-in-the-middle attacks is one of the major benefits of using SSL encryption.

The preceding steps generate two files:

newkey.pem This file contains the private key for your LDAP server. You'll move this file to an appropriate location later.

newreq.pem   This file contains the public key and is your certificate request which you must sign to produce a certificate to identify your LDAP server!

To sign the certificate:

1. At the terminal prompt, use the CA tool to do the job. Enter the following command:

    ```
    misc/CA -sign
    ```

2. At the terminal prompt, enter the "PEM pass phrase" password that you chose earlier and press Enter. Confirm the signing when asked to do so by typing **y** and pressing Enter.

You have created a signed certificate, which can be found in the file `newcert.pem` in the current directory.

Now that you've created a private key and obtained a signed certificate containing a public key, all you need to do is copy the CA certificate, the newly signed LDAP server certificate, and the LDAP server's private key to the `/etc/openldap` directory:

1. Copy the CA certificate to the LDAP configuration files directory:

    ```
    cp demoCA/cacert.pem /etc/openldap/cacert.pem
    ```

2. Copy the LDAP server's private key to the LDAP configuration files directory:

    ```
    cp newkey.pem /etc/openldap/slapdkey.pem
    ```

3. Copy the LDAP server's private key to the LDAP configuration files directory:

    ```
    cp newcert.pem /etc/openldap/slapdcert.pem
    ```

This allows them to be more conveniently referenced from the various LDAP configuration files.

When you installed OpenLdap, a special user, with the name `ldap` was automatically born. This built-in account, is what is actually performing the work behind the scenes. In this example, we'll change the ownership of the `*.pem` files so that only this special built-in user account (again, named `ldap`) has access.

```
chown ldap /etc/openldap/*.pem
chmod a-rwx,o+r /etc/openldap/*.pem
```

Setting up a Certification Authority is a lot of work, but it allows you to use the full security capabilities of OpenLDAP. Heck, it's better than moving cleartext passwords around the network. You can also reuse the Certification Authority to create certificates for secure intranet websites and other SSL-enabled applications.

WARNING
If you make a mistake during this section and need to recreate a certificate, you'll need to revoke the original certificate first before the Certification Authority software will allow you to create it again. To revoke a certificate, just enter the following command: **openssl ca -revoke certfilename.pem**.

Now you're ready to move on to configuring the server software itself.

About *chmod* and *chown*

chmod is a very useful command for setting permissions. That gabble of letters after chmod can be read as follows:

(a)ll users should not (-) have (r)ead, (w)rite, or e(x)ecute permission(,) but the (o)wner of the file should (+) have (r)ead permission. These rules are applied consecutively, so that the owner is again given read permission after everyone's permissions are conveniently wiped out.

Use the command man chmod for more information.

chown is the Unix command to set the ownership of a file. The username that follows chown becomes the owner of the file. You can also specify a group to own the file by placing a period (.) between the username and the group.

See man chown for more information.

Configuring the OpenLDAP Server Software

In Chapter 1, it took several steps to create Windows' directory service (Active Directory). At this point, you're ready to leverage the previous step of creating a certificate to finally configure Linux's OpenLDAP, which will be configured in five steps:

1. You'll set up the slapd.conf file that contains technical details about the OpenLDAP server, such as the type of password encryption to use and just enough additional information to "bootstrap" a new LDAP database.

2. You'll configure the ldap.conf file, which gives LDAP client applications running on your server—including, for instance, the Webmin LDAP administration module itself—enough information to make a connection to the LDAP server.

3. You'll launch the LDAP server and ensure that it always starts at boot time.

4. You'll create the uppermost objects in the LDAP database hierarchy: the organization (o) object and organizational unit (OU) objects to contain Unix users and groups.

5. You'll use Webmin to create and manage individual users and groups. Unfortunately, however, Webmin isn't ready to manage OUs. We'll give you some other options for that.

 Be sure to save a copy of your slapd.conf. To rename your original file, we suggest you simply type **mv /etc/openldap/slapd.conf /etc/openldap/slapd.old**.

slapd.conf: Essential Server Settings

Your system will already contain an /etc/openldap/slapd.conf file. In short, our suggestion is to throw it out and use what we're providing here. (A fully commented version of our version of the file is available on the book's website (www.WinLinAnswers.com) if you don't want to type it in by hand.)

```
include          /etc/openldap/schema/core.schema
include          /etc/openldap/schema/cosine.schema
include          /etc/openldap/schema/inetorgperson.schema
include          /etc/openldap/schema/nis.schema

allow bind_v2

pidfile          /var/run/slapd.pid
argsfile         /var/run/slapd.args

TLSCACertificateFile /etc/openldap/cacert.pem
TLSCertificateFile /etc/openldap/slapdcert.pem
TLSCertificateKeyFile /etc/openldap/slapdkey.pem

security ssf=1 update_ssf=112 simple_bind=64

database         bdb
suffix           "dc=ldap,dc=corp,dc=com"
rootdn           "cn=root,dc=ldap,dc=corp,dc=com"
directory        /var/lib/ldap

index objectClass                      eq,pres
index ou,cn,mail,surname,givenname     eq,pres,sub
index uidNumber,gidNumber,loginShell   eq,pres
index uid,memberUid                    eq,pres,sub
index nisMapName,nisMapEntry           eq,pres,sub
```

Here's what each line means:

- The lines beginning with include define the various types of objects that will be allowed in our LDAP database. For instance, nis.schema defines objects that correspond to information you would otherwise deliver via NIS.

- allow bind v2 allows a more modern version of the LDAP protocol to be used.

- pidfile and argsfile record the process ID and initial parameters passed to the slapd server.

- The prefix TLS refers to Transport Layer Security, a newer term for SSL (Secure Sockets Layer), the same protocol that protects secure web shopping sites. These three lines point to the Certification Authority's own signature (`cacert.pem`), the publicly advertised certificate of the LDAP server (`slapdcert.pem`), and the private key of the LDAP server (`slapdkey.pem`).

 Note the slight differences in spelling: TLSCACertificateFile refers to the Certification Authority's certificate file, while TLSCertificateFile refers to your LDAP server's own certificate file. TLSCertificateKeyFile refers to the file containing the server's private key, with which it encrypts outgoing traffic.

- The line that starts with `security` instructs OpenLDAP that *only* secure connections to the server are permitted. This ensures that passwords aren't going across the wire in cleartext.
- `database bdb` states that you will be using the Berkeley Database (BDB) for the storage of data. BDB is a simple, lightweight, open-source database that integrates easily into applications like OpenLDAP, which require a simple data store but not the complexity of a full SQL database.
- The line that starts with `suffix` specifies the top, or *root*, of the LDAP tree. In other words, you can't store LDAP objects higher in the tree than this. Every object in this database will be contained within `dc=LDAP,dc=corp,dc=com`.
- The line that starts with `rootdn` specifies the name of the administrative root user (analogous to the Unix root user). It must be specified in the configuration file rather than the database itself. This avoids a "chicken and egg" problem, since you must have the authority to create the first object in the database. Note that the root user has unlimited privileges to modify (not just query) the database.
- `directory` specifies the location, `/var/lib/ldap`, where the actual database will be stored.

You must also specify a password for this LDAP root administrator, of course. You take care of this with the `slappasswd` command, which generates an encrypted password that you can paste into `slapd.conf`. This is definitely preferable to an unencrypted password in the configuration file!

To create an LDAP administrator root password and add it to the `slapd.conf` file:

1. At the command prompt, enter **slappasswd**.
2. When prompted, provide the same password twice. For our examples, we used **p@ssw0rd**. You'll be presented with a password hash, such as

    `{SSHA}bxC3A8HilcOFEx32/Lloa/4YVwDalqUH`

3. To complete the root-password-setting process, add the following line into `slapd.conf`:

    `rootpw {SSHA}bxC3A8HilcOFEx32/Lloa/4YVwDalqUH`

Of course, be sure to copy and paste the response *you* received from `slappasswd` in place of ours.

Leveraging LDAP Authentication While Logging onto the Server

When you log on the server, you'll want to authenticate to the LDAP database you've built. You'll be acting as an LDAP client, even though the LDAP server happens to run on the same computer. So, in addition to server configuration, linserv1.corp.com must also be configured correctly to allow LDAP client software to work.

The easiest way to set up LDAP authentication is for you to first use Fedora's graphical configuration tools, which conveniently turn on LDAP authentication in a variety of configuration files you would otherwise have to modify by hand.

Then you'll turn your attention to the configuration file for LDAP clients. Since the Fedora tools don't set up that file quite the way you need, you'll make a few modifications to that file after you're done using the Fedora tools.

To turn on LDAP authentication support for logins while on your server:

1. From the Applications menu, choose System Settings ➢ Authentication. The "Authentication Configuration" dialog will appear.

2. You will default to the "User Information" tab within the "Authentication Configuration." Check the "Enable LDAP Support" box. Select the "Configure LDAP" button. Set the LDAP server name to **linserv1.corp.com**, check the "Use TLS to encrypt connections" check box, set the "LDAP search base DN" field to **dc=LDAP,dc=corp,dc=com** and then click the "OK" button.

3. Select the "Authentication" tab. Select the "Enable LDAP Support" check box.

4. Click "OK" to save the changes and close the "Authentication" window.

At this point, the settings in /etc/ldap.conf are probably sufficient for unencrypted LDAP. If you're just authenticating to the server from itself, this is sufficient. However, since you plan to authenticate logins from workstations, you need full encryption.

To slightly complicate matters, there are *two* LDAP client configuration files, /etc/ldap.conf and /etc/openldap/ldap.conf. Apparently this situation exists to allow the LDAP utilities and the authentication system to have *different* LDAP configurations, but in practice this leads to nothing but confusion and wasted hours of testing!

You can solve this problem by taking advantage of one of the nicest features of Linux and Unix in general: the symbolic link.

Enter the following commands, as root:

```
mv /etc/openldap/ldap.conf /etc/openldap/ldap.conf.orig
ln -s /etc/ldap.conf /etc/openldap/ldap.conf
```

From now on, attempts to read either filename will yield the contents of /etc/ldap.conf, giving you a single place to correctly configure all LDAP client parameters for the system.

Next, open /etc/ldap.conf with your text editor and make sure it matches the following, in the order shown; make any modifications as needed. Comments and blank lines are not shown:

```
host linserv1.corp.com
uri ldaps://linserv1.corp.com
base dc=ldap,dc=corp,dc=com
```

```
pam_password md5
tls_checkpeer yes
tls_cacert /etc/openldap/cacert.pem
```

Here's what each line means:

- `host linserv1.corp.com` tells the client piece (on the server) to connect to the default LDAP port (389) on `linserv1.corp.com` (the server itself). You'll support connections both this way, with SSL negotiated later, and on the pure SSL port described next.

- `uri ldaps://linserv1.corp.com`: the server then insists that the client "switch on" SSL encrypted communications, a feature known as "start_tls." The second line presents an alternative: the client may also connect to the "LDAPs" (LDAP over SSL) port (636), using SSL from the very beginning (if the default port does not respond). This is the method that Windows clients will use later in this chapter.

- `base dc=ldap,dc=corp,dc=com` tells the client piece (on the server) where in the directory to start looking for your username.

- `pam_password md5` tells the client piece (on the server) to use MD5 password hashing (a popular and strong password hashing algorithm).

- `tls_checkpeer yes` tells the client piece (on the server) to insist that the server's certificate is valid before continuing.

- `tls_cacert /etc/openldap/cacert.pem` tells the LDAP client on the server where to find the Certification Authority's public key certificate. Without knowing this, the client cannot verify the signature and your LDAP SSL certificate will be rejected.

Your LDAP client settings on the server are now complete. This means you can begin to use LDAP tools on this server to populate your LDAP database with data, just as soon as you launch the LDAP server program itself.

Starting the LDAP Service

At this point, you need to start the LDAP server daemon and ensure that it also launches at every reboot. To do this:

1. Open a terminal window and ensure you are root.

2. Enter the following commands:

   ```
   chkconfig --add ldap
   service ldap start
   ```

Mini-Checkout: Making Sure TLS Encryption Is Set up Correctly for LDAP

You've done quite a bit already. Let's stop and review a bit:

- You opened up ports 389 and 636 in the firewall.

- You created your own Certification Authority.

- You created and signed a certificate for your LDAP server.

- You performed initial configuration of the LDAP server by creating the file `/etc/openldap/slapd.conf`.

- To authenticate the server to itself, you configured `LinServ1` as an LDAP client by using Fedora's Authentication tool and by editing `/etc/ldap.conf`. You created a symbolic link from `/etc/openldap/ldap.conf` to `/etc/ldap.conf` so that all LDAP clients see the same settings.

- You launched the LDAP server and configured Fedora to start the LDAP server again on each reboot.

You can verify your success at this point using the `ldapsearch` command. `ldapsearch` is a utility that acts as an LDAP client and requests information from the LDAP server. You will use the `-x` option, which specifies that you want to use LDAP "simple authentication." Simple authentication theoretically passes a username and password as cleartext, but in this case you are just binding anonymously. To verify that you can connect successfully to the LDAP server, use the following command:

```
ldapsearch -x -ZZ
```

This command should produce output ending in:

```
result: 0 Success
# numResponses: 0
# numEntries: 0
```

If you do not see `result: 0 Success`, review the output for clues to the problem. Make sure your TLS options are set correctly in `ldap.conf` and that the LDAP server key and certificate are installed properly. Then try the command again with the `-d 2` option added to produce even more detailed debugging output.

Initializing the LDAP Database

Once LDAP is installed, there are exactly zero user accounts (other than the root account you specifically created earlier.) You need to create the root of the LDAP database. First, you need to tell it our organization, or "o" name. You'll create `ldap.corp.com`.

Next, you need a place, an organizational unit (OU), to hold your first gaggle of users. You'll create two OUs, one called Users and one called Groups. Guess what you'll be placing inside each?

Wouldn't it be great if you could just fire up Webmin and get started adding user accounts? Too bad you cannot. You need to bootstrap LDAP with the barest amount of initial organizational information. After that, you can use Webmin for ongoing administration. At this point, you need to create the "parent" organization and organizational unit objects in which to store those account objects.

There is a simple plain text format for describing LDAP objects called LDAP Directory Interchange Format (LDIF). Just fire up your favorite text editor and create an LDIF file called `/tmp/linserv1.ldif`. You need to define your organization and your first two OUs. Therefore, enter:

```
dn: dc=ldap,dc=corp,dc=com
o: linserv1.corp.com
```

```
dc: ldap
objectClass: dcObject
objectClass: top
objectClass: organization

dn: ou=Users,dc=ldap,dc=corp,dc=com
objectClass: top
objectClass: organizationalUnit
ou: Users

dn: ou=Groups,dc=ldap,dc=corp,dc=com
objectClass: top
objectClass: organizationalUnit
ou: Groups
```

Take the file you just created and create the root of the LDAP tree with two OUs using the ldapadd utility. Type the following all on one line:

```
ldapadd -x -W -D "cn=root,dc=ldap,dc=corp,dc=com"  -f /tmp/linserv1.corp.com
```

Here's the breakdown of the commands:

- The -x option specifies "simple" authentication, which sends the password in cleartext. You're covered because you are encrypting the entire conversation via SSL.

- The -W option forces you to enter a password at a password prompt.

- The -D option specifies an account to use for binding. At this point, the only available account is the LDAP root account you specified in slapd.conf. Changes can only be made by the root account.

- The -f specifies the LDIF file to import, /tmp/linserv1.corp.com.

Now you need to verify that you have a simple LDAP hierarchy. You'll use the ldapsearch command. To dump the LDAP hierarchy, type **ldapsearch -x** (where -x has the same significance as with ldapadd).

You should receive a plain-text, LDIF-format representation of the same information you inserted into the database. If not, double-check your slapd.conf and ldap.conf files carefully. Take special care to make sure you set up the **rootpw** option correctly in slapd.conf. Then restart slapd with the command:

```
service ldap restart
```

Using Webmin to Manage OpenLDAP Server Graphically

While you have to suffer through the command for initial configuration, you needn't suffer additionally past this point for ongoing administration. Fortunately, there is a Webmin module for this purpose.

Installing the LDAP Users and Groups LDAP Module

First things first: get Webmin to talk to your LDAP server.

To install the Webmin module for LDAP:

1. Log into Webmin and click the "Webmin" button, then "Webmin Configuration."

2. Next, click the "Modules" button, select the "Install Standard Module" radio box, and click the "…" button next to it.

3. From the list of modules that appears, select "LDAP Users and Groups." Then click "Install Module" to carry out the installation.

4. A progress display will appear. When the installation of the module has completed, click "LDAP Users and Groups" at the end of the installation status page.

From now on, you'll always find "LDAP Users and Groups" within Webmin's "System" button, as shown in Figure 2.8.

Configuring the LDAP Users and Groups LDAP Module

You need to tell Webmin where we want to store users and groups. Remember, you've already used an LDIF file with `ldapadd` to create your "base" location for users and groups. All you have to do is tell Webmin where those locations are.

To specify the base locations for users and groups:

1. Using Webmin, select System ➤ LDAP Users and Groups.

2. Select the "Module Config" tab, as shown in Figure 2.9.

FIGURE 2.8   You can easily get to the "LDAP Users and Groups" button from the main "System" button (at the top).

FIGURE 2.9 The Module Config can be hard to find. After you select "LDAP Users and Groups," it will be hiding in a little tab.

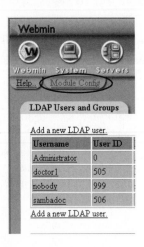

3. On the "Configuration options for LDAP Users and Groups" screen, shown in Figure 2.10, look for the "LDAP Use TLS?" radio button and select "Yes" to enable encryption. You've already made this a requirement for all LDAP connections.

4. At "Bind to LDAP server as," click the radio box next to the entry blank, then enter:

   cn=root,dc=ldap,dc=corp,dc=com

5. For "Credentials for bind name above" enter the same LDAP root password you entered when running the LDAPpasswd utility (**p@ssw0rd**, in our examples).

6. For "Base for users," select the radio box next to the text field and enter:

   ou=Users,dc=ldap,dc=corp,dc=com

   This is the dn (distinguished name) you chose earlier for the organizational unit that will contain Unix user accounts in your LDAP database.

7. For "Base for groups," select the radio box next to the text field and enter:

   ou=Groups,dc=ldap,dc=corp,dc=com

8. Under "Other objectClasses to add to new users" be sure to add the word **account**, which is necessary to avoid a "no structural class for object" error. Every object in an LDAP database must have at least one structural class that provides its context in relation to other types of objects.

9. For "Encryption method for passwords," select "LDAP MD5."

10. Finally, click "Save."

FIGURE 2.10   You're ready to move on to creating users and groups!

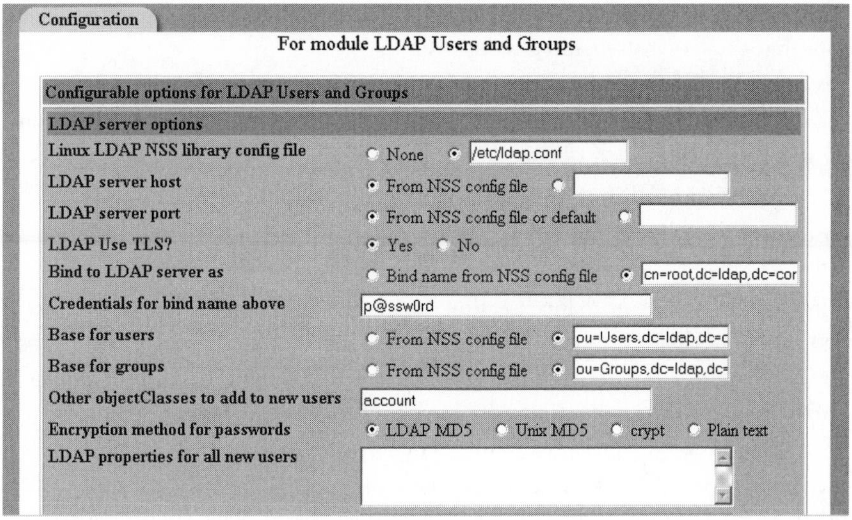

Administering Users and Groups Using LDAP Users and Groups Module

You've already got your Users OU. And that's great. But here's where Webmin falls down a bit. It doesn't seem to have any native way of creating additional OUs or sub-OUs within existing OUs, and that's a crying shame. To see what can do the job, see the sidebar "Other Graphical Interfaces to OpenLDAP." For now, you're going to continue using Webmin (heck, it's already installed) and make sure your OpenLDAP server is functioning properly. If, you later want to install one of the other recommended tools, go for it! There's nothing stopping you.

In this example, you'll create two Linux groups, doctors and nurses and put them in the OU named Groups.

Begin by adding two LDAP groups called doctors and nurses. To create LDAP groups using Webmin:

1.   While in Webmin, click the "System" icon on the Webmin toolbar. Select "LDAP Users and Groups" from the icon list.

2.   Click "Add a new LDAP group," then enter **nurses** in the "Group" name field. The defaults are acceptable for the remaining options. Now click "Create." Repeat this process for the **doctors** group.

You'll create users in a minute, but first you have a bug to squash. In the version of the Webmin LDAP module that you tested, the Webmin "LDAP Users and Groups" module does not immediately list your new groups as potential primary groups for new users, even though it lists them as secondary groups! If you see this problem, there is a simple workaround. First, restart Webmin, which kicks it in the pants. To do this, click the "Webmin" button (upper-left corner of the screen), then "Webmin Configuration." Scroll down the page that follows and click the "Restart Webmin" button.

The restart only takes a moment and allows Webmin to correctly recognize the newly created groups that the server itself can already see.

Now, to create LDAP users:

1.   Using Webmin, click the "System" button, then the "LDAP Users and Groups" button.

2.   On the "LDAP Users and Groups" page, you should see the two new groups listed. Click "Add a new LDAP User" to add your first LDAP user.

3.   On the "Create User" page, enter the username **nurse1** and the real name **Nurse One**. Click the "Normal Password" radio button and enter **p@ssw0rd** next to it.

4.   In the "Group Membership" section, locate the "..." browse button next to "Primary group" and click `nurses` in the list that appears.

5.   You can accept the defaults for the remaining queries; in particular, "create home directory" should already be checked. Now, click "Create."

You have added our first user to the LDAP database.

Repeat the process for `nurse2`. Then repeat the process for `doctor1` and `doctor2`, selecting "`doctors`" as the group for these. In short, you should have four accounts in two groups, like this:

User	Group
nurse1	nurses
nurse2	nurses
doctor1	doctors
doctor2	doctors

Viewing Your New LDAP Users with *getent passwd*

Your users and groups are ready to test! You could just configure the Linux client and start logging in via LDAP authentication, but it's prudent to have a little stop along your journey and check in. You need to make sure the accounts you created with Webmin are being seen by the server.

The `getent` command, a convenient utility, prints out the users and groups available from *all* authentication systems configured for this machine, including the LDAP server on your system. If you created any users with NIS and left NIS enabled in the Fedora authentication tool, you'll see those as well. On `LinServ1`, enter the following command to dump out information about all users:

```
getent passwd
```

Other Graphical Interfaces to OpenLDAP

As a one-stop-shop tool, Webmin can't be beat to configure lots of different aspects of Linux. However, for LDAP-specific tasks, there some alternative choices that specialize in manipulating your day-to-day LDAP tasks. Because none of these packages are inside Fedora, each has its own way of installing so be sure to carefully read the notes on the download pages. Here are our two cents about our experiences of installing and running each:

Luma: http://luma.sourceforge.net/   Because I was using the GNOME desktop, I found Luma is a little clunky to work with. It has various preinstalled plug-ins that work independently against the LDAP database. I couldn't create an OU or move users around between OUs. You need to have the KDE development tools installed for this package to install, along with the most current version of the Python scripting language. If you're already using KDE, you might find it easier to install than I did, but you'll still need to install the KDE development libraries as well as a possible upgrade of Python.

Directory administrator: http://diradmin.open-it.org/index.php   I tried installing rpms for RedHat 9 but had no luck. I re-downloaded the whole source and, per their suggestion, tried to create an rpm from that source. That failed. Then I tried compiling the whole package from the source. That worked, but it couldn't find the icons. Once I made a symbolic link to help the program finds its icons, it did work and had a charming wizard to get me started. Once going, the interface was keen and allowed me to change all sorts of properties about the user (including both Unix and Windows attributes), but I still couldn't create an OU or move users around LDAP. Overall impression: better than the Webmin module but not being able to create OUs is a bummer.

PhPLDAPAdmin: http://www.phpldapadmin.com/   This tool requires you to have an Apache web server up and running first. I didn't try to test it, but there's a spectacular live demo available at the website that really shows this tool off. The tool allows an administrator to create OUs as well as Windows and Linux user accounts and a bunch of other types of LDAP objects. For $50, it appears to be a steal, and includes support and a user-community. In all, looks like a real winner.

LDAP Administrator 3.1: www.ldapadministrator.com   Here's a twist: use a Windows application to manage OpenLDAP. That's the case with Softerra's LDAP Administrator 3.1. It'll manage Active Directory, too, so it's a nice one-stop-shop. However, it's a little on the geeky side— you'll have to get familiar with the specific attributes you might want to manage—but it's got some nice reporting functionality, and the interface can't be beat. It's $215 for a license and worth it. If you're trying to manage both Active Directory and OpenLDAP (or another LDAP server), give this a look. They also have a 100 percent free tool that allows a read-only inspection of your LDAP directories.

The response you receive should end with the following lines:

```
nurse1:x:505:503:Nurse One:/home/nurse1:/bin/sh
nurse2:x:506:503:Nurse Two:/home/nurse2:/bin/sh
doctor1:x:507:504:Doctor One:/home/doctor1:/bin/sh
doctor2:x:508:504:Doctor Two:/home/doctor2:/bin/sh
```

If `getent passwd` doesn't list the `nurse` and/or `doctor` accounts:

- Try the `ldapsearch -x` command. At the end of the output, you should see information about the `nurse` and `doctor` accounts. If so, be sure to reread the section (verifying along the way) "Leveraging LDAP Authentication While Logging onto the Server."

- If `ldapsearch` does not list the new accounts, then you most likely received errors during Webmin administration as well. Go back and check your work in the "Initializing the LDAP Database" section.

Authenticating Linux Clients to the OpenLDAP Server

Next, you need to find out if you can get your Linux client system, `LinCli1`, to authenticate using the LDAP service on `LinServ1`. To do so, you'll configure `LinCli1` to request authentication from the server's LDAP database.

Earlier, you configured your server (`LinServ1`) to use its own LDAP service for authentication. Now, you'll tell `LinCli1` to use `LinServ1` for LDAP lookups.

To enable a Linux client to authenticate via LDAP:

1. While on `LinCli1`, from the Applications menu, select System Settings ➢ Authentication. The "Authentication Configuration" dialog will appear.

2. You will default to the "User Information" tab. Check the "Enable LDAP Support" box.

3. Select the "Configure LDAP" button. The "LDAP Settings" dialog appears. First, select the "Use TLS to encrypt connections" check box. Then, set the LDAP Search Base DN to **dc=ldap,dc=corp,dc=com** and the LDAP server name to **linserv1.corp.com**.

4. Click the "OK" button to return to the "Authentication Configuration" dialog.

5. Select the "Authentication" tab and check the "Enable LDAP Support" box. Then click the "Configure LDAP" button. The "LDAP settings" dialog appears, as shown in Figure 2.11. Again, select the "Use TLS to encrypt connections" check box and set the LDAP Search Base DN to **dc=ldap,dc=corp,dc=com** and the LDAP server name to **linserv1.corp.com**.

6. Click "OK" to close each dialog to complete the task.

Next, since you've opted for a properly secured LDAP server, you'll need to tell your Linux client to definitely use encryption. As previously stated, there are two possible locations client LDAP programs might look: `/etc/ldap.conf` and `/etc/openldap/ldap.conf`.

In the section "Leveraging LDAP Authentication While Logging onto the Server," you used a symbolic link to make one file point toward the other, thus eliminating the problem. Do that same thing again here on the `LinCli1` client.

FIGURE 2.11   Be sure to configure the "LDAP Settings" dialog twice: once for the "User Information" tab, and once here, on the "Authentication" tab.

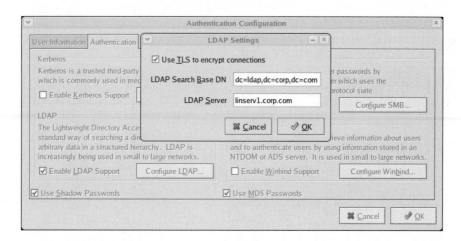

To create a symbolic link on your client, type the following commands:

```
mv /etc/openldap/ldap.conf /etc/openldap/ldap.conf.orig
ln -s /etc/ldap.conf /etc/openldap/ldap.conf
```

Now make sure /etc/ldap.conf contains the following settings in the order shown:

```
host linserv1.corp.com
uri ldaps://linserv1.corp.com
base dc=ldap,dc=corp,dc=com
pam_password md5
tls_checkpeer yes
tls_cacert /etc/openldap/cacert.pem
```

> You might want to look through the whole /etc/ldap.conf file. The file should be mostly comments. However, if even one stray line is uncommented, you will be unsuccessful. In other words, triple-check ldap.conf and ensure the only uncommented lines are the ones you add, and make sure it looks like our example here.

If you need a refresher of what each setting in /etc/ldap.conf means, see the section "Leveraging LDAP Authentication While Logging onto the Server."

Finally, you'll need to install the CA certificate for your own Certification Authority on the client. To do so, just copy the file /etc/openldap/cacert.pem from LinServ1 to LinCli1, installing it in the same place on LinCli1. Why do you copy the CA certificate, and not the LDAP server's certificate? As explained earlier, the value of a Certification Authority is that a single CA certificate can be used to validate *many* server certificates.

When a client connects to the LDAP server, the LDAP server presents its certificate. The client verifies the signature on the SSL certificate using the public key in `cacert.pem`.

The `scp` command is a convenient way to copy a file from one Linux system to another. The syntax is very similar to `cp`, with the addition of a simple syntax to specify the username and hostname on each end; usually, of course, one end is a local file or path in which to put that file.

First, you'll need to open up the SSH port on the firewall. That's because `scp` is built "on top" of SSH, the secure shell often used for remote access to the shell prompt. This is simpler for SSH than for some services because there is a convenient check box for it. From the Applications menu, select System Settings ➤ Security Level. On the "Firewall Options" tab, in the "Trusted Services" list box, check "SSH." Then click "OK" to put the change into effect.

You need to copy a file from the server to the client (while logged in at the client), so execute this command as root on `LinCli1`:

```
scp root@linserv1.corp.com:/etc/openldap/cacert.pem /etc/openldap
```

Here's the breakdown of the command:

- The source filename is the first parameter. You need to tell `scp` the credentials of the username on the source server: *username@server*. The colon marks the end of the hostname and the beginning of the directory name to which the file should be copied, in this case, `/etc/openldap/cacert.pem`.

- The destination filename is then given, in this case, `/etc/openldap`.

You will be prompted for the root password on `linserv1.corp.com`, which we have set to p@ssw0rd in the examples.

> scp can be used to copy files in either direction. scp also supports the -r option, which allows directories and their contents to be copied recursively. In general, most options of cp behave the same way in scp. Convenient, isn't it?

When the file copying operation is complete, make sure the permissions and ownership of the file are correct on the receiving end by executing the following commands as root on `LinCli1`:

```
chmod a+r,o+rw /etc/openldap/cacert.pem
chown ldap /etc/openldap/cacert.pem
```

The `chmod` command permits all users to read the certificate file (a+r). You allow this because you want applications on the client to start LDAP conversations with the server in order to verify passwords as needed. The `chown` command, as previously explained, grants ownership of a file to a particular user, in this case to the `ldap` user.

Finally, as before, verify your configuration using the `getent` command:

```
getent passwd
```

If all goes as expected, you'll see a list of usernames that ends in `nurse1`, `nurse2`, `doctor1`, and `doctor2`.

> If you don't see these new users listed, double-check your settings and make sure you created the symbolic link between /etc/ldap.conf and /etc/openldap/ldap.conf correctly. If you still have no joy, check the firewall settings on the server and verify that getent passwd still works there. (You *did* test it on the server the first time, right?)

Now, the final step: ensuring that home directories will be created for LDAP users the first time they log into this particular client.

Earlier, we said that there are three typical ways users log on and interact with the system: the shell, encrypted shell (via SSH), and the GNOME interface, Therefore, you need to tell each of these authentication mechanisms how to create home directories. The line you'll add is:

```
session     required     pam_mkhomedir.so skel=/etc/skel umask=0077
```

Simply append the preceding line to the following three files:

- /etc/pam.d/login
- /etc/pam.d/sshd
- /etc/pam.d/gdm

Again, each file control policies for how clients log on to the Linux machine. The /etc/pam.d/login is for plain-text console and serial logins, /etc/pam.d/sshd is for SSH-encrypted shell logins, and /etc/pam.d/gdm is how most users graphically log on via the Fedora GNOME desktop.

That's it! You're ready to try an actual LDAP login. The computer must be restarted to thoroughly reinitialize the authentication interfaces with the new pam settings. Once finally rebooted, try logging in with the username nurse1 and the password p@ssw0rd. You should receive a message notifying you that a home directory has been created for this account, and then your desktop should appear as normal. That's it—you've achieved Linux-to-Linux LDAP bliss!

If Logins from Linux Clients Don't Work

Here are a handful of things to try if you are unable to get your Linux clients to authenticate to your Linux LDAP server:

- Try the ldapsearch -x command on LinCli1 and LinServ1. Do you see the doctor and nurse accounts on one machine but not another? If so, review your /etc/ldap.conf on the computer that isn't working.

- Ensure the firewall settings on the server correctly pass ports 389 and 636 through as described in the "Firewall Passthrough" section earlier.

- Double-check your entries in the Authentication tool (which you found inside in the "System Settings" submenu) and make sure your /etc/ldap.conf changes are kosher. Sometimes the Authentication tool will overwrite portions of this file and append unwanted material to the end.

- Reboot the Linux client again. It can't hurt.

Authenticating Windows to OpenLDAP via SSL

If you want to have Windows clients use your Linux OpenLDAP directory, you can allow it. But out of the box, Windows doesn't natively "speak" plain LDAP; it speaks NTLM to old-school Domain Controllers and Kerberos to an Active Directory Domain Controller.

We've already discussed how to inject additional (or alternate) methods of authentication into the interactive logon process via pGina, and pGina has a plug-in module for LDAP.

On your test Windows client, be sure you have pGina installed as specified earlier. Once installed, there are two main steps to having Windows authenticate to OpenLDAP:

- Introduce the CA certificate to Windows so that your Certification Authority and all certificates you choose to sign with it can be recognized. This is required before you can communicate with the OpenLDAP server via SSL.

- Configure pGina to communicate to your OpenLDAP server via SSL.

Importing the CA Certificate to Your Windows Clients

First, you'll need to copy the SSL certificate from the Linux server. Since SSH is already installed on the Linux server, we suggest that you use a user-friendly Windows scp (secure copy) client, such as winscp (available from winscp.sourceforge.net), to copy the file from /etc/openldap/cacert.pem on LinServ1 to the desktop of your Windows client system.

Once you have the public certificate copied to the Windows client, you're almost there. The certificate is just a text file and should look something like this (although it's cut short here to save space):

```
-----BEGIN CERTIFICATE-----
MIIDBjCCAm+gAwIBAgIBADANBgkqhkiG9w0BAQQF
MBMGA1UECBMMUGVubN5bHZhbmlhMRUwEwYDVQQH
BgNVBAoTCGNvcnAuY29tMRYwFAYDVQQDEw1sZGFw
MTE1NDUxM1oXDTA2MDEyMTE1NDUxM1owZjELMAkG
DFB1bm5zeWx2YW5pYTEVMBMGA1UEBxMMUGhpbGFk
b3JwLmNvbTEWMBQGA1UEAxMNbGRhcC5jb3JwLmNv
AAOBjQAwgYkCgYEAyzAapLWPTEH2OATd65dHyFKj
-----END CERTIFICATE-----
```

The file coming from Linux is cacert.pem. Of course, things are different in the Windows world, so you must rename the file to cacert.cer (it's the .cer part of the name that's important). You can see the certificate placed on the Windows desktop in Figure 2.12.

Once you double-click "cacert.cer," you'll open the certificate. In the "General" tab of the Certificate, click "Install Certificate." This will open the "Certificate Import Wizard" as also shown in Figure 2.12

Now you just have to tell Windows where to store the certificate. Don't just blast on through, accepting all the defaults here. There are particular steps you must take to put the certificate in the right place. To install the certificate on your XP system:

1.   At the "Welcome to the Certificate Import Wizard" screen, click "Next."

FIGURE 2.12   After you double-click the "cacert.cer" file, you can install the certificate. Just follow the instructions in the text carefully.

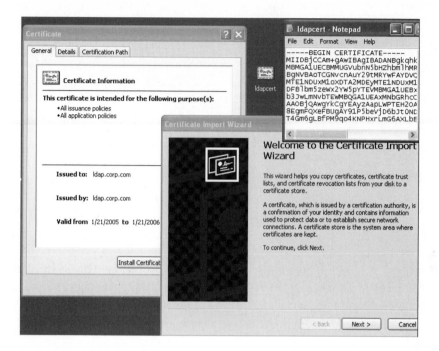

2.   Select "Place all certificates in the following store" (do not select "Automatically select the certificate store").

3.   Click "Browse."

4.   Check the "Show physical stores" check box.

5.   Drill down to "Trusted Root Certification Authorities" and then highlight "Local Computer," as shown in Figure 2.13. Click "OK."

6.   At the Certificate Store screen, select "Next."

7.   At the final page of the Wizard, select "Finish."

You have now introduced the certificate to Windows.

To Configure pGina to Authenticate to OpenLDAP via SSL

Be sure you're logged in as a local administrator. To configure pGina to perform encrypted LDAP logins:

1.   Download and install the required plug-in(s). In this example, we downloaded the LDAP plug-in (not the LDAP Groups plug-in) from here: http://pgina.xpasystems.com/plugins/LDAPauth.php.

2.   Select the pGina configuration tool by selecting Start ≻ Programs ≻ pGina ≻ Configuration Tool.

FIGURE 2.13 Click the "Show physical stores" check, then drill down to "Local Computer."

3. Select the "Plugin" tab. Click the "Browse" button and select "LDAPauth_plus.dll" (which was installed in step 1 in c:\pGina\plugins\LDAPauth). Once selected, the Plugin Path will confirm your selection, as shown in Figure 2.14.

4. On the "Plugin" tab, select the "Configure" button to open the "LDAPAuth" screen. Here are the settings you'll need to choose:

LDAP Method Click "MultiMap Mode."

LDAP Server Enter the name of the server, linserv1.corp.com.

Prepend Type uid= as shown in Figure 2.14. Every user's DN (distinguished name) will start with uid=.

Use SSL Because your server is set up to accept secure communications via SSL certificates, ensure this is checked. Leaving it unchecked will result in a failure to authenticate.

Contexts For now, all your LDAP users are stored in the users container. Enter the full path to the users container: ou=users,dc=ldap,dc=corp,dc=com and then click "Add Context." The context will be added in the big open box as shown in Figure 2.14.

5. Click "OK" to close pGina's LDAPAuth screen. Click "OK" to close pGina's configuration.

6. Reboot your Windows XP machine (logging off isn't enough).

Next time you press Ctrl+Alt+Del, you should be able to log in with one of the newly created LDAP users, such as doctor2, with a password of p@ssw0rd.

FIGURE 2.14   pGina is using LDAPAuth plug-in; the LDAP server and context are added, as well as checking "Use SSL."

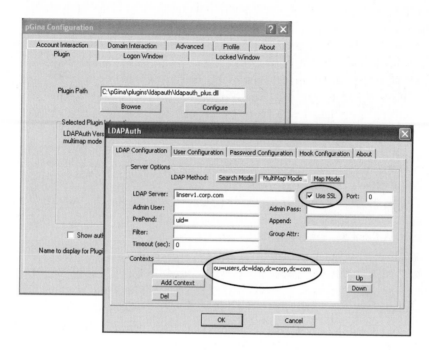

If it doesn't work, here are some things to try and/or revisit:

- From the XP machine, check to make sure you can ping linserv1.corp.com. Without DNS resolution, you won't get very far. You might have to add an A record entry into the DNS server. Alternatively, you can use a static hosts file entry.

- Make sure you followed the instructions for installing the certificate exactly as specified. Again, when installing the certificate, you didn't just take the defaults, you had to make some choices.

- Did you check the "Use SSL" check box as shown in Figure 2.14? Again, your server requires all traffic to be encrypted. It simply won't accept unencrypted traffic.

- Are you allowing ports 636 and 389 to flow outward? Windows firewall doesn't restrict outbound communication, but if you're using a third-party Windows firewall, make sure you're not somehow squelching these required outbound ports.

- Some advanced help in troubleshooting the certificate is available on the pGina website at http://pgina.xpasystems.com/plugins/LDAPauth.php, specifically in the section "How do I know if my LDAP server's SSL certificate is correctly recognized on my computer?"

- See the earlier section "Troubleshooting pGina" for three more tips that might additionally help.

Checkout: Using OpenLDAP for Your Authentication

In this previous section, you just set up your Linux machine to be an OpenLDAP server. You authenticated both Linux Clients and Windows Clients to OpenLDAP.

Here's a quick rundown of how you did it.

To configure your Linux OpenLDAP Server:

- If you're using the firewall, you adjusted the firewall settings to allow TCP ports 389 (unencrypted LDAP traffic) and 636 (encrypted LDAP traffic) through.

- You created a Certification Authority, generated a private SSL certificate (to store on the server), and created a public certificate (to store on the workstations).

- You configured the OpenLDAP server configuration file (`slapd.conf`) and told it what certificates to use, that you want to use encryption, and the name of the root user and the LDAP directory (`ldap.corp.com`).

- You used the `slappasswd` to generate a password hash for the OpenLDAP root user. Then you added that password hash into the `slapd.conf` file. This helped you get OpenLDAP started without any real users yet.

- You told the server to start using LDAP when you log on directly to it. First, you used the graphical "Authentication Configuration" dialog to specify that you want to start using LDAP.

- Then you did a little trick using symbolic links to fool Linux into thinking there were two LDAP client configuration files (when, in reality, you were centralizing on one).

- You configured the server's LDAP client via the `ldap.conf` file. You told the server to use the LDAP server to authenticate you (naturally); you also told it what kind of password encryption you'll use and where the private certificate is.

- You started the LDAP server and ensured it launches at every reboot. You did that with `chkconfig --add ldap` and `service ldap start`, respectively.

- You created your first organization (`linserv1.corp.com`) and two OUs: `Users` and `Groups`. You did this by hand with an LDIF text file. You then used `ldapadd` to import the file and create the objects.

- You instructed Webmin where to place users and groups in the two OUs you created for OpenLDAP. You used Webmin to create some initial users and groups. Webmin isn't the ideal tool for the long run, but for initial testing it'll do. (Better tools are phpLDAPAdmin and LDAP Administrator).

To configure your Linux Client to use OpenLDAP:

- You used the graphical "Authentication Configuration" to specify the LDAP server and base DN.

- You did a little trick using symbolic links to fool Linux into thinking there was only one LDAP configuration file (when, in reality, there were two).

- You configured the client's LDAP settings via the `ldap.conf` file. You told it to use the LDAP server to authenticate you; you also told it what kind of password encryption you'll use and where the private certificate is.

- You copied the private cert from the server to the client.
- You changed the three usual login methods to authenticate to your LDAP repository. These three usual methods are the shell, the encrypted SSH shell, and the graphical GNOME interface.

To configure your Windows client to use OpenLDAP:

- You loaded pGina on your Windows client.
- You loaded the pGina LDAP plug-in.
- You configured the pGina LDAP plug-in by telling it the LDAP server name and the correct base DN, and specifying that it use SSL encryption.

Authentication to Samba as a PDC

Samba is a suite of tools that helps Linux pretend to be a Windows machine, at least for authentication and file and print services. That is, you can run Samba on a Linux machine and share files to Windows clients or run Samba on a Linux machine and grab files on an existing Windows server.

Samba takes its clever name from the protocol that's used under the hood for file transfers: Server-Message-Block, or SMB. Samba isn't just available for Linux; it's available for a litany of non-Windows operating systems—be sure to check out www.samba.org for the complete list.

We'll be exploring Samba backward and forward in the upcoming chapters in this book. In this chapter, you'll perform just one major magic trick with Samba: you'll make it look, act, and quack like a Windows NT 4 PDC (Primary Domain Controller) and authenticate your Windows ducklings, er, clients.

 It is also possible to authenticate Linux clients *directly* to a Samba PDC (or NT 4 PDC). We don't cover that in this chapter. However, we do have a related sidebar in Chapter 3, "Making Linux Clients Authenticate to a PDC." In general, however, authenticating Linux clients to a Samba PDC doesn't make sense. That's because complete Unix user and group ID information is more easily available from NIS or LDAP, running on the very same Linux server.

Before we go on and you fall in love with Samba, here are the two major shortcomings (as we see it) to making your Linux servers pretend to be NT 4:

- No Active Directory–based Group Policy for Windows 2000, Windows XP, and Windows 2003 clients. For us, this is a showstopper in a production environment. Group Policy is a major force in Windows management—and with a bajillion Windows clients out there—so not being able to use Group Policy to manage your Windows clients puts a damper on Samba's usefulness as a Domain Controller.
- While you can make Samba server pretend to be both a NT 4 PDC (which you'll do here) and NT 4 BDC (which we're not going to show at all), there are real issues:
  - Samba cannot be the BDC of a *real* NT 4 PDC.

- Samba cannot be a BDC when the domain is Active Directory. Not even when the Active Directory is in "mixed mode," which would normally allow NT 4.0 BDCs!

In other words, Samba can *only* be a BDC when the PDC is a Samba server. This is a real drag, as it makes branch office deployments of Samba when the main office is Active Directory a real challenge. Samba 3.0's maximal usefulness as a Domain Controller can be seen in Figure 2.15. This diagram is for example; this isn't how we're going to configure it.

In essence, while pretending to be a Domain Controller, Samba 3 is capable of one thing: pretending to be NT 4. While this might be sufficient for older Windows clients and any kind of Linux client, the loss of enterprise-quality identity management is painful. That is, having "pockets" of micro-directories in your enterprise is a hassle you don't need. However, depending on what you need to do with it, Samba might just be the ticket, so we'll present it here.

 We'll also be exploring Samba in Chapter 4 as a file server. Indeed, it can integrate quite nicely with existing Active Directory and can be a very useful additional free file server when you need it.

Samba is capable of operating as a fully functional Windows NT 4–style PDC. Before you use it as such, however, you should ask yourself a question: in what kind of repository do you want to store the actual accounts? You have oodles of options...pick one:

- `smbpasswd` files: similar to classic Linux `/etc/passwd` files.

- `tbdsam` databases: Samba's own "Trivial DataBase" format, introduced with Samba 3.*x*. Reasonably fast but not suitable for replication, so this is a good choice only when a single domain controller is sufficient.

- LDAP repositories: use `ldapsam` as the access mechanism.

- MySQL repositories: use `mysqlsam` as the access mechanism.

- `Xmlsam` repositories: use a text-based file with XML content.

With so many choices, what's best?

Option 1: tdbsam (can be easier)   `smbpasswd` and `tbdsam` are easiest to set up. Neither even tries to replace `/etc/passwd`. Instead, they extend it. The `smbpasswd` back end uses a `smbpasswd` file that adds a Windows password hash but doesn't extend `/etc/passwd` further than that. However, `smbpasswd` has fallen out of favor, and `tdbsam` is becoming more popular. This is because `smbpasswd` does not scale well to large numbers of users and does not provide for storage of additional Windows-specific information about users, groups, or computers. The `tdbsam` back end, on the other hand, is powerful enough to store all the information you might need for a real domain controller... if you're working in a vacuum with just one domain controller, that is. `tdbsam` is not recommended for more than 250 users, according to the Samba development team. And using `tdbsam` doesn't provide a way to build Linux-based BDCs for your Linux-based PDC, so it doesn't scale very well. It also can't build on your existing work with LDAP for Linux client authentication. However, if you're flipping through this book and you're in a hurry to build a stand-alone PDC, `tdbsam` is likely to be your choice. However, bear in mind that certain projects later in the book will only work by going forward with the LDAP option.

FIGURE 2.15   Here's how Samba might integrate into your environment.

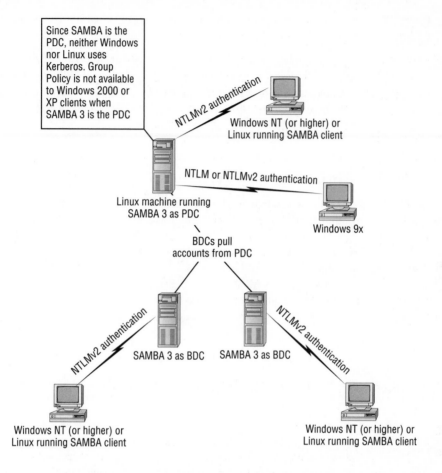

Since SAMBA is the
PDC, neither Windows
nor Linux uses
Kerberos. Group
Policy is not available
to Windows 2000 or
XP clients when
SAMBA 3 is the PDC

NTLMv2 authentication

Windows NT (or higher) or
Linux running SAMBA client

NTLM or NTLMv2 authentication

Windows 9x

Linux machine running
SAMBA 3 as PDC

BDCs pull
accounts from PDC

NTLMv2 authentication

SAMBA 3 as BDC   SAMBA 3 as BDC

NTLMv2 authentication

Windows NT (or higher) or
Linux running SAMBA client

Windows NT (or higher) or
Linux running SAMBA client

Option 2: OpenLDAP (more robust and scalable)   You can store the accounts in OpenLDAP
or another LDAP server with the ldapsam Samba back end. Since LDAP databases are easy to
replicate, it is possible to build BDCs when you choose this method, and OpenLDAP is a genuine database built for lots and lots of accounts. Also, if you've been following along up until
this point, you've already built an OpenLDAP database and you can leverage that work. That
is, you can make the OpenLDAP database the place where the accounts live for Samba, *and
those same accounts are already valid for your Linux LDAP clients.* We strongly recommend
LDAP for large deployments.

In the next two big sections, we'll examine both methods. But, then, we'll configure the
robust LDAP method. In real life, you wouldn't do both on the same server, so don't do so here.
Our suggestion is to pick a method (Option 1 or Option 2) and stick with it.

In this book, we're not going to be discussing the other three possible ways to configure Samba account databases. That is, we're not going to cover smbpasswd files, MySQL repositories (via mysqlsam), or Xmlsam repositories. If these options interest you, you can check out www.samba.org/samba/docs/man/Samba-HOWTO-Collection/. This is also a useful guide for the myriad of options you can stick in a smb.conf file (explored in a moment.) Unlike many Samba HOWTOs on the Net, this official HOWTO stays reasonably up to date with changes in the Samba 3.*x* series.

Option 1: Samba Storing Accounts in *tdbsam*

The Samba project has its own simple database format, called TDB. tdbsam is the name of the Samba back-end module that allows TDB to be used as a repository for user accounts.

If you're gung-ho about using the tdbsam back end, we've got a how-to on our website at www.winlinanswers.com/ for how to do this. However, for this book, we recommend you stick with ldapsam as the back-end and continue on by implementing Option 2, below. Doing a good job with tdbsam is nearly as much work, especially if you already built an LDAP authentication system earlier in this chapter. And the end result doesn't scale well, or integrate as well with certain aspects of the e-mail system we'll build in Chapter 6.

Option 2: Samba Storing Accounts in OpenLDAP

In this section, you'll set up a Samba PDC to use an LDAP database back end for better scalability.

In practice, you'd use either the tdbsam *or* LDAP as the back-end. So if you've already gone up to our website, and used the downloadable documentation to implement the tdbsam back end, no need to proceed here.

If you want to use the more robust LDAP, doing so is easier than you might think, thanks to the work you already did earlier in this chapter to enable LDAP authentication for Unix clients. You can reuse all of that work as part of your Samba PDC. In other words, you'll be using your LDAP server as a back end to store the actual account information, as shown in Figure 2.16. As an added benefit, Linux clients can continue to authenticate directly to the LDAP server using the same accounts that are valid on Windows workstations.

The same "LDAP Users and Groups" Webmin module you used earlier can also be used to administer Samba domain accounts! In fact, LDAP accounts you already created can be "upgraded" to allow Samba authentication. But first, there are a few housekeeping chores you must attend to.

FIGURE 2.16   Internal architecture of your Samba PDC

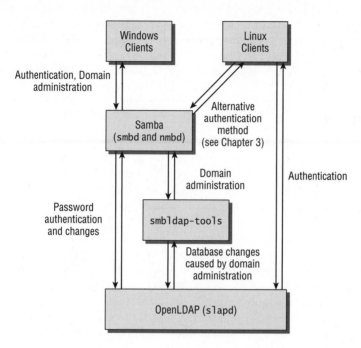

In the previous section, you built a complete authentication system based on a popular LDAP server called OpenLDAP. Additionally, to make sure your passwords weren't being sent around in the clear, you used SSL encryption based on certificates issued by a Certification Authority so your clients and your OpenLDAP server could securely communicate.

Adjusting the Firewall to Allow Samba Traffic

Much like LDAP, Samba is compatible with Fedora's standard firewall software, but it is necessary to open up a few additional ports. Specifically, you must open ports 137 (for NetBIOS browsing), 138 (for NetBIOS name service), 139 (for file and printer sharing), and 445 (for Windows 2000, XP, and Windows Server 2003 without the NetBIOS helper). To do so, follow these steps:

1. From the "Applications" menu, select System Settings ➢ Security Level.

2. If "Disable firewall" is selected, change the setting to "Enable firewall."

3. Add the following to the end of the current contents of the "other ports" list:

   `137:udp, 138:udp, 139:tcp, 445:tcp`

4. Click "OK" to complete the process.

Directly authenticating users to LDAP is a reasonable solution for Linux-based networks. If you also have Windows, you can certainly use the pGina plug-in for Windows workstations, but you don't need to with Samba. Samba can act as a PDC, and use your OpenLDAP server as an accounts repository. Why bother? Because a Samba PDC pretends to be a Windows NT 4.0 PDC and therefore you needn't modify any Windows clients to authenticate right to it. There's no need to reconfigure every Windows client with, say, pGina to make the magical connection. All the client workstations need to do is join the Samba domain—exactly as they would join an NT 4 domain.

Adding *samba.schema* to OpenLDAP

To store Windows account information in OpenLDAP, you need a slightly enhanced set of structure and syntax definitions—a different *schema*. For instance, in the Samba/Windows world, each account contains a flag that indicates whether an account is a user account (for a person) or machine account (for a workstation). Unix accounts make no operational distinction between users and workstations, so the OpenLDAP schema files do not contain an attribute for the associated flag.

Out of the box, OpenLDAP knows how to handle Linux accounts because there's a convenient definition of what a Linux account looks like. This is contained within the file /etc/openldap/schema/nis.schema. You told OpenLDAP to use this definition via an include directive in the /etc/openldap/slapd.conf file. In other words, you taught OpenLDAP how to handle Unix accounts. Now you need to tell it how to handle Windows accounts.

OpenLDAP *doesn't* include an out-of-the-box schema that defines the additional characteristics that make Windows accounts different. Fortunately, however, the Samba software *does* include a ready-to-go samba.schema file. Once plugged into your OpenLDAP server's /etc/openldap/schema directory, your existing OpenLDAP server will be ready to rock for Windows accounts.

Nothing's easy. Things are complicated just a little bit by the fact that the samba.schema file is in the Samba documentation directory...and there is a Samba documentation directory for each version of Samba that has previously been installed. When you updated your packages in Chapter 1, you most likely wound up with at least two Samba documentation directories: one for the version that came on the CD and one for the latest official version from Fedora. As of this writing, the current version is version 3.0.10, which places the Samba documentation in the /usr/share/doc/samba-3.0.10 directory. Your Samba version is most likely more recent than ours.

Use the ls -d command to list *all* of the Samba documentation directories, making it easy to pick out the newest version.

 The -d option for the ls command specifies that directories should be listed by name only, without descending to list their contents.

To take care of these tasks, just follow these steps:

1. Add the following line to /etc/openldap/slapd.conf, immediately following the last include line already present:

    ```
    include          /etc/openldap/schema/samba.schema
    ```

2. Locate your Samba documentation directory:

    ```
    ls -d /usr/share/doc/samba-*
    ```

Make note of the most recent version number if you see more than one, and substitute that version for 3.0.10 in the step that follows.

3. Copy the samba.schema file from the Samba documentation directory to /etc/openldap/schema:

```
cp /usr/share/doc/samba-3.0.10/LDAP/samba.schema /etc/openldap/schema
```

Speeding up Samba/OpenLDAP Performance

Performance is also important. The OpenLDAP server can always answer any query by searching through its entire database, one item at a time. But if you have a bajillion accounts in your OpenLDAP database, it makes sense to perform an index ahead of time.

index directives in /etc/openldap/slapd.conf already speed up requests such as "give me the account object for the username fred." But Samba may also need to look up a workstation quickly by its SID (security identifier). To all this, you'll add an index directive to speed up such common Windows requests.

Add the following additional line to /etc/openldap/slapd.conf, following the last index line already present in that file:

```
index sambaSID,sambaPrimaryGroupSID,sambaDomainName    eq
```

Restarting OpenLDAP with the Samba Changes

You can now restart the OpenLDAP service with these changes by executing the following command at the terminal prompt as root:

```
service ldap restart
```

"Glue" for Samba and LDAP: The *smbldap-tools*

Samba ships with the built-in capability to consult an LDAP database for user authentication—but there's more to operating a full-fledged PDC than simply fielding ongoing user authentication requests.

For a Windows workstation to be happy, it has to be a member of a domain. It doesn't have to be a Windows domain—it can be a Samba domain pretending to be a Windows domain. But in either case, the Windows machine must be able to join the domain in the usual Windows way without the manual intervention of an administrator on the server itself. Additionally, a domain administrator might also want to create and administer user accounts via Windows-based domain administration tools, and the PDC should handle these requests correctly as well.

You would think that these capabilities would be built right into the Samba package. But they're not. The authors of Samba followed a very Unix philosophy: each program should do one job well. Samba's primary job is to speak "Windows." Its secondary job is to interface with *other* programs that do things like managing accounts and storing directory information. You're using LDAP to ultimately store your accounts, but others may choose completely different back ends. Since Samba doesn't implement the back-end, it must provide a way to specify programs that should be run to carry out each of the back-end tasks when they are needed.

Since LDAP is the back end, you can take advantage of a ready-made suite of programs for those back-end tasks. Implemented as a collection of scripts written in the Perl programming language, the smbldap-tools suite provides the necessary "glue" between Samba and LDAP. While the name "tools" might suggest programs that the administrator runs personally, for the most part this is not the case. Most of the smbldap-tools are meant to be run automatically by Samba. For instance, every time an administrator sits down at a workstation and joins that workstation to the domain, Samba automatically starts up the command smbldap-adduser with a special -w option that specifies a workstation account is being added rather than a regular user account. That tool then adds an object representing the new workstation in the LDAP database. Without the ability to do this, a Samba server can't accommodate adding a new workstation or other administrative tasks in the standard Windows way using tools Windows administrators are familiar with. You would constantly need manual administrator interaction on the server itself—not to mention that the standard Windows dialog boxes to join a domain wouldn't work. And that's no fun. Hence, you'll employ the smbldap-tools to make sure all of the standard Windows dialogs for administering a domain work properly with your Samba domain.

Preparing for the *smbldap-tools* Installation

While a copy of these scripts is included with Samba, the latest and greatest version is maintained by the generous folks at Idealx, who offer the tools at http://samba.idealx.org. We recommend you use the latest version directly from Idealx; our instructions are based the latest version we could get a hold of.

To obtain and install the smbldap-tools, just follow these steps:

1. Access the URL http://samba.idealx.org/dist/.

2. Download the latest version in .tar.gz format. You'll see an example of the right file in Figure 2.17. As of this writing, the latest version is smbldap-tools-0.8.6.tgz. (An rpm file is available, but we cannot recommend using it because of dependency error messages that could not be satisfactorily resolved with the rpm command as of this writing. In other words, we couldn't get it to work properly.)

3. Copy this file to /usr/local/src on LinServ1. If you download the file to a Windows machine, we suggest copying the file to LinServ1 using the free, user-friendly "WinSCP" Windows scp program (available from http://winscp.sourceforge.net).

4. Change the directory with the cd /usr/local/src command.

5. A .tgz file is a file that has been "tarred," meaning that many files have been accumulated together into a single archive, and then "gzipped," a Unix file format closely related to the .zip format common on Windows systems. To unpack the contents of the file and change the current directory to the newly unpacked directory, you can use the tar command. Pass three options, z, x, and f. z indicates that the input file is gzipped, x indicates that files should be extracted (read) from the input file, and f indicates that input is from a file rather than from an old-fashioned backup tape drive:

```
tar -zxf smbldaptools-0.8.6.tgz
cd smbldaptools-0.8.6
```

See the ".tar.gz, gzip, gunzip, and tar" sidebar for more information about gzip, gunzip, and tar.

FIGURE 2.17   Downloading this latest version of the smbldap-tools

Name	Last modified	Size
Parent Directory	16-Dec-2004 21:57	-
ChangeLog	18-Jan-2005 13:46	11k
INSTALL	17-Jan-2005 09:28	5k
LATEST-IS-SMBLDAP-TOOLS-0.8.6	18-Jan-2005 13:12	0k
old-versions/	18-Jan-2005 13:10	-
smbldap-tools-0.8.5-3.tgz	28-Oct-2004 12:54	269k
smbldap-tools-0.8.6-1.noarch.rpm	17-Jan-2005 09:28	92k
smbldap-tools-0.8.6-1.src.rpm	17-Jan-2005 09:28	275k
smbldap-tools-0.8.6.tgz	17-Jan-2005 09:28	271k
smbldap-tools.pdf	10-Feb-2004 10:30	197k

.tar.gz, gzip, gunzip, and tar

The Linux/Unix philosophy generally calls for simple utilities that do a single job well. This is why data compression and the archive creation were traditionally handled by two different tools in the Linux world.

gunzip filename.gz is the reverse of gzip filename. While gzip filename produces a compressed file called filename.gz, gunzip filename.gz restores the original and deletes the compressed version. Unlike .zip, .gz is a simple container format for a single file only.

tar -xf filename.tar is the reverse of tar -cf filename.tar [filename list]. While tar -cf filename.tar [filename list] builds a new .tar archive containing all of the specified files, including subdirectories of any directories in the list, tar -xf filename.tar extracts and restores all of the files found in the .tar file. Unlike gzip and gunzip, tar -cf and tar -xf do *not* delete the original files or the .tar file, respectively.

In recent years, the z option was added to tar as a convenience; it automatically invokes gunzip on the fly to take care of unzipping compressed data before extracting files from the archive. When the z option is used, the .tar.gz or .tgz file is *not* replaced with a .tar file. Instead, tar skips ahead to extracting the actual contents of the archive.

Teaching Samba How to Encrypt Passwords

The latest versions of the smbldap-tools can encrypt Samba passwords directly, which is a nice performance boost over previous versions that relied on a separate program to do this. However, since the smbldap-tools are written in the Perl programming language, you need to install the optional "Crypt::SmbHash" Perl module to make this feature work. Fortunately, the Perl community maintains a central repository of such modules called the CPAN (Comprehensive Perl Archive Network).

Fedora includes a helpful up2date-like tool called cpan for installing the latest versions of such modules, and it provides a fairly painless way to install any widely recognized enhancement for Perl. You can learn more about Perl by visiting www.perl.org. For more information about CPAN, see www.cpan.org.

To install the "Crypt::SmbHash" Perl module:

1. Execute the cpan command:

```
cpan
```

If you have never used cpan before on LinServ1, you may be asked if you wish to manually configure it. You can answer no to this prompt; the automatic configuration is quite effective.

2. When the cpan> prompt appears, enter the following command to install the "Crypt::Smb-Hash" Perl module:

```
install Crypt::SmbHash
```

3. When the cpan> prompt returns, quit cpan with this command:

```
quit
```

Installing the *smbldap-tools* on Your System

You're nearly ready to install the smbldap-tools utility programs. Before you do, you'll need to change two settings in a Perl source code file that all of those utilities share in common, smbldap_tools.pm.

Don't panic when you open the file. Although this file contains Perl programming language code, you *don't* need to know Perl to understand what needs to be changed. All you need to do is open the file with your preferred text editor, locate two directory names that are set incorrectly for your system, and fix them.

Then, since the file contains Perl code that is used by more than one Perl program, you will install it in a place where *all* of the smbldap-tools utilities (and any other interested Perl programs) can find it. Once you do this, all of the smbldap-tools will be able to easily learn where their configuration files are. For the record, the standard directory for such things is /usr/lib/perl5/site_perl, a directory deliberately set aside for Perl libraries and modules like smbldap_tools.pm that are not part of cpan.

To make the necessary changes we described, you copy the tools to the /usr/local/sbin directory. For the record, this directory is the standard location for utilities intended for the root user but not part of the standard Fedora distribution.

To customize and install the smbldap-tools:

1. Recall that you used the cd command to enter the directory smbldaptools-0.8.6. To perform the copy, enter the following command

```
cp smbldap-* /usr/local/sbin
```

2. Edit the file smbldap_tools.pm. Near the top of this file, you'll find these two settings:

```
my $smbldap_conf =
"/etc/smbldap-tools/smbldap.conf";
```

```
my $smbldap_bind_conf =
"/etc/smbldap-tools/smbldap_bind.conf";
```

Make sure the directory names in the quotation marks are exactly as shown. If not, change them to match the preceding code. This ensures that the utilities can find their configuration files properly.

3. Install the smbldap_tools.pm file where Perl scripts can automatically find it:

```
cp smbldap_tools.pm /usr/lib/perl5/site_perl
```

That's it for installation! Time to move on to the configuration files.

Configuring the *smbldap-tools*

Now it's time to create the configuration files for the smbldap-tools. These contain the information that the smbldap-tools must know in order to communicate with your LDAP database. For instance, just like any other LDAP client, the smbldap-tools must know what host the LDAP server runs on, what port number it responds on, whether to use SSL encryption, and so forth. In addition, the smbldap-tools must have the right credentials to make changes to the LDAP database because the smbldap-tools carry out administrative tasks, such as creating new account objects.

The smbldap-tools include a pair of sample configuration files. They're great and you'll leverage them as a starting point, but you'll modify them to work with *your* particular LDAP configuration.

We'll do it in two steps:

1. Copy in the provided sample files.

2. Modify those sample files that will teach smbldap-tools about your OpenLDAP configuration.

Copying in the Sample *smbldap-tools* Configuration Files

To set up the configuration files, first carry out the following preparatory steps, continuing to work in a terminal window while logged on as root.

1. cd to the directory where you untarred the smbldap-tools:

```
cd /usr/local/src/smbldaptools-0.8.6
```

2. To create the configuration file directory, use mkdir:

```
mkdir /etc/smbldap-tools
```

3. Copy the provided configuration files to this directory:

```
cp *.conf /etc/smbldap-tools
```

Now you're ready to edit the smbldap-tools configuration files, giving the tools critical information they need to access and administer the LDAP database.

smbldap.conf: smbldap-tools Settings

There are essentially two categories of settings found inside `smbldap.conf`.

One category of settings tells the software where the LDAP sever is, on what port it responds to connections, whether to use SSL, what certificate authorities to trust, and so on. The `smbldap.conf` file spices this up a little by allowing for the possibility of *separate* LDAP servers. In large environments, you might have one LDAP server just for write requests and a whole bunch of additional LDAP servers just for read requests. The configuration file calls these servers *master* and *slave*. The distinction is somewhat similar to that between a Windows PDC and a Windows BDC, but for the sake of example we'll keep things simple. That is, you've only got one LDAP server, which will provide for both read and write requests, so you'll set the "master" and "slave" options *exactly the same*. For instance, set `masterLDAP` to `linserv1.corp.com` and `masterPort` to 389 (the standard TCP port number for LDAP), and set `slaveLDAP` and `slavePort` the same way—again, you do not have a separate LDAP server *just* for read requests.

The second type of setting in `smbldap.conf` has to do with the way various Windows logon issues should be handled. For instance, should a particular home directory on the server be mapped as a network drive? Should a special Windows batch file be executed on the workstation every time a user logs on? Since this chapter is concerned with authentication, we'll expand on these settings later and use only safe default answers for now.

To set up `smbldap.conf` for your environment:

1. Open /etc/smbldap-tools/smbldap.conf in a text editor.

2. Set the LDAP server host and port options as follows:
    ```
    slaveLDAP="linserv1.corp.com"
    slavePort="389"
    masterLDAP="linserv1.corp.com"
    masterPort="389"
    ```

3. Turn on SSL encryption (also called TLS) when talking to the LDAP server:
    ```
    ldapTLS = "1"
    ```

4. Tell the tools to always verify the LDAP server's certificate:
    ```
    verify = "require"
    ```

5. Give the tools the location of the CA certificate:
    ```
    cafile="/usr/share/ssl/demoCA/cacert.pem"
    ```

6. Set the LDAP suffix, just as in /etc/ldap.conf:
    ```
    suffix="dc=ldap,dc=corp,dc=com"
    ```

7. Leave the following defaults for other options, most of which we'll discuss in later chapters:
    ```
    userSmbHome=""
    userProfile=""
    userScript="%U.cmd"
    mailDomain="corp.com"
    userHomeDrive="H:"
    ```

The remaining options may be left unchanged, except for the SID option, which you'll change later when we've launched our Samba server and learned its unique Windows SID (security ID). Since the server doesn't actually have a SID until the Samba server runs for the first time, it makes sense to delay setting this option.

smbldap_bind.conf: Credentials for Talking to the LDAP Server

`smbldap_bind.conf` is another required file for Samba to talk to your LDAP server. It contains the credentials the LDAP server expects you to present before allowing you to read and write information. Just as in `smbldap.conf`, there are separate master and slave settings available for writing and reading. And as before, you will set them exactly the same, as you'll use the same LDAP server for reading and writing.

The masterDN option sets the distinguished name of the LDAP root user, which should match the rootDN option you previously set in `/etc/openldap/slapd.conf`. The masterPW option sets the password associated with the LDAP root user. The slaveDN and slavePW options will be set identical to these. Note that since this file must contain the root LDAP password, its permissions should be set carefully. Yes, you read that right—you need to embed the sensitive LDAP password inside this file. To put a little bit of security upon it, you'll restrict access to who can read this file so you can sleep (at least a little better) at night.

To set up the LDAP credentials for the `smbldap-tools`:

1. Edit `/etc/smbldap-tools/smbldap_bind.conf` to match the following:

    ```
    slaveDN="cn=root,dc=ldap,dc=corp,dc=com"
    slavePw="p@ssw0rd"
    masterDN="cn=root,dc=ldap,dc=corp,dc=com"
    masterPw="p@ssw0rd"
    ```

2. Set the permissions of `/etc/smbldap-tools/smbldap_bind.conf` so that only the root user can read the LDAP server password it contains:

    ```
    chmod a-rwx,o+r /etc/smbldap-tools/smbldap_bind.conf
    ```

The `smbldap-tools` are now installed and configured. You're ready to use them to populate the LDAP database with essential Windows networking-related accounts and other settings.

Populating the LDAP Database with Samba Objects

Earlier you adjusted your LDAP schema to include the definitions of Samba objects. Now it's time to actually create common Samba objects that should be present on all Windows-compatible systems, such as the Administrator account. You'll also create the Computers organizational unit, which will store machine trust accounts for workstations that are members of the domain.

Conveniently, the `smbldap-tools` distribution comes with a command to do all of this for us! Execute the following command as root:

```
/usr/local/sbin/smbldap-populate
```

This command will warn you that the Users and Groups organizational units already exist; it may generate Perl programmer-oriented warnings as well, as shown next. Neither of these is cause for concern. These acceptable warning messages are shown below for your reference:

```
Using builtin directory structure
Use of uninitialized value in pattern match (m//) at /usr/local/sbin/smbldap-
populate line 118.
Use of uninitialized value in concatenation (.) or string at /usr/local/sbin/
smbldap-populate line 126.
Use of uninitialized value in concatenation (.) or string at /usr/local/sbin/
smbldap-populate line 126.
Use of uninitialized value in string at /usr/lib/perl5/site_perl/smbldap_
tools.pm line 169.
Use of uninitialized value in string at /usr/lib/perl5/site_perl/smbldap_
tools.pm line 169.
adding new entry: dc=ldap,dc=corp,dc=com
failed to add entry: Already exists at /usr/local/sbin/smbldap-populate line
389, <GEN1> line 2.
adding new entry: ou=Users,dc=ldap,dc=corp,dc=com
failed to add entry: Already exists at /usr/local/sbin/smbldap-populate line
389, <GEN1> line 3.
adding new entry: ou=Groups,dc=ldap,dc=corp,dc=com
failed to add entry: Already exists at /usr/local/sbin/smbldap-populate line
389, <GEN1> line 4.
```

You may wish to verify that the information was successfully added to the LDAP database. You can do so with the following command:

```
ldapsearch -x | less
```

> The `less` command will display another page of output every time you hit the space bar. When you reach the end of the output, press the q key to quit `less`.

You should see references to the Administrator and Nobody accounts as well as the Computers organizational unit. If not, double-check your `slapd.conf` file carefully and review any error messages not just shown that were received from `smbldap-populate`. Then restart the OpenLDAP server with the `service ldap restart` command and run `smbldap-populate` again.

There is one more critical object that must be created in the LDAP database. Most administrative tasks, including the joining of workstations to a domain, must be carried out by the administrative user. By convention, this user is named `administrator` in the Windows world. Samba conveniently remaps `administrator` to the root account via the file `/etc/samba/smbusers`. But there's one catch: when LDAP is used as the password database, it isn't enough for root to exist only as a regular Unix account in the server's `/etc/passwd` file, root must also exist in the LDAP database. Otherwise, attempts to join the domain will fail with mysterious, unhelpful error messages.

Take care of this chore using the `smbldap-passwd` command:

```
/usr/local/sbin/smbldap-passwd root
```

Enter root's password correctly twice to confirm the change. In theory, you could now eliminate root's entry from `/etc/passwd`, but we strongly discourage you from doing so as the option of logging in locally as root is critical when LDAP servers behave badly.

Configuring Samba Itself

Now that the back-end LDAP database is ready to rock, you are at last ready to configure Samba itself! Samba is configured via the file `/etc/samba/smb.conf`. Although a stock version is provided with your Fedora system, we strongly recommend that you replace it with the version presented here and on our website.

In our examples, we have already made the changes necessary to accommodate operation as an NT primary domain controller rather than a simple workgroup server.

Web-Based Interfaces to Configure Samba: SWAT and Webmin

Editing the `smb.conf` file by hand isn't the only way to configure Samba. It's also possible to configure Samba using a Webmin module. In addition, the Samba team offers its own web-based user interface, SWAT.

So why are we editing `smb.conf` by hand? Because initial Samba configuration is a task we do only once. So we don't save much repetitive labor by doing it through a web-based interface. In addition, there is a compelling reason not to. Most of the Samba documentation, online and in print, discusses configuration file options by name. Understanding how these option names relate to text fields and radio buttons in a "friendly" web-based interface can be difficult. So if you have a problem and need support, you're going to need to understand the configuration files. That means it's best to speak the language from the beginning.

In later chapters, we *will* use Webmin's Samba Windows File Sharing module to speed up simpler and more repetitive tasks, like adding and modifying file shares. We chose to go with Webmin consistently throughout the book for simplicity.

Samba's SWAT interface does present options by their "real" names in the configuration file. But there isn't an enormous difference in convenience between SWAT and editing a text file, especially for the one-time task of initially setting up your configuration file. SWAT is definitely worth a look, though. You can learn more about it here: `www.samba.org/samba/docs/man/swat.8.html`

Again, the best reference for `smb.conf` configuration files is "The Official Samba-3 HOWTO and Reference Guide," available at `http://us1.samba.org/samba/docs/man/Samba-HOWTO-Collection`.

A little later in the chapter, we'll give you the full configuration of our suggested `smb.conf` file, but before we present that, here's a breakdown of the decisions that went into each setting in our `/etc/samba/smb.conf` file, broken up into logical sections:

- Prologue
- Windows Networking Settings
- "Back End Database" LDAP Settings
- Logging Options: Where to Send the Bad News

Prologue   In principle, `smb.conf` can have options in many different categories. In practice, all of the options we use fall into the global category. The first line of `smb.conf` informs Samba that we are about to list options in the global category, and should always be `[global]`.

Windows Networking Settings   Options in this section have to do with Windows networking issues. What should the domain be called? What networks are allowed to connect to it? How should the Samba server it identify itself to workstations? Do you want the various behaviors associated with a PDC, as opposed to a BDC or mere workgroup server? Should encrypted passwords, required by out-of-the-box modern versions of Windows, be required by Samba? All of these questions are answered by the options in the following list.

- The `workgroup` option is used for both domains and simple workgroup servers. We set this to `corp`, the name we chose for our Windows NT-compatible Samba domain.

- The `hosts allow` option limits the IP addresses that are allowed to connect to the server. The syntax used here is simple: to allow all addresses in our class C local network, 192.168.2, we specify using the odd syntax of `192.168.2.`. Similarly, to allow loopback connections from the server itself, we specify `127.` (*All* IP addresses with the first byte set to 127 are reserved for a machine that wishes to talk to itself, although in practice only `127.0.0.1` is frequently used.) So, when typing in this particular line be sure to type it in exactly as shown. Specifically, you want to enter in 192.168.2(period)(space) 127(period).

- The `server string` option allows workstations to tell inquisitive users what server software is being used. We chose to proudly announce our Samba server, but you can choose a more or less interesting response if you prefer.

- The `security` option determines the type of security model used by Samba. For a domain controller, this option is set to `user` because our primary goal is user authentication.

- We set the `encrypt passwords` option to yes. This option is almost a historical footnote at this point. Prior to the release of Windows 98, Windows workstations were quite comfortable with keeping passwords as plain text on the server. With the arrival of Windows 98, unencrypted passwords began to require registry changes on each workstation. Since the release of Windows 98, encrypted passwords have moved from an option to a default to a requirement. This option should always be set to `yes` on a modern Samba server.

- `min passwd length` sets the minimum length of a password in characters. You may find that three characters is far too short. Feel free to set a higher minimum.

- `domain logons` is a crucial option for operation as a PDC or BDC: without it, the server would not accept logons from client workstations. We set this option to `yes`.

- `domain master` is another PDC-related option. In Windows, the PDC is the domain-master browser. Setting this the same here would be a functional equivalent. The domain-master browser is responsible for combining browse lists from all of the Ethernet subnets involved that have Windows clients on them. Since this is how a real Windows PDC works, we set it to `yes`.

- `preferred master` indicates that the Samba server should be the Windows networking "master browser" for this local subnet. We set this option to `yes`. This does not guarantee that Samba will be the master; it only forces an "election" to choose a master browser at the time the Samba server starts up. It is not necessarily a problem for another server in the domain to be the master for the subnet on which our Samba domain master server is located. We just want to make sure one is chosen promptly at startup time. This option also implicitly turns on the `local master` option, which indicates that the server *can* be a Windows networking master browser for the local subnet.

- We set the `wins support` option to `yes`. This option specifies that the Samba server should act as a WINS (Windows Name Service) server. This allows Windows or Samba clients to register their IP addresses and have other clients look them up. It's a nice touch if no Windows server is already performing this chore. If this Samba server is the only server on the network, always set this option to `yes`. If there are multiple servers present, make sure only one is a WINS server.

"Back End Database" LDAP Settings   What sort of database should you use to store passwords? For us, the answer is LDAP. Where is that database? How is it structured? Where should information about users, computers, groups, and Windows SIDs be kept? Should the LDAP connection be encrypted? In the following list, you see the options that resolve these questions.

- The `passdb backend` option specifies what sort of database should be used to store passwords, as well as the URI (Uniform Resource Identifier) where that database can be reached. We're using LDAP as a back-end repository, so our value for this setting begins with `ldapsam:` to specify the LDAP Samba back end. This is followed by `ldaps://linserv1.corp.com/`, which is understood to mean that an LDAP server is listening on the encrypted LDAP-over-SSL port (636) on the server `linserv1.corp.com`.

- `LDAP passwd sync` is a necessity when working with encrypted passwords and using an LDAP back end, which we are. Recall that Unix and Windows use different techniques for encrypting passwords. Samba needs to store the new password in both formats. We set `LDAP passwd sync` to yes to accomplish this.

- The `ldap ssl` option specifies that our LDAP connection should be encrypted via SSL.

- The `ldap admin dn` option specifies the credentials of the LDAP root user, which Samba needs in order to change passwords, an administrative task that it performs directly. You have already seen other administrative tasks that are performed via the `smbldap-tools`.

- The `ldap suffix` option is identical in purpose to the suffix option in `/etc/openldap/slapd.conf`, as covered earlier, and we also set it to `ldap suffix = dc=ldap,dc=corp,dc=com`.

- `ldap group suffix`, `ldap machine suffix`, and `ldap user suffix` should specify three distinct LDAP organizational units (OUs) in order to avoid name collisions between users, groups and computers. We set them to `Groups`, `Computers`, and `Users`, respectively, matching the existing layout in our LDAP database.

- `ldap idmap suffix` can share the same organizational unit with `ldap user suffix` because Windows SIDs are not valid Windows usernames and vice versa. Since a Windows SID will never be the same as a Windows username, there's no risk of the one overwriting the other. The `smbldap-tools` were designed with this assumption in mind, so we'll follow Idealx's recommended practice by setting this to `Users`.

Logging Options: Where to Send the Bad News Options in this section are concerned with the logging of error messages, warnings, and diagnostic messages.

- The `log level` option determines how much information will be included in error log files (see the later section "If Samba Doesn't Work," for more information on how to take advantage of the error logs). We set this to 2 because it causes most useful debugging information to be logged without completely swamping the log file in detail.

- The closely related `log file` option determines where error messages, warnings, and diagnostic messages related to a particular workstation should be logged. Replacing the `%m` wildcard with the IP address of the workstation. `/var/log/samba/%m.log` is a good choice because `/var/log/samba` is the standard place to log Samba-related activity.

"Glue" Options: Connecting the *smbldap-tools* to Samba

The options in the preceding section allow Samba itself to talk to LDAP in order to verify and change passwords. As we've described, there are a bunch of additional administrative tasks that Samba doesn't do on its own. The Samba maintainers made a wise decision to break these tasks out, allowing the administrator to plug in tools of their own choosing.

We've already chosen the `smbldap-tools`, which do a comprehensive job of implementing all of these functions. There's a lot of "under the hood" stuff going on here. It should be noted that the `smbldap-tools` can be run manually or plugged into scripts of your own. This section provides a useful introduction to their capabilities.

For readability's sake, we chose not to use full paths in this section. All of the `smbldap-tools` scripts are located in `/usr/local/sbin/`, and that prefix does appear in the actual configuration file. You will also note wildcards such as `%u` and `%g`. Samba automatically replaces these with the actual user (`%u`) and group (`%g`) names involved in each request before executing the script in question.

- `add user script` is executed each time a new user should be added and should be set to `smbldap-useradd -a -m '%u'`. This instructs smbldap-useradd to add a new user.
  - The `-a` option specifies that a Windows account should be created.
  - The `-m` option indicates that a home directory should be created.

- The `'%u'` option specifies the username specified by the Windows domain administrator who made the request. Placing %u between single quotes ensures that the Bash command shell does not try to misinterpret any special characters in the username with possibly unwanted consequences. Samba itself takes care of making sure there are no back-ticks (`` ` ``) in the username that might otherwise ruin this security precaution.

- Similarly, `delete user script` is executed when a user should be removed. In this case, we use `smbldap-userdel` and pass it the name of the user to delete, again via the %u wildcard.

- `add group script` performs a similar task: adding a new group; `smbldap-groupadd` is used. The -p option indicates that a Windows group should be added, and the username is passed in the same way via `'%u'`.

- `delete group script` is similar to `delete user script`; `smbldap-groupdel` is used. The username is passed in via `'%u'`.

- `add user to group script` takes care of adding a user to a group; the script `smbldap-groupmod` is used. The -m specifies that a user should be added to a group. The user and group names are then substituted in using the %u and %g wildcards.

- `delete user from group script` removes a user from a group. The script `smbldap-groupmod` is again used, but with different options. The -x option specifies that a user should be removed from a group, and the user and group names are again substituted in using the %u and %g wildcards.

- `set primary group script` sets the primary group for a user. This is the group that will initially own any files created by the user unless the user expressly specifies otherwise. The `smbldap-usermod` script is used, with the -g option specifying that the default group should be changed, and the group and usernames (in that order for this particular command) are substituted in using the %g and %u wildcards.

- `add machine script` runs every time a new workstation joins the domain. The `smbldap-useradd` script is used, but the -w option clarifies the situation by asking the script to add a workstation account rather than a regular user account.

Listing 2.1: *Isetc/samba/smb.conf*

```
[global]
# Set our domain name
workgroup = corp


# Lock out people not on the local LAN. Optional.
# Also allow local loopback (127.)
hosts allow = 192.168.2. 127.


#So, when typing in the hosts allow line (above), be sure to type it in exactly
as shown. Specifically, you want to enter in 192.168.2(period)(space)127(period)


# Identify our software
```

```
server string = Samba Server

# Security mode should be "user" for a domain controller
security = user

# We must encrypt passwords to talk to
# modern versions of Windows
# without registry hacks, and we want to
#do that anyway
encrypt passwords = yes

# Set a reasonable minimum password length
min passwd length = 3

# Crucial options to enable operation as a PDC
domain logons = yes
domain master = yes
preferred master = yes
wins support = yes

#Talk to LDAP via SSL to obtain account information
passdb backend = ldapsam:ldaps://linserv1.corp.com/
# Sync our passwords with the ldap database
ldap passwd sync = yes

ldap ssl = yes
ldap admin dn = cn=root,dc=ldap,dc=corp,dc=com
ldap suffix = dc=ldap,dc=corp,dc=com
ldap group suffix = ou=Groups
ldap machine suffix = ou=Computers
ldap user suffix = ou=Users
ldap idmap suffix = ou=Users

#Scripts run to carry out domain administration tasks
add user script = /usr/local/sbin/smbldap-useradd -a -m '%u'
delete user script = /usr/local/sbin/smbldap-userdel '%u'
add group script = /usr/local/sbin/smbldap-groupadd -p '%g'
delete group script = /usr/local/sbin/smbldap-groupdel '%g'
add user to group script = /usr/local/sbin/smbldap-groupmod -m '%u' '%g'
delete user from group script = /usr/local/sbin/smbldap-groupmod -x '%u' '%g'
set primary group script = /usr/local/sbin/smbldap-usermod -g '%g' '%u'
```

```
add machine script = /usr/local/sbin/smbldap-useradd -w '%m'
#Log enough information to debug problems but not so much as to swamp us
log level = 2

# Log errors where Fedora normally does; one
# log file per client IP address
log file = /var/log/samba/%m.log
```

Cluing Samba in to the LDAP Root Password

Once the Samba configuration file is ready, you need to make the Samba server aware of the root password for the LDAP database. This is because, while you leverage the smbldap-tools for most administrative tasks, Samba handles password changes internally. For historical reasons, this information is stored in a special file called secrets.tdb that Samba creates in /etc/samba. You do this task using the smbpasswd command and passing the -w option, which indicates that you want to set the password needed to make changes to the LDAP database:

```
smbpasswd -w p@ssw0rd
```

You should receive the following response:

```
Setting stored password for "cn=root,dc=ldap,dc=corp,dc=com" in secrets.tdb
```

To continue with Samba configuration, you must now launch the Samba server to determine its SID.

Launching the LDAP-Based Samba Server for the First Time

To start the Samba server and to ensure that it is restarted at the next reboot, enter the following commands as root. The first command ensures that the two Samba server daemons, smbd and nmbd, are always launched at boot time. The second launches the Samba servers now:

```
chkconfig --add smb
service smb start
```

You can now determine the Windows SID (security identifier) of the server using the net command. As you may recall, the smbldap-tools need this information to operate correctly, and you were not able to add the SID option to smbldap.conf earlier because you had not yet generated a SID by starting Samba for the first time. To learn the server's SID, use the following command:

```
net getlocalsid
```

If your Samba server launched successfully, this should produce output similar to the following. Note that the name of your individual server appears rather than corp, the NT domain name you have chosen. This is not cause for concern.

```
SID for domain LINSERV1 is:
S-1-5-21-3084340505-2073876770-3452236727
```

Now, edit the file /etc/smbldap-tools/smbldap.conf and change the SID setting to match what you received (*don't* just copy our example):

SID="YOURSIDGOESHERE"

The smbldap-tools are now ready to handle administration requests such as joining a workstation to a domain.

Using Webmin to Administer LDAP User Accounts for Samba

You're nearly ready to join a true Windows client to your Samba domain! To make that truly useful, you'll first need to enable Samba login for each of your existing LDAP users and configure the Webmin LDAP Users and Groups to do so automatically for newly created users in the future.

Configuring the Webmin LDAP Users and Groups Module for Samba

Follow these steps:

1. Log into Webmin. Then click the "System" button, followed by the "LDAP Users and Groups" button.

2. You will note that the display now includes several new users, including the standard Windows account Administrator and the machine trust account linserv1$. The Groups list has also been expanded quite a bit with a collection of standard Windows groups.

3. Click the "Module Config" link to access the Configuration page.

4. Set the "other objectClasses to add to new users" field to **account sambaSamAccount**, as shown in Figure 2.18. Note that this means that all newly created LDAP accounts will support Samba domain logins.

5. Scroll down to "Samba account options." To the right of "LDAP object class for Samba users," make sure "sambaSamAccount" is present. This is needed to allow upgrading existing accounts to Samba support.

6. To the right of "Domain SID for Samba3," paste in your SID as received from the net getlocalsid command.

7. Scroll to the end of the page and click "Save."

Now you're ready to upgrade your user accounts to support Samba.

Upgrading and Adding LDAP Samba-Enabled Accounts with Webmin

You'll also need to retrofit your existing LDAP users to support their new lives as Samba users. After you do that, we'll demonstrate how to add a new account with Samba support.

To upgrade an existing account from the "LDAP Users and Groups" main page, click the user "doctor1." On the page that follows, click the radio box next to "Normal password' and enter **p@ssw0rd** again in the field to the right of the radio box, as shown in Figure 2.19. This is necessary because Unix and Windows both encrypt passwords via a one-way function that does not allow the original password to be recovered. As a result, the Samba password database cannot be automatically populated using the existing LDAP-MD5 password. When upgrading to Samba, administrators have solved this problem by issuing new passwords to all users or by requiring each user to come to a central workstation and reset their password.

FIGURE 2.18   Webmin settings to support Samba accounts in LDAP Users and Groups

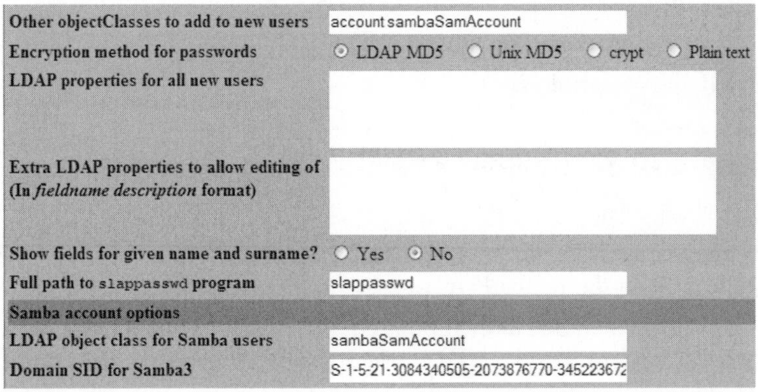

Other objectClasses to add to new users	account sambaSamAccount
Encryption method for passwords	⊙ LDAP MD5 ○ Unix MD5 ○ crypt ○ Plain text
LDAP properties for all new users	
Extra LDAP properties to allow editing of (In *fieldname description* format)	
Show fields for given name and surname?	○ Yes ⊙ No
Full path to `slappasswd` program	slappasswd
Samba account options	
LDAP object class for Samba users	sambaSamAccount
Domain SID for Samba3	S-1-5-21-3084340505-2073876770-345223672

FIGURE 2.19   Upgrading an existing LDAP account to support Samba

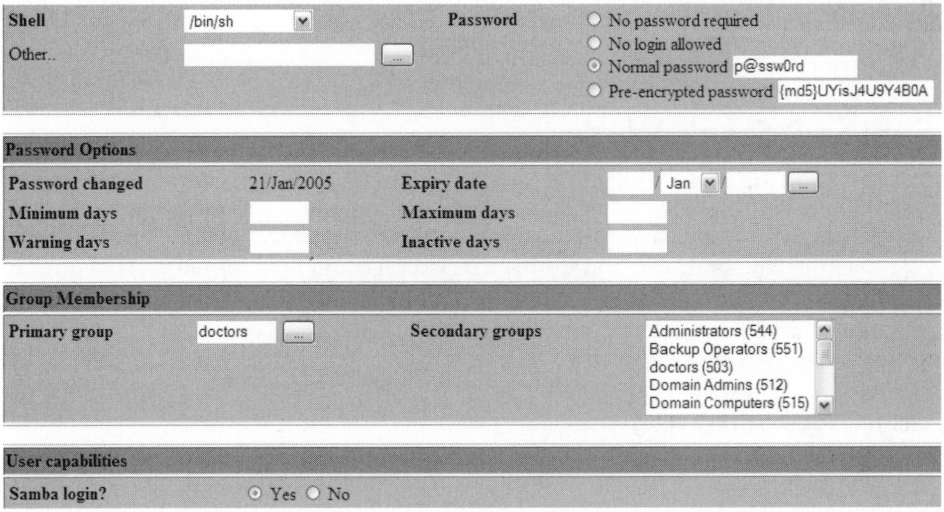

Shell	/bin/sh	Password	○ No password required
Other..			○ No login allowed
			⊙ Normal password p@ssw0rd
			○ Pre-encrypted password {md5}UYisJ4U9Y4B0A

Password Options

Password changed	21/Jan/2005	Expiry date	/ Jan ▼ . [...]
Minimum days		Maximum days	
Warning days		Inactive days	

Group Membership

Primary group	doctors [...]	Secondary groups	Administrators (544)
			Backup Operators (551)
			doctors (503)
			Domain Admins (512)
			Domain Computers (515)

User capabilities

Samba login?	⊙ Yes ○ No

WARNING   If you do not reset an existing user's password when adding Samba support to their account, they will not be able to authenticate from a Windows workstation.

Now, scroll down to "User capabilities" and press the radio button labeled "Yes" next to the "Samba login?" This allows doctor1 to authenticate from a Windows workstation. Scroll to the end of the page and click "Save." Repeat this process for doctor2, nurse1, and nurse2.

Adding a new account with Samba support is easy: just follow the same procedure described earlier in this chapter to add a new LDAP account. Thanks to your configuration changes, all new accounts will automatically support Samba. You can verify this by adding a `doctor3` account.

That's it—your LDAP-based Samba PDC is ready to use! Continue with the next section to learn how to verify its operation.

Joining the Samba Server to Its Own Domain

You now have a Samba PDC! Your first test will be a simple loopback test: joining the Samba server to its own domain. While not required for the server to function, this is a useful way to verify your work. To join the Samba PDC to its own domain, just follow these steps:

1. Join the server to its own domain with this command. Enter root's password when asked for it:

    ```
    net join
    ```

2. You should receive a response similar to the following, after several seconds' delay:

    ```
    [2005/01/25 13:16:01, 0] utils/net_ads.c:ads_startup(186)
     ads_connect: Confidentiality required
    Joined domain CORP.
    ```

If Samba Doesn't Work

If you run into trouble, here are some things to try.

Are all of your services properly started?   Be sure to verify that the `ldap` (if you are using LDAP rather than tdbsam), `smb`, and `winbind` services have all been started without error messages. If you don't happen to have the output of your `service ldap start` and `service smb start` commands in your terminal window's scrollback, there is a convenient way to restart them. The restart option to the service command shuts down a service first, then starts it again:

```
service ldap restart
service smb restart
```

If you forgot to start one or more of these, the service command will complain that the shutdown process failed. This, of course, you may safely ignore. However, if you receive a "FAILED" response for starting one or more of the services, you'll need to go back and review the relevant section of this chapter. If all of the services start successfully and you still can't join your own domain, carefully verify your work in `smb.conf` and make sure you created the root user in the LDAP database or tdbsam database as described earlier.

Did you check your log files?   If the preceding suggestion doesn't resolve your problem, there are more sophisticated ways to learn what went wrong. Most Linux services, including those you're working with, log error messages and warnings via a central service called syslog. syslog, in its standard configuration on Fedora Linux, logs most error messages to the file `/var/log/`

messages, rotating out the oldest contents of the file over time. It is also possible to configure syslog to log error messages from different services to different places and to ignore some messages entirely. Under Linux, syslog does the same job that the event log does under Windows.

The good news is that /var/log/messages is a simple text file. The bad news is that it can be very large. Fortunately, Linux offers a handy command to view only the last few lines of a text file, tail. By default, tail displays the last ten lines of a text file, for example:

```
tail /var/log/messages
```

You can also display a larger number of lines. To display 100 lines, just specify -100 as the first option. You can specify any desired number of lines in this way:

```
tail -100 /var/log/messages
```

Samba also logs error messages, warnings, and general diagnostic output in three additional locations:

```
/var/log/samba/smbd.log
/var/log/samba/xxx.xxx.xxx.xxx.log
```

xxx.xxx.xxx.xxx should be replaced by the IP address of the workstation involved. Oddly enough, you may also see a log file with the hostname rather than the IP address of the workstation, so look for both. You can learn quite a bit by using the tail command on these files as well.

Did you Google?   When all else fails, try searching Google for the error message you received. And this might seem ridiculously obvious, but we've done it ourselves: when pasting error messages into the Google search window, *do not* include any portions that are clearly unique to *your* network and circumstances—specifically, your IP addresses, the current date and time, and the names of any workstations and servers involved will clearly not appear in any Samba discussion forums and FAQs on the Web. Searches that include such search terms will fail.

Using NT 4 Old-School Tools to Manage Samba Users and Computers

Remember, Samba is now set up to pretend to be an NT 4 Domain Controller. And, since monkey see, monkey do, you're in luck. That is, you can utilize the old-school Windows NT 4 User Manager for Domains and Server Manager for Domains (seen in Figure 2.20) to manage your Users and Computers, respectively, in Samba (but only when it's a PDC). And thanks to our careful work in smb.conf, this works identically with your tdbsam-based Samba PDC and your LDAP-based Samba PDC.

Doing this is easy, but you have to get the tools—and you have to get the *right version* of the tools. Here's the deal: don't download them from Microsoft. Why? Because these updated tools, when run against Samba servers, *don't* work. Why not? I have no idea.

FIGURE 2.20   The User Manager in Windows NT 4

Instead, the correct course of action is to find an old NT 4 Server CD-ROM and rip out the tools by hand. The files will be in the i386 directory in compressed format. All you need to do is use the expand command on two files: usrmgr.ex_ and svrmgr. For example, you'll type:

```
expand usrmgr.ex_ c:\usrmgr.exe
expand srvmgr.exe c:\srvmgr.exe
```

When you do, you'll have two uncompressed and ready-to-run files in your c:\ directory. Once you run them on your Windows machine, you'll be able to manage your Samba domain just like in the NT 4 days! We got files work that were a usrmgr.exe of size 299,280 (date 7/26/1996) and a svrmgr.exe 211,216 (date 7/26/1996).

One weird byproduct about these tools is that after you, say, delete a user using svrmgr.exe, you might not immediately see the update without pressing F5 for a refresh. When you do, you should see your change reflected.

Joining a Windows Workstation to the Domain

You're just one step away from successfully authenticating a Windows user via your Samba PDC! First, you'll need to join a Windows workstation to the domain.

On a Windows XP machine, you'll do this by right-clicking "My Computer" and selecting "Properties." Then, on the "Computer Name" tab, click the "Change" button. Select the "Domain" radio button and enter the name of the Samba domain—**CORP**.

When prompted, enter administrative credentials: `administrator` for the username and `p@ssw0rd` for the password. When you do, you'll be rewarded as shown in Figure 2.21.

FIGURE 2.21   Here you can join the Samba CORP domain.

Logging into a Windows Workstation via Samba PDC Authentication

Now you're ready to log in! Just log out of your XP workstation and log back in with the username `doctor1` and the password `p@ssw0rd`. After a few moments, a desktop for `doctor1` should appear in the usual fashion. Congratulations! In the next chapter, we'll extend the usefulness of authenticating in this manner by adding shared home directories that allow users to access the same files regardless of which workstation they have chosen to work with.

Checkout: To Create a Linux PDC

Here's a review of what you accomplished:

- You made a choice about how to create your Linux PDC: to either use the `tdbsam` "trivial database" back end to store user accounts, or to leverage OpenLDAP.

- On our website (`www.WinLinAnswers.com`), we have steps which allow you to use `tdbsam` to hold your accounts. If you chose this route for your Samba PDC, you:

  - Configured Webmin's Samba module to correctly edit user and group information in a way that is compatible with `tdbsam`

  - Configured the Samba server to operate as a PDC and use the `tdbsam` database as a back end in which to store account information

  - Installed `change-group-membership.pl`, a Perl script that can correctly change group membership settings for users in response to requests from the NT administration tools on Windows clients

  - Using Webmin, upgraded existing Linux accounts to support Samba authentication and set up automatic synchronization so that future accounts will automatically be Samba-enabled

- If you leveraged the existing OpenLDAP server configuration by following our steps in this book, you:

  - Expanded the database schema to support Windows account information needed by Samba

  - Configured Samba to build efficient indexes for Windows SIDs (security identifiers)

  - Installed and configured the `smbldap-tools`, which provide the necessary "glue" to allow Samba to carry out domain administration tasks when a Windows domain administrator remotely requests it (such as doing the dirty work when a new workstation joins the domain)

  - Populated the LDAP database with standard Windows networking objects, such as the Administrator account

  - Configured the Samba server to operate as a PDC and use the LDAP database as a back end in which to store account information

  - Configured the Samba server to use the smbldap-tools for administration tasks

  - Using Webmin, upgraded your LDAP user accounts to support Samba authentication

- In both scenarios, you:

  - Joined your own Linux PDC to its own `corp` domain

  - Joined a Windows workstation to the `corp` domain

  - Successfully logged into the `corp` domain from the Windows workstation

Final Thoughts

Linux has a powerful array of possible authentication mechanisms. Heck, we haven't even explored them all. But we have visited the ones you'll likely find in most networks.

Getting them set up can be a chore, but you only have to get them set up once. Getting both Linux and Windows clients to leverage your preferred authentication mechanism can be another chore, but it's very rewarding when it's done.

In the next chapter, we'll turn the tables a bit. You'll leverage Active Directory as the "go to" point for authentication. Turn the page to see how to do it!

3

Authenticating Linux Clients to Active Directory

In the last chapter, we talked about using Linux to house the user accounts. When our Windows or Linux clients logged on, they had three ways of getting authenticated on the network:

NIS server   Old and crusty, but still in heavy use. There are native NIS clients on Linux, and third-party NIS clients for Windows.

OpenLDAP server   Offers much better security and the potential for a hierarchical namespace. Again, there are native OpenLDAP clients on Linux and third-party add-in LDAP clients for Windows.

SAMBA server   Allows Windows clients to authenticate to Linux servers without third-party software on the client. In one scenario, we built this on top of our OpenLDAP server. This gave us the best of both worlds. Linux clients authenticated directly to LDAP, and unmodified Windows clients authenticated to Samba. In an alternative scenario, we configured Samba without OpenLDAP. Samba without OpenLDAP is an acceptable solution when all clients run Windows and the network is not expected to grow to a size that requires backup domain controllers.

In this section, we'll turn the tables a bit. We'll use Active Directory as the "go to" place to authenticate our users. We'll do so in two major ways:

- We'll use Active Directory out of the box. Here, we'll have both native XP clients authenticate directly to Active Directory (easy!), as well as Linux clients authenticating directly to Active Directory. We'll do it using only the tools contained within Windows and Linux. This is called the *Winbind* method.

- We'll extend Active Directory to house special Linux user and group data with Microsoft's "Services for Unix" toolkit. Then we'll contact Active Directory via LDAP but ultimately authenticate using Kerberos.

We'll also explore some third-party tools which make this whole business easier. These tools hook into both Active Directory and Linux to help them talk more easily.

Preparing Active Directory for User Logins

You already set up Active Directory in Chapter 1. When you did, you created a centralized repository for user, group, and computer accounts to be authenticated to. In this chapter, we'll start to leverage that repository and make it worth the money you paid for it.

Now is a great time to create some sample user accounts in some sample OUs (organizational units). Otherwise, we'll have no user accounts to authenticate against (other than the `administrator` account).

Creating Active Directory Organizational Units (OUs)

First, we'll create our OUs, then we'll put some sample users inside. To create our OUs:

1. Log on to your Windows Active Directory server as the domain administrator. Select Start ➢ Programs ➢ Administrative Tools ➢ Active Directory Users & Computers.

2. Right-click the domain name (`ad.corp.com`) and select New ➢ Organizational Unit, as shown in Figure 3.1.

3. In the "New Object – Organizational Unit" dialog, enter **Sales** .

Repeat these steps and create another OU for Marketing and another for Human Resources.

FIGURE 3.1 Create two new OUs: Sales and Marketing

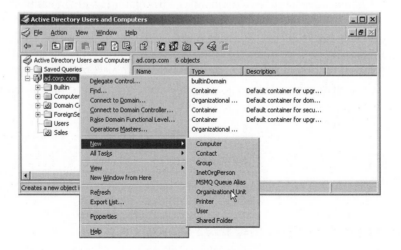

Creating Active Directory User Accounts

It's easy to create Active Directory users. Simply right-click the OU in which you want to create your users and select New ➢ User. Then, follow the wizard to create your first user.

1. In the Sales OU, create two users: salesperson1 and salesperson2.

2. In the Marketing OU, create two users: marketperson1 and marketperson2.

3. In the Human Resources OU, create two users: HRperson1 and HRperson2.

   Be sure to give everyone the same password. For this book, we'll stick with **p@ssw0rd** We'll use these users a bit later.

Creating Active Directory Group Accounts

It's also easy to create Active Directory groups. Simply right-click the OU in which you want to create the group and select New ➢ Group. Then follow the wizard to create your first user. In the Sales OU, create a group named SalesGroup.

To add salesperson1 and salesperson2 to that group, press Shift and click both salesperson1 and salesperson2, right-click and select "Add to a group," then choose the new SalesGroup you created.

Repeat by creating MarketingGroup and adding marketperson1 and marketperson2 to it. Additionally, create HRGroup and add HRperson1 and HRperson2 to it.

We'll use the SalesGroup a bit later in this chapter and the others in the next chapter.

Authenticating Windows Clients to Active Directory

To authenticate Windows clients to Active Directory, the computer account has to be "joined" to the domain. You should have already done this in Chapter 1 during setup, but if you weren't able to perform this step for some reason, here's how to do it.

Joining Windows XP Machines to Active Directory

Select Start, then right-click My Computer and select "Properties." Select the "Computer Name" tab, then click the "Change..." button. At the "Computer Name Changes" screen, select the radio button labeled "Domain:" then enter the name of the domain. You can enter either **AD** (the short name) or **ad.corp.com** (the Fully Qualified Domain Name); then press Enter. Enter your administrative credentials to join the domain, then reboot.

If you're having trouble joining the domain, be sure to check the client's IP address, subnet mask, and DNS settings. Specifically, make sure the client machine is using the IP address of windc1.ad.corp.com (192.168.2.226) as the "Preferred DNS server."

Logging into Active Directory from Windows XP

There's nothing special that you need to do to authenticate Windows Clients to Active Directory. On rebooting your Windows XP machine, you'll be asked to select the domain to authenticate to in the Ctl+Alt+Del drop-down, as shown in Figure 3.2.

FIGURE 3.2 Use the "Log on to:" drop-down to select the domain.

Using Standard Active Directory for Linux Authentication (via Winbind)

Just now, we joined a Windows XP computer to the ad.corp.com. domain. We'll assume the name was xppro1 (the same name we recommended you use in Chapter 1). This enables users in Active Directory to sit down at an Windows XP machine and log on to Active Directory. You can see this in Figure 3.3.

FIGURE 3.3 Windows and Linux clients can both bind to an Active Directory domain.

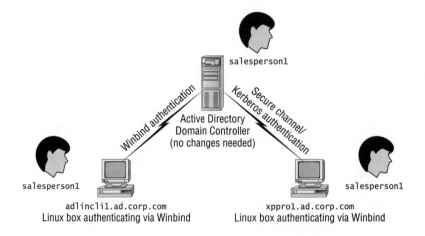

Linux machines can leverage Active Directory as the "go to" source for their account information. That is, you can have an Active Directory user sit down at a Linux machine and log on. This is likely desirable if you already have Active Directory; leveraging centralized account information is a good thing.

As we stated, in this chapter we're going to present two main ways of leveraging Active Directory for your Linux clients. In this first section, we'll be exploring Winbind (a subset of the Samba tools.) Winbind is great because it requires *no* changes to Active Directory. For those seeking to integrate Linux into an environment where changes to the Windows server are politically or practically impossible, that's *very* good news.

Now, here's the bad news about Winbind: it's tricky to set up Winbind correctly, and support for it in the Red Hat/Fedora GUI tools is incomplete at best. We'll spend some quality time navigating some command-line steps and performing a gaggle of edits to some configuration files.

Also, Winbind can cause consistency and security problems, as shown in the sidebar "How Winbind Fakes Linux User IDs (and How It Can Hurt)." Specifically, problems can occur where Linux users on Linux client machines attempt to copy files back and forth among themselves using a Linux-based NFS server. Problems can also occur if Winbind's Windows-to-Linux user ID mapping data is lost for any reason. See the sidebar for more information about this issue.

Go ahead and utilize this section on Winbind if you simply cannot convince your Active Directory administrator to embrace Microsoft's Services for Unix 3.5. The solution we highlight later in the chapter, in the "Extending Active Directory with Unix/Linux Information" section, is a much more complete, more robust, and ultimately more maintainable solution. However, it does require some cooperation from both the Linux and Windows sides to make it work.

How Winbind Fakes Linux User IDs (and How It Can Hurt)

Winbind helps Linux client systems be a member of a Windows domain. And when the full cooperation of the Windows administrator is not available, Winbind can't be beat. That's because a Linux client running Winbind looks like a real Windows client from the server's point of view.

But making a Linux client look like a Windows client introduces a thorny problem. Windows 2003 doesn't have a native capability (out-of-the-box) to store Linux user IDs in the same format as Linux. Windows uses a two-part user ID combination called a Security Identifier, or SID. SIDs can also identify groups and computers, but for right now, let's concentrate on users. A user SID might look like S-1-5-21-2460136348-1980938915-682000001-512

The SID is made up of a domain identifier and unique relative identifier, called a RID. The complete SID uniquely identifies a user, but it contains too much information to "fit" in the space of a normal Unix UID. A Unix UID is just a flat number, like 1002.

In the general case, a Windows SID can't be stuffed into a Linux UID. So when a Windows user logs on to a Linux machine, Winbind tries to cope. Winbind arbitrarily invents a local UID for each Windows user who logs in. Then Winbind maintains a table of which Windows user logged in and what local Linux UID they're arbitrarily getting. Here's the problem: Each Winbind-enabled Linux machine maps these local Linux UIDs *separately* to Windows users.

In most cases, though it's a bit sloppy, it usually works. As long as the Windows user (logging onto a Linux machine) transfers files through a Windows or Samba file server, there's no problem. But these safeguards can be circumvented in at least two cases (that we know of):

Case 1: Joe and Jane Arbitrarily Get the Same UID from Two Different Linux Workstations

The Linux clients attempt to use a Linux-based NFS (Network File System) server to share files. (We'll explore NFS in more detail in the next chapter, so bear with us.) NFS identifies users by UID and expects that UIDs will be consistent between computers. With most centralized authentication systems, that would be a reasonable expectation, but since Winbind assigns user IDs to Windows SIDs on a *per-workstation basis,* the following scenario can occur. There are two Linux workstations involved, adlincli1 and adlincli2:

- Jane logs into adlincli1 for the first time. Winbind on adlincli1 arbitrarily assigns her the UID 5010.

- Jane creates files and copies them to the NFS server. These files now belong to UID 5010 on the NFS server. She sets the permissions so that the files should only be readable by her.

- Joe logs into adlincli2 for the first time. Winbind on adlincli2 arbitrarily assigns the UID 5010 to him. Remember, Winbind's UID mappings are independent on *every Linux workstation*.

- Joe attempts to access Jane's files on the NFS server and *succeeds*, because he has the same UID.

We really don't want Joe to see Jane's files, but because they are arbitrarily assigned the same UID on their local Linux machine, the security is circumvented. NFS doesn't magically prevent this.

Case 2: User ID Mappings Are Lost on a Workstation

Imagine now that a month goes by. The administrator accidentally deletes the location on the Linux workstation that holds the Windows user to Linux UID mapping table. Specifically, the location is /var/cache/samba.

Samba is successfully reinstalled, but the user ID mappings (stored in /var/cache/samba) have been lost.

The system shows that many files on the hard drive belong to UID 5010, but which Windows user does this correspond to? Nobody knows.

To recover from this, the system administrator asks each Windows user to log in to `adlincli1`. But doing so creates a *new* UID mapping. The user IDs will not match their old values. The old mapping, having been lost, can only be recovered the hard way: the system administrator must manually reassign files to the new UIDs.

Ouch!

Samba, theoretically, offers a way to centrally manage SID to UID mappings through a central LDAP server, but there are currently no standard tools for making that magic happen.

Our recommendation to alleviate this problem is a one-two punch using free stuff. Later, in the section "Extending Active Directory with Unix/Linux Information," we'll show you how to do it using:

- Microsoft's Services For Unix 3.5 (with Active Directory). This will get us Linux account information inside Active Directory. We'll also describe in general how Windows 2003/R2 has similar functionality (and what you'll do when you're ready for Windows 2003/R2).

- Fedora's LDAP authentication mechanism to ask Active Directory for account information. Because Active Directory will be enhanced to additionally store Linux user IDs directly, we'll be in clover.

Before we continue, there is some additional hope on the horizon. Some ultramodern versions of Winbind and Samba offer the option of determining the Unix user ID based on the Windows RID of the user.

Since the Windows RID is unique *within the domain* (and takes the same basic "flat" format as a Linux UID), Winbind wouldn't have to arbitrarily make up any ol' ID. It could just determine what Joe and Jane's Windows RIDs were and use them as Linux UIDs. If you choose to research this option, the new mechanism in Samba that supports this is called `idmap_rid`.

This could be a very attractive option for environments containing only one Windows domain, but it falls apart in multidomain environments because the RID for a user Harold in the CORP domain might be the same RID as a user Gary in the FLORP domain. There would be no way to distinguish Gary's files from Harold's files when present on a single Linux client.

As of this writing, `idmap_rid` is not standard in Fedora Linux. If you want to go at it alone, it's conceivable that you could compile your own SAMBA which includes the `idmap_rid` module. However, that's impractical for a variety of reasons—mostly because SAMBA is frequently updated for security reasons, and you'd have to recompile that extra feature into Samba each and every time.

In short, `idmap_rid` looks promising and clears up some issues, and there is an excellent chance it will be standard in future revisions of Fedora Linux. But it is not standard equipment at this time.

By the end of this section on Winbind, you'll have your Linux clients authenticating directly to an Active Directory domain—using only the tools found inside the box. It's not pretty, but it works.

Before you begin, let's make sure you have the supplies you need for our journey:

- You must have an Active Directory Domain Controller to talk to! In our examples, that server is called `windc1.ad.corp.com`.

- You'll need a Linux client you want to authenticate via Active Directory. If you don't have a machine that fits the bill, you'll need to spend some time creating one using the basic steps outlined in Chapter 1. Here's a tip: use a hostname for the Linux client that makes sense for its intended use. For instance, in our examples, we'll be going with the name `adlincli1.ad.corp.com` for this Linux client workstation that is going to authenticate to Active Directory.

- Regardless of how you name the client, it *must* be in the `ad.corp.com` subdomain. Otherwise, domain membership simply will not work.

authconfig: The First 90 Percent of the Journey

Fedora's authconfig tool can do 90 percent of the work associated with permitting the use of Active Directory domain logins on your Linux client workstation using Winbind. (Of course, figuring out the remaining 10 percent is what makes grown men cry. *Not* that I'm saying that happened while writing this book.)

First, open a terminal window and type **su -** to log in as root.

Next, run the command `authconfig`, which will present a reasonably friendly CUI (character user interface) with keyboard-driven dialog boxes. Although you must walk through these dialog boxes using the arrow keys, the Tab key, the spacebar, and the Enter key (rather than the mouse), they are otherwise roughly as friendly as regular GUI tools.

 WARNING   A similar GUI-based tool *does* exist in Fedora, but unfortunately it does not complete as large a percentage of the task at hand. We're sure it'll be nice when it's finished! In the meantime, `authconfig` command can do the job properly.

`authconfig` will display two lists. On the left is a list of sources of user information; these resources are consulted to determine a user's full name, user ID, group ID, and so forth. On the right is a list of valid authorities to authenticate a user's password. By default, Fedora fetches user information from the traditional Unix /etc/passwd, /etc/shadow, and /etc/group text files. When "Use Shadow Passwords" is checked, then password hashes are stored in the more secure /etc/shadow file instead of /etc/passwd. When "Use MD5 Passwords" is checked, the modern MD5 hashing algorithm is used instead of the old Unix "crypt" hashing algorithm. These two should remain checked, because, at a bare minimum, we still need to be able to log into the workstation as the local root user for maintenance when network authentication is not available.

What we want to do now is add the option of logging in by an additional method. In the list on the left, put a check (a "star" really) next to "Use Winbind." In the list on the right, put a check next to "Use Winbind Authentication." You'll see this shown in Figure 3.4. Then move to the Next button and press Enter.

In the "Winbind Settings" screen, shown in Figure 3.5, you'll specify information about your Active Directory configuration.

Here's how to set up the "Winbind Settings" screen:

- Security Model: Select "ADS."

- Domain: Enter the short NetBIOS "Windows NT" name of your Active Directory domain. In our examples, it's **AD**.

- Domain Controllers: Enter the Fully Qualified DNS name of an Active Directory server. In our example, this is **windc1.ad.corp.com** .

FIGURE 3.4 Use the "Authentication Configuration" screen to select both "Use Winbind" and "Use Winbind Authentication" options

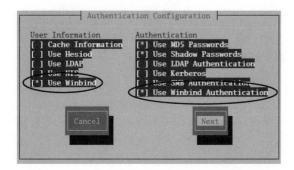

FIGURE 3.5 Use these Winbind Settings to specify your Active Directory and shell information.

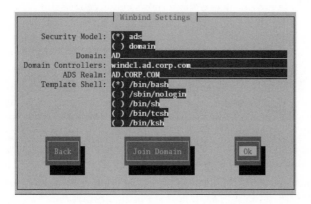

- ADS Realm: Enter **AD.CORP.COM** in this field.

- Template Shell: We suggest you leave this set to /bin/bash, but if you have a different Unix shell standard at your organization, that's fine too. This field is necessary because an unmodified Active Directory does not contain information about the preferred Unix command-line shell of each user.

When you are satisfied with your selections as shown in Figure 3.5, click the "OK" button (not that tempting "Join Domain" button—just "OK").

Although a "Join Domain" button is provided, we do *not* recommend using it because authconfig does not provide particularly enlightening feedback as to whether it works or not!

There's Something about PAM

While the authconfig tool looks good, it doesn't quite do the entire job. Although it configures most of the crucial authentication-related files in the system correctly, the system still doesn't have what it needs to create local home directories for users. Without a local home directory, login attempts for any user will fail. We can take care of that problem by modifying two of the configuration files used by PAM, the "pluggable authentication modules" system. The PAM standard allows anyone to add support for a new way of authenticating users. All applications that support PAM will automatically take advantage of it. A related standard, NSS, allows anyone to add support for a new way of looking up user information, also referred to as *directory services*. Let's get a clearer understand of both PAM and NSS.

What Are PAM and NSS?

Once upon a time, Unix systems could only look up account information or authenticate users by looking at the local Linux computer's /etc/passwd file (and its relatives). In more recent years, a variety of network-based directory services have come into being, including NIS, Active Directory, and LDAP. All of these provide account information in a centralized way. Additionally, you might choose to use more than just one of these systems to store user account information, so your enterprise's account information could be distributed across many of these centralized systems.

Unfortunately, many Unix applications continued to stubbornly expect their answers from the /etc/password file. It was clear that standardized interfaces to centralized account information and user authentication were required.

Two standards emerged as a result: one for authentication and one for directory services. PAM (Pluggable Authentication Modules) is the new universal authentication interface for Unix. Anyone can create a new authentication method by writing a suitable PAM module for it, and all Unix applications that support PAM will automatically support it.

A second modern Unix standard, NSS (Network Service Switch), provides a way to tell applications which directory service they should use to look up user information.

PAM and NSS make adding support for LDAP user authentication and directory services much easier. We simply use the `pam_ldap` and `nss_ldap` modules. These provide Linux with the ability to perform authentication and directory searches, respectively, via an LDAP server. We won't have to grapple with these modules ourselves. Instead, we use the Fedora Authentication tool, which configures them for us under the hood in the `/etc/pam.d` configuration files.

Configuring PAM To Create Home Directories As Needed

Linux is all about choice. Because of that, you can log on to Linux in any number of ways. Specifically, you can log on via:

- The normal desktop GUI (such as `gdm`—the GNOME Display Manager)
- Text-based Linux virtual consoles
- ssh secure remote logins

When you do log on via one of these methods, a home directory needs to automatically be created. No home directory equals nowhere to keep user information. Since Linux doesn't have a registry or a notion of user profiles, the home directory is crucial. PAM has a separate configuration file for all three methods of logging on to the system, so in all three cases, we need to tell PAM how to create a home directory if it does not already exist. And—you guessed it—someone has written a PAM module for that!

PAM is configured via text files in the `/etc/pam.d` directory. If you take a quick look inside that directory, you'll see a configuration file for any number of ways someone could "log on" to this server.

We only need to make changes to three files inside the `/etc/pam.d` directory: `gdm`, `login`, and `sshd`. We'll tell these files to create home directories for users. We need to add the following line to each file:

```
session required pam_mkhomedir.so skel=/etc/skel umask=0077
```

For more information on `skel` and `umask`, check out the "About `skel` and `umask`" sidebar in Chapter 2.

Use your preferred text editor (launched as root) and edit the first file, `/etc/pam.d/gdm`.

The `/etc/pam.d/gdm` file should look something like Figure 3.6 when you're done adding your one line at the end of the file.

FIGURE 3.6   Edit `/etc/pam.d/gdm` to add the last line as shown.

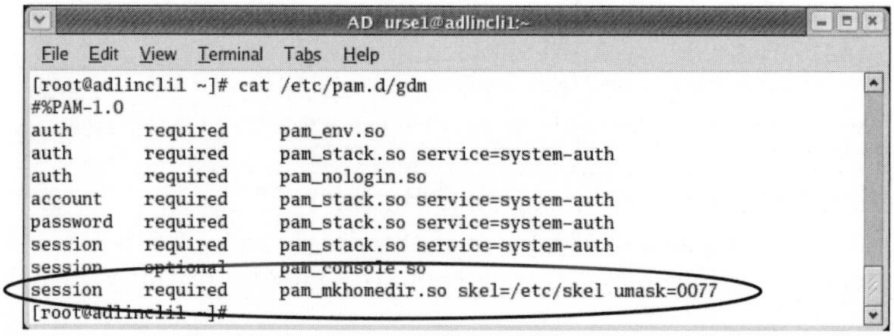

Next, use your text editor and modify /etc/pam.d/login.

WARNING While inside this file, you may see a comment which says to leave the last line as is. If yours says this, enter the line circled in Figure 3.6 just *before* the comment.

When done, it should look like Figure 3.7.

Finally, edit /etc/pam.d/sshd. Enter the same line as before to the end of the file. When finished, it will look something like Figure 3.8:

We're almost there!

Just two more steps are required:

- A bit of client-side Samba configuration to specify what a home directory path should look like for each user

- A command to actually *join* the Active Directory domain

Samba/Winbind Configuration

Samba, as previously mentioned, is a suite of services and client applications that provide Windows file-sharing protocols to Linux clients and servers. Winbind (the thing that gets us authenticated to Active Directory) is part of the Samba suite. Most people think of Samba as a technology that can serve up files and printers. And, sure, we'll be doing that on our servers in the upcoming chapters on file and print serving. But here, Samba configuration is still required on the Linux client to tell Fedora exactly where to create home directories when users log on via Active Directory.

It's all configured via the /etc/samba/smb.conf configuration file.

As a first step, we'll need to create a parent directory that houses our users' home drives, and we'll do it in a smart way. That is, we'll choose a top-level directory that specifically avoids conflicts should we add additional Active Directory domains later.

FIGURE 3.7 Edit /etc/pam.d/login to create home directories for command-line logins.

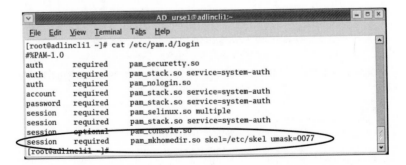

FIGURE 3.8   Edit the /etc/pam.d/sshd file to tell it how to create home directories

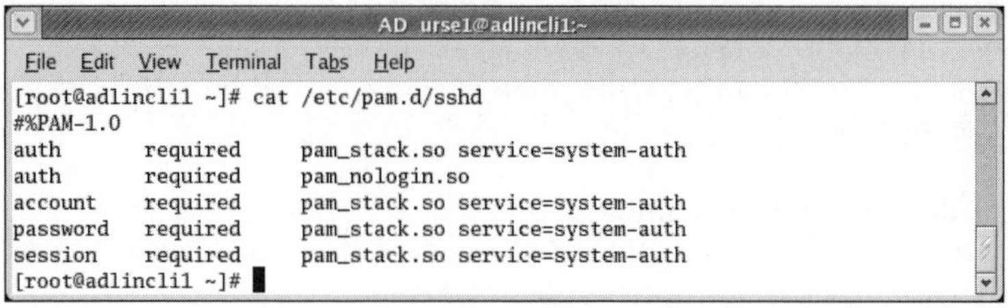

```
AD urse1@adlincli1:~
File  Edit  View  Terminal  Tabs  Help
[root@adlincli1 ~]# cat /etc/pam.d/sshd
#%PAM-1.0
auth        required        pam_stack.so service=system-auth
auth        required        pam_nologin.so
account     required        pam_stack.so service=system-auth
password    required        pam_stack.so service=system-auth
session     required        pam_stack.so service=system-auth
[root@adlincli1 ~]#
```

So, as root, at the command line, execute the following command:

```
mkdir /home/AD
```

In a real-world environment you will replace AD with the Windows NT-style "short" name of your Active Directory domain in all caps. Yes, that's right: IN ALL CAPS. If you try it with lowercase (as many commands and syntaxes in Linux are), it won't work. So in our case, all Active Directory user's home directories will conveniently be tucked away in /home/AD.

Now, we'll need to set the permissions on the new /home/AD directory so that everyone can list its contents (in order to find their own home directory) but only root can modify it. This is straightforward using the familiar chmod command. Here we grant read and "execute" permissions to everyone and write permissions only to root. For a directory, "execute" permission is required in order to access subdirectories:

```
chmod a-rwx,a+rx,u+rwx /home/AD
```

Next, edit /etc/samba/smb.conf with your text editor while running it as root. To the section of the file that begins with the line:

```
[global]
```

add the following line:

```
template homedir = /home/%D/%U
```

The %D variable is replaced with the NT-style short Windows domain name, and the %U variable is replaced with the Windows user logon name in lowercase. Thus, a user successfully logging in as AD\salesperson1 will receive the home directory /home/AD/salesperson1. The pam_mkhomedir module we added to the login configuration files will take care of creating user home directories for those who have not logged into this particular workstation previously.

Now, restart the Winbind service using the following command, as root:

```
service winbind restart
```

Joining the Linux Computer to the Active Directory Domain

Once the preceding steps are completed, we are almost ready to join our Linux computer to the Active Directory domain. Just a few things to triple-check first:

- Make sure the system clocks on the client and the Active Directory server are in close agreement. Joining a domain simply won't work without it.

- Make sure the DNS name of the computer you are joining to the domain is a part of the `ad.corp.com` subdomain (example: `adlincli1.ad.corp.com`). A name such as `client.whatever.com` will not work, because the Active Directory is looking for `ad.corp.com` not `whatever.com`.

As root at the command line, enter the following command:

```
net ads join -U administrator
```

Of course, if your Active Directory server does not have an administrative account called `administrator`, you will substitute the appropriate username.

When prompted, enter the password of the administrative user, which is `p@ssw0rd` in our examples.

Congratulations, you have joined a Linux computer to an Active Directory domain. You can verify your success by checking for the new computer in "Active Directory Users and Computers" on the Active Directory server. If you don't see it, double-check the two bullet points mentioned above: the system clocks must be in sync, and the Linux computer must be in the `ad.corp.com` subdomain. Then try the join again.

Logging into Active Directory via Winbind

This is it, the moment of truth: time to log in to Linux using an Active Directory account! Log out of your current session to return to the "gdm login" screen. Then, assuming you are following our examples with regard to domain and usernames, log in with the username `AD\salesperson1` and the password `p@ssw0rd`.

If all goes well, you will receive a notice explaining that a home directory has been created for `AD\salesperson1`, and your login should then complete in the usual fashion. Your Linux client workstation now accepts any login that is valid for your Active Directory domain.

If All Does Not Go Well

We suggest the following steps to resolve or determine the cause of any problems you may have when logging in:

- Make sure your Active Directory server is successfully validating logins for actual Windows XP clients. Always rule out the obvious!

- Verify that the system clock of the Linux workstation and the Active Directory server are in agreement.

- Make sure the workstation's full name includes the `ad.corp.com` suffix.

- Reboot the Linux workstation to ensure that all relevant services have been restarted.

- Use the `tail /var/log/messages` command immediately after a failed login attempt to learn more about the nature of the error.

- Bill Boswell's excellent article "Linux-Windows Single Sign-On" in the January 2005 edition of redmondmag.com is the source for much of the information in this section. Bill was instrumental in making this section possible. You can find his article at: `www.redmondmag.com/columns/article.asp?EditorialsID=858`.

- Although documentation tends to lag behind the capabilities of the Samba suite, the Samba website at `www.samba.org` is a crucial primary source of information on Samba-related issues.

Extending Active Directory with Unix/Linux Information

In the previous section, we saw that Linux clients can authenticate to an unmodified Active Directory server. While it's an interesting technical feat, this technique has limitations. Specifically, keeping Unix user IDs and group IDs consistent among Linux systems is a challenge when an unmodified Active Directory server is used for authentication.

So the answer is simple: modify Active Directory so it can get to understand Linux a bit better.

The "big picture" goal is to leverage Active Directory as the "go to" source for account information. Then the idea is that you can change the password in just one place: Active Directory. Storing Linux account information in Active Directory is the goal. Except there's one big problem: out of the box, Active Directory doesn't have the ability to store Unix user, group, and computer account information.

For Windows accounts, Active Directory knows just what to do. It has specific placeholders for things like username, group name, home directory, office phone, etc. However, Active Directory simply doesn't have placeholders for lots of Linux account attributes. Specifically, the two main things we need to teach Active Directory about are Unix user IDs (UIDs) and group IDs (GIDs).

Beyond that, Active Directory also needs to be taught about a location for Linux home directories, which login shell any particular user should use, and a whole lot more.

In short, Active Directory needs to be taught how to embrace Unix user, group, and computer account information. For it to do that, we'll need to extend the Active Directory schema. You extend the schema based on which version of Active Directory you are running.

- If your domain is Windows 2000 or Windows 2003, download and install the free Services for Unix 3.5 installation from Microsoft.

- If your domain is Windows 2003/R2 (or you're about to upgrade from Windows 2003 to Windows 2003/R2), then upgrade your Active Directory to the Windows 2003/R2 schema. The Windows 2003/R2 schema specifically includes attributes suitable for storing Unix/Linux account information.

Let's better understand how these paths are different.

Possible ways to extend Active Directory

As of this writing, Windows 2003 is out, and Windows 2003/R2 is close at hand. To that end, you may be rearing to go install Windows 2003/R2 when it comes out, or you might wait a while until your other system administrator pals have taken the plunge. So, depending on the road you take, you'll need to know precisely how to extend Active Directory to get Unix/Linux account information inside.

If You Have Windows 2000 and Windows 2003: Extend the Schema via SFU 3.5

In this chapter, we're about to inspect and install Microsoft's Services for Unix 3.5. It's a free add-in to Windows 2000 and Windows 2003 that allows Windows to embrace all sorts of Unix-like functionality; it can be downloaded at www.microsoft.com/sfu.

You should always download the latest version of SFU 3.5. There have been updates to SFU 3.5 since its release to support Windows 2003 + SP1, but older SFU 3.5 CDs (which you might have picked up a trade show) might have problems.

One of the main facets of SFU 3.5 is that it automatically extends the Active Directory schema so that Unix and Linux attributes can be tucked inside. Once SFU 3.5 is installed on a Domain Controller (which we'll do in a little bit), the Active Directory schema is extended to support the necessary attributes used to support Linux accounts. When this happens, Active Directory will have the information it needs if it wants to act as a NIS server. Yes! It's true. For more information on this added capability, see the sidebar "Really? Active Directory as a NIS Server?"

For a complete list of what's updated in the Active Directory schema, check out a document from Microsoft titled "Windows Services for UNIX 3.0: Schema Changes for Server for NIS" at http://tinyurl.com/6wcu7.

Note, even though the name of the document says "Windows Services for Unix 3.0" it's still 100 percent valid for SFU 3.5.

If You Have Windows 2003/R2: Extend the Schema via Windows 2003/R2

If you're taking the plunge to Windows 2003/R2, that's great. And one of Windows 2003/R2's key advertised features is that it has Unix Identity Management built right into it. In other words, when you upgrade a Windows 2003 domain to Windows 2003/R2 (or build a Windows 2003/R2 domain from scratch) your Windows 2003/R2 domain will have a schema that automatically has placeholders for Unix/Linux accounts.

These placeholders are similar, but not exactly the same as what SFU 3.5 (and SFU 3.0) perform. In short, and to be blunt, the SFU 3.5 schema updates are proprietary. Microsoft has publicly expressed how the Windows 2003/R2 schema updates are RFC compliant. Specifically, they are RFC 2307 compliant. RFC 2307 defines a set of classes and attributes for storing NIS information in LDAP.

The goal of RFC 2307 is to have a unified way to describe how to extend modern LDAP to contain old-and-crusty NIS data. For instance, you might need to extend another LDAP server, like an old Sun iPlanet (now with the impossible name Sun Java System Directory Server), Netscape Directory Services (or whatever they'll call it), or, yes, Active Directory!

Here's the deal—the RFC 2307 extension that Windows 2003/R2 employs are RFC 2307 compliant. But here's the kicker—it doesn't employ the entire set of RFC 2307. Yes, that's right. Windows 2003/R2 employs an *incomplete set* of the RFC 2307. What does this mean for you? Likely not much, unless you have a third party LDAP server that is looking for an RFC 2307 attribute in Active Directory that Windows 2003/R2 doesn't support.

In the downloadable web appendix, we'll specifically demonstrate how to install the Windows 2003/R2 schema, as well as take on the other main parts of this chapter going forward with Windows 2003/R2 (instead of just Windows 2003.) We'll also show you what happens if you've already committed to Windows 2003 and SFU 3.5, then decide to do an upgrade to Windows 2003/R2.

Services for Unix 3.5 Components and Installation

For the rest of this chapter, we're going to assume you're working with Windows 2003 (and not Windows 2003/R2.) To that end, Services for Unix (SFU) 3.5 allow Windows 2000 and 2003 to embrace all sorts of Unix-like functionality. Remember, you should always download it at www.microsoft.com/sfu.

We'll explore some of the functionality explored within SFU 3.5 here because it has ramifications about authentication. We'll explore other functionality in later chapters because they deal with other tools, components, and other utilities that aren't germane to authentication.

So, since we're here anyway, we'll install SFU 3.5 with all the components we'll be talking about in the book.

A bunch of great "how-to" articles on SFU 3.5 is available at www.microsoft.com/technet/interopmigration/unix/sfu/default.mspx. Note that SFU 3.5's main enhancements over SFU 3.0 are mostly performance- and cluster-specific. In other words, the technical articles for SFU 3.0 are likely just as valid for SFU 3.5.

What Does SFU 3.5 Have to Offer?

Here's a rundown of what SFU 3.5 contains. With a price tag of $0.00 is a pretty good deal:

Server for NIS   This component allows a Windows 2000 or Windows 2003 Domain Controller to pretend to be a master NIS server. It can also pretend to be a slave NIS server but only to other Domain Controllers with the NIS Server components running—not to Unix NIS master servers. Using this component, you can get rid of all your Unix NIS servers and centralize NIS account information in Active Directory. Why is this good? See the sidebar titled "Really? Active Directory as a NIS Server?"

Password Synchronization   This suite of tools helps keep collections of Windows and Linux computers up-to-date with password changes on either platform. We'll briefly touch on these features at the end of the chapter.

NFS Client, Server, Gateway, and Client for PCNFS and User Name Mapping   A suite of tools that runs on a Domain Controller that allows a Windows user to transparently view files contained within Unix/Linux NFS shares. This is explored more in Chapter 4.

Base Utilities   If you're already familiar with the Unix/Linux set of commands, (e.g., `ls`, `cat`, `grep`, and more), this is the perfect addition. We'll reexamine the base utilities in Chapter 7.

Telnet Server and Telnet Client   Telnet Server is already built in to both Windows 2000 and Windows 2003. However, loading this software on a Windows 2000 machine gives you a more enhanced version. SFU installs a Telnet Server and Client that operate in both stream and console mode (useful if your Unix application requires it). We won't be exploring the Telnet Server or Telnet client in this book.

Development Tools   SFU 3.5 includes tools for compiling existing Unix software for which the source code is available in order to make that software work on Windows. We'll talk in more detail about this in Chapter 10.

Note that you can load SFU 3.5 on Windows 2000 and higher, but not all features are available unless you install SFU 3.5 on a server and/or a Domain Controller. Specifically, here's what you won't get:

- If you load SFU 3.5 on a Windows 2000 or Windows XP workstation, neither Gateway for NFS nor Server for NIS will install.

- If you load SFU 3.5 on a member server (not a Domain Controller), Server for NIS will not install.

SFU 3.5 Installation

The installation of SFU 3.5 is pretty straightforward. However, there is one key point you need to be aware of before you run the installation program.

As we described, SFU 3.5 has the ability to pretend to be a NIS server. It does this by maintaining Linux accounts in Active Directory. That's the good news. The bad news is that Linux accounts are looking for information about those accounts that aren't "built-in" to Active Directory. Hence, we need to *extend* the schema of Active Directory. This is a one-time, irreversible operation. Many large corporations make schema changes part of their change-management process. A lot of smaller companies just go for it, usually without incident, but we would be remiss if we didn't express that this is a permanent, one-way change. However, for the examples in this book, we're going to need to have implemented the schema change, so that's what we're going to do here. In practice, there's very little likely to go wrong.

Really? Active Directory As a NIS Server?

It's true that you can make an Active Directory Domain Controller respond as if it were a Unix NIS server. Why would you ever want to do this? There are a slew of reasons why you might consider this strange combination:

- Your Unix clients remain untouched (as they think they're still talking to a Unix NIS server). However, they do need to rebind to the Active Directory/NIS server.

- Old and crusty Unix NIS servers can be decommissioned.

- Active Directory replication does the hard work of (securely) replicating user accounts around. The "NIS master" role can be played by all Active Directory servers as a result of the multimaster replication capabilities of Active Directory, eliminating a single-point-of-failure inherent to NIS. Active Directory replication is far more robust—and far more bandwidth friendly—than traditional NIS map propagation.

- User provisioning for both Windows and Linux clients would be through one unified tool: Active Directory Users and Computers. You could argue that this lowers costs and simplifies workflow.

In short, this is a low-risk solution that saves some money, increases robustness, and offers a unified tool (Active Directory Users and Computers) and some quality-of-service improvements.

If the idea is so wonderful, why aren't we describing in detail how to do it? Because, in reality, there are larger gains from migrating from NIS and converting those accounts to either Active Directory or OpenLDAP than from keeping NIS around any longer than necessary. However, making a larger jump like this does mean greater risk during the transition.

It might sound like a good idea to leverage this "Active Directory as a NIS server" as a stepping stone to get all your Unix accounts directly into Active Directory. Indeed, you can do this, but be aware that this path could be fraught with peril. In a nutshell, there are a lot of manual steps you need to get right.

A better choice is to perform a migration from NIS to Active Directory or OpenLDAP. Here's how you might go about performing that sort of project (which is beyond the scope of this book). For free advice:

- A Google search for "NIS to LDAP Migration" yields plenty of hits. There seem to be lots of scripts that profess to migrate NIS data directly to LDAP.

- Check out Microsoft's excellent document "Solution Guide for Windows Security and Directory Services for Unix" at http://go.microsoft.com/fwlink/?LinkID=23115.

There are also some commercial options I know that will help you leave NIS behind and go straight to an LDAP directory:

- PADL Software has a NIS/LDAP gateway product for sale at www.padl.com/Products/ NISLDAPGateway.html. Quoting from its website, "It permits existing NIS clients to transparently use LDAP to resolve user, group, and host information."

- Vintela's VAS product (also discussed later) has a set of tools to help convert NIS tables directly to Active Directory. Check out www.vintela.com.

- Centrify (at www.centrify.com) also has tools to help you convert NIS to Active Directory.

Before we leave this section, there is one aspect of Active Directory running as a NIS server that we must leverage in order to be successful. We'll explore that in Chapter 4 when we explore file sharing. Specifically, we must "ask" the Active Directory running as a NIS server to help us determine which user on Linux "maps" to which user in Active Directory. This is all part of the User Name Mapping service, which must interface with Active Directory running as a NIS server. Stay tuned.

Again, don't proceed if you have Windows 2003/R2. If you do, please download and read the web appendix, which discusses how to proceed.

Now that you understand what SFU 3.5 will do to our Active Directory schema, we're ready to roll. To install SFU 3.5 on our Windows 2003 DC (with the options needed for this book):

1. Start the SFU 3.5 installation program (SfuSetup.msi).

2. At the "Welcome" screen, click "Next."

3. At the "Customer Information" screen, enter your name and the organization name.

4. At the "License and Support Information" screen, accept the agreement and click "Next."

5. At the "Installation Options" screen, select "Custom Installation" and click "Next."

6. At the "Selecting Components" screen, drill down to Windows Services for Unix ➤ NFS ➤ Gateway for NFS. Change the defaults so that component is additionally loaded, as shown in Figure 3.9. Additionally, the "Client for NFS" must, unfortunately, be disabled as also seen in Figure 3.9. Again, we'll need to load the NIS server components of SFU 3.5 for this book. They need to be loaded in order to extend the schema. Additionally, they're used in the next chapter in conjunction with the User Name Mapping service.

7. At the "Security Settings" screen, you have two options: "Enable setuid behavior for Interix programs" and "Change the default behavior to be case sensitive." For our examples, we don't require either of these settings to be checked. (With these options, you decide how Windows should handle case-sensitivity.)

8. Next, you'll see the "User Name Mapping" screen. We're going to use this feature in the next chapter, so select the "Network Information Service (NIS)" button and click "Next."

9. You'll next see screen 2 of "User Name Mapping." Select your Windows domain name from the drop-down (in our case it's "AD"). Leave the "NIS domain name" field blank. Also, leave the "NIS Server name:" field blank. Click "Next" to continue.

10. At the "NIS/Password Synchronization" screen, you'll get a warning stating that schema changes are irreversible. For the purposes of this book, we'll need the changes, so click "Next" to continue.

11. At the "Install Location" screen, select where you want to install SFU 3.5 The defaults are fine ("c:\SFU"), so click "Next."

At this point, SFU 3.5 will install. When completed, you'll likely be asked to reboot. Do so, and you'll be ready to continue.

How to Unix-Enable Your Active Directory Users and Groups

Now that SFU 3.5 is fully installed, you can Unix-enable your Active Directory users and groups. It's easy. To get started, just fire up Active Directory Users and Computers. Then, to Unix-enable a user account, we must first have a Unix-enabled group account.

Unix-Enabling an Active Directory Group

Using Active Directory Users and Computers, double-click the SalesGroup we created earlier in the chapter. You'll see a new tab labeled "Unix Attributes," as shown in Figure 3.10.

FIGURE 3.9 Avoid installing the "Client for NFS" and the "Password Synchronization" features, but do install the "Gateway for NFS."

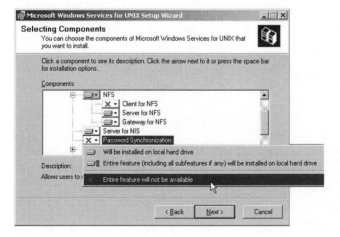

FIGURE 3.10 You can Unix-enable an Active Directory group.

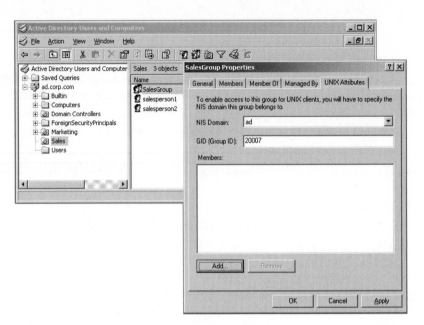

To Unix-enable the group, simply pull down the drop-down in the NIS domain box to select your Active Directory. When you do, Active Directory will automatically assign a GID (group ID) for this Active Directory group that's also now a Unix group.

Unix-Enabling an Active Directory User

Earlier in the chapter, we created `salesperson1` and `salesperson2` in the Sales OU. Double-click the `salesperson1` account and select the "Unix Attributes" tab, as shown in Figure 3.11.

To Unix-enable the user, simply pull down the drop-down in the NIS domain box to select your Active Directory. When you do, Active Directory will automatically assign a UID (user ID) for this Active Directory group that's also now a Unix user.

While you're here, you can select "`SalesGroup`" in the "Primary group name/GID" field. This field is only populated with Active Directory groups that have Unix attributes such as we just set up with the `SalesGroup`.

Using Extended Active Directory for Linux Authentication

In the immediately preceding section, we enhanced our Active Directory sever by installing Microsoft Services for Unix (SFU). Or perhaps you downloaded the web-appendix and learned how to extend the schema using Windows 2003/R2.

FIGURE 3.11   You can Unix-enable your users and specify which Unix-enabled groups they are members of.

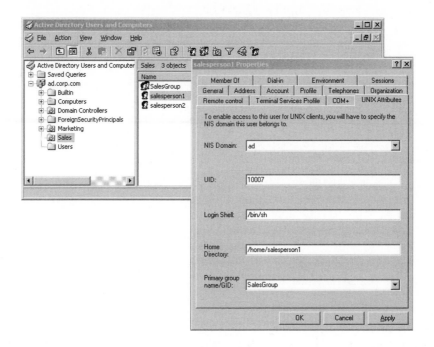

Active Directory is now aware of Unix user IDs and group IDs and has provisions to store them for each user and group account. That means we can authenticate Linux clients directly against Active Directory without worrying about file ownership inconsistencies when files are moved from one Linux client to another, because Active Directory is the sole arbiter of user and group IDs. This is a great improvement over the Winbind-based approach we discussed earlier. For the full gist of this, see the sidebar earlier, titled "How Winbind Fakes Linux User IDs (and How It Can Hurt)."

But how does the Linux client obtain the Unix user ID (UIDs) and group IDs (GIDs) from the Active Directory server? Since those fields are not part of the traditional Windows networking protocols, Linux's Winbind (which emulates those protocols) can't grab the goods. Handily for us, Active Directory responds to LDAP queries and, because we can use our Linux client to make LDAP queries to Active Directory, we can just *ask* for those UIDs and GIDs.

Setting the Stage for Active Directory/LDAP Requests and Authentication

In the last chapter, we authenticated a Linux LDAP client to a Linux LDAP server in the section "Authenticating Linux Clients to the OpenLDAP Server." When we did this, the OpenLDAP client components on `linclil.corp.com` made contact with the OpenLDAP server components on `linserv1.corp.com`. In one fell swoop, we looked up our user account and authenticated directly to OpenLDAP. Nice.

Now our goal is to get the OpenLDAP client components on a brand new machine, `adldaplincli1.ad.corp.com`, and have it talk to the Active Directory on `windc1.ad.corp.com`, as shown in Figure 3.12.

FIGURE 3.12   How a Linux client authenticates to an Active Directory with extended Unix attributes

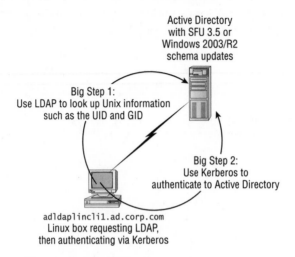

Active Directory
with SFU 3.5 or
Windows 2003/R2
schema updates

Big Step 1:
Use LDAP to look up Unix information
such as the UID and GID

Big Step 2:
Use Kerberos to
authenticate to Active Directory

`adldaplincli1.ad.corp.com`
Linux box requesting LDAP,
then authenticating via Kerberos

But "talking" to Active Directory isn't enough. There are two big steps the Linux client needs to perform:

Step 1   Find the user account in Active Directory and grab the UID and GIDs (and other information home directory paths) stored therein. We'll configure the client pieces of OpenLDAP on `adldaplincli1.ad.corp.com` to make contact to Active Directory to do this.

Step 2   Authenticate to Active Directory. We'll use a robust protocol that Active Directory uses to do the same task: Kerberos. This is a very strong protocol that protects all authentication traffic.

If we're really feeling frisky, we can go the extra mile and encrypt the LDAP traffic whenever we ask Active Directory to find our user accounts (in that first step).

Step 1 is the easy part. It'll be similar to what we did in Chapter 2's "Authenticating Linux Clients to the OpenLDAP Server." Step 2 is the new part. We'll simply configure our Linux client to authenticate directly to Active Directory's Kerberos server components. The optional "extra mile" of encrypting the initial LDAP traffic is the hard part. You'll see why a bit later.

About Kerberos Authentication

Kerberos is a standard for authenticating and authorizing users. Built into Microsoft's Active Directory at a fundamental level, Kerberos is also used by Linux and other operating systems.

Kerberos is highly secure and also has other advantages beyond simple login authentication. One of the most interesting is that Kerberos makes it much easier to implement "single sign-on," allowing a user access to many services after they log on without the need to present a password over and over again.

Unfortunately, most popular Linux applications are not yet "kerberized," so we won't benefit much from the single sign-on feature in this book. For the purposes of this chapter, the most important feature of Kerberos is its ability to authenticate logons in a highly secure fashion, but it's worth bearing in mind that additional benefits will appear as more and more applications such as web browsers and file sharing clients are "kerberized."

Kerberos is a complex beast, and multiple books have been written about the protocol. For our purposes, here are the three fundamental crib notes:

- First, a Kerberos server is properly known as a "KDC" (Key Distribution Center). The term "KDC" appears in the Fedora authentication configuration dialogs, so we'll try to be consistent and use that term.

- Second, a KDC plays host to a Kerberos "realm," which has a name of its own. A single Kerberos server could, in theory, be the "go to" server and host many different collections of security principals without name conflicts (as long as they all belonged to different realms.) In practice, however, an Active Directory domain's Kerberos realm name *always* matches the Active Directory domain name, but IN ALL CAPS. And that's important. Entering the Kerberos realm name in lowercase (as it typically appears in Windows) will simply not work.

- Third, a Kerberos "admin server" is a KDC that has the power to change passwords on a user's behalf. It is possible to create distributed "master" and "slave" KDCs, and in that situation we might specify a separate "admin server." But for our purposes in this book, the admin server is the same as the KDC.

WARNING

If you have not extended the Active Directory schema with Microsoft Services for Unix (SFU) 3.5, or Windows 2003/R2, you'll need to do that now as described earlier.

To pull this off, we'll refine our two "big steps" into five ministeps:

1. We'll add a user account to the Active Directory server purely for LDAP browsing purposes. The issue here is that Active Directory always requires us to authenticate at the LDAP level as a user before we can make any directory queries, so we'll create a special account for that purpose.

2. We'll set up our Fedora Linux workstation to use LDAP "user information" directory services. The Fedora GUI does about 90 percent of the work.

3. We'll set up the workstation to use Kerberos authentication and specify the name of the Kerberos KDC (Key Distribution Center). The Fedora GUI takes care of this step for us very neatly.

4. We'll reconfigure /etc/ldap.conf, allowing Linux to interoperate correctly with Active Directory. There are a few extra settings needed to account for differences between Active Directory and other LDAP user account directories. (See Chapter 2 for an introduction to /etc/ldap.conf.)

5. We'll make sure that home directories can be created as needed.

Then we'll be ready to log in to Active Directory using LDAP and Kerberos! Hold on to your seats! (And people think we lead boring lives.)

Setting up a User Who Can "Touch" Active Directory

In order for Linux clients to search Active Directory via LDAP for user accounts to utilize, you have to make a choice. You could "dumb down" Active Directory and allow "anonymous" LDAP traffic. You have to change the way the Active Directory reacts to queries. This is called the "heuristics" of the directory service. KB article 326690 describes how to modify the Active Directory heuristics to allow anonymous queries."

A better solution is to just tell our Linux clients about a regular user account for which we provide a password in the LDAP configuration file. Insecure? Maybe a little bit, but this user account won't really be able to *do* anything. The account will have no privileges other than be able to make LDAP queries. This special account will authenticate using LDAP "simple authentication."

Here's the bad news: simple authentication sends the user's password in cleartext. Because of this, at the end of this chapter, we'll go the extra mile and encrypt the LDAP traffic. So let's go ahead and create this special account that will enable LDAP lookups.

In this example, we'll create an Active Directory user account called dirsearch:

1. Select Start ➢ Programs ➢ Administrative Tools ➢ Active Directory Users and Computers.

2. Right-click the "Users" folder, and select New ➢ User.

3. Follow the wizard to create your first user. You can fill in any name you want in the "First name" and "Last name" and "Full name" fields. Just be sure to enter **dirsearch** in the "User logon name" field.

4. Be sure to enter the same password as usual: **p@ssw0rd**

5. Once the user is created, double-click the account and select the "Account" tab. Check "User cannot change password" and "Password never expires."

Configuring the LDAP Client with the Fedora Authentication Tool

Rather than use one of the Linux clients that we configured previously, before proceeding, we'll create a brand-spankin' new Fedora Core 3 client so we're sure to avoid interactions with other authentication methods. The goal of this Linux client is to authenticate to Active Directory using LDAP. In our examples, we'll call this fresh machine `adldaplincli1.ad.corp.com` (think of that as "*active directory ldap linux client #1*").

We need to tell our new Linux client to look up user information using LDAP and to perform authentication with Kerberos. We'll use the Authentication tool, accessed via the "System Settings" submenu of the "Applications" menu. This was covered at length in Chapter 2.

Configuring LDAP User Information

To configure the Fedora Core 3 Authentication tool to perform lookups using LDAP:

1. On your Linux client machine, from the Applications menu select System Settings ➢ Authentication. The "Authentication Configuration" dialog will appear.
2. You will default to the "User Information" tab. Check the "Enable LDAP Support" box.
3. Select the "Configure LDAP" button. The "LDAP Settings" dialog appears. Then, set the LDAP Search Base DN to **dc=ad,dc=corp,dc=com** and the LDAP server name to **windc1.ad.corp.com** . Do not check "Use TLS to encrypt connections" at this time. We'll reexamine that issue in the "Securing Active Directory LDAP Traffic" section. You can see these settings in Figure 3.13.
4. Click "OK" to return to the "Authentication Configuration" dialog. Now you're ready to configure Kerberos authentication.

Configuring Kerberos Authentication on the Client

Fedora makes setting up Kerberos authentication easy. Just follow these simple steps to configure Kerberos authentication with your Active Directory server. Again, we'll be performing these steps on the `adldaplincli1.ad.corp.com` client. To configure the Linux client for Kerberos authentication to Active Directory:

1. If you have not already done so, access the Fedora Authentication tool as described in the previous section.
2. Click the "Authentication" tab.
3. Check the "Enable Kerberos Support" box.
4. Click "Configure Kerberos"; you'll see the "Kerberos Settings" dialog.
5. In the "Realm" field, enter **AD.CORP.COM** in ALL CAPS (as shown in Figure 3.14).
6. In the "KDCs" field, enter **windc1.ad.corp.com** .
7. In the "Admin Servers" field, enter **windc1.ad.corp.com** . Note that we'll leave the two check boxes for DNS entries unchecked. That's because we're specifying the entries instead of asking the system to try to find them.

FIGURE 3.13   Enter the name of the Active Directory distinguished name (dn) and the Active Directory server name.

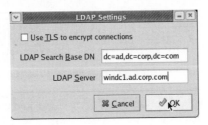

FIGURE 3.14   Enter the Active Directory name and the name of our Active Directory Domain Controller in the Kerberos Settings in the Authentication tool.

8. Click "OK" to exit the "Kerberos Settings" dialog.

9. Click "OK" to exit the Authentication tool.

Achieving Compatibility with SFU-Enhanced Active Directory

If we were using an ordinary Linux-based LDAP server, we'd be nearly done at this point. However, there are a few important differences between Active Directory and the OpenLDAP server we built in the previous chapter.

First, we need to spell out the key differences in /etc/ldap.conf settings when communicating with an Active Directory server (versus an OpenLDAP server).

In this section, we'll introduce each /etc/ldap.conf option that provides compatibility with Active Directory's LDAP support. Here, we need to:

- Tell Linux which Active Directory account to utilize for searching.

- Tell Linux which fields to use in Active Directory.

- Tell Linux where to dig up a user's account information.

- Tell Linux where to start searching for users in Active Directory.
- Tell Linux where to locate the "username" field in Active Directory.
- Speed up Active Directory searches.

Then we'll present a complete `/etc/ldap.conf` file that uses these features to successfully obtain user information via an SFU-enhanced Active Directory server's LDAP interface.

 Panic not if you're using the Windows 2003/R2 schema. Simply download the web appendix for how to achieve the same level of compatibility with a Windows 2003/R2 schema.

Tell Linux Which Active Directory Account to Utilize for Searching

By default, Active Directory does not allow "anonymous bind" via LDAP. That means that clients must log into the LDAP interface of Active Directory with a valid username and password; that's why we created our `dirsearch` user in the Active Directory. Our goal is to present that `dirsearch` user's LDAP "distinguished name" when needed so we can touch Active Directory.

The two lines we'll need to add to the `/etc/ldap.conf` file are

```
binddn cn=dirsearch,cn=Users,dc=ad,dc=corp,dc=com
bindpw p@ssw0rd
```

You'll see these in the final `/etc/ldap.conf` file at the end of this section.

Tell Linux Which Fields to Use in Active Directory

As previously described, there are dueling standards for extending Active Directory's schema: the SFU 3.5 way and the Windows 2003/R2 (RFC 2307) way. (See the section titled "Possible ways to extend Active Directory".)

Since in this chapter, we're demonstrating the schema extensions of SFU 3.5, we need to teach Fedora Core 3 how to leverage the SFU 3.5 schema attributes.

When Services for Unix extends the Active Directory schema, the new attributes are prefixed with `msSFU30`. Yes, that's right. They're msSFU30 even though we're working with SFU 3.5. So, for instance, the Unix home directory field in an Active Directory extended with SFU 3.5 is known as `msSFU30HomeDirectory`.

Fortunately, `nss_ldap` supports a technique called *schema remapping*. This allows us to tell the Linux system that the `homeDirectory` field can be found in the `msSFU30HomeDirectory` field when talking to an Active Directory server. We accomplish this using the `nss_map_attribute` option in `/etc/ldap.conf`. Here are the key lines we'll add to `/etc/ldap.conf`. Again, you'll see the complete file at the end of this section.

```
nss_map_attribute uid sAMAccountName
nss_map_attribute uidNumber msSFU30UidNumber
nss_map_attribute gidNumber msSFU30GidNumber
nss_map_attribute loginShell msSFU30LoginShell
```

```
nss_map_attribute gecos name
nss_map_attribute homeDirectory msSFU30HomeDirectory
nss_map_objectclass posixGroup Group
nss_map_attribute uniqueMember member
nss_map_attribute cn sAMAccountName
```

Tell Linux Where to Dig up a User's Account Information

Active Directory also calls the account object, which contains all information about an account, by a different name. In a typical Unix LDAP directory, the account object would be called a posixAccount, and the "shadow password" information would be in a similar object called a shadowAccount; Active Directory, however, has a single type or *class* of object, called a user, that serves both purposes.

We'll use the nss_map_objectclass option to tell Linux where the account information it expects can be found in Active Directory. Here are the key lines we'll add to /etc/ldap.conf. Again, you'll see the complete file at the end of this section.

```
nss_map_objectclass posixAccount user
nss_map_objectclass shadowAccount user
```

Tell Linux Where to Start Searching for Users in Active Directory

The nss_base_passwd, nss_base_shadow, and nss_base_group options are similar to the base option we've discussed previously.

They must be identical to or "beneath" the base. They indicate where in the LDAP hierarchy nss_ldap should start looking for user, shadow password, and group objects. Here are the key lines we'll add to /etc/ldap.conf:

```
nss_base_passwd dc=ad,dc=corp,dc=com
nss_base_shadow dc=ad,dc=corp,dc=com
nss_base_group  dc=ad,dc=corp,dc=com
```

For instance, in our example, all three are set to dc=ad,dc=corp,dc=com. This allows all users in any part of the Active Directory LDAP database to log into this workstation.

You might want to set the base to a *lower* point in the LDAP hierarchy, such as a particular department's organizational unit. Although beyond the scope of this book, creatively restricting the nss_base_passwd, nss_base_shadow, and nss_base_group options and the base option can improve performance and help to enforce policy. Or you might want to restrict the search to just one portion of the LDAP tree, say, an OU (organizational unit) such as Sales. This could be an effective way to restrict the use of a workstation exclusively to salespeople.

Such restrictions can also improve performance by avoiding the need to exhaustively explore tens of thousands of accounts for each login attempt when the only people who should be using a particular workstation are salespeople. Such a restricted setting might look like: nss_base_passwd ou=Sales,dc=ad,dc=corp,dc=com

But in our case, we want to search the whole Active Directory domain.

Tell Linux Where to Locate the "username" Field in Active Directory

The user logs on by entering a username. What field in the LDAP schema should be searched for a match with that username? The key line we'll add to /etc/ldap.conf is

```
pam_login_attribute sAMAccountName
```

We use the pam_login_attribute option to set this to sAMAccountName, which is the Windows "username" field. This allows users to log into Linux workstations using the same username they would use on a Windows workstation.

Speed up Active Directory Searches

We've covered the bare necessities, but there's one more option that will help keep us out of trouble. One additional line we'll want to add is

```
pam_filter objectcategory=User
```

By setting pam_filter to objectcategory=User, we ensure that our LDAP search doesn't waste time or generate bogus results by trying to match usernames to objects that don't contain account information at all. While it may seem unlikely that such objects will have a sAMAccountName field, they certainly *could*, and we speed up our search by skipping them.

Note that there are many attributes with darn similar names. Specifically, be very careful and set pam_filter to objectcategory=User (and not to objectclass=User). These are not the same. Specifically the User object class includes computer objects. Setting it to objectcategory=User specifically hones in just on user objects.

The Complete */etc/ldap.conf* File for a Linux Client to Authenticate Using LDAP to Active Directory with SFU 3.5

In this chapter, the goal is to provide LDAP authentication against an SFU-enhanced Active Directory server (in our case, windc1.ad.corp.com). Our Active Directory domain name is ad.corp.com, and to search Active Directory via LDAP we're leveraging a basic user account named dirsearch (with the password p@ssw0rd). Each of these options is explained in the preceding section.

Listing 3.1 shows the full /etc/ldap.conf file. We'll have this file available for download on www.WinLinAnswers.com.

For additional information about /etc/ldap.conf, see Chapter 2.

Listing 3.1: */etc/ldap.conf* for LDAP Authentication against Active Directory

```
# Here, we'll use unencryupted LDAP port 389. ("ldap")
uri ldap://windc1.ad.corp.com

base dc=ad,dc=corp,dc=com
binddn cn=dirsearch,cn=Users,dc=ad,dc=corp,dc=com
bindpw p@ssw0rd

nss_base_passwd dc=ad,dc=corp,dc=com
nss_base_shadow dc=ad,dc=corp,dc=com
nss_base_group  dc=ad,dc=corp,dc=com

nss_map_objectclass posixAccount user
nss_map_objectclass shadowAccount user
nss_map_attribute uid sAMAccountName
nss_map_attribute uidNumber msSFU30UidNumber
nss_map_attribute gidNumber msSFU30GidNumber
nss_map_attribute loginShell msSFU30LoginShell
nss_map_attribute gecos name
nss_map_attribute homeDirectory msSFU30HomeDirectory
nss_map_objectclass posixGroup Group
nss_map_attribute uniqueMember member
nss_map_attribute cn sAMAccountName
pam_login_attribute sAMAccountName
pam_filter objectcategory=User
```

Making Home Directories on the Fly

We've configured the Linux workstation to use LDAP and added the crucial options to achieve compatibility with SFU-enhanced Active Directory. There's only one step to go.

When a new user logs into a particular workstation for the first time, that user doesn't have a local home directory yet. As you saw in Chapter 2, a user can log in via three methods:

- The shell
- Encrypted shell (via ssh)
- The GNOME interface

We address this by adding the pam_mkhomedir.so module to the sshd, gdm, and login files in /etc/pam.d. See Chapter 2 (in the "Authenticating Linux Clients to the NIS Server" section) for a detailed discussion of this step.

Briefly, the procedure is:

1. As root, open the file `/etc/pam.d/sshd` with your text editor.

2. Add the following line to the end of the file:

   ```
   session      required      pam_mkhomedir.so skel=/etc/skel umask=0077
   ```

3. Repeat steps 1 and 2 for `/etc/pam.d/gdm` and `/etc/pam.d/login`.

Logging into Active Directory Using Linux via LDAP

We're there! Log out of your Fedora workstation and log in again as `salesperson1` with the password p@ssw0rd.

You should receive a message explaining that a home directory has been created for `salesperson1`, and your desktop should then appear as normal.

Congratulations!

Your Linux workstation is now authenticating against an Active Directory server.

Thanks to Microsoft Services for Unix, the Active Directory server now provides centralized management of Linux user IDs and group IDs, as well as all other account information—and Windows workstations can log on with the very same accounts!

If It Doesn't Work

Here are some suggestions if it doesn't go quite as planned:

1. Be sure that Windows workstations can log into the Active Directory domain using the same credentials you are testing on your Windows workstation. It bears repeating: always, always rule out the obvious.

2. Make sure you installed Microsoft Services for Unix 3.5 on the Active Directory server as described in the section "Services for Unix 3.5 Components and Installation."

3. Did you create the `dirsearch` and `salesperson1` accounts on the Active Directory server? If not, do so following our instructions.

4. Double-check your `/etc/ldap.conf` file to make sure it matches our configuration.

5. As root, try the command `su - salesperson1`. This opens a new shell running as `salesperson1` rather than root. Root can switch to any other user at any time, so you will not be prompted for a password. You should receive an illuminating error message if this command fails. If it succeeds, you'll be returned to the prompt logged in as `salesperson1`, so type **exit** to return to root's shell prompt. When this command succeeds but logon attempts still fail, it is likely that you are not logging in with the right password.

6. Add a new line to `/etc/ldap.conf` to help you debug: just add a single line (anywhere) that says **debug 1** . Then try step 5 again. You should receive quite a bit of debugging output, which may shed some light on the problem. Be sure to remove that line afterward.

7. As recommended at the end of Chapter 2, use the command `tail -20 /var/log/messages` to check for error messages relevant to the logon process.

8. Always try Google searches for error messages you receive.

Checkout

To authenticate a Linux client via the LDAP interface of an Active Directory server:

1. We installed Microsoft Services for Unix.

2. We created a `dirsearch` account in the Active Directory for LDAP binding purposes. We also created a user account named `salesperson1` for testing purposes.

3. We used the Fedora Core 3 GUI Authentication tool to enable LDAP authorization and authentication and specified the Active Directory server as the LDAP server.

4. We customized our `/etc/ldap.conf` file to enable compatibility with Active Directory's significantly different LDAP schema.

5. We added support for creating home directories on the fly using `pam_mkhomedir.so`.

The Extra Mile: SSL Encryption of LDAP Traffic between Linux and Active Directory

We are using Kerberos to encrypt the crucial authentication traffic: user logons and password changes. But it is also sometimes desirable to encrypt less critical LDAP directory services traffic like user listings, home directory paths, full usernames, and so forth.

It is possible to encrypt LDAP traffic using SSL, just as we did when working with a Linux-based LDAP server, but there are some challenges in our path. Since the directory services traffic is of much less concern than password authentication, this is only an "extra mile" security precaution. If you want to, you can skip it—but if you have the time and are very security conscious, then go for it.

The goal is to encrypt LDAP traffic using SSL. To enable SSL encryption of LDAP traffic between Linux clients and Active Directory, we must do three things:

- Determine whether the Linux client has a new enough version of the OpenLDAP client software. An incompatibility between older versions of the OpenLDAP client software and Active Directory makes SSL encryption between the two impossible. As of this writing, Fedora Core 3 with the available official updates still includes the older version of OpenLDAP, so read that section very carefully before proceeding.

- Enable SSL on the Active Directory server. This involves creating a domain controller certificate and a Certification Authority on the Windows server, much as we did on the Linux server in the last chapter. Windows and Active Directory make this easy.

- Configure the Linux client's `/etc/ldap.conf` file to use SSL and recognize the Windows-based Certification Authority.

Ensuring the OpenLDAP Client Supports SSL with Active Directory

Let's jump right to the end of the story and tell you what we found when we first ran these experiments. We configured the OpenLDAP client and enabled it for SSL encryption. The good news was that we found that the OpenLDAP client talks to Active Directory, and the traffic is encrypted! Yay! Except: Fedora freaks out, and the connection just hangs forever. Ouch!

Of course, the first thing we did was to re-run Fedora's up2date to ensure we had the latest version of OpenLDAP client (and sever) pieces. A new version downloaded, but it wasn't enough to stop the hanging.

Here's the good news: this problem *has* been fixed in OpenLDAP version 2.2.23, which is available directly from www.openldap.org. Buuut...unfortunately, the latest OpenLDAP has not been integrated into Fedora Core 3 yet. As of this writing, it's not available to download via up2date.

Here's where you make a decision about where to go:

Option 1   Give up now. It's not a huge deal if LDAP traffic goes unencrypted. What goes unencrypted are lookups into Active Directory. However, the only kinda-bad news is that the dirsearch account's password will be sent across in cleartext.

Option 2   Wait until Fedora Core 3's up2date makes OpenLDAP 2.2.23 available or wait until Fedora Core 4 (which should incorporate version 2.2.23 of OpenLDAP).

Option 3   Install OpenLDAP 2.2.23 from source. We provide the gory instructions below. And if you do need to upgrade it, you'll also need to rebuild nss_ldap, which is not obvious at first glance.

Again, this is a known problem and has been fixed in later versions of OpenLDAP, but as of this writing Fedora Core 3 doesn't yet incorporate this later version.

Does your version of Fedora Core have OpenLDAP 2.2.23 or higher? Let's find out.

How to Find Out If Your OpenLDAP Is New Enough

Here's a command that will tell you whether *your* version of OpenLDAP is new enough to do the job correctly:

```
ldapsearch -V
```

The first line of output should resemble this:

```
ldapsearch: @(#) $OpenLDAP: ldapsearch 2.2.23  (Mar 10 2005 15:08:18) $
```

Note the version number in boldface. With versions older than 2.2.23, we do *not* recommend trying to enable SSL on Linux clients communicating with Active Directory via LDAP.

Fedora Core 4 is slated to include OpenLDAP 2.2.23. If Fedora Core 4 is in your hands, you should be able to use SSL LDAP connections without problems between Fedora and Active Directory.

The Hard Way: How We Verified That Version 2.2.23 or Better Will Work

If Fedora Core 3 doesn't yet offer OpenLDAP 2.2.23 as of this writing, how do we know that version will work? Because we manually upgraded OpenLDAP with unofficial Fedora rpms built by a third party and then rebuilt `nss_ldap` from source code. We do not recommend that you attempt this yourself unless you are *very* comfortable installing system software from source code and you have already verified that your newer, fully updated Fedora system does not already have OpenLDAP 2.2.23.

Here are the steps we performed. Again, *we don't recommend you follow this procedure* unless you are very comfortable upgrading system software *and* you trust the source of the rpms you use. This is *not* intended to be an exhaustive guide to installing from source. It is intended to be helpful to experienced users who want to be able to reproduce our tests.

1. We located a source of unofficial Fedora Core 3 rpms for OpenLDAP 2.2.23 at `http://openldap.prolocation.net/`.

2. We downloaded and installed all of those rpms except for the openldap-servers-sql rpm, which had an unresolved dependency and is not used in our system. We used the following command to install each rpm, overwriting files installed by the official Fedora OpenSSL rpm. The `--force` option allows us to overwrite existing files with the contents of the unofficial rpm:

   `rpm -i --force rpmfilename rpmfilename etc.`

3. We upgraded OpenLDAP. Shouldn't we be finished? Nope! Unfortunately, `nss_ldap` is "statically linked" to OpenLDAP, meaning that we must recompile `nss_ldap` from source code to take advantage of the upgraded OpenLDAP libraries on the system. We obtained an "SRPM" (source code rpm) for the `nss_ldap` Fedora package. Source rpms allow us to rebuild binary rpms from source code while still saving a great deal of time compared with building from non-Fedora-specific source code packages. That's because the source rpm "knows" exactly where Fedora keeps configuration files, libraries, data files, and so on. When building from non-Fedora sources we must configure all of those things manually. We fetched the SRPM from the following location, a mirror of Fedora Core 3:

   `http://mirror.web-ster.com/fedora/core/3/SRPMS/nss_ldap-220-3.src.rpm`

4. Once we had the SRPM, we were able to build binary rpms of `nss_ldap` linked to the new version of OpenLDAP using this command:

   `rpmbuild --rebuild nss_ldap-220-3.src.rpm`

   This builds ordinary "binary" rpms and places them in the folder `/usr/src/redhat/RPMS/i386`.

5. Now we finish the job by installing our new `nss_ldap` binary rpms with these commands:

   `cd /usr/src/redhat/RPMS/i386`
   `rpm -i --force nss*.rpm`

After completing these steps, you will be able to use a secure LDAP connection. The URI in the `ldap.conf` file will specifically start with `ldaps` (instead of `ldap`) to signify that the connection is secure.

When testing this, be sure to keep a root shell open so that you can undo it if you are not successful. Otherwise your attempts to log in as root and fix the problem will fail when the LDAP connection to the server "hangs" indefinitely.

Enabling SSL for LDAP on the Active Directory Server

Active Directory supports LDAP over SSL, and SSL requires the use of certificates between the client and server. This means you need a Domain Controller x.509 certificate at every domain controller.

To acquire these, we'll need to create an Active Directory Certification Authority. Now, here's the deal: the advice in this section is for testing purposes only.

Creating your Active Directory–based Certification Authority (CA) can be a really, really big deal in your environment. This is definitely not something that should be done by winging it. The definitive guide in this subject area is by Brian Komar in his book titled *Microsoft Windows Server 2003 PKI and Certificate Security* (MS Press, 2004). Again, we're winging it here for the sake of these examples; but you shouldn't!

Once we create the Enterprise CA, all Domain Controllers in the domain will automatically enroll for a Domain Controller certificate, and that will enable them to use LDAP over SSL.

To create an Enterprise CA on a Windows 2003 server, perform the following steps:

1. Select Start ➢ Control Panel ➢ Add or Remove Programs. Once the "Add or Remove Programs" applet appears, select "Add/Remove Windows Components."

2. Select the check box for "Certificate Services" as shown in Figure 3.15. When you do, you'll be warned that installing a CA prevents you from disjoining this computer from the domain. Select "OK."

FIGURE 3.15   For these examples, you'll be installing an Active Directory Certificate Server. In the real world, don't run out and do this without thinking about it first.

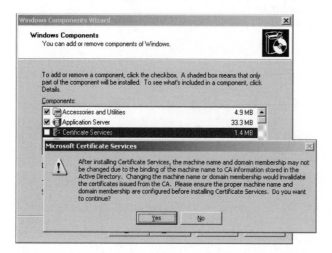

3. In the "Windows Components Wizard" at the "Windows Components" screen, click "Next." When you do, you'll be prompted for the "CA Type." Select "Enterprise root CA." You can leave the "Use custom settings to generate the key pair and CA certificate" box unchecked.

4. At the "CA Identifying Information" screen, you'll have to enter one or two pieces of information in order to create a Certification Authority. This is what will enable us to create certificates later. It's a good idea to give this a name that makes sense, say, **ADCERTAUTHORITY**. An example of our choices is shown in Figure 3.16. When ready, click "Next."

5. At the "Certificate Database Settings" screen, you can specify where Windows will keep the database and log files. Leave the settings at the default and select "Next."

6. You may be prompted to temporarily stop the IIS server. Select "Yes" if prompted.

7. You may also be prompted to allow Active Server Pages to be enabled for IIS. Select "Yes" if prompted.

Once finished, you have two options to embrace the new certificate:

- You can open a command prompt, and type the command **gpupdate /force**. This should force it to get the certificate.

- If that doesn't work after about 15 minutes, then I suggest you reboot your Active Directory Domain Controller.

After either of these steps, port 636 should be available to accept encrypted Active Directory traffic.

FIGURE 3.16 Enter some identifying information about your Active Directory CA.

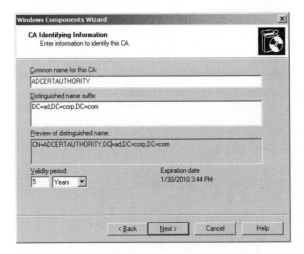

To Confirm Active Directory Can Accept SSL Traffic

One of the tools in the Windows 2003 Support Tools is called LDP and can help you ensure that SSL traffic is ready to be accepted by Active Directory. You can load the Support Tools by double-clicking the `suptools.msi` file in the `\support\tools` directory of the Windows 2003 CD-ROM. Once you do that, you're ready to go.

To confirm that you can make an SSL connection:

1. Select Start ➤ Run, type **ldp** , and click "OK."

2. Once LDP launches, select Connection ➤ Connect. In the "Connect" window, type **windc1.ad.corp.com** in the "Server" field, as shown in Figure 3.17. Change the "Port" field from 389 to 636 and check the "SSL" check box. Leave the "Connectionless" check box unchecked.

3. You should receive a message that demonstrates you have connected to the Domain Controller. Using LDP, select Connection ➤ Bind. Enter our `dirsearch` username and **p@ssw0rd** as well as our domain name, **ad.corp.com** , as shown in Figure 3.18, and click "OK."

FIGURE 3.17 Use LDP to connect to the Active Directory server with port 636.

FIGURE 3.18 Bind to Active Directory using the `dirsearch` account you created earlier.

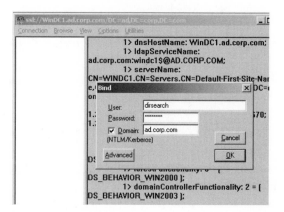

4. You should get some text in the big gray window that demonstrates that you are authenticated as the `dirsearch` user. It might look something like this:

    ```
    res = ldap_bind_s(ld, NULL, &NtAuthIdentity, 1158); // v.3
        {NtAuthIdentity: User='dirsearch'; Pwd= <unavailable>; domain =
    'ad.corp.com'.}
    Authenticated as dn:'dirsearch'.
    ```

5. Using LDP, select View ➢ Tree. Leave the "BaseDN" field blank and click "OK." In the left pane, you should be able to browse Active Directory's OU structure. And you're doing so, encrypted over port 636.

To Export the Certificate for Linux Clients

Once your CA is in place and ready to accept SSL traffic over port 636, you need to get a copy of the Certification Authority certificate to your Linux clients. This tells the Linux clients to trust the Domain Controller certificate issued by the CA. To do this, we'll use the super-secret Certificates snap-in. (It must be a secret, because there is no evidence of it on the Start Menu.)

  To load the Certificates snap in:

1. Select Start ➢ Run and type **MMC**

2. At the naked MMC console, select File ➢ Add/Remove Snap-in. Click "Add," and at the "Add Standalone Snap-in" dialog, select "Certificates" (not "Certification Authority").

3. At the "Certificates snap-in" dialog, you'll be asked which kind of certificates you want to manage. Select the "Computer account" radio button and click "Next."

4. At the "Select Computer" screen, select "Local Computer," then click "Finish."

5. Back at the "Add Standalone Snap-in" dialog, click "Close."

6. Back at the "Add/Remove Snap-in," click "OK."

  Now you'll have the chance to export the public certificate of the Certification Authority (which is valid for all authentications against Active Directory).

  To export the necessary certificate:

1. From the "Console Root," drill down to Certificates (Local Computer) ➢ Personal ➢ Certificates, as shown in Figure 3.19.

2. Right-click the "ADCERTAUTHORITY" certificate (not the certificate of the Domain Controller) and select All Tasks ➢ Export. The Certificate Export Wizard appears. At the "Welcome" screen of the wizard, click "Next."

3. At the "Export Private Key" screen, select "No, do not export the private key" and click "Next."

4. At the "Export File Format" screen, select "Base-64 encoded X.509 (.CER)." This produces a text file that is readable by Linux clients. Click "Next."

5. Browse to where you can easily get to the file for copying. Give it a filename such as `ADCERT1.cer`. Click "Next."

6. At the final screen of the wizard, click "Finish."

FIGURE 3.19   Export your Active Directory certificate.

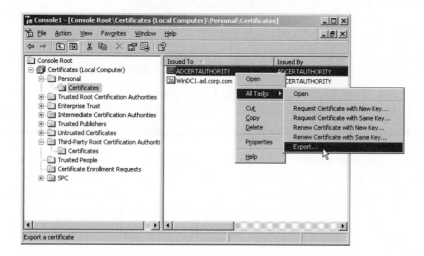

At this point, you'll have to get that certificate over to each of your Linux clients. One method is to use a downloadable tool called psftp. It's an SSH-encrypted way to send files from Windows to Linux machines. You can download psftp from `http://tinyurl.com/2r4w`.

Here's how it looks to use psftp to transfer the certificate from Windows to, say, the Linux machine named `adlincli1`:

```
C:\downloads>psftp lincli1.corp.com
login as: root
The server's host key is not cached in the registry. You
have no guarantee that the server is the computer you
think it is.
The server's rsa2 key fingerprint is:
ssh-rsa 1024 55:ba:b6:0e:bb:fe:d5:d6:d8:e3:7a:48:e4:f4:ef:ee
If you trust this host, enter "y" to add the key to
PuTTY's cache and carry on connecting.
If you want to carry on connecting just once, without
adding the key to the cache, enter "n".
If you do not trust this host, press Return to abandon the
connection.
Store key in cache? (y/n) y
Using username "root".
root@lincli1.corp.com's password:
Remote working directory is /root
psftp> cd /etc/openldap
Remote directory is now /etc/openldap
```

```
psftp> put adcert1.cer
local:adcert1.cer => remote:/etc/openldap/adcert1.cer
```

The adcert1.cer is now in the Linux machine's /etc/openldap directory.

Configuring the Linux OpenLDAP Client to Use SSL

Configuring the Linux client to support an SSL-encrypted connection to the Active Directory LDAP server requires just three changes to /etc/ldap.conf. First, we'll change the uri setting from an insecure ldap:// URI to a secure ldaps:// URI. Second, we'll tell the client to be sure to verify the server's SSL certificate with the tls_checkpeer option. And third, we'll use tls_cacert to tell the client about our Windows-based Certification Authority. Although we have covered the tls_cacert option before, it is worth mentioning that we are using the Enterprise Certification Authority we created on our Active Directory server as our Certification Authority (CA), while in Chapter 2 we used a Linux-based CA.

In any real-world enterprise, having just *one* CA is probably the best choice. After all, not having to install many certificates on each client is the purpose of having CAs. However, for the purposes of this book, it is worthwhile to show how CAs are created and used on both Linux and Windows. It's also worth mentioning that Windows Enterprise Certificate Authorities will *automatically* create server certificates for all Active Directory Domain Controllers (which is super sweet). Not to mention that Windows 2003 CA's perform auto-enrollment to clients and a whole lot of other features. In short, a Windows CA provides a compelling advantage. If you choose to have only one CA, it might be easiest to choose Windows, at least until the process of administering a CA on Linux becomes significantly more user friendly.

We're ready to secure our LDAP connections. To enable SSL for LDAP connections to Active Directory, follow these steps:

1. To enable SSL encryption, replace this line of /etc/ldap.conf:

   ```
   uri ldap://windc1.ad.corp.com
   ```

   with the following line (the only difference is ldaps versus ldap):

   ```
   uri ldaps://windc1.ad.corp.com
   ```

2. Add the following two lines at the end of the file:

   ```
   # Verify the server's certificate
   tls_checkpeer yes
   # CA Certificate for verification of server certificate
   tls_cacert /etc/openldap/adcert1.cer
   ```

That's it! Your Linux-to-Active-Directory LDAP traffic is now encrypted with SSL. You can verify this by logging into the client, but we *strongly recommend* that you do the test the following way, just in case you made a mistake and your version of OpenLDAP isn't really new enough to do this:

1. Keep your existing root shell open. You will need it to back out your changes by switching back to an ldap:// URI in /etc/ldap.conf if your attempts to log on hang indefinitely.

2. Use the `ssh` command to start a remote logon attempt from the workstation to itself. `ssh` is a useful way to remotely and securely access the shell on other Linux workstations and servers, but we can also use it to connect to the same computer as a useful test. The `-l` option specifies the user we wish to log in as and is followed by the hostname of the system to log into. For convenience, we are using the special name `localhost`, which always refers to the *same* computer you are coming from:

```
ssh -l salesperson1 localhost
```

Enter the password when prompted. If your logon is successful, great, you're done! If not, you can debug the problem using exactly the same suggestions made earlier under "If It Doesn't Work" in the "Logging into Active Directory using Linux via LDAP" section. In addition, make sure that you:

1. Enabled SSL on the Active Directory server

2. Exported the Certification Authority's certificate

3. Copied the certificate to the Linux client and placed it in the same location that the `tls_cacert` option is set to

4. Verified that your version of OpenLDAP is version 2.2.23 or later

Commercial Interoperability Products

There are several commercial, third-party solutions that can help make the integration of Active Directory and Linux clients easier. We've already seen the open-source `nss_ldap` and `pam_ldap` modules, and how they can help to connect Linux machines to Active Directory. These are standard in Fedora Core 3 and other popular Linux distributions.

The commercial products we'll describe are

- VAS by Vintela, Inc.
- DirectControl by Centrify Corporation

WARNING It should be noted that the third-party software companies have provided some of the information in this section to us. In short, be sure to test-evaluate any solution before purchasing.

The goal in this section is to leverage Active Directory as the "go to" source for account information. After installation, the idea is that you can just change the password in once place: Active Directory.

NOTE Both commercial products we list here have to complete with the open-source `nss_ldap` and `pam_ldap` modules which, as we have seen, are built-in to Fedora Core 3. For the record, it should be noted that `nss_ldap` and `pam_ldap` were originally created by PADL Software Pty Ltd., who can be found at `http://www.padl.com/`.

VAS by Vintela

Vintela Authentication Services (VAS) is a commercial product from Vintela which aims to centralize Active Directory authentication from a wide variety of Linux and Unix clients. A native binary package is available for most Linux and Unix distributions (as opposed to hand-carving PAM configuration files as we've done throughout this chapter). Additionally, this company has recently received a financial blessing from Microsoft.

Some of the main features VAS includes and notes as reasons it is superior to PADL's offerings are:

- Native binary packages for a wide variety of Unix/Linux platforms
- A consistent command-line interface across all platforms
- Nested Group Support (without recursive LDAP calls)
- Native Windows installer and MMC snap-in
- Ability to load another Vintela product, VGP (Vintela Group Policy), to support Group Policy on Unix and Linux systems
- Disconnected mode for caching credentials when offline
- Additional single-sign on support
- NIS Compatibility mode for easy integration with automounter utilities and legacy NIS apps
- Support for multiple Unix identities per Active Directory user

In Figure 3.20, you can see VAS in action.

You can download a trial of VAS at www.vintela.com/products/vas/.

From what I can see, the competition between Vintela and the in-the-box solution seems pretty fierce. Multiple comparisons to PADL Software Pty Ltd., the company behind nss_ldap and pam_ldap, are made on the Vintela website, in the FAQ (www.vintela.com/products/vas/vasfaq.php) and in multiple places within a paper available at www.vintela.com/support/docs/vas/2.6/VAS_Myths.pdf

PADL does acknowledge that VAS might have the upper hand, but it weighed in its two cents about Vintela's positioning vis-à-vis PADL's nss_ldap, which you can read at www.padl.com/Articles/ClarificationonVintelaAut.html.

DirectControl by Centrify

DirectControl by Centrify is another commercially available third-party tool to centralize administration and authorization. DirectControl has the noted distinction of not requiring a schema change (unlike FU 3.5, Vintela's VAS, and nss_ldap).

DirectControl has a "zones" philosophy that enables administrators to take multiple Unix/Linux usernames and UIDs from different systems and map them directly to one Active Directory account. You can see DirectControl's interface in Figure 3.21. Additionally, Centrify's DirectControl product has some Group Policy functionality built into the product.

You can learn more about DirectControl by Centrify at www.centrify.com/index.htm.

FIGURE 3.20   Vintela's VAS

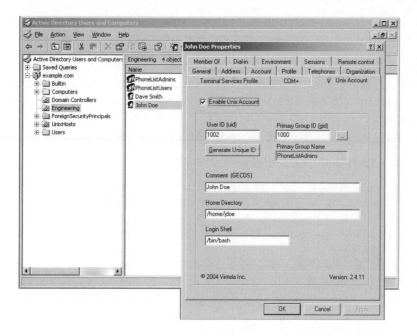

FIGURE 3.21   Centrify's DirectControl

Synchronized Peer Directories

In this chapter and the last chapter, we've tried to highlight the most useful cases where Linux clients can authenticate to Active Directory and where Windows clients can authenticate to Linux directory services, such as NIS, SAMBA, and OpenLDAP. The point is to work toward some semblance of single-sign-on.

However, it's certainly possible that we didn't hit on your particular need. Specifically, you might not be able to get Windows to authenticate to Linux or Linux to authenticate to Windows. In these cases, you'll need a way to synchronize different peer directories. Here is a rundown of several other ways to accomplish a single-sign-on in mixed environments.

Using a Metadirectory Service

In the best case, you would simply have one directory store for your entire company. You'd use either Active Directory or, say, OpenLDAP as the *one* source of company-wide user-based information.

Except that's not always realistic. The problem is, your company's phone switch likely doesn't know how to talk to Active Directory or OpenLDAP. Neither does your company's payroll system or the security system the employees use to buzz themselves into the building.

The goal of a metadirectory is to take multiple account stores, such as Active Directory, OpenLDAP, your phone system, your human resources system, etc., and have them all talk with each other. It's a very ambitious goal, but the payout can be great. But be careful: one slip-up and you could be dumping bad data into multiple systems.

There are many metadirectory systems to consider:

Microsoft MIIS   You can find Microsoft's MIIS at `www.microsoft.com/technet/security/topics/identity/idmanage/default.mspx`.

Novell's Nsure Identity Manager 2.0 (formerly DirXML)   At last check, even though DirXML was going though a name change, it could still be found at `www.novell.com/products/dirxml/`.

Sun ONE Meta-Directory 5.1   You can find out about Sun's product at `www.sun.com/software/products/meta_directory/home_meta_dir.xml`.

SimpleSync   SimpleSync's product is fairly inexpensive compared to the competition, and it's easy to set up. You can find it at `www.cps-systems.com`.

Open Source?   For now, there doesn't seem to be an open-source metadirectory solution in the works. Stay tuned. Those late-night basement coders are always cooking up something new.

SFU 3.5's Password Synchronization Suite

We loaded this when we loaded SFU 3.5 earlier. The goal is to keep collections of Windows and Linux computers up-to-date should a user's password change on either the Windows or Linux side. There are pieces of code that run on Windows computers and pieces of code that run on Linux computers.

This is a useful set of components but *not* if you're ultimately planning on utilizing Active Directory as a centralized directory store. This set of tools is ultimately useful when you *don't* have Active Directory and just have a collection of Windows machines in a workgroup that you want to synchronize with a collection of Linux machines. If you do use this suite, there are components that run on every machine, both Windows and Linux. Should you change your password on a Linux machine, a notification will be sent to all of the Windows machines that you specify. Should you change your password on a Windows machine, all Linux computers that you specify will get the notification of the update. A useful document for its use is at www.microsoft.com/technet/interopmigration/unix/sfu/psync.mspx, or you can find it at the shortened URL http://tinyurl.com/3vw3k.

Final Thoughts

Getting Windows and Linux machines to talk isn't an easy task. The previous chapter and this chapter demonstrate these two systems definitely come from different worlds. Indeed, the only thing they have in common is TCP/IP, and thank heavens for that. It's not a cakewalk to get Linux clients authenticating to Active Directory. In this chapter, we explored three major ways to get the job done:

- We used the Winbind method, and joined the Linux workstation to the domain. We did this without modification to the Active Directory schema.

- We modified the schema using SFU 3.5 or used the partial RFC 2307 schema built into Windows 2003/R2. We connected the client using LDAP and Kerberos. We also went the extra mile and showed you how to encrypt LDAP traffic if you wanted to.

- We explored commercial options to make the job easier. These options included packages you could load on your client systems, or metadirectory programs to synchronize your different account repositories.

Hopefully, you've been able to get a lot out this chapter and make the initial authentication to Active Directory happen. We simply couldn't go over each and every possible way to authenticate Windows to Linux and Linux to Windows. However, one of the best references I've located on the subject is *Solution Guide for Windows Security and Directory Services for Unix*, which is free and downloadable from http://go.microsoft.com/fwlink/?LinkID=23115.

4

File Sharing between Windows and Linux

Both Windows and Linux have a "native" way of sharing files over a network. In this chapter we'll first explore those native ways. Then we'll show how to access files served by a Windows system from a Linux client and vice versa. Of course, some combinations work better than others, so along the way we'll suggest what we feel the best options are in each scenario.

As you'll see in this chapter, NFS (Network File System) is the traditional file-sharing solution on Linux. NFS is still in heavy use and is probably the best option in a pure Linux environment. Making Windows clients talk to Linux NFS servers is also possible, and we'll demonstrate that. However, since Samba can offer up Windows-compatible shares via Windows SMB (Server-Message-Block), the best Windows-client to Linux-server file sharing solution is Samba.

With that in mind, here is what we want to do:

- Use Windows to create file shares to store files and
    - Have Windows clients see and open the files
    - Have Linux clients see and open the files
    - Have Windows clients use Windows shares for home directory and roaming profile storage
- Create Linux file shares using Samba (which look like Windows SMB shares). Account validation will come from Samba and OpenLDAP (appearing to Windows clients as a PDC). Then, we'll
    - Have Windows clients see and open them
    - Have Windows clients use Samba shares for home directory and roaming profile storage
- Create Linux file shares using Samba but have account validation from Active Directory. In other words, we'll create a domain member file server running on Linux. Then we'll have Windows clients see and open those shares.
- Leverage NFS mount points on Linux and Windows. Here, we'll
    - Have our Linux clients see and open them, including using them for home directory storage
    - Have our Windows clients open and see them (via a centralized method)
    - Have our Windows clients open and see them (individually from each Windows XP machine)
    - Create a centralized home drive (in Linux, home directory) for users who log on to both Windows and Linux

Of course, we'll get started by introducing the basics: Linux clients talking with Linux servers and Windows clients talking with Windows servers. Setting up Windows SMB shares is a fairly easy task. Having Windows clients talk to them is also, as expected, pretty easy. Let's go through a quick file sharing test.

To create a share on our Windows 2003 server:

1. Click Start ➢ My Computer and select a drive to store the data on. You might only have one drive letter set up (C) so go ahead and double-click that drive if it's the only choice available.

2. While the C: drive is open, select File ➢ New ➢ Folder and give the folder the name `WinShare1`.

3. Right-click "`WinShare1`" and select "Sharing and Security." The "`WinShare1` Properties" window will appear as shown in Figure 4.1.

4. Click the "Permissions" button and the "Permissions for `WinShare1`" window will appear (also shown in Figure 4.1.)

5. For now, leave the default Windows 2003 permissions on the share (that is, Everyone can read the files contained within the share), so click "OK."

6. At the "`WinShare1` Properties" page, click "OK."

FIGURE 4.1   You can set permissions directly on each Windows share.

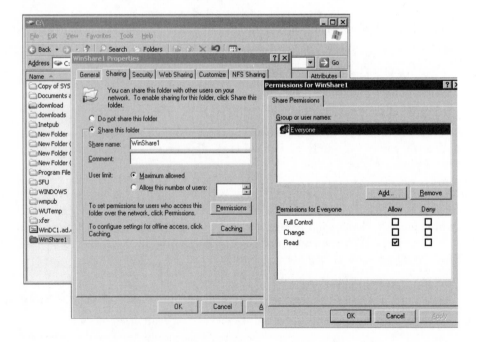

At this point, WinShare1 is shared. Right now, there's nothing in it. Double-click the WinShare1 directory, then right-click the white space and select New ➢ Text Document. Create two documents for later use: winfile1.txt and winfile2.txt. While you're here, you might as well add a sentence or two of text to each file, so you can read it later. We'll leverage these files when we perform our integration testing.

Having Windows Clients Utilize Windows File Shares

As expected, it's pretty easy to have a Windows client utilize a Windows share. To test, let's first log on as salesperson1 at our Windows XP machine—xppro1.

There's a multitude of ways for us to browse to the Windows shares. Let's take the most straightforward. To see Windows shares from a Windows client:

1. Click Start ➢ My Computer. In the "Other Places" heading, select "My Network Places."

2. Next, locate and click "Entire Network," still in the "Other Places" heading.

3. Select "Microsoft Windows Network." You will see a list of the available domains, including AD, the NetBIOS name of ad.corp.com. Double-click "AD."

4. Now you will see the names of the machines within the AD domain. Double-click "Windc1" to see the shares it contains.

5. Double-click "WinShare1" to see the files and folders within the share. Double-click any file to open it, as shown in Figure 4.2.

It was easy to make Windows clients connect to a Windows server. What's next—and more interesting—is to have Linux clients make a connection to Windows file shares.

FIGURE 4.2   You can see the files in the share on Windc1.

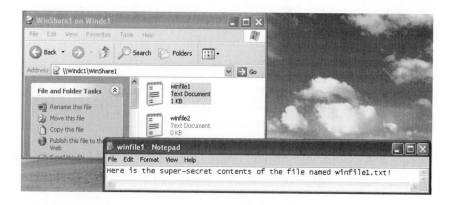

Having Linux Clients Utilize Windows File Shares

Samba has been around for a while and it works well. As a general rule, client-side access to Windows file shares is well supported in Linux, as long as you use the command line. But if you want a user-friendly GUI, there are a few significant snags. Fortunately, we've sorted through the available options so that you don't have to.

There are two basic ways Linux clients can access Windows file shares. Some applications "speak" the Windows SMB protocol directly. Most such applications do so by using the `libsmbclient` library, which is part of the Samba suite. Examples of such applications include the Nautilus file manager, which is a standard part of the GNOME desktop we are using in Fedora.

The alternative is to take advantage of one of two drivers that add SMB file sharing capabilities directly to the Linux kernel. This approach allows applications to see files on a Windows file server as part of the Linux file system without any direct support for SMB in the application. The two SMB kernel drivers, both of which are included in Fedora Core 3, are known as `smbfs` and `cifs`. The `smbfs` driver works well with file shares offered by Windows NT and older versions of Windows, but it does not support *SMB signing*, a security mechanism designed to prevent nefarious types from potentially hijacking your SMB sessions. SMB signing was an optional step that could be added for protection with Windows NT shares and Windows 2000 shares. However, with Windows 2003 shares, SMB signing became mandatory by default, although SMB signing can still be turned off on the Windows 2003 server to loosen security. An additional overview of SMB signing and how to turn it on or off for various operating systems can be found by checking out MSKB 887429.

Fortunately, `smbfs` has been replaced by `cifs`, a driver that supports SMB signing and interoperates with the latest versions of Windows in their default configurations. `cifs` is named for the "Common Internet File Sharing" initiative, an effort to create a standard file sharing protocol based on SMB. We mention both drivers because a variety of older file browsing applications for Linux still use `smbfs` "under the hood." That's why those applications have difficulty talking to Windows 2003 file servers.

We'll discuss the advantages and disadvantages of these two basic approaches in more detail as we go along.

We're almost ready to start taking advantage of SMB file sharing from our Linux client. But first, we'll need to improve our standard Linux user authentication by adding Kerberos to the mix. Without it, user-friendly Linux software has a great deal of trouble connecting to Windows 2003 Server shares.

Kerberos Authentication and Windows File Sharing

As discussed in Chapter 3, Kerberos is a standard for authenticating users and is built into Microsoft's Active Directory at a fundamental level. It's also used by Linux (and other operating systems).

Why Kerberos Authorization Will Be Brilliant (and Standard)…Eventually

Kerberos has one key advantage: when a user authenticates to a Kerberos-aware client, the Kerberos server verifies that the client is a valid "security principal" (in this case, a user). Then the server hands back a special temporary access key called a *TGT (Ticket Granting Ticket)*. The TGT can then be presented to obtain tickets to many different services during the user's session.

The client can present the TGT for entry to many different services offered by the server or by an entire Active Directory domain. For instance, it is not necessary to present usernames and passwords over and over when mounting different shares. The TGT allows the client to obtain valid tickets for entry to any of the "rides" in the Active Directory "theme park" for as long as the user is logged in. No more redundant password prompts! Exciting, isn't it?

The Bad News: It's Not Quite That Convenient Yet

As of this writing, in our tests with Fedora Core 3 and Windows 2003, GNOME desktop applications like Nautilus still prompt for a username and password each time you connect to a new share, even if Kerberos is used for logon authentication. However, if we don't use Kerberos authentication at all, connection to shares offered by Windows 2003 server fails altogether with an error message.

The Good News: This Problem Will Be Short-Lived

What's the conclusion? It's in our short-term and long-term best interest to turn on Kerberos authentication now. Without it, Nautilus browsing of shares on Windows 2003 server does not work.

Experimental code for full Kerberos support in Nautilus is already appearing in the GNOME development process. When that version of Nautilus becomes part of the Fedora Core distribution—possibly even by the time this book is in your hands—the need for the redundant logons will disappear…if you follow our advice and set up Kerberos authentication now.

How to Set up Kerberos Authentication

We'll set up Kerberos authentication just as we did in Chapter 3 for the `adldaplinclil` system. Follow these steps to enable Kerberos authentication on `adlinclil`:

1. From the "Applications" menu, select System Settings ➤ Authentication.
2. When the Authentication tool appears, click the "Authentication" tab.
3. Check the "Enable Kerberos Support" box.
4. Click "Configure Kerberos" to get the "Kerberos Settings" dialog box.
5. In the "Realm" field, enter **AD.CORP.COM** in ALL CAPS (as shown in Figure 4.3).
6. In the "KDCs" field, enter **windc1.ad.corp.com** .
7. In the "Admin Servers" field, enter **windc1.ad.corp.com** .
8. Click "OK" to exit the "Kerberos Settings" dialog box.
9. Click "OK" to exit the Authentication tool.

FIGURE 4.3 Enter the Active Directory NAME and the name of our Active Directory Domain Controller in the Kerberos Settings dialog in the Authentication tool.

Domain Logons and Kerberos Don't Quite Get Along

One more little snag. Recall that in the previous chapter when we configured Active Directory authentication using Winbind, the user was required to enter a logon name with a domain prefix, such as **AD\winuser1** . Well, Linux Kerberos authentication doesn't understand logons where the username contains a domain prefix.

But this doesn't have to be a deal breaker for us. We'll tell Winbind to *always* use the name of the workstation's domain (**AD**) so the user doesn't need to provide one. This way, Kerberos can authenticate the user and Winbind can get details about the user.

 This works great if you just have one Active Directory domain. However, it breaks down a bit if you have multiple domains, because users will be unable to specify which Active Directory domain they want to log on to. This could be a major problem if you have roaming users who use computers in multiple domains to log in. With any luck, support for domain separator characters in usernames will improve throughout Linux in the future.

We'll have to make one small change to /etc/samba/smb.conf. Edit that file with your preferred text editor and add the following line:

```
winbind use default domain = yes
```

If there is already a line that begins with "winbind use default domain", be sure the setting after the equal sign is yes.

Restart Winbind with the following command, as root:

```
service winbind restart
```

Verifying Kerberos Authentication

How do we test it? Easy! Just log on as the Active Directory user salesperson1, with the password p@ssw0rd.

If your logon fails, double-check that you

- Entered the Kerberos realm name in ALL CAPS when you configured AuthConfig
- Entered the KDC and admin server names correctly

If your logon still fails, check /var/log/messages for additional diagnostic information. If all went well, we're ready to move on to accessing SMB shares from our Linux desktop.

Testing Kerberos Authentication

As of this writing, the best-known application that takes advantage of Kerberos authentication at logon time is a command-line tool called smbclient. This tool is part of the Samba suite.

smbclient is similar to the old command-line FTP client. After you have completed the previous steps, go ahead and log in as salesperson1. You can then experiment with the command smbclient //windc1/winshare1 -k, which will log into the share winshare1 on the windc1 server without prompting for a username and password.

Once connected, try the ls command to list files. Note that smbclient never prompts you for a username or password. Why? Because it's Kerberized and beautiful. Soon this single-sign-on capability will be standard in GNOME applications as well.

Using Windows File Shares

You can allow Linux clients to utilize Windows shares in two main ways.

Browsing   When you need spur-of-the-moment access to a particular Windows share. This is where a GUI is most helpful.

Mounting   Your best choice when you need a particular share to be available all the time. Not unlike the "map network drive" option in Windows, mounting an SMB share makes it visible in the Linux file system as a new subdirectory. The biggest advantage is that other Linux applications can use the share without any special code.

It is possible to mount a share automatically every time the Linux machine boots up or to mount a share every time a user logs in. This allows a user's home directory to reside on the Windows server. Like roaming profiles for Windows, this enables Linux client users to roam from workstation to workstation and see the same files and environment.

We'll explore some of the ways you can visit Windows-land from a Linux machine.

Quick Visits to Windows-land: Browsing SMB Shares with Linux

Browsing SMB shares with Fedora Linux is easy enough now that we've done the grunt work of setting things up.

Pull down the "Applications" menu and select "Network Servers" to bring up a list of *all* network file servers the client can "see" on the network. For instance, you'll see stuff being shared via Windows-style SMB, and, once we set it up, stuff we export using NFS (described and implemented later). It can take a while to populate the network server windows, though, so be patient.

For now, double-click "Windows Network" to proceed to a list of available domains, which will be similar to the display shown in Figure 4.4. Now double-click the **ad** domain to browse the servers in our domain. This pops up another window listing those servers, also shown in Figure 4.4. Finally, double-click "WINDC1" to list the shares available on our main Windows 2003 server.

Now we'll open up the share we created earlier in this chapter by double-clicking "WinShare1." As soon as we do that, we'll be prompted for our username, password, and domain name as shown in Figure 4.5. Enter **salesperson1**, **p@ssw0rd**, and **ad**, respectively. Then check the "Save password in keyring" box. This allows Fedora to store your domain logon information in a special encrypted "keyring" file so that it can be automatically reused. Although this is not as convenient as using proper Kerberization, it will save us from entering credentials again the next time we browse the share.

The credentials in the keyring are not updated when users change their Active Directory passwords; the user must update the keyring credentials manually the next time the share is accessed following a password change. The client will prompt the user for the password again and give the user a new opportunity to save it in the keyring.

FIGURE 4.4   Browsing domains via the "Network Servers" window, then browsing our Active Directory domain, then browsing the available shares on WinDC1.

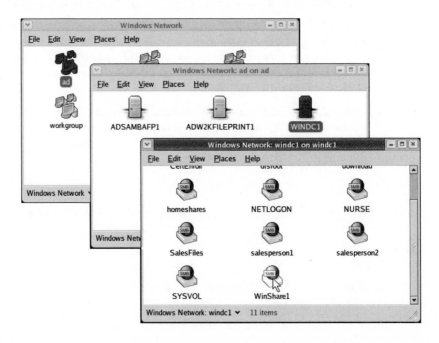

FIGURE 4.5   You can use the "Save password in keyring" option to avoid having to re-enter credentials for each share.

When you're finished, click "OK." You will be prompted for, yes, another password (see Figure 4.6)! Now, don't scream—not too loudly, anyway. This password only has to be given once per session; it's used to control access to the keyring. Enter a password and click "OK." (We used **p@ssw0rd** in our tests.) A window opens displaying the files in the share.

To demonstrate access to a file on the WinShare1 share, double-click "winfile1.txt." This launches the standard GNOME text editor, gedit, but before we can read the file we'll have to answer one last security-related prompt.

gedit and the Nautilus file manager are two separate applications, and GNOME doesn't allow a new application to access passwords stored in your keyring until you grant permission to that application.

When you see the "Allow application access to keyring?" prompt, click "Always Allow" to add gedit to the list of programs that can use passwords saved in the keyring. At last you'll see the contents of winfile1.txt displayed in gedit, as shown in Figure 4.7.

Congratulations, we've been on safari in Windows land for SMB!

FIGURE 4.6   Users are asked to set a password for their individual keyring.

FIGURE 4.7 You can browse and open the file on Windows shares. This simple file opens with Linux's gedit.

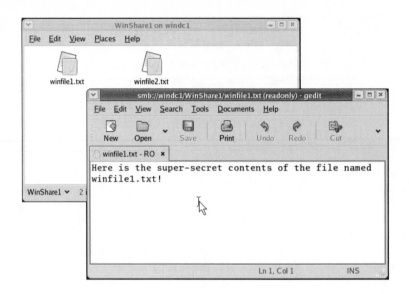

Alternative SMB Browsers and Mounters

Nautilus is a fine, general-purpose file manager that also happens to work with SMB shares. It's also smart enough to work with the requirement that shares on Windows 2003 use SMB signing by default.

The file manager for KDE, Konqueror, also handles SMB shares about as well as Nautilus.

In your travels, you might come across other utilities that promise the allure of browsing and mounting SMB shares. But beware: that tool might not be able to look within Windows 2003 shares if it depends on older tools that don't support SMB signing. The message you receive is hysterical: "SMB signing is mandatory and we have disabled it." It's specifically funny to me because I would expect them to say, "We don't have support for it" or, "We haven't enabled it." It sort of reminds me of that video game which declared "All your base are belong to us" — but I digress. Regardless, most alternative SMB browsing tools won't work with Windows 2003 signed shares.

Here's a list of tools we tested. None are part of Fedora Core 3 installation, but you can download them and get them going in no time—but again, be aware of the limitations in browsing SMB-signed shares.

gnomba This application's homepage is the mightily sparse page at `http://gnomba`
`.sourceforge.net`, but I was able to download a Fedora Core 2–specific rpm for an easy
install from `http://dag.wieers.com/packages/gnomba/`. (Yes, I did say Fedora Core 2, but
it installed and worked just fine.) It worked, and I could poke around, buuuut...it couldn't
show me any shares on Windows 2003 machines.

linneighborhood This application seems to have lost its support some time back. It's a shame,
too; it's quite cute. The homepage for Linneighborhood is `http://www.bnro.de/~schmidjo/`,
but I was able to download a Fedora Core 3–specific rpm for an easy install from `http://`
`dag.wieers.com/packages/linneighborhood/`. It worked and I could poke around, buuuut...it
couldn't show me any shares on Windows 2003 machines.

smb4k The homepage for smb4k is at `http://smb4k.berlios.de/`, but I was able to download
a Fedora Core 3–specific rpm for an easy install from `http://dag.wieers.com/packages/smb4k`.
The first time you run it at the command line takes a little while, and then a little green and blue
computer icon appears next to the "Up2Date" exclamation in the upper right-hand corner. Just
click it and it drops down to open. It worked and I could poke around, buuuut...it couldn't show
me any shares on Windows 2003 machines.

To summarize, these tools aren't prepared to talk with Windows 2003 shares that use the
default of SMB signing. Nautilus is, however, so we continue to recommend that you use that.
You could disable Windows 2003 SMB signing, but it's not recommended. With that in mind,
stay away from these tools until you see that they explicitly support SMB signing.

Automatically launching gedit is a fine solution for text files, but what if we needed to look
at a different kind of file? Nautilus and other GNOME applications support SMB file sharing
directly without actually "grafting" the share into the Linux file system, but non-GNOME
applications won't necessarily understand what to do with one of their files on an SMB share.

We can work around this problem by copying files to the local drive, working with them
there, and copying them back. For instance, it's not overly difficult to drag a Microsoft Word
document from the "Windows Network" window to the desktop, double-click it there, edit it
in OpenOffice, save it, and drag it back. But doing this kind of thing on a regular basis becomes
aggravating. That's why it is often preferable to mount an SMB share to make it appear as part
of the Linux file system. All applications can automatically use it, not just those that are
GNOME-aware or otherwise speak SMB themselves.

Long-Term Stays in Windows-land: Mounting SMB Shares with Linux

Browsing with Nautilus is a useful for learning what's out there and making the occasional
quick visit, and for working with files that a GNOME application fully supports, it can be a
complete solution. However, if you need to get to the same files on SMB shares over and over,
especially when you want to use a non-GNOME application, you need a better plan.

Mounting an SMB Share

You want to "mount" the share so that it *appears to be part of the local file system*. This way, every application on the local workstation believes the file is local (and automatically understands how to work with it).

> This is analogous, sort of, to mapping a drive letter in Windows. Some Windows applications are smart enough to handle UNC paths, such as *server**share name*, but even the most poorly designed Windows application can handle a mapped drive letter when opening and writing to files. In Linux, mounting an SMB share offers exactly the same benefits. The application doesn't need to know how to handle SMB shares in order to be useful. Just point the application toward the "mount point" that you're about to create, and you'll be in clover.

It takes two pieces of information to mount a share:

- The UNC path of the share. Thanks to our explorations with Nautilus, we already know that the share named `WinShare1` is located on the server `Windc1`. (Case is not really significant here, but we'll use the same uppercase and lowercase letters we saw while browsing.)

- Where we want to mount the share locally. The Linux command-line utility `mount` can "graft" the share into the file system using an empty folder as a mount point.

Let's mount the `Windc1\WinShare1` share onto our `salesperson1`'s desktop. That allows us to marry the convenience of desktop access with the power of a mount from the command line.

The `mount` command is actually the same utility that Linux uses to mount all types of file systems, including CD-ROM drives, flash media, even stuff located elsewhere on the local hard drives. The general syntax for mount is

```
mount -t <filesystem type you are mounting> <what you want to mount> <where you
want to mount it>
```

But first things first: Let's create a folder on our desktop where we can mount the share. We'll place the *mount point* at /home/AD/salesperson1/Desktop/WinShare1. The `mount` command requires an existing, empty directory, so we'll first create this directory with the `mkdir` command as follows:

```
mkdir /home/AD/salesperson1/Desktop/WinShare1/
```

Now that we have the directory prepared, we're ready to formulate the `mount` command and provide it the key things it needs to know:

- The `-t` option tells mount what type of file system we want to work with. As discussed earlier, we should use the `cifs` driver to talk to Windows 2003 servers, so we'll give `cifs` as the value for the `-t` option.

- We'll also need to specify the full name of the share. This is done much the same as on a Windows system, except that the usual Unix slash (/) character is used in place of the Windows backslash character (\). The full name of the share is `//Windc1/WinShare1`.

- SMB file systems require logon credentials. Local and NFS file systems don't, so we need to pass some extra options to the `mount` command that most file systems wouldn't require. The `-o` option allows us to pass a series of additional options through mount, directly to the `mount.cifs` program that does the dirty work. We'll use this feature to pass the Windows username by providing `user=salesperson1` as the value for the `-o` option. We could also supply the password by adding a comma and `pass=p@ssw0rd` after the user information, but because it's a best practice to avoid putting passwords on the command line, we'll leave off the password and allow mount to ask us for it.

WARNING   Why do we avoid placing passwords on the command line? Because Linux is a multiuser operating system. All users have access to the process table (via the `ps -aux` command), which lists the commands that are currently running. If another user happened to spot our command while it was executing, they would learn our SMB password! Because you may use your Linux system in a multiuser fashion somewhere down the road, it's best to stick to the most secure practices.

At the terminal prompt, *as the root user*, enter the following command:

```
mount -t cifs //Windc1/WinShare1 /home/AD/salesperson1/Desktop/WinShare1/ -o
user=salesperson1
```

You will be prompted for `salesperson1`'s password. Enter **p@ssw0rd** and press Enter.

You should be returned to the prompt with no further output. If you do receive an error message, double-check that you created the directory with the `mkdir` command and that the username and share name arguments are correct. (Make sure you used the Unix slash and not the Windows backslash!)

Now that we have a mapped share, how do we take advantage of it? We already have! Just take a look at your desktop and double-click the "`WinShare1`" folder. Inside, you'll find `winfile1.txt` waiting for you. Additionally, you can also open this file from *any* Linux application that browses for files, such as OpenOffice (as we'll explore in Chapter 9). This is the key advantage of mounting shares instead of just browsing them.

Unmounting a Share

If you want to stop accessing the share, you can unmount a share using the `umount` command (yes, the command is `umount`, not `unmount`). As root, you'd enter the following command:

```
umount /home/AD/salesperson1/Desktop/WinShare1/
```

However, an annoying quirk of the GNOME desktop may prevent you from unmounting the share. Since folders within the desktop are generally kept open internally by Nautilus, you will probably receive a "Device is busy" error if you try this command, although the share will still unmount properly when you shut down the workstation. If this behavior bothers you, you might prefer to use a mount point that is not inside the Desktop folder.

Buying a Condo in Windows-Land: Mounting SMB Shares at Boot Time

You've seen how to graft an SMB/CIFS share into the Linux directory structure. What if we wanted to make a Windows SMB share visible to all users who logged on to our Linux machine every time we boot the machine? For example, perhaps we have a share containing read-only files that *all* company employees should see—employee manuals in PDF format, for instance. Wouldn't it be nice to have this material visible in a standardized place (say, /mnt/<smb_sharename>) so that all users could get to it easily?

To do this, we'll tell Linux to mount the SMB share at boot time, and voilà! All users will be able to see the share.

Linux file systems are automatically mounted when you boot your workstation via a configuration text file called /etc/fstab, which lists all of the file systems with their mount points and mount options. However, /etc/fstab isn't a great choice for SMB. That's because mounting an SMB share requires a password, and /etc/fstab is readable by *all* users on the workstation. We need to exercise some restraint in handling the password.

So how can we set up the share to be mounted automatically? Well, we already know the Bash shell commands for mounting a share. With just two additional commands, we can mount the share without ever putting the password on the command line of a program *or* typing it at a prompt. Once you know how to do that, we can turn those four commands into a Bash "shell script," a simple program much like a Windows .BAT batch file. By tying that script into the sequence of things that happen when the computer boots up, we can automatically mount our share on every boot.

The mount.cifs "back end" supports an alternative way of providing the password. By setting the PASSWD "environment variable," which is visible only to the shell script we're writing, we can provide mount.cifs with the password without using the command line or answering a prompt. Bash supports setting environment variables—just like Windows .BAT batch files do—but the syntax is a little bit different. First, we set the variable with a simple variablename=value command. Then we must "export" the variable with export variablename. This makes the variable visible in the environment for commands, like mount, that we launch from Bash. Finally, we run mount in the usual way, and no password prompt is needed.

These four commands, when given as root, will do the job:

```
PASSWD=p@ssw0rd
export PASSWD
mkdir -p /mnt/WinShare1/
mount -t cifs //Windc1/WinShare1 /mnt/WinShare1/ -o user=salesperson1
```

In our example, we mount the share with the privileges of the salesperson1 user. That's fine for a demonstration, but in a production environment you should use a Windows user created just for this purpose. That user should have no other unnecessary privileges and a password that doesn't change or expire.

After executing these commands, the contents of `WinShare1` are visible at `/mnt/WinShare1/`. You can verify this with the `ls` command, which will list the files present in `WinShare1`:

```
ls /mnt/WinShare1/
```

We have the commands we need to do the job. Now all we need to do is turn them into a Bash shell script. A shell script is nothing more than a series of shell commands, one per line—you already know how to write one! The only things you need to do differently are

1. The first line must be `#!/bin/sh`. This tells Linux what program to use to interpret the rest of the commands in the file. For Bash, we traditionally use `/bin/sh`, which is the name of the original Unix `sh` shell that Bash imitates and replaces. You can also put `#!/bin/bash` here if you prefer.

2. After you create the file, you need to make it executable with the `chmod` command. In this case, because the file contains a password, we don't want *anyone* except root to be able to read it.

We're ready to create our shell script! With your preferred text editor, create the file `/usr/local/sbin/mountwinshare` and type the following:

```
#!/bin/sh

PASSWD=p@ssw0rd
export PASSWD
mkdir -p /mnt/WinShare1/
mount -t cifs //Windc1/WinShare1 /mnt/WinShare1/ -o user=salesperson1
```

Now we'll use the `chmod` command to deny all access, except for execution by root. Of course, root can always read and write a file, but it never hurts to be thorough.

```
chmod a-rwx,o+x /usr/local/sbin/mountwinshare
```

Finally, make sure the file belongs to root using the `chown` command:

```
chown root /usr/local/sbin/mountwinshare
```

At this point, typing `/usr/local/sbin/mountwinshare` as root should mount the share at `/mnt/winshare1` without the need for any password entry on your part. However, we still haven't tied it into the startup sequence for when your Linux machine reboots.

Linux has a powerful and complex system for deciding what happens at boot time and in what order. Fortunately, we don't need to understand it thoroughly to add one little command! The file `/etc/rc.d/rc.local` is a shell script in its own right, and it is there for your benefit. Fedora runs it last, after everything else that must happen at boot time.

All we need to do is add one command to the *end* of `/etc/rc.d/rc.local`:

```
/usr/local/sbin/mountwinshare
```

That's it! Try rebooting the adlincli1 workstation. Log into the desktop as any user you wish, then feel free to use the Nautilus desktop file manager or the ls command at the command line to verify that you can see the contents of the share at /mnt/winshare1.

Mounting Shares at Logon Time, *or* Why We Don't Show Linux Home Directories Mounted on a Windows Server Using SMB

We've shown how to mount a share from the command line as needed. And we've shown how to mount a share at boot time. But you'll note that we haven't yet shown how to mount a share each time the user logs on. In particular, we haven't shown how to mount a Linux user's home directory from a Windows file server.

Alas, there are sound reasons for that. Is it possible? Barely, but we can't recommend it, at least not at this time. However, we'll point out areas where improvements are coming quickly and will likely fill this gap in the near future.

Why *can't* we mount shares automatically when users log on? After all, Windows clients can easily mount "home drives" and other mapped drives configured for that user. Well, there are two ways that can be done under the hood. Let's look at why Linux options that attempt to cover both of those methods don't quite stand up to serious use at this time. We'll also point out the most effective alternatives available at this time.

The First Method: Mount a smb/cifs Share Re-Using the Linux User's Logon Credentials
This is how Windows NT 4 does it. The user's logon information is first presented for authentication and then presented *again* to file servers to map drives. There *is* an implementation of this for Linux called pam_mount, and it works by plugging in an additional PAM module, like the pam_mkhomedir module we configured in Chapter 3. Because it is part of the Pluggable Authentication Module system, pam_mount can see the user's credentials and reuse them to mount shares. Unfortunately, in our tests, we were unable to make pam_mount a happy and stable part of the Fedora environment. While we were able to configure it to mount drives in our tests, we could not reliably convince Fedora to *unmount* drives when logging out of sessions. An unrelated problem with the current version of the cifs file system prevents the mounting of two shares from the same server as two *different* users. So a second Linux user can't log on and get to his home share on Windows, even after the first logs out. Equally bad, when logging in via the regular Fedora desktop, we were *prompted twice for the password*—exactly the thing we wanted to avoid by installing pam_mount! To try to get this to work, we went the extra mile and installed it from source code, but it still couldn't do the job. In general, the PAM subsystem needs more tender loving care from the Linux community before this method can be relied on. If you're interested in experimenting, you can find more information about pam_mount at: www.flyn.org/projects/pam_mount/

The Second Method: Kerberos Authorization   We've set up Kerberos authentication on our Linux clients, so we ought to be able to mount Windows shares without a password prompt, right? Every Windows 2000 and 2003 server uses Kerberos, right? Absolutely right! Unfortunately, the cifs file system driver has not yet been Kerberized. This is particularly unfortunate in the short term, because it would otherwise offer a very simple solution to the problem. For the long term, though, we've verified that Kerberos authentication does eliminate the need for a password in the Samba suite's smbclient tool, a simple command-line application similar to an FTP client. We saw this earlier in the "Testing Kerberos Authorization" section. This is small consolation today, as it doesn't yield a particularly practical solution. However, it does show that Samba has all of the necessary pieces of plumbing just waiting to be put together. All that is required is for Kerberos to be integrated into Samba's cifs file system driver so that mount -t cifs can work without a password. This should lead quickly to a clean and elegant solution. As of today, however, the pieces haven't been put together yet.

The Icing on the Cake: Symbolic Links Don't Work   Both the GNOME and the KDE desktop environments like to create symbolic links from the user's home directory to places outside of it. In theory, cifs can represent symbolic links even though Microsoft's file systems don't use them. In practice, support for symbolic links is very limited and they cannot "point" outside of the share, so both of the major desktop environments will refuse to run properly when the user's Linux home directory is an SMB share.

As of Today: the Best Workaround Available   We've seen that the GNOME desktop does support Samba. And the GNOME keyring system means that, in practice, users won't need to provide credentials to their Windows shares *every* time, although it is not as clean as Kerberization would be. As we've pointed out, GNOME will soon be fully Kerberized. When that happens, "single sign-on" to Windows shares will be a reality, at least for GNOME-enabled applications. This is expected to happen soon.

But stay tuned. We *can* make a unified home drive (for Linux, home directory) for both Linux and Windows clients, it's simply going to take a little elbow grease with NFS. That's coming up a little later in the "Leveraging NFS on Your Servers" section.

Samba as a PDC: File Sharing, Roaming Profiles

In Chapter 2, we learned how to create a Linux-based PDC. When we did this, it created our own NT 4–style domain named CORP. Our Linux Samba PDC, linserv1, provides authentication services to unmodified Windows clients. linserv1 also authenticates Linux clients via LDAP.

In this section, you'll see how the same Linux server can also offer file shares, including "home drives" and roaming profiles, to Windows users. We'll set this up using Samba's SMB file sharing support. Later in this chapter, we'll show you how to provide equivalent file access to Linux users via NFS. In this scenario, Windows servers are out of the picture for both file sharing and authentication.

Figure 4.8 shows how we'll use Samba to share files and home directories to both our user accounts which reside on the Samba PDC. These users can log on to either a Windows or Linux client and get to the same files.

Sharing Folders with Samba

Since Samba's smbd server process is already up and running and providing authentication services on linserv1 for the CORP domain, adding SMB shares is a snap. All it takes is a few clicks in our favorite administration tool, Webmin. But first, we'll need to create something to share.

Our Linux server, linserv1, has two groups of users in its LDAP database: doctors and nurses. If you chose not to complete the LDAP exercises in Chapter 2, be sure to create the local users and groups shown in the following table:

User	Primary Group
doctor1	doctors
doctor2	doctors
nurse1	nurses
nurse2	nurses

See "Using Webmin to Manage OpenLDAP Server Graphically" in Chapter 2 to ensure you created the appropriate user and group accounts.

FIGURE 4.8   Linux and Windows client computers can authenticate to Samba as a PDC and share files.

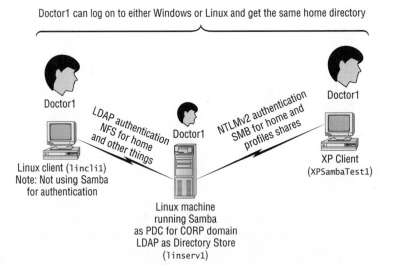

Let's assume we have a need to make certain files available to everyone who relates to these two groups. We want nurses to see nursing files. We want doctors to see doctoring files.

We'll create directories for each of these groups with the following simple commands, all but two of which you've seen before. Be sure to execute these as root:

```
mkdir /doctorfiles
echo "It worked" > /doctorfiles/test.txt
chgrp -R doctors /doctorfiles
chmod a+r,g+rw /doctorfiles

mkdir /nursefiles
echo "It worked" > /nursefiles/test.txt
chgrp -R nurses /nursefiles
chmod a+r,g+rw /nursefiles
```

We now have directories called `/doctorfiles` and `/nursefiles` that are writable by all doctors and all nurses, respectively, and readable by everyone. Now we'll demonstrate how to share them using Samba. To access the "Create File Share" page, follow these steps:

1. Log into Webmin as usual.

2. Click the "Servers" button.

3. On the "Servers" page, click the "Samba Windows File Sharing" button.

4. On the "Samba Windows File Sharing" page, click "Create a New File Share."

5. The "Create File Share" page appears, as shown in Figure 4.9.

The Create File Share page prompts us for information about the new share. Let's create our share for `doctorfiles`. The entries we place here are seen in Figure 4.9.

Share name   This is the label that users see when browsing. Enter **doctorfiles**   here.

FIGURE 4.9   You can use Webmin to create a Samba share.

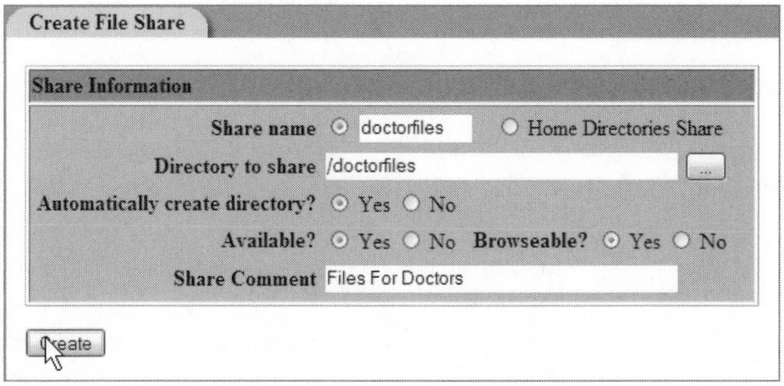

Directory to share   This is the directory we are going to share. In our case, we're sharing right off the root (/). Enter **/doctorfiles**   here.

Automatically create directory?   If the directory doesn't exist, Webmin can automatically create it for us. Since we've already created it manually, selecting "Yes" here has no effect.

Available?   This is useful if we wish to create a share without enabling it right away. Select "Yes" here to make the share immediately available.

Browseable?   This determines whether users can see the share when browsing the available shares on the server. Not advertising a share doesn't provide real security, but it can help to keep clueless users from trying to access unauthorized files. We will advertise this share. Select "Yes" here.

Share Comment   This is a comment that's displayed when the share is browsed. Enter **Files for Doctors**   here, and then click "Create."

The main "Samba Windows File Sharing" page now reappears, featuring our new share in the list of existing shares. To create our second share, click "Create a new file share" again and repeat the preceding steps, substituting **nurse** for doctor in every case.

That's it! Nothing left to do but try it out. Return to the Windows XP client that you joined to the Samba-based CORP domain in Chapter 2 (in our examples and our diagram in 4.8, we're calling it XPSambaTest1).

Log in as doctor1. The account will be validated by the Samba server. Then follow the steps covered earlier in this chapter in the "Having Windows Clients Utilize Windows File Shares" section, browsing the CORP domain instead of the AD domain. You'll be able to access the doctorfiles share and read and write the file test.txt in the doctorfiles share. If you log in as nurse1, you'll find that you can read the file but can't write to it. That's because we created the file to be readable by everyone but writable only by members of the doctors group.

Sharing Home Drives and Roaming Profiles with Samba

Now that you understand the basics of creating SMB shares with Samba, it's time to move on to more exciting stuff! Windows NT file sharing offers the potential for users to have roaming profiles and network home drives.

Roaming profiles   Allow users to hop from Windows machine to Windows machine and see their desktop and such on each machine.

Home drives   Allow users to plunk down files that belong only to them and put them on a network share.

I cover roaming profiles and best practices therein in my book *Group Policy, Profiles and IntelliMirror for Windows 2003, Windows XP, and Windows 2000* (Sybex, 2004). Come to www.GPanswers.com for help on this subject in a pure Windows environment.

We'll set these up now. Ideally, you'll want to isolate your users' home drives and profile shares such that a user cannot poke around inside their profile. The goal is to hide the profile out of plain sight where confused users won't stomp on the files inside. We'll take care of that chore in the next section.

Home Drives with Samba

Samba offers a convenient way to set up home drive shares on a per-user basis. Normally, when we create a share with a particular name, such as `salesstuff`, Samba expects us to also specify the name of the directory to be shared. However, when a share specifically named `homes` is present in the `/etc/samba/smb.conf` file, special behavior is activated in Samba. When a user named `doctor1` attempts to mount a share called `doctor1`, Samba automatically connects that share to the Linux home directory of `doctor1`. On `linserv1`, that directory is `/home/doctor1`. Presto, instant home drive! As you'll see later in this chapter, when `doctor1` logs in from a Linux client, she'll see exactly the same files via NFS. Cross-platform nirvana!

So how do we set it up? Well, remember that "Home Directories Share" radio box we didn't use in Figure 4.9? It's time to go back and take advantage of it:

1. Log into Webmin.

2. Access the "Create File Share" page as described earlier.

3. Select the "Home Directories Share" radio box.

4. Leave the "Share name" and "Directory to share" fields *empty*.

5. Leave "Automatically create directory" set to "Yes."

6. Make sure "Available?" is set to "Yes."

7. Make sure "Browseable?" is set to "Yes."

8. Enter **Home Directory** in the "Share Comment" field.

9. Click "Create."

FIGURE 4.10   Creating home directory shares with Webmin

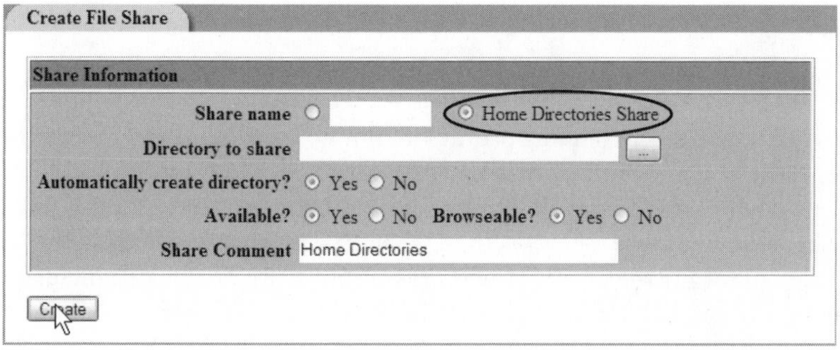

Roaming Profiles with Samba

At this point, we *could* log right into our XP workstation as, say, `doctor1` and take advantage of our home drive, which Samba automatically mounts as drive Z by default. Typically, however, administrators assign alternate drive letters, such as H in lieu of Z.

If this interests you, you can change the drive letter by setting the `logon drive` option in `/etc/samba/smb.conf` to a specific drive letter, like this:

```
logon drive = H:
```

However, we're going to wait on that a bit. If we log in now, our roaming profile will be created as a subdirectory of our home drive, called `profile`, which puts it right where the average user can see it. Unfortunately, when some users see a folder they don't recognize, their first impulse is to delete it! A better solution is to place the profile in a *separate* share, which is *not* mounted with a drive letter, where the user won't casually stumble across it.

Creating the Roaming Profiles Share

How do we pull off this stunt? By adding a profile share. All we need to do is follow the usual steps, except that we won't make this share browseable. This makes it highly unlikely that any user will stumble across their own profile and delete it. Of course, we use Linux file permissions to prevent them from tampering with anyone *else's* profile at all.

To make the share, just do the following:

1. Log into Webmin.

2. Access the "Create File Share" page, as described earlier.

3. Enter **profile**   in the "Share name" field and make sure the radio box to the left of it is selected.

4. Enter **/profiles**   in the "Directory to share" field.

5. Leave "Automatically create directory?" set to "Yes."

6. Make sure "Available?" is set to "Yes."

7. This time, make sure "Browseable?" is set to "No."

8. Enter **Profiles**   in the "Share Comment" field.

9. Click "Create."

Telling Clients to Use the Profiles Share

Now we have a share to store roaming profiles in. But how do Windows clients know to store their profiles there and not on the home drive? When a user logs into a Windows PDC, the PDC tells the client where the profile can be found. The great news is that Samba fully supports this. The mildly annoying news is that Webmin doesn't provide us with a convenient place to set the "hint" for the client. However, we can easily do it by changing one line of `/etc/samba/smb.conf` by hand.

The Samba configuration file offers an option called `logon path`. This option is used to tell every Windows client that logs on to the PDC where their roaming profile can be found. There's just one problem: a separate roaming profile directory is needed for every user. Fortunately,

Samba allows us to use the special variable %U to represent *the name of the user who is logging on*. This means that we can specify \\linserv1\profile\%U as the logon path, automatically storing profiles in the correct place for *each* user.

Edit /etc/samba/smb.conf with your preferred text editor and add the following line. Please note that if an existing setting for the logon path option exists, you should change the logon path setting to this one:

```
logon path = \\linserv1\profile\%U
```

To activate this change, we'll need to restart the Samba smbd process as root with the service command:

```
service smb restart
```

Are we ready to go? Not quite yet! One hurdle remains. Don't worry, we'll clear it, with room to spare.

Creating User Subdirectories in the Profiles Share

At this point, we have a profiles share on our Samba server and users logging in to the Samba-based CORP domain can find it, but there is one little problem. We need a subdirectory in that share for each and every user. We also need those subdirectories to have the right permissions so that only the correct user can modify them.

Wouldn't it be nice if account administration tools on Linux made the profiles directory for us? Alas, they don't. That's because Linux doesn't have separate concepts of home drives and user profiles.

Why *doesn't* Linux have separately stored user profile directories? Because instead, Linux has "dotfiles." Filenames that begin with a period, such as .bashrc, are not listed by the ls command unless a special -a option is used to show *all* files. GUI-based file browsers for Linux also tend to respect this convention. Such files are typically used to hold user configuration information, analogous to a Windows user profile, in such a way that clueless users are not tempted to delete it.

To do the job right, all we need is a simple tool that regularly checks for users who don't have a subdirectory in /profiles. Then that tool just creates the missing subdirectory. We've written exactly that tool for you as a simple script in the Perl programming language. This isn't a programming book, so if you're not a programmer don't fret. We're not going to expect you to know anything about it; we're just giving you this script for your use.

We won't go line by line through makeprofiles.pl. As we mentioned in Chapter 2, teaching Perl is well beyond the scope of this book. Consider makeprofiles.pl a "ready-to-run" application like any other we use in this book. Because it's quite short, however, we'll present the full listing at the end of this section in Listing 4.1. You can also pick up a fully commented copy from our website at www.winlinanswers.com. Just look for the makeprofiles.pl script.

> **Why Perl**
>
> Perl has come up earlier in the book, but we haven't had an opportunity to tell you why it comes in handy for jobs like this and why, as a Linux system administrator, you might want to pick up a good book on Perl and master the basics.
>
> The executive summary is this: Perl has all of the good features of the Bash shell and most other Unix command-line tools, easily accessible as part of a single programming language. Some people consider Perl unfriendly because it is *possible* to write ugly, unmaintainable Perl code—but that's true in most languages. It is also very possible to write simple, elegant Perl scripts that do exactly what we want, in a hurry. Our makeprofiles.pl script is a good example of that. (But not a modest one, apparently.)

Once you have downloaded or typed the script, mark it as executable by the owner (root), so that Linux knows it is a program to be run:

```
chmod o+x /usr/local/sbin/makeprofiles.pl
```

Now we'll need to create profiles for the first time. Just execute this command to create our profile subdirectories:

```
/usr/local/sbin/makeprofiles.pl
```

If all goes well, you will see no output. No output is good, since when we have this job running automatically, any output that would normally go to the screen will be emailed to us automatically. No errors = no emails, and that's a good thing. If you receive error messages, verify that you typed or downloaded the script correctly, then try again.

Once you have run the script successfully, you can use the ls -l command to verify that profile subdirectories for individual users were created:

```
ls -l /profiles
```

The output should include the following, among other lines for users we're not concerned with:

```
drwx------   2 doctor1   doctors  4096 Feb 16 00:58 doctor1
drwx------   2 doctor2   doctors  4096 Feb 16 12:52 doctor2
drwx------   2 nurse1    nurses   4096 Feb 16 12:53 nurse1
drwx------   2 nurse2    nurses   4096 Feb 16 12:54 nurse2
```

We don't need to discuss every aspect of ls -l output here, but note the third and fourth columns. These are the names of the user and group that own each directory. Note that makeprofiles.pl correctly created the directories as the property of the appropriate users and their default groups. Also, take a look at the first column:

```
drwx------
```

Here's how this breaks down:

- The first character, d, means we're looking at a directory rather than a file.
- The next three characters represent the read, write, and execute permissions for the *owner* of the directory—rwx means that the owner has full control over the directory.
- The next three characters represent the permissions for the *group* that owns the directory. Dashes mean the group has no rights here, which is correct: no one but doctor1 should be able to alter her profile.
- The last three characters represent permissions for all other users, who of course should have no rights here either.

We now have profile directories that are ready to use. But what happens when we create new users in the future? How will they get profile subdirectories? Easy! We'll just schedule a cron job to run once an hour, creating folders for users who don't already have them. For complete information about how to do this, see the "Scheduling Tasks with cron" sidebar next. Here's the crontab entry you'll need:

```
0 * * * * perl /usr/local/sbin/makeprofiles.pl
```

 If your system has thousands of users, running this script every hour may be impractical. You may find the performance impact more acceptable if you run it once a day. Just replace the "*" in the second position with a 0, and the script will run at zero hours and zero minutes (midnight) every day. If you have *very* large numbers of users, you'll want to consider modifying the "LDAP Users and Groups" Webmin module to make profile directories *as users are added*. This avoids the need to scan the entire user database for users who still need a profile directory. Easier said than done, but if you're a programmer, the world is your oyster.

Scheduling Tasks with *cron*

The cron service allows each user to specify jobs to be run at various times of day, days of the week, and so on. You can set this up by first fetching a listing of any existing cron jobs for the user root:

```
crontab -l > /tmp/jobs.root
```

The crontab -l command outputs a list of the scheduled jobs for the current user, and the > character indicates that the output should be written to the filename that follows rather than to the terminal window. /tmp, the temporary folder, is a good place for files we won't be needing permanently, particularly if they do not contain secure information. When running commands as root it is always a good idea to be careful not to overwrite existing files in whatever the current working directory may be.

Next, edit the file /tmp/jobs.root with your favorite text editor and add the following line at the end:

```
0 * * * * perl /usr/local/sbin/makeprofiles.pl
```

The last part is the command we want to execute every hour. But what about the zero and the asterisks? Those * characters occupy each of the following places: minutes, hours, days of the month, months of the year, and days of the week. Leaving an * rather than specifying a number indicates that the job should be run every time. For instance, 30 2 * 2 * executes a job at 2:30 in the morning every Tuesday. With five * characters, a job is run once per minute, all day, every day. In this case, we've configured cron to run our command at the top of the hour (zero minutes after the hour), every hour of every day.

Finally, submit the file as the new crontab file for the user root using the following command:

```
crontab /tmp/jobs.root
```

Logging onto Our New Home Drive and Roaming Profile

That's it! Just sit down at the XP workstation you joined to the corp domain (in our examples XPSambaTest1) and log on as doctor1. You'll discover an H: drive, which is your new home drive and contains the same files regardless of which workstation you log into. You'll also discover that your profile (containing desktop settings and other personal registry items) follows you from workstation to workstation.

Listing 4.11: *makeprofiles.pl*: a Perl Script to Create */profiles* Subdirectories for Users as Needed

```perl
#!/usr/bin/perl -w

my $line;

mkdir("/profiles/", 0755);

open(USERS, "/usr/bin/getent passwd|");
while ($line = <USERS>) {
        my ($name, $password, $uid, $gid) = split(/\:/, $line);
        if ($name !~ /^[\w\ \-\+]+$/) {
                next;
        }
        if (-e "/profiles/$name") {
                next;
        }
```

```
    if (($uid =~ /^\d+$/) && ($gid =~ /^\d+$/))
    {
            mkdir("/profiles/$name", 0700);
            chown($uid, $gid, "/profiles/$name");
    }
}
close(USERS);
```

Nitrobit: Group Policy for Samba Where There Is No Active Directory

One way of using the material in this section would be to walk away from Active Directory and have nothing but NT 4 functionality on a Linux Samba Server. Again, a Samba 3 server can only act like an NT 4 PDC, not an Active Directory server.

Because of this, the crown jewel of Active Directory (in my opinion) is lost if you walk away from Active Directory and "downgrade" to a pure Samba domain acting as an NT 4 domain. That crown jewel is Group Policy.

You might be familiar with my Sybex book *Group Policy, Profiles and IntelliMirror for Windows 2003, Windows XP, and Windows 2000* (2004), which covers the ins and outs of Group Policy, troubleshooting, and more. You can check it out at www.GPanswers.com (hope you don't mind the little commercial). That aside, Group Policy is a super-powerful tool to help you centrally control many aspects of your Windows client and server environment, including desktop settings, software deployment, security, and a lot more.

However, one adventurous company, Nitrobit is making an interesting promise: Group Policy for Samba where there is no Active Directory. The idea is that you set up your Samba server with an OpenLDAP back end (just as we did in the last chapter) and Group Policy Objects are stored inside OpenLDAP and downloaded by Windows 2000, Windows 2003, and Windows XP clients.

Of course, adding Nitrobit doesn't get you a lot of the other major Active Directory features such as pure Kerberos authentication, delegation of control, a full PKI, Remote Installation Services, a full LDAP directory that is extensible, and more and more and more.

Again, if you're sticking with Active Directory as your main source for authentication, this product won't do you much good. However, if you're planning on ditching Active Directory in lieu of Samba and OpenLDAP, and want to keep delivering Group Policy to your clients, then check out www.nitrobit.com.

Integrating Linux Samba File Servers into Windows Active Directory

Linux is free. And its being free is a great reason to build a free server that lets us share files out and serve an existing Windows environment. Additionally, we can then.configure it so both Linux and Windows clients can easily get to the files on those servers.

But just plunking in a Linux server as a stand-alone file server isn't ideal. Better than that is to have it act like any ol' Windows member server. That way, once users authenticate to Active Directory, they can seamlessly access files on this new Linux server.

In this section, we'll explore the multiple steps it takes get a Linux Samba server to be as integrated as possible into an existing Active Directory. At the end of this section, this server will be a full-fledged member server with integrated authentication to Active Directory, as shown in Figure 4.11.

FIGURE 4.11 You can validate to Active Directory as any user and gain access to SMB shares hosted on Windows or Linux servers.

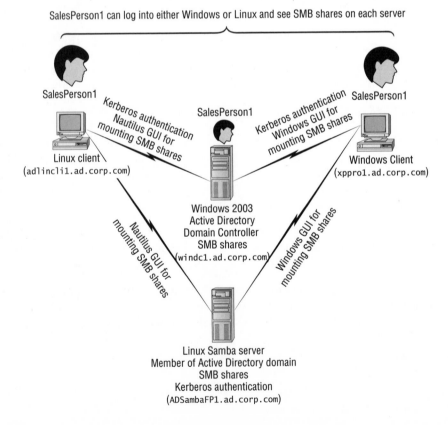

To pull it off, we'll need to do the following:

- Create a new Fedora Core 3 Linux server called `adsambafp1` because using our existing crop of servers can get messy. We'll also use this server in the next chapter to help out with printing.

- Add a DNS record on the Windows server so that the hostname `adsambafp1.ad.corp` `.com` can be resolved to an IP address.

- Configure Samba to recognize domain logons by verifying Kerberos tickets from Kerberized clients (and NT 4–style credentials from other clients). That is, when either a Windows or Linux client presents a Kerberos ticket (or authorized credentials that are valid for the domain), we want to make sure Samba accepts them. We can do this with Webmin.

- Configure Samba to offer a share. We can do this with Webmin also.

- Configure Fedora Linux to accept logons by Active Directory domain users. Before we can allow ownership of files by domain users, we'll need to make sure the operating system "sees" those users. We'll do this by turning on Winbind authentication via the Fedora Authentication tool.

- Start `smbd` and `winbindd` (the two Linux daemons that need to be running to perform the magic) and configure Fedora Linux to restart them on every reboot.

- Join the server to our Active Directory domain and start offering up the `research` share to interested parties.

    Ready? Let's get started! We'll take on one major step at a time.

Installing Linux on *adsambafp1*

We've previously installed Linux on the `linserv1` server. For `adsambafp1`, we'll install exactly the same Fedora packages. Refer to Chapter 1 for the installation procedure. Here, we'll specify only the differences from the installation procedure for `linserv1`, as follows:

- In the "Edit Interface eth0" dialog box of the "Network Configuration" screen, give our new server its own distinct IP address: **192.168.2.211** .

- In the "Hostname" section of the "Network Configuration" screen, set the hostname to **adsambafp1.ad.corp.com**   .

- In the "Miscellaneous Settings" section of the "Network Configuration" screen, set the primary DNS server to **192.168.2.226**   (which is our Active Directory Domain Controller `Windc1.ad.corp.com`).

    Oh, and don't forget to install Webmin on `adsambafp1`. We'll need it to configure Samba for file sharing in this chapter and for printing in the next chapter. The steps for installing Webmin can be found in Chapter 1, in the "Leveraging Webmin" section.

Adding a DNS Record for *adsambafp1*

On `windc1.ad.corp.com`, add a DNS "A" record resolving `adsambafp1` to `192.168.2.211`. To do so, simply fire up the DNS manager in Windows. It's located in Start ≻ Programs ≻ Administrative Tools ≻ DNS. In the zone for the `AD.corp.com` domain, right-click and select New ≻ A Record.

When finished, you should be able to ping `adsambafp1.ad.corp.com` from `WinDC1.ad.corp.com`.

Configuring Samba as a Domain Member

Now we're ready to start configuring Samba as an Active Directory domain member. Follow these steps to get started:

1. Log into Webmin as usual, except of course that you will use the following URL for the new server:

   `https://adsambafp1.ad.corp.com:10000/`

2. Click the "Servers" button.
3. Click the "Samba Windows File Sharing" button on the "Servers" page.
4. On the "Samba Windows File Sharing" page, click "Windows Networking."

Configuring Samba's Windows Networking Options with Webmin

At this point, the "Windows Networking Options" page will appear. We'll be configuring it to match Figure 4.12. Let's discuss each option and the reasons for our choices:

FIGURE 4.12   Configuring Samba's Windows networking options with Webmin

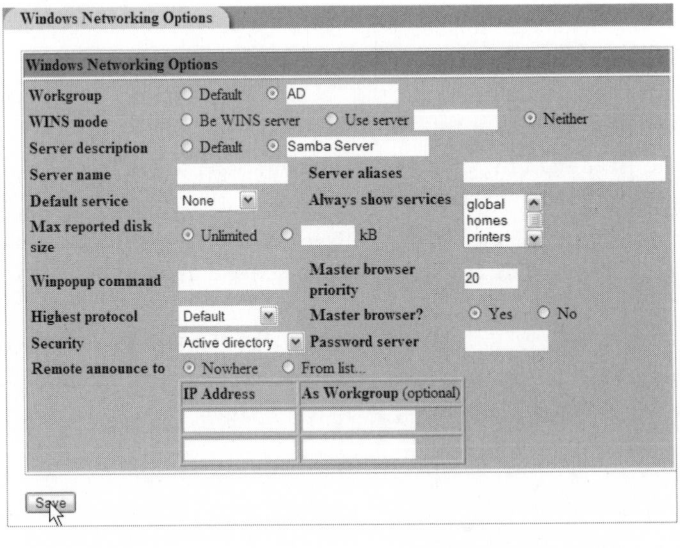

Workgroup   Samba uses the terms "workgroup" and "domain" interchangeably; if the machine is joined to or serving a domain, then this option refers to the domain. We set this option to **AD**, the "short name" of our Active Directory domain.

Server name   This field can be left blank because Samba will correctly use the hostname, `adsambafp1`.

Security   We set this field to **Active directory**   to ensure that all logons are verified by the Active Directory server. (When clients use Kerberos, the server can verify that a Kerberos ticket is valid without actually talking to the Active Directory server again every time.)

The remaining options can be left at their default settings as their use is rarely necessary and beyond the scope of this book.

Once you have completed your settings, click the "Save" button to continue.

Configuring Samba's Winbind Options with Webmin

Winbind is the Samba component that verifies login credentials against an Active Directory Domain Controller or NT PDC. You met Winbind previously in Chapter 2. There we used it to verify Linux client logons against an Active Directory Domain Controller. Here, our goal is just a little bit different: to verify "logons" to our Samba file server against an Active Directory Domain Controller. (By logons, we really mean "touches" to our Samba file server from Active Directory users.)

By accepting Active Directory domain logons, we can separate the task of authentication from the task of file sharing. That enables us to keep the benefits of running an Active Directory server on Windows while still reducing costs by running individual file servers on Samba.

To configure Samba's Winbind options, click the "Winbind Options" button. The Winbind Options page will appear. The correct choices are shown in Figure 4.13. Let's take a look at the individual options and our reasons for choosing them:

FIGURE 4.13   You'll want to configure your Samba file server's Winbind options as shown here.

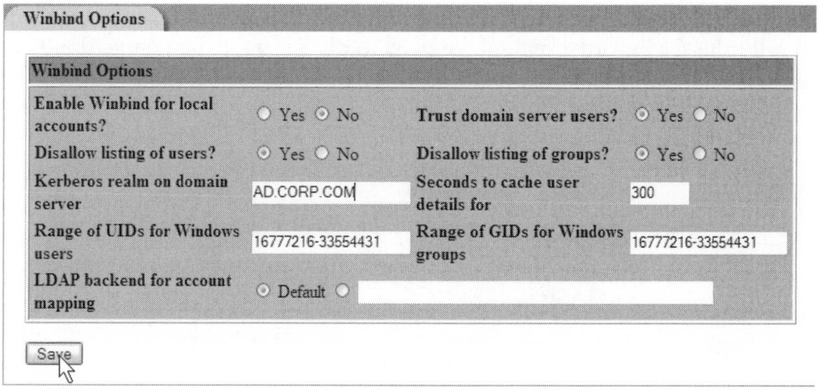

Enable Winbind for local accounts? This option would allow clients to log on using local Unix account names on the server. Our goal is to allow only domain logons, so we set this option to "No."

Trust domain server users? This allows our server to accept domain logons, which is exactly what we set out to do! We set this option to "Yes."

Disallow listing of users? Allowing clients to list the names of other users reduces security and is not our job as a domain member file server. We should leave such functions to the Active Directory Domain Controller. Set this option to "Yes."

Disallow listing of groups? Again, allowing clients to list the names of user groups reduces security and is not our purpose as a domain member file server. Set this option to "Yes."

Kerberos realm on domain server As you saw earlier in this chapter, every Active Directory domain is also a Kerberos realm by the same name, in ALL CAPS, so the correct setting is **AD.CORP.COM**

Range of UIDs for Windows users As explained in Chapter 3, Samba must "invent" Unix user IDs for each Windows user. The ranges specified here allow for millions of users and are well outside any popular range of IDs for local Unix users.

Range of GIDs for Windows groups As explained in Chapter 3, Samba must also "invent" Unix group IDs for each Windows group. Again, the ranges specified here allow for millions of groups and are well outside any popular range of IDs for local Unix groups.

The remaining options come into play only for stand-alone servers that offer logons other than those offered by the Active Directory Domain Controller. They can be left at their default settings.

Once you have completed your settings, click the "Save" button to continue.

Turning on Winbind Authentication

Samba has now been taught to "understand" Active Directory domain users and groups, but the rest of the operating system doesn't. In other words, we can't leverage Linux tools to manage our Active Directory users. For example, that means we can't yet use the chown command to "give" files to domain users.

We can fix this easily, however. All we need to do is use the Authentication Configuration tool to enable Winbind authentication. We've seen this tool several times before. To set up your Samba file server to adhere to Winbind authentication:

1. From the "Applications" menu, select System Settings ➢ Authentication tool and wait for it to appear.

2. In the "User Information" tab, check "Enable Winbind Support."

3. Click the "Authentication" tab.

4. Verify that "Enable Winbind Support" is checked here also.

5. Click "OK."

Your system is now ready to recognize Windows users and groups and map them to user and group ID numbers.

Launching *smbd* and *winbindd*

The underlying work that we've set in play is really performed by two running Linux daemons: smbd and winbindd. These running programs implement the two major parts of a Samba server: the actual file sharing and Windows-compatible user and group management.

 The extra "d" on the end stands for "demon" or "daemon," a traditional name for Unix programs that continue to operate in the background. You've already seen an example of this in the name daemon—named.

We've configured the settings these programs rely on. Now we're ready to start them up with the service command and install them for automatic launch on the next boot with the chkconfig --add command. We've seen these commands before:

```
service winbind start
service  smb start
chkconfig --add winbind
chkconfig --add smb
```

Our Samba server processes are up and running. Now we're ready to join the Active Directory domain.

Joining the Active Directory Domain

Our next task is to join our server to the Active Directory domain. Webmin provides a button for this, but in our analysis, under the hood it seems to be using Samba commands more appropriate for an NT 4–style domain. We recommend that you instead join the domain at the command line with the net ads join command, which you saw previously in Chapter 3 when we joined Linux workstations to an Active Directory domain. Use this command to join the domain:

```
net ads join -U administrator
```

When prompted for the password, enter **p@ssw0rd**

Your server is now a member of an Active Directory domain. You can verify this in two ways:

The *wbinfo* command   Use the wbinfo command. wbinfo is a handy utility that fetches information from Winbind. In this case, we'll use the -t option, which verifies that our server and the Active Directory Domain Controller share a "trust secret" that proves we are a member of the domain. Try this command:

```
wbinfo -t
```

You will receive the following output:

```
checking the trust secret via RPC calls succeeded
```

Now, let's verify that we can see the list of valid users for the domain. We can do that using the -u option of the wbinfo utility. Use the following command:

```
wbinfo -u
```

The output you receive will include these two familiar users:

```
AD\salesperson1
AD\salesperson2
```

Active Directory Users and Computers   On your Domain Controller, fire up Active Directory Users and Computers and dive into the Computers folder. You should see the name of the computer you just joined to the domain. In our case, it's adsambafp1.

Best of all, you should now be able to see your server when browsing the domain from the desktop of any domain member workstation or the Domain Controller itself using Network Neighborhood (on Windows) or Network Servers (on Linux).

Creating and Using Shares with Windows ACL Support

We're almost ready to serve up shares on our Active Directory domain member server. In fact, our server *is* ready to provide shares now, and serve files, as long as we don't mind some limitations on the permissions we can set on those files. At this point, we can offer the typical Unix model: separate read, write, and execute permissions for the owner of the file, users in the group that owns the file, and everyone else.

However, as Windows administrators know, Windows offers a much richer set of permissions for files and directories. Thanks to Windows ACLs (Access Control Lists), it is possible to set specific permissions on a single file or directory for any number of users and groups. For instance, we can decree that users in AD\SalesGroup should have read, write, and execute access, and allow users in AD\MarketingGroup to read and execute only, while still locking out everyone else.

Are we prevented from doing this with Samba? Not at all! What many Windows and Linux administrators don't know is that modern versions of Linux, including Fedora Core 3, also support ACLs, and Samba has the smarts to translate between Windows ACLs and the POSIX (Portable Operating System Interface) ACLs supported by Fedora, on the fly.

NOTE   POSIX is a standard that allows applications to run the same across all platforms. For instance, you can have a POSIX-compliant application on Linux and bring it over to Windows (once SFU 3.5 is installed). Applications need to be recompiled for the new host operating system, but they'll run just the same if they stick to features covered by the POSIX specification. Included in the POSIX specification is how to handle lots of things like ACLs.

Translating Windows ACLs to POSIX ACLs is great, but there's a small catch. Windows ACLs are more general in their capabilities. For instance, in Windows, a file can be *writable* but not *deletable* by a given user. When Samba encounters an ACL that ACLs on the Linux side can't fully express, Samba copes by translating the portions that do make sense in both systems. For the most part, this works beautifully. Just bear in mind that your ACLs may look slightly different if you examine them again after having set them from Windows. The actual meaning should be the same, though, as long as what you are trying to do can be expressed fully as a combination of "read," "write," and "execute" permissions.

 There are additional options to fine-tune the behavior of Windows ACLs in Samba, including the ways in which Windows ACLs are mapped to POSIX ACLs. You can find more information about these via the man smb.conf command.

Enabling ACLs in the Linux EXT3 File System

Before we can take advantage of POSIX ACLs, we'll need to enable them on our file system. The EXT3 ("third extended") file system used by default in Fedora Linux *does* support ACLs, and so does the operating system kernel that ships with Fedora. However, as of this writing, Fedora Core 3 does not turn on ACL support on the root file system by default at boot time. And, because ACL support is relatively new in Fedora, it is not currently something we can turn on through the "System Settings" submenu. Instead, we'll need to add a flag to the configuration file that controls file systems in Linux, /etc/fstab, and reboot the system.

/etc/fstab is a simple text file containing one line for each file system mounted by Linux. Each line consists of five space-separated fields. Although you don't need to understand all of the fields in detail, briefly, the fields of an /etc/fstab entry are as follows:

1. The device to be mounted.
2. The existing, usually empty directory where it should be attached to the file system.
3. The type of file system, such as nfs or ext3.
4. Optionally, a comma-separated list of flags to be passed to the file system, such as rw for read/write access and acl to enable ACLs.
5. Optionally, a 1 to indicate that the file system should be included in backups or a 0 to indicate it should not be.
6. Optionally, a 1 to indicate the file system should be checked for errors when deemed appropriate, or a 0 to indicate it should not be.

In this case, we're concerned with the following entry:

```
/dev/VolGroup00/LogVol00 / ext3 rw 1 1
```

As mentioned, the rw flag in the fourth field means that the file system should be mounted with full read and write access. We need to add an additional flag, acl, to indicate that we want ACL support on this file system. The corrected line is

```
/dev/VolGroup00/LogVol00 / ext3 rw,acl 1 1
```

After we complete this change and save the file, it is necessary to reboot the system. This is because we want to change the way the root file system is mounted, and the root file system is where the Bash shell and desktop GUI tools we're using are located. Making this change without a reboot is relatively complex, while rebooting is a simple solution.

Here are the steps to enable ACLs on Fedora's root file system:

1. As root, edit the file `/etc/fstab` on `adsambafp1`.

2. Locate this line. You may see `rw` in place of `defaults`:

   `/dev/VolGroup00/LogVol00 / ext3 defaults 1 1`

3. Change it to read as follows:

   `/dev/VolGroup00/LogVol00 / ext3 rw,acl 1 1`

4. Save your changes and exit the editor.

5. Reboot `adsambafp1`.

Creating the Research Share with Webmin

Reboot complete? Great! Now we're ready to make a share available. This part is straightforward and Webmin does all the heavy lifting. To create a share called `research` in which to keep files for sales and marketing people, we use the "Create a new file share" link on the "Samba Windows File Sharing" page of Webmin. Then we fill out the "Create File Share" page as shown in Figure 4.14. For a more detailed discussion, refer to "Sharing Folders with Samba," earlier in this chapter.

FIGURE 4.14   Creating the research share with Webmin

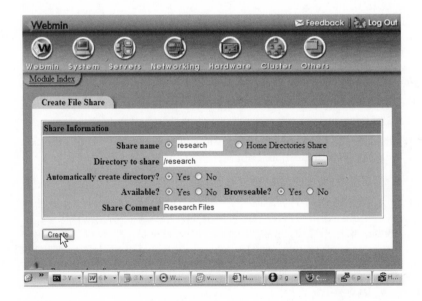

Now that we have created the share, we must be sure to make it writable. By default, as we've mentioned, a Samba share is read-only. Clicking "Create" returned us to the "Samba Windows File Sharing" page. Click "research" in the "Share Name" column. This will bring you to the "Edit File Share page." Click "Security and Access Control." The "Edit Security" page appears. *Make sure you set "Writable?" to "Yes."* Scroll to the end of the page and click "Save." The "Edit File Share" page reappears. Click "Save" again to return to the "Samba Windows File Sharing" page. The research share is ready for use.

Enabling ACL Inheritance in Samba

There's one more adjustment to be made to the Samba configuration. This one involves an option that Webmin doesn't know about as of this writing, so we'll need to add a line to `/etc/samba/smb.conf` and tell Samba to reload its configuration file.

The option we want to enable controls the way ACLs are "inherited" from the parent folder when a new folder is created within it. This matters because our goal is to create a share where *all* files are under the full control of salespeople, readable by marketing, and inaccessible to anyone else—but if we don't turn on inheritance, these properties won't be "passed down" from the `/research` folder to newly created folders within it.

To turn on inheritance of ACLs and restart Samba, follow these steps:

1. Add the following line to `/etc/samba/smb.conf`, in the [global] section, before the sections for individual shares such as [home]:

    ```
    map inherit acls = yes
    ```

2. Make sure Samba reloads its configuration file with this command:

    ```
    service smb reload
    ```

Setting Initial Permissions and Ownership of the Research Share

To make things interesting, we'll decree that members of the Active Directory group `AD\SalesGroup` can read and write to the share, members of `AD\MarketingGroup` can only read it, and everyone else except the administrator will have *no* access. This wouldn't be possible with old-fashioned Unix permissions. Fortunately, we can now use ACLs, and we can use our Windows client to set them with beautiful friendly dialog boxes instead of the Linux command line.

Before we do that, though, we need to solve a "chicken-and-egg" problem. Linux doesn't allow any user to set or change ACLs on a directory except for (a) the root user or (b) the owner of the file. But our Windows domain users are not root, and when first created by Webmin, the `/research` directory belongs to root. So at the Linux command line, we'll give ownership of that directory to a domain user who belongs to `AD\SalesGroup`. Then we'll log into our Windows client as that user to do the *really* interesting ACL stuff.

We can use the `chown` command to grant ownership of files to domain users just as we would with regular Unix users. There is one catch: we need to "escape" the backslash (\) character that separates the domain from the username with an extra backslash (\), which is why you'll notice a double slash on the `chown` command line. This is intentional.

We'll also save some time and effort by setting the initial permissions on /research so that only the owner, AD\salesperson1, has any access to the file to begin with. That way, when we do start setting ACLs, the effect will be more obvious.

To give the /research directory to AD\salesperson1 and set the initial permissions, follow these steps:

1. Open a terminal window and become root with the su command if you did not log in as root.

2. Use this command to set ownership:

   chown AD\\salesperson1 /research

3. Use this command to set permissions:

   chmod a-rwx,u+rwx /research

Now we're ready to log into our Windows client and set up the rest of the permissions we want in a user-friendly and elegant way. We *could* set up the permissions we want entirely on the Linux server side using the setfacl command, but we'll be using a Windows client instead. After all, our goal is to demonstrate that Windows machines can set ACLs and the Samba server will respect them. However, see the sidebar "Setting ACLs from the Linux Command Line" for more information about how the setfacl command could be used to accomplish the same thing.

Setting ACLs from the Linux Command Line

setfacl is the Linux command to set ACLs on a file or directory. When started with the -m option, it "modifies" the ACL set for a particular user or group.

The next option to setfacl is broken into three parts, separated by colons (:).

The first part is a single letter, either u or g, indicating whether we wish to set an ACL for a user, for a group, or for all others who do not match another ACL.

The second is the name of the user or group.

The last is the actual set of permissions to assign, using the r, w, and x characters with the same meanings as in the chmod command.

These four commands would give the folder the permissions we want. As a starting point, we use a simple chmod command to establish that no one should have access to the file. Then we use ACLs to grant access to the two groups:

```
chmod a-rwx /research
setfacl -m g:SalesGroup:rwx /research
setfacl -m g:MarketingGroup:rx /research
```

The `setfacl` command has additional options. For more information, type `man setfacl` at the Linux command line.

You will note that we don't specify the domain name when referring to `SalesGroup` and `MarketingGroup` in the preceding commands. That's because in our tests `setfacl` didn't handle slashes in domain usernames correctly. The commands work as they are written if we include the following line:

```
use default domain = yes
```
in the file:

```
/etc/samba/smb.conf
```

Setting `use default domain = yes` has a downside, though: it rules out setting permissions for users in *other* trusted domains. We hope that support for the "\" domain separator character in commands like `setfacl` will improve in the near future. There is also a `winbind separator` Samba option that can be used to set a different separator character instead of "\", but you may find that alternative separator characters also cause difficulties with some commands. Check out the `man smb.conf` command for more information.

Setting ACLs with the Windows GUI

Now we're ready to log into our Windows client and set up our ACLs just the way we want them for the `research` share. First, we'll log into the `xppro1` workstation as the AD domain user `salesperson1`. Then we'll browse the network neighborhood and locate the research share on the `adsambafp1` server. Once we're there, we'll edit the properties of the research directory and set up access control just the way we like it. Then we can do some simple tests as `salesperson2`, `marketperson1`, and `hrperson1` to verify that our actions have the desired effects.

When we set ACLs on the main folder of a share, we receive a warning message from Windows. That's because, on a true Windows file server, changing ACLs on a folder affects all of the existing files in the folder. But the share is currently empty and there are no existing files whose permissions would be disturbed by the change. Even if there were, Linux wouldn't automatically change the permissions and ACLs of existing files in the folder. But Windows doesn't know that, so it warns us anyway.

WARNING In our tests, ACLs looked great in the Windows GUI while initially setting them, but we did have one frustrating problem when re-opening the "Security" tab of the "Properties" window later: `SalesGroup` and `MarketingGroup` appeared as SIDs rather than as user-friendly names. For instance, `SalesGroup` appeared as `S-1-5-21-875667829-2241442456-3328505926-1130`. However, the actual *behavior* of the ACLs was completely correct, and the `getfacl` command on the Linux side shows that the correct access controls are in force. We hope this apparent Samba issue will be resolved in the near future.

Here is a summary of what we aim to accomplish by setting ACLs on the `research` share:

- `salesperson2`, or another member of the `SalesGroup`, should be able to read and write files.

- `marketperson1`, or another member of the MarketingGroup, should be able to read files but not write to them.

- `hrperson1` and other members of neither group should not be able to access *any* files.

Follow these steps to set up ACLs for the research folder using the Windows GUI:

1. Log on to the `xppro1` workstation as the AD domain user `salesperson1`.

2. Select Start ➢ My Computer.

3. Select the text in the "address" field at the top of the "My Computer" window and type **\\adsambafp1**

4. Press Enter. A list of shares available on `adsambafp1` appears.

5. Right-click the research share.

6. Choose "Properties" from the menu.

7. Click the "Security" tab.

8. Click the "Add..." button.

9. The "Select Users, Computers or Groups" dialog box appears. Enter **AD\SalesGroup** in the "Enter the object names to select" field and click "OK." AD\`SalesGroup` now appears in the "Group or user names" list in the "Properties" dialog box.

10. Select "AD\`SalesGroup`."

11. In the "Permissions for `SalesGroup`" list, check the "Allow" box next to "Full Control" as shown in Figure 4.15.

12. Click "Apply."

13. The message box in Figure 4.16 appears. Click "Yes."

14. Repeat steps 9–15 for AD\MarketingGroup. This time, instead of "Full Control," check the "Read," "Execute" and "List Folder Contents" boxes.

15. Click "OK" to exit the "Properties" window.

Browsing Our Shares from a Windows Workstation

You can now browse into the AD domain and then onto our new server using the normal network browsing features of any domain member workstation. The procedure is no different from that for exploring shares on a domain member server that runs Windows; that's the point, after all! But here's one way to access the research share:

1. Select Start ➢ My Computer.

2. Select the text in the "address" field at the top of the "My Computer" window and type **\\adsambafp1**

3. Press Enter. A list of shares available on `adsambafp1` appears.

4. Double-click the `research` share.

The `research` share will allow you to store and retrieve files normally, provided that you are logged in as `salesperson1` or another member of the `SalesGroup`. You'll be able to read files if you are logged in as a member of the `MarketingGroup`. You will have no access at all if you are logged on as a member of another group. That's exactly what we set out to achieve!

A final note: you can also browse your shares from the `adlinclil` Linux workstation just as you browsed shares on `windc1`. This works because the Linux client `adlinclil` and our new server `adsambafp1` are both members of the AD domain.

If It Doesn't Work

Here are some things to check out if you have unexpected problems:

- *Be sure the system clocks agree.* Kerberos is very picky about the current time; there must be close agreement between the machines involved.

- *Double-check your configuration settings.* Did you skip one of the Webmin configuration pages?

- *Be sure to enable ACLs in* `/etc/fstab`. Did you forget to reboot after this step?

- *Restart* `smbd` *and* `winbindd`. After correcting any oversights, you'll need to restart the `smbd` and `winbindd` processes. You can do so with the following commands:

```
service smb restart
service winbind restart
```

FIGURE 4.15 Setting an ACL on the Samba Server via a Windows client

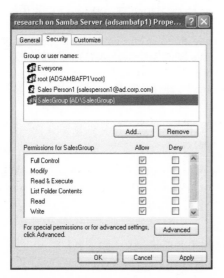

FIGURE 4.16 Confirmation message when changing ACLs on the root folder of a share

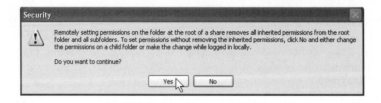

Leveraging NFS on Your Servers

Linux supports many ways to share files. As you've just seen, we can leverage Samba to pretend to be a part of an existing Active Directory domain.

The other major way it can share files is via the Network File System (NFS). In this section, we'll set our Linux server to be an NFS server. Then we'll have our Linux clients connect, as well as our Windows clients.

Additionally, SFU 3.5 has the ability to act as an NFS server. That way, your existing Linux clients can connect to it and mount shares just as if it were a real Unix NFS. And here's the best part yet: your Active Directory users can use the same home drive (on Linux, home directory) when they log on with either a Windows or Linux client computer. How amazingly cool is that? Well, you're going to find out firsthand.

The diagram in Figure 4.17 shows how Linux and Windows clients can connect to Linux NFS servers or Windows servers running the NFS services that comes in SFU 3.5.

Note that you might not ever *need* to offer up an NFS mount directly to a Windows client. That is, you *could* just use Samba (as shown in the last section) to offer up a Linux directory as an SMB share. Why then would you ever need to make an NFS export and have Windows clients see it using Windows NFS tools? It takes an extra step to load Windows NFS tools on the client, so why bother?

Because you could have a situation where the NFS is already perfectly set up on the Linux or, especially, legacy Unix server and you have no desire to run any Samba server components on that server. In that case, it would be necessary to have Windows see those native NFS shares somehow; you'll see how to do that next.

Setting up a Linux NFS Server

NFS is the original, old-school Unix/Linux way to share files, and there are good reasons why it is still the most common way to share files in a pure Unix environment. NFS has a number of things going for it:

- It's very simple.

- It handles Unix users, groups, and permissions easily.

- Because it's so simple, most implementations are compatible with one another.

FIGURE 4.17   Linux and Windows clients can be set up to directly connect to servers exporting NFS.

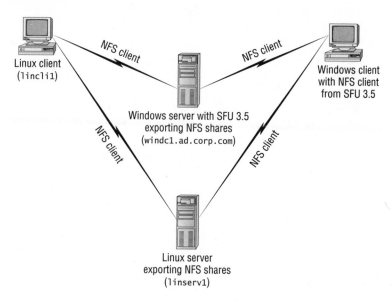

Of course, NFS has some significant disadvantages too:

- It "trusts" machines based on their IP address.
- Users are not authenticated by a central server.
- User and group IDs must be the same on every client.

Considering the Flaws of NFS

Are these flaws critical? It comes down to this: If you can reasonably ensure that users on Linux machines cannot change their IP addresses or obtain root access, then NFS is an acceptable choice—and even if Windows clients are involved, NFS can still sometimes be acceptable.

However, since NFS uses a "trusted host" model, where workstations are individually responsible for limiting access to particular files to the correct users, *every workstation must be secured carefully*. It is critical that both Linux and Windows clients be kept thoroughly up to date with security patches and antivirus updates.

Don't let us give you the impression that NFS has *no* security capabilities. Here are four ways you can help secure NFS:

- You can lock down a share to clients on the local network only using a network address and a netmask (which we strongly recommend). See the upcoming note.
- You can lock down NFS access to individual IP addresses.
- You can serve up read-only shares. This is useful because for many less secure applications, making sure that a rogue client can't delete files is sufficient.

- Although NFS doesn't require users to authenticate, an NFS server need not blindly trust clients to act as *any* user. You can and should configure NFS to prohibit clients from acting with the privileges of the root user. This makes attacks more difficult.

Setting up NFS Exports

Assuming we've decided that NFS is suitable for what we need to do, how do we configure NFS "exports" (analogous to Windows shares)? Webmin to the rescue—it does a great job setting up NFS!

We'll begin by sharing the /home directory of linserv1. Then we'll configure a Linux client computer (lincli1) to use this exported directory instead of its own /home directory. Actually, if we had a bunch of Linux client machines, we would want to do this on all on them. That way, whenever users bounce from Linux machine to Linux machine, they always receive their home directory centrally from the server. Sort of like a Windows roaming profile, as shown earlier in this chapter.

Once set up, any user can log into any workstation and see their own files, just as they left them. As Martha Stewart would say, "That's a good thing."

Later, we'll also share two other directories to demonstrate how to use NFS in other scenarios.

Exporting Home Directories via NFS

To export /home via NFS, follow these steps:

1. Log into Webmin as usual. As a reminder, use your favorite web browser to connect to https://linserv1:10000 and provide root credentials.

2. Click the "Networking" icon

3. Click the "NFS Exports" icon.

4. Click "Add a New Export."

5. The "Create Export" page will appear (see Figure 4.18).

6. In the "Directory to export" field, enter /home.

7. You want to activate the NFS export. Next to "Active?", ensure "Yes" is selected.

8. To the right of "Export to," select the "Network" radio button.

9. In the "Network" field, enter **192.168.2.0** .

10. In the "Netmask" field, enter **255.255.255.0** .

11. The remaining default selections are acceptable and should match Figure 4.18; see the sidebar "Other NFS Options via Webmin" for more information about what they do.

12. Click "Create" to create the new export.

13. The "NFS Exports" page reappears. The /home export should be listed (see Figure 4.19).

14. Click "Apply Changes."

How do network addresses and netmasks work? In our case, the network address is 192.168.2.0, and the "netmask" is 255.255.255.0. NFS will compare the IP address of the client to the network address we specify. If the corresponding byte of the netmask is 255, that byte must match in the client address and the network address. If the corresponding byte of the netmask is 0, that byte doesn't have to match. Allowing only the last byte to vary in our situation keeps out machines not on the local LAN. The NFS server actually requires the individual bits that are set in the netmask to match (255 and 0 are not the only acceptable values), but subnet addressing is beyond the scope of this book.

The /home export is ready to go! Soon we'll examine how to mount /home from our Linux client workstation. First though, we'll export two additional directories to demonstrate how NFS can be used to create read-only shares.

Other NFS Options via Webmin

What do the remaining options do?

- Setting "Clients must be on secure port?" to "Yes" prevents rogue client applications running as a non-root user on a Linux client from making their own rogue NFS requests. This is only effective if the root account on that particular Linux client hasn't been compromised.

- Setting "Access mode" to "Read/write" allows users to write to their home directories.

- Setting "Deny access to directory?" makes the share active but unusable.

- Setting "Trust remote users" to "Everyone except root" prevents *any* client from acting as the root user with full control over the exported directory.

- Selecting "None" for "Don't trust UIDs" and "Don't trust GIDs" forbids clients from acting as additional Unix user IDs and group IDs other than root.

- "Treat untrusted users as" determines what happens if a client tries to act as root or another forbidden NFS user. The "default" selection causes a request to work with a file as root to be treated as a request from the user "nobody," and it fails unless that file's permissions allow that action for *all* users.

- Turning on "Immediately sync all writes" would prevent the NFS server from delaying write operations for the sake of performance. We'll accept the default for this option. Samba's default behavior is not to immediately sync all writes.

FIGURE 4.18 You can leverage NFS to create an export of /home on linserv1.

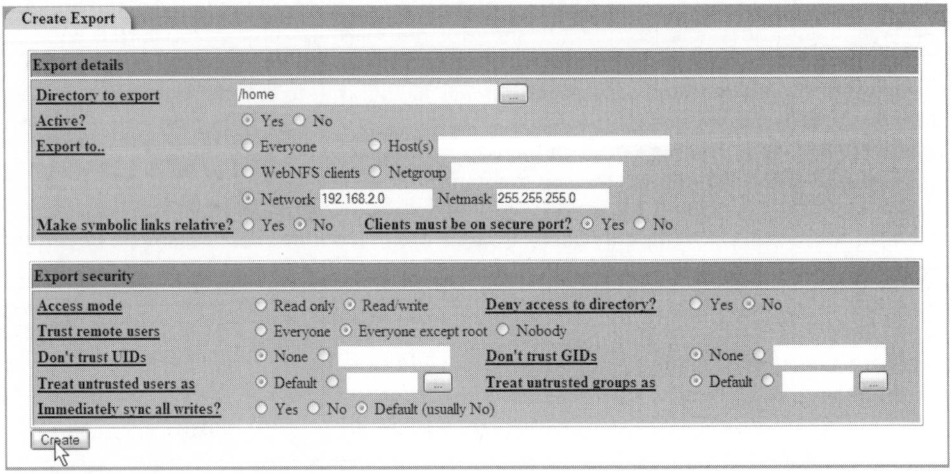

FIGURE 4.19 The NFS Exports page shows our new /home export. Click "Apply Changes" to make it take effect.

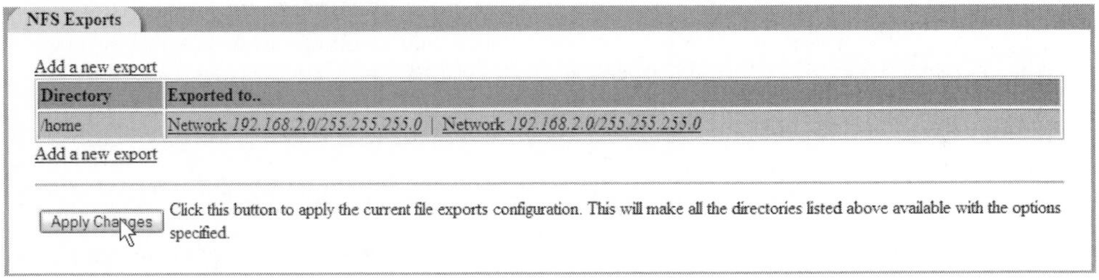

Exporting Read-Only Directories via NFS

Why export directories on a read-only basis? It's not uncommon to have a large number of legacy files that all users are permitted to access. You may also want to export them to client workstations that are not well secured and cannot be trusted not to delete or modify them. Since NFS does not authenticate individual users, this is a serious concern. Making the files read-only provides you with a little bit of security (at least they cannot be written to).

Our Linux server, linserv1, has two types of users in its LDAP database: doctors and nurses. Let's assume we have a need to make certain files available to everyone related to these two groups. We'll create directories for each of these groups with the following simple commands, all but two of which you've seen before. Be sure to execute these as root:

```
mkdir /doctorfiles
echo "It worked" > /doctorfiles/test.txt
```

```
chgrp -R doctors /doctorfiles
chmod a+r,g+rw /doctorfiles

mkdir /nursefiles
echo "It worked" > /nursefiles/test.txt
chgrp -R nurses /nursefiles
chmod a+r,g+rw /nursesfiles
```

The chgrp command, like the chown command, changes the ownership of a file but in this case, it sets the *group* that owns the file rather than the user. Just as with chown, the -R option recursively changes group ownership of the directory and all of its contents.

The echo command (which also exists in Windows), simply outputs the text it receives as an argument to standard output. The > character, as you have seen, redirects standard output to a file. So we've created two little text files containing one line of text each. We'll use these to verify that our NFS mounts are successful.

Now, we'll create read-only NFS mounts for these directories. The procedure is almost identical to that for exporting /home, but there are some differences.

To create a read-only NFS mount:

1. Log into Webmin as usual.

2. Click the "Networking" icon.

3. Click the "NFS Exports" icon.

4. Click "Add a New Export."

5. The "Create Export" page will appear.

6. In the "Directory to export" field, enter **/doctorfiles**   .

7. Make sure "Yes" is selected next to "Active?"

8. To the right of "Export to" select the "Network" radio button.

9. In the "Network" field, enter **192.168.2.0** .

10. In the "Netmask" field, enter **255.255.255.0** .

11. To the right of "access mode," select "Read only."

12. The remaining default selections are acceptable.

13. Click "Create" to create the new export.

14. The "NFS Exports" page reappears. The /doctorfiles export should be listed (as shown previously in Figure 4.19).

15. Click "Apply Changes."

16. Repeat these steps, substituting /nursefiles for /doctorfiles.

We now have two read-only NFS exports, which are available to everyone. Now, how do we access these exported directories from a Linux client? That's the topic of the next section.

Connecting Linux NFS Clients to Linux NFS Servers

We've got the pieces in place on the server side. We're ready to set up a Linux client so that both home directories and the read-only exports are mounted over NFS. How do we set up the client side?

We're pleased to report that the task is remarkably easy to accomplish. Mounting our NFS exports requires only four steps:

- We will log into the lincli1 workstation directly *as root*. The root account has its home directory in a separate location outside of /home, so root won't be disrupted by the change when we switch to the NFS-mounted home directories.

- We will create the mount points for each export. That is, we'll create a directory where we can hang each NFS export.

- We will add one line describing each export to /etc/fstab, the system-wide table of file systems that are mounted on every reboot.

- We will use the mount -a command to mount any file systems in /etc/fstab that are not already mounted. In this case, that means our new NFS mounts.

Let's go through the steps in detail and get this show on the road!

Logging in Directly as root

We'll start by logging in directly as root. If you are currently logged into the desktop of a non-root user, log out now. It's not good enough to simply use su, because we're about to replace our local home directories with an NFS mount, pulling the rug out from under any non-root user currently logged in! root, fortunately, has its home directory in /root where the mount won't affect it. This is good practice since we may still need root access to the client if the NFS server goes down.

Now log back in to the graphical console as root and proceed to the next step.

Creating the Mount Points

Next, we'll create mount points for all three exports. As you have seen, the Linux mount command requires an existing, typically empty local directory as a "mount point" to attach the server's export to. To take care of the two read-only shares, just enter these commands:

```
mkdir /doctorfiles
mkdir /nursefiles
```

But what about the /home share? Well, we already have a /home directory with local files for the accounts we've used in previous experiments. We could use that nonempty /home directory as a mount point, but that can get confusing fast. We won't know if we're really succeeding if the mount fails—we'll have stuff in the directory already. To avoid confusion, we'll rename the original /home directory and create a new, empty /home as our NFS mount point.

If anything does go wrong with the NFS mount, we'll know immediately, as we'll see an empty /home directory! Use these two commands:

```
mv /home /home-old-local
mkdir /home
```

Now we have all three mount points we'll need to mount the NFS exports from the server.

Adding the Mounts to */etc/fstab*

We could set up our NFS mounts right now from the command line, using `mount -t nfs`. However, the goal is to mount /home, /doctorfiles, and /nursefiles automatically all the time. As you've already seen, the file /etc/fstab is a list of mounts that are remounted every time the system reboots. This is where we'll add entries to take care of our NFS mounts.

There are entries for many types of file systems in /etc/fstab, and some of them take complex options. NFS mounts are very simple, however. We need to specify only three things: the export we want to mount, the local mount point, and the file system type. We specify the export very simply; all we have to do is identify the server and the exported path on the server, separated by a colon (:):

```
servername:/exportpath
```

The mount point parameter is just the path of the mount point we created with the `mkdir` command. The file system type, of course, is `nfs`. (As we said, it's very easy.) Just add these three lines to the end of /etc/fstab:

```
linserv1.corp.com:/home /home    nfs
linserv1.corp.com:/doctorfiles /doctorfiles    nfs
linserv1.corp.com:/nursefiles /nursefiles    nfs
```

Accessing the NFS Mounts Now

We're already finished, in a way. We could reboot `linclil` right now and the NFS mounts would come right up. But there's no need to wait for a reboot. Just use the `mount -a` command to mount them right now. The -a option specifies that "all" file systems in /etc/fstab should be mounted, if they are not mounted already. Just type

```
mount -a
```

If the mount command works properly, the shell prompt will reappear with no further messages. If you do receive errors, check to be sure that

- You created the mount points.
- `linserv1` is up and running, /doctorfiles and /nursefiles exist on `linserv1`, and /etc/exports has been set up correctly on `linserv1`.
- The `nfs` service has been started on `linserv1` with the command `service nfs start`.

Verifying Your Success

Once you have completed the mount command without errors, you can verify your success easily. First, type

```
ls /home
```

Instead of the empty mount point directory we created locally, you will see the contents of the server's exported /home directory. That list will include /home/doctor1, /home/doctor2, /home/nurse1, and /home/nurse2.

Now log out of lincli1 as root and log back on as the user named doctor1. You can use your home directory and GNOME desktop on the server just as you would use a local home directory. Also try the command

```
ls /doctorfiles
```

You will be able to see the file test.txt, which we created on the server listed among the contents.

Congratulations: you have successfully configured an NFS client and server. Once you set up all of your Linux client systems to mount home directories via NFS, users will be able to log into any workstation and find their usual files, settings, and so on—just like Windows users utilizing home drives and roaming profiles.

If you choose to use the same Linux server additionally acting as a Samba-based PDC and file server, doctor1 can find her documents on the server when she logs on from a Windows workstation *or* a Linux workstation. Now *that's* interoperability.

Having Windows Clients Locate NFS Servers

Now that you've seen our Linux clients connect to NFS mounts, we should also demonstrate how to do the same for our Windows clients. There are two ways to make Windows client machines see NFS exports that live on Linux servers:

- Use the Windows 2003 server as a gateway for our Windows clients that translates incoming Windows SMB requests to NFS mounts. This software is part of SFU 3.5 and runs on the Windows 2003 server. Indeed, we already installed SFU 3.5 on our server, and when we did, we suggested that you also install the NFS gateway (see Figure 3.8 in Chapter 3).

- Trot out to each and every Windows client system and load SFU 3.5 and select the "NFS Client" during the installation. That way, Windows clients can connect directly to the machines which are exporting NFS shared files.

Connecting Windows Clients via NFS Gateway

In this example, we'll tell our Windows 2003 server (Windc1.ad.corp.com) to accept inbound SMB connections and re-route them as NFS connections. In other words, we'll map what looks like an SMB share to an existing NFS mount. That's the point of the gateway for NFS from SFU 3.5. A diagram of this can be seen in Figure 4.20.

FIGURE 4.20   You can use SFU's NFS Gateway to make existing NFS exports on Unix and Linux appear as if they were regular SMB.

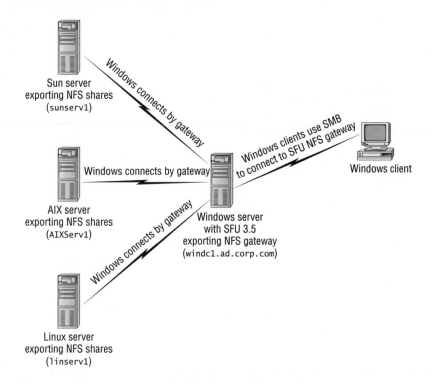

To start, log on as administrator to the Windows 2003 Domain Controller. Select Start ➢ All Programs ➢ Windows Services for Unix ➢ Gateway for NFS Configuration as shown in Figure 4.21.

When you select the icon, you'll be presented with the "Gateway for NFS Shares" screen. Here, you'll set up the name for the SMB share (which appears as an inbound Windows connections) as well as the name of the NFS mount.

In Figure 4.22, you can see we've entered **LINNURSEFILES** as the SMB share on Windows, and we've entered the name of the NFS mount (in typical Windows notation) as **\\linserv1 \nursefiles**.

The "Drive" letter designation is optional. Additionally, you can use the "Users" part of the interface to restrict how many clients can connect, and you can use the "Permissions" button to specify who can perform what rights once connected to the share. For instance, perhaps you want only the members of the Human Resources Group in Active Directory (HRGroup) to see the files contained within that sensitive Linux export. If desired, go ahead and click "Permissions," remove "Everyone," and specify that only the HRGroup should have, say, "Read" access.

Once you're satisfied, click the "Connect" button to initiate the gateway between the LINNURSEFILES Windows SMB share and the \\linserv1\nursefiles NFS mount. You might be prompted with a warning if your SMB share name is longer than eight characters, as Windows 9x and clients cannot view long share names.

To check out your work, from a Windows client simply browse to \\Windc1\LINNURSEFILES. Inside, you should see the files we placed inside when we originally created the NFS mount points, as shown in Figure 4.23.

FIGURE 4.21 The Gateway for NFS Configuration application has its own icon. It's not part of the SFU console.

FIGURE 4.22 Input the name that should appear as the SMB share in the "Share Name" field and the name of the existing NFS resource in the "Network Resource" field.

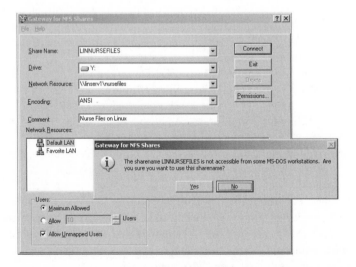

FIGURE 4.23   Windows clients can now connect to the NFS resource as a plain ol' SMB share.

Connecting Windows Clients Directly to NFS

The preceding scenario cannot be beat. That is, you set up one little piece of code on your Windows 2003 server and all your Windows clients can magically map NFS mounts via a standard Windows share.

This works great, until you have hundreds of clients pounding down that one server's door to get to the NFS mounts. Ouch, that could be painful for that one poor box. Instead, you could put a NFS client piece directly on the clients that need it. That way, your poor Windows 2003 server doesn't take all the pounding—each client machine individually asks the NFS server for a connection.

Here's how to do that. First, run the SFU 3.5 setup program on your Windows XP client machine. (You can refer to download and initial setup instructions in Chapter 3.)

A "standard" SFU 3.5 installation will install the NFS client on your Windows XP machine. You can accept all the defaults during the Installation Setup Wizard. Once loaded, you're ready to browse NFS mounts from Windows XP.

To see Windows shares from Windows clients loaded with the SFU 3.5 NFS client software:

1. Select Start ➢ My Computer and in the "Other Places" heading, select "My Network Places."

2. Next, locate and click "Entire Network," still in the "Other Places."

3. Select "NFS Network." From the list, double-click "Default LAN."

4. Inside Default LAN, double-click "LinServ1" to see the NFS mounts it contains.

5. You should be able to see the NFS mounts we created. Click inside, say, the nursefiles mount and you'll be able to see and open the files we put inside.

Leveraging NFS Exports on Your Windows Server for a Unified Windows and Linux Home Drive

In Chapter 3, you loaded SFU 3.5 on your Domain Controller. When you did this, you performed several key functions. When loading SFU 3.5, you

- Extended the Active Directory schema to allow for Unix attributes to reside in Active Directory. For instance, a user's UID and a group's GID can now be manipulated in the user's or group's "Unix Attributes" tab.

- Told Active Directory to answer to NIS queries. Now that SFU 3.5 is installed on your Domain Controller, it can respond to Unix computers asking for the attributes specified on the "Unix Attributes" tab.

- Loaded (but haven't yet configured) a service called the "User Name Mapping" service. This will come in handy here, as it's a critical piece of the magic required to make the dream of unified home directories a reality. You'll see how this fits in the story in a bit.

- Loaded (but haven't yet configured) the server for NFS. This allows us to take any directory we want and export it as an NFS mount.

To create a unified home directory for our Active Directory users when they log on to Windows or Linux, we need a battle plan. Here it is:

- We'll create a home share for our Active Directory users.

- We'll share that home share via SMB for when Active Directory users log on to Windows.

- We'll leverage the server for NFS and export that *very same directory* as a NFS mount. This way our Linux clients can see the exact same directory.

In other words, our Windows clients will connect to the directory via SMB, and our Linux clients will connect via NFS. It'll be beautiful.

In Figure 4.24, you can see what should happen: a user whose account is in Active Directory, say, salesperson1 can log on to either a Linux client (which is a domain member) or a Windows client (which is a domain member).

There's one extra step in the equation: the User Name Mapping service. However, we'll cross that bridge when we come to it.

Creating, Sharing (via SMB), and Exporting (via NFS) a Unified Home Directory — Oh, and Securing It Too

As we stated, we need to create a unified place on our server for our users to store their junk, er, files. To that end, on our Windows 2003 server we'll create a normal directory using Explorer and we'll call it homedirs. This can be any place you like. A best practice is to put it on a volume that isn't the system (that is, the C) drive. However, for example purposes, feel free. Once created, we need to also share the directory via SMB so our Windows clients can easily access it.

Finally, we'll change the NTFS permissions on that directory so we can set up individual users reading their own directories later.

FIGURE 4.24   You can create unified home drives by using Windows 2003, SMB shares, and NFS exports.

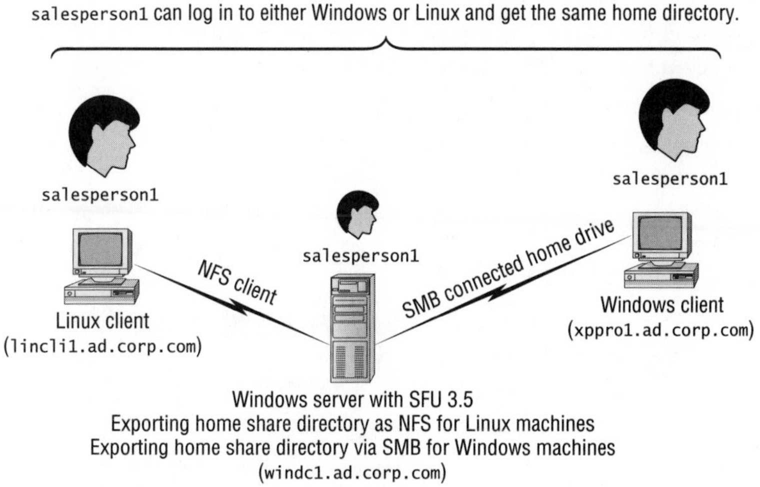

salesperson1 can log in to either Windows or Linux and get the same home directory.

salesperson1

salesperson1

salesperson1

NFS client

SMB connected home drive

Linux client
(linclil.ad.corp.com)

Windows client
(xpprol.ad.corp.com)

Windows server with SFU 3.5
Exporting home share directory as NFS for Linux machines
Exporting home share directory via SMB for Windows machines
(windc1.ad.corp.com)

Sharing *homedirs* via SMB

Don't panic when, in a moment, we set Authenticated Users to have Change and Read rights on this new SMB share. That's because we'll also set up NTFS permissions on the files and folders *inside* this directory, which will ultimately keep Windows users writing only where they should.

To create the directory and share via SMB:

1. Log on to Windows 2003 as administrator.

2. Select Start ➢ My Computer and select the C: drive.

3. Select File ➢ New and enter a name for the directory, say, **homedirs** .

4. Right-click over the new directory and select "Sharing and Security."

5. On the Sharing tab, click the "Share this folder" button, as shown in Figure 4.25. By default the "Share name" field will be the same name as the directory. This is recommended as this is also the name we will use when using NFS in a moment.

6. Click the "Permissions" button (not shown in the figure). You'll see the Permissions for the share. By default, a Windows 2003 share is Everyone: Read. Change so the access is Authenticated Users: Change and Read, as shown in Figure 4.25.

7. Select "OK" to return to the properties of the homedirs directory.

Here, the homedirs directory is shared out to Everyone: Full Control. Don't worry: your users will be protected by NTFS permissions, which will be stronger than these initial share-level permissions.

FIGURE 4.25   You can set the permissions on the home directory share so Authenticated Users has Change access.

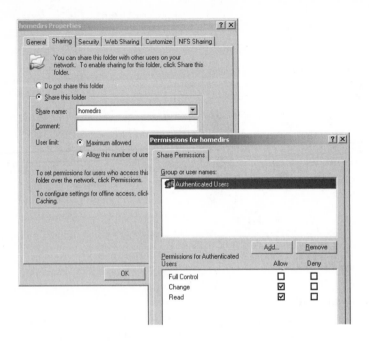

Exporting *homedirs* via NFS

Now you're ready to also export the directory via NFS. You can do this via the "NFS Sharing" tab on the properties of the directory. Before we do, however let's recall one undeniable tenet of NFS: NFS's security is based on what machine connects to the export. This is very archaic, but that's the breaks, so don't panic when, in a moment, we set all machines to be able to Read and Write to this export. That's because we'll also set up NTFS permissions on the files and folders themselves inside this directory, which will ultimately keep Linux users writing only where they should.

   To export the homedirs directory via NFS:

1. Select the "NFS Sharing" tab, which is in the properties of the homedirs page. Click the "Share this folder" button. By default the "Share name" field will be the same name as the directory. This is recommended as this is also the name we just created via SMB sharing.

2. By default the "Allow anonymous access" is unchecked. This is good—leave it unchecked, as it's not needed.

3. On the "NFS Sharing" tab, click the "Permissions" button. The "NFS Share Permissions" dialog appears as shown in Figure 4.26.

4. By default "ALL MACHINES" have "Read-Only" access. You need to change this so that "ALL MACHINES" have "Read-Write" access. Perform this change by pulling down the drop down next to the "Type of access" and selecting "Read-Write."

5. Additionally, be sure to select the "Allow root access" check box. This is a highly important step and should not be missed. This will permit Linux clients to map to this directory when they start up. In the next section, we'll make sure we have a root user in Active Directory who can actually perform the connection.

6. At the NFS Share Permissions screen, click "OK" to return to the homedirs properties

7. At the homedirs Properties screen, click "OK."

Securing the *homedirs* Directory via NTFS

Last, but not least, we have to configure NTFS permissions on the underlying homeshares directory. Click the "Security" tab, and you'll see that the Users group has a whole lot of access. This doesn't work for us; we don't want Johnny User seeing what Sally Admin is doing. We'll remove the Users group from having access here, which will force us to explicitly designate permissions just to those users who need permissions where they need them. However, it's a little tricky to remove Users from this default access. Let's do that now. To remove Users from accessing the homedirs folder:

1. If not already done, click the "Security" tab in the homedirs properties.

2. Click the "Advanced" button to bring up the "Advanced Security Settings for homedirs."

3. Uncheck the "Allow inheritable permissions from this object and all child objects. Include these entries explicitly defined here" check box. The "Security" dialog will appear asking how you should handle permissions. Select Copy. At the "Advanced Security Settings for homedirs" click "OK.

FIGURE 4.26 On the NFS tab, "Allow anonymous access" is not needed. On the "NFS Share Permissions" dialog box, ensure the "Allow root access" is selected.

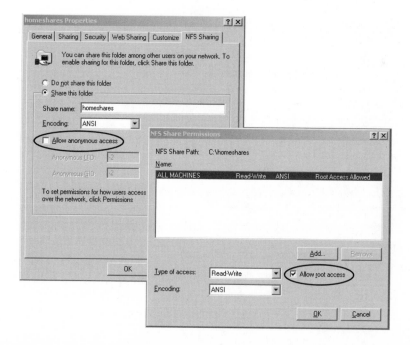

4. At the homedirs Properties page, select the Users group and click "Remove."

5. Click "OK" to close the homedirs properties.

Creating an Active Directory root User

In the last step, you selected "Allow root access" for the NFS share. Without it, your Linux clients will not be able to mount the NFS share. This is because every Linux client has an account named root and has a UID of 0. But Active Directory doesn't know about this, however, so we have to train Active Directory to have a root user and give it the UID of 0.

To do this, you've got two choices:

- Using Active Directory Users and Computers, select any existing user for instance, the administrator account select the "Unix Attributes" tab, and enter **UID 0** .

- Or create a completely new garden-variety Active Directory user and name it root. Then select the "Unix Attributes" tab and enter **UID 0** .

These do the exact same thing. Note that the Active Directory root user need not be an administrative account.

When you're done, your root user's "Unix Attributes" tab should look similar to Figure 4.27. Note, in our case we're arbitrarily selecting a Primary group. It can be whichever Unix-enabled group you like.

FIGURE 4.27 Active Directory needs to know who your Linux UID 0 account should be. We suggest you create a new user named root and specifically grant it UID 0.

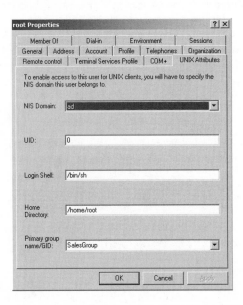

Mapping Active Directory User Accounts to Unix UIDs

Let's take a look at the big picture again for a moment. Imagine for a second that we are the user named `salesperson1` whose account lives in Active Directory. Recall that we specifically Unix-enabled this account by going to the "Unix Attributes" tab and entering a Unix UID.

Remember, the goal is to log in on the Linux client and have the Linux client automatically know who we are and what rights we have. You might think that because we authenticated directly to Active Directory that Active Directory would automatically tell the Linux client what the UID of `salesperson1` is. But it doesn't.

In order for the Linux client to know the UID within Active Directory of `salesperson1`, the Linux client has to query the NIS server that you set up on your Domain Controller. You got that right: Active Directory is pretending to be a NIS server, and the Linux client queries that database to discover what the UID is. Strange but true.

You can ensure that your Active Directory Domain Controller is masquerading as an NIS server while inside the "Services for Unix" console. Figure 4.28 shows the "Server for NIS" heading and the NIS server it's running as. Note the name in our case is **ad** (that's a lowercase **ad**), which will become extraordinarily important to know in a moment.

 WARNING If you don't see the name of your Active Directory NIS server when you double-click the "Server for NIS" heading, you might not have that component loaded properly. Go to the Add/Remove Programs applet in Control Panel, locate the Services for Unix entry, choose to install additional components, and load the NIS server.

When `salesperson1` logs on to the Active Directory/NIS server, another service called the *User Name Mapping* service kicks into high-gear. It says: "Holy cow! `salesperson1` is trying to log on to NIS. Let me check inside Active Directory to see what the UID is set to." In other words, as long as you log on as `salesperson1`, you'll be automatically able to locate the UID from Active Directory when asking via NIS—and it's all thanks to the User Name Mapping service.

It's a bit convoluted, but it works.

FIGURE 4.28   The User Name Mapping service maps Active Directory accounts with Unix Attributes over to the Active Directory NIS server components.

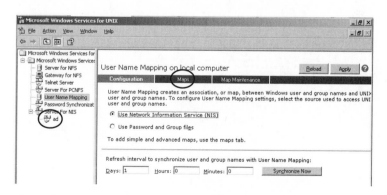

We simply need to configure the User Name Mapping service once, then forget about it forever. There is one very weird aspect of the User Name Mapping service. By default, it only updates once every day. For instance, if you create a brand spankin' new Active Directory user and enter the Unix Attributes such as the UID, any queries to NIS requesting the UID of the user will not be valid until up to 24 hours later. This can be a troubleshooting nightmare: you set up a new user, provide the Unix Attributes, then pull your hair out wondering why you have no permissions!

You can manually specify a synchronization at any time with the "Synchronize Now" button as shown in Figure 4.29. Better yet, change the refresh interval to one that makes more sense to your environment. Note that synchronization can have some network impact on your environment because it sends all data about every account to all Domain Controllers which are running the SFU 3.5, so be careful in how you set this value.

Additionally, there are various ways to configure the User Name Mapping server. The simplest and easiest is via what is called "Simple Mapping." It basically means, "When I see user salesperson1 logging in from Linux, it means he's UID 10007."

Here's how to set up the User Name Mapping service to use Simple Mapping:

1. Select Start ➢ All Programs ➢ Windows Services for Unix ➢ Services for Unix Administration. The Microsoft Windows Services for Unix console appears.

2. Select the "User Name Mapping" section.

3. Select the "Use Network Information Service (NIS)" radio button if it's not already selected.

4. Change the refresh interval to something that makes more sense. Again, the quicker you refresh, the more network traffic to other Domain Controllers you'll generate. In our test lab, we only have one Domain Controller, so setting this value to move quicker will have no consequence other than burn a few CPU cycles.

5. Click the word "Maps," as shown circled in Figure 4.29.

6. In the "User Name Mapping on local computer" dialog, select the "Simple Maps" check box. The "Windows domain to NIS domain mapping" dialog box appears, as shown in Figure 4.29.

FIGURE 4.29   In the "NIS domain name" field, you must enter the exact NIS domain name you are using for the Active Directory NIS.

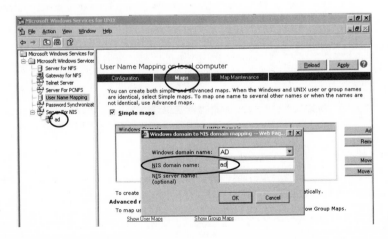

7. The Windows domain name "AD" is automatically filled in. Here's the trick: when entering the "NIS domain name," be sure it matches the precise case you see in the NIS domain under "Server for NIS." Click "OK."

8. In the upper-right corner of the "Maps" screen, select "Apply."

At this point, you've done it. However, for an extra test, select the "Show User Maps" hyperlink and scroll down to the bottom of the page to locate the "Display simple maps in Mapped users list" check box, as shown in Figure 4.30.

If you haven't clicked the "Apply" button in the upper-right corner, be sure to do so, as you could lose all your settings if you do not. At this point you can close the SFU 3.5 console.

Securing the Underlying *homedirs* Structure

Earlier, you set the homedirs directory so that mere mortal user accounts cannot read, write, or do much else. However, you do need to add one particular user for access: your Active Directory root user you created earlier with the UID of 0.

In the "Security" tab of the homedirs properties, you need to explicitly add in the new Active Directory root user you created and grant this user "Read & Execute," "List Folder Contents," and "Read" permissions, as shown in Figure 4.31.

Remember how earlier, when setting up NFS permissions, you selected "Allow root access"? Well, root access was only granted to mounting the share. When it actually comes to seeing what's inside, you'll have no joy until you explicitly add root so it can "see" what's inside this directory. Additionally, you need to add "Authenticated Users" to the list and give them "List Folder Contents" permissions. Yes, this means that all users will be able to see each others' home directories—but in the very next step we're going to prevent them from being able to see *inside* each others' home directories.

FIGURE 4.30   The "Display simple maps in Mapped users list" check box demonstrates that queries to NIS will return Unix UIDs stored in Active Directory.

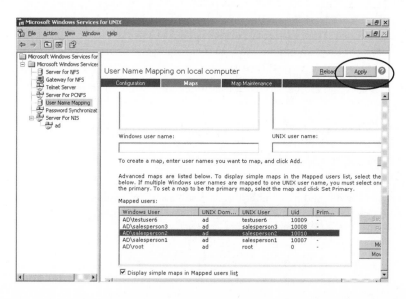

FIGURE 4.31   Your Active Directory root user needs to have "Read & Execute", "List Folder Contents," and "Read" access on the homedirs directory. You also need to add "Authenticated Users" and give them "List Folder Contents" permissions.

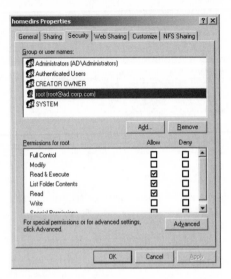

Securing a Directory for Each Active Directory User

Now you're ready to create specific directories for each user inside your new homedirs share you created earlier. In Figure 4.32, we can see two hand-created directories—salesperson1 and salesperson2—for testing. The goal is to set the permissions so that only the designated user, and the Administrators group can dive in and use the files.

However, by default each home directory you create for a user will inherit the permissions from the homedirs directory above it, and this directory has too many permissions. Specifically, it allows Authenticated Users "List directory contents" and allows the Active Directory root user "Full Access." We're going to remove those two entries at the user's specific folder level. To configure an individual user's home directory:

1. If not already done, create a directory with the same name as a user inside the homedirs directory.

2. Right-click the directory and select "Sharing and Security." Select the "Security" tab to bring up the NTFS security properties of the directory.

3. Click the "Advanced" button to bring up the "Advanced Security Settings".

4. Uncheck the "Allow inheritable permissions from this object and all child objects. Include these entries explicitly defined here" check box. The "Security" dialog will appear asking how you should handle permissions. Select "Copy." At the "Advanced Security Settings for homedirs" screen, click "OK".

5. At the "Properties" page for the directory, select "Authenticated Users" group and click "Remove." Additionally, select the Active Directory root user and click "Remove."

6. Click the "Add" button, and in the "Select Users, Computers, or Groups" dialog box, enter the name of the user who will own the home directory.

7. Grant the user "Full Control" rights, as seen in Figure 4.32.

8. Click "OK" to close the properties of the specific home directory.

Repeat these steps for each user you wish to create a unified home directory for.

Setting Windows Users in Active Directory to Use SMB Home Drives

Setting up each user to use their new home drive in Windows is easy. Just fire up Active Directory Users and Computers, select the "Profile" tab, and enter the full SMB share and path.

For instance, as shown in Figure 4.33, we're connecting H: to \\windc1\homedirs\salesperson1.

The next time salesperson1 logs on to xppro1.ad.corp.com, the user will automatically have the H: drive mapped and it will be all his! salesperson1 can, for instance, launch Windows Notepad and create a text file, saving it to drive H: as myfirsthomefile.txt, as shown in Figure 4.34.

You'll note that this figure includes some unfamiliar filenames beginning with a "." character. We're jumping ahead in time a little bit here, showing you what the home drive will look like after salesperson1 has also logged on from a Linux workstation (that's coming right up.) Linux doesn't have separate home and profile folders. Instead, Linux keeps profile settings in files beginning with a period, commonly referred to as "dotfiles." Linux knows not to display these in the file browser by default. So users who switch between the two operating systems will need to be educated to leave these "dotfiles" in peace.

FIGURE 4.32   Specifically grant each user access on their own home directory.

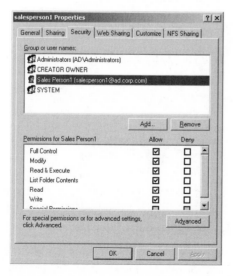

FIGURE 4.33 Use the "Profile" tab in "Active Directory Users and Computers" to specify which drive letter to map to the user's home directory. Be sure to specify the UNC path name for the homedirs share, including the user's specific directory.

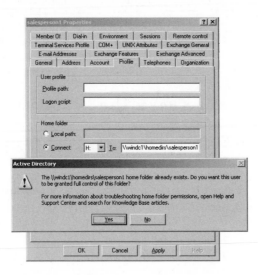

FIGURE 4.34 salesperson1's home drive, as seen from a Windows workstation. All of salesperson1's files are visible, including files created in Linux.

Configuring Linux Clients to Use NFS Home Drives

This time the easy part is on Linux! Or rather, it's easy if you have already completed Chapter 3. Here we make one key assumption: *you will use the same Linux client system that you created in Chapter 3 to demonstrate the use of LDAP authentication with Active Directory.*

This is *not* `adlinclil`.

This is quite important. For this procedure to work, your Linux client must "see" the same user IDs that the Windows NFS server is seeing, and that means your client must fetch user IDs via LDAP from Active Directory, as covered in Chapter 3 in the section "Using Extended Active Directory for Linux Authentication." So if you haven't created that client system yet, go back and do it now. We will call this client system `adldaplinclil.ad.corp.com` to avoid confusion with `adlinclil.ad.corp.com`.

To configure `adldaplinclil.ad.corp.com` to use the `/homedrive` NFS export of the Windows server, just refer to the "Connecting Linux NFS Clients to Linux NFS Servers" section of this chapter. The procedure is *exactly* the same, except for one small difference in `/etc/fstab`. We need to specify the Windows server rather than the Linux server, and the `/homedirs` export rather than the `/home` export.

When following the instructions in that section, be sure to replace the line:

```
linserv1.corp.com:/home /home    nfs
```

with this line:

```
windc1.ad.corp.com:/homedirs /home    nfs
```

When you have completed the procedure, you'll be able to log in as the user `salesperson1` or any other Unix-enabled user in the AD domain.

Congratulations! You have successfully unified your home directories for Windows and Linux workstations. A user can now log in as `salesperson1` on a Linux client and see the files created under Windows, as shown in Figure 4.35. Also refer to Figure 4.34 to see how this looks from the Windows side.

FIGURE 4.35   `salesperson1`'s home drive, as seen from a Linux workstation. All of `salesperson1`'s files are visible, including files created in Windows.

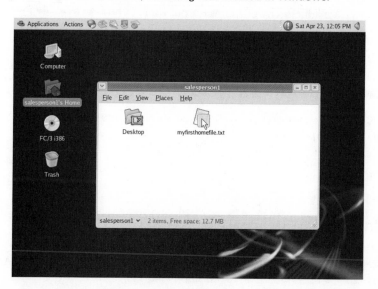

Creating a Unified DFS Space

Now that you have your Windows and Linux servers talking, it might be nice to have all clients be able to easily find all shares in your network. You do this by leveraging Windows 2003's DFS, or Distributed File System. The idea behind DFS is that it provides a "share of shares," or central clearinghouse of shares for users to find.

Therefore, you can tell all your users to surf one network location, then easily browse down the hierarchy of shares that you set up.

DFS Types

There are two kinds of DFS types you can create.

Stand-alone DFS   A stand-alone DFS can be hosted on a Windows 2003 (or Windows 2000) server or even a Samba server. However, the problem with this design is that if the particular server the DFS is hosted on should go down or become otherwise unavailable, users trying to use the DFS will not be able to. Therefore, a much better approach is to leverage the existing Active Directory and make your DFS more fault-tolerant. We won't be demonstrating how to do this on either a Windows or Samba server.

Active Directory Integrated DFS   Active Directory Integrated DFS allows you to host the DFS within Active Directory, and because it's in Active Directory, the information about the DFS is replicated to all Domain Controllers. Therefore, if any one Domain Controller should fail, you've got other Domain Controllers picking up the slack and hosting the DFS. This is what we'll set up.

Note that Active Directory Integrated DFS can be set up to allow for replication of the data within the shares. We are not attempting to perform that in this simple demonstration. The idea here is that we want to create a hierarchy of shares for our users to browse to easily find stuff.

At the end of this section, we'll point you toward some heavy-duty DFS documentation for you to play with those advanced features.

Implementing a DFS for Our Active Directory Users

Let's briefly recall our story line: our Active Directory domain is `ad.corp.com`, and we have three OUs with users and groups inside:

- Sales
    - `salesperson1`
    - `salesPerson2`
    - `salesGroup` (which contains `salesperson1` and `salesPerson2`)
- Marketing
    - `marketPerson1`
    - `marketPerson2`

- marketgroup (which contains `marketperson1` and `marketperson2`)
- HR
  - `HRperson1`
  - `HRperson2`
  - `HRGroup` (which contains `HRPerson1` and `HRPerson2`)

When you're done, users will be able to create "pockets" for your users. Here are two examples of when this can be immediately useful:

- Human Resources can immediately locate `\\windc1.ad.corp.com\WinShare1` and the nurses' files (located on the Linux NFS server). (Remember, the nurses' files are now available via SMB as `\\windc1\linnursefiles` via the NFS gateway we set up earlier.)
- Sales can immediately locate `\\windc1.ad.corp.com\WinShare1` and `\\adsambafp1\research`.

In both cases, you just tell your Human Resources and Sales users to surf to `\\ad.corp.com\dfsroot`, and they'll immediately be able to locate what you want them to see.

In this example, we'll set this up only for Sales, but you can repeat as you wish for Human Resources or anything else. To set up a DFS for Sales:

1. Select Start ➢ Program Files ➢ Administrative Tools ➢ Distributed File System. The Distributed File System Manager tool will start.

2. In the left pane, right-click over the words "Distributed File System" and select "New Root." The New Root Wizard appears. Click "Next" to proceed past the "Welcome" screen.

3. At the "Root Type" screen, select "Domain root" and click "Next."

4. At the "Host Domain" screen, ensure `ad.corp.com` (or whatever your domain name is called) is selected and click "Next."

5. At the "Server name" screen, browse for or enter **windc1.ad.corp.com**   and click "Next."

6. At the "Root Name" screen, enter a name, such as **dfsroot** , provide a comment, and click "Next." Everyone will see this comment when they connect to your DFS hierarchy.

7. At the final screen of the wizard, click "Finish."

Now, you will see your DFS root underneath the words "Distributed File System" in the left pane. You're ready to start hanging nodes and shares. A node is just a made up space for your users to look for stuff. For instance, we're about to create a node called "Sales", but there isn't anything in Active Directory that equates. Underneath Sales, we'll hang `\\windc1.ad.corp.com\WinShare1` and `\\adsambafp1.ad.corp.com\research` so that they're easily found. To create nodes and hang shares off them:

1. Right-click over the DFS root you just created and select "New Link." The "New Link" dialog box appears.

2. In the "New Link" dialog, enter a link name that consists of the node name, a backslash (\), and what you want the share to be presented as. For instance, we want to create a node named Sales and initially hang `\\windc1.ad.corp.com\WinShare1` from it. So, in the

"Link Name" field, we enter **Sales\WinShare1** . Heck, you could enter **Sales\ Anythingyouwanted** and that's what users would see. In the "Path to target (shared folder)" field, enter **\\windc1.ad.corp.com\WinShare1** , as shown in Figure 4.36.

Repeat these steps to create additional links to hang \\adsambafp1.ad.corp.com\research so it appears under a node named Sales. Again, in the "Link name" field, be sure to specifically type **Sales\ *whatever you want to call it*** to have it be neatly tucked in under a node called Sales.

For instance, let's imagine you want to create a node just for Human Resources. You would just repeat these steps to create additional links to create a fake "Human Resources" node. Then, underneath that you would hang resources that matter to Human Resources, say WinShare1 (located on \\windc1.ad.corp.com\WinShare1) and the nurses' files (\\windc1\linnursefiles).

See how easy it is to specify the nurses' files now? Remember, under the hood those nurses' files are really NFS exports, but because we installed the NFS gateway on WinDC1, it's supereasy to refer to them as the SMB share \\windc1\linnursefiles.

So, again, in the Link name, be sure to specifically type **HR*whatever you want to call it*** to have the stuff you want be neatly tucked in under a node called HR.

When you're finished, your Distributed File Manager should look something like the topmost window in Figure 4.37. Here, you can see that the fake Human Resources node is there with nurses' files and WinShare1 hanging off of it. The fake Sales node has also been created with Research and WinShare1 hanging off of it.

Additionally, in the other windows in Figure 4.37, you can see what users see if they "surf" the \\ad.corp.com\dfsroot structure you created. It's easy for them to spot either HR or Sales and then choose the path via the fake node they need. Then, inside either HR or Sales, it's easy to find the shares you created (representing them with whatever names you choose).

FIGURE 4.36 You can create fake "nodes," like Sales, just by typing in the word "sales." Then enter a backslash (\) and what you want to call the share name. What you call it needn't have any relation to the underlying share name.

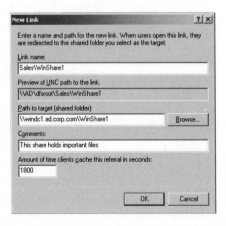

FIGURE 4.37 The DFS manager helps you sculpt your DFS so you can present a unified view for your shares (as seen in the other windows).

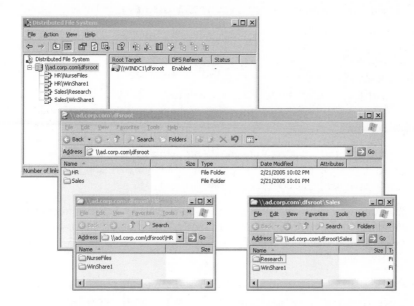

The best part is that the underlying share and NTFS permissions (on Windows) and the POSIX permissions (on Linux) keep the people out who should be out. This is a great way to unify your people and let them easily find the stuff that matters just for them.

For more information on Windows DFS, check out the following:

- www.microsoft.com/windows2000/techinfo/howitworks/fileandprint/dfsnew.asp

- www.microsoft.com/windows2000/techinfo/planning/fileandprint/dfssteps.asp

- www.microsoft.com/windowsserver2003/technologies/fileandprint/file/dfs/default.mspx

Again, DFS has a lot more features (such as replication services) that we aren't exploring here. For more information the DFS services that Samba provides, check out the following:

http://us2.samba.org/samba/docs/man/Samba-HOWTO-Collection/SambaHA.html

Final Thoughts

Making Linux and Windows share files can really be a challenge. As we've explored, the Linux camp is diligently working on making Linux more compatible with Windows. Ideally, full Kerberization of all key file services (especially for Samba) will occur. That way, a user who logs into a Linux machine using an Active Directory domain account will have 100 percent seamless integration with existing Windows file servers across the entire domain, only needing to log on once.

But as of today, it just isn't there. For the time being, file sharing between Linux and Windows definitely works, but the potential for true single-sign-on for Linux clients remains largely unrealized. Redundant password prompts abound and currently the "keyring" features are only a band-aid. Kerberization is the wave of the future.

I'm not saying we should give up hope. There's plenty of additional resources to check out when it comes to Kerberos and interoperability. And initial support for it has already appeared in the latest development versions of the GNOME desktop on which Fedora's desktop is built.

Kerberos Wrap-up

We've seen Kerberos in the last several chapters. And, at this point in the book, we'll be putting Kerberos to bed. Here are some suggested avenues for additional reading about the potential for Kerberos interoperability that we weren't able to delve in to.

Windows 2000 Kerberos Authentication   This document introduces how Kerberos is implemented on Windows 2000 (and Active Directory in general). The material here is largely kosher for Windows 2003 as well. Find the doc at www.microsoft.com/windows2000/techinfo/howitworks/security/kerberos.asp.

Windows 2000 Kerberos Interoperability and Step-by-Step Guide to Kerberos 5 (krb5 1.0) Interoperability   These documents really show you how to perform cross-realm compatibility with an existing Kerberos realm. Start at www.microsoft.com/windows2000/techinfo/howitworks/security/kerbint.asp and continue onward to www.microsoft.com/windows2000/techinfo/planning/security/kerbsteps.asp.

Centralized User Management with Kerberos and LDAP   If you're planning on using LDAP as the repository for the accounts and want a second opinion on how to Kerberize it, a great article is at www.samag.com/documents/s=9494/sam0502a/0502a.htm.

5

Printer Sharing between Windows and Linux

Ah, printers. They're the enterprise's necessary evil. They consume paper, toner, time, and patience. And oftentimes our enterprises have a lot of printers. Maybe it would be better if we had fewer? Or, if not fewer, we could at least get more people printing on the printers we do have.

That's what this chapter is about. That is, you can leverage your existing Linux or Windows printer investment and share it.

Then the fun begins.

As with previous chapters, we'll ensure things are set up and working first by making our Windows clients talk to printers on Windows servers and our Linux clients talk to printers on Linux servers. In Figure 5.1, you can see our intended design. That is, we want to have a Windows 2003 server host a printer and also have our Linux server host a printer. Then, we want to have our Windows and Linux clients be able to print to whichever printer we want.

Leveraging Windows Printers

Setting up a Windows printer has been made easier over the years. In our examples, we'll physically attach a printer to our Windows server. In addition, you might have other options, such as printer that is "networkable" via, say, an HP Jetdirect or similar *print server device*. We can't possibly go over all the potential options out there—there are just too darn many printer manufacturers with their own ways of doing things. However, we'll try to show you how to best prepare for those cases as you consult the manuals for the printers and their accompanying networking devices.

To get started, we'll physically attach our printer to our Windows server's parallel port. Our printer is a Canon BJC-7000.

Setting up a Windows Printer

First things first: Let's tell our server about our new printer. We'll do this in four steps.

1. We'll load the appropriate Windows drivers onto our server machine.

FIGURE 5.1   We will be setting up our Linux Samba server and our Windows 2003 server to share printers and have our Windows and Linux clients print to them.

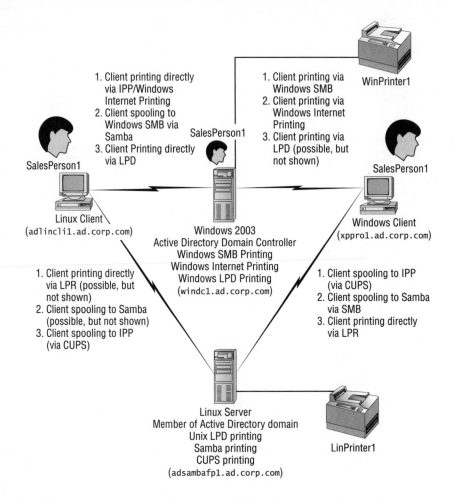

1. Client printing directly via IPP/Windows Internet Printing
2. Client spooling to Windows SMB via Samba
3. Client Printing directly via LPD

1. Client printing via Windows SMB
2. Client printing via Windows Internet Printing
3. Client printing via LPD (possible, but not shown)

WinPrinter1

SalesPerson1

SalesPerson1

SalesPerson1

Linux Client
(adlincli1.ad.corp.com)

Windows Client
(xppro1.ad.corp.com)

Windows 2003
Active Directory Domain Controller
Windows SMB Printing
Windows Internet Printing
Windows LPD Printing
(windc1.ad.corp.com)

1. Client printing directly via LPR (possible, but not shown)
2. Client spooling to Samba (possible, but not shown)
3. Client spooling to IPP (via CUPS)

1. Client spooling to IPP (via CUPS)
2. Client spooling to Samba via SMB
3. Client printing directly via LPR

Linux Server
Member of Active Directory domain
Unix LPD printing
Samba printing
CUPS printing
(adsambafp1.ad.corp.com)

LinPrinter1

2. Then, we'll share the printer so Windows computers and Linux computers running Samba can find it.

3. We'll enable Windows' *Internet Printing*, otherwise known as IPP (Internet Printing Protocol), which will allow for both Windows and Linux clients to simply point to a web address to find the printer.

4. We'll enable "old-school" Unix printing support via the LPD (Line Printer Daemon) protocol.

Loading Windows Printer Drivers

We'll tell Windows to maintain the spooler (which holds jobs in queue as they go to the printer) here on our server, `windc1.ad.corp.com`. But be forewarned, the vocabulary the wizard uses can be a bit misleading. We'll explain this as we go.

To set up a new Windows printer:

1. Select Start ➢ Control Panel ➢ Printers and Faxes ➢ Add Printer to initiate the "Add Printer Wizard." Once the wizard starts, click "Next."

2. At the "Local or Network Printer" dialog select "Local printer attached to this computer." This is because in our examples we have physically attached the printer to the server via parallel port. However, note that you would use this same option to connect to HP Jetdirect or other networkable printer devices because even though those devices are over the network, the spooler (or software that holds the queue for printing) resides on *this* box. This can be confusing because the other option, "A network printer, or a printer attached to another computer" seems very tempting—but don't use it. You'd use that option to print to a printer that was already set up on another server.

3. In the "Local or Network Printer" dialog, you also have the option to "Automatically detect and install my Plug and Play printer." I suggest you leave this check box disabled. In the upcoming dialogs you'll be able to specify which drivers are best suited to use.

4. At the "Select a Printer Port" dialog, select the "Use the following port," select the "LPT1" setting, and click "Next."

5. At the "Install Printer Software" dialog, select the manufacturer and printer model. In our example, we chose "Canon Bubble-Jet BJC-7000." Windows has built-in drivers for this printer. Then click "Next."

6. At the "Name your Printer" screen, you can enter a name for the printer. Clear out the suggested name and enter **WinPrinter1** and click "Next."

7. At the "Printer Sharing" screen, you can give it a share name for others to see. By default, Windows truncates the name so all clients can handle it—including Windows *9x* and all ancient computers. However, we're assuming you have no ancient machines in our pretend world, so go ahead and change the name back to WinPrinter1 and click "Next."

8. At the "Location and Comment" screen enter something that might be appropriate, like **1st floor by the coffee machine**; you might also enter a comment such as who tends to the supplies and other care and feeding. When ready, click "Next."

9. At the "Print Test Page" we always select "Yes." That way, we know Windows actually sees the printer.

Enabling Windows Internet Printing (IPP)

Windows and Linux share a modern, neat way of offering printing services to clients. It's an Internet standard called IPP, or Internet Printing Protocol, and it's documented in the Internet Printing Protocol (IPP) in RFC 2910. The idea is that if you know a web page address (e.g., `http://<something>`), you'll be able to print to the printer. RFC 2910 says that printer traffic will come over port 631 (as opposed to the normal port 80 traffic for http).

Everything in Windows that involves anything http means that Windows IIS needs to be configured. At installation time, we recommended that you install IIS on your Windows server, so you should be ready to go here. If you haven't loaded IIS, you'll have to do that now. Again, IPP is optional but very neat, and we'll be setting it up so our Windows and Linux clients will know the web address of our printers and be able to be off and running.

Here's the trick, though. Windows doesn't call it IPP, they have their own name: Windows Internet Printing. In addition, Microsoft's Windows Internet Printing doesn't use the standard port 631—it uses regular ol' port 80. According to Microsoft, this is because the original RFC didn't specify a port, and that's what Microsoft wrote to. Now the RFC specifies port 631, but Microsoft was already committed to port 80. This really isn't a problem, though it might be nice if Microsoft had an easy-breezy way to make Windows Internet Printing completely support the RFC standard. But they don't. So, as we go along in this journey, we'll tell our Linux clients how to use Windows Internet Printing over port 80 so the Windows server can pick up the traffic, run with it, and start printing.

Let's configure it now.

Installing IIS and Internet Printing (If Not Previously Performed)

The first step in using IPP is to ensure that Windows IIS and the Internet Printing extension is installed. To install IIS (or to check if it's installed):

1. Select Start ≻ Control Panel ≻ Add or Remove Programs.

2. Select "Add / Remove Windows Components."

3. In the list of components, double-click "Web Application Server" and select the "Internet Information Services (IIS)" check box.

4. Double-click the "Internet Information Services (IIS)" entry to see the optional components underneath. Ensure "Internet Printing" is selected, as shown in Figure 5.2.

5. Click "OK" to close the "Internet Information Services (IIS)" screen. Click "OK" to close the "Application Server" screen.

6. Click "Next" to continue at the Windows Components screen.

7. Click "Finish," then close Add/Remove Programs

Verifying Windows Internet Printing Is Installed

You just verified that IIS with the "Internet Printing" option is installed. So, theoretically, Windows Internet Printing is ready to go. However, it's always best to confirm that it's enabled. To confirm Windows Internet Printing is enabled:

1. Select Start ≻ Programs ≻ Administrative Tools ≻ Internet Information Services Manager (IIS).

2. Drill down to Windc1 ≻ Web Services Extensions. Ensure "Internet Printing" is present and has a status of "Allowed."

Setting up IIS to Allow Windows Internet Printing from Linux Clients

By default the only clients who can print via IPP are (who woulda guessed?) Windows clients. If we want Linux clients to be able to print using Windows Internet Printing, we need to open up additional access to "anonymous access."

FIGURE 5.2   Use Add/Remove Programs to install "Internet Printing."

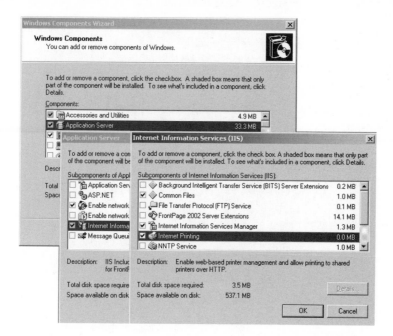

Enabling anonymous printing allows a Linux user to send bazillions of pages of print jobs to any printer hosted by the Windows print server. As it stands now, Windows users can already do this, but you should know what you're getting into.

Allowing access to Anonymous opens up a potential security issue. This is because Anonymous will have read/write access to the spool files.

To do this:

1. In the IIS manager, drill down to WinDC1 ➤ Web Sites ➤ Default Web Site ➤ Printers. Right-click "Printers" and select "Properties."

2. Select the "Directory Security" tab. In the "Authentication and access control" section select "Edit" to open the "Authentication Methods" dialog.

3. In the "Authentication Methods" dialog, select "Enable anonymous access" and ensure "Integrated Windows authentication" is enabled, as shown in Figure 5.3. You can leave everything else the same.

4. Click "OK" to return to the "Printers Properties" dialog.

5. Click "OK" to return to the IIS Manager. Close the IIS Manager.

FIGURE 5.3 You can secure IIS to allow authentication in a number of ways. Here, we suggest you specify only "Integrated Windows authentication."

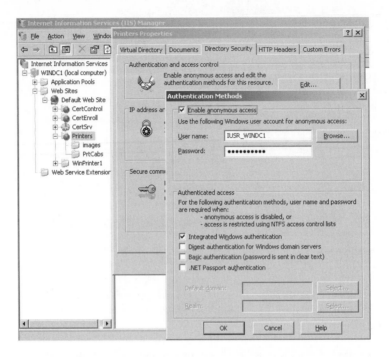

 You can also control access to Internet printers based on the IP address (as opposed to user credentials). To specify which computers can use the printers, in the Printers Properties screen, select "Edit" under "IP address and domain name restrictions."

Preparing for Older Clients

As time marches on, newer and better ways to do things come along. Printing is definitely one of those things that have gotten easer and better over time. However, there might be occasions when you have Windows or Linux clients that are stuck in the stone age. Consequently, you need to configure your server so your older clients can still print. Let's make some adjustments to our Windows servers so our older Windows clients can print. Additionally, we'll set up a service on our Windows server so that older Unix (and Linux) clients can print using an older protocol called LPD.

Preparing for Older Windows Clients

Modern Windows clients need little preparation to start printing with Windows servers right away. However, if you have old and crusty clients such as Windows 9x or Windows NT 4 lying around, it might be in your best interest to enable those computers to automatically download the drivers from this Windows server.

To do that, right-click over the printer definition in the Printers applet in Control Panel and select "Properties." In the "Sharing" tab, select "Additional Drivers" (in the lower right side). Then select the category of driver you want to additionally install, such as Windows NT 4.0. Note that in Figure 5.4, no older client drivers are actually selected.

Once you select the additional drivers, you'll be prompted for the files. This is where the pain can occur. That is, you need to dig up the drivers from either the old NT 4 CD-ROM or download them from a manufacturer's website—or maybe they don't exist at all.

Preparing for Older Unix/Linux Clients

As you're about to see, we'll want our Linux clients to print to Windows servers via modern methods, such as the traditional Windows printing protocol (SMB, the same protocol used for Windows file sharing in Chapter 4) or the newer Windows Internet Printing.

However, the original old-school way to print from Unix to Unix was via a client-side program called Line Printer Request, or "LPR," which sent data to a Unix server running "LPD" or Line Printer Daemon. This method is falling by the wayside but is still in heavy use, especially on legacy systems. To that end, Windows can pretend to run LPD. That way, older Unix and Linux clients that don't want to (or cannot) print via one of the new-school ways can still interoperate and print.

FIGURE 5.4   If desired, you can add automatic downloading driver support for older Windows clients.

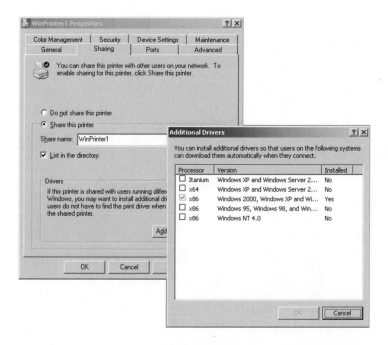

So we'll teach Windows to run the LPD (via a service called "Print Services for Unix") so an older Unix or Linux machine needn't change in any way to print to Windows. Again, this isn't the preferred method—it's here for completeness. Additionally, the "Print Services for Unix" are not part of the Services for Unix 3.5 we loaded in earlier chapters. "Print Services for Unix" are just a regular, built-in part of Windows 2003 and Windows XP.

To enable Print Services for Unix:

1. Select Start ➤ Control Panel ➤ Add or Remove Programs.

2. Select "Add / Remove Windows Components."

3. In the list of components, double-click "Other Network File and Print Services" and select the "Print Services for Unix," as shown in Figure 5.5.

4. Click "OK" to return to the Windows Components screen and click "Next" to continue.

5. Click "Finish" when finished.

Performing Printing Tests

Now that our Windows server is all set up to accept print jobs from Windows and Linux clients, let's do some testing.

FIGURE 5.5   "Print Services for Unix" is built into Windows 2003 and Windows XP and enables LPD printing.

Printing from Windows Clients

There are several ways you can locate printers from a Windows client:

Using Active Directory   We'll be exploring this option later, but here's the short story. Once SMB printers are available (either from Windows or Linux Samba), they can be "published" in Active Directory. Then our Active Directory–aware clients can easily find them, connect to them, and print to them.

Using Network Neighborhood to browse   You can, if you like, browse for SMB printers using Network Neighborhood. Just browse, browse, browse, find the printer and double-click it to load the drivers. You'll get a chance to do this later.

Using \\\servername\printername   We'll explore this in this chapter. That is, we'll just enter the name of the server and the printer and, voilà! We'll be printing in no time.

Using Windows Internet Printing   This method of printing allows us to take advantage of the new Windows Internet Printing we just set up. We can point our Windows clients to the printer using only a web-browser. We'll also explore this in this chapter.

Using \\\servername\printername

The most common way to connect to a Windows printer is by opening the "Printers and Faxes" applet in Control Panel and selecting "Add a printer" to start the "Add Printer Wizard."

At the "Local or Network Printer" screen, you'll be able to select "A network printer, or a printer attached to another computer." You'll then have the option to "Connect to this printer (or to browse for a printer, select this option and click Next)," as shown in Figure 5.6. Either type the name of the printer (**\\\windc1\WinPrinter1**   ), or leave it blank and click "Next" and browse for the printer.

Note that browsing for the printer is different from searching for the printer. Browsing relies on Windows' Browser service. Searching, as we'll perform at the end of the chapter, relies on records within Active Directory that we can search for.

When ready, enter the name of the server and printer as shown in Figure 5.6 and click "Next." You will be asked if you want to make this the default printer. Click "Next" to say yes, then click "Finish" to close the wizard.

NOTE   At the "Local or Network Printer" screen, instead of selecting a network printer you can browse for a printer. To do this, select the option "Connect to this printer" option and click "Next"—but note that browsing for the printer is different from searching for the printer. Browsing relies on Windows' Browser service. Searching, as we'll perform at the end of the chapter, relies on records within Active Directory that we can search for.

Using Windows Internet Printing

Another way to connect to the printer on WinDC1 is to use the Windows Internet Printing we set up earlier. To connect to a printer from an XP client:

1.   Fire up Internet Explorer.

FIGURE 5.6 You can enter the SMB name of the printer in the "Add Printer Wizard."

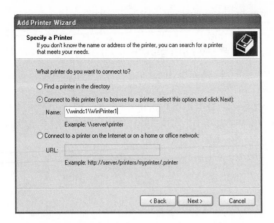

2. Enter the address in the form of **http:// *<server_name>*/printers**, such as **http://windc1/printers**. A list of shared printers on the server appears.

3. Click the name of the printer. You'll see several possible "Printer Actions." Select "Connect to this printer," as shown in Figure 5.6, and you'll be prompted to add the printer as shown in Figure 5.7.

 You already installed the printer in the previous step, so re-installing it here won't have any effect.

You can now try to send a test print to the printer!

FIGURE 5.7 Windows Internet Printing offers an easy way to connect to printers.

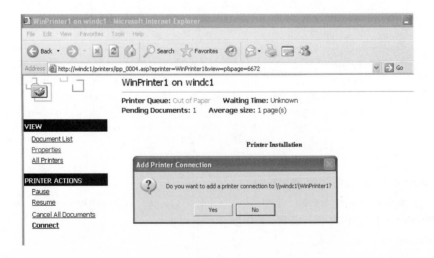

Printing to Windows Servers from Linux Clients

Of course, Windows to Windows printing should "just work." The fun part starts when Linux clients try to print to Windows server. There are three ways they can do this:

Printing via LPD   Linux can talk old school to Windows (which is happy to talk old school, too).

Printing via SMB   Linux can send native SMB printing requests to Windows machines—just like the majority of Windows clients do.

Printing via Internet Printing (IPP)   Since we just set up Windows Internet Printing, it might be nice to use it. Again, note that Windows uses port 80 (where the RFC specifies port 631), so we have to tell our Linux clients to *use* port 80 and not 631.

Linux Clients Printing to Windows LPD

As stated, the old-fashioned way to print on Unix is called LPD. It's still well supported by modern Linux distributions. When you have a modern Linux client *and* a modern Windows server, you're not likely to use it because you have the (better) options of using IPP and/or SMB printing. However, for completeness, let's ensure that our Windows can embrace Linux printer jobs and utilize LPD.

We'll configure our Linux client (which is a member of our Active Directory), `adlincli1`, to print via LPD. Rather than Webmin, we'll use Fedora's standard printer configuration tool, which does a good job. Indeed, the Printer Queue Setup Wizard is quite friendly to work with. In general, the standard Fedora tools work well enough for client tasks, so we chose not to install Webmin on our clients.

In the Unix world, historically everything was printed in a common lingua franca known as the Postscript language, and the old-school Unix-to-Unix way of printing would be to just choose a generic Postscript driver. This clever technique sidesteps the worry about specific printer drivers on every Unix client system; we'll further explore this curiosity later.

However, in *this* case, we need to tell our Linux client about the proper printer driver we need because our target machine is a Windows print server. We'll select the BJC-7000 specifically (when we come to that step). To configure our Linux client machine to print a Windows LPD server:

1. From the "Applications" menu, drill down to System Settings ➢ Printing. Wait for the "Printer configuration" tool to appear.

2. Click the "New" button to add a new print queue.

3. Click "Forward" on the explanatory page that follows.

4. On the "Queue name" page, enter **WinPrinter1ViaLPD**   in the "Name" field. In the "Short description" field, enter **Windows Printer One Via LPD**   or another descriptive name that you like. Click "Forward."

5. On the "Queue type" page, pull down the "Select a queue type" menu and pick "Networked Unix (LPD)," as shown in Figure 5.8.

6. The "Server" and "Queue" fields appear. Enter **windc1** in the "Server" field and **WinPrinter1**   in the "Queue" field. Click "Forward."

7. On the "Printer model" page, pull down the "Manufacturer" menu and pick "Canon." Then scroll through the list of models and pick "BJC 7000." Click "Forward."

8. The "Finish, and Create the New Print Queue" page appears. Click "Finished."

9. When asked whether you wish to print a test page, click the "Yes" button. A test page will emerge from your printer after a short delay.

For a more interesting test, we also suggest launching OpenOffice Writer from the "Office" section of the "Applications" menu. Create a simple document and pick "Print" from the "File" menu. Be sure to select "WinPrinter1ViaLPD" as the printer to use, then click "Print" in the "Print" dialog to send your test document to the Windows-hosted printer.

FIGURE 5.8   Once your Windows server has LPD set up, you can choose LPD printing as an option.

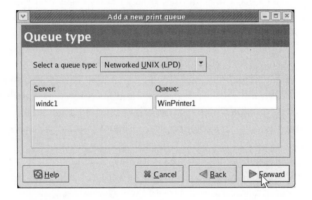

Linux Clients Printing via Samba to Windows SMB

Linux can also handle printing to native Windows SMB printer shares, thanks to Samba. The process is just as smooth as the just-demonstrated LPD (and quite similar), though there is one snag.

You'll choose this option when you have control over your Linux clients but can't change (or don't want to change) much on the Windows server. In cases like these, printing directly to Windows via Linux SMB printing support is ideal.

When you have the option of setting up Windows Internet Printing on the Windows server, the case for SMB isn't quite as strong. Given a choice between the two, Windows Internet Printing is probably the easiest way to go. That's because IPP is an open standard; the rules aren't likely to change.

Since SMB is not a fully open and documented standard, there's always a chance that a new version or service pack of Windows will exercise features the Samba team hasn't seen before. That makes SMB printing a moving target, which can lead to temporary but annoying problems for Samba file sharing and printing. In addition, in our tests we had difficulty printing test pages from the Fedora printer configuration tool, although printing from actual applications worked fine. True, SMB printer sharing offers the ability to install drivers automatically, but those drivers are for Windows only, so they don't help your Linux clients support new printers. Active Directory does offer a searchable database of printers, but as of this writing, Fedora's printer configuration tool doesn't support searching it. Given these facts, we think your best choice is to set up Windows Internet Printing. However, when you can't, SMB printing from Linux is a fine alternative.

Setting up `adlincli1` to print via SMB isn't difficult. Once again, we'll use Fedora's standard printer configuration tool. The Printer Queue Setup Wizard works fine for SMB printing, except for a problem we observed in our tests of the "print a test page" feature.

1. Pull down the "Applications" menu and drill down to System Settings ➢ Printing. Wait for the printer configuration tool to come up.

2. Click the "New" button to add a new print queue.

3. Click "Forward" on the following page.

4. On the "Queue name" page, enter **WinPrinter1ViaSMB** in the "Name" field. In the "Short description" field, enter **Windows Printer One Via SMB** or another descriptive name that you like. Click "Forward."

5. On the "Queue type" page, pull down the "Select a queue type" menu and pick "Networked Windows (SMB)."

6. A list of shares appears. If the server you want appears, great—click the arrow to the left of it to display a list of shares and double-click the shared printer you want. The "Authentication" dialog should appear with the "Workgroup," "Server" and "Share" fields already filled in. If it does not, as in our tests, click the "Specify" button.

7. If not already done, set the "Workgroup" field to **AD**, as shown in Figure 5.9.

8. If not already done, set the "Server" field to **WinDC1**.

9. If not already done, set the "Share" field to **WinPrinter1**.

10. Set the "User name" field to **administrator**.

11. Set the "Password" field to **p@ssw0rd**

FIGURE 5.9   Select your Windows queue and then enter your Active Directory credentials.

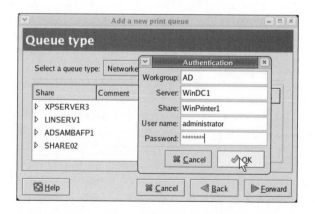

For the record, Windows applications that provide SMB print services are kerberized. That means, theoretically, you shouldn't have to enter your username and password when printing from Windows clients to Windows servers. However, the Linux client GUI isn't quite there yet with kerberization. So, when printing from Linux to Windows clients, you will likely still need to enter your credentials. See Chapter 4 for more information about kerberization.

12. Click "OK" to dismiss the "Authentication" dialog.

13. Note that `WinDC1` is added to the list of servers if it was not previously detected. Make sure "WinPrinter1 (Specified)" is selected beneath it.

14. Click "Forward."

15. On the "Printer model" page, pull down the "Manufacturer" menu and pick "Canon." Then scroll through the list of models and pick "BJC 7000." Click "Forward."

16. The "Finish, and Create the New Print Queue" page appears. Click "Finished."

17. When asked whether you wish to print a test page, you may click the "Yes" button. However, in our tests, this did not produce a successful test page—but actual printing from applications worked just fine.

For a more meaningful test, especially if the test page feature does not work for you, we suggest launching OpenOffice Writer from the "Office" section of the "Applications" menu. As in the previous example, create a simple document and pick "Print" from the "File" menu. Be sure to select "WinPrinter1ViaSMB" as the printer to use, then click "Print" in the "Print" dialog to send your test document to the Windows-hosted printer.

Linux Clients Printing via IPP to Windows Internet Printing

Leveraging Windows Internet Printing is the best bet for supporting Linux clients printing to Windows servers because Windows Internet Printing is compatible with the Internet Printing Protocol (IPP), an open standard. Again, however, it should be noted that the genuine RFC 2910 standard clearly states that the printing traffic is required (in big ALL CAP letters) to utilize port 631, whereas Windows Internet Printing only supports port 80 by default. To be fair, it is possible to add an additional virtual "website" listening on port 631 to your IIS configuration, but this ought to happen right out of the box when IPP is installed. We'll continue configuring `adlincli1` and have it print to our Windows servers via IPP/Windows Internet Printing.

Windows Internet Printing printers don't advertise their existence in a way that makes it easy for Fedora clients to browse them. By contrast, you'll see later that when we set up printers on Fedora that Fedora goes the extra mile and broadcasts their existence. This allows for users on Fedora to more easily find Fedora printers. Windows clients can browse or search for Windows Internet Printing printers if they are published in Active Directory, but this doesn't currently help Fedora clients.

So Fedora clients won't be able to just "find" Windows printers via Windows Internet Printing. We need to manually type the path and server where the printer is located the first time we use such a printer. And, since Windows Internet Printing normally responds on port 80 while Fedora's expectation is to deliver on port 631, we'll need to properly instruct the client about the required port change.

Let's jump right to the end of this little story by taking a look at the dialog box we'll enter our printer information into, as shown in Figure 5.10. (Don't worry, we'll describe all the step-by-steps in a second.)

FIGURE 5.10   Printing to a Windows server with Windows Internet Printing requires you to specifically enter the port number (80) and the printer path.

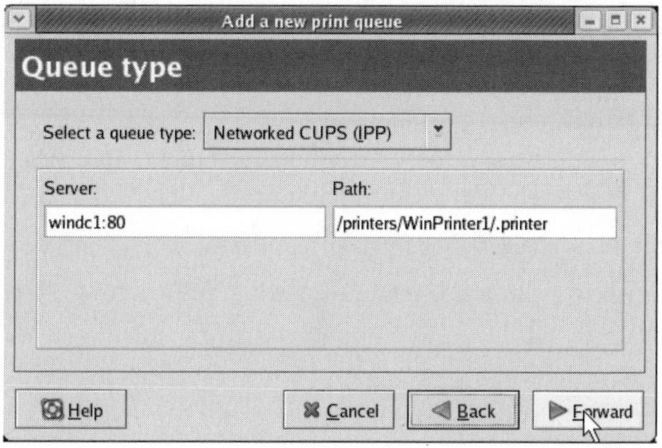

To talk to a Windows Internet Printing server, we need to know three pieces of information:

Server   The "Server" field will always look like this

```
servername:80
```

In our example, the server name is WinDC1, so the correct setting is:

```
WinDC1:80
```

Path   The "Path" field will always look like this:

```
/printers/printername/.printer
```

In our example, the printer name is WinPrinter1, so the correct setting is:

```
/printers/WinPrinter1/.printer
```

The `/printers/` prefix is necessary because Windows Internet Printing is delivered by the web server, which may have other uses. So printers don't belong in the top folder. The `/.printer` suffix is a common convention and mandatory when using Windows Internet Printing.

Now we know enough to set up our Fedora system as a client of Windows Internet Printing. To have our Linux client print to Windows via IPP:

1. Pull down the "Applications" menu and drill down to System Settings ➢ Printing. Wait for the "Printer configuration" tool to appear.

2. Click the "New" button to add a new print queue.

3. Click "Forward" on the explanatory page that follows.

4. On the "Queue name" page, enter **WinPrinter1ViaIPP** in the "Name" field. In the "Short description" field, enter **Windows Printer One Via IPP** or another descriptive name that you like. Click "Forward."

5. On the "Queue type" page, pull down the "Select a queue type" menu and pick "Networked Unix (CUPS)."

6. The "Server" and "Queue" fields appear. Enter **WinDC1:80** in the "Server" field (note that we specify port 80). Enter **/printers/WinPrinter1/.printer** in the "Path" field (see Figure 5.10). Click "Forward."

7. On the "Printer model" page, pull down the "Manufacturer" menu and pick "Canon." Then scroll through the list of models and pick "BJC 7000." Click "Forward."

8. The "Finish, and Create the New Print Queue" page appears. Click "Finished."

9. When asked whether you wish to print a test page, click the "Yes" button. A test page will emerge after a short delay.

As in the previous scenarios, we also suggest using OpenOffice Writer to carry out a more interesting test. Be sure to select "WinPrinter1ViaIPP" as the printer to use.

Leveraging Linux Printers

The LPD (Line Printer Daemon protocol) and the associated `lpr` command formed the core of the Linux print spooling system for many years. Even today, the `lpr` command and the LPD remote printing protocol are still available as part of the modern Linux/Unix printing system.

This more modern system is called CUPS (Common Unix Printing System). CUPS is implemented by the `cupsd` daemon, and it also speaks the more modern IPP protocol (Internet Printing Protocol). To understand how Linux printing works today, it is necessary to understand a few things about the history of printing on Linux and Unix systems.

Understanding Linux Printing

For many years Unix printing facilities were heavily oriented toward plain-text, 80-column printing. Later, Adobe's Postscript language became the standard Unix answer to the question of attractively formatted printing. Those who wanted to print attractive documents in a portable way were advised to purchase a Postscript printer with a built-in interpreter for the Postscript language. The popularity of Postscript printers for use with Macintoshes made this a reasonable choice, and Unix systems were generally high-end workstations, so the higher price of Postscript printers was not an issue.

At the time when Postscript printers were most popular, placing the smarts to interpret the Postscript language in the printer made sense because Postscript is a high-level, human-readable language that can describe a page in a very sophisticated way. Ten years ago, translating that language into dots on a page required a large percentage of any computer's resources.

Printing to Network Print Servers

Of course, in today's office environment and even in the home, printers are not always connected directly to a Linux or Windows server. Instead, printers are often connected directly to the network via a device called a dedicated print server. The sole function of a dedicated print server is to accept a stream of printer commands from print clients and to communicate those commands to the attached printer.

However, even though a printer has a dedicated print server, it still needs support from a general purpose computer running Windows or Linux to provide temporary print job storage and to host additional management features too complex to store in the limited memory of the network print device.

Printing to a dedicated print server from Windows is generally straightforward because manufacturers provide Microsoft with drivers for their network print devices along with drivers for their printers. But what about Linux?

IPP-Compatible Print Servers

As it turns out, most print server manufacturers today support IPP in their latest products, and they support it in just the way Fedora Linux expects: on port 631. That means that we can add a queue for such a printer using the "Networked Unix (CUPS)" queue type in Fedora's printer configuration tool. Not all such boxes advertise themselves on the local network, so you will usually need to enter the print server's IP address and a printer path. Windows users also need to do this using the Internet Printing feature of the Add Printer Wizard. The exact server IP and printer path information to use is readily available in the documentation of each print server. Standalone print servers offer a web-based configuration interface, which can be operated with equal ease from Linux- and Windows-based web browsers.

Examples of IPP-compatible print servers on the market as of this writing include the Linksys WPS54GU2, which offers a wireless network interface and support for both parallel and USB printers. Another similar unit is the Netgear PS101NA, a less expensive device with a wired Ethernet interface and a parallel printer port.

HP Jetdirect Print Servers

One type of dedicated print server requires special mention, the Hewlett-Packard Jetdirect printer server. It's possible to print to newer Jetdirect print servers using IPP, but you can also print from Linux to a Jetdirect print server using HP's own Jetdirect protocol.

Newer models of Jetdirect printer servers offer a browser-based configuration interface that can be accessed from any operating system. Once the printer server has been configured, you can click the "New" button in the Fedora printer configuration tool and select the "Networked Jetdirect" queue type on the first page of the wizard. When prompted, enter the IP address of the Jetdirect box in the "Printer" field and leave the port number set to 9100 to talk to a standard Jetdirect box. The rest of the steps are identical to those for a local printer.

Of course, not all printers understood Postscript even at the height of its popularity. Cheaper printers in general rarely had Postscript interpreters built in. These printers instead "spoke" much simpler languages like HP's PCL (Printer Command Language) or Epson's ESCP2 (named for the escape sequence of characters that enabled it). These languages were interpreted at the host computer so that only control characters were sent to the printer itself. Using these printers on a Linux system required an open-source page rendering solution.

Matters grew worse with the introduction of Winprinters, which were (and sometimes still are) printers that, to save a few pennies, do not offer even the rudimentary smarts to handle a language like PCL or ESCP2. Instead, the computer to which they are attached is required to micromanage printing, right down to the precisely timed transmission of rows of pixels. The specifications for these printers were rarely made available to open source developers. Generally speaking, no one much cared for Winprinters because they put considerable and largely unnecessary demands on the host computer. They also couldn't be easily moved to computers running alternative operating systems.

Today, computers have CPU and memory to spare, and an open-source Postscript interpreter, called Ghostscript, is a standard part of every Fedora Linux system. Ghostscript supports many different printer languages on the back end, including hundreds of printers that do not speak Postscript natively (and even quite a few Winprinters!). Ghostscript accepts Postscript as input and renders a bitmap of the actual pages. Then it feeds the results to the printer in its native control language. If Ghostscript supports your printer, or it speaks Postscript natively, then you can attach that printer to a Linux system.

Why Linux Printing and Windows Printing Are Different

All Windows applications use a single interface to the operating system to create graphics called the *GDI (Graphics Device Interface)*. GDI draws stuff on the screen, and it's also what's used to help stuff get printed on the page.

While it's true that there can be differences between printer drivers and on-screen graphics drivers, in a general sense Windows programmers can write one set of code both for the screen and the printer.

Because Windows is so popular, it wasn't difficult for Microsoft to convince printer manufacturers to create GDI printer drivers. Even Postscript printers have GDI drivers, which translate GDI API requests to Postscript commands. We'll take advantage of that fact later, when we wish to print from Windows clients to Linux servers *without* the need for a printer-specific print driver on each Windows client.

On the Linux side, the situation is different. Linux applications draw to the *screen* using the X Window System or libraries, like GNOME's gtk library, which are built on top of it.

However, the X Window System was not originally intended for printing (although some support for printing was added very recently). Linux and other Unix systems use Adobe's Postscript printer language for printing tasks. Applications, or the development libraries they rely on, must provide separate code for on-screen graphics and Postscript printer graphics. That's why Postscript-compatible printers, as well as the free Ghostscript interpreter software that permits non-Postscript printers to handle Postscript, hold such key roles in Linux printing.

Linux-Compatible (and Not-So-Compatible) Printers

Does this mean that every printer works with Linux? Well, no. Some Winprinters continue to provide only a proprietary and undocumented interface. Since their manufacturers will not release information to the Ghostscript developers, nothing can be done to support those printers.

The good news is that virtually all "business-class" printers (such as most modern laser printers) work well with Linux. In addition, certain printer manufacturers have been particularly generous in their support of Linux. Thanks to HP's thorough and detailed support, virtually all of HP's printers are highly Linux-compatible, even including home-oriented multifunction inkjet models such as the HP PSC 2175. HP provides a driver called `hpijs` that does the back-end work to make this possible, and `hpijs` is a standard part of Fedora Linux.

Epson has made a similar effort, and most current Epson printers are also highly Linux-compatible via Epson's gnome-print driver. And although most of the low-end inkjet Lexmark printers are not particularly Linux-friendly, Lexmark's business-class laser printers are thoroughly supported.

Of course, we need more precise information to decide whether a specific printer is suitable for Linux. How can we most easily sort out the compatible printers from the rest? The website `www.linuxprinting.org` offers both a compatibility database and a list of recommended printers for Linux at:

`www.linuxprinting.org/printer_list.cgi`

If you're shopping for a new printer specifically for your Linux system, compatibility should be your first consideration. You can find Linux printer recommendations at:

`www.linuxprinting.org/suggested.html`

How Linux Printing Works Today

Nearly all modern Linux applications generate Postscript code when asked to print a document. Sometimes they do this directly, other times via printing APIs supported by gtk or KDE's Qt library. The Postscript code is then sent to CUPS, often via the `lpr` command. If the printer does not reside on the same computer, the Postscript code is delivered to the print server via IPP.

CUPS maintains a queue of print jobs for each printer. This way, the application can continue operating in the foreground while printing tasks are carried out in the background. In the background, CUPS then launches a printer driver.

Printer drivers consist of a .ppd file and, if the printer does not natively speak Postscript, a filter program as well. The filter program is usually a simple wrapper shell script that launches Ghostscript with appropriate parameters for the printer. The filter program is responsible for translating Postscript (or occasionally simple plaintext) input to the native language of the printer. Finally, this raw printer-friendly data is fed to the printer by CUPS, either via the USB port or an old-fashioned parallel port interface. See Figure 5.11 for a diagram of the Linux printing architecture.

FIGURE 5.11 The Linux printing architecture

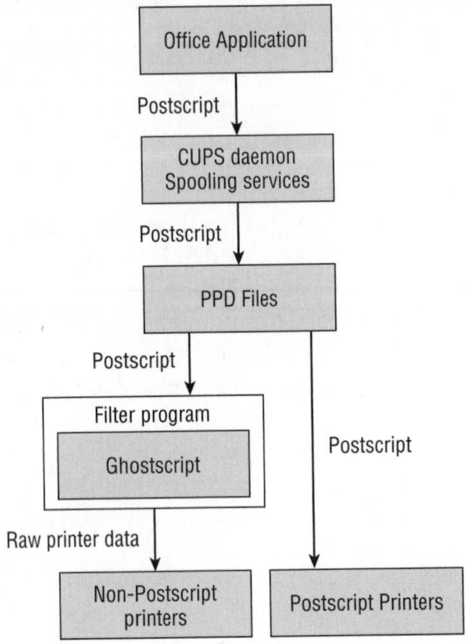

Printing from Windows: Postscript vs. Native Drivers

Figure 5.11 shows how Linux printing works in a pure Linux environment. But Linux can also accept print jobs from Windows clients. Windows print jobs can arrive via LPD, IPP, or SMB. LPD and IPP are natively supported by CUPS with no additional configuration. SMB is supported by Samba, which passes all printing requests through to CUPS.

Individual Windows clients have printer drivers that output the native language of the printer, or an intermediate, Windows-specific language that is more compact for transmission over the network. Windows print servers then interpret the intermediate language and pass the result to the printer. So what happens when Windows clients talk to Linux print servers? There are two ways to approach the problem.

Postscript Printing from Windows to Linux

A Windows client can print to a Linux server using a Postscript driver, just as a Linux client would. This means that you can load any ol' Postscript printer driver on all your Windows systems (like an Apple Color LaserWriter 12/600), instead of the "real" printer model name and number...and you're off to the races. This assumes that your printer has similar physical capabilities to the Postscript printer the driver is intended for, especially the same paper size.

We'll do this later in several steps and talk more about the process as we do it. However, the best news is that once one Windows client system is all set up, we can automatically tell our

Linux server what to tell new Windows clients when *they* want to print. In other words, other clients will pick up the printer type information saved on the server and avoid even the need to pick a driver.

Additionally, you might have some old-and-crusty printer that doesn't have proper "networking" drivers available. If the printer is supported by Ghostscript, then the printer can *always* be shared over the network. For instance, you could take that $50 low-end inkjet printer and get it on your network. That's cool.

Raw Printing from Windows to Linux

Using a Postscript driver does have one disadvantage. Sometimes printer drivers offer special features, like specifying the printer resolution or how much ink is available in the ink well or stapling options. Those features can't usually be supported if we use the Postscript approach.

When these features are essential for our application, we need to use the correct native Windows printer driver. To do that reliably with a Linux print server, we've found it is best to create a separate *raw* printer queue with the Fedora printer configuration tool. Creating a raw queue, instead of a queue for a specific model of printer, tells CUPS not to try to interpret the data it receives from the client in any way. Instead of trying to determine whether the data is Postscript code, CUPS will pass it directly to the printer without modification. In this chapter, we'll demonstrate the raw queue approach with SMB, but bear in mind that we could also use it with IPP or LPD.

Understanding Linux Printer Device Names

Last but not least, before we start configuring printer queues on a Linux server, you should understand how physical printer devices are labeled in Linux. Since we're using a parallel printer that is not automatically detected by Fedora Linux, we'll need to tell Fedora to which port we've connected it. Windows calls the first parallel printer port LPT1, the second port LPT2, and so on.

Linux calls these devices /dev/lp0, /dev/lp1, and so forth. Just remember that the Linux printer device names start from zero, not from one, and you'll be in great shape.

As for USB, Fedora Linux can automatically detect quite a few USB printers when they are connected. For instance, Fedora Core 3 automatically detects an HP PSC 2175 printer and offers to create a queue for it. However, it is sometimes useful to add a second queue for the same printer. In fact, we need this capability to support both a raw queue for Windows clients with native drivers and a Postscript queue for Linux clients, so it does help to be able to recognize a USB printer device name when you see one in the printer configuration tool.

USB printer devices are called /dev/usb/lp0, /dev/usb/lp1, and so forth. And because USB devices can identify themselves by name, the printer configuration tool will also display the model name to the right of the device name.

Setting up a Linux Printer

Now that you know what's going on "under the hood" and why, we're ready to start printing via a Linux server. We'll begin by attaching a printer to our Linux domain member server, `adsambafp1.ad.corp.com` (refer back to Figure 5.1).

Here are the short-term goals for this section:

- We'll configure CUPS and Samba to support IPP, LPD, and SMB (Windows) printing on two queues, one a typical CUPS queue expecting Postscript, the other a raw queue intended for use with Windows clients.

- We'll demonstrate Linux-to-Linux printing via IPP over the Postscript-friendly queue.

- Finally, we'll "go for the gold" and demonstrate Windows-to-Linux printing by all three methods. Here, we'll show how to use both the Postscript-based queue and the raw printer queue. For those interested in the raw approach, we'll also look at how to support Windows click-and-print automatic downloading of printer drivers via SMB with Samba, and we'll show how to publish Samba SMB printers in Active Directory.

First, we'll physically attach our printer to our Linux server's parallel port. However, unlike in our Windows examples, the printer we'll use is a Canon i560. We use this printer because we want to demonstrate click-and-print driver downloading. Since the driver for the BJC-7000 printer we used earlier is standard in Windows XP, there is nothing to download, so the i560 is a much better demonstration of that feature.

However, Fedora Linux doesn't ship with a driver specifically for the Canon i560, so how will we support it on the Linux side in the CUPS-and-Postscript case? The answer is that the Canon i560 is backward compatible with the Canon BJC-7000, so we'll use the BJC-7000 driver on Linux. However, on the Windows side, when we're ready to demonstrate SMB printing with a native printer driver and a raw queue, we'll use the "real" i560 driver to create an interesting test case for automatic driver downloading.

Now we need to tell the server about the printer we've attached to it. We'll also need to deal with the sharing issues just mentioned. We'll do this in three main steps:

1. We'll use the Fedora printer configuration tool to add a new queue, or *spool*, for the printer we've just connected. We'll tell Fedora that the printer is connected to the local parallel port, /dev/lp0, and we'll configure this queue to translate Postscript print jobs to the printer's native language. At the same time, we'll enable sharing of the printer via IPP and LPD. Later, we'll demonstrate IPP with both Windows and Linux clients and LPD with a Windows client.

2. We'll add an additional raw spool that accepts raw printer data and forwards it directly to the printer. We'll configure Samba to offer SMB printing via this raw spool; we'll do this using Webmin. Later, we'll demonstrate how to use this printer share with a Windows client.

3. We'll configure the Linux server to support click-and-print driver downloading. Later, we'll demonstrate that capability with two Windows clients: one to upload the driver for the first time and another to show that driver downloading works.

Adding a Postscript Spool for Our Printer

To add and share a new spool for the Canon i560 printer that accepts Postscript print jobs, just follow these steps. Bear in mind that we must use the older (but compatible) Canon BJC-7000 driver. That's because no driver specifically for the Canon i560 is included with Fedora or available on www.linuxprinting.org as of this writing.

 What if we needed to use a printer that wasn't supported by Fedora? We'd check www.linuxprinting.org for an appropriate driver. www.linuxprinting.org offers PPD files for many printers. These can then be imported into the CUPS printing system using the "Import PPD" option on the "Actions" menu of the Fedora printer configuration tool.

1. Pull down the "Applications" menu and drill down to System Settings ➤ Printing. Wait for the printer configuration tool to appear.

2. Click the "New" button to add a new print queue.

3. Click "Forward" on the explanatory page that follows.

4. On the "Queue name" page, enter **LinPrinter1**   in the "Name" field. In the "Short description" field, enter **Linux Printer One**   or another descriptive name that you like. Click "Forward."

5. On the "Queue type" page, pull down the "Select a queue type" menu and pick "Locally-connected" as shown in Figure 5.12.

6. In the list box beneath that menu, select "/dev/lp0." Then click "Forward."

7. On the "Printer model" page, pull down the "Manufacturer" menu and pick "Canon." Then scroll through the list of models and pick "BJC 7000." Click "Forward."

8. The "Finish, and Create the New Print Queue" page appears. Click "Finished."

9. When asked whether you wish to print a test page, click the "Yes" button. A test page will emerge after a short delay.

10. Leave the printer configuration tool on the screen in order to continue with the next section.

Adding a Raw Spool for Our Printer

The spool we just created is useful for Linux clients, as well as for Windows clients using Postscript printer drivers. However, sometimes we want to use special features of a native Windows printer driver. Here are the steps to create a raw spool that accepts print jobs from Windows clients using the native Canon i560 printer driver:

1. Pull down the "Applications" menu and drill down to System Settings ➤ Printing. Wait for the printer configuration tool to appear.

2. Click the "New" button to add a new print queue.

3. Click "Forward" on the explanatory page that follows.

FIGURE 5.12 Adding a local printer to a Linux server

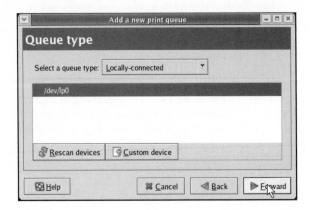

4. On the "Queue name" page, enter **LinPrinter1Raw** in the "Name" field. In the "Short description" field, enter **Linux Printer One Raw Spool** or another descriptive name that you like. Click "Forward."

5. On the "Queue type" page, pull down the "Select a queue type" menu and pick "Locally-connected."

6. In the list box beneath that menu, select "/dev/lp0." Then click "Forward."

7. On the "Printer model" page, pull down the "Manufacturer" menu and pick "Generic." Then scroll through the list of generic printer types and print "Raw Queue." Click "Forward."

8. The "Finish, and Create the New Print Queue" page appears. Click "Finished."

9. When asked whether you wish to print a test page, click the "Yes" button. A test page will emerge after a short delay.

10. Leave the printer configuration tool on the screen in order to continue with the next section.

Sharing Printers via IPP and LPD with CUPS

The Common Unix Printing System (CUPS) is now aware of the printer and ready to accept jobs for it in two formats, raw and Postscript. Now, it's time to share the printer via IPP. We will also lock this printer down so only specific client computers can print to it. We will choose to only allow local computers to print to this printer.

Lastly, we'll enable old-fashioned LPD printing as well, just in case we have some old Unix machine that needs to print.

To configure our Linux server to enable printing via IPP and LPD:

1. Pull down the "Applications" menu and drill down to System Settings ➢ Printing. Wait for the printer configuration tool to appear.

2. Make sure "LinPrinter1" is selected in the list of printer queues in the printer configuration tool's main window.

3. Pull down the "Action" menu and pick "Sharing".

4. The "Sharing Properties" dialog appears. Make sure the "Queue" tab is selected. Check the box labeled "This queue is available to other computers." This enables IPP printer sharing.

5. To lock the printer down so that only certain client computers can print to it, select the "Allowed Hosts" list box and make sure "All Hosts" is selected. Then click "Remove," followed by "Add" to display the "Add allowed hosts" dialog.

6. Click the "Network Address" radio button.

7. Now we'll specify the local network address to prohibit computers on other networks from printing to this printer. In the first field beneath "Network Address," enter **192.168.2.0** . This is the network address that is allowed to access the printer.

8. In the second field, to the right of the first, enter **255.255.255.0** . This is the network mask. A zero for the last byte means that clients with addresses beginning with 192.168.2 and ending with any byte are allowed to print.

9. Click "OK."

10. Click the "General" tab.

11. Click the radio box labeled "Enable LPD protocol."

12. Click "OK."

13. Choose "Quit" from the "Action" menu or just click the "X" button in the upper-right corner to close the printer configuration tool.

14. When the message "Do you want to save the changes you have made to your printer configuration?" appears, be sure to click "Save."

15. Repeat steps 1–14 for LinPrinter1Raw. Be sure to select "LinPrinter1Raw" rather than "LinPrinter1" when repeating step 2.

Sharing Printers via SMB with Samba

Now that the Fedora printer configuration tool has configured CUPS to drive the printer, we'll add support for native Windows SMB printing via LinPrinter1Raw. Samba takes care of this chore for us, and Webmin provides a friendly way to set it up. Samba makes it especially easy by allowing us to set up a special "all printers" share that is automatically understood to mean "share all of the connected printers in the same way."

Why do we share *both* of the print spools? Isn't LinPrinter1Raw the only appropriate spool for Windows clients? Well, no. We *can* use a Postscript queue with Windows SMB clients if we want to. All we have to do is choose a Postscript printer driver instead of the Canon i560 driver on the client side. In this chapter, though, we'll use Postscript drivers for LPD and IPP printing and the native Canon i560 driver for SMB printing. Just bear in mind that you're not required to do it that way.

Samba needs a *spool directory* to store print jobs in. Conveniently, Fedora ships Samba with a ready-made directory for this purpose: `/var/spool/samba`. We'll just specify this directory when prompted for the spool directory.

Follow these steps to complete the process:

1. Log into Webmin with the username `root` and the password `p@ssw0rd` at the URL: `https://adsambafp1.ad.corp.com:10000/`.

2. Click "Servers."

3. Click "Samba Windows File Sharing."

4. On the "Samba Windows File Sharing" page, click "Create a new printer share."

5. On the "Create Printer Share" page, select "All Printers Share."

6. Leave the "Unix Printer" menu set to "Default."

7. Set "Spool Directory" to `/var/spool/samba`

8. Set "Available" to "Yes."

9. Set "Browseable" to "Yes."

10. Set "Share Comment" to "All Printers."

11. Click "Save."

LinPrinter1, LinPrinter1Raw, and any other printer queues you add to the server are now set up to be automatically shared via SMB so that Windows clients can use them in a familiar way. But before we demonstrate that, we'll improve matters even more by adding support for click-and-print printer driver uploading and downloading.

Setting up Samba to Enable Windows Click-and-Print Driver Downloads

Microsoft's click-and-print system is a neat trick: clients can automatically download drivers from the server. Windows servers simply dish out the driver when the client asks. It all happens in the background and it's magical.

Samba has the same ability. All we have to do is create a Samba file share called `print$` and create a single subdirectory in it. We call that subdirectory `W32X86` because Windows XP clients understand this to mean "drivers for Windows 2000 and/or Windows XP."

We'll map the share to the local directory `/usr/local/samba/windrivers` on the server. As mentioned previously, `/usr/local` is the correct parent directory for a directory created by the local administrator for a purpose not specific to one user. We'll also create the `W32X86` subdirectory to actually house the Windows XP drivers.

We can create the whole subdirectory path in a single command, thanks to the `-p` option of `mkdir`. The `-p` option causes `mkdir` to create any parent directories that do not already exist, instead of generating an error.

We will also need to secure the share properly. We don't want ordinary domain users to be able to delete or tamper with drivers, but we do need to allow the `administrator` user to upload drivers. We will arrange this by restricting write access to the share only to `administrator`. Webmin provides a friendly way to set this up. Samba implements these settings "under the hood" through settings in the file named `/etc/samba/smb.conf`.

There are a few more steps that must be taken, just once, from a Windows client to actually upload the drivers to the `print$` share. We'll show those steps later when we demonstrate SMB printing to Linux from a Windows client.

To prepare the Samba server to accept Windows print drivers:

1. At the command line, execute the following command:

    `mkdir -p /usr/local/samba/windrivers/W32X86`

2. Log into Webmin with the username `root` and the password **p@ssw0rd** at the URL: `https://adsambafp1.ad.corp.com:10000/`, if you haven't already.

3. If you are not already at the Windows File Sharing page, click "Servers," then "Samba Windows File Sharing."

4. Click the "Create a new file share" link. The "Create File Share" page appears.

5. Make sure the radio box next to "Share name" is selected. In the "Share name" text field, enter **print$** .

6. In the "Directory to share" field, enter **/usr/local/samba/windrivers/W32X86** .

7. Click the "No" box for "Automatically create directory?"

8. Click the "Yes" box for "Available?"

9. Click the "Yes" box for "Browseable?"

10. In the "Share Comment" field, enter **Click And Print Drivers** .

11. Click "Save."

12. `print$` should appear in the list of shares. Click `print$`.

13. The "Edit File Share" page appears. Click "Security and Access Control."

14. Make sure "Writable" is set to "No."

15. On the "Read/Write Users" line, enter **AD\administrator** .

16. Verify that "Guest Access" is set to "None" and "Limit to possible list" is set to "No."

17. Click "Save." The "Samba Windows File Sharing" page will reappear.

18. Scroll to the bottom of the page and click "Restart Samba Servers."

That's it—the server is configured! Time to test our new printing capabilities.

Performing Printing Tests

Our Linux server is now ready and willing to accept print jobs from both Windows and Linux clients. Let's test that out.

Printing from Linux Clients

Printing from Linux to Linux is, of course, very straightforward. The process is made especially easy because a CUPS server broadcasts its existence to systems on the local network. That makes CUPS IPP printing as convenient on Linux as SMB printing is on Windows. We don't have to use the Add a New Queue Wizard at all.

We're going to use `adsambafp1`, our Linux Active Directory domain member server, for our printing tests. We'll use `adlincli1`, our Linux domain member client, for our client-side tests.

But bear in mind that Active Directory plays no role in this and the procedure would be exactly the same in a pure Linux environment.

Everything we need to do can be accomplished with the Fedora printer configuration tool on `adlinclil`.

To configure our Linux client to print to a Linux server:

1. Pull down the "Applications" menu and drill down to System Settings ➢ Printing. Wait for the printer configuration tool to appear.

2. Click the "New" button to add a new print queue.

3. Click "Forward" on the explanatory page that follows.

4. Double-click the right-pointing arrow next to "Browsed queues."

5. LinPrinter1 appears in the list. Select it with the mouse.

6. Pull down the "Test" menu and pick "CUPS Test Page." Click "Yes" after the page appears successfully.

As before, we suggest using OpenOffice Writer to carry out a more interesting test. Select "LinPrinter1" as the printer to use. Notice that we didn't have to explicitly add this printer, since it is automatically detected on the local network.

Before we move on, there are two scenarios that we're not going to specifically cover in step-by-steps, and you might be asking yourself why not.

CUPS can only automatically find printers on the same subnet. What if I need to print to a CUPS printer that isn't on the same LAN?   It is possible to set up automatic relaying of printer browsing information between CUPS hosts on separate subnets. However, the relevant options, BrowsePoll and BrowseRelay, are not currently supported by the Fedora GUI. Currently configuration files must be edited by hand to implement this. We simply don't have space to address this in detail in this book, but you can learn more with this command:

```
man cupsd.conf
```

We can also, of course, add a CUPS printer manually. To do that, we would follow the same steps used earlier to add a queue for a Windows Internet Printing shared printer. The only difference would be in the "Server" field, which would not require the :80 at the end. That's because the CUPS IPP server listens on port 631, the default IPP port, instead of port 80. This is also good to know in certain types of VPN environments and other situations where "broadcasting" does not work.

What about printing from Linux clients to Linux servers using LPD or SMB?   We don't really recommend either when you have control over both the client and the server. IPP is both modern and an open standard. However, when an older Unix server that cannot be upgraded offers an LPD server, you may find it useful to follow exactly the same procedure we demonstrated earlier to print to a Windows server using LPD. Printing from Linux to Linux with SMB is not the best option, but it can be accomplished following the same procedure we used to print from Linux to Windows using LPD.

Printing from Windows Clients

Printing from Windows clients to Linux servers can be accomplished in three ways:

- We'll examine printing from Windows clients to Linux servers via IPP first. This requires minimal effort to set up and can be done in no time flat. We think, over the long haul, you'll use this option the most.

- Next, we'll examine printing from Windows clients to Linux servers via the native SMB printing protocol of Windows. Since we're here anyway, we'll also show how to upload printer drivers to enable click-and-print functionality for other clients on the network.

- The last method demonstrates something you likely won't use much. That is, you'll force your Windows client into talking the "old and crusty" LPD-style of printing, and your Linux print server will happily oblige. We demonstrate this primarily to show how Windows clients can print to legacy Unix LPD print servers that can't be upgraded to CUPS. It's also handy for those with archaic Unix LPD *clients*, although this book naturally focuses on Windows-and-Linux combinations.

Windows Clients Printing via IPP to Linux

Printing via IPP from Windows to Linux isn't difficult. We just need to know the correct URL for the printer. A Windows client can't automatically detect the URL using the web browser as it would if the server were running Windows Internet Printing.

There's a simple way to specify the right URL. When printing to a CUPS server via IPP, the correct URL will always look like this:

`http://`*servername*`:631/printers/`*printername*

servername, in our case, is adsambap1. and *printername* should be LinPrinter1, so the correct URL is:

`http://adsambafp1:631/printers/LinPrinter1`

Communicating with a printer via IPP to a Linux CUPS server also requires that we manually select a printer driver on the Windows side. When we do, we need to make a choice. We can choose a Postscript printer, which will work well with the LinPrinter1 spool, or we can choose to install the Canon i560 driver software from Canon's website or driver CD-ROM, which will work correctly with the LinPrinter1Raw spool.

For this example, we'll go with Postscript. This is always a good bet when talking to a Linux print server. To convince Windows to use a Postscript driver, we select Apple from the Manufacturer list. Then we select Apple Color LaserWriter 12/600 from the Printers list. The Apple Color LaserWriter 12/600 is a true Postscript printer, one that accepts Postscript as its native language. So Windows will send Postscript to CUPS, believing it is destined for a true Postscript printer, and CUPS will automatically recognize it and translate it to the native language of our actual printer using Ghostscript.

Now you know everything you need to know to make IPP work between Windows and a Linux CUPS server. To configure our Windows client to print via IPP to a Linux server with a generic Postscript driver:

1. Open the "Printers and Faxes" applet in Control Panel and select "Add a printer." This launches the "Add Printer Wizard" as we've seen before.

2. At the "Local or Network Printer" screen, select "A network printer, or a printer attached to another computer." Then click "Next."

3. On the page that follows, select the radio box labeled "Connect to a printer on the Internet or on a home or office network." In the "URL" field, enter the following:

   `http://adsambafp1:631/printers/LinPrinter1`

4. Click "Next." The client will talk to the server for a moment and then the "Select the manufacturer and model of your printer" dialog will appear.

5. Select "Apple" from the manufacturers list. Select "Apple Color LaserWriter 12/600" from the Printers list. Click "Next" to move on.

6. You will be asked whether to make this the default printer; click "Yes" or "No" as suits your preference.

7. Click "Finish" on the confirmation screen to end the wizard.

8. You can now test actual printing using the "Print" option on the "File" menu of an application such as Microsoft Word. Just select "LinPrinter1" from the list of printers available when printing.

Windows Clients Printing via SMB to Linux

SMB is, of course, the traditional, native printing protocol of Windows. Not surprisingly, convincing Windows clients to print via SMB to a Linux server running Samba isn't hard to do. However, for a bit of "extra credit," we'll set up *click-and-print*. That way, when other Windows clients stumble on this printer, they will automatically download the drivers and be good to go!

How does click-and-print work? When a Windows client prints to a Windows print server, the client automatically downloads the printer drivers from the print server. This happens transparently to the user. Very elegant.

But what if a client running Windows 98 tries to print to a print server running Windows Server 2003? After all, the new Windows XP / Windows 2003 printer drivers won't work with old Windows 98.

Windows provides a practical workaround. An administrator can install the printer on a Windows 98 machine then configure the client to print to the Windows 2003 server. This causes the server to automatically upload the Windows 98 drivers. From that point on, *the Windows 98 drivers are available to any Windows 98 client who uses that print queue on the server.*

Linux print servers use a similar trick to support Windows clients. Think of a Linux Samba print server as a Windows server that runs an exotic version of Windows that doesn't support regular Windows XP / Windows 2003 printer drivers. Just as in the Windows 98 / Windows 2003 scenario, the answer is to upload the drivers from a Windows XP client. You as the administrator can install a printer on a Windows machine, then upload the drivers to the Linux print server where they are available to any other Windows clients who print to that print server.

So here, we'll do the job in two steps, as shown in Figure 5.13.

First, we'll log on to a client workstation as a domain administrator in order to install the driver locally on that one workstation and then upload it to the Linux print server to be shared. Next, we'll log on to a separate client workstation as an ordinary user, who will discover that the driver automatically downloads when they first access the printer via the print server. All other users will experience the same benefit. That's *click-and-print*.

Of course, to demonstrate driver uploading, we need to use a printer driver that doesn't come with Windows as "standard" equipment. So for this test, we'll use a real Canon i560 driver that we downloaded from Canon's website. We'll have to install this driver on our first Windows client. To do this, we'll run Canon's installation program, then quit at the point where it would otherwise begin searching for a printer connected directly to the client. It's a bit confusing, but the installation program does install the driver before that point, and that's all we need.

Printer driver installation programs can be a bit baffling when it comes to installing a driver you intend to upload to a network server. That's not surprising, since with a true Windows print server you would run the installation program on the server itself. If step 2 later in this section doesn't work well for your model of printer, we suggest connecting the printer directly to the first client and fully installing the driver software. *Then* you can move the printer to the server and continue with the steps.

FIGURE 5.13   We'll leverage a Windows workstation to upload any required printer drivers to our Linux server. Then we'll log on to another Windows workstation and watch the drivers automatically download.

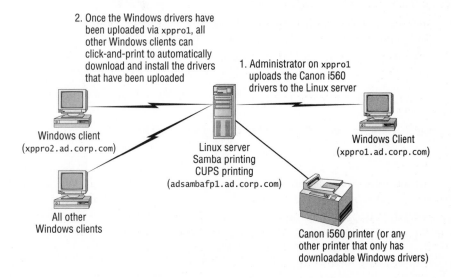

Keep in mind that we could have chosen to use a Postscript printer driver for SMB as well. If we had, there would be no need to set up click-and-print because the Postscript driver ships as standard equipment with Windows. However, since printer drivers occasionally have desirable features that can't be reached conveniently through the Postscript driver, it's worthwhile to demonstrate how to use native drivers and click-and-print as well.

Ideally, before you begin, we suggest that you configure a *second* XP client system if you don't have one just lying around. It's on this new XP client system that we'll actually witness the proper downloading of the driver (which we're initially loading on xppro1 and uploading to our Linux Samba server).

If you want to have another machine handy, here are our suggestions. Follow exactly the same procedure you followed for xppro1 except:

- The hostname should be xppro2.

- The IP address should be 192.168.2.115.

Once xppro2 is ready, we can demonstrate SMB printing and click-and-print driver downloading.

First things first: let's get our printer drivers loaded on our first client machine (xppro1). Then, we'll upload them via Samba for our other clients, such as xppro2, to utilize.

To load our printer drivers onto our Windows XP system:

1. Make sure you are logged in as AD\Administrator.

2. Install the Canon i560 driver software on xppro1 from the printer manufacturer's CD or website. When you reach the point where the installation program says it is trying to detect a printer connected to the local computer, click "Cancel."

3. Open the "Printers and Faxes" applet in Control Panel and select "Add a printer." This launches the "Add Printer Wizard" as we've seen several times before.

4. At the "Local or Network Printer" screen, select "A network printer, or a printer attached to another computer." Then click "Next."

5. On the page that follows, select the radio box "Connect to this printer (or to browse, for a printer, select this option and click "Next")." Then click "Next" to browse for the printer.

6. A list of print servers will appear, including ADSAMBAFP1. Double-click ADSAMBAFP1 to make LinPrinter1Raw visible and select it with the mouse as shown in Figure 5.14. Then click "Next."

7. A message box will appear saying that "the server for the printer does not have the correct driver installed." Click "OK" to manually select the correct driver on this first client.

8. The "Select the manufacturer and model of your printer" dialog will appear. Select "Canon" from the manufacturers list. Select "i560" from the Printers list. Click "Next" to move on.

9. You will be asked whether to make this the default printer; click "Yes" or "No" as suits your preference.

10. Click "Finish" on the confirmation screen to end the wizard.

11. You can now test actual printing using the "Print" option on the "File" menu of an application such as Microsoft Word. Just select "LinPrinter1" from the list of printers available when printing.

Using xppro1, we've added the printer queue to ADSAMBAFP1—but we're not done yet. Next, we need to take advantage of click-and-print by uploading the Canon i560 driver to the Samba print server. We do this via the "Sharing" tab of the "Properties" dialog for LinPrinter1Raw. While we're there, we can also list the printer in Active Directory to enable searches for the printer. Just follow these steps:

1. Open the "Printers and Faxes" applet in Control Panel.

2. Right-click "LinPrinter1Raw" and pick "Properties."

3. Click the "Sharing" tab.

4. If you wish, enable the "List in the directory" setting. This enables searches for this printer in Active Directory. We'll talk more about enabling searching for Active Directory in the next major section.

5. In the "Drivers" box, click "Additional Drivers."

6. From the list of driver types, check the box for "Intel Windows 2000 or XP" (Intel-compatible processors are in all typical Windows office PCs).

7. Click "OK."

8. A "Copying Files" progress box will appear while the drivers are uploaded to the server.

9. Click "Close."

FIGURE 5.14   Selecting LinPrinter1Raw from the Samba server via SMB browsing on a Windows client

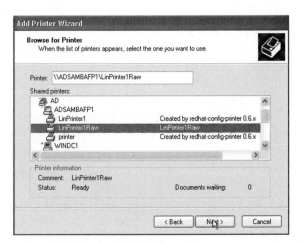

Our first client is now ready to print to LinPrinter1Raw. More importantly, we can now add a second client without the need to manually install the Canon i560 driver. It's time to demonstrate that.

Now we're ready to try a new client and see if it will automatically download the drivers from our Samba server. To test the automatic driver downloads from our Samba server:

1. Log in as any domain user. `AD\salesperson1` is a reasonable choice.

2. Open the "Printers and Faxes" applet in Control Panel and select "Add a printer" to launch the "Add Printer Wizard."

3. At the "Local or Network Printer" screen, select "A network printer, or a printer attached to another computer." Then click "Next."

4. On the page that follows, select the radio box labeled "Connect to this printer (or to browse, for a printer, select this option and click "Next")." Then click "Next" to browse for the printer.

5. A list of print servers will appear, including ADSAMBAFP1. Double-click ADSAMBAFP1 to make LinPrinter1Raw visible and select it with the mouse as shown in Figure 5.14. Then click "Next."

6. A "Copying Files" progress box will appear. The driver software will download from the server automatically. This is click-and-print at work.

7. You will be asked whether to make this the default printer; click "Yes" or "No" as suits your preference.

8. Click "Finish" on the confirmation screen to end the wizard.

9. You can now test actual printing using the "Print" option on the "File" menu of an application such as Microsoft Word. Just select "LinPrinter1Raw" from the list of printers available when printing.

Again, the amazing thing here is that we're using a Linux Samba print server to serve up Windows print drivers to Windows boxes. Now that's slick.

Windows Clients Printing via LPD to Linux

Before we can print via LPD from a Windows client, we need to install the "Print Services for Unix"—exactly as we performed earlier as shown in Figure 5.5.

LPD support in the Windows "Add Printer Wizard" has a strange approach. That is, we must add the printer as a "Local printer attached to this computer," and then we set up a remote LPD port. That's because, technically, the initial spooling of the print job happens here—on this local system. This isn't very intuitive, but it does work well.

Here's the procedure:

1. Be sure to have the "Print Services for Unix" installed. Again, this is found in the Add/Remove Programs applet and is described earlier in Figure 5.5.

2. Select Start ➢ Control Panel ➢ Printers and Faxes ➢ Add Printer to initiate the Add Printer Wizard. Once the wizard starts, click "Next."

3. At the "Local or Network Printer" screen, select "Local printer attached to this computer" and be sure to de-select the "Automatically detect and install my Plug-and-Play printer" box. Then click "Next."

4. On the "Select a Printer Port" page, click the "Create a new port" box and select "LPR Port" from the menu. Click "Next" to move on.

5. The "Add LPR compatible printer" dialog appears. Enter **adsambafp1.ad.corp.com** in the "Name or address of server providing lpd" field. Enter **linprinter1** in the "Name of printer or print queue on that server" field. Then click "OK."

6. At the "Install Printer Software" dialog, select the Manufacturer and Printer model. We'll stick to our Postscript approach in this example, so select Apple as the manufacturer and Apple Color LaserWriter 12/600 as the model. Then click "Next."

7. At the "Name your Printer" screen, you can enter a name for the printer. Replace the suggested name with **LinPrinter1ViaLPR**, then click "Next."

8. At the "Printer Sharing" screen, you can give a share name for others to see. This might seem strange, but it's actually a fine idea if you wish to "re-export" the printer via SMB. Well, it might not be a fine idea from a Windows XP machine, but if this were a Windows 2003 print server, this might be a fun idea. Once you do so, other clients can access the printer via traditional SMB Windows network printing without the need to additionally go through the hassle of installing the "Print Services for Unix" LPD driver.

9. At the "Location and Comment" screen enter what you like. When ready, click "Next."

10. At the "Print Test Page" prompt, select "Yes" to verify that we added the printer successfully.

What We Accomplished with Linux Printers

We've done quite a few nifty things with our Linux printer.

We shared it via IPP, using CUPS. That's the best way to share the printer with Linux clients, and it can also be used with Windows.

We also shared the printer via SMB, the traditional method of sharing printers with Windows clients. We showed how to use a raw queue to make sure print jobs from native Windows drivers are passed without modification to the printer. We also demonstrated how to list the printer in Active Directory and deliver native drivers automatically over SMB using click-and-print. Not bad for a free operating system!

We also made it available via LPD, which is convenient for archaic Unix clients and demonstrates what Windows clients need to do when talking to an archaic Unix server.

Leveraging Active Directory

Active Directory is a robust directory service. We've already leveraged it for user authentication, but Active Directory can also be used to locate printers in a central directory.

We can tell Active Directory about the various SMB printers we have—both Windows and Samba—and be able to enjoy an easily searchable method of connecting right to them. Once we connect, downloading the drivers is already happening automatically, as shown in the last section.

In this section, we're specifically concerned with getting all the printers we know into Active Directory, as well as having both Windows and Linux clients search Active Directory to find the printers in the most expeditious manner possible.

Here's the bad news, though: There's no great way (that we know of) to allow for Linux clients to perform an easy-breezy search of Active Directory to find printers. Maybe someday, but not today. However, at least we can give our Windows clients the ability to search Active Directory and easily pick the printer they want to, even if it lives on a Samba server.

Publishing Printers into Active Directory

The mechanism we'll use to get printers as records in Active Directory is called *publishing*. When we publish a printer, we simply make it available in Active Directory to search. It's a snap to publish a printer once you have the queues set up. In our previous examples, we set up three queues:

WinPrinter1   This was created on `windc1.ad.corp.com`. It uses normal print drivers and offers automatic downloading of drivers.

Linprinter1   This was created on `adsambafp1.ad.corp.com`. This queue is ready and willing to accept Postscript input and give it to CUPS, which takes care of rendering pages in the printer's native language via Ghostscript and ultimately feeds those pages to the printer.

LinPrinter1Raw   This was also created on `adsambafp1.ad.corp.com`. This queue expects clients to use regular Windows printer drivers, and it will pass the data on in raw form to CUPS, which will spit it back up to the printer. Like WinPrinter1, this queue supports automatic downloading of native Windows printer drivers.

Here, we have one queue that lives on a Windows server and two that live on a Samba server. The goal is to have all three be searchable in Active Directory.

Automatically Publishing Printers in Active Directory

When we added WinPrinter1 to `windc1.ad.corp.com`, Windows 2003 went the extra mile for us and published the printer in Active Directory. We didn't need to tell it to, it just did. We can see this by right-clicking over the printer's icon and clicking the "Sharing" tab, as shown in Figure 5.15.

Unchecking the "List in the directory" check box (and clicking "OK") will make the printer not show up when Active Directory searches are performed. However, this does not prevent the browse, browse, browse method using Network Neighborhood.

Manually Publishing Printers in Active Directory

Using the properties of the printer dialog is one way to add printers so that they are searchable within Active Directory. Another way is to manually publish printers in Active Directory.

To publish printers manually in Active Directory:

1. Select Start ➢ Programs ➢ Administrative Tools and then select "Active Directory Users and Computers."

FIGURE 5.15 The "Sharing" tab determines if the printer should be listed in Active Directory.

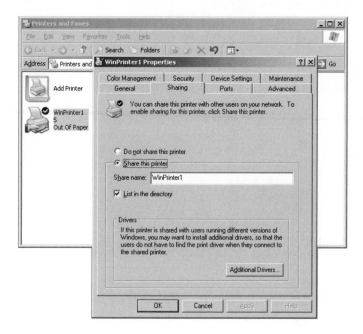

2. Pick a location in Active Directory where you want to publish the printer. This can be just about anywhere inside Active Directory, and in most cases location isn't really that important. One option is to create an OU that just contains published printers, but that's at your option. Once decided, right-click the OU and select New ➢ Printer. The "New Object – Printer" dialog appears.

3. In the "New Object – Printer" dialog, enter the queue name. For instance, if you want to publish LinPrinter1 from ADSAMBAFP1, enter the SMB name, **\\adsambafp1\linprinter1** as seen in Figure 5.16.

4. Click "OK," and it will validate that the queue exists. Then it will put it into Active Directory.

Once performed, Active Directory will represent the printer with an icon within the OU you specify. If you're feeling particularly frisky, you can set certain attributes about these printers in Active Directory, such as the location, if it's color-capable, if it can print dual sided, and more. All you need to do is to select the properties of the entry. The resulting screen can be seen in Figure 5.17.

This way you can make it easy to search Active Directory for particular printers with particular attributes.

At this point you should repeat these steps for the other queue you created: LinPrinterRaw. That way, if someone on a Windows client wants to print to the printer using the native Windows drivers, they can easily search for it in Active Directory and have the drivers automatically download.

FIGURE 5.16   You can add any SMB printer to Active Directory to make it searchable.

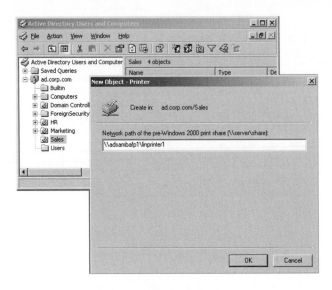

FIGURE 5.17   You can select and enter attributes that can help users search for specific printers.

It should be noted that the "Location" field has a super-secret special super power to help Active Directory clients locate printers. I simply don't have room to go into it all here, but I've written it up in detail. To read the article, come to my website at www.moskowitz-inc.com/writing/articles.html and look for "October 2002: (Feature): Printer Magic." You'll find it in no time.

Searching for Printers in Active Directory

Searching for Printers in Active Directory should be easy as punch. And it is, for both Windows and Linux clients.

The good news is that it's easy to find and start using printers when the client is Windows. The bad news is that there's no easy-breezy way to start using printers from our Linux clients after we find them in Active Directory.

Finding Printers in Active Directory with Windows Clients

To find printers in Active Directory from your Windows machines:

1. Log in as any domain user. AD\salesperson1 is a reasonable choice.

2. Open the "Printers and Faxes" applet in Control Panel and select "Add a printer" to launch the "Add Printer Wizard."

3. At the "Local or Network Printer" screen, select "A network printer, or a printer attached to another computer." Then click "Next."

4. At the "Specify a Printer" screen, select "Find a printer in the directory" and click "Next." The "Find Printers" dialog appears.

5. At the "Find Printers" dialog, you can specify "Find Now" to select all printers or click the "Features" tab to select printers with specific features you want to display, such as only those which print in color. Once done, click "Find Now" as seen in Figure 5.18.

6. Double-click the printer you want to add, and the wizard will continue as normal.

Finding Printers in Active Directory Using Linux Clients

On the Linux side, no GUI tools currently exist for this purpose. But we have verified that one *can* find the relevant information the hard way, by making an LDAP query from the Linux command line. And that means a friendly GUI for that purpose is very possible. So with any luck, an enterprising Linux coder will soon create a GUI to search for printers in Active Directory and add queues for them on a Fedora Linux client.

FIGURE 5.18   Just find the printer you want, double-click it, and go!

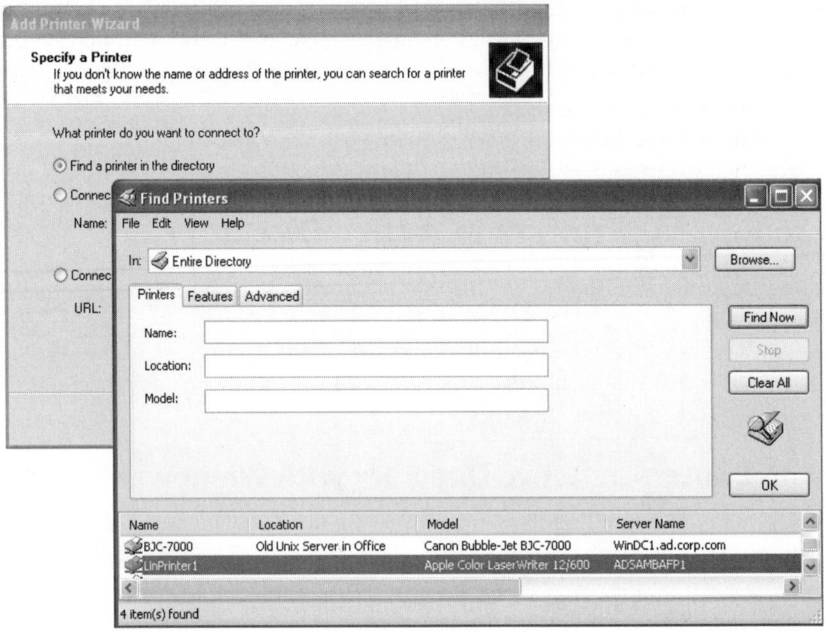

Here's the command we used to successfully list published printers from the command line of adldaplincl1.ad.corp.com, which is already configured to communicate with the LDAP server on windc1.ad.corp.com:

```
ldapsearch -x -D "cn=dirsearch,cn=Users,dc=ad,dc=corp,dc=com" -w p@ssw0rd
objectClass=printQueue
```

This command binds to the Active Directory LDAP server using the usual credentials from Chapter 3 and, using the filter objectclass=printQueue, prints information about all published printers. There's quite a bit of information there, but the most interesting fields are uNCName (for printers shared via SMB) and url (for printers shared via IPP). For instance, this command:

```
ldapsearch -x -D "cn=dirsearch,cn=Users,dc=ad,dc=corp,dc=com" -w p@ssw0rd
objectClass=printQueue | grep -i uNCName
```

Outputs the following in our tests:

```
uNCName: \\WinDC1.ad.corp.com\WinPrinter1
uNCName: \\ADSAMBAFP1\LinPrinter1Raw
uNCName: \\ADSAMBAFP1\LinPrinter1
```

Armed with this information, we suspect it won't be long before someone decides to add a friendly GUI for this purpose to Fedora Linux.

Final Thoughts

Printer interoperability is a main selling point in getting Windows and Linux to play nicely. It's one of those features that users just expect to work all the time. If you can leverage the printers you have, you'll be the big hero.

Both Windows and Linux do a great job in working with standards for printing. The main standards that are supported on both sides are LPR/LPD for older-style Unix printing, SMB printing for Windows/Samba, and IPP. As mentioned previously, Windows' IPP doesn't use the RFC compliant port of 631, it uses port 80, so be sure to compensate, as we've specified in the chapter.

Samba does a great job in setting up new printers and automatically allowing driver downloads when necessary. Windows does a great job in making it easy to search for printers in Active Directory.

In all, it's a match made in printer heaven.

6

Practical Windows Exchange and Linux Postfix E-mail Integration

In Chapter 1, we described a very typical evolution of many companies. Let's briefly revisit and adorn the story of what happens in many typical companies. We'll review the story in three acts:

Act I: It arrives

- Unix arrives. Then Linux arrives. The Unix/Linux camp "owns" DNS for `corp.com` and provides a myriad of services to the Unix/Linux user base.

- Windows comes next. Along with it come NT domains, then Active Directory domains.

Act II: E-mail abounds

- Linux e-mail services are used to support the installed Linux user base. The Linux administrator sets up a simple e-mail server (which is precisely what we'll do in this chapter). All the Linux users get e-mail addresses such as *user*@corp.com.

- Windows users also want e-mail services. At first they try the simple e-mail services on Linux, but then they give Exchange a try. During the testing, the CEO falls in love with the centralized message storage, shared calendaring, and public folders in Exchange. Exchange gets anointed as the standard for most of the organization. However, even though Exchange is installed in `ad.corp.com`, the CEO wants all Exchange users to have e-mail addresses in the form of *user*@corp.com.

Act III: Growth and stagnation

- Active Directory becomes the primary account storage for all users whether they utilize Windows or Linux.

- The CEO wants everyone to use Exchange e-mail whenever possible.

- Some Linux users have work processes that require them to continue to use the Linux e-mail server.

Let's pause for a second and take a look at Figure 6.1, which demonstrates this current state of affairs. That is, two camps, two e-mail servers, and not much else. We're going to be setting up this scenario in this chapter and solving the associated interoperability problems.

We have several major problems to solve:

- We need a way to unify our mail so that everyone has a `corp.com` e-mail address, which will present some challenges:

  - The CEO wants Exchange to be the primary method of e-mail for `corp.com`, but Exchange e-mail "lives" in `ad.corp.com`.

  - The Linux e-mail server currently hosts mailboxes for a bunch of users who already have `corp.com` e-mail addresses and who cannot move off the Linux e-mail server.

- Spam and e-mail viruses are flowing in from the Internet at an alarming rate. You need to set up an inexpensive e-mail spam and anti-virus gateway.

FIGURE 6.1 Both Windows and Linux camps have independent e-mail systems that don't really talk to each other.

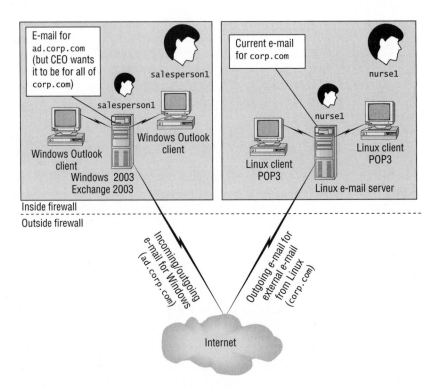

We'll work through this scenario in several steps and grow our e-mail environment to make use of the best features in Exchange and Linux e-mail:

- We'll set up Linux as a departmental e-mail server for `corp.com`.

- We'll install Exchange.

- We'll set up another Linux machine to act as a unified *gateway* between our Linux and Windows e-mail servers as well as make it an anti-spam and anti-virus gateway to the Internet.

  This is going to be fun!

Linux As a Departmental Mail Server

Linux can serve as a departmental mail server. To demonstrate this, we'll turn `linserv1.corp.com` (the Linux-based authentication and file server we built over the last several chapters) into a Linux-based mail server that hosts mailboxes and provides access to Linux and Windows e-mail clients.

Recall that in Chapter 2, we loaded OpenLDAP on `linserv1.corp.com` and created several LDAP users: `nurse1`, `nurse2`, `doctor1`, and `doctor2`. The idea was that these users logged on via Linux's LDAP client, via Windows and pGina's LDAP client, or even via ordinary Windows NT-style authentication as part of a Samba-based Linux PDC.

These same LDAP accounts that we created in Chapter 2 will now also be valid destinations for e-mail. It will be easy for these users to send and receive e-mail from Windows clients such as Microsoft Outlook and Eudora as well as Linux clients such as KMail, Balsa, Evolution, and Mozilla Thunderbird.

Several mail server software programs are available for Fedora Linux. These are divided into three categories:

Mail Transfer Agent (MTA) software   Responsible for e-mail delivery. MTAs are what most people mean by "mail servers." These are programs that deliver e-mail from one server to another. When you send e-mail, your client software hands the message off to an MTA, and your client software's responsibility ends there. The MTA is responsible for managing a queue of outgoing messages and delivering them to other MTAs for other domains. The MTA is also responsible for delivering incoming mail from local clients and other MTAs to individual user mailboxes.

Post Office Protocol (POP) software   The original option for users to download their e-mail. POP does not offer an option of keeping multiple folders on the server. There is just one inbox. Typically users download and delete all messages from the inbox each time they check mail.

Internet Message Access Protocol (IMAP) software   Another popular way for e-mail clients to get their e-mail. We prefer IMAP to POP because IMAP allows users to leave their mail at the server so they can access their mail from multiple locations. Also, IMAP users can have multiple mail folders on the server, making it simpler to create structured individual storage.

We chose to use Postfix for the MTA, which is a change from the default Fedora MTA, Sendmail. See the sidebar "Why We Chose Postfix" for the reasons we're changing.

For POP and IMAP services, we're using Fedora's standard Dovecot POP/IMAP server.

Why We Chose Postfix

By default, when you install a mail server, Fedora Linux installs the Sendmail MTA. Sendmail is a fine mail server with a long history and a strong reputation.

However, we prefer Postfix.

That's because Postfix is ultimately simpler to configure and is not weighed down with features relating to archaic mail protocols that are no longer used, such as UUCP. Considerable experience has taught us that Postfix is every bit as robust and a great deal easier to work with than Sendmail.

Finally, Postfix is the recommended mail server component for the OpenXChange project, an open-source Exchange alternative that is still under development. While OpenXChange is not ready for inclusion as a recommended solution in this book, it is a promising project and we aim to use components that are compatible with it.

Installing Postfix on *linserv1.corp.com*

Since Fedora installed Sendmail rather than Postfix by default when we originally configured `linserv1.corp.com` in Chapter 1, we'll take a moment to correct that problem by installing the MTA of our choice. At the same time, we'll make sure that other required packages are installed. We'll use the Add/Remove Applications tool, which we've seen several times before. Follow these steps to install Postfix on `linserv1.corp.com`:

1. Pull down the "Applications" menu.

2. Select System Settings ➢ Add/Remove Applications.

3. There will be a delay while the Add/Remove Applications tool determines what packages are already installed.

4. When the "Add or Remove Packages" screen appears, scroll down to "Mail Server," make sure the appropriate box is checked, and click "Details."

5. If the "Extra Packages" list is not expanded, click the triangle to expand it.

6. Check the box for "Postfix."

7. Check the box for "Dovecot" if it is not already checked.

8. Click "Close."

9. Click "Update."

Configuring Postfix on *linserv1.corp.com*

We're ready to configure Postfix to serve as our MTA. We can do that using Webmin, which provides a friendly interface to all but one of the options we need to configure.

Stopping Sendmail and Starting Postfix and Dovecot

First we'll tell Fedora to stop running Sendmail (both now and on future reboots) and to start running Postfix as well as the Dovecot POP/IMAP server. We do this with the familiar chkconfig and service commands. As root on linserv1.corp.com, enter these commands to disable Sendmail and enable Postfix:

```
chkconfig --del sendmail
service sendmail stop
chkconfig --add postfix
chkconfig postfix on
service postfix start
chkconfig --add dovecot
chkconfig dovecot on
service dovecot start
```

Leveraging Webmin to Configure Postfix

Now we're ready to use Webmin to do most of our configuration work. For the most part, Fedora's standard installation of Postfix works well for our needs. Postfix is pretty bright. It automatically recognizes all valid accounts on linserv1.corp.com and accepts e-mail for all of them. Remember, we're already using linserv1.corp.com for some LDAP accounts, as well as for accounts in /etc/passwd. Postfix will accept e-mail for any of these accounts and deliver it to mailboxes set up in the /var/spool/mail directory, creating them on first use.

Dovecot is configured right out of the box to allow users to check their mailboxes using any POP or IMAP client.

We need to leverage Webmin to do three things:

1. We'll configure Postfix to add an @corp.com address to outgoing mail. That way messages to the outside world appear to come from nurse1@corp.com, not nurse1@linserv1.corp.com.

2. We'll tell Postfix to accept incoming mail for the whole corp.com domain, not just for addresses @linserv1.corp.com.

3. We'll tell Postfix to accept incoming e-mail over all network interfaces, including the local network interface. By default, Postfix accepts mail only from the server itself, which is not very useful yet! But it's easy to fix.

To configure Postfix as a departmental mail server, follow these steps:

1. Log into Webmin on linserv1.corp.com using the usual URL: https://linserv1.corp .com:10000.

2. Click "Servers."

3. Click "Postfix Configuration."

4. Click "General Options."

5. For "What domain to use in outbound mail," pick "Use domainname," as shown in Figure 6.2.

6. For "What domains to receive mail for," pick "Whole domain."

7. Scroll down to locate "Network interfaces for receiving mail" and pick "All" as shown in Figure 6.3.

8. Scroll down and click "Save and Apply."

Now the Linux-based departmental mail server is ready to test!

Testing the Linux-Based Departmental Mail Server

Testing the mail server is straightforward. Any e-mail client that supports POP or IMAP can be configured to work with linserv1.corp.com. Just set the following options as shown in the e-mail client program of your choice. Preferably, you should try this on a workstation in the corp.com organization (Windows or Linux.) But the connection should work regardless of what domain your client machine is a member of.

Here are the general options to specify using your e-mail client:

Option	Setting
Incoming Mail Server	linserv1.corp.com
Outgoing Mail Server	linserv1.corp.com
Incoming Server Type	IMAP
Account Name	nurse1
E-mail Address	nurse1@corp.com
Real Name	Nurse One

FIGURE 6.2   Using Webmin to configure the "What domain to use in outbound mail" and "What domains to receive mail for" options for the Postfix departmental mail server

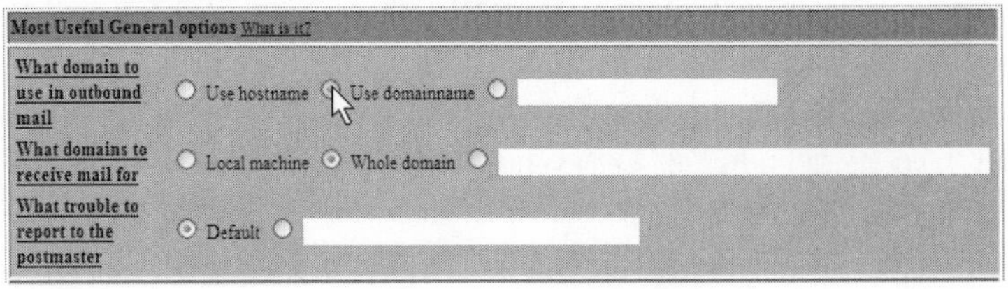

FIGURE 6.3   Using Webmin to configure the "Network interfaces for receiving mail" option for the Postfix departmental mail server

 In Chapter 2, we created accounts named nurse1, nurse2, doctor1, and doctor2 in the "Administering Users and Groups LDAP Users and Groups LDAP Module" section. If you did not do so then, refer back to that section and take care of it now. To successfully complete *all* of the exercises in this chapter, it is necessary to store these accounts in an LDAP database as described in Chapter 2.

Yes, you may use POP if your e-mail client does not support IMAP. We recommend IMAP because of its support for keeping multiple personal e-mail folders on the server. Virtually all modern e-mail clients support IMAP.

Now set up a second e-mail client on a second workstation, accessing the nurse2 account:

Option	Setting
Incoming Mail Server	linserv1.corp.com
Outgoing Mail Server	linserv1.corp.com
Incoming Server Type	IMAP
Account Name	nurse2
E-mail Address	nurse2@corp.com
Real Name	Nurse Two

Now you're ready to send e-mails back and forth between nurse1 and nurse2. Just send messages from nurse1@corp.com to nurse2@corp.com and vice versa.

Installing Exchange (a Quick-Start Guide)

Exchange installation is a big deal that shouldn't be undertaken lightly. There are a lot of steps involved. A *lot*. Heck, there are whole books just about Exchange, and installation is a big chunk of those books. The following are some of the best books on Exchange installation and care and feeding.

- *Learning Exchange Server 2003* by Bill Boswell (who is also the technical editor of this book), Addison-Wesley 2004, www.amazon.com

- *Mastering Microsoft Exchange Server 2003* by Barry Gerber, Sybex 2003, `www.sybex.com`
- *Microsoft Exchange Server 2003 With SP1* by Tony Redmond, Digital Press 2004, `www.amazon.com`

To that end, we're *not* going to step through an entire Exchange install—and we're certainly not going to describe detailed administration, care and feeding, or many other very important day-to-day topics. Our goal here is Linux integration. We will, however, point out specific configuration options we've chosen along the way and add some commentary to some installation steps.

Exchange Editions

Exchange Server comes in two flavors, Standard and Enterprise, and it's a devil of a time trying to figure out on Microsoft's website what the difference between them is. Here is a table that spells out which version does what:

Feature	Exchange Standard Edition	Exchange Enterprise Edition
Storage Space	Maximum 16GB	Basically unlimited
Multiple store support	No (only one storage group with one mailbox store and one public folder store)	Yes (up to four storage groups with up to 20 mailbox and public folder stores)
Interoperability	No x.400 support	x.400 support included
High Availability	No clustering support	Clustering support

For the purposes of this book, you can't go wrong with either Exchange version. You can have Microsoft send you a trial CD, or you can download the bits yourself. Track down a trial version at `www.microsoft.com/exchange/evaluation/trial/default.mspx`.

Server Setup Suggestions

In the real world, you'd work with an Exchange expert to help you plan your server configuration. There's a lot of robust hardware you can choose from: Intel Xeon or AMD Opteron processors, RAID arrays, tape backup, UPS, etc. For our purposes, we're not that picky. In our test lab, we'll be setting up Exchange on a simply configured machine:

- Windows 2003 preloaded and joined to the `ad.corp.com` domain. We'll call it `Exchange2003.ad.corp.com`.
- Pentium 4, 800Mhz
- 512MB of RAM
- A disk to hold the Exchange mailbox databases; we'll choose a D: drive with 8GB free

And that's it.

Again, when it comes to planning your real Exchange setup, be sure to check out the references at the beginning of the section.

Extending the Active Directory Schema for Exchange

Exchange and Active Directory work together. You simply cannot have Exchange without Active Directory. This is because Exchange stores all of its configuration and mail routing information in Active Directory. To that end, the Active Directory schema must be extended to accept the Exchange object classes and attributes. To do this, two things must occur:

- You must perform the schema extension as a member of the `Schema Admins` group. The Administrator account in `corp.com` is a member of this group by default.
- You must perform the schema extension on the Domain Controller which holds the "Schema Master" role. `windc1.ad.corp.com` will have this role by default.

Again, because this isn't an Exchange-specific book, we cannot delve into each of these topics in detail. The simplest way to extend the schema is to kick off Exchange setup.

First Time Running Setup: Extending the Schema for the Forest

On `windc1.ad.corp.com`, log in as Administrator, insert the Exchange Server CD into the CD-ROM reader and run `setup /forestprep`. This will extend the schema. This step needs to be done only once, and it affects all domains.

When you run this step, you'll be asked which account will be the "Full Exchange Administrator." In our examples, we'll stay with the default of the domain Administrator account.

Second Time Running Setup: Extending the Schema for the Domain

Stay logged on at `windc1.ad.corp.com` as Administrator. From the Exchange Server CD, run `setup /domainprep`. This will extend the schema attributes for the `ad.corp.com` domain specifically. If you had more than one domain, you would perform this step multiple times.

Third Time Running Setup: Installing Exchange on the Exchange Server

Log on to the server you designated as the Exchange server. In our examples, we'll use a machine named `Exchange2003.ad.corp.com`. Insert the Exchange CD-ROM and double-click "Setup" to run the rest of the setup graphically.

Follow the bouncing ball. That is, select the "Exchange Deployment Tools," then follow the guided installation to install your first Exchange 2003 server. You've already performed some of the steps (i.e., Forestprep and Domainprep), and it suggests some other tests for good measure. The final step helps you launch the graphical Installation Wizard setup. In our examples, we'll be installing Exchange to the D: drive (instead of the C: drive) and we'll create a new Exchange Organization called CORP.

Common Exchange Tasks

As stated, we simply don't have room to go over all the possibilities on configuring Exchange. However, to get you started, you should know how to use two tools: Active Directory Users and Computers (to mail-enable your users) and the Exchange System Manager (ESM) console.

Using Active Directory Users and Computers to Mail-Enable Accounts

Now that Exchange is loaded, a whole lot of "nothing" has happened. That is, in order for users to actually get Exchange mail, you have to *mailbox-enable* their accounts. You do this using Active Directory Users and Computers. Specifically, right-click a user's account and select "Exchange Tasks," as shown in Figure 6.4.

A wizard launches and presents some options. Specifically, you're after the "Create Mailbox" option. You can zip through the wizard, taking the defaults, and a user will be configured to have a mailbox on the Exchange server.

Use this process to mailbox-enable `salesperson1` and `salesperson2`.

Note that the "Exchange Tasks" fly-out menu in Active Directory Users and Computers is only available on machines on which you've loaded the Exchange System Management Tools. Of course, you did that on the machine running Exchange 2003 but not on `windc1.ad.corp.com`. I suggest you use the Exchange Setup Wizard to also install the Exchange System Management Tools on `windc1.ad.corp.com`, as shown in Figure 6.5.

FIGURE 6.4 Use Active Directory Users and Computers and right-click any user for their "Exchange Tasks."

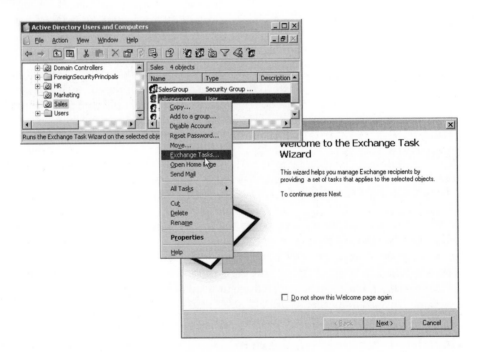

FIGURE 6.5 To get the "Exchange Tasks" fly-out on Active Directory Users and Computers at the domain controller, load the Exchange System Management Tools where you do your management.

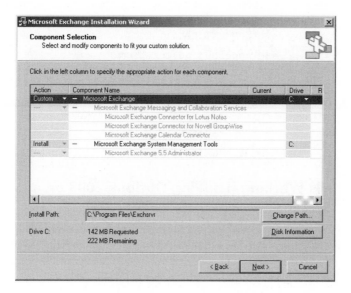

Enabling Pop and IMAP Access to Exchange for Linux Clients

Not every environment has a separate Linux mail server for Linux clients to talk to. In some cases you may wish to allow Linux or other non-Windows clients to check mail directly on an Exchange server. We can easily enable this by turning on support for POP and IMAP on the Exchange server. Although this doesn't grant Linux clients access the full rich collaboration capabilities that you get by running Outlook with Exchange, it works well for simply reading e-mail.

We'll enable support for POP and IMAP with four commands on the command line of our Exchange server. Using a command prompt, type:

```
sc config pop3svc start= auto
sc config imap4svc start= auto
sc start pop3
sc start imap4
```

Note, that there's a space after the equal sign in the preceding code.

Windows refers to these protocols as POP3 and IMAP4 to distinguish them from older versions of POP and IMAP.

Linux clients can now talk to the Exchange server exactly as they would talk to a Linux-based mail server. Here are the general options to specify in your Linux e-mail client:

Option	Setting
Incoming Mail Server	`exchange2003.ad.corp.com`
Outgoing Mail Server	`exchange2003.ad.corp.com`
Incoming Server Type	IMAP4
Account Name	`salesperson1`
E-mail Address	`salesperson1@ad.corp.com`
Real Name	Sales Person One

Testing Exchange Is Working (Loading Outlook 2003 on a Windows Client System)

The most efficient way to make sure Exchange is working properly is to install Outlook 2003 on a Windows XP system. Outlook is part of Microsoft Office 2003. If you don't have a licensed copy, you can download a trial version of the whole Office 2003 Standard Edition (which includes Outlook) from www.microsoft.com/office/trial/default.mspx.

 After you've installed Outlook and/or Office, be sure to update it at www.officeupdate.microsoft.com to install the latest patches.

Once Outlook is loaded on your client machine—say, xppro1.ad.corp.com—you'll be able to configure Outlook for two users: `salesperson1` and `salesperson2`. Then, while logged on as `salesperson1`, you can send mail to `salesperson2` and vice versa.

The first time you fire up Outlook for each user, you'll be prompted with a wizard to help you get the user connected to the Exchange server.

After you configure Outlook, the main window opens. Create a new e-mail message; clicking the "To" button opens the Global Address List (GAL) from which you can select one or more recipients, as shown in Figure 6.7.

Try sending e-mails back and forth from `salesperson1` and `salesperson2`.

Unified Linux and Exchange Delivery (with Anti-Spam and Anti-Virus)

In the current configuration, doctors and nurses are getting e-mail from the Postfix MTA on `linserv1.corp.com`. Their addresses are similar to `nurse1@corp.com`.

FIGURE 6.6 In Outlook setup, enter the name of the Exchange server and the user's name.

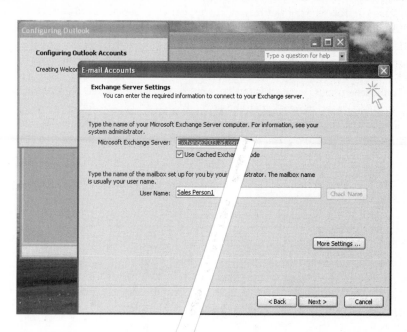

FIGURE 6.7 Use the Global Address List to locate Exchange-enabled users.

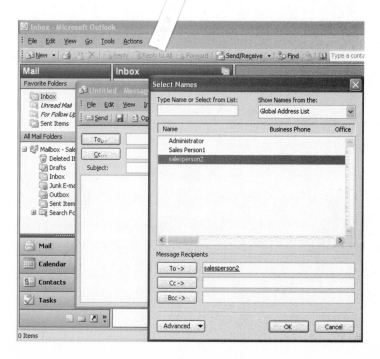

The Sales, Human Resources and Marketing staffs are getting e-mail from Exchange on Exchange2003.corp.com. Their addresses are similar to salesperson1@ad.corp.com.

Even though we want the majority of our users on Exchange, we need to keep the Linux Postfix mail server serving our doctors and nurses.

It's time to unify the e-mail domains, so we need a new server that can route incoming e-mails from the Internet and route them to the correct e-mail server. Incoming e-mails will go to Exchange2003.ad.corp.com or linserv1.corp.com or get bounced back to the sender because there is no valid recipient on either system.

In Figure 6.8, you can see the new system we want to introduce outside the firewall. We want this system, named mail.corp.com, to both route e-mail to the mail server (Exchange or Postfix) that hosts the recipient's mailbox and prescrub incoming e-mail for spam and viruses.

FIGURE 6.8   We'll create mail.corp.com outside the firewall to clean incoming mail and route mail to the correct e-mail server.

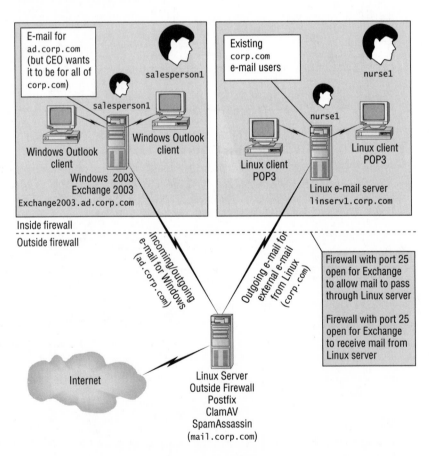

To do this, we'll need to take several steps:

1. We'll reconfigure Exchange a bit. Right now Exchange thinks its users have addresses `@ad.corp.com`, but we want everyone to have an `@corp.com` address. Also, right now Exchange assumes any e-mail address in its own domain that it can't find in Active Directory is a bad address. We need to tell Exchange to forward such messages to the `mail.corp.com` server for possible delivery to the Linux departmental server.

2. Similarly, we'll reconfigure Postfix on the departmental Linux server a bit. So far, the Postfix departmental server assumes any e-mail address in its own domain that it can't find in LDAP or `/etc/passwd` is a bad address. We need to tell Postfix to forward such messages to the outside `mail.corp.com` server for possible delivery to the Exchange server.

3. We'll bring up our new `mail.corp.com` server outside the firewall. Of course, we'll install it with the services we want to configure such as having its own Postfix MTA. We'll discuss the role of `mail.corp.com` in more detail in the next section.

4. We'll install anti-spam and e-mail anti-virus packages on `mail.corp.com`. That way, we kill the bad e-mail as soon as it gets sent to our company, before it even makes it inside.

5. Finally, we'll make sure that when mail comes in to `mail.corp.com`, it is specifically routed to the e-mail server where the users can pick up their mail. Mail for Exchange users must be recognized as such and forwarded to Exchange. Mail for users on the Linux departmental server must be correctly forwarded to that server.

What a Front-End MTA Does for Us

We already have perfectly good Linux and Exchange MTAs. Why do we need a front-end MTA?

We could, if we wanted, set up anti-virus and anti-spam services on both the departmental Postfix server and the Exchange server. But we don't have to. Instead, we'll create a *front-end* server that collects all the incoming e-mail, scrubs it of viruses, labels spam as spam, and sends the clean e-mail to our internal *back-end* e-mail servers. This has three major benefits:

- It greatly reduces the load on the back-end mail servers. You'll be able to stuff more users on any given server because you won't have to worry about the overhead of running anti-spam or anti-virus on your internal mail servers.

- A clean Exchange MTA is a healthy Exchange MTA. To that end, it's best to scrub e-mail *before* it hits the Exchange MTA, to maximize MTA health and maximize uptime.

- If you pay for anti-spam or anti-virus, you're reducing your costs because you only have to load it one time—on the front-end server.

In addition, we can set up `mail.corp.com` to verify that mail has legitimate addresses before forwarding messages to the back-end servers. In other words, if the mail is going to bounce anyway because the user doesn't exist, we'll have it bounce right away instead of making one of our back-end servers process it.

Besides setting up anti-spam and anti-virus, the main goal of the front-end MTA is to solve the problem of coexistence between Exchange and Linux back-end mail servers in the same organization. Both back-end mail servers think they serve users with `@corp.com` e-mail addresses. And they do. But we need a way to route the incoming mail from the outside world to the back-end server that actually has the correct mailbox for the specific @corp.com user. We also need to be able to route mail from our Exchange users to our Linux users and vice versa.

We'll do all this using four main components:

The Postfix mail server We've already met this piece of software. In this case we'll use Postfix as an e-mail router and cleaner instead of delivering messages directly to mailboxes on the server.

The SpamAssassin spam filter SpamAssassin is a mail filter that "identifies spam using a wide range of heuristic tests on mail headers and body text," according to the SpamAssassin home page at http://spamassassin.apache.org.

The ClamAV e-mail virus filter ClamAV is a virus detection and removal tool supported by an active open source community. You can learn more about ClamAV from the ClamAV home page at www.clamav.net.

MailScanner This bridges the gap between Postfix, SpamAssassin, and ClamAV. Spam-Assassin and ClamAV include their own simple methods of integration with Postfix, but these methods assume you won't be using both. MailScanner provides the ability to integrate any number of mail-scanning programs with Postfix. For good measure, it has some spam and virus detection capabilities of its own. For more information, visit the MailScanner home page at www.mailscanner.info/.

All of the above are free, open-source software packages.

However, we still have one bridge to cross. We need a way for mail.corp.com to "know" which users have mailboxes on Exchange and which users have mailboxes on the Linux mail server. We need a way for mail.corp.com to route to our back-end servers appropriately. To that end, we custom-wrote a Perl script to determine the correct back-end server for any given recipient. And that script can be used to route mail to any combination of Exchange and Postfix back ends, not just the specific configuration shown in this chapter.

WARNING This script will work great only if you're using LDAP-based accounts on linserv1.corp.com. Otherwise, there's no way for mail.corp.com to find out which addresses belong to the Linux back-end MTA. LDAP is the key to sharing that information between the servers. If you didn't set up LDAP-based authentication in Chapter 2, this is the time to go back and do so. Specifically, check out the "Setting up an OpenLDAP Server on Linux" section of Chapter 2.

Here's one big word of caution: you must complete all the steps in this section and through the end of this chapter. These guidelines are provided to you as a whole package and shouldn't be performed piecemeal. During these steps, mail will stop routing properly until you're finished because we're about to tell both the Postfix departmental server and the Exchange server to route mail to mail.corp.com—before it even exists.

Exchange Reconfiguration Tasks

To meet our aforementioned goals, we need to reconfigure Exchange a little bit differently than it comes out of the box. Here's what we're going to do:

Make the Exchange Server send and receive mail as if it were *corp.com*   As it stands, all users on Exchange have e-mail addresses like `salesperson1@ad.corp.com`. We need to train Exchange to allow users to have e-mail addresses that show just `@corp.com`.

Force Exchange to send all mail to our *mail.corp.com* server   We could allow Exchange to send outgoing e-mail directly to the Internet. But by forwarding these messages to the `mail.corp.com` front-end MTA, we gain the benefits of virus scanning for our outgoing mail. If an outbreak of e-mail viruses occurs within the local network, it's nice to know it won't be propagated to other companies and customers. Scanning your outgoing mail for viruses is good PR!

Force Exchange to send e-mail for unrecognized addresses in *corp.com* to the *mail.corp.com* server   When an Exchange user (such as `salesperson1`) sends out an e-mail, it might be destined for someone on the Linux Postfix departmental mail server (such as `nurse1`). The `mail.corp.com` server will be configured to automatically distinguish between e-mail for Exchange users and e-mail for Linux users. So we'll forward messages for users in the `corp.com` domain that the Exchange server doesn't recognize to `mail.corp.com` and let `mail.corp.com` figure out whether they are intended for the Linux departmental server or simply invalid addresses. Without this change, Exchange assumes it is the one and only arbiter of who can get e-mail in the `corp.com` domain and drops messages for non-Exchange users.

Making Exchange Server Pretend to Be *corp.com*

As it stands, Exchange thinks it's sending and receiving mail as `ad.corp.com`. But when `salesperson1` hands a business card to people she meets, it says `salesperson1@corp.com`. Therefore, we need to teach Exchange to send and receive mail as if it were responsible for message routing in `corp.com`.

To configure Exchange to do this, the tool you'll use is the Exchange System Manager. To make Exchange send and receive mail as `corp.com`:

1. Select Start ➢ Program Files ➢ Microsoft Exchange and select System Manager.

2. Drill down to Corp (Exchange) ➢ Recipients ➢ Recipient Policies and find Default Policy in the right-hand pane.

3. Right-click Default Policy and select "Properties."

4. Click the "E-mail Addresses (Policy)" tab, and click "New."

5. In the "New E-mail Addresses" dialog, select "SMTP Address" and click "OK."

6. In the "SMTP Address Properties" dialog, in the "Address" field, enter **@corp.com**, select "This Exchange Organization is responsible for all mail delivery to this address," and click "OK."

7. Back at the "E-Mail Addresses (Policy)" tab, click the new `@corp.com` address you just created and select "Set as Primary." `@corp.com` will be bolded to let you know it's now the primary address, as shown in Figure 6.9. Click "OK" to continue.

8. You'll be asked to update your current batch of users with e-mail addresses. You should select "Yes," as you've already assigned e-mail @ad.corp.com addresses to `salesperson1` and `salesperson2`. Note that this doesn't always take effect right away. Be patient. Within a few minutes, the new addresses will appear in Active Directory Users and Computers.

Making Exchange Server Use a Smart Host

In our world, we want to ensure that all mail the Exchange server sends and receives goes through the mail.corp.com front-end server. To do this, we'll tell Exchange to only send via a *smart host*.

To configure Exchange to send e-mail via a smart host:

1. Select Start ≻ Program Files ≻ Microsoft Exchange and select "System Manager."
2. Drill down to Corp (Exchange) ≻ Servers ≻ *<your server name>* ≻ Protocols ≻ SMTP.
3. Right-click the "Default SMTP Virtual Server" entry and select "Properties."
4. In the "Default SMTP Virtual Server Properties" page, select the "Delivery" tab.
5. On the "Delivery" tab, select "Advanced." In the "Advanced Delivery" page, as shown in Figure 6.10, enter **mail.corp.com** in the "Smart host" field.
6. Click "OK" on the "Advanced Delivery" page.
7. Click "OK" on the "Delivery" tab, to close that as well.

FIGURE 6.9   Add a primary and alternate destination address in the Default Policy Properties.

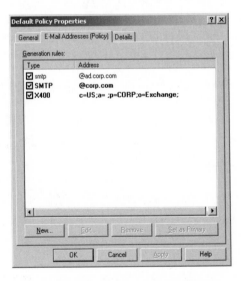

FIGURE 6.10   Setting `mail.corp.com` as a smart host forces all mail to be routed out to `mail.corp.com`.

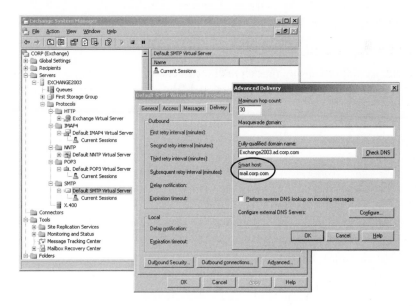

Making Exchange Forward Mail It Cannot Process

All of our internal Active Directory users will use Exchange to process their e-mail. However, as we've stated, some users in our organization won't be using Exchange; they'll be using `linserv1.corp.com` as a Linux Postfix e-mail server.

This presents a problem. Everyone in the organization has an e-mail address in the form of *user*@corp.com. What happens if an Exchange user sends e-mail to someone at `corp.com` but they aren't an Exchange user? That is, we need to tell Exchange what to do if it doesn't have the e-mail address for the user. In our case, we'll want to send all mail to `mail.corp.com`—our gateway machine—which will then figure out which server the e-mail is destined for and route it appropriately.

To set this up, just click the "Messages" tab in the "Default SMTP Virtual Server Properties" page. In the last entry, "Forward all mail with unresolved recipients to host" enter **mail.corp.com**, as shown in Figure 6.11.

Postfix Departmental Server Reconfiguration Tasks

Right now, the Postfix departmental server thinks it is the one and only mail server for `corp.com`. We need to adjust the departmental server's configuration a bit so that it can coexist with the Exchange server. We also want to configure the departmental server to take advantage of the spam- and virus-filtering capabilities of our front-end MTA, `mail.corp.com` for outgoing messages as well. We'll do most of this using Webmin. One final step is not supported by Webmin's Postfix module, so we'll just edit the Postfix configuration file directly for that one change.

FIGURE 6.11 Enter `mail.corp.com` as the destination address for forwarding unresolved e-mail.

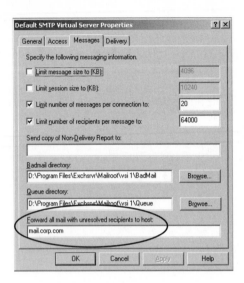

First, we'll change the way outgoing mail is delivered. Right now, `linserv1.corp.com` delivers e-mail destined for domains other than `corp.com` directly to other MTAs. However, since we plan to create a front-end mail server that can filter out spam and viruses, it makes sense to subject our own outgoing e-mail to the same scans. After all, if internal workstations are compromised by viruses and become virus transmitters themselves, there's no reason to allow those machines to damage the organization's reputation by allowing their messages through. So we'll set the "Set outgoing e-mail via host" option in Webmin to `mail.corp.com`, the hostname of the front-end mail server we will configure later in this chapter.

Second, we'll tell the Postfix departmental server what to do with e-mail messages for addresses in the `corp.com` domain that do not have corresponding valid Linux accounts. For instance, when a Linux Postfix user, such as `nurse1`, tries to send e-mail to an Exchange user, such as `salesperson1`, we want that message to be forwarded to our new box—`mail.corp.com`. This server handily solves the routing problem because `mail.corp.com` will be configured to correctly deliver messages to the right back end, either Linux or Exchange. Passing the messages through `mail.corp.com` also permits `mail.corp.com` to limit the spread of spam and viruses, stopping them at the gate between Linux and Exchange, in case of an outbreak of e-mail-virus-afflicted workstations in either camp.

We'll arrange this using the "Optional transport for unknown recipients" option of Webmin. A *transport* in Postfix is a way to deliver e-mail to a specific destination. A complete transport involves a protocol and, if delivery is not to the local server itself, a mail server (MTA) name. In this case, the protocol we want to use is SMTP (the Simple Mail Transfer Protocol, used by all MTAs to communicate with one another). The mail server we want to pass the message on to is `mail.corp.com`. Postfix configuration files separate these two things with colons, like this:

`smtp:mail.corp.com`

That's exactly how we'll describe the transport we want when we set that option in Webmin.

Finally, we need to let the Postfix departmental server know that it is not the sole and final authority on who has a valid e-mail address in the `corp.com` domain. Unless we do that, setting up the "Optional transport for unknown recipients" feature does us no good, because the server will discard e-mails for unknown recipients as junk mail.

By default, Postfix checks a list of "local recipient maps" to figure out what addresses are valid. Instead of allowing it do this, we'll set this option to an empty value. That tells Postfix not to discard e-mails for addresses it doesn't recognize. We'll set this directly in the Postfix configuration file, `/etc/postfix/main.cf` because this option cannot be set via Webmin.

Now we're ready to reconfigure Postfix based on what we just described. To reconfigure the Postfix departmental server to use `mail.corp.com` as a front-end MTA, follow these steps:

1. Log into Webmin as usual at `https://linserv1.corp.com:10000/`.

2. Click "Servers."

3. Click "Postfix Configuration."

4. Click "General Options."

5. Scroll down and locate "Send outgoing mail via host." Select the right-hand radio box and enter **mail.corp.com**   .

6. Scroll down and click "Save and Apply."

7. Click "Local delivery."

8. Locate the "Optional transport for unknown recipients" option. Select the right-hand radio box and enter **smtp:mail.corp.com**   in the text entry field.

9. Scroll down and click "Save and Apply."

10. With your favorite text editor, open `/etc/postfix/main.cf` and replace any existing setting for the local recipient maps option with the following, or add it at the end of the file if it does not already appear:

    ```
    local_recipient_maps =
    ```

11. Effect this change `/etc/postfix/main.cf` by restarting the Postfix server with the following command, as root:

    ```
    service postfix restart
    ```

Setting up a DNS MX Record for *mail.corp.com*

Before the outside world can deliver mail to *anyone*@`corp.com`, we'll need to set up an MX (mail exchanger) DNS record for the front-end MTA. This is the DNS record that allows other hosts on the Internet to figure out where to send e-mail intended for the `corp.com` domain.

When someone outside of `corp.com` wants to send e-mail to, for instance, **salesperson1@corp** **.com**, they transmit the message to their own outgoing MTA. But exactly how does their MTA figure out what MTA to deliver the mail to? That's where MX records come in: MX records in DNS allow MTAs to use a DNS query to figure out where e-mail should go.

We'll add an MX record for the `corp.com` domain and set the MTA in that record to `mail.corp.com`.

Webmin can help us out with this task. All we have to do is use the Webmin module BIND DNS Server to add a new MX record. There's not much to it, just two things to know:

- The domain to which e-mail is being delivered is referred to, a bit confusingly, as the "Name" field.

- We'll need to set a priority for the MX record. This is very useful when there are multiple MX records for a domain because MTAs will automatically try the highest-priority MTAs first. In our case, there's just one MX record, so we'll arbitrarily choose a priority of 100.

To add an MX record for `mail.corp.com` in the `corp.com` domain, follow these steps:

1. Log into Webmin on `linserv1.corp.com` (the DNS server) as usual, at `https://linserv1.corp.com:10000/`.

2. Click "BIND DNS Server."

3. Click "`corp.com`" under "Existing DNS Zones."

4. Click "Mail Server (MX)".

5. The "Mail Server Records" page appears with the subheading "Add Mail Server Record."

6. In the "Name" field, enter **corp.com** .

7. In the "Mail Server" field, enter **mail.corp.com** .

8. In the "Priority" field, enter **100**.

9. Leave "Time-To-Live" set to the default.

10. Click "Create."

11. Click "Return to Zone List."

12. Click "Apply Changes."

Our MX record is ready! You can verify this with the `dig` command, which can be used to make a variety of DNS queries. Use the following command:

```
dig -t mx corp.com
```

The response should be, in part:

```
;; ANSWER SECTION:
corp.com.               3600    IN      MX      100 mail.corp.com.
```

If not, make sure you clicked "Apply Changes" to restart the DNS server.

Now we're ready to actually create the `mail.corp.com` system.

Installing Fedora on the Front-End Mail Server with the Postfix and SpamAssassin Packages

For Fedora installation instructions, follow those given in Chapter 1 for `linserv1.corp.com`, with the following changes:

1. The hostname should be `mail.corp.com`

2. The IP address of the server will be a valid, fixed Internet IP address, *not* part of an internal network such as `192.168.2.x`. In our examples, we'll use the IP address `10.1.1.10`. Of course, you will use a real Internet IP address assigned to your organization.

3. The DNS server name will be `192.168.2.202` (the IP address of `linserv1.corp.com`). This ensures that `mail.corp.com` will be able to resolve hostnames within the local network.

4. When you reach the package selection step, for the mail server option, click the "Details" link to display a full list of available packages.

5. Make sure the optional SpamAssassin and Postfix packages are selected. If not, check the box next to each.

6. Uncheck the box next to the Sendmail server. We are using Postfix instead of Sendmail.

When you have completed the initial installation, make sure you also fetch security updates and other fixes by running up2date. Mail servers are particularly vulnerable to security risks and should be kept up to date to guard against newly discovered attacks. Double-click the exclamation point icon the upper-right corner and follow the steps given in Chapter 1 to update your system.

Now we're ready to install the ClamAV virus filter.

Installing Clam Anti-Virus

The best way to obtain the ClamAV anti-virus software for Fedora Core 3 is to visit the ClamAV website at `www.clamav.net`. This way, you can seek out providers of rpms whose work has been acknowledged by the ClamAV team and used by many others.

We will also take the time to download a cryptographic key that verifies the identity of the person who packaged the rpm. This helps us to verify that the rpm has not been tampered with.

We followed these steps to obtain an rpm of ClamAV compatible with Fedora Core 3:

1. Go to the URL `www.clamav.net/`.

2. Under the "Downloads" heading, click "binary packages and ports."

3. Under the "Red Hat -- Fedora" heading, follow the "Fedora3" link, which currently leads to `http://crash.fce.vutbr.cz/crash-hat/3/clamav/`.

4. Click "clamav-0.83-1.i386.rpm" (the version number will vary; this is the current version number as of this writing, but you should download the latest available or latest stable release).

5. Save or copy that file to `/tmp` on `mail.corp.com`.

We could install the rpm now, but we would receive a warning like this one:

```
warning: clamav-0.83-1.i386.rpm: V3 DSA signature: NOKEY, key ID 6cdf2cc1
```

This is because the rpm file was cryptographically signed with a key that `mail.corp.com` doesn't already have on file. So RPM can't verify the origin of the software. We can improve on this situation by downloading the author's cryptographic key, which we can locate by browsing the top directory of the `http://crash.fce.vutbr.cz` site. To install the key of the person who packaged this rpm, Petr Kristof, just use the `rpm --import [URL]` command to fetch the key and install it:

```
rpm --import http://crash.fce.vutbr.cz/Petr.Kristof-GPG-KEY
```

When successful, this command produces no output in the terminal window. If you receive warnings or errors, try opening the same URL with your web browser. If you don't have success doing that, we recommend that you visit `http://crash.fce.vutbr.cz/` and check whether the key file's name has been changed.

Now we're ready to install the rpm, and any other rpm signed by Petr Kristof, without warning messages:

```
rpm -i clamav-0.83-1.i386.rpm
```

As mentioned before, your version number will most likely differ because ClamAV development is ongoing.

ClamAV is now installed on your system. Earlier, we installed SpamAssassin as part of the process of installing Fedora on `mail.corp.com`. Now, we'll install MailScanner, the software that integrates SpamAssassin and ClamAV with Postfix.

The default installation of ClamAV works perfectly for our needs and doesn't require any configuration changes, so we don't use Webmin to modify the ClamAV configuration in this book. However, a ClamAV module for Webmin is available. For more information, visit `http://wbmclamav.labs.libre-entreprise.org/`.

Installing MailScanner

We have an MTA, a spam filter, and a virus filter. Aren't we finished? Well, no. Like most Linux applications, SpamAssassin and ClamAV attempt to do just one job and do it well. That job is reading the e-mail you hand off to them and deciding whether it contains spam or viruses.

These packages do *not* provide a robust, high-performance interface to various specific MTAs. That's where MailScanner comes into the picture. MailScanner can integrate any number of different e-mail filters with the MTA of our choice—in this case, Postfix.

 There *are* ways to integrate SpamAssassin or ClamAV with Postfix without using MailScanner or a similar program, but these methods assume you only need one or the other. When you want to use them together with good overall performance, you need MailScanner or a comparable program such as amavis.

MailScanner is easy to install. It's written in Perl and requires an assortment of Perl modules. The authors have packaged those with an installation script that automatically installs all of these requirements.

To install MailScanner, follow these steps:

1. Browse the MailScanner website, at:

   `http://www.sng.ecs.soton.ac.uk/mailscanner/`

2. Click "Downloads."

3. Under the "Stable" heading, click "Version 4.39.6-1 for RedHat and Mandrake Linux (and other RPM-based Linux distributions)." The version number you see will probably be newer; download the latest stable version.

4. Move the downloaded file, `MailScanner-4.39.6-1.rpm.tar.gz` (the version number will vary), to `/tmp` on `mail.corp.com`.

5. As root, change your current directory to `/tmp`:

   `cd /tmp`

6. Unpack the gzipped tar file with the following command, which we've seen before:

   `tar -zxf MailScanner-4.39.6-1.rpm.tar.gz`

7. Change directories into the newly created `MailScanner-4.39.6-1` directory (the version number you see will probably be different):

   `cd MailScanner-4.39.6-1`

8. Using a text editor, skim the README file for newer instructions, just in case the installation process has changed.

9. Install the software with the following command:

   `./install.sh`

At the end of the process you will see instructions to activate the software. Those are intended for Sendmail; however, so don't try to follow them. We'll take care of configuring MailScanner for use with Postfix later.

Configuring Postfix As a Front-End MTA

Postfix has many, many configuration options. It's well beyond the scope of this chapter to attempt to cover them all. For a complete treatment of Postfix, see *The Book of Postfix: State-of-the-art Message Transport* by Ralf Hildebrandt and Patrick Koetter (No Starch Press, 2005, ISBN 1-59327-001-1). Also, see the Postfix website at `www.postfix.org`.

Fortunately, a standard installation of Postfix on Fedora Core 3 includes reasonable default settings for most options. Here we will concern ourselves only with those that must be changed from the default configuration to create our front-end MTA. However, we'll present our entire, working Postfix configuration file at the end of this section for completeness, with the options we added or changed listed first.

All Postfix configuration files are found in the directory `/etc/postfix`. The "master" configuration file for Postfix is `/etc/postfix/main.cf`. This is where all of the configuration choices are made. Some options refer to additional files or databases that contain, for instance, lists of domains to reject mail from, aliases to accept mail for, and so on.

The `main.cf` file has a very simple format. Blank lines and lines beginning with a # are ignored. All other lines take the following form:

```
option = value
```

Some options accept multiple values, separated by commas. In many cases the value will be a reference to another text file or to a database that we'll create a bit later using a Postfix command called `postmap` You'll see examples of this next.

inet_interfaces

By default, Fedora sets this option to `localhost`. That means that mail is only accepted from the server itself. We, of course, are creating a front-end MTA that accepts mail from the rest of the world, so we'll want to accept mail on the Ethernet interface also. We can do this by setting `inet_interfaces` to `all`.

mydestination

This option determines the domains and hostnames that the server accepts incoming mail for. If we were building a typical standalone mail server that delivered mail to local POP mailboxes, we would want our domain, `corp.com`, to be on that list. However, in this case, we intend to relay mail for `corp.com` to the Exchange server behind the firewall...after we clean it of viruses and spam, of course. The only addresses we should regard as local are `localhost`, `localhost.localdomain`, and `localhost.corp.com`. These are typically used to deliver notices of system activity to the local system administrator. We'll set this option to `localhost.$mydomain, localhost.localdomain, localhost`. Postfix automatically replaces `$mydomain` with `corp.com` without our changing the configuration file if our domain name changes.

relay_domains

Once upon a time, most mail servers cheerfully forwarded e-mail for third parties. The mail server for `corp.com`, for example, would have typically accepted a message "From:" `jane@examplecompany.com`, addressed "To:" `doug@exampleschool.edu`, and simply forwarded it on to the mail server for `exampleschool.edu`. Nowadays, this behavior is known as *open relay*. Because an open relay can be used to forward unlimited amounts of spam, many sites have harsh filtering policies that refuse *all* e-mail from servers known to be open relays. That's why we must be very careful to specify which domains we really do want to relay e-mail for. By default, postfix relays mail only for hosts it is the final destination for. Since our front-end MTA is not the final destination (the Exchange server or departmental Postfix server is), we must explicitly state that mail for `corp.com` should be relayed. This is one of the areas where the Webmin GUI for Postfix is currently inadequate for our purposes.

transport_maps

By default, Postfix is configured as the final destination for e-mail, delivering it to POP mailboxes on the server's hard drive. We, of course, are forwarding mail to the Exchange server and departmental Postfix server instead. How exactly do we do that? By creating a transport *map*, a text file that specifies where mail for `corp.com` should be delivered. We introduced the idea of a Postfix *transport* in the previous section. Though we used Webmin in that section, transports are described in the same way in the configuration file.

We'll create the text file `/etc/postfix/transport`, which should contain "rules" in this format, one per line:

```
emailaddress smtp:hostname
```

Rules like this specify that mail for *emailaddress* should be forwarded via SMTP (the Simple Mail Transfer Protocol) to *hostname*. A typical rule for a user on the Exchange back-end server would be:

```
salesperson1@corp.com smtp:exchange2003.ad.corp.com
```

and a typical rule for a user on the Linux Departmental Mail Server back end would be:

```
nurse1@corp.com smtp:linserv1.corp.com
```

Postfix uses map files like this for many purposes. Notice that the rule consists of a *key* (the domain name) on the left and a *value* (the mail delivery instructions) on the right. All Postfix map files are made up of key/value pairs like this. Once we create or edit an existing map file, we'll need to *publish* it using the `postmap` command. Publishing the file creates a database in which Postfix can look up the value for any key much more quickly than scanning a text file over and over would allow. We use the `postmap` command this way:

```
postmap /etc/postfix/transport
```

We then use the `transport_maps` option in `main.cf` to point to the `/etc/postfix/transport file` as our source of transport map information, by setting the value for this option to `hash:/etc/postfix/transport`. The term *hash* indicates that the actual data should come from a .db file published by the `postmap` command. The filename specified, `/etc/postfix/transport`, is that of the text file, but the `hash:` prefix allows Postfix to locate the actual data in `/etc/postfix/transport.db`.

Does this mean we'll have to maintain `/etc/postfix/transport` by hand? Thankfully, no! We've written a Perl script which does that job automatically, rebuilding `/etc/postfix/transport` every hour. The script, `build-transport-maps.pl`, fetches information about valid e-mail accounts from *both* the Linux-based Departmental Mail Server *and* the Active Directory server and builds a complete map file that allows our front-end MTA to correctly deliver mail to both sets of users. We present this script in detail later in this section.

relay_recipient_maps

We'd like Postfix to take care of discarding e-mail for bogus addresses that don't actually exist on Exchange or on our departmental Postfix server. This will save wear and tear on our back end servers. But if our front-end MTA isn't the final destination for e-mail, how can we tell good addresses apart from bad?

Postfix has an option, `relay_recipient_maps`, which allows us to specify all of the valid e-mail addresses for the `ad.corp.com`. By setting this option to point to a file containing a database of valid e-mail addresses, we enable our front-end MTA to correctly recognize legitimate recipients. E-mail for all other recipients is bounced back to the sender without forcing the Exchange server to deal with it. No matter how good our spam filters are, there will always be junk mail that slips by them, but many (if not most) of these messages will be intended for bad e-mail addresses, and we can completely eliminate the need for Exchange to deal with those messages.

We set this option to `hash:/etc/postfix/recipients`. But how can we keep an up-to-date list of every valid e-mail address in that file? Surely that's impractical! Again, fortunately, we don't have to do it by hand. As explained, we've written a Perl script which does that job automatically, rebuilding both `/etc/postfix/transport` and `/etc/postfix/recipients` every hour. The script, `build-transport-maps.pl`, fetches information about valid e-mail accounts from *both* the Linux-based departmental mail server *and* the Active Directory server and builds a complete list of valid e-mail recipients, as well as a transport map that allows our front-end MTA to correctly deliver mail to either set of users.

header_checks

Postfix provides several ways to check e-mails for telltale signs of spam and other important markers. One of these is the `header_checks` option; this option points to a map file. Each rule in the map file consists, as usual, of a key and a value. Each key is a *regular expression*, a pattern that matches something that may or may not appear in the header lines of an e-mail message. Each value indicates what should be done with a message that matches the regular expression.

We'll set the `header_checks` option to point to a map file called `/etc/postfix/header_checks:`, as follows:

```
header_checks = regexp:/etc/postfix/header_checks
```

In that file, we'll place a single rule which requires Postfix to place any messages that contain a `Received:` header "on hold" by moving them to the hold queue. Since *all* e-mail messages contain a `Received:` header, this is really a way of placing all messages on hold. We do this so that every incoming message finds its way to the hold queue, where we will configure MailScanner to pick up messages and scan them for spam and viruses. The single rule we'll place in `/etc/postfix/header_checks` is

```
/^Received:/ HOLD
```

Unlike `/etc/postfix/recipients`, we don't publish this file with the `postmap` command. That's because Postfix needs to look at *all* of the rules in the file, not just one, so there's no performance benefit to be gained by creating a database index.

Most of this regular expression is fairly obvious: the pattern to be matched appears between the slashes. The ^ character matches the beginning of a line. For complete information about regular expressions, see *Mastering Regular Expressions, 2nd Edition* by Jeffrey E. F. Friedl (O'Reilly Press, 2002, ISBN: 0-596-00289-0.) Also see the excellent Wikipedia entry at `http://en.wiki-pedia.org/wiki/Regular_expression`.

MailScanner will take care of moving good messages from the hold queue to the incoming queue so that Postfix can continue the process of delivering them.

Listing 6.1: `/etc/postfix/main.cf` for the `mail.corp.com` front-end MTA

```
queue_directory = /var/spool/postfix
command_directory = /usr/sbin
daemon_directory = /usr/libexec/postfix
mail_owner = postfix
inet_interfaces = all
mydestination = localhost.$mydomain, localhost, localhost.localdomain
unknown_local_recipient_reject_code = 550
relay_domains = corp.com
alias_maps = hash:/etc/aliases
alias_database = hash:/etc/aliases
header_checks = regexp:/etc/postfix/header_checks
debug_peer_level = 2
debugger_command =
    PATH=/bin:/usr/bin:/usr/local/bin:/usr/X11R6/bin
    xxgdb $daemon_directory/$process_name $process_id & sleep 5
sendmail_path = /usr/sbin/sendmail.postfix
newaliases_path = /usr/bin/newaliases.postfix
mailq_path = /usr/bin/mailq.postfix
setgid_group = postdrop
html_directory = no
manpage_directory = /usr/share/man
sample_directory = /usr/share/doc/postfix-2.1.5/samples
readme_directory = /usr/share/doc/postfix-2.1.5/README_FILES
transport_maps = hash:/etc/postfix/transport
relay_recipient_maps = hash:/etc/postfix/recipients
```

We're almost ready to move on. But first, we need to configure a script that will provide us with regularly updated `/etc/postfix/recipients` and `/etc/postfix/transport` files.

WARNING   Although we have configured Postfix itself as a front-end MTA, we did so in a way that requires us to also configure MailScanner and the rest of the tools described in the sections that follow. Be sure to follow through and complete the remaining sections before expecting your front-end MTA to operate properly.

Installing and Configuring the *build-transport-maps.pl* Script

To review, the ultimate goal is to have incoming e-mail on `mail.corp.com` and for that e-mail to be routed to either `linserv1.corp.com` or `exchange2003.ad.corp.com`—depending on where the real destination mailbox is.

To that end, we've written a Perl script entitled `build-transport-maps.pl`. It does three things:

- It identifies valid Exchange e-mail addresses by fetching a list of valid e-mail addresses from Active Directory.

- It identifies valid Postfix departmental server e-mail addresses by fetching a list of valid LDAP accounts from the OpenLDAP server on `linserv1.corp.com`.

- It uses this information to rebuild the `/etc/postfix/recipients` and `/etc/postfix/transport` files, then rebuilds the relevant Postfix databases using the `postmap` command. This allows the Postfix server on `mail.corp.com` to recognize an updated list of valid e-mail addresses and forward messages to the correct back-end mail server for each.

The script is presented at the end of this section as Listing 6.3 and can also be found on our website at `www.winlinanswers.com/`.

To begin, copy the script and put it in a file named to `/etc/postfix/build-transport-maps.pl` on `mail.corp.com`.

Next, using a text editor, we'll need to set up a configuration file for the script. The configuration file name is `/etc/postfix/build-transport-maps.conf`. This file should have three section headings: `[global]`, `[Exchange Mail Server]`, and `[Linux Mail Server]`. The complete configuration file is presented in Listing 6.2.

> Options in `build-transport-maps.conf` are set using a familiar *name = value* syntax. Option names are not case-sensitive.

Global Options (designated with a *[global]* heading)

The first line in your `/etc/postfix/build-transport-maps.conf` file should have a line that reads:

```
[global]
```

The global category contains just one option, `domain`. This is the domain name to be added to valid account names to produce an e-mail address. In our case, the correct setting is `corp.com`, so that line of the configuration file looks like this:

```
domain = corp.com
```

Back-End Options (Designated with *[Exchange Mail Server]* and *[Linux Mail Server]* Headings)

Here is what the [Linux Mail Server] heading should look like in /etc/postfix/build-transport-maps.conf:

```
[Linux Mail Server]
name = Linux Mail Server
#May be specified more than once
uri = ldaps://linserv1.corp.com/
base = dc=ldap,dc=corp,dc=com
filter = (&(objectclass=account))
smtpserver = linserv1.corp.com
attr = uid
```

Here is what the [Exchange Mail Server] heading should look like:

```
[Exchange Mail Server]
name = Exchange Mail Server
#May be specified more than once
uri = ldaps://windc1.ad.corp.com/
base = dc=ad,dc=corp,dc=com
binddn = cn=dirsearch,cn=Users,dc=ad,dc=corp,dc=com
bindpw = p@ssw0rd
filter = (&(sAMAccountName=*)(mail=*))
smtpserver = exchange2003.ad.corp.com
attr = name
```

Two options, binddpw and binddn, are optional for Linux but required for Active Directory. This is because Active Directory *requires* authentication before making directory service queries.

Here's a breakdown of each value and how it can be set:

name   The name option specifies the name of the back end as it will appear in any error messages from build-transport-map.pl. We set it to Linux Mail Server for the Linux option group and to Exchange Mail Server for the Exchange option group.

uri   The uri option, which may be given more than once for a single back end, specifies the LDAP server address to connect to. It's similar to the uri option in /etc/ldap.conf, as discussed in Chapters 2 and 3.

For the Linux back end, the correct setting is ldaps://linserv1.corp.com; which establishes a secure connection on the secure LDAP port, port 636.

For the Windows back end, the correct setting is ldaps://windc1.ad.corp.com if the mail.corp.com front-end server meets the requirements for secure LDAP connections from Fedora Linux to Active Directory, as explained in Chapter 3, specifically the section titled "The Extra Mile: SSL Encryption of LDAP Traffic between Linux and Active Directory."

If the version of OpenLDAP installed on `mail.corp.com` is too old, use `ldap://windc1.ad.corp.com` (not `ldaps://`) to establish a nonencrypted connection on port 389. Since only account names are being transmitted, this is an acceptable risk (but encryption is preferable).

Giving this option more than once on separate lines provides fault tolerance. That is, the script will contact the first URI, then the second, and so on until a successful connection is made. If *all* URIs fail for any back end, the script will produce an error message and exit without updating maps.

base The `base` option specifies LDAP search base beneath which the search for accounts should be conducted. This is identical to the `base` option in `/etc/ldap.conf`. See Chapters 2 and 3 for extensive coverage of this subject.

filter Not every object in an LDAP database is an e-mail account. The `filter` option, similar to the `filter` option in `/etc/ldap.conf`, is used to limit the search to relevant objects. For Linux, we set this to `(objectclass=account)`, which matches all account objects in the LDAP database because accounts are always part of the `account` LDAP object class. For Exchange, we set it to `(&(sAMAccountName=*)(mail=*))`, which matches accounts in Active Directory that possess both a logon name and an e-mail address. * matches any value, and & specifies that all of the additional conditions within the enclosing parentheses must be true. A detailed discussion of LDAP filters is beyond the scope of this book; see Randy Franklin Smith's article, "LDAP Filters," on the Windows IT Pro website for more information at `www.windowsitpro.com/Windows/Article/ArticleID/38949/38949.html`.

smtpserver What is the final destination of the mail? The `smtpserver` option answers this question. We set this to `linserv1.corp.com` for the Linux back end and to `exchange2003.ad.corp.com` for the Windows back end.

attr The `attr` option specifies the name of the LDAP attribute that holds the account name. This is the logon name that can be followed with `@corp.com` to arrive at an e-mail address. This is needed because the different back ends have different LDAP schemas, as you saw in Chapters 2 and 3. For Linux, the correct setting is `uid`. For Windows, it is `name`.

binddn The `binddn` option specifies the distinguished name of the LDAP user to authenticate to the LDAP server as. This is used with the Active Directory server, where we configured a low-security user named `dirsearch` for this purpose in Chapter 3. For the Exchange back end, we set this option to `cn=dirsearch,cn=Users,dc=ad,dc=corp,dc=com`. We don't use this option with the Linux LDAP server because it is configured to allow anonymous queries.

bindpw The `bindpw` option specifies the password of the LDAP user we will authenticate to the LDAP server as. This is used with the Active Directory server, where we configured a low-security user named `dirsearch` for this purpose in Chapter 3. For the Exchange back end, we set this option to `p@ssw0rd`. We don't use this option with the Linux LDAP server because it is configured to allow anonymous queries.

We've finished configuring `build-transport-maps.pl`. We're almost ready to test it. But first, we need to install the Net::LDAP Perl module from CPAN, which `build-transport-maps.pl` needs to communicate with Active Directory and the OpenLDAP server on `linserv1.corp.com`.

We've used the `cpan` command to install such modules before. Follow these steps to install Net::LDAP:

1. Make sure `mail.corp.com` has Internet access. The `cpan` command installs modules over the Net from the central Perl module repository.

2. As root, enter the command:

    `cpan`

3. At the `cpan>` prompt, enter

    `install Net::LDAP`

    and press Enter.

4. If CPAN detects that other modules on which Net::LDAP depends are also not installed, it will offer to add them to the list of modules to install. Say yes to any such prompts. If CPAN detects that Net::LDAP is already up to date, skip to step 6.

5. The installation will begin and will take about a minute or so.

6. When the `cpan>` prompt reappears, type:

    `quit`

    Press Enter to return to the shell prompt.

Just one task left before we can test the script. We must make the script executable with the following command, executed by root:

`chmod 700 /etc/postfix/build-transport-map.pl`

While we're at it, we will also limit access to the script's configuration file to the root user. There shouldn't be other users running free on a dedicated front-end server like `mail.corp.com`, but "defense in depth" is always the best strategy:

`chmod 600 /etc/postfix/build-transport-maps.conf`

Now we can test it by executing it:

`/etc/postfix/build-transport-map.pl`

If all goes well, this will produce no output at the shell prompt. That's because `build-transport-map.pl` is typically run from cron, and programs that generate output when run from cron result in e-mail to the user. We don't want root to be bombarded hourly by e-mails indicating that everything is fine. We *do* want root to get e-mail when things don't work, and `build-transport-map.pl` does complain in such situations.

If you see error messages, or if the script does not end and return to the shell prompt within two minutes, check all of the following:

1. Do you have both the Linux mail server back end and the Exchange mail server back end up and running? If not, start them now.

2. Did you follow the LDAP exercises in Chapter 2 as part of creating the Linux server `linserv1.corp.com`? If not, you won't be able to set up a separate front-end MTA because a list of valid addresses can't be easily obtained over the network.

3. Are you using an ldaps: URL to communicate securely with Active Directory? If you are, did you verify that your version of OpenLDAP is new enough as described in Chapter 3? If not, use an ldap: URL instead.

If the script completes successfully, you can verify that the `/etc/postfix/transport` and `/etc/postfix/recipients` files were updated by examining them with a text editor. `/etc/postfix/transport` should look like this:

```
Administrator@corp.com   smtp:exchange2003.ad.corp.com
salesperson1@corp.com    smtp:exchange2003.ad.corp.com
salesperson2@corp.com    smtp:exchange2003.ad.corp.com
salesperson3@corp.com    smtp:exchange2003.ad.corp.com
salesperson4@corp.com    smtp:exchange2003.ad.corp.com
doctor1@corp.com         smtp:linserv1.corp.com
doctor2@corp.com         smtp:linserv1.corp.com
nurse1@corp.com smtp:linserv1.corp.com
nurse2@corp.com smtp:linserv1.corp.com
```

And `/etc/postfix/recipients` should look like this:

```
Administrator@corp.com   OK
salesperson1@corp.com    OK
salesperson2@corp.com    OK
salesperson3@corp.com    OK
salesperson4@corp.com    OK
doctor1@corp.com         OK
doctor2@corp.com         OK
nurse1@corp.com OK
nurse2@corp.com OK
```

Finally, we need to install a cron job to run this script once each hour. The crontab entry we'll need is

```
0 * * * * /etc/postfix/build-transport-maps.pl
```

We introduced cron jobs and how to install them in Chapter 4. See the "Scheduling Tasks with cron" sidebar in that chapter for details.

We've completed the configuration of Postfix. Now we're ready to configure MailScanner to bridge the gap between Postfix and the two virus and spam filter programs.

Listing 6.2: /etc/postfix/build-transport-maps.conf

```
[global]
domain = corp.com

[Linux Mail Server]
name = Linux Mail Server
#May be specified more than once
uri = ldaps://linserv1.corp.com/
base = dc=ldap,dc=corp,dc=com
filter = (&(objectclass=account))
smtpserver = linserv1.corp.com
attr = uid

[Exchange Mail Server]
name = Exchange Mail Server
#May be specified more than once
uri = ldaps://windc1.ad.corp.com/
base = dc=ad,dc=corp,dc=com
binddn = cn=dirsearch,cn=Users,dc=ad,dc=corp,dc=com
bindpw = p@ssw0rd
filter = (&(sAMAccountName=*)(mail=*))
smtpserver = exchange2003.ad.corp.com
attr = name
```

Listing 6.3: /etc/postfix/build-transport-maps.pl

```perl
#!/usr/bin/perl -w

#All settings appear in
#/etc/postfix/build-transport-maps.conf,
#nothing to change here.

use strict;

my %options;
if (!open(IN, "/etc/postfix/build-transport-maps.conf")) {
    die "Can't open /etc/postfix/build-transport-maps.conf";
    }
my $label = '[global]';
my $line;
while ($line = <IN>) {
```

```perl
    # Remove comments...
    $line =~ s/\#.*$//;
    # And skip blank lines, including lines made blank by
    # removing comments
    if ($line =~ /^\s*$/) {
        next;
    }
    # Start new labeled section
    if ($line =~ /\[([\w\s\.\-\+]+)\]/) {
        $label = $1;
        $label =~ tr/A-Z/a-z/;
        next;
    }
    my ($name, $val) = split(/\=/, $line, 2);
    $name =~ s/^\s+//;
    $name =~ s/\s+$//;
    $name =~ tr/A-Z/a-z/;
    $val =~ s/^\s+//;
    $val =~ s/\s+$//;
    if ($label eq "") {
        die "All options must appear within a section, did you forget
[global]?\n";
    }
    push @{$options{$label}{$name}}, $val;
}
close(IN);
my $domain = @{$options{'global'}{'domain'}}[0];

my @serverTypeNames = keys(%options);

my @serverTypes;

my @required = (
    "name",
    "base",
    "filter",
    "addr",
    "smtpserver",
    "uri"
);
```

```perl
my %required;

my $r;
for $r (@required) {
   $required{$r} = 1;
}

my @scalar = (
   "name",
   "base",
   "binddn",
   "bindpw",
   "filter",
   "attr",
   "smtpserver"
);

my @list = (
   "uri"
);

my $sn;

for $sn (@serverTypeNames) {
   if ($sn eq "global") {
      next;
   }
   my $s = { };
   my $item;
   for $item (@scalar) {
      if (defined($options{$sn}{$item})) {
         $$s{$item} = (@{$options{$sn}{$item}})[0];
      }
      if ($required{$item} && (!defined($$s{$item}))) {
         die "Required option $item missing for $sn";
      }
   }
   for $item (@list) {
      $$s{$item} = $options{$sn}{$item};
      if ($required{$item} && (!defined($$s{$item}))) {
```

```
            die "Required option $item missing for $sn";
        }
    }
    push @serverTypes, $s;
}

# Talk to both OpenLDAP and Active Directory to create
# a transport map forwarding mail for Linux users to
# one destination and Exchange users to another.
# Also build a combined list of all valid recipients
# for easy filtering of unsolicited junk mail without
# troubling the internal servers.

use Net::LDAP;

my $s;

open(RECIPIENTS, ">/etc/postfix/recipients.new");
open(TRANSPORT, ">/etc/postfix/transport.new");

for $s (@serverTypes) {
    my $ldap;
    my $uri;
    for $uri (@{$$s{'uri'}}) {
        $ldap = Net::LDAP->new($uri);
        if ($ldap) {
            last;
        }
    }
    if (!$ldap) {
        die "Could not contact any LDAP URIs for " ,
            $$s{'name'} , "\n" ,
            "To avoid inconsistencies no maps will be updated.";
    }
    my $bind;
    if ($$s{'binddn'}) {
        # Bind as a specific user (simple authentication)
        $bind = $ldap->bind(
            dn => $$s{'binddn'},
            password => $$s{'bindpw'});
```

```perl
    } else {
       # Anonymous bind
       $bind = $ldap->bind;
    }
    if ($bind->code()) {
       die "Bind error: error:", $bind->code(), "\n",
          "No maps will be updated on this pass.\n";
    }
    my $search = $ldap->search(base => $$s{'base'},
                     filter => $$s{'filter'},
          attrs => $$s{'attr'});
    my $entries = $search->count;
    if ($entries < '1') {
       print STDERR "Warning: zero accounts found for ", $$s{'uri'}, "\n";
    }
    my @entries = $search->entries;
    my $e;
    for $e (@entries) {
       my $m = $e->get_value($$s{'attr'});
       # Ignore orphaned Exchange mailboxes with
       # raw SIDs instead of user names
       if ($m =~ /\{/) {
          next;
       }
       my $smtpServer = $$s{'smtpserver'};
       print RECIPIENTS "$m\@$domain\tOK\n";
       print TRANSPORT "$m\@$domain\tsmtp:$smtpServer\n";
    }
    # Unbinding
    $ldap->unbind;
}
close(RECIPIENTS);
close(TRANSPORT);

unlink("/etc/postfix/recipients");
rename("/etc/postfix/recipients.new", "/etc/postfix/recipients");
system("/usr/sbin/postmap /etc/postfix/recipients");

unlink("/etc/postfix/transport");
rename("/etc/postfix/transport.new", "/etc/postfix/transport");
system("/usr/sbin/postmap /etc/postfix/transport");
```

Configuring MailScanner: Anti-Spam and Anti-Virus Capabilities for Your Front-End MTA

MailScanner's job is to scan e-mail messages using filter programs like SpamAssassin and ClamAV. When we configured Postfix, we added a rule to move all incoming mail to the hold queue. Now we need to configure MailScanner to pick up mail arriving in that queue, scan it for spam and viruses, and return clean e-mail back to the Postfix incoming queue for delivery to the Exchange server or departmental Postfix server.

Why We Didn't Use Webmin for MailScanner

A Webmin module for MailScanner is currently in beta and can be found at `http://lushsoft.dyndns.org/mailscanner-webmin/`.

We chose not to rely on this module because it is still in beta, it is not one of the official Webmin modules on `www.webmin.com`, and as of this writing, the author recommends making backups of the MailScanner configuration file before using it. Also, the configuration changes needed in the MailScanner configuration files really aren't that difficult to make manually. Still, the MailScanner Webmin module is under active development and certainly worth taking a look at.

MailScanner's file has far too many configuration possibilities to list in detail here, and the default settings are reasonable. We'll cover only the options that need to be changed in order to use MailScanner with Postfix, SpamAssassin, and ClamAV. Consult the MailScanner documentation at `www.sng.ecs.soton.ac.uk/mailscanner/` for additional information.

All MailScanner configuration files are found in the directory `/etc/MailScanner/`. The main configuration file for MailScanner is called `/etc/MailScanner/MailScanner.conf`. All of the settings we need to change can be found here.

Similar to other configuration files, `MailScanner.conf` has a simple format: blank lines and lines beginning with a # are ignored, and all other lines take the following form:

`option = value`

Now, we'll examine each option that must be changed or set for the first time.

Run As User   In Linux, as in Windows, programs always run as a particular user. Since we want MailScanner to pick mail up from and return it to Postfix queues, we'll need to run MailScanner as the `postfix` user, so we'll set this option to equal `postfix`.

Run As Group   Similarly, we want to run the program with the correct group ID so that files are created with the correct group ownership for Postfix, so we also set this option to `postfix`.

Incoming Queue Dir   We need to pick up mail from the Postfix hold queue. We accomplish this by setting this option to `/var/spool/postfix/hold`.

Outgoing Queue Dir   When we have successfully scanned an e-mail message, we need to return it to Postfix. We do that by dropping it off in the incoming queue, so we'll set this option to `/var/spool/postfix/incoming`.

MTA   The rules for picking up and dropping off messages in mail queues vary from MTA to MTA, so we need to specifically tell MailScanner we are using Postfix by setting this option to `postfix`.

SpamAssassin User State Dir   SpamAssassin is often run on behalf of particular Linux users. In this configuration, MailScanner will be running it only as the Postfix user to filter all mail before it ever reaches individual users. However, we don't want to clutter up the Postfix user's home directory, `/var/spool/postfix`, with SpamAssassin-related data files. To avoid this, we'll specify an alternative location, `/var/spool/MailScanner/spamassassin`, and we'll use the `mkdir` and `chown` commands to make sure this directory exists and belongs to the Postfix user and group.

Use SpamAssassin   By default, SpamAssassin is turned off in MailScanner. We activate it by setting this option to `yes`.

Spam Actions   What should MailScanner do when it believes it has detected spam? By default, MailScanner delivers the message anyway and tags the message with an extra header line to make it easy for client software to sort spam messages into a separate bulk folder or delete them if the end user chooses. The extra header line looks like this:

```
X-yoursite-MailScanner-SpamCheck: spam, (additional text, which varies)
```

Since no spam detection software is perfect, and there is always a possibility that *real* e-mail will occasionally be mislabeled as spam, we recommend that you stick with this default approach. However, if you prefer, you can set the Spam Actions option to `delete`. This causes e-mails that are considered highly likely to be spam to be deleted entirely and not delivered at all.

Configuring MailScanner to Use ClamAV

MailScanner is compatible with a wide variety of virus scanners. We'll need to specify the virus scanner we wish to use, ClamAV.

MailScanner has a separate configuration file with specific settings for each virus scanner. This file is called `/etc/MailScanner/virus.scanners.conf`. In this file, one line for each virus scanner determines what script should be run to scan for viruses and under what directory the virus scanner can be found. The first field on each line is the name of the virus scanner. The second is the path to a script, usually a wrapper installed by MailScanner that runs the real virus scanning tools in turn. The third is the parent directory under which the actual virus scanning programs can be found.

We will need to make one small change to this file. MailScanner assumes by default that the ClamAV tools are installed in subdirectories of `/usr/local`, such as `/usr/local/bin`, but the ClamAV rpm installed those programs in subdirectories of `/usr`, such as `/usr/bin`. So we'll need to edit `/etc/MailScanner/virus.scanners.conf` and change the following line:

```
clamav    /usr/lib/MailScanner/clamav-wrapper/usr/local
```

to read as follows:

```
clamav    /usr/lib/MailScanner/clamav-wrapper/usr
```

We have successfully created a front-end MTA. Now we're ready to start it up!

Launching MailScanner and Postfix

Now we can launch MailScanner and Postfix at the same time. Since the startup script for MailScanner also automatically launches Postfix, we'll tell Fedora *not* to separately launch Postfix and MailScanner.

Use these commands to configure Fedora to automatically launch MailScanner and Postfix together at startup and to start them now:

```
chkconfig --del postfix
service postfix stop
chkconfig --add MailScanner
chkconfig MailScanner on
service MailScanner start
```

We're up and running! Time to send some test messages.

Testing Our Front-End MTA

Our front-end MTA serves several purposes. We should test it in all three roles:

- As an e-mail router that directs messages to the correct back end

- As an anti-virus filter that strips out virus attachments

- As a spam filter that marks spam for convenient filtering by clients.

Testing the Front-End MTA As an E-mail Router

Using an Exchange client such as Outlook on xppro1.ad.corp.com, send a test e-mail to nurse1@corp.com. This is the simplest way to test the front-end MTA from *within* the local area network. That's because the nurse1 account is not an Active Directory/Exchange account. It is an OpenLDAP account with a mailbox that lives on linserv1.corp.com.

If you have:

- Correctly configured Exchange to forward messages for unrecognized addresses in corp.com to mail.corp.com

- Correctly configured mail.corp.com to act as a front-end MTA

- Verified that linserv1.corp.com has LDAP users

then the e-mail message should arrive at the Exchange server but be immediately forwarded to mail.corp.com (as Exchange cannot deliver it to anyone it knows about). mail.corp.com then recognizes it as a valid recipient on the linserv1.corp.com Linux Postfix server and delivers it there.

You can verify this by checking your e-mail with the IMAP client you configured in the "Linux as a Departmental Mail Server" section of this chapter.

Now let's try it in reverse! Just click "Reply" to that e-mail from your Active Directory/ Exchange user. The reply should arrive at the `linserv1.corp.com` Postfix server but be immediately forwarded to `mail.corp.com. mail.corp.com` then recognizes it as a valid recipient on the Exchange server and delivers it there.

You can verify this by checking your e-mail with the Outlook client on `xppro1.ad.corp.com`.

Troubleshooting E-mail Routing Problems

What if it doesn't work? Well, you have three MTAs: the Linux back end, the Linux front end, and the Exchange back end. Every one of them produces useful error logs that you can examine to learn more about the nature of the problem. For Exchange, take a look at the Application log in the Windows event viewer tool.

For the Linux MTAs, look at the file `/var/log/maillog`. Similar to `/var/log/messages`, `/var/log/maillog` contains errors, warnings, and event notifications specifically from MTAs and the POP/IMAP server. Use the `tail` command, as used in Chapter 4, to view the most recent entries in the file. That will give you the information you need to determine which of these categories the problem falls into:

If the Linux back end rejects messages for Exchange users   Double-check the `relay_ recipient_maps` option setting in `/etc/postfix/main.cf` on `linserv1.corp.com` and make sure that "Optional transport for unknown recipients" was set correctly in Webmin (or just set it as the `fallback_transport` option directly in `/etc/postfix/main.cf`).

If the Exchange back end rejects messages for Linux users   Make sure you followed the steps in the "Making Exchange Forward Mail It Cannot Process" section.

If the Linux front-end MTA rejects messages for either back end   Make sure you followed the debugging suggestions at the end of the "Installing and Configuring the `build-transport- maps.pl` Script" section.

If messages get stuck on the *mail.corp.com* front-end server   Double-check that you have fully configured ClamAV, SpamAssassin, and especially MailScanner. If MailScanner is not running, then mail will never move out of the hold queue and become eligible for delivery.

Even if all goes well in your tests, you may wish to examine `/var/log/maillog` on `mail.corp.com` to verify that you see indications of MailScanner scanning messages, as shown below:

```
Apr  1 20:09:25 mail MailScanner[3724]: New Batch: Scanning 1 messages, 877 bytes
Apr  1 20:09:28 mail MailScanner[3724]: Virus and Content Scanning: Starting
Apr  1 20:09:30 mail MailScanner[3724]: Requeue: 79ACFC1C0.2682C to 5E9F4C1DB
Apr  1 20:09:30 mail postfix/qmgr[3626]: 5E9F4C1DB:
from=<root@localhost.localdomain>, size=718, nrcpt=1 (queue active)
Apr  1 20:09:30 mail MailScanner[3724]: Uninfected: Delivered 1 messages
```

Testing the Front-End MTA As an Anti-Virus Filter

How can we verify that our anti-virus scanner is working properly? We could infect one of our workstations with a virus that generates outgoing virus e-mails. But to quote the European Institute for Computer Antivirus Research (EICAR), that's "rather like setting fire to the dustbin in your office to see whether the smoke detector is working." The results are meaningful, but the risks are not worth it.

Fortunately, there's a better way. EICAR, a nonprofit alliance of organizations concerned about computer viruses, offers a "test virus." The EICAR virus is a simple Windows executable called eicar.com, which just prints a message and exits.

Technically, of course, that means it's not a virus at all because it doesn't attempt to propagate itself. So what is the EICAR virus good for? Well, all good anti-virus scanners include the EICAR virus in their database of viruses to watch out for. And that means that a correctly configured anti-virus scanner should detect the eicar.com file and remove it when it is attached to an e-mail message. If your scanner detects eicar.com, it is correctly configured and should also detect known malicious viruses.

Let's try it out and see what happens! All we have to do is send a message from an Exchange user to a Linux user and attach a copy of the test virus file. That forces a round trip to mail.corp.com where the anti-virus scanner resides. Messages *between* Exchange users are immediately delivered by the Exchange server and don't see the anti-virus scanner. Similarly, e-mail messages between the departmental Postfix server are immediately delivered by the Postfix MTA. After all, the primary purpose of the anti-virus scanner is to detect viruses sent by users in the outside world.

Here are the steps to follow to test the ClamAV anti-virus scanner:

1. Log on to the xppro1 workstation as salesperson1.

2. Temporarily disable any virus scanning software you might have installed on xppro1.

3. Using Internet Explorer, download the file www.eicar.org/download/eicar.com to xppro1 and save it to disk as eicar.com.

4. Using Outlook, send an e-mail message to nurse1@corp.com, sending the file eicar.com as an attachment.

5. Using an e-mail client configured to check the nurse1 account via POP or IMAP, check for new messages for nurse1. The message should arrive after approximately one minute, *without* the virus attachment.

6. Use the tail command to peek at the /var/log/maillog file on mail.corp.com. You should see output similar to the following:

```
Apr  2 21:21:06 mail MailScanner[17816]: Virus and Content Scanning: Starting
Apr  2 21:21:09 mail MailScanner[17816]: /var/spool/MailScanner/incoming/
17816/./94A78C1C4.24FF5/eicar.com: Eicar-Test-Signature FOUND
Apr  2 21:21:10 mail MailScanner[17816]: Virus Scanning: ClamAV found 1
infections
Apr  2 21:21:10 mail MailScanner[17816]: Infected message 94A78C1C4.24FF5
came from 192.168.2.202
```

```
Apr  2 21:21:10 mail MailScanner[17816]: Virus Scanning: Found 1 viruses
```
Apr 2 21:21:10 mail MailScanner[17816]: **Filename Checks: Windows/DOS Executable (94A78C1C4.24FF5 eicar.com)**
```
Apr  2 21:21:10 mail MailScanner[17816]: Other Checks: Found 1 problems
Apr  2 21:21:10 mail MailScanner[17816]: Requeue: 94A78C1C4.24FF5 to
DB63FC1EE
Apr  2 21:21:10 mail postfix/qmgr[3626]: DB63FC1EE: from=<nurse1@corp.com>,
size=1343, nrcpt=1 (queue active)
Apr  2 21:21:10 mail MailScanner[17816]: Cleaned: Delivered 1 cleaned
messages
```

7. Re-enable the anti-virus software on xppro1, if any.

Congratulations, your anti-virus scanner is successfully removing virus attachments!

A one-minute delay to receive an e-mail message might reasonably make you wonder if MailScanner is fast enough. The answer is that MailScanner is capable of scanning many messages quickly in a single batch. While the delay before the scanning of a new batch begins is approximately one minute, MailScanner *doesn't* use a whole minute to scan each e-mail message.

If eicar.com is not correctly detected as a virus, consider the following issues:

1. Did you install ClamAV?

2. Did you edit /etc/MailScanner/virus.scanners.conf to enable the use of ClamAV?

Testing the Front-End MTA As a Spam Filter

We can use a similar method to test whether the spam-detection capabilities of SpamAssassin and MailScanner are operating properly. Quality spam detection software includes support for a special string of characters called the GTUBE (Generic Test for Unsolicited Bulk E-mail). Any e-mail message that contains this string of characters should be recognized as spam.

In our default configuration of MailScanner, that means your message will have added the following header line:

```
X-yoursite-MailScanner-SpamCheck: spam, <additional text, which varies>
```

To see this additional header line, you will need to turn on display of *all* e-mail message headers in your e-mail client.

If you chose to set the "Spam Action" option in /etc/MailScanner/MailScanner.conf to delete, then messages containing the GTUBE should not be delivered at all.

Here are the steps to follow to test your anti-spam configuration with the GTUBE:

1. Log on to the xppro1 workstation as salesperson1.

2. Using Outlook, send an e-mail message to nurse1@corp.com. You should include the following line in your e-mail:

```
XJS*C4JDBQADN1.NSBN3*2IDNEN*GTUBE-STANDARD-ANTI-UBE-TEST-EMAIL*C.34X
```

You can also conveniently copy and paste the GTUBE from `http://spamassassin`
`.apache.org/gtube/`.

3. Using an e-mail client configured to check the `nurse1` account via POP or IMAP, check for
   new messages for `nurse1`. The message should arrive after approximately one minute *with*
   the extra header identifying it as spam. If you set the Spam Action option in `/etc/`
   `MailScanner/MailScanner.conf` to `delete`, the message will not arrive at all.

4. Use the `tail` command to peek at the `/var/log/maillog` file on `mail.corp.com`. You
   should see output similar to the following:

   ```
   Apr  2 22:15:18 mail MailScanner[18910]: New Batch: Scanning 1 messages, 1282
   bytes
   Apr  2 22:15:19 mail postfix/smtpd[20459]: disconnect from
   unknown[192.168.2.203]
   Apr  2 22:15:20 mail MailScanner[18910]: Spam Checks: Found 1 spam messages
   ```

We have now verified that the spam-filtering capabilities of MailScanner and SpamAssassin
are working properly.

If the GTUBE is not detected as spam, look into the following issues:

1. Did you install SpamAssassin?

2. Did you set "Use SpamAssassin" and "SpamAsssassin User State Dir" correctly in `/etc/`
   `MailScanner/MailScanner.conf`?

3. Did you type all the right characters of the GTUBE e-mail correctly? If you're unsure, copy
   and paste the e-mail found at `http://spamassassin.apache.org/gtube/gtube.txt`.

Final Thoughts

Linux does mail, and Exchange does mail. Many organizations are going to want to choose something that enables rich collaboration. Today, the big winner here is Exchange. Soon, however, up
and comers in the Linux world will be OpenXChange (at `http://www.openxchange.org/`) and
Hula (at `http://hula-project.org/`). We checked these two packages out, but in our estima-
tion they just weren't ready for prime time coverage yet.

There are a percentage of people who are looking to expunge Exchange in lieu of some Linux-
based alternatives. The credible alternatives at this time are not free packages, however. A good
article that details the Linux alternatives can be found at `http://www.networkworld.com/`
`news/2005/040405-linux-email.html`

Regardless, for today, most people are trying to contend with existing Linux e-mail and integrating it with the corporate Exchange environment. In this chapter, we've provided a unified
way of bridging the gap between the two.

With one new server, we've been able to route mail between Linux and Exchange mail servers, create a front-end MTA to route incoming mail from the Internet to the correct mail server,
discard messages for invalid recipients, filter spam, and quash viruses.

All this before Exchange or the Linux back end has to lift a finger!

Pretty good for free software, no?

7

Application and Desktop Compatibility

Most people have Windows 2000 or Windows XP as their primary desktop operating system, but we have a handful of friends who have Linux as the primary operating system on their laptops.

The Windows folks we know need to get the occasional Linux application to peacefully co-exist with Windows and, more frequently, the Linux folks need to get Windows applications running on Linux. So the idea of getting Linux applications to run on Windows and Windows applications to run on Linux is becoming an increasingly hot topic.

With that in mind, how can we do that?

There are a handful of ways we can approach this problem. We could

- Use software *meant* to work the same way on Windows as it does on Linux (and vice versa). That is, the software was written to look, act, and feel the same way regardless of what operating system it's running on. The Firefox web browser and the OpenOffice suite are good examples of this.

- Create a *virtual machine* environment and basically pretend to have a whole other machine inside our real machine. We can run Linux on our Windows machines (and run the applications we need inside) or Windows on our Linux machines (and run the applications we need inside).

- Run a program that enables Windows to run applications meant for Linux, or vice versa. This differs from the virtual machine approach in that the application can "see" the normal file system of the host operating system and interoperates a bit more naturally with other applications.

We'll explore some other desktop and application issues along the way. Specifically, we'll discuss how Windows users can have a very decent Linux-like environment. We'll also discuss some of the more popular methods for handling Office productivity.

Making Windows Run Linux Applications

The Windows desktop application world and the Linux desktop application world don't collide all that often. For instance, you hardly hear, "Hey! I got this *killer* Linux desktop application. Too bad you can't run it in Windows—har har!" Arguably, it's because Microsoft's desktop percentage is something like 97 percent to Linux's 3 percent (from data found at Linuxplanet—www.linuxplanet.com/linuxplanet/reports/5381/1/).

That doesn't mean you won't need to run Linux applications on Windows occasionally; it's just that the need doesn't often arise. However, it's likely you'll find yourself needing to more and more.

In this section, we'll describe several ways that Windows users can leverage existing Linux applications.

OpenCD 2

Linux power-users have quasi-standardized a collection of tried and true applications to get their jobs done. These applications have a good reputation for working as advertised, are relatively bug free, and are 100 percent cost-free. So far, the deal is pretty sweet! However, until recently it was difficult for Windows users to access that same battery of software.

There's a very interesting project called the OpenCD project (at www.theopencd.org/). Here's the idea: round up the best-of-breed Open Source software and make it run natively in Windows. Yes, they're ready-to-run Windows applications, already in heavy use in the Linux world, and they're 100 percent cost-free.

The added bonus is that if you run the same application on your Linux desktop, you'll have nearly zero interoperability concerns. The applications on the OpenCD that run in Windows will, of course, output exactly the same data files that would be readable by their Linux counterparts.

OpenCD 2 contains a bunch of very useful software. We'll be exploring one of the applications it contains, OpenOffice, later in the chapter. You'll also find GIMP (a hugely popular graphics editor) and Audacity (a hugely popular audio editor), among others. To see a list of all the applications OpenCD 2 contains, just go to the website, and click "The Programs" in the menu on the left.

Unix Tools within Windows

Even Windows users like the power tools that are inherent to the Linux operating system. The Linux command-line tools simply cannot be beat. To that end, there are two sets of tools you might want to check out to help you add a little Linux flair to your daily Windows life: SFU 3.5 and Cygwin.

SFU 3.5 Tools and Shells

Microsoft's Services For Unix (SFU) includes a suite of command-line tools, ported to Windows. You already loaded SFU 3.5 on your `windc1.ad.corp.com`, the Windows domain controller, but you can also load SFU 3.5 on your Windows XP machine. If you followed along in Chapter 4, you did that to get an NFS client on our Windows XP machine. When you did this, you also loaded the SFU 3.5 command-line tools, including some Unix-style shells and a Perl interpreter.

All about the X Window System

Before loading SFU 3.5 on additional machines just for the tools, be sure to read the next section on Cygwin, an open source collection of free tools that also has a lot to offer , including an "X server" program.

But what *is* an X server? Well, the X Window System (often referred to simply as "X") provides graphics capabilities to Linux and Unix applications. Without it, you're stuck in Plain Text Land.

For historical reasons, X is very much a client/server system. The system displaying the user interface runs a piece of software called an *X server*, which responds to X protocol requests from the actual applications, which are known as *X clients*. An X application program can be run on one system and the user interface can be displayed on a completely separate system. Of course, they can also run on the same system.

The client/server terminology is used because GUI applications connect to the X server and make requests to display things and receive user input; this is certainly a client/server model, but it does lead to confusion because people aren't used to running things called "servers" on client workstations. The following graphic is helpful to understanding this.

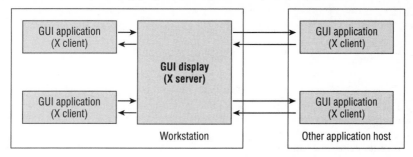

These days, the application and the user interface are nearly always on the same workstation. When they aren't, it's not uncommon to use a lightweight solution like VNC (Virtual Network Computing, discussed in Chapter 8) to achieve remote display, instead of the older X protocol. However, the terminology and the underlying architecture are still with us.

Because SFU 3.5 doesn't include an X server program, it means that Unix applications that feature a GUI can't be immediately ported to Windows using SFU without a separate X server program. A free version is available from Startnet:

`www.starnet.com/xwin32LX/get_xwin32LX.htm`

Hummingbird's eXceed product also does the job:

`www.hummingbird.com/products/nc/exceed/`

It is even possible to use the X server that comes with Cygwin, an alternative to SFU that we'll discuss later, to provide a display for Unix GUI applications running on SFU. At that point, however, you may as well just run your Unix application on Cygwin instead of SFU and be done with it.

SFU may meet your needs if your primary concern is command-line Unix compatibility, but it is not the most complete collection of free Unix tools available for Windows.

SFU 3.5 Commands for Windows

SFU has a variety of popular Linux commands. Here's a quick table:

Function	DOS/Windows Command	Unix/Linux Command
Take a directory listing	`dir`	`ls`
Copy files	`copy`	`cp`
Display a file	`type`	`cat`
Delete a directory	`rmdir`	`rmdir, or rm -r`
Set attributes	`attrib`	`chmod`
Change ownership	`subinacl as extra-download`	`chown`
Unpack a TAR file	None	`tar`
Print domain name	None	`pdomain`
Display processes	None	`ps -al`
Search for text	`find`	`grep`
Search for files by name, date, etc.	`dir /b /s`	`find`

The University of Minnesota Supercomputing Institute offers an excellent table of Unix and Windows command-line equivalents, as well as GUI ways to do the same tasks. You can find the table at `www.msi.umn.edu/llsda/ntunix.html`.

SFU 3.5's Shells for Windows

SFU also ships with two popular Unix-style shells that run under Windows. Specifically, the `ksh` (Korn shell) and `csh` (C shell). The idea is that if you already have Linux or Unix shell scripts that are working properly, you can just copy them over, and they'll work, assuming that all of the Unix utilities they rely on are included in SFU, of course.

If you have some experience with Unix shell scripts, you may question whether scripts written for the standard Unix `sh` shell, on which the POSIX standard for shell behavior is based, will really run on `ksh`. The answer is yes. Like the Bash shell more commonly found on Linux systems, `ksh` includes all of the features of `sh` and aims to be highly backward compatible.

To experiment with `ksh`, select Start ➢ All Programs ➢ Windows Services for Unix ➢ Korn Shell. A command shell window will open, and the Unix-style $ prompt will appear.

Once inside, you'll have a wide range of Unix command-line programs to play with. For instance, you can run sh shell scripts and Perl scripts just as you would in Linux, often without any modification. However, if your script doesn't run perfectly, Microsoft does have some recommendations for porting sh shell scripts at www.microsoft.com/technet/interopmigration/unix/sfu/pshscrpt.mspx.

> Alternatively, you can use the csh shell, also accessed from the "Windows Services for Unix" submenu of the Start menu. We don't recommend csh for beginners because it is not an implementation of the POSIX shell standard, but csh it is useful for old-school Unix users who already have csh commands memorized "in their fingertips."

What if you want Linux compatibility for more than just scripts? What if you want to port full-scale applications? SFU can also be used for this purpose.

Interop Toolworks

InteropSystems offers a collection of additional open source software packages ready to use with SFU. The package is commercial, currently offered for $40. You could in principle compile these yourself with the compiler tools provided with SFU, but sometimes it makes sense to pay for convenience.

It should be noted, though, that many of these utilities and most of the other software in the Interop Toolworks toolkit come in the Cygwin suite described in the next section.

You can locate the Interop Toolworks toolkit at www.interopsystems.com/InteropToolworks.htm.

Cygwin Linux-Compatible Environment

A complete set of ported Linux tools is available from Cygwin, a subsidiary of Red Hat. (For the record, most people pronounce Cygwin "sig-win.")

The Cygwin project describes itself as "a Linux-like environment for Windows." Indeed, installing Cygwin is rather like installing a Linux distribution—but a little different. There are no hard drives to partition of course, but a similar GUI is used to pick and choose packages from various categories, as shown in Figure 7.1.

The Cygwin installer makes it easy to download packages over the Internet. A full installation of Cygwin includes the gcc compiler, which you'll find essential if you decide to try recompiling Linux applications for the Cygwin environment from the source code.

Cygwin relies on the Bash shell. The Bash shell is no more or less "standard" than the ksh shell in SFU, but Bash on Cygwin does have exactly the same keyboard shortcuts and other user-friendly touches that Linux Bash users expect to find.

Cygwin includes the X Window System, which lies beneath the GUI of most user-friendly Linux applications. Even better, Cygwin also includes the GNOME environment on which the Fedora desktop we've used in this book is based. In general, Cygwin is the most Linux-like environment you can have on Windows without actually running Linux.

FIGURE 7.1   Selecting packages to install with the Cygwin setup program

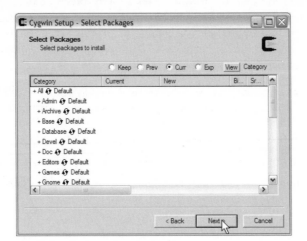

You can install Cygwin by following the current instructions on the Cygwin home page, at `www.cygwin.com/`.

Cygwin's Shells for Windows

Cygwin uses the Bash shell by default, which is normally the default choice on Linux. Cygwin also offers many additional shells, including `tcsh`, a more user-friendly version of `csh`. You might understandably raise an eyebrow at the idea of a "user-friendly" Unix shell. `tcsh` and Bash are considered more friendly because they support the use of arrow keys to recall recently used commands, command completion with the Tab key, and similar features missing from the `csh` and `sh` legacy shells with which they are backward compatible.

Once you have installed Cygwin, you can launch a Bash shell by selecting Start ≻ All Programs ≻ Cygwin ≻ Cygwin Bash Shell. The Unix-style `$` prompt will appear.

As in the SFU `ksh` shell, you can run existing Unix shell scripts and Perl scripts very well in the Cygwin environment. In addition, because the package includes an X Window System server and support for GNOME applications, it's simpler to port Linux applications that feature a graphical user interface.

Porting Applications with Cygwin

What if you want Linux compatibility for more than just scripts? What if you want to port full-scale applications? Cygwin can also be used for this purpose. Intriguingly, with Cygwin, it is possible to mix Windows code and Linux code in the same program.

Wholesale Linux (and PC) Emulation on Windows

If you can't find the Linux application you want to run for Windows, why not simply make Windows *run* Linux? That's the approach several pieces of software take.

The first category will pretend to create an entire working PC inside your PC. Yes, you heard that right. The idea is that if you can emulate an entire PC inside your own PC, you can run any operating system you want—say, Fedora Core 3—and simply install the applications you want inside this virtual machine!

To that end, I (Jeremy) have written several articles on PC virtualization technology that we encourage to check out:

"A Virtual Machine Primer"   This article describes what PC virtualization is all about and how it got started:

```
http://mcpmag.com/features/article.asp?editorialsid=429
```

"A Virtual Shootout"   This article describes specifics about the two leading products in this space: Virtual PC and VMware. We'll make some additional notes about each in the next two section.

```
http://mcpmag.com/features/article.asp?EditorialsID=428
```

By reading these articles before continuing, you'll get a handle on terminology and why you'd care to possibly take this approach.

Microsoft's Virtual PC and Virtual Server

Virtual PC and VirtualServer are two products from Microsoft. For what they do, they're very reasonably priced.

On Virtual PC, Microsoft doesn't specifically support Linux inside the virtual machines. We've done it, though. It *works*, it's just not supported. In other words, Microsoft only wants you to run Windows within Windows. That doesn't really help you here. Therefore, we cannot in good conscience recommend Virtual PC for running Linux virtual machines (guests) within your real Windows machine (the host).

Note that Microsoft also produces Virtual Server, which is the bigger, badder server version of the tool and is similar to Virtual PC. The good news is that certain Linux distributions are supported within Virtual Server (once Virtual Server's SP1 is applied). However, for the casual user running Windows XP on their desktop, Virtual Server running Linux isn't the answer, as it only runs under Windows 2003 and won't run under Windows XP. However, in a test lab environment where you have access to Virtual Server, it would make a fine choice for testing Linux while running Windows.

You can download a 45-day trial version of Virtual PC at `www.microsoft.com/windows/virtualpc/default.mspx`.

You can download a 180-day trial version of Virtual Server at `www.microsoft.com/windowsserversystem/virtualserver/evaluation/trial/default.mspx`. Be sure to load Virtual Server's SP1 if it's not specifically included in the download.

VMware

VMware Workstation 5 is VMware's latest PC virtualization product. It has full support for running Linux within Windows. VMware also has executables that run on Linux! (So we'll mention VMware again in a little while when we talk about how to get Windows applications to run under Linux.) You can see a screenshot of VMware in Figure 7.2. Here we're running Windows XP as our "real" operating system (again, called the "host") and Fedora Core 3 as a virtual machine (sometimes called the "guest").

One of the most important aspects of using VMware effectively and efficiently is that after the virtual machine is installed, you must load the VMware tools inside the virtual machine. These tools are not strictly required, but they provide increased speed, stability, time synchronization with the host computer, and (with Windows) the ability to drag-and-drop files from the host's desktop to a guest's desktop.

Loading the VMware tools when your guest machine is Windows is a no-brainer and works perfectly every time. However, in our example here, our guest is a Fedora Core 3. While Red Hat products are fully supported with VMware, Fedora Core 3 is only quasisupported.

Because of this, the prescribed instructions to load the VMware tools don't quite work perfectly with Fedora Core 3 machines as guests. However, we have found that with Fedora Core 3 only one small additional step is required to make things work properly. Other distributions may require more elaborate workarounds; see the sidebar "Installing Other Linux Distributions On VMware" for more information.

FIGURE 7.2   VMware Workstation for Windows running Fedora as a guest

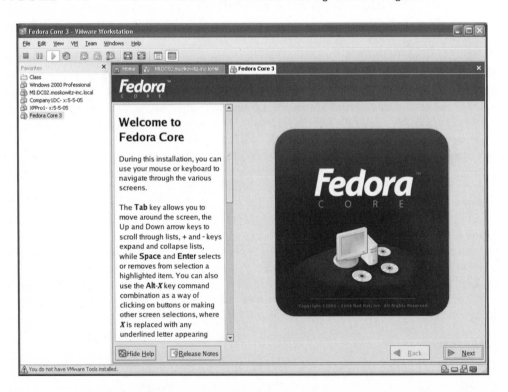

When Fedora Core 3 is a VMware guest, you'll encounter the following issues:

- Installing Fedora Core 3 from downloaded CD-ROM ISO images is a bit of a pain. There is a lot of switching between the various ISOs during installation time. You'll solve this by downloading a DVD-ROM image of Fedora instead. This works just as well in VMware's virtual CD-ROM drive, and only one ISO file is needed during installation.

- When creating a guest machine, VMware doesn't have a category to specifically create a "Fedora Core 3" guest in the same way it has options for other specific operating systems, Selecting Red Hat Linux works fine, as long as we address the other issues on this list.

- As mentioned, installing the VMware tools is the most important thing we can do to maintain a fast and stable Fedora Core 3 guest. The VMware tools aren't specifically compatible with Fedora Core 3. That is, the tools don't come with a precompiled kernel module for the Linux kernel version included with Fedora Core 3. Fortunately, the VMware tools installer is smart enough to compile a new module to work with our kernel. But this option is only available if we specifically install the "Development Tools" (under the "Development" heading) when we install Fedora. These include the necessary "C" language compiler and other software needed to compile a kernel module.

- There are several issues to overcome when trying to run VMware tools using versions older than VMware Workstation 5. If you want to get the tools running in, say, VMware GSX 3.2 or Workstation 4.5, definitely visit our web site at www.winlinanswers.com

VMware has instructions on how to load the tools on web site at http://tinyurl.com/9d47r for both VMware 5.0 and other version of VMware (like GSX 3.2 and VMware Workstation 4.5). These instructions are general guidelines for various Linux distributions. However, here is what we did to get Fedora Core 3 to run as a guest operating system. Here, we'll present instructions for 5.0 (see our web page at www.winlinanswers.com for tips on how to get VMware Workstation 4.5 and GSX 3.2 to run a Fedora guest):

1. Download a DVD-ROM installation image of Fedora Core 3 from `http://fedora.redhat.com/`.

2. Create a new VMware virtual machine. Specify Red Hat Linux as the guest operating system.

3. Install Fedora Core 3 from the DVD image. When selecting packages, make sure you include the "Development Tools" (under the "Development" heading during installation). You do not have to include the X11 development packages.

4. When you have completed the installation process, log in as root.

5. Inside the VMware application, pull down the "VM" menu and choose "Install VMware Tools." This puts a fake CD-ROM in the drive of the Fedora Core 3 guest.

6. At a command prompt, type `ls /media/cdrom` to see a list of files on the VMware tools CD. Note the name of the RPM package. In our version, the file name is `VMwareTools-5.0.0-13125.i386.rpm`. Note, if you see a lot of gobbeldy-gook when you take an listing of CD-ROM, we've found a reboot (and a re-log on) helps kick it in the pants.

7. At a command prompt type `rpm -i /media/cdrom/{name_of_rpm_package_you_got_in_the_last_step}.rpm`

8. Once the previous command finishes, start the VMware installation script:

`vmware-config-tools.pl`

9. The installation script will ask a variety of questions. You may accept the default for each of these by pressing Enter, and we recommend that you do so. However, toward the end of the script, you're asked which screen resolution suits you. Choose whichever you want, say, 800x600 or 1024x768.

The VMware tools are now installed, but you have two more steps. You need to run it the first time, then also tell the tools to run every time you graphically boot.

To run it the first time, open a command-prompt and type `vmware-toolbox`. When you do, you'll be able to check out the various VMware options. The most meaningful being on the first page to allow for time synchronization with the host. Note that the mouse is now allowed to freely move between the Fedora Core 3 guest and the host machine. Click Close to close the `vmware-toolbox`.

Now, we need to make the `vmware-tools` (a service) run at every startup we make graphically. To do this we can use the `system-config-services` command. Once running select Action | Add Service. Simply type in `vmware-tools` (not vmware-toolbox) and click OK. You've now added the vmware-tools to automatically be run in the background every time the machine boots graphically.

We have found that failing to install the VMware tools makes both the guest operating system and the host operating system much slower and makes the guest less stable, so we strongly recommend installing them as specified above.

Once the tools are installed, reboot your Fedora Core 3 machine and ensure the tools are working. You'll know they're working if you can freely move the mouse in and out of the virtual machine.

Bochs

There's a free alternative to commercial virtualization software. There are several projects, in fact, but only one can run Windows XP or Windows 2003 at present. That solution is called Bochs and can be found at `http://bochs.sourceforge.net/`. You can see a Windows XP machine running Bochs in Figure 7.3.

Installing Other Linux Distributions on VMware

There are other incompatibilities that can arise between the assumptions made by the VMware installation script and the reality of various Linux distributions. This is especially true with versions of VMware prior to 5. These incompatibilities generally have to do with the names and locations of files and applications. Specifically, in addition to the /dev/mouse problem, older VMware installers assume that Linux is using the X Window System software provided by the XFree86 organization. However, most distributions now install an alternative distribution of the X Window System from x.org. Unfortunately older versions of the VMware installer don't automatically catch this distinction and fail to configure the GUI correctly.

Fixes for these problems are available. The following discussion thread on the VMware website provides solutions:

`www.vmware.com/community/thread.jspa?threadID=8923&messageID=99653`

(The URL is also shortened as `http://tinyurl.com/4tpne`.)

Of course, using VMware 5 is the easiest way to resolve these difficulties, and could be a free upgrade for you depending on your circumstances.

FIGURE 7.3   Bochs is a virtual machine emulator that runs in Windows or Linux. Inside a Bochs guest, you can run Windows or Linux.

The most important limitation of Bochs, and one that should be mentioned right up front, is performance. Simplifying a bit, VMware and Virtual PC simulate the peripherals attached to the computer. And so does Bochs. But VMware and Virtual PC execute the actual guest operating system application code natively on the real processor with speed that approaches that of a real PC. Bochs doesn't. Bochs *simulates* the processor, one machine language instruction at a time, which is very, very slow. Orders of magnitude slower than a real PC. There is a project to bring VMware-like native code execution to Bochs, but as of this writing the project has been stalled for quite some time for lack of funding. See www.plex86.org/ for the latest on this effort.

Also, compared with VMware or Virtual PC, Bochs is a lot clunkier. Specifically, the GUI for setting up a virtual machine is lacking. In fact, it's a simple command text box, although it does get the job done.

Another problematic limitation of Bochs: communicating between the host PC and the guest PC can be difficult. Although Bochs supports virtual networking similar to that of VMware, in practice it is quite difficult to configure. In VMware, it just works.

For light duty, Bochs may be useful, but for tasks that require a virtual machine with performance in the same ballpark with the real, host machine, Bochs is not a good choice. Unless you're running Windows XP on a non-Intel-compatible architecture that can't run VMware, which is a very rare scenario (and you would know if it applied to you), Bochs is probably not a practical choice.

coLinux

The guys over at www.colinux.org have an interesting approach. The idea is to port the Linux kernel so it just *runs* on Windows. The Linux kernel becomes an application within the Windows operating system. You can try this on your xppro1.ad.corp.com machine if you like.

There are five major steps to getting coLinux running on your Windows box:

- Preloading a special network driver, Winpcap
- Downloading and installing coLinux on Windows and downloading a coLinux guest image
- Unpacking a coLinux guest image
- Downloading a swap file
- Configuring the .XML file which describes our intended setup

Finally, we'll be able to run coLinux.

Loading Winpcap

To try coLinux out, you first need to load Winpcap, a free packet capture library for Windows. coLinux uses it to trick out your Windows network card so the coLinux installation can see it. You can get it at http://winpcap.polito.it/ or http://winpcap.mirror.ethereal.com/.

Do this before proceeding.

Downloading and Installing coLinux and Downloading a coLinux Guest Image

You'll be asked several questions during your installation. In our tests, at the "Selected components to install" screen, we chose to load everything.

Here's our advice: Do not accept the default suggestion of installing to c:\program files\coLinux during the installation. Instead, choose to install coLinux at c:\coLinux, and you'll be much happier. This is because the default configuration file assumes you will choose c:\coLinux. Additionally, since you'll have to fire it off (later) at the command line, you'll be happier doing so from within c:\coLinux rather than c:\program files\coLinux. No one enjoys using the cd command to access long paths with spaces.

Next, during the installation, you're asked which distribution you want to run: Debian or Gentoo. Our familiar Fedora Core 3 isn't currently supported by coLinux. In our tests, we chose Debian.

The selected distribution is downloaded to your coLinux installation directory. However, it is compressed in the high-compression .bz2 format and you'll need to unpack it. Under Linux, you would just use the bunzip2 command, but because we're in Windows we'll use the WinRAR archiving utility to solve this particular chicken-and-egg problem.

Additionally, during the install, you'll be prompted to load a third-party, downloadable Windows network driver. This is required for coLinux networking support. WinRAR can be found at http://www.rarlab.com/ if you choose to use it for unpacking as we did.

Downloading a Swap File

The next step is to download a Linux swap file. The idea is that coLinux writes its temporary stuff to the swap file, and coLinux needs its own swap space, independent of the Windows swap file. Here, you can download a swap file representing how much swap space you want to allocate to coLinux. Download the swap files from `http://gniarf.nerim.net/colinux/swap/`.

For now, put the .bz2 file in the same directory as the rest of your coLinux. In our testing, we chose the `swap_128Mb.bz2` file.

Unpacking Your Distribution and Swap File for coLinux

The quickest way to unpack .bz2 files is by using WinRAR, available from `www.rarlab.com/`.

Unpack the two .bz2 files you downloaded, one for the distribution and one for the swap file. This produces files by the same names, minus the .bz2 extension. You will end up with files named `Debian-3.0r2.ext3-mit-backports.1gb` and `swap_128Mb`. We unpacked these to directories with the same names as their corresponding files.

Configuring the .XML Settings File

In your coLinux directory, there's a file named `default.colinux.xml`. Windows Notepad can't edit this; you'll need to use Windows Wordpad. Inside, you'll see a bunch of configuration parameters. In order to make this work, we simply had to find some default text and replace it with our situation. Here's a quick list of what to find and what to replace it with if you have followed our instructions exactly for installing coLinux thus far.

1. Find the line that says:

   ```
   <block_device index="0" path="\DosDevices\c:\coLinux\root_fs"
   enabled="true" />
   ```

   Append it so it points directly at your unpacked Debian file. Specifically, ours now says:

   ```
   <block_device index="0" path="\DosDevices\c:\coLinux\Debian-3.0r2.ext3-
   mit-backports.1gb\Debian-3.0r2.ext3-mit-backports.1gb" enabled="true" />
   ```

2. Find the line that says:

   ```
   <block_device index="1"  path="\DosDevices\c:\coLinux\swap_device "
   enabled="true" />
   ```

   Edit it so it points directly at your unpacked 128MB swap file. Specifically, ours now says:

   ```
   <block_device index="1" path="\DosDevices\c:\coLinux\swap_128Mb\swap_
   128Mb" enabled="true" />
   ```

3. Find the line that says:

   ```
   <memory size="64" />
   ```

   Change it so it says:

   ```
   <memory size="128" />
   ```

Running coLinux

To fire up coLinux, at a Windows command prompt, first change to the `c:\coLinux` directory. Then run the command `colinux-daemon -c default.colinux.xml`. coLinux will boot. At the end of the boot process, you should see the display shown in Figure 7.4.

FIGURE 7.4 The top window shows Debian Linux running under coLinux. The bottom window is the monitor, which shows any errors during startup or runtime.

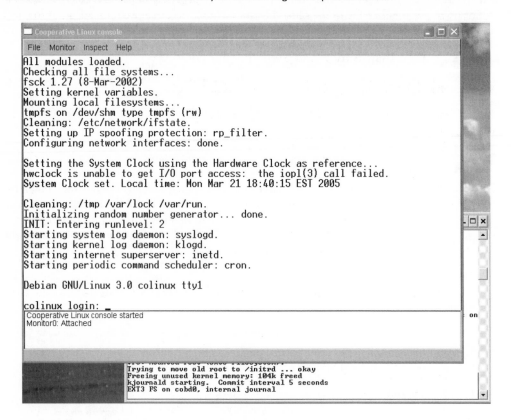

You can log in as root with root as the password.

There's a lot to be said for coLinux. It's possible for coLinux to successfully run a full GUI environment, and it also supports virtual networking more smoothly than Bochs. In addition, initial support for accessing the host file system (accessing, for instance, the C:\ drive of the host machine) has been added. coLinux is very promising and well worth a try. It's not a complete solution for power administrators today, but it's certainly a decent up-and-coming solution. A pretty good community forum and more detailed installation instructions can be found at http://wiki.colinux.org.

Making Linux Run Windows Applications

Linux is gaining application support. That is, there are more and more native applications that you can just load on Linux and be as productive as you are when running them on Windows.

However, there are still tons more applications on Windows than Linux. Therefore, you might find yourself in a situation where you want to run a Windows application while on your Linux machine. In this section, we'll explore ways to get your Linux machine running Windows applications. There are multiple techniques to make that magic happen, so, let's discuss what they are.

Wholesale PC Emulation within Linux

As you saw on the Windows side, there are several applications that will basically present a whole "fake" virtual environment for you to play in. There are three main options that allow Linux to have Windows virtual machines: VMware, Bochs and Win4Lin.

 Note that there are plenty of other virtual machine software options for Linux. However, only the three noted here can specifically also run Windows. The rest seem only to allow additional Linux instances and instances of other open source operating systems to run within Linux. That's because they rely on the fact that very small modifications to a guest operating system's kernel can make it vastly easier to virtualize. A keen observation but not helpful when you don't have the source code of the guest operating system at your disposal. For more information, see the sidebar "Other Virtual Machine Technologies for Linux."

VMware

You already saw VMware running on Windows to provide a running Linux machine. VMware also has packages for many Linux distributions that will allow you to run Windows within Linux. This is an excellent option because Windows never knows it's running under Linux at all; it just thinks it's running on its own machine. This is in contrast to what you'll see a bit later when we demonstrate solutions that try to intercept each application's API calls and execute them in a Linux context.

Don't forget one important element when using VMware. Obviously, VMware costs a bit of money ($199 U.S.). More importantly, each instance of Windows you run (or commercial Linux distribution) requires a license. Other solutions (like WINE, described later) don't require a license because they're simply emulating Windows. However, with VMware, you really *are* running Windows, and hence, need a Windows license. Of course, you could use a free evaluation version of Windows and pay no licensing fee. However, evaluation editions of Windows usually expire within 180 days.

Bochs

As we described earlier, Bochs is a simulated PC, and Bochs can be hosted by Linux, so you might be interested in running Windows XP under Bochs. As it turns out, that *is* possible. However, Windows XP is *extremely* slow under Bochs. Again, that's because Bochs simulates the entire PC, including the processor itself, instead of executing the actual application code directly on the processor. The resulting performance is orders of magnitude slower than a real machine.

If you are running Linux or another flavor of Unix on a non-Intel-compatible platform, such as a Sun workstation, Bochs is your best option because it can simulate the entire processor. For such systems, VMware is not an option. But for any conventional PC, Bochs is a *very* slow choice. You can find more information about Bochs at `http://bochs.sourceforge.net/`.

The Bochs home page does not mention Windows XP compatibility. However, we did find confirmation of it and a suggestion regarding necessary settings in the Bochs documentation at `bochs.sourceforge.net/doc/docbook/user/guest-winxp.html`.

Win4Lin

Win4Lin is a commercial package that lets you run a full instance of Windows on top of Linux. Most interesting for our purposes, at a price tag of about $120, is the recently released Win4Lin Pro version of the product. This version can run Windows 2000 or XP. What makes it different from VMware is that the hardware isn't fully virtualized in the same way. VMware emulates a whole computer; Win4Lin emulates just enough to get Windows up and running and supplies Windows with special device drivers to get the rest of the services it needs from the host Linux operating system. Win4Lin is currently also a bit cheaper than VMware. In Figure 7.5 you can see Win4Lin actively loading Windows XP.

FIGURE 7.5   Win4Lin is a commercial application capable of running Windows XP within Linux.

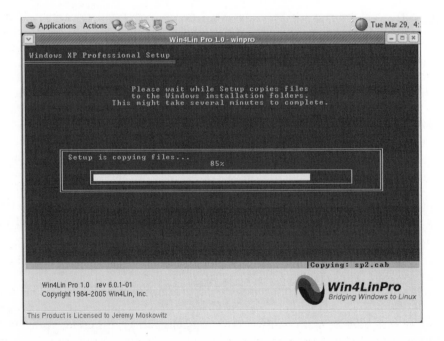

Other Virtual Machine Technologies for Linux

There are other virtual machine technologies available for Linux. However, most of the others we've encountered will run Windows. That is, many of them are only capable of running Linux and other flavors of Unix within Linux, and that's a subject for another day. However, here are some of those others for your perusal:

- Plex86: www.plex86.org/

- FreeOSZoo: www.freeoszoo.org/download.php

- XEN: www.cl.cam.ac.uk/Research/SRG/netos/xen/ and www.xensource.com

- UML (User Mode Linux): http://user-mode-linux.sourceforge.net/

The XEN project in particular is interesting because Microsoft Research was one of the original supporters of the project. At one point, XEN was capable of running Windows. However, since XEN's design relies on the idea that the guest operating system actively cooperates with XEN, and Microsoft has withdrawn from the project, XEN is unfortunately not an option today that runs Windows.

Binary-Compatible Windows emulation on Linux

In the Linux world there are a crop of solutions that, in essence, do the same thing. That is, they allow for a Windows application to run, unchanged, on a Linux client. Of course, you need a license for each application you want to install. But actually running the application as if it were running within Windows is really very neat. And, since there's no real Windows running, there's no Windows license to buy.

The next few sections run down the solutions that make this magic happen.

WINE

WINE stands for "WINE Is Not [an] Emulator." It intercepts the Windows API calls made by an application. The rest of the application code runs natively on the processor. WINE is part of Fedora Core 3, which makes it very easy to use. In Figure 7.6, we simply copied Windows XP's sol.exe program over to our Fedora Core 3 machine. Then we simply ran `wine sol.exe` and up popped Windows XP's Solitaire.

WINE is being improved all the time, but it does have some shortcomings. Specifically, it's quite hard to get applications like MS Office installed. However, there are several options to make that easier. One option is to use a free add-on called Winetools, which is basically a menu-driven installer to get a gaggle of popular applications easily loaded. It prepares your Linux system with a myriad of must-haves including the right Windows system font, a "fake" Windows drive, and more. For instance, applications running under WINE can be configured to see Linux file systems easily, unlike instances of Windows running under VMware. Note that when we ran Winetools on our Fedora Core 3 installation, it said our version of Linux wasn't "recognized" but seemed to work nonetheless.

FIGURE 7.6   WINE is part of Fedora Core 3, which makes it handy for running simple Windows applications.

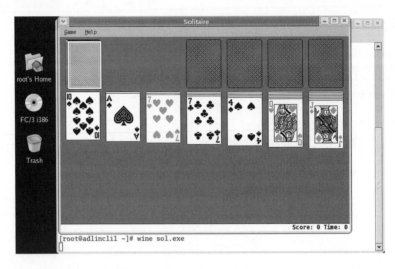

As we mentioned, WINE is being updated all the time so, even though it's part of Fedora Core 3, you might wish to update it with the latest available download—especially if you plan to really take advantage of Winetools. You can download WINE and Winetools from www.winehq.com/site/download.

WINE can also be used as a tool for porting Windows applications to Linux as native applications. That's an option open to developers with access to the Win32 source code of the applications.

CrossOver Office by Codeweavers

Admittedly, WINE is a bit rough around the edges. It works as advertised, but installation of applications could be improved. Winetools helps, but things could still be better.

To that end, a commercial product called CrossOver Office is available from a company named Codeweavers. In fact, they have three versions:

CrossOver Office Standard   The basic package. Allows for MS Office and a whole lot of other Windows applications to run right on Linux.

CrossOver Office Professional   Same as Standard but has Enterprise-level deployment ability (so you won't have to run around manually installing the software on every desktop).

CrossOver Office Server   Helps make a Linux server act like a Windows terminal server and serve up Windows applications. (There'll be more on terminal servers in the next chapter, but we won't be able to specifically explore this product.)

We tested the Professional version, at a cost of about $75. CrossOver Office Professional has three main ways to run: you can allow applications to run only for the root user, allow the users on the system to set up their own applications, or have the root user install the applications for specific users on the system.

CrossOver Office excels in installation of Windows software. In Figure 7.7, you can see a partial list of the supported software. Once selected, the process is entirely wizard driven. In our tests, we ran the Office XP installation (Office 2003 was not supported at this writing). The wizard performed some downloads, found the CD-ROM, and bing-bang-boom, installed Office XP.

Genuine Microsoft Software Program May Thwart Efforts of WINE, CrossOver Office, Win4Lin and Others

Microsoft has a major problem with piracy, so they want to be sure that the people who get updates to their software are legitimate users of those systems. To that end, Microsoft started the Genuine Microsoft Software program, which you can read about at www.microsoft.com/genuine/.

For some downloads, Microsoft asks that you execute a little piece of code on your Windows machine. Out pops a little validation code that you paste into the Window to demonstrate your authenticity.

The point of this is to keep the bad guys out the loop—that is, prevent the bad guys from getting access to Microsoft's free updates. Makes sense. However, the Genuine Microsoft Software Program also has the potential for knocking out the efforts of WINE, CrossOver Office, and Win4Lin.

Specifically, in an article at WineHQ.com (http://tinyurl.com/3v3ny) the author specifically demonstrates how Windows products running on WINE are prevented from being eligible for the Genuine Windows download service.

FIGURE 7.7   CrossOver Office makes it easy to install all sorts of Microsoft and non-Microsoft applications.

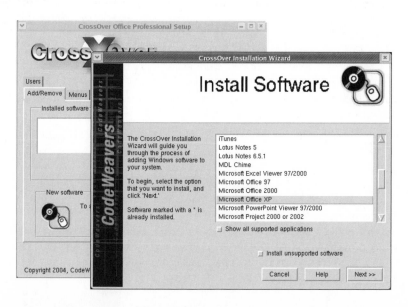

Cedega by transgaming.com

CrossOver Office builds on WINE to make easy installation and runtime for productivity applications. Similarly, Cedega by transgaming.com does the same thing for games. That is, Windows games run 100 percent unchanged. A huge list of supported Windows games is available from the transgaming community site at `transgaming.org/gamesdb` (yes, `.org`).

Making Nice at the Office

Arguably one of the most important tasks in day-to-day computing that can be accomplished is the creation and sharing of simple office documents. The problem is, those tasks aren't simple. It takes entire suites of software to run a modern office.

In this section we'll survey several office suites. Of course, there's the big one: Microsoft Office, which, of course, runs on Windows. But there are others that can run on Windows—and also on Linux. Along the way, we'll see if they play nicely with each other, or need a little work.

Additionally, in the last chapter, we explored connecting Outlook to Exchange. That was easy to do, but connecting Linux to Exchange is another potential hurdle, which we'll overcome in this section.

Microsoft Office vs. StarOffice vs. OpenOffice

MS Office is the big kid on the block, but there are other third-party office options. In particular, the 100 percent free open source office solution called OpenOffice (available at `www.openoffice.org`) is a remarkably complete office suite with a substantial degree of Microsoft Office compatibility.

Also available is StarOffice from Sun Microsystems for a reasonable $70 or so. You can check it out at `www.sun.com/software/star/staroffice/index.xml`. StarOffice is built on the base code of OpenOffice but has some additional polish around the edges. Specifically, StarOffice includes a database program, a WordPerfect filter, and some other doodads. There is an excellent comparison available at `www.sun.com/software/star/openoffice/docs/SO_Comparison_OOo.pdf` (which is also shortened to `http://tinyurl.com/6pycj`).

Additionally, TechTarget.com has a nice list of questions and answers about the various office suites at `http://tinyurl.com/5vefm`.

Opening OpenOffice

Installing OpenOffice couldn't be easier. In fact, it's built in to Fedora Core 3. The main parts of OpenOffice are Calc (a calculator with formula support), Draw (a drawing/publishing program), Impress (for presentations), Math (a spreadsheet program), and Writer (for word processing).

Getting started with OpenOffice is easy too—it's right on the Applications ➢ Office menu, as shown in Figure 7.8.

FIGURE 7.8   OpenOffice is in the Fedora Core 3 distribution, so once you install Fedora Core 3 with our recommended package selections, OpenOffice is right there.

OpenOffice is a very well put together suite of tools that does the job pretty much as advertised. However, in our tests, the main difficulties were in exchanging documents back and forth between OpenOffice and MS Office.

Specifically, PowerPoint files loaded up just fine in OpenOffice, but all the elements weren't translated perfectly. That is, no PowerPoint animations came across. Additionally, some of the text on the pages wasn't aligned or in the right places. Lastly, a common background didn't make its way across either. These are issues we're sure the OpenOffice team is working toward fixing. However, in real life, these would be immediate showstoppers from getting OpenOffice adopted within an enterprise. That is, if you cannot 100 percent interoperate with MS Office, the suite is basically no good for anyone wishing to e-mail files to the rest of the world on MS Office. In short, your testing should include sending sample files back and forth (making changes along the way) between Microsoft Office and OpenOffice before you decide if the compatibility it achieves is good enough for your needs.

There are other issues that make OpenOffice somewhat problematic for power users. In our testing, we had difficulty getting Windows macros to run (as they are based on VBScript, unsupported in OpenOffice). We also had trouble exchanging document templates.

Still, if your goal is to work with an occasional Word or Excel document on Linux and then use "Save As" to save your document in the Word or Excel format for Windows users in your office, OpenOffice can definitely be used in this role. As we mentioned, macros are currently a big exception, and if you are required to use macro-driven VBScript applications built on top of Office, OpenOffice is not an option.

It should be noted that heavyweight Novell has its own version of OpenOffice available, which you can learn more about at `www.novell.com/products/desktop/features/ ooo.html`. We didn't test it, but they claim to be able to support macros and quell some other additional MS Office compatibility concerns.

StarOffice 8

As mentioned, StarOffice 8 does include some features beyond those found in OpenOffice, so it's well worth checking out. However, we ran into significant snags with the default installation process on Fedora Core 3.

We'll show you a simple step to overcome the installation problem and, if you're really interested in what those steps do and why they work, you'll find the sidebar "How We Resolved StarOffice 8 Beta Installer Problems" intriguing.

How We Resolved StarOffice 8 Beta Installer Problems

StarOffice 8 beta ships with a Java-based installation system, wrapped inside a shell script. It's the largest shell script you'll ever see! Once upon a time, many Unix applications were distributed as "shar archives," shell scripts with the actual software binaries to be installed encoded in the script itself. Users would just download the .sh file and run it with the sh command (sh is the name of the original Unix shell with which Bash is 100 percent compatible, and the sh command is still available for backward compatibility). This format is still occasionally used today instead of an .rpm file when software is meant to run on many different Linux distributions, and that's what Sun has chosen to do with StarOffice 8 beta.

So all you should have to do is download the enormous 204MB .sh file and run it with the sh command, right? Ideally, yes. Unfortunately, as of this writing, the installation program fails on Fedora Core 3 with rather inscrutable error messages. However, the process gets far enough to unpack the files that make up the installation and, as it turns out, it's mostly a big ol' pile of .rpm files.

First we tried installing all of the rpms at one go, with the following command:

```
rpm -i *.rpm
```

That didn't quite do it because one of the rpms is specifically for SUSE Linux and refuses to install in a non-SUSE environment.

A simple workaround is to rename the one offending rpm `staroffice-suse-menus-8.0.0-78` `.noarch.rpm` to `staroffice-suse-menus-8.0.0-78.noarch.old`.

Then, run `rpm -i *.rpm`, and it'll work.

Here is the procedure we followed to successfully install StarOffice Beta 8 on Fedora Core 3:

1.   Download StarOffice Beta 8 for Linux or the latest StarOffice release for Linux from Sun's website:

```
http://www.sun.com/software/star/staroffice/beta/
```

2.   Run the installer you just downloaded:

```
sh so-8-beta-bin-linux-en-US.sh
```

3. Accept the default location of /var/tmp/unpack_staroffice when asked where to unpack the software.

4. The installer may succeed if Sun has addressed the problems by the time you read this. If the installation succeeds, great! If not, continue with the remaining steps.

5. Change to the directory where the rpms were unpacked:

   `cd /var/tmp/unpack_staroffice/RPMS`

6. Rename the one unused rpm, `staroffice-suse-menus-8.0.0-78.noarch.rpm` to `staroffice-suse-menus-8.0.0-78.noarch.old` by typing:

   `mv staroffice-suse-menus-8.0.0-78.noarch.rpm staroffice-suse-menus-8.0.0-78.noarch.old`

7. Finally, install all rpms with `rpm -i *.rpm`.

StarOffice is installed! Start up StarOffice by selecting Applications ➢ Office ➢ "StarOffice 8 Writer. You can see StarOffice 8 in action in Figure 7.9.

Accessing Exchange with a Web Browser

So far you've seen two potential alternatives to Microsoft Office. However, neither of these includes an e-mail client, let alone one with support for group scheduling and other calendar features found in Microsoft Outlook.

FIGURE 7.9   StarOffice 8 Writer running on the Fedora Linux desktop

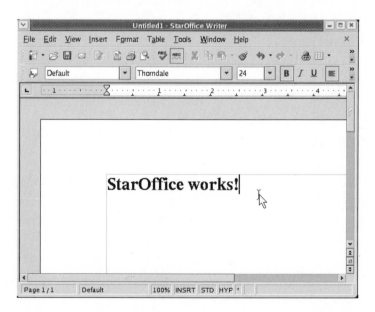

How can we fill this gap? The simplest option: Microsoft Exchange offers a very good web interface. Not only does this provide e-mail access, but also calendaring, contacts, and so forth. This interface is called Outlook Web Access (OWA), and you only need a web browser to get to it.

Microsoft has chosen to implement two web interfaces, depending on the web browser connecting to it. A "premium" interface and a "basic" interface are automatically chosen. The premium interface, which comes close to the full feature set of the Outlook application, appears only when Internet Explorer is detected. The basic interface is presented to all other browsers. While some support for calendaring and contact management is included, it is not as complete or as friendly as the premium interface.

Accessing Outlook Web Access is simplicity itself. Just access `http://exchange2003.ad.corp` `.com/exchange/` and log in with your Active Directory username and password when prompted. You can do so from Firefox on a Linux client. It doesn't get much easier than that. See Figure 7.10 for an example of the appearance of the basic interface of Outlook Web Access as shown when running Firefox on a Linux client.

FIGURE 7.10 Accessing the Exchange server via Outlook Web Access with the Firefox browser on a Linux Client

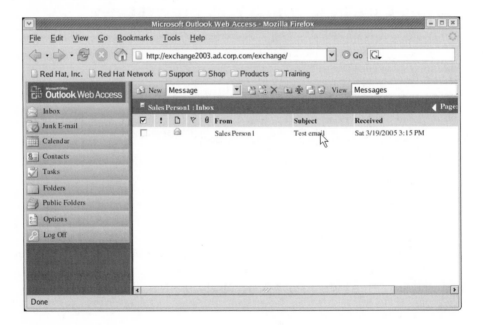

Evolution

Evolution is a full Linux e-mail client. This application has strong support for Exchange, including scheduling and contacts as well as the obvious e-mail features.

Evolution is sponsored by Novell, so it's built in to Novell's desktop product. You can find out about that at `www.novell.com/products/desktop/features/evolution.html`.

The Evolution project is open source, managed as part of the GNOME project, and the official community development site can be found at `http://gnome.org/projects/evolution/`.

Evolution is included as "standard equipment" with Fedora Core 3. Evolution, out of the box, can connect to a variety of mail server types. In the last chapter, we set up IMAP services on Exchange. Theoretically, you could simply pull your mail via IMAP from the Exchange server. However, Evolution's secret weapon is that it also has WebDAV support. WebDAV, which stands for "Web-based Distributed Authoring and Versioning," is a set of extensions to the HTTP protocol used by web browsers and servers. WebDAV extends HTTP by adding support for collaborative editing and version control of files by a large number of users. Microsoft added support for WebDAV access to Exchange in Exchange 2000. Evolution takes advantage of that support to provide Exchange compatibility. That opens the door to groupware features, such as appointment scheduling, that can't be implemented with IMAP alone. However, Fedora Core 3 doesn't install the connector by default when installing Evolution.

We can add the Evolution Exchange connector using the familiar Add/Remove Applications tool by following these steps on the `adlincli1.ad.corp.com` Linux system:

1. Select Applications ➤ Settings.

2. Choose the Add/Remove Applications tool.

3. Scroll down to "Graphical Internet" and click "Details."

4. On the "Extra Packages" list, check "Evolution Connector."

5. Click "Close" to return to the "Package Management" screen.

6. Click "Update." After a delay, the "Completed System Preparation" dialog appears.

7. Click "Continue" to begin the installation process.

8. Insert CDs when and if prompted, as usual.

9. Click "OK" when the installation is complete.

10. Click "Quit" to leave the Add/Remove Applications tool.

Now log out of the desktop environment and log in as any Active Directory user you like—for instance, `salesperson1`.

Since the Exchange connector is now installed, you can launch Evolution from the Application menu and select Internet ➤ Mail.

Configuration occurs when you fire up Evolution the first time. This wizard-driven process happens separately for each user who wants to use Evolution. The first main screen of the wizard can be seen in Figure 7.11.

There are several pages of the wizard, depending on the configuration options. In Figure 7.11, we've entered in the name of the Exchange server and provided our user's name.

Evolution, unfortunately, is not yet kerberized and does not attempt to use the credentials of a user who has authenticated against Active Directory when logging into the desktop environment, so you will be prompted for a password. You will also be prompted for quite a bit of other information that an Outlook user would never have to provide manually, such as the global catalog server name.

In Figure 7.12, we've configured the global catalog server and the Active Directory server, `windc1.ad.corp.com`, are one and the same. However, you only need to provide this information once.

FIGURE 7.11 Once the Evolution-Exchange connector is installed, Microsoft Exchange is an available server type.

FIGURE 7.12 Specifying the global catalog server on the second page of the Evolution Exchange Connector Account Setup Wizard.

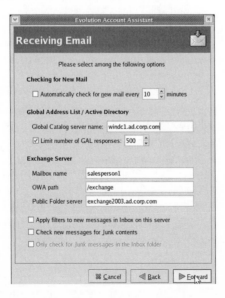

The last two pages of the wizard are very easy: just accept the default settings on the "Sending E-mail" and "Account Management" pages.

When you complete the wizard, click "Send/Receive" to fetch your mail from the Exchange server. Congratulations, you've integrated a Linux client into a Microsoft Exchange environment!

Note that, to see your Exchange email, you'll need to expand `salesperson1@corp.com` in the tree of folders on the left. Then expand "Personal Folders" and finally "Inbox". By default, Evolution displays salesperson1's mail spool on the local workstation, which is not what we want.

Linux-Hosted Calendaring Servers

We feel as if there was a meeting in the last four or five years, and we missed it. In this meeting, people all agreed to take the noun "calendar" and turn it into the verb "calendaring." Collectively, we could have used the word "scheduling" but apparently that word wasn't "techy" sounding enough.

Anyway, calendaring is a big deal, and Exchange is King of the Calendar. That is, many organizations count on Exchange to schedule their people in various meetings and meeting rooms. And, as you saw in the last example, the Evolution connector does a good job making Linux talk with the backend Exchange box. The Evolution client can manipulate calendar information stored on Exchange, including "free/busy" appointment lists. Outlook Web Access provides an alternative way to access this information.

When your servers run Windows, Outlook and Exchange make up the definitive calendar solution. Outlook Web Access and/or Evolution provides the Linux client piece of the puzzle. But what about Linux-hosted and cross-platform alternatives to Exchange? Sometimes, these alternatives are called *groupware*, usually to refer to Exchange-like mail plus calendaring solutions.

There are several open source efforts to provide a full alternative to Exchange Server. None of these are quite as mature as we'd like, and none are officially part of Fedora Core 3 as of this writing. In addition, since the open source groupware solutions tend to be made up of many different open source components, installation is challenging. Each of the Linux calendaring servers we looked at requires particular versions of many packages, including specific versions of databases, MTAs, and POP servers. That means installing far too many non-Fedora packages from source code. For now, we present an overview of these options to fill you in on what's happening in the Linux-hosted calendaring world.

OpenGroupware

The OpenGroupware project, also known as OGO (not to be confused with the handheld device of the same name), aims to produce "the leading open source groupware server to integrate with the leading open source office suite products and all the leading groupware clients running across all major platforms." OpenGroupware offers an Outlook connector, ZideStore, raising the possibility of hosting all calendars on the Linux side. OpenGroupware also offers a demonstration CD based on the Knoppix distribution of Linux. You just put the CD in the PC, boot from the CD, and off you go. Nothing is written directly to disk, which makes trying out OpenGroupware significantly simpler than experimenting with the other projects mentioned here. You can find more information about the OpenGroupware project at `www.opengroupware.org/`.

Kolab

Kolab is another groupware server project, seeking to provide full and equal support for the KDE desktop's Kontact client, Outlook (with a connector called Toltec), and a web interface. The Toltec Connector software is proprietary software with a price tag, as of this writing.

Kolab was originally launched by a group of German companies who received a contract with the German government to develop a better cross-platform calendaring solution. That particular contract has ended, but Kolab development continues as an open source project. You can find more information about Kolab at www.kolab.org/.

Hula

The creators of the Hula project are "focused on building a calendar and mail server that *people love to use*," instead of "a 'groupware server' that managers want to deploy." To that end, they have emphasized simplicity and, at this stage, a primarily web-based interface. They have also emphasized scalability. The Hula project claims to support large numbers of concurrent users on a single server.

However, Hula is not mature calendaring software. As of this writing, Hula supports calendaring only for web-based access, and there is no active project to create an Outlook connector for Hula.

Hula deserves points for a single-rpm installation and very few dependencies. Documentation is still in the early stages. You can learn more about Hula at www.hula-project.org/.

Novell has also recently announced that they are throwing developmental resources toward Hula, so this may be one to watch.

OpenXChange

The OpenXChange project, which is also backed by Novell, is intended to become a full-fledged alternative to Microsoft Exchange. In fact, OpenXChange now offers an Outlook connector, making it a potentially viable alternative to Exchange for those with a mixture of Linux and Windows clients.

The Outlook connector is not open source and, as of this writing, it is unclear what the final terms will be when a stable, production-quality version of OpenXChange is released. OpenXChange also works with Linux groupware clients such as KDE's Kontact, but OpenXChange is not convenient to install on Fedora Core 3 systems and documentation remains immature and incomplete. However, the recent release of the Outlook connector shows that OpenXChange development is very active and great things can be expected in the near future. You can learn more at www.open-xchange.org/ (note the hyphen).

Linux Client and Stand-Alone Calendar Software

Of course, not every organization uses a shared calendaring solution. If your needs extend only to individual private calendars, you have several Linux-based options. Windows users will typically use Outlook, but they may also use the free, cross-platform Sunbird calendar software as described in this section. We'll look at each of the major offerings. Doing so also gives us a chance to say more about clients we've mentioned previously with regard to particular groupware servers they support.

Evolution

Evolution, as mentioned earlier, is an open source calendar and e-mail client included with Fedora Core 3. Evolution can manage local calendars as well as Exchange-hosted calendars and so deserves mention here.

Sunbird

This Mozilla project, which stands behind the Firefox browser, has more recently launched an effort to create a new standalone calendar program. Sunbird is still in an early version as of this writing, but already offers stable releases with good local calendar support. It is also possible to publish calendars to a WebDAV server and to subscribe to calendars published by others in this way, creating a simple "poor man's groupware" solution. More information about Sunbird is available from `www.mozilla.org/projects/calendar/sunbird.html`.

Kontact

Kontact is the KDE project's e-mail and calendaring client. Kontact can interoperate with several groupware servers, including Kolab and OpenXChange. Some support for Microsoft Exchange is provided, but Kontact's support for Exchange is both incomplete and unsupported as of this writing. To learn more about Kontact, you can visit `www.kontact.org/`.

Final Thoughts

Applications are king. That is, users won't want to work on a platform like Windows or Linux unless the applications they use are available on that platform. As you saw, there are lots of ways to bring those non-native applications over to Windows or Linux and use them.

Office suite compatibility is an ongoing issue that should not be dealt with lightly. The Linux office suites have some catching up to do for full compatibility. Until this is 100 percent rectified, MS Office will still be the big man on campus.

Finally, calendaring is coming of age. MS Exchange is currently the most robust way to achieve company-wide shared calendaring. You can connect to MS Exchange from Linux today via Outlook Web Access or the Evolution connector. Additionally, if you're interested in alternative collaboration solutions, Linux collaboration solutions are on the way.

8

Remote, Terminal, and Assisted Computing for Windows and Linux

Getting up from your desk is a real drag. Who knows *what* other work someone is going to ask you to do if you venture out of your safe and cozy cubicle confines. In our ideal world, we'd never get up, and people would serve us flat food and deliver it under the door. But I digress.

There are many times when you might want to operate a computer remotely, without being in the same room or at least not sitting at the same desk.

What's more, operating a computer remotely isn't just about convenience. It can also be about centralizing applications on a single server, with workstations providing a keyboard, mouse, and display but not running applications directly.

Remote, Terminal, and Assisted Computing Terms and Definitions

Let's define some terms that will help us as we sally forth through this chapter:

Remote computing   You might want to access a server in the basement and do an administrative task that would otherwise require access to the console. We'll call this *remote computing*.

Terminal computing   You might want to centralize your applications on a single *terminal server* (sometimes known as an *application server*) with numerous users logging on from simple, interchangeable PCs, or specialized terminal devices. The terminal server is going to actually run the application for us, but we'll just remotely connect to it. It's a lot like remote computing, but on a larger, multiuser scale. We'll refer to this as *terminal computing*.

As we said, terminal computing's main job is to centralize applications on the server, but secondarily, it's to keep users out of each other's lives. That is, when Johnny is remotely using the server at the same time as Sally, they don't see the same desktop and they don't interfere with each other's activities. Terminal computing allows multiple users to log into the same server *completely independently* of one another and without interfering with one another. We'll get a feel for this a bit later.

> When client workstations are used *exclusively* for terminal computing, they are sometimes referred to as "thin clients." The term is particularly popular for workstations designed expressly to be used with a terminal server and not as standalone PCs.

Assisted computing   You might want to help another user solve a problem with their PC while they watch and learn. This differs from remote computing in that you are remotely operating the same display they can see. That is, you're sharing the same console—except you're not sitting in the user's lap. We'll call this *assisted computing*.

Windows and Linux can deliver all three kinds of "computing at a distance" just described. Because this book is all about integrating Windows and Linux together in the same organization, in this chapter we'll focus on solutions that allow Linux to remotely access Windows and vice versa.

To avoid confusion in this chapter, let's embrace a second set of definitions.

The host   The computer to which we are remotely connecting.

The guest   The computer we are physically typing and moving the mouse on. It controls stuff happening on the host.

If you were to buy a book specifically on, say, Microsoft Terminal Services, you wouldn't find these definitions. Indeed, you might think the words *server* and *client* would be most appropriate. However, the terms *server* and *client* are confusing in this context because users frequently connect remotely to both client workstations (for instance, to provide assisted computing) and to server systems (for terminal computing or remote administration). Except it's a "server" program that accepts your connection, and it's a "client" program that makes the outbound connection. Because of this, for the rest of this chapter, we'll reserve the terms *server* and *client* to refer only to specific software that plays a server or client role, such as VNC server software. We'll stick with *host* as the computer we're operating, and *guest* as the computer we're operating it from.

Let's examine the two main situations: Windows connecting to Linux under various conditions and Linux connecting to Windows under various conditions.

What tools help us connect a Linux guest to our Windows host?   For remote computing (to make a connection to a server in a basement or in the server room), we'll use the Remote Desktop feature of Windows, which relies on the RDP (Remote Desktop Protocol). RDP clients are available for both Windows and Linux guests and work quite well.

For assisted computing (when someone needs help), it would be great to use Microsoft's Remote Assistance feature, but unfortunately the Linux RDP client currently doesn't support this. Fortunately, VNC (Virtual Network Computing) works quite well for assisted computing purposes and is widely available for both Windows and Linux, so we'll use VNC in this scenario.

For terminal computing (logging into a terminal server to do all or most of your computing tasks on the server, instead of installing applications on the local desktop), we'll use the Remote Desktop application in exactly the same way we use it for remote computing. Of course, we'll have to deal with licensing issues to permit numerous users to log on at the same time.

What tools help us connect a Windows guest to our Linux host?   What about the opposite situation: Windows guests accessing a Linux host? Here VNC is always the answer. Linux doesn't have an application that can accept RDP requests and, since VNC guest (or *viewer*) applications are easy to find for Windows, they make a great choice. We'll demonstrate how to accomplish remote, assisted, and terminal computing with VNC on a Linux host.

See the sidebar "RDP Versus VNC: Which Is Better?" for a more detailed discussion of the pros and cons of RDP and VNC.

RDP Versus VNC: Which Is Better?

RDP has certain advantages over VNC that usually make it the superior choice for remote computing when the host computer runs Windows.

There are currently no production-quality RDP host programs for Linux, although a guest application *is* available, and we will use it for Linux-to-Windows remote and terminal computing in this chapter.

The following table shows how RDP and VNC stack up in several feature areas. We'll discuss each of these feature areas in more detail. In many cases, workarounds are available for the shortcomings of VNC.

Feature	RDP	VNC
Built-in encryption	X	
Optimized application integration	X	
Sound	X	
Printing	X	
Linux hosts supported		X
Most guest devices		X
Open standard		X
Multiple spectators		X

Built-In Encryption RDP is secure out of the box. Encryption is built into the RDP protocol. Currently most VNC guest and host applications *do not* support encryption all by themselves, but that's not the whole story. The initial logon is secure, at least in an assisted computing configuration, but otherwise pretty much all other data goes across unencrypted. In a terminal computing configuration, the logon prompt itself is just another remotely displayed Linux application, so that is not encrypted either. However, since connecting to Linux host via RDP isn't an option, we'll show you how to encrypt a VNC connection to a Linux host by routing it over a secure `ssh` shell connection from a Windows guest. Or, if you don't want to "roll your own encryption," there are commercial VNC products that offer built-in encryption (available for both Windows and Linux) from RealVNC (`www.realvnc.com`). There is also the option of encrypting the entire network connection with a VPN (Virtual Private Network), as discussed in Chapter 9.

Optimized Application Integration RDP is tightly integrated into Windows. That means that incoming RDP connections to Windows have a lesser impact on the host than incoming VNC connections. Also, applications like Microsoft Internet Explorer are "RDP-aware" and can automatically choose to behave in a more network-friendly manner. Specifically, if you pull down the "Tools" menu of Internet Explorer and select "Internet Options," you'll notice this option, turned off by default: "Force offscreen compositing even under Terminal Server." What this means is that, by default, Internet Explorer is smart enough to deliver web pages to the screen in a slightly different way for the benefit of terminal server users. (The option exists to give users a way to force Internet Explorer to behave exactly the same as it would at the console. It's a bit confusing because turning this option on *disables* something.) No similar "remote-awareness" exists in, for instance, Firefox for Linux.

Sound and Printing When you connect an RDP host to an RDP guest, you can redirect the sound from the host so it plays on your guest. Ditto for printers physically attached to the guest when connecting a Windows RDP guest to a Windows RDP host. Right now, the Linux RDP client implements only sound. Of course, this is only an issue if you care about sound or about printing to a device attached to the guest computer. VNC does support the basic "system beep" bell sound. Alternative solutions to the printing problem exist, such as making the guest printer visible through network printing techniques discussed in Chapter 5.

Linux Hosts Supported Host software for VNC is available for non-Windows hosts. VNC host software (usually referred to as a "VNC server") is readily available for a very wide range of operating systems. As stated, on Windows, RDP is king, and RDP servers for non-Windows systems are rare, because the RDP specification is not freely available.

Most Guest Devices VNC guest software is available for a staggering range of devices, including Palm Pilots, Java-based cell phones, and other similar equipment. RDP guest applications do exist for some lightweight devices, especially those that run Windows CE. It should be noted that an RDP client is available from Microsoft for Mac OS X. The Linux client, `rdesktop`, has also been ported to several other operating systems, including Mac OS X.

Open Standard The Linux rdesktop RDP guest application does not currently offer redirected local printing. Printing is not supported in VNC either, but there are other ways around this problem (such as sharing the local printer over the network). Still, this brings up a larger issue: the challenge of maintaining full-featured compatibility with a closed standard. As of this writing, the RDP 5.0 specification is only available from Microsoft under a nondisclosure agreement (NDA). Since NDAs are incompatible with open source licenses, they usually cannot be signed by contributors to open source software like the rdesktop guest application. As with Samba, the added burden of reverse engineering makes full-featured compatibility harder to achieve.

Multiple Spectators In an assisted computing scenario, many VNC guests can connect to the same VNC host. Obviously, this is impractical if everyone is moving the mouse, but there is no limit on the number of "view-only" guests who may observe what is happening. This is potentially useful in training scenarios. Windows Remote Assistance supports only one guest at a time.

Remote, Terminal, and Assisted Computing for Windows Hosts

A Windows XP or Windows 2003 machine is "over there" and you want to use it as if you were sitting in front of it. What are you going to do? Again, that's the idea of remote computing. When we're on a Windows or Linux guest, we'll show you how to connect to that machine in the basement that doesn't have a keyboard, monitor, or mouse.

Additionally, Windows 2003 servers can house applications, such as Microsoft Office or your own home-grown application, and run them on behalf of dozens of guests. This is the terminal computing scenario. We'll show you how to do that, as well as talk about the major add-on here, Citrix.

Finally, when a user logs on to a Windows XP or Windows 2003 machine and runs into difficulty, they have the ability to ask for help. This is the "assisted computing" feature we mentioned earlier. Alas, the Linux RDP guest application isn't smart enough to accept such a call for help from a Windows host, at least not yet. We'll show you how to work around this problem using VNC.

Remote Computing for Windows Hosts

Remote computing is built right in to Windows XP and Windows 2003. You do have to turn it on, however. Microsoft made this a feature that you turn on only if you need it, and for good reason. Turning off remote access features by default is always a sensible security practice.

In this section, we'll first demonstrate Windows-to-Windows remote computing, just to make sure it's all working properly. Then, we'll set our sights on how a user on our Linux guest adlincli1.ad.corp.com or any other Linux client can remotely log on and interact with a virtual desktop on the host windc1.ad.corp.com, one of our Windows servers. Since windc1.ad.corp.com happens to be a Domain Controller, we'll have to take an extra step or two to enable remote computing on it.

Enabling Windows Remote Desktop on a Windows Host Computer

Windows XP and Windows 2003 can remotely connect to one another. To make this happen, the following pieces must be in place:

- Windows Remote Desktop must be enabled on the Windows host.

- If the Windows host is joined to Active Directory, the right user must be expressly granted rights to log on remotely.

In our example here, we'll enable Remote Desktop on `windc1.ad.corp.com` (but it can be any Windows XP or Windows 2003 system). To enable Remote Desktop for a Windows host:

1. Click the "Start" menu.

2. Right-click "My Computer" and select "Properties."

3. Select the "Remote" tab.

4. Check the "Enable Remote Desktop on this computer" box, as shown in Figure 8.1.

FIGURE 8.1 You can enable Remote Desktop for either Windows XP or Windows 2003 systems.

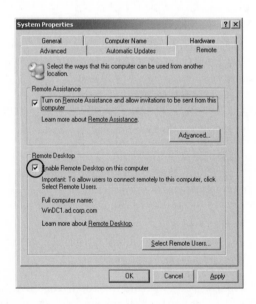

From here, you should now click the "Select the Remote Users" button and add the users you want to allow to connect to this system. By default the Administrator is the only one with remote access, but as you can see in Figure 8.2, we've added `salesperson2` and `salesperson3`.

FIGURE 8.2   Here, add in the users to which you explicitly want to grant remote access.

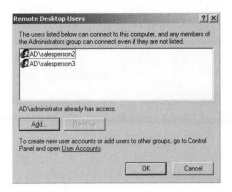

If this Windows host was a regular file server or a Windows XP machine, you'd be done. But because windc1.ad.corp.com is a Domain Controller, there's an extra security measure in place to ensure that mere mortals cannot log on there. This is because of the extra-sensitive nature that Domain Controllers have. In real life, you wouldn't normally be granting salesperson3 the ability to log on via Remote Desktop to your Domain Controller. No, no, no. That would be bad. However, WinDC1 is the only Windows 2003 server in our lab, so together, we'll be bad, bad, bad and circumvent Windows' security to allow salesperson3 to log on. If you don't do this step, when you try to make a connection (using the steps in the next section), you'll get the error shown in Figure 8.3.

FIGURE 8.3   This is the error you will receive unless you expressly add the users you want to allow to remotely connect to a Domain Controller.

To specifically enable RDP connections for users logging on to Domain Controllers:

1. Log on to the Domain Controller as Administrator.

2. Select Start ➢ Programs ➢ Administrative Tools ➢ Terminal Services Configuration.

3. Click the "Connections" folder, and in the right-pane, right-click the item called "RDP-Tcp," as shown in Figure 8.4. Select properties to open up the "RDP-Tcp Properties" dialog, also shown in Figure 8.4.

4. Click the "Permissions" tab and then click the "Add" button. Add the Active Directory user you want to specifically allow access to this Domain Controller. In the Permissions list, select User Access in addition to Guest Access. This permits the user to obtain information about the session, send messages to users in other sessions, and connect to another session. Then click "OK."

FIGURE 8.4   Because this is a Domain Controller, you need to expressly add the users (or groups) of users you want to allow to remotely connect.

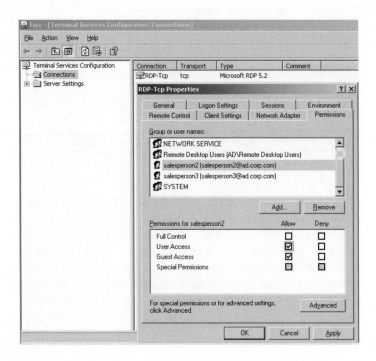

You'll get a message saying that changes you've just made will only take effect for the next time someone remotely connects. Click "OK," then proceed.

Ensuring Windows XP Can Connect via RDP to Windows 2003

To connect to `windc1.ad.corp.com` as `salesperson2` or `salesperson3`, simply log on to any Windows XP machine as anyone. Then select Start ➢ All Programs ➢ Accessories ➢ Communications ➢ Remote Desktop Connection, as shown in Figure 8.5. You'll get a window called "Remote Desktop Connection," also shown in Figure 8.5.

In the Remote Desktop Connection applet, clicking "Connect" after adding the computer you want to connect to performs the magic. At that point, you'll be able to provide your credentials and virtually be there.

Connecting a Linux Guest to a Windows Host (Installing *rdesktop* and *tsclient*)

When Linux needs to connect to a Windows host, our Linux workstation requires appropriate software. Handily for us, Fedora includes everything we need. All we have to do is install it using the familiar Add/Remove Applications tool, which we've seen many times in this book.

FIGURE 8.5 The Remote Desktop Connection applet lets you remotely connect via RDP to other Windows machines.

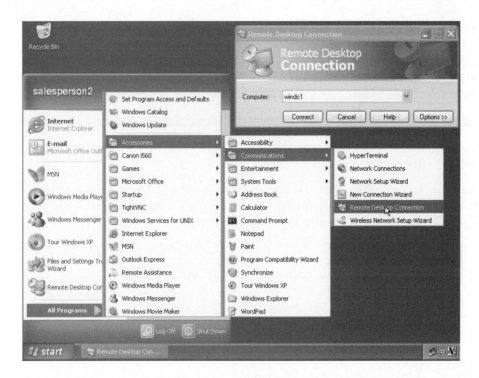

In the course of this chapter we will use three Linux client applications:

rdesktop   Is used for RDP connections. It's analogous to the Windows Remote Desktop client we just played with.

vncviewer   Is used for VNC connections. We won't be using this right away, but since we're here installing software anyway, there's no time like the present to install this one too.

tsclient   Is the "terminal services client" that acts as a convenient front end to both of the preceding and launches the appropriate one as needed. While it doesn't integrate as tightly with `rdesktop` and `vncviewer` as we'd like, it does make them easier to start. And installing `tsclient` on a Fedora system automatically installs `rdesktop` and `vncviewer` as well, which saves us a few check boxes of effort.

To install `tsclient` and `rdesktop` on `adlincli1.ad.corp.com`, follow these steps:

1. Select ➢ Applications ➢ System Settings ➢ Add/Remove Applications.

2. Scroll down to the "System" category and click the "Details" link to the right of "System Tools."

3. Check the box next to "`tsclient`." This automatically installs `rdesktop` and `vncviewer` as well.

About the Citrix ICA Client for Linux

Citrix makes software that rides on Windows Terminal Services to add a slew of additional features. It can provide load balancing features, centralized application deployment features, and a super-duper protocol called ICA (Independent Computing Architecture) that is more efficient than Microsoft's RDP. For instance, ICA performs better with video than RDP does, and it supports individual application sharing (instead of having to share a whole honkin' desktop).

The Linux application `tsclient` appears to have support for acting as a front end to the Citrix ICA client for Linux, if it is installed. However, in our tests, this did not work. Apparently, the current version of `tsclient` passes command-line arguments that the current version of the Linux ICA client does not like.

You can, however, run the Citrix ICA client directly if you need it. It is not included with Fedora Linux, but you can download an rpm of the official Linux client from www.citrix.com. Once you install that rpm with the usual rpm installation command:

```
rpm -i rpmfilename.rpm
```

you can then configure and use the client with the following command:

```
/usr/lib/ICAClient/wfcmgr
```

For more information, see the Citrix website.

---

4. Click "Close" to return to the "Package Management" screen.

5. Click "Update." After a delay, the "Completed System Preparation" dialog appears.

6. Click "Continue" to begin the actual installation process.

7. Insert CDs when prompted, as usual.

8. Click "OK" when the installation is complete.

9. Click "Quit" to leave the Add/Remove Applications tool.

That's it! We now have the `tsclient` (Terminal Server Client) software available on our Linux guest computer. Now we're ready to make our first connection as a guest.

Connecting a Linux Guest to a Windows Host with Terminal Server Client

We have everything we need to make a terminal computing connection between Linux and Windows with the `rdesktop` guest application via the Terminal Server Client front end. Let's take the plunge!

In our example, we'll connect to `windc1.ad.corp.com`. The Terminal Server Client software calls this the "Computer:" field. We'll log on as the Active Directory user `salesperson1` with the usual password. Since Terminal Server Client and `rdesktop` are smart enough to understand Windows authentication domains, we'll specify that this user is in the AD domain. In this scenario, we'll assume that the user is an administrator logging on to carry out administrative tasks on `windc1.ad.corp.com` without the need to physically sit in front of it. Other users can also log on remotely, as long as they have been granted this right on the server.

One annoyance you'll be sure to notice: the "Password:" field in Terminal Server Client isn't good for much. In our experiments, both `rdesktop` and `vncviewer` prompted us separately for a password regardless of what we entered in the Terminal Server Client password field, so you can save yourself some typing and leave that field blank. Or, if you like, test it out to see if this has been improved in later updates of Fedora Core 3 or 4.

To make an RDP connection from a Linux guest to Windows Remote Desktop on a Windows host, follow these steps:

1. Select ≻ Applications ≻ Internet ≻ Terminal Server Client.

2. The "General" tab of the "Terminal Server Client" dialog box appears as shown in Figure 8.6. In the "Computer:" field, enter **windc1.ad.corp.com** .

3. Set the "Protocol:" pull-down menu to "RDP."

4. In the "User Name:" field, enter **administrator** .

5. Leave the "Password:" field blank (you will be prompted later). In the "Domain:" field, enter **AD**.

6. Leave the "Client Hostname:" and "Protocol File:" fields blank. Click "Connect."

After a few moments (or a bit longer if your connection is not over a local network), you should see a standard Windows logon prompt with the password field blank. Enter **p@ssw0rd** and click "OK" to log on.

Shortly thereafter, you will see `salesperson1`'s desktop on `windc1.ad.corp.com`, as shown in Figure 8.7. Just click in the "Terminal Server Client" window to interact with the remote desktop exactly as if you were sitting at the console of `windc1.ad.corp.com`.

When you are finished, log out of the Windows desktop as you normally would. Alternatively, you can disconnect by clicking the "X" (close window) button in the upper-right corner, in which case the desktop remains available for reconnection.

 You can configure how Windows hosts react to disconnected sessions by using the "Sessions" tab as seen in Figure 8.4.

Terminal Computing for Windows 2003 (Windows and Linux Users Running Windows Applications Remotely)

Recall the preceding remote computing examples (where we allowed `salesperson2` and `salesperson3` to connect to our Windows 2003 server). When we did this, Windows permitted a maximum number of two connections to our server. That's right: a maximum of two. That's because remote computing is really meant to let administrators remotely manage their boxes in the basement or the server cabinet.

FIGURE 8.6   Making a Windows Remote Desktop connection from Linux to Windows using the Terminal Server Client application. The "Password" field didn't seem to do much for us in our experiments.

FIGURE 8.7   Remote computing: accessing a Windows host from a Linux guest workstation using RDP and the rdesktop application, started from Terminal Server Client

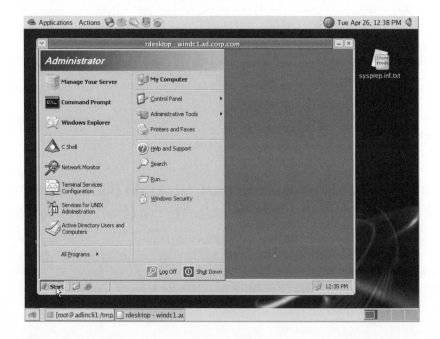

Terminal computing is a logical extension of remote computing. You can think of terminal computing as "more users doing remote computing." It provides true multiuser access, even to the same application. Five users can log in to separate accounts, and each can run Microsoft Word to edit their own documents, without interfering with one another. Windows does support this, but it's optional. In Figure 8.8, you can see how to optionally add the licensed Terminal Server components of Windows:

1. On Windows 2003, make sure you're logged in as Administrator

2. Select Start ➤ Control Panel ➤ Add/Remove Programs.

3. Select "Windows Components."

4. In the "Windows Components" screen, select "Terminal Server" and "Terminal Server Licensing."

FIGURE 8.8 Since Windows Terminal Services is an optional component, you must also add licensing services somewhere on your Windows network.

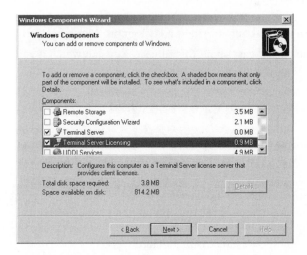

Space prevents us from delving in to setting up Windows Terminal Server and Terminal Server Licensing. However, here are some references to you get on your journey if you want to set up a full-fledged Windows Terminal Server:

Windows Terminal Services by Christa Anderson, Sybex 2002   www.sybex.com.

Terminal Services Home Page on TechTarget   Lots of good stuff, including a lot by the well-known Terminal Services goddess, Christa Anderson: http://tinyurl.com/77eme.

Brian Madden   Brian is a one-man Terminal Services deity. There are books, training classes, and more at www.brianmadden.com/

Again, this is a licensed option. If multiuser terminal computing of Windows and Linux clients is desired, you must pay up. No licenses mean no love, though there is an initial grace period of 120 days to get compliant. Afterward, the server will reject requests to open simultaneous connections if a license server is not available that has been configured to dispense Terminal Server Client access licenses.

Also available is the third-party Citrix Metaframe that rides on top of Windows Terminal Services both technically and for licensing. Yes, that's right. If you want the features of Citrix Metaframe, you need to first license your clients for Windows Terminal Services, then also pay for the Citrix Metaframe licenses. Citrix provides a gaggle of add-on features, the two biggest being their leaner ICA protocol and their ability to manage a lot of applications over a large number of servers. Be sure to check them out at www.citrix.com.

Assisted Computing for Windows Hosts (Linux Users Helping Windows Users)

When a Windows XP user needs help, there's a built-in function called "Remote Assistance" that enables the distressed user to get help from another Windows XP user.

This is a lengthy and interesting subject, but the Linux RDP client doesn't support it, and since we're mostly interested in where Windows and Linux collide, that's what we'll explore here. However, you can learn more about Windows XP's Remote Assistance here:

- A while ago I (Jeremy) did a webcast about this subject. You can watch it at http://tinyurl.com/c2a26. (Be sure to disable any pop-up blockers beforehand.)

- Microsoft has a step-by-step guide to Remote Assistance at www.microsoft.com/technet/prodtechnol/winxppro/maintain/rmassist.mspx (or, get to it via the shortened URL http://tinyurl.com/4aw3g).

- Microsoft's Remote Assistance FAQ is at www.microsoft.com/windowsxp/using/helpandsupport/rafaq-general.mspx (or, get to it via the shortened URL http://tinyurl.com/b7vc3).

Microsoft's Remote Assistance relies on "invitations" to the person providing the help, and Linux's rdesktop guest application does not know how to interpret these. So, in mixed Windows and Linux environments (where you want folks on Linux machines to help out Windows users), Microsoft's built-in Remote Assistance isn't going to work.

Instead, we recommend setting up the Virtual Network Computing (VNC) software in advance of the problem. This software works great for assisted computing purposes, so we'll use it instead.

In this section, we'll demonstrate how a user (salesperson1) on a Windows machine can get help from a user (salesperson2) on a Linux machine, using VNC.

We'll specifically discuss VNC on Linux later, but it's worth noting that VNC is available for *many* systems, including Macs. That includes clients for handheld devices from many vendors. You can find more information about VNC for other operating systems at this page, maintained by RealVNC but offering links to many other sites: www.realvnc.com/resources.html.

Requirements for Assisted Computing on Windows Hosts

Now, we're ready to get up so that our Linux clients can remotely assist our Windows boxes. To make assisted computing happen from a Linux guest to a Windows host, the following pieces must be in place:

- VNC server software must be installed on the Windows host. There are several distributions of VNC software for Windows. The package we'll use is called TightVNC. See the sidebar "VNC Distributions for Windows and Other Platforms" for a comparison of the two most common VNC packages for Windows.

- The firewall on the Windows host must be adjusted to allow connections on the VNC port, which is TCP port 5900.

- The `vncviewer` VNC guest application and the `tsclient` front-end software that makes it more convenient to use must be installed on the Linux guest. If you followed the "Remote Computing for Windows Hosts" section, these packages should already be installed. If you did not, refer to the section "Connecting a Linux Guest to a Windows Host (Installing `rdesktop` and `tsclient`)".

VNC Distributions for Windows and Other Platforms

Each of these packages includes both a Windows server and a Windows client. In both cases, Linux clients and servers are also available, but we'll use the perfectly adequate VNC client and server included with Fedora on the Linux side.

RealVNC   RealVNC is directly descended from the original AT&T Laboratories VNC software. RealVNC "free edition" is available free of charge under the terms of the GNU General Public License (GPL). The Personal Edition, which is not free, offers fully encrypted sessions. The Enterprise Edition also supports Windows authentication, avoiding the need for a separate VNC password. More information about RealVNC is available from www.realvnc.com/

TightVNC   TightVNC is an alternative open source distribution of VNC, specifically focused on reducing the bandwidth requirements. TightVNC also offers improvements to the user interface for configuring VNC clients and servers. TightVNC is a good example of open source licensing at work. The original VNC was released under the GPL, so the authors of TightVNC were able to improve on it and share their work under the same free license. TightVNC compresses the data stream more than other VNC products, which can be important over dial-up links. This benefit only comes into play if the client and server both run TightVNC. If they run different versions, the connection still works but falls back to features included in the original VNC protocol, which still works just fine, especially for local network and broadband Internet connections. We will be using TightVNC in this chapter because all of its features are available free of charge. More information about TightVNC is available from www.tightvnc.com/. However, if you fall in love with what VNC has to offer and your budget permits, we recommend you check out the RealVNC Enterprise Edition. Since it can use Active Directory for authentication, you won't have an additional password to remember—and built-in encryption is also an extra-nice thing to have.

Installing and Configuring TightVNC on the Windows Host

We'll set up the TightVNC host software on xppro1.ad.corp.com and use the standard Fedora vncviewer guest application on adlincli1.ad.corp.com to access the desktop of the other computer, providing live assistance to a console user who can also see everything that is happening. While we're at it, we'll find it convenient to also install the TightVNC guest software (known as the VNC "viewer"), which we'll use later in this chapter.

For installation purposes, we'll log on to xppro1.ad.corp.com as the Administrator, who has the necessary privileges to install applications. Then we'll download and install the Tight-VNC software from the TightVNC website. After TightVNC is installed and running as a service, we can log in normally as any user, and it will always be possible to log on and provide assistance via VNC with the appropriate password.

TightVNC uses a password to control who gets access to remotely control or view your PC. If these passwords get into the wrong hands, it could be the start of a very bad day for you. The password is encrypted on the network but only obfuscated on the local hard drive. And an obfuscated password is just as bad as a plaintext password, so TightVNC Server isn't likely a true enterprise solution. Our suggestion is to check out the Enterprise Edition of RealVNC, which hooks in to Active Directory and can specify which Active Directory users can take control.

Setting up the TightVNC host software, known as the TightVNC Server, is very straightforward. There are just two decisions to be made:

Do we want to run TightVNC as a Windows service?   Windows services, like Linux daemons, run in the background and are always present on the system. This is useful when we want VNC logons to always be possible on a particular system. We'll choose to enable this option in our walkthrough. It is also possible to launch the TightVNC Server application on an as-needed basis from the Start menu.

What password scheme do we want?   TightVNC has two potential passwords: one for remote control and the other for "view-only" access. In our upcoming example, we'll suggest the same password for both, but you may choose to offer view-only access for training purposes. There is no hard limit on the number of "spectators" simultaneously watching a VNC session. For our tests, we used the password p@ssw0rd, but in a production environment your VNC password should be well-chosen and kept secure. Remember that the VNC password provides full access to the console.

   If the Administrator is logged into the console, the VNC password is as good as the Administrator password! Choose accordingly.

To install TightVNC on xppro1.ad.corp.com, follow these steps:

1. Log on to xppro1.ad.corp.com as Administrator.

2. Launch Internet Explorer.

3. Access the website www.tightvnc.com.

4. Click "download" to proceed to the download page.

5. Click the link to download the setup program for the latest stable version. As of this writing, it's `tightvnc-1.2.9-setup.exe`.

6. A list of mirror download sites appears. Find the mirror closest to your location and click the download link at right (not the name of the company hosting the mirror).

7. Save the file `tightvnc-1.2.9-setup.exe` to disk when prompted.

8. When the download is complete, launch `tightvnc-1.2.9-setup.exe`.

9. The TightVNC Setup Wizard will appear. Click the "Next" button to leave the introductory screen.

10. On the "Information" screen, review the license terms and click "Next."

11. On the "Select Destination Directory" screen, click "Next" to accept the default installation location.

12. On the "Select Components" screen, leave the server, viewer, and documentation options checked, and click "Next."

13. The "Select Start Menu Folder" screen appears. Click "Next" to accept the default name, "TightVNC."

14. On the "Select Additional Tasks" screen, check "Register TightVNC Server as a system service" and "Start or restart TightVNC service." Click "Next" to proceed.

15. Review the "Ready to Install" screen and click "Install."

During the final steps of the installation process, you may see messages indicating that the "WinVNC" service has been installed. This message is left over from the open source WinVNC code on which TightVNC is based.

16. The message "The WinVNC Service was successfully registered" will appear. Click "OK."

17. The message "WARNING: This machine has no default password set. WinVNC will present the "Default Properties" dialog now to allow one to be entered." will appear. Click "OK."

18. The "WinVNC: Default Local System Properties" dialog appears, as shown in Figure 8.9. Set the "Password:" field to `p@ssw0rd`. Also set the "Password (view only):" field to `p@ssw0rd`.

19. Click "OK" to dismiss the dialog.

20. The "Completing the TightVNC Setup Wizard" screen will appear separately while you are still working with the dialogs of the TightVNC Server service. That happens because the service is running as a separate application. You may click "Finish" on this screen at any time.

Firewall Configuration for VNC on the Windows Host

Our Windows host is ready to accept VNC connections, but since Windows XP/SP2 disables most inbound connections with the Windows Firewall, we need to take some action.

FIGURE 8.9   Setting up the TightVNC host software to allow Linux guests to assist the user of a windows host

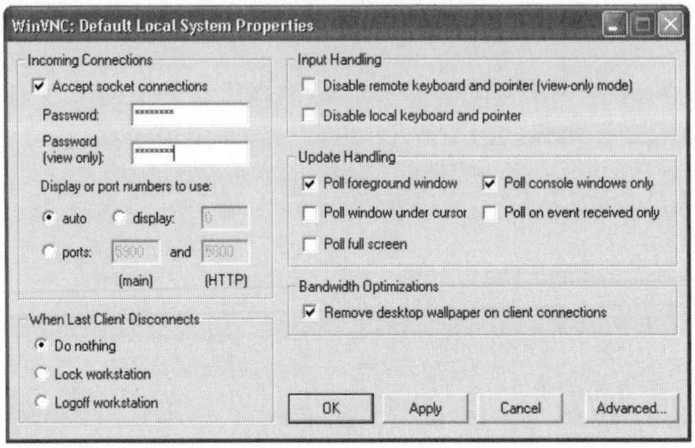

Inbound RDP connections (which we discussed earlier) aren't a problem. This is because Windows Firewall expressly permits these connections. However, for VNC we'll need to explicitly tell Windows to open the VNC port. The standard VNC port number is TCP port 5900.

To allow VNC connections through the firewall on xppro1.ad.corp.com, follow these steps:

1.   Select Start ≻ Control Panel.

2.   Double-click "Windows Firewall."

3.   Select the "Exceptions" tab.

4.   Click "Add a Port."

5.   The "Add a Port" dialog appears, as shown in Figure 8.10. In the "Name:" field, enter **VNC**.

6.   In the "Port number" field, enter **5900**.

7.   Select the "TCP" option.

8.   Click "OK" to dismiss "Add a Port."

9.   Click "OK" again to close "Windows Firewall."

Connecting a Linux Guest to a Windows Host with VNC

We're ready to demonstrate how a Linux user can assist a Windows user with VNC. The Windows host is already configured to allow this, and the Linux guest already has the necessary guest applications.

The vncviewer VNC guest application and the tsclient front-end software that makes it more convenient to use should already be installed on the Linux guest. If you followed the "Connecting a Linux Guest to a Windows Host (Installing rdesktop and tsclient)" earlier, these packages will already be installed. If you did not, be sure to go back before continuing.

We'll encounter one minor annoyance when making the connection. Although Linux's Terminal Server Client front-end application supports VNC as the transport, any password entered in Terminal Server Client is *not actually passed* to the vncviewer VNC guest application. Frustrating, but livable. We'll just skip entering the password in "Terminal Server Client's Connection" dialog and wait until we are prompted for it separately by vncviewer.

FIGURE 8.10   Adding a firewall rule allowing traffic on the VNC port 5900 to reach the Windows host

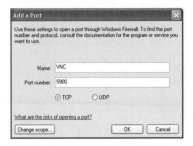

Here are the steps to make a VNC connection from a Linux guest to our Windows host, so that `salesperson1` (on Linux) can assist `salesperson2` (on Windows):

1. Log out of `xppro1.ad.corp.com` as Administrator and log back in as `salesperson2`.

2. Log into `adlincli1.ad.corp.com` as `salesperson1`.

3. On `adlincli1.ad.corp.com`, select ➢ Applications ➢ Internet ➢ Terminal Server Client.

4. The "General" tab of the "Terminal Server Client" dialog box appears as shown in Figure 8.11. In the "Computer:" field, enter **xppro1.ad.corp.com**   .

5. Set the "Protocol:" pull-down menu to "VNC."

6. Leave the "User Name:" "Password:" and "Domain:" fields blank. Also leave the "Client Hostname:" and "Protocol File:" fields blank. Click "Connect."

FIGURE 8.11   When VNC is used as the transport for Linux's Terminal Server Client application, the password field isn't passed through to the VNC viewer, so we leave that field blank. We will be prompted for the password separately later.

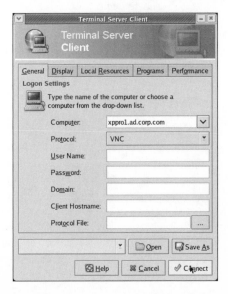

7. The "VNC Authentication" dialog appears, as shown in Figure 8.12. Enter the VNC password that you set in the "TightVNC Default Local System Properties" dialog and press Enter. The "Username" field is not used with TightVNC, so it is disabled.

FIGURE 8.12 Entering the VNC password is a separate step when making a VNC connection from Linux to Windows using the Terminal Server Client application.

8. The Windows desktop appears, as shown in Figure 8.13. `salesperson1` can now use the keyboard and mouse to operate the host Windows desktop while `salesperson2` observes from his seat at the host console.

9. When `salesperson1` is through assisting `salesperson2`, she can disconnect by clicking the "X" (close window) button in the upper-right corner of the `vncviewer` window.

We've succeeded in accessing Windows hosts from Linux guests, both for assisted computing and for remote computing. As far as the Linux guest is concerned, the solution for terminal computing is the same as that for remote computing. But what about the opposite scenario? How can Windows guests access Linux hosts? The short answer: VNC (again!). Read on for the long answer!

FIGURE 8.13 Assisting the user of a Windows host from a Linux guest workstation using VNC and the Terminal Server Client application

Remote, Terminal, and Assisted Computing for Linux Hosts

Like Windows, Linux hosts have built-in support for assisted computing and remote computing.

The traditional answer to the remote computing question is to use an X server on the guest machine. While that is certainly a viable solution, we feel VNC is a better answer when the guest machine runs Windows. See the sidebar "Why VNC Instead of an X Server?" for the reasons we made this choice.

For terminal computing, Linux servers can embrace a wonderful free tool that makes them act as Terminal Servers. We'll briefly explore this download called the LTSP project.

Additionally, we'll come back to VNC to explore assisted computing. We'll demonstrate how to use a VNC guest application on a Windows guest machine to provide assistance to a Linux user.

Why VNC Instead of an X Server?

As explained in Chapter 7, X server software is available for Windows, and the X Window System was originally designed with remote computing in mind. So why did we choose to use VNC instead of the X Window System? We were persuaded by the following advantages:

- VNC guest applications are freely available and easy to install on Windows workstations. Compare this with the relatively complex installation procedure for the free Cygwin X Server software.

- VNC places minimal demands on the guest computer.

- VNC works much better over slow links. The X Window System protocol was designed for use on local area networks and does not perform as well over long-distance links. VNC is well-optimized for slow links and also performs quite well on local area networks.

- Actually, when we use VNC to access Linux hosts, we *are* benefiting from the X Window System. Under the hood, the VNC host application on Linux is a specialized X server program called Xvnc, which maintains a "virtual screen" and translates activity on that screen to the VNC protocol.

Running an X server on the guest does have one advantage: since the server does not have to maintain a virtual screen for each user, the per-user impact on the server is somewhat reduced. The virtual screen for each guest user requires approximately 2MB of memory. We feel this is an acceptable price to pay for a straightforward remote computing solution with excellent low-bandwidth performance, especially given the memory capacity of modern Linux servers.

Remote Computing for Linux Hosts

In this section, the idea is that we have `linserv1.corp.com`, which lives in the server room. Whenever we (the administrators) want to connect to it, we'll simply remotely connect to it.

Actually, what we'll set up here is good for more than just remote computing. It also covers the needs of terminal computing. With Linux, there are no per-user licensing issues to address. All we have to do is set things up right the first time. So first, we'll configure the system to accommodate remote and terminal computing. Then we'll demonstrate remote computing. Following that, we'll talk briefly about various aspects of terminal computing for Linux hosts.

A bit later, we'll move on to assisted computing. That is, if we want to connect to a Linux desktop system to remotely control an active session, we can do that too. Unlike remote and terminal computing for Linux hosts, which are essentially the same thing, assisted computing is quite a bit different on the host side. So we'll configure it separately when we come to that.

Let's set things up so that `xppro1.ad.corp.com` (or any other Windows client) can remotely log on and interact with a virtual desktop on the host, `linserv1.corp.com`, a Linux server.

Requirements for Remote Computing on Linux Hosts

Here are the pieces we must put in place before we can make a VNC remote computing connection to a Linux host from a Windows guest:

- The TightVNC guest or "viewer" software must be installed on `xppro1.ad.corp.com`. If you completed the exercises in the "Assisted Computing for Windows Hosts" section, you will already have this software installed on `xppro1.ad.corp.com`. If not, refer to "Installing and Configuring TightVNC on the Windows Host." If you are not interested in allowing Linux guests to access the Windows host via VNC, you may leave the "Server" option unchecked on the "Select Components" screen discussed in step 12.

- The Linux VNC host software for remote computing, `vncserver`, must be installed. This has already been taken care of as part of our installation of Fedora Linux in Chapter 1. `vncserver` is the name of a front end that starts a special X server for VNC known as Xvnc. Xvnc maintains a virtual screen and describes changes on that screen to the VNC guest it is connected to. Assisted computing is handled a bit differently, which we'll describe in an upcoming section.

- Normally, the Linux VNC host application displays the same shared desktop to all connected guests. This is handy for assisted computing and training situations, but it's not what we want for remote computing. Instead, we'll configure Fedora to accept incoming VNC guest connections on port 5900 and start a separate `vncserver` process, with its own virtual desktop, to talk to each one. We'll do this using a standard Linux daemon called `xinetd`. `xinetd`'s purpose is to accept connections on a variety of ports and start appropriate programs to handle each of those connections in an orderly and controlled manner.

- A Fedora Linux server, such as `linserv1.corp.com`, is perfectly capable of accepting logons from more than one X server, not just the one that drives the console of the server itself. That includes the special Xvnc X server for VNC users. The same logon prompt that you see when you sit down right at the console can also be accessed via VNC. However, for security reasons, this is not turned on out of the box. On Fedora, the logon prompt is displayed by a program called gdm, the GNOME Display Manager. We'll reconfigure gdm to accept requests to display the logon prompt on VNC guest displays as well as the console. To do that, we'll have to make a few changes to /etc/X11/gdm/gdm.conf, the main configuration file for gdm. Then we'll restart gdm to make those changes take effect.

- Optionally, we can encrypt the VNC connection. Unlike RDP, freely available VNC host and guest applications do not support encryption. Fortunately, the ssh "secure shell" protocol that Linux users use to log on securely at a plain-text terminal prompt has a remarkable feature. In addition to providing a terminal window, ssh can be used to forward traffic on any TCP port, *encrypting that traffic as it travels over the* ssh *connection.* That means we can encrypt our VNC connection by routing it through a freely available ssh client for Windows, even though the TightVNC guest application knows nothing about encryption. As mentioned earlier, encrypted VNC can also be achieved using nonfree, closed-source VNC host and guest software from RealVNC (www.realvnc.com), which some may find more convenient if price is not a concern. And routing *all* of your workstation's traffic over a VPN (Virtual Private Network), as described in Chapter 9, is also an option.

- We must allow traffic on TCP port 5900, the VNC port, through the firewall on linserv1.corp.com.

Configuring *xinetd* to Accept VNC Connections and Launch VNC Sessions

Linux has a great VNC host application called Xvnc. It is very powerful on its own, with the ability to accept connections over the network, verify the guest's password, and so on. For remote computing alone, that might be acceptable. That is, if you don't mind having yet another password to take care of.

But Xvnc all on its own isn't quite right for terminal computing. To accommodate both remote and terminal computing, Xvnc needs a little help. That's because the built-in, stand-alone network capabilities of Xvnc are only suited to single-user remote computing. It's easy to start up a copy of Xvnc that accepts connections to a specific user's desktop for very simple remote computing. However, any additional connections, if allowed, see that *same* desktop in an assisted computing-like fashion, and to achieve remote computing in a way that scales right up to terminal computing, we need *separate* desktops for everyone.

So how do we get out of this pickle? We need a program that can accept connections on Xvnc's behalf and start up a *separate* copy of Xvnc for every logon session. That program is called xinetd.

xinetd is a standard Unix/Linux daemon that accepts connections on a variety of ports and takes care of launching applications to do the actual "talking" on those connections. The applications in question can be simple programs that simply read from standard output and write to standard output, like any shell command does. xinetd does all the tricky network stuff, freeing the application to focus on its core competency. Just another example of the Unix philosophy: simple, single-purpose applications working together. In our case, xinetd will be responsible for accepting VNC guest connections on port 5900 and launching the Xvnc host application to handle that connection appropriately. Even though Xvnc offers its own networking capabilities, it also has a -inetd command-line option to integrate with xinetd instead and let xinetd "do the driving" on the network.

Sure, it's a bit confusing, but a good hard look at Figure 8.14 should set you straight in no time.

FIGURE 8.14   VNC traffic from xppro1 travels over the network to TCP port 5900 on linserv1. xinetd accepts the traffic and routes it to the correct Xvnc session for that particular user.

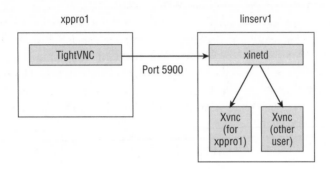

 Experienced Unix users may be wondering about the relationship between xinetd and the older inetd software. xinetd is a modern, vastly more flexible replacement for inetd.

But how will we configure xinetd? Handily for us, a Webmin module is available for xinetd. We'll install the official xinetd module for Webmin and use it to configure xinetd to do what we need it to do. Under the hood, Webmin will create a file for our new VNC service in /etc/xinetd.d. You can learn more about the gory details by reading the official documentation. Just use the man xinetd and man xinetd.conf commands.

Here are the steps to add the Xvnc module to Webmin:

1. Log into Webmin as usual at the URL https://linserv1.corp.com:10000/.

2. Click "Webmin Configuration."

3. Click "Webmin Modules."

4. Click the radio button to the left of "Standard module from www.webmin.com" and enter **xinetd** in the text field to the right. Alternatively, you may click the "..." browsing link at the far right and select **xinetd** from a list.

5. Click "Install Module."

Now that xinetd support has been added to Webmin, we're ready to configure xinetd to accept connections from VNC guests. We'll need to give xinetd the following information:

- A name for the xinetd "service" we are creating.

- The port number on which connections should be accepted, which will be 5900, the standard VNC port.

- The type of network protocol we are using. VNC is a TCP-based protocol, so we'll select TCP.

- Whether to wait for the service to finish before allowing further connections to it. We want to allow multiple remote users (terminal computing), so we'll choose not to wait.

- The correct command line to start a VNC host session for the guest to talk to. We'll launch /usr/bin/Xvnc. As we've mentioned earlier, Xvnc is a special X server that is specifically designed to maintain a virtual screen and communicate with a VNC guest. We'll need to pass several options to Xvnc. We've done the heavy-duty work to discover the required options; you can learn more yourself with the man Xvnc command. We'll launch /usr/bin/Xvnc, but also add the following command-line switches:

-inetd   Signals that Xvnc has been launched from xinetd (or another inetd-like program) and should not attempt to listen for network connections itself. Instead, it can simply "talk" to its standard input and output. xinetd provides the "plumbing" to connect this to the actual guest's network connection.

-query localhost   Tells Xvnc to ask the gdm display manager for a logon prompt. Xvnc queries for a logon prompt using a protocol called XDMCP (X Display Manager Control Protocol). This way, our guests will see the standard graphical gdm logon prompt we see every time we log onto the console.

-SecurityTypes None   Prevents VNC from demanding a separate, redundant password of its own. Normally Xvnc would expect the guest to supply a password much as the Windows VNC host software does, but that doesn't provide a way to log on as the user of your choice. So we shut off this feature in favor of a gdm logon prompt as explained previously.

-once   Configures Xvnc to shut down any programs left running by the user when the user breaks the connection. Ordinarily, VNC host sessions stick around and can be connected to again. That's a convenient feature for some purposes, but not for a terminal computing situation. When a user disconnects, we want to reclaim the memory and other resources they were using right away.

-geometry 800x600   Specifies that we want an 800×600-pixel virtual desktop. You don't have to stick with this setting. It suited our purposes while writing the book, but you could also specify 1024×768 or an even higher resolution. It is also possible set up *multiple* Xvnc services with different names and listening on different port numbers, which pass different settings for the -geometry option. (VNC guest applications support connections to any port, not just the default port 5900.)

-depth 16   Specifies that the virtual desktop should support 16-bit color (65,536 colors). It is possible to save some memory and bandwidth by specifying -depth 8 (256 colors), but the reduction in the quality of the user experience is dramatic. It is also possible to specify 24- or 32-bit color, but the improvement is not great and the cost in memory and network bandwidth is considerable.

Using Webmin, follow these steps to configure xinetd for VNC:

1. Log into Webmin as usual at the URL https://linserv1.corp.com:10000/.
2. Click "Networking."
3. Click "Extended Internet Services."
4. On the "Extended Internet Services" page, click "Create a new Internet service."
5. The "Create Internet Service" page appears, as shown in Figure 8.15.

FIGURE 8.15 Configuring the VNC service in the Webmin Extended Internet Services (xinetd) module

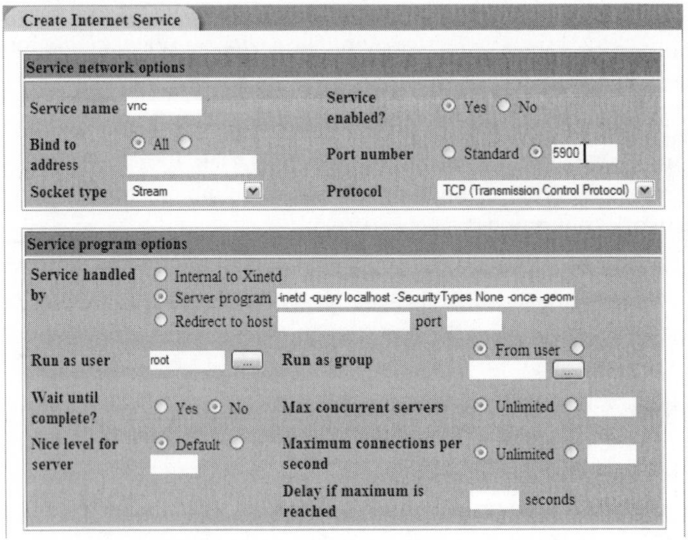

6. In the "Service name" field, enter **vnc** .

7. For "Service enabled?" select the "Yes" option.

8. "Bind to address" should already be set to "All." For "Port number," select the second radio button and enter **5900** in the text field.

9. "Socket type" should already be set to "Stream." For "Protocol," select "TCP (Transmission Control Protocol)."

10. "Service handled by" should already be set to "Server program." To the right of "Server program," enter the following command line:

    ```
    /usr/bin/Xvnc -inetd -query localhost -SecurityTypes None -once -geometry
    800x600 -depth 16
    ```

11. In the "Run as user" field, enter **root** .

12. You may accept the defaults for the remaining options on the "Service program options" portion of the page. But don't close the page yet—there's more to do!

We're almost done configuring the VNC service for xinetd. There's one task remaining: deciding who is allowed to connect. We'll configure xinetd to accept connections from the server itself (127.0.0.1, as we've mentioned before) and from the local network. All addresses beginning with 192.168.2. are part of the local network. When configuring xinetd, we specify that we want to include the entire 192.168.2 subnet by specifying 0 (a zero) for the final part of the address. So, you'll enter **192.168.2.0** .

Why do we need to allow connections from the server itself? Later in this chapter we'll discuss how to encrypt a VNC connection from a Windows guest. Such connections are forwarded using an ssh secure shell connection. Then the ssh server program (sshd) on linserv1.corp.com makes the final unencrypted connection to xinetd, also on linserv1.corp.com. This is secure because the connection never leaves the server. As a result, the "last mile" of the connection appears to be coming from the server itself, which is always the address 127.0.0.1. Those who plan to allow *only* connections secured in this way may choose to leave out the subnet address, 192.168.2.0, but we recommend leaving it in at least to complete these exercises.

Using Webmin, continue with these steps to limit access to VNC, save your work, and put the new xinetd changes into effect:

1. Scroll down to the "Service access control" portion of the page, as shown in Figure 8.16.

FIGURE 8.16   Completing the configuration of the VNC service in the Webmin xinetd module by restricting access to the local subnet and securely forwarded connections

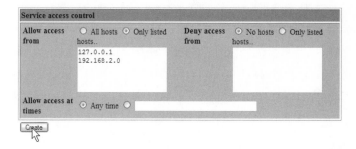

2. Select the "Only listed hosts" option to the right of "Allow access from."

3. Leave "Allow access at times" set to "Any time."

4. Click "Create" to add the new service and return to the "Extended Internet Services" page.

5. Click "Apply Changes" to put these settings into effect.

Configuring *gdm* to Accept Remote Logons

We have the pieces in place to create a new VNC host session each time a guest connects on port 5900, and the Xvnc X server that we launch for this purpose is all set to display the usual logon prompt.

Are we done? Almost! Xvnc is asking nicely for a logon prompt using the XDMCP protocol, but the gdm display manager refuses such requests by default. We'll need to adjust that setting.

Also, when remote logons *are* allowed, gdm displays a less glamorous logon prompt than usual to save network bandwidth. In our tests, that really isn't necessary on a local network or even over a broadband or DSL connection. So we'll also configure gdm to display the "normal" Fedora logon screen in all cases.

Finally, there's the question of how many connections to allow. 50 connections will require a bare minimum of 100MB of RAM and a practical minimum of 500MB with interesting applications in use, because of the demands of the applications themselves. The memory requirements could quite possibly be even higher, depending on the applications being used (web browsers and OpenOffice can use quite a bit of memory). We used a setting of 50 users, but you might prefer to set a lower limit. In addition, gdm sets an upper limit on the number of connections from a single host (IP address). *If you plan to follow along later and secure your VNC connections with* ssh, *It is crucial to disable the limit on connections from a single host* by setting it the same as the upper limit on all connections. That's because connections forwarded via ssh appear to come from the server itself. By default, only two would be allowed at a time.

Follow these steps on linserv1.corp.com to configure gdm to accept a significant number of remote connections and present the standard Fedora logon prompt:

1. Applications ➢ System Settings ➢ Login Screen. The "General" tab of the "Login Screen Setup" tool will appear, which we will configure to match Figure 8.17.

FIGURE 8.17   Configuring gdm to display the standard Fedora logon prompt to VNC guests

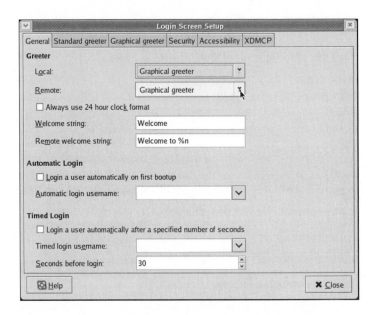

2. Beneath "Greeter," change the setting for "Remote:" to "Graphical greeter" and click the "XDMCP" tab, which we will configure to match Figure 8.18.

3. Check the "Enable XDMCP" box.

4. Set "Maximum remote sessions" to 50.

5. Be sure to also set "Displays per host" to 50.

6. Click "Close." Your changes will be applied immediately.

You have completed the configuration steps necessary to permit remote VNC logons. Now we'll demonstrate how to log on to Fedora Linux from a Windows workstation using a VNC guest application.

FIGURE 8.18   Configuring gdm to allow remote display of the logon prompt and to allow a sufficient number of simultaneous users on secure connections that appear to come from the server itself

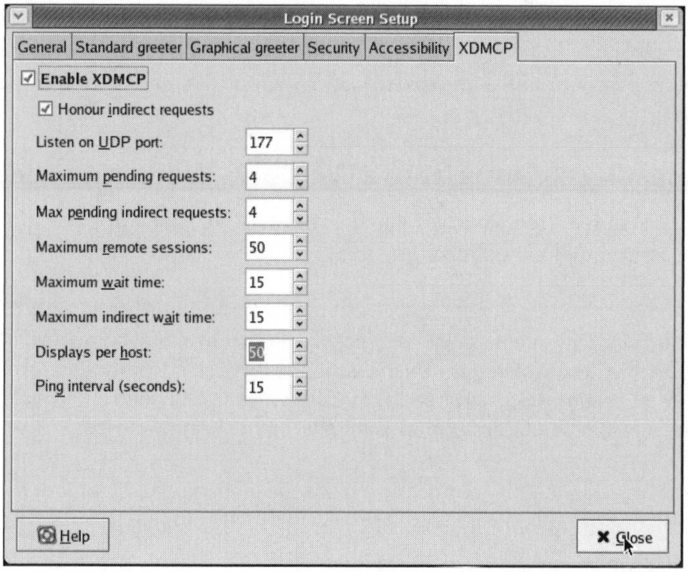

Configuring the Fedora Firewall to Allow VNC Traffic

The Fedora firewall blocks VNC traffic by default. Guests can't communicate with the host if their traffic is blocked. We'll open up TCP port 5900 using Fedora's familiar "Security Level" tool which we have used several times in this book. Just follow these steps to open up TCP port 5900 in the Fedora firewall:

1. Select Applications ➢ System Settings ➢ Security Level.

2. In the text field labeled "Other ports:" you will see a comma-separated list of ports and port types (UDP or TCP). Add **5900:tcp** to the end of the list.

3. Click "OK" to complete the adjustment. When asked to confirm, click "Yes."

Remotely Connecting to Linux from a Linux Workstation via VNC

For our first test, we want to make sure a Linux client can connect to our Linux host machine. That's easy to do, because we have already installed the Terminal Services Client and vncviewer guest applications on adlincli1.ad.corp.com. To access a remote desktop on the host linserv1.corp.com from the guest adlincli1.ad.corp.com, follow these steps:

1. Log into adlincli1.ad.corp.com as salesperson1.

2. On adlincli1.ad.corp.com, select Applications ➢ Internet ➢ Terminal Server Client.

3. The "General" tab of the "Terminal Server Client" dialog box appears as shown previously in Figure 8.11. In the "Computer" field, enter **linserv1.corp.com**   .

4.   Set the "Protocol" pull-down menu to "VNC.". Leave the "User Name," "Password" and "Domain" fields blank. Also leave the "Client Hostname" and "Protocol File" fields blank.

5.   Click "Connect."

6.   The standard gdm logon prompt appears. Log on as nurse1 with the password p@ssw0rd. The Linux desktop of nurse1 appears in a VNC window.

Okay, so logging on from Linux to Linux is easy enough. But what about Windows-to-Linux remote computing?

Remotely Connecting to Linux from a Windows Workstation via VNC

We're ready to log on! All we need to do now is fire up the VNC guest application on xppro1.ad.corp.com and make a connection.

   The TightVNC guest or "viewer" software must be installed on xppro1.ad.corp .com. If you completed the exercises in the "Assisted Computing for Windows Hosts" section, you will already have this software installed on xppro1. If not, refer to "Installing and Configuring TightVNC on the Windows Host."

Follow these steps to make a VNC connection from the guest xppro1.ad.corp.com to the host linserv1.corp.com:

1.   Log on to xppro1.ad.corp.com as salesperson1.

2.   Select Start ≻ All Programs."

3.   Select the "TightVNC" group.

4.   Select "TightVNC Viewer (Fast Compression)." If connecting over a slow link you may prefer to select "(Best Compression)."

5.   The "Connection details" prompt will appear. Enter **linserv1.corp.com**   in the "VNC server" field, as shown in Figure 8.19. Click "OK."

6.   After a few moments, the Linux desktop will appear in a window within your Windows desktop, displaying the standard Fedora logon prompt, as shown in Figure 8.20. Log in as the user nurse1 with the password p@ssw0rd.

7.   Shortly thereafter, the desktop of nurse1 will appear, as shown in Figure 8.21. You may interact normally with the Linux desktop as long as the mouse remains within the window. When you are through working with Linux, log out in the usual fashion or just close the VNC window.

FIGURE 8.19   Opening a VNC connection to linserv1.corp.com from xppro1.ad.corp.com using the TightVNC Viewer VNC guest application

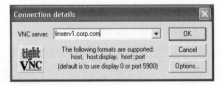

FIGURE 8.20 Logging on to `linserv1.corp.com` from `xppro1.ad.corp.com` using the TightVNC Viewer VNC guest application

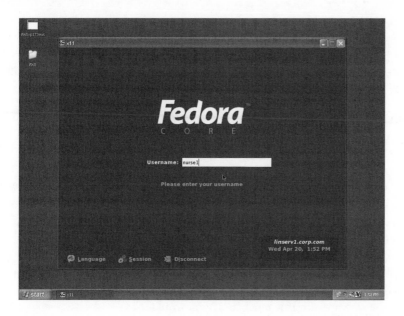

FIGURE 8.21 `nurse1`'s Fedora Linux desktop on `linserv1.corp.com`, as shown via VNC guest application on `xppro1.ad.corp.com`

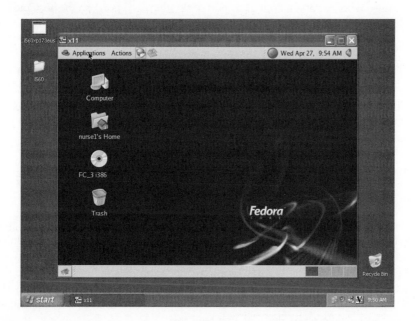

Going the Extra Mile: Securing Windows-to-Linux VNC Connections with *ssh*

As we've mentioned, VNC traffic isn't automatically encrypted. The built-in VNC password prompt, at least, does not transmit the password in cleartext, but we lose this benefit when we use gdm and the standard Fedora logon prompt instead. That's because when we use gdm, we're remotely displaying the standard Fedora logon program itself just as we would remotely display any another application, and it suffers from the same lack of encryption as everything else. Fortunately, there's a way we can regain network security for the logon process *and* encrypt the entire session into the bargain. This brings VNC's security into the same ballpark with that offered by RDP. The two main ways to encrypt VNC traffic are

- Creating a VPN. The beauty of VPNs is that they encrypt *all* of your traffic. With a VPN in place, there is no need to worry about encryption of individual programs' traffic (like our VNC host and guest applications). We'll show how to create VPNs in the next chapter.

- ssh—the same secure shell protocol that Linux administrators often use to log on remotely with a plain-text terminal window. We'll use this here. We'll also use PuTTY, a free, open-source ssh client for Windows, to pull off this trick.

Like most ssh clients, PuTTY provides more than simple plain-text terminal capabilities. In addition, PuTTY can be configured to forward or "tunnel" any TCP port number on the machine running PuTTY to any port on the machine to which the user has logged on with PuTTY, encrypting the forwarded traffic much as a VPN would.

However, ssh port tunneling isn't as elegant or all-encompassing as a full-fledged VPN because the process is not transparent. To make an ssh-encrypted VNC connection from xppro1.ad.corp.com to linserv1.corp.com, we first need to configure PuTTY on xppro1 to forward connections from port 5950 on xppro1 to port 5900 (the VNC port) on the host and log onto linserv1 with PuTTY. Then we launch the TightVNC guest application as we normally would, except that we connect to port 5950 on localhost (a hostname which always means "the computer we're working on") instead of connecting directly to linserv1.corp.com.

Confused? In short, we're routing our VNC viewer's traffic through a preprocessor (PuTTY) which encrypts the data via ssh. Then, as the traffic is shot across the wire, it's decrypted on the Linux server by sshd, which then passes the data to xinetd and finally Xvnc. See Figure 8.22 for a helpful diagram.

 We chose port 5950 rather than the usual port 5900 to forward our outgoing VNC traffic to because this leaves open the option of running a VNC host application on port 5900 on xppro1. Indeed, we've done that in this chapter.

There's one major hassle with this setup: you have to log on twice, once with PuTTY and then again when the Fedora logon prompt appears in the TightVNC guest application. Unfortunately, this problem currently cannot be avoided without resorting to inadvisable solutions such as keeping passwords saved permanently on the workstation. We're hoping a future version of the TightVNC guest application will integrate more tightly with PuTTY, removing the need to log on more than once. Since both are open source projects, this is a project an Enterprising Linux Guru™ may take on by the time you read this.

FIGURE 8.22   Traffic from the TightVNC guest application is handed off to PuTTY, which is listening on port 5950 on xppro1. The traffic is then encrypted, forwarded to the ssh daemon on linserv1, unencrypted, and finally forwarded on to the VNC port (5900) on linserv1.

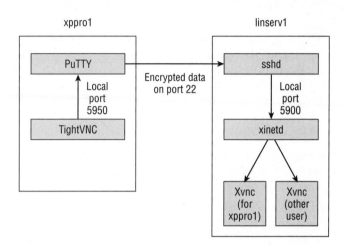

    Again, RealVNC offers commercial VNC software for both Windows and Linux with built-in support for encryption. These tools are certainly worth your consideration. Visit www.realvnc.com for more information about them.

Before we can proceed, we'll need to install PuTTY. We recommend obtaining PuTTY from the website of its author Simon Tatham, as in the following steps. Follow these steps to install the PuTTY ssh client on xppro1.ad.corp.com:

1. Log on to xppro1.ad.corp.com as the Administrator.

2. Access the PuTTY home page: http://www.chiark.greenend.org.uk/~sgtatham/putty/.

3. Click the "Download" link.

4. On the PuTTY Download Page, scroll down until you locate the heading "A Windows-style installer (x86 only) for everything except PuTTYtel."

5. Click the download link under the heading for the installation program for the current version of PuTTY. As of this writing, the filename is putty-0.58-installer.exe, but this can be expected to change.

6. Save the PuTTY installation program to disk.

7. Launch the PuTTY installation program.

8. The "Setup" window appears. Click "Next" to move on from the introductory screen.

9. The "Select Destination Location" screen appears. Click "Next" to accept the default location.

10. The "Select Start Menu Folder" screen appears. Click "Next" to accept the default setting.

11. Click "Next" to accept the defaults for the "Select Additional Tasks" screen.

12. The "Ready to Install" screen appears. Click "Next" to complete the installation of PuTTY.

13. The "Completing the PuTTY Setup Wizard" screen appears. Click "Finish" to exit the installation program.

Now that we have PuTTY, our `ssh` client, we're ready to forward VNC connections securely with it. Follow these steps on `xppro1.ad.corp.com` to configure an `ssh` connection that forwards VNC traffic:

1. Select Start ➢ All Programs.

2. Select the "PuTTY" group.

3. Select the "PuTTY" application.

4. The "PuTTY Configuration" dialog appears, with the subheading "Basic options for your PuTTY session." We will configure it to match Figure 8.23. In the "Host Name (or IP address)" field, enter **linserv1.corp.com** .

5. The "Port" field should already be set to 22, and the "Protocol" field should already be set to "SSH." Find the "Connection" heading in the tree control at left. Beneath it is an "SSH" subheading, and beneath this you will find "Tunnels." Click "Tunnels" to begin configuring secure tunneling for VNC.

6. "Options controlling SSH port forwarding" appears at the top of the right-hand portion of the dialog. We will configure these options to match Figure 8.24. For "Source Port," enter **5950**.

FIGURE 8.23 Configuring the PuTTY ssh client application on the Windows PC xppro1.ad.corp.com to connect to linserv1.corp.com

FIGURE 8.24 Configuring the PuTTY ssh client application to "tunnel" VNC connections from the local port 5950 to port 5900 on linserv1.corp.com

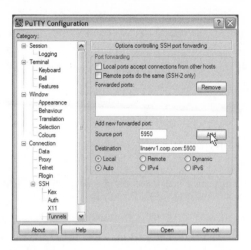

7. For "Destination," we must enter both a host and a port number, separated by a colon: **linserv1.corp.com:5900** .

8. The remaining options should be left at their defaults. Click "Session" at the top of the tree control at left. "Basic options for your PuTTY session" reappears.

9. In the text field beneath "Saved Sessions," enter **linserv1.corp.com (VNC)** .

10. Click "Save" to retain these settings for convenient future reuse.

11. Close the window. (Alternatively, we could click "Open" at this point to immediately open our first connection.)

Once you have configured PuTTY, you can launch a secure shell connection at any time, creating a tunnel for VNC traffic. First, however, we'll need to adjust the firewall on linserv1.corp .com to make sure that ssh traffic is being allowed in. (You may have already done this if you are using ssh for administrative tasks.) VNC traffic normally enters the system on port 5900, but when tunneled via ssh it arrives on the ssh port, which is port 22. If the ssh connection can't be established on port 22, nothing can be tunneled through it.

Follow these steps to allow ssh traffic through the Fedora firewall on linserv1.corp.com:

1. Select Applications ➢ System Settings ➢ Security Level.

2. Check the "ssh" box beneath "Trusted Services."

3. Click "OK" to complete the adjustment. When asked to confirm, click "Yes."

We're finally ready to go! To open a secure VNC connection, follow these steps on xppro1.ad.corp.com:

1. Select Start ➢ All Programs.

2. Select the "PuTTY" group.

3. Select the "PuTTY" application.

4. Double-click "linserv1.corp.com (VNC)" in the list box beneath the words "Saved Sessions."

5. The PuTTY terminal window appears, displaying a login: prompt. Log on as nurse1 with the password p@ssw0rd.

6. A Linux shell prompt appears. You may now minimize (not close) the PuTTY terminal window.

7. Select Start ➢ All Programs.

8. Select the "TightVNC" group.

9. Select "TightVNC Viewer (Fast Compression)." If connecting over a slow link you may prefer to select "(Best Compression)."

10. The "Connection details" prompt will appear. Enter **localhost::5950** in the "VNC Server" field. Note how the nomenclature is two colons between localhost and the port number.

11. Click "OK." After a few moments, the Linux desktop will appear in a window within your Windows desktop, displaying the standard Fedora logon prompt, exactly as shown earlier in Figure 8.20. The difference, of course, is that your Fedora logon will be securely encrypted, as will all of your VNC activities.

Terminal Computing for Linux Hosts via LTSP

Do you want to allow a roomful of users sitting at Windows workstations to log on and access remote desktops on a Linux terminal server? We're already there! The steps we followed earlier to set up remote computing on the Linux host linserv1.corp.com were carefully chosen to accommodate multiple users. And under Linux, there is *no* per-user licensing to worry about. Just fire up VNC connections from multiple workstations. The number of simultaneous desktops is limited only by the memory available on the server.

There are alternative approaches, though, which can further reduce the power needed on the client side. They can be worthwhile if the cost of client hardware is an extremely important issue for you. One of these is the Linux Terminal Server Project (LTSP), which we'll address only briefly because this is a Windows-and-Linux interoperability book.

LTSP is all about getting diskless machines (that is, no hard drive, booting stripped-down Linux *over the network*) talking to Linux hosts. There's not a lot of Windows action there. We're also not going to spend a lot of time talking about Linux guests talking to Linux hosts. We will, however, give you some pointers toward ways to make LTSP work with *Windows* hosts.

LTSP, despite its name, is *not* the Linux equivalent of Windows Terminal Services. We already set that up in the "Remote Computing for Linux Hosts" section, purely using software included with Fedora Linux. LTSP provides remote logon capabilities too, but LTSP's real claim to fame is the power to boot diskless, low-power machines over the network, load a minimal Linux kernel and system on the fly, and do all the computing on the server.

Of course, under normal circumstances, LTSP is a Linux-specific animal on both the guest and the host side. That is, the server runs Linux plus LTSP. The clients, when turned on, use a simple program in a "boot ROM" chip on the Ethernet card to download a Linux kernel.

However, it is also possible for LTSP thin clients to use `rdesktop` to access Windows terminal servers. It is not a standard and fully supported configuration, but it is theoretically possible to boot LTSP thin client workstations from a Windows server.

Why would anyone want to do this? Well, LTSP's memory requirements on the client are very low and the disk space requirement, of course, is zero.

On the negative side, configuring a Windows host to remotely boot LTSP thin clients, while possible, is far from straightforward. Also, `rdesktop` is not currently a standard part of the LTSP package and must be added separately using third-party patches that are not in sync with the latest versions of LTSP as of this writing. In addition, the network boot process trusts that the Linux kernel it is downloading to the thin client is legitimate, so the local network must be trustworthy. In this book, we have emphasized solutions in which encryption for better security and authentication is at least a possibility. That's why, for instance, we advocate SSL-encrypted LDAP instead of the familiar but insecure NIS in Chapter 2.

Finally, bear in mind that "low requirements" is a very relative phrase! Those five-year-old Pentium III systems your employer is throwing out are perfectly capable of acting as thin clients based on Fedora Linux, and we'll tell you exactly how to do that without LTSP in a note called "Fedora as a Thin Client" which we'll make available on `www.WinLinAnswers.com`. So LTSP's advantages are questionable unless you are desperate to wring some use out of 486-era hardware.

For more information about LTSP, see the following resources:

- The LTSP home page, which will get you up and running with LTSP initially in a pure Linux environment and offers links to Linux-to-Windows tips for LTSP: `www.ltsp.org/`

- The "Configuring Windows 2000/2003 For Etherboot" page, which discusses the fine points of convincing your LTSP thin clients to boot over the network from a *Windows* server rather than from a Linux server: `http://diet-pc.sourceforge.net/windows/etherboot-w2k.html`

- LTSP patches for Windows support: `www.wilisystem.com/`

Turning Windows Workstations into Thin Clients of a Linux Host

We've mentioned that on WinLinAnswers.com, we'll provide instructions on how to set up a simple Fedora Linux client as a thin client of a Windows terminal computing host. We've also written another document which explains how to do the opposite: set up a simple Windows client as a thin client of a Linux terminal computing host.

It's done using a VNC client configured to start as soon as Windows finishes booting up. You can find that in the online downloads for this chapter at `www.WinLinAnswers.com`.

Assisted Computing for Linux Hosts

You've seen how to log on to a Linux host remotely via VNC, using a Windows guest workstation as a graphical terminal.

You've also seen remote computing where the guest user logs on to their own desktop session.

But how do we set up assisted computing on a Linux workstation so that one employee can help another to resolve a problem? Having a user log on via gdm logon prompt isn't right for this purpose. We want to *share* the current user's session at the console, not log on separately. Fortunately, Fedora includes a very straightforward assisted computing feature akin to Windows Remote Assistance but based on VNC. That feature is called Remote Desktop, and Windows guests can easily connect to it.

Earlier, we presented how salesperson1 (on the Linux workstation adlincli1.ad.corp.com) could assist salesperson2 (on the Windows workstation xppro1.ad.corp.com).

Now it's time for salesperson2 (on Windows) to return the favor by assisting salesperson1 with her Linux workstation.

> **WARNING**   The following experiments will likely not work when the target Linux machine is really contained within VMware. In our tests, Fedora's Remote Desktop was incompatible with virtual machines running the VMware 4 tools for Linux. Fedora Remote Desktop computing relies on a special extension to the standard Fedora X server. When VMware's tools are loaded, VMware replaces the X server with a special VMware-friendly version. Remote computing works fine on "real" machines, and on VMware machines on which the Linux tools have not yet been installed.

Requirements for Assisted Computing on Linux Hosts

Again, we want to have our Windows machines make contact with our Linux machines and offer help. We need to set up our Linux machines so they can accept the help from a Windows user.

- The TightVNC guest or "viewer" software must be installed on xppro1.ad.corp.com. If you completed the exercises in the "Assisted Computing for Windows Hosts" section, you will already have this software installed on xppro1. If not, refer to "Installing and Configuring TightVNC on the Windows Host."

- As described in the previous section, traffic on the VNC port (port 5900) must be allowed through the Fedora firewall on linserv1.corp.com. If you did not do this already, refer to "Configuring the Fedora Firewall to Allow VNC Traffic."

- The host in question must not already be configured as a remote computing host according to the directions in the preceding section. The reason is that we configured linserv1.corp.com to accept VNC remote computing connections on port 5900, for convenience because port 5900 is the default. Unfortunately, Fedora Remote Desktop insists on responding on port 5900. So if we want to do both, remote computing needs to change ports. See the sidebar, "Fedora Remote Desktop and Remote Computing on the Same Host" for information about how to make that happen.

Fedora Remote Desktop and Remote Computing on the Same Host

In the "Remote Computing for Linux Hosts" section, we chose to listen for remote computing connections on port 5900 because 5900 is the default port for VNC, and terminal computing should be as easy to log into as possible. Typing alternate port numbers is a pain.

Unfortunately, Fedora Remote Desktop can only respond on port 5900. Which means the two come into conflict. Normally this is not a problem, because assisted computing is rarely needed on a server.

However, those who wish to support both at once can do so by moving remote computing to an alternative port number. To do so, you need only do two things:

1. Replace port 5900 with port 5901 when following the configuration instructions in the "Remote Computing for Linux Hosts" section.

2. When connecting from the Windows guest, specify the alternate port number as well as the hostname. Note the unique double-colon syntax:

    `linserv1.corp.com::5901`

Again, though, there is usually little reason to use assisted rather than remote computing on a server.

Enabling Fedora Remote Desktop on *adlincli1.ad.corp.com*

To accept `salesperson1`'s help, `salesperson2` first needs to set up Fedora's Remote Desktop feature. To set up Fedora Remote Desktop on `adlincli1.ad.corp.com`, follow these steps:

1. Log into `adlincli1.ad.corp.com` as `salesperson2`.
2. Select ➢ Applications Preferences ➢ Remote Desktop.
3. The "Remote Desktop Preferences" dialog appears. We will configure it as shown in Figure 8.25. First, check the "Allow other users to view your desktop" box.
4. Check the "Allow other users to control your desktop" box.
5. Keep the "Ask you for confirmation" box checked. Optionally, you may also require a password.
6. Click "Close" to allow your settings to take effect.

Connecting to Fedora Remote Desktop from a Windows Workstation

We're almost there. All we have left to do is open a connection with the TightVNC guest application on `xppro1.ad.corp.com`. An `ssh`-encrypted connection may be used, following the instructions in the "Going the Extra Mile: Securing Windows-to-Linux VNC Connections with `ssh`" section and simply substituting `adlincli1.ad.corp.com` for `linserv1.corp.com` in each case. Or a simple unencrypted VNC connection may be made.

FIGURE 8.25   Configuring Fedora's Remote Desktop feature to accept VNC assisted computing connections

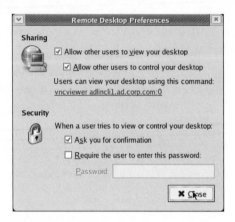

Follow these steps to open a VNC connection from xppro1.ad.corp.com to adlincli1.ad.corp.com:

1.   Log on to xppro1.ad.corp.com as salesperson1.

2.   Select Start ➤ All Programs.

3.   Select the "TightVNC" group.

4.   Select "TightVNC Viewer (Fast Compression)." If connecting over a slow link you may prefer to select "(Best Compression)."

5.   The "Connection details" prompt will appear. Enter **adlincli1.ad.corp.com**   in the "VNC Server:" field. Click "OK."

6.   At the console of adlincli1.ad.corp.com, salesperson2 will see a dialog asking whether they wish to allow the remote connection, as shown in Figure 8.26. She can accept the connection by clicking "Allow."

FIGURE 8.26   Accepting an assisted computing connection with Fedora's Remote Desktop on adlincli1.ad.corp.com

After a few moments, `salesperson2`'s Linux desktop will appear in a VNC window on `salesperson1`'s screen. `salesperson1` can now assist her with the task in question, and both users will have access to the keyboard and mouse until `salesperson1` disconnects or `salesperson2` logs out of `adlincli1.ad.corp.com`.

Final Thoughts

Remote computing, terminal computing, and assisted computing are all technically similar, but they each serve very different purposes:

- Remote computing enables us to connect to the server in the basement or the desktop down the hall.

- Terminal computing is all about centralizing applications on a single server with multiple users getting access to those applications at the same time while retaining their unique settings.

- Assisted computing has a more modest goal: allowing a "co-pilot" to temporarily assist in the operation of a particular system by sharing a view of the desktop and providing both parties with access to the keyboard and mouse.

You've seen how these goals can be achieved in a cross-platform environment. Linux guests can access Windows hosts, and Windows guests can access Linux hosts. Either operating system can be used simply as a "thin client" for accessing the other.

VNC-based remote and assisted computing for Linux isn't quite up to the standard set by RDP on Windows. RDP integrates encryption, local printing and sound into the experience. The free versions of VNC don't really do these things yet. However, it is likely that we'll see encryption, at least, as a standard feature in open-source VNC guest and host applications before long.

Terminal computing on Linux deserves special mention for the lack of licensing costs. The only thing that limits the number of guests connected to a Fedora terminal computing host is the memory and computing power of the server. The Linux Terminal Server Project also deserves an acknowledgment here. The LTSP.org project is alive and kicking with some great developers and support. We have met these guys firsthand, and they're super-charged about their project. Their enthusiasm is really catching.

9

Windows and Linux Network Interoperability

In this chapter, we'll take on several major network integration tasks. First, as an appetizer, we'll describe what is necessary to get a Windows Active Directory up and running (again), this time using a Linux server as the DNS server. We'll also show how to use a Linux branch office server as a DNS server and make it talk to our main Windows DNS servers.

In our "salad" course, we'll do a little Samba upgrade and show you how to get a Linux domain trusted by an Active Directory domain. This comes in handy for our "main dish."

As our main dish in this chapter, we'll configure Windows 2003's RRAS server to act as a VPN server that permits Linux and Windows users to connect remotely and act as if they were local nodes on our network.

Integrating Windows and Linux DNS

In Chapter 1, we took a whirlwind tour of setting up Windows and Linux servers. Then, on our Linux server, we create a *delegated subdomain* that allowed our Active Directory to play in its own "sandbox" of ad.corp.com. Next, on our Windows server, we ran the dcpromo command and got our Active Directory up and running in ad.corp.com.

In Chapter 1, we demonstrated the ideal way of integrating Active Directory and Unix/Linux DNS. That is, we hardly integrated at all. We gave Active Directory its own sandbox using its own DNS servers to house the required Active Directory records, and we gave the Unix/Linux users their own sandbox in corp.com to house their DNS resource records. The delegated subdomain from the Linux-hosted root DNS server makes the two domains, corp.com and ad.corp.com, play together nicely.

If at all possible, you should do your production DNS setup this way, with separate DNS domains for Active Directory and Linux.

Housing Active Directory DNS Records on Linux DNS Servers

In the first chapter, we set up Active Directory to "own" its own DNS. This is almost certainly the best way to go, from Microsoft's perspective. They kind of have a good point. Here are a handful of reasons why setting up Active Directory–integrated DNS specifically for Active Directory is a good idea:

- If you decide to implement a Linux BIND server, you need to be careful to choose one which also implements DNS Security, or DNSSEC. Even if you specify to lock down updates so that they're received only from Windows Domain Controllers, it's possible for a rogue administrator or rogue process on those DCs to register resource records without any kind of intervention.

- Active Directory–integrated zones give security to dynamic updates. That is, when the workstation re-registers via DHCP their IP address, Active Directory–integrated DNS can ensure those updates are really being changed by the client, not someone pretending to be the client.

- Active Directory–integrated zones also avoid the problem of a single point of failure. That is, because every Active Directory Domain Controller is writable, there's no one place that the DNS data *must* be written to be propagated.

If the preceding points don't persuade you to embrace the Microsoft best practice, then, yes, it is possible to set up an Active Directory domain so it doesn't "own" its own DNS. Rather, you can set up Linux to house the required Active Directory DNS records and have all clients use the Linux DNS servers (which run BIND DNS). Why would you want to do this? Many organizations already have BIND DNS servers and expert BIND administrators. Many places ask themselves, "Why should we bother creating a whole 'parallel' DNS structure, if our existing BIND DNS structure is already great?"

As it turns out, there are technically only a few things that the BIND DNS server needs to handle in order to be Active Directory–compatible.

Our Fedora Linux server is running BIND version 9, which is compatible with Active Directory DNS records right out of the box, including the use of underscores in resource record names. See the sidebar "If You're Using an Older DNS" for more background about these issues.

The best news is that Webmin supports everything we need to do in order to enable effective storage of Active Directory DNS records in BIND 9. All we have to do is enable dynamic updates so that the Active Directory server can "push" DNS changes to our BIND server on the fly.

Here's what we want to accomplish. We want to set up a new Active Directory domain in the same forest as `ad.corp.com`. We'll call it `peerad.corp.com`. The first Domain Controller in `peerad.corp.com` will be called `peerdc1.peerad.corp.com` and, in our examples, will have the IP address 192.168.2.240.

To create a new Active Directory domain, we'll first need a new DNS domain. We'll configure our Linux DNS server, `linserv1.corp.com`, to house the `peerad.corp.com` resource records.

Happily, we can do so using Webmin's "BIND DNS Server" module, which makes the procedure rather painless. All we need to do is create a new DNS zone for the `peerad.corp.com` subdomain and edit the options for that zone to enable DNS updates from 192.168.2.240, which is the IP address of `peerdc1.peerad.corp.com`, the new Active Directory Domain Controller for the `peerad.corp.com` domain. There's just one extra step: with updates coming from Active Directory on the fly, the BIND server (`named`) needs to be able to write those updates to disk. However, for security reasons, `named` does not run as root. Instead, it runs as a special user called `named`. Only root has permission to write to the DNS zone files kept in `/var/named` and `/var/named/chroot/var/named`.

Existing symbolic links from the first directory allow named to work identically, regardless of whether it is running in a special `chroot jail` mode in which `/var/named/chroot/var/named` appears to be `/var/named` from BIND's perspective. We'll fix permissions in both directories to cover either mode of operation.

Fortunately, the `named` user is a member of the special `named` group, and that group owns the directories in question, so we can use a simple `chmod` command to grant `named` the power to write to them.

Follow these steps to create the `peerad.corp.com` DNS zone on `linserv1.corp.com`:

1. Log into Webmin as usual at the URL `https://linserv1.corp.com:10000/`

2. Click "Servers."

3. Click "BIND DNS Server."

4. Click "Create master zone." The "Create Master Zone" page appears as shown in Figure 9.1.

5. In the "Domain name/Network" field, enter **peerad.corp.com**.

6. In the "E-mail address" field, enter **root@corp.com**.

7. Accept the defaults for the remaining options and create the new DNS zone by clicking "Create." The "Edit Master Zone" page appears. You can save some effort by leaving this page open for the steps that follow.

FIGURE 9.1   Creating a separate DNS zone for the `peerad.corp.com` subdomain on `linserv1.corp.com`

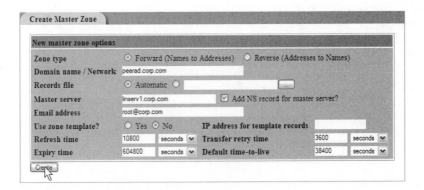

Follow these steps to configure linserv1.corp.com to accept DNS updates from the Active Directory Domain Controller:

1. Give the named group write access to the DNS data directories:

   chmod g+w /var/named/chroot/var/named
   chmod g+w /var/named

2. Log into Webmin as usual at the URL https://linserv1.corp.com:10000/.

3. Click "Servers."

4. Click "BIND DNS Server."

5. Click "peerad.corp.com" to access the "Edit Master Zone" page.

6. Scroll down and click "Edit Zone Options." The "Zone Options" screen appears. We will configure it as shown in Figure 9.2.

7. For "Allow updates from" enter **192.168.2.240**. This is the IP address of the peerdc1.peerad.corp.com.

8. Leave the remaining settings as shown in Figure 9.2.

9. Click "Save" to return to the "Edit Master Zone" page.

10. Click "Apply Changes."

If you have used earlier versions of BIND, you may wonder why we aren't configuring BIND to specifically tolerate unusual hostnames used by Active Directory, such as _kerberos, which begin with underscores. This was an issue in BIND 8. However, BIND 9, included with Fedora Core 3, accepts such names out of the box. That's because, eventually, the RFC that specifies acceptable DNS characters evolved to allow underscores. BIND 9 embraces this new standard and no special configuration is required to accept them. BIND 8 users can make the necessary configuration change by setting "Check Names?" to "Ignore" on the "Zone Options" page, instead of leaving it set to "Default" as shown in Figure 9.2, where we are able to leave this option set to "Default" because BIND 9 has no need for it.

FIGURE 9.2 Be sure to specify the Active Directory Domain Controller from which to accept records—in our case, 192.168.2.240, peerdc1.peerad.corp.com.

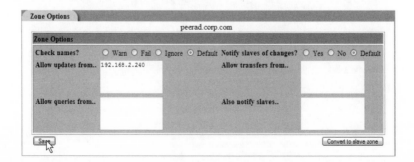

When it's finished, your new Active Directory structure will look like Figure 9.3. You will have the new `peerad.corp.com` subdomain integrated into the existing `corp.com` domain.

Bringing up a New Active Directory Domain

In this section, we'll bring up a new Active Directory domain, a peer to `ad.corp.com`. We'll call it `peerad.corp.com`. Again, the goal is to support this Active Directory domain using DNS running on `linserv1.corp.com`.

At this point, you can refer to the steps back in Chapter 1 in the "Installing Your Active Directory" section when we brought up `windc1.ad.corp.com`, the first Domain Controller in `ad.corp.com`. There is only a handful of differences in the domain configuration. Here's a brief rundown:

- The server name is different. We suggest `peerdc1`.

- In our examples, we're assigning the IP address of 192.168.2.240 to `peerdc1`.

- During the Domain Controller Promotion wizard (DCPROMO), when you get to the "Domain Controller Type" screen, select "Domain controller for a new domain." When you get to the "Create a new domain" screen, choose "Domain tree in an existing forest." Enter **peerad.corp.com** as the new domain name, as shown in Figure 9.4.

- Configure the TCP/IP properties for the network interface on `peerdc1` to use `linserv1` (192.168.2.202) as the DNS server.

FIGURE 9.3 peerad.corp.com will be a new domain whose DNS records will "live" upon linserv1.corp.com.

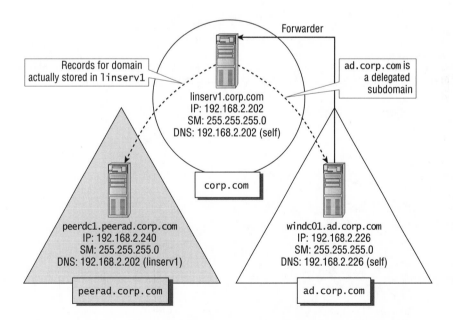

Again, you needn't keep the DNS service running on the Domain Controller. The DNS records are all going to be housed on `linserv1.corp.com`.

Once you've finished the Domain Controller Promotion Wizard and restarted the server, the DNS resource records for `peerad.corp.com` will be placed into the `corp.com` zone. If you get an error message, such as in Figure 9.5, or if you get anything else that expresses that DNS records cannot be written upon `linserv1.corp.com`, be sure you've made the `/var/named` and `/var/named/chroot/var/named` folders writable and enabled updates from 192.168.2.240 on the Linux side.

FIGURE 9.4   Your new peer domain will be called `peerad.corp.com`.

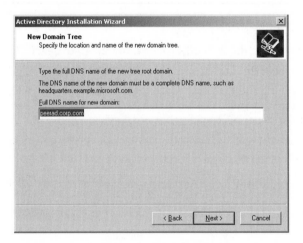

FIGURE 9.5   If you get a DNS-related error message like this one, be sure that BIND's data directories are writable and that 192.168.2.240 is allowed to send updates to `linserv1.corp.com`.

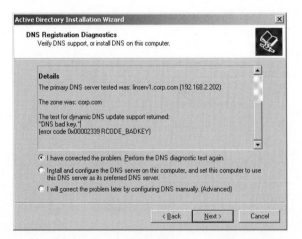

Verifying Active Directory DNS Records within Linux

Now that you've brought up `peerad.corp.com` (with `peerdc1` as the only Domain Controller in it), you're ready to make sure the appropriate Active Directory DNS records got created in the `peerad.corp.com` zone that lives on `linserv1.corp.com`.

But how can we tell if peerdc1.corp.com's resource records successfully made it into the new zone? We can browse the DNS records in the `peerad.corp.com` zone using Webmin. However, Webmin only shows us the contents of the zone file, `peerad.corp.com.hosts`, which was created automatically by Webmin when we created the new zone. It doesn't interrogate the DNS server on the fly for this information. This is an issue because `peerad.corp.com.hosts` is not rewritten on the fly right away when updates arrive from the Active Directory server. Instead, for efficiency reasons, changes received on the fly are written to a "journal" file called `peerad.hosts.corp.com.jnl`.

We can work around this problem by asking the DNS server to restart. When Webmin asks the DNS server to shut down and restart gracefully, the DNS server *does* rewrite the `peerad.corp.com.hosts` file as a final step before exiting. (The DNS server also does this on a periodic basis while running, so that the `.jnl` file doesn't grow forever.) Once we do that, it's a cinch to view the DNS records with Webmin.

We'll verify our success by checking the `peerad.corp.com` for service address (SRV) records, which specify the hosts that provide various services such as Kerberos and LDAP. We certainly didn't set these up, so their presence indicates that DNS updates are happening successfully.

To verify that DNS updates for the `peerad.corp.com` domain are being accepted successfully by `linserv1.corp.com`'s BIND DNS server, follow these steps:

1. Log into Webmin as usual at the URL `https://linserv1.corp.com:10000/`.

2. Click "Servers."

3. Click "BIND DNS Server." The "BIND DNS Server" page appears.

4. Scroll to the bottom of the page and click "Apply Changes." This restarts the BIND DNS server. The "BIND DNS Server" page reappears.

5. Click "`peerad.corp.com`" to access the "Edit Master Zone" page.

6. Click "Service Address" to view the "Service Address Records" page.

7. This page should contain records similar to those shown in Figure 9.6.

If you don't find any records in the listing, be sure that BIND's data directories are writable and that 192.168.2.240 is allowed to send updates to `linserv1.corp.com`.

FIGURE 9.6 Displaying service address records to verify that DNS updates from Active Directory have been accepted by `linserv1.corp.com`

Name	TTL	Priority	Weight	Port	Server
kerberos.tcp.Default-First-Site-Name. sites.dc. msdcs.peerad.corp.com.	Default	0	100	88	peerdc1.peerad.corp.com.
ldap.tcp.Default-First-Site-Name. sites.dc. msdcs.peerad.corp.com.	Default	0	100	389	peerdc1.peerad.corp.com.
kerberos.tcp.dc. msdcs.peerad.corp.com.	Default	0	100	88	peerdc1.peerad.corp.com.
ldap.tcp.dc. msdcs.peerad.corp.com.	Default	0	100	389	peerdc1.peerad.corp.com.
ldap.tcp.pdc. msdcs.peerad.corp.com.	Default	0	100	389	peerdc1.peerad.corp.com.
kerberos.tcp.Default-First-Site-Name. sites.peerad.corp.com.	Default	0	100	88	peerdc1.peerad.corp.com.
ldap.tcp.Default-First-Site-Name. sites.peerad.corp.com.	Default	0	100	389	peerdc1.peerad.corp.com.

Setting up a Linux Branch Office DNS Server

One of the other ways you might choose to integrate Windows and Linux DNS is to have a Linux server be a secondary DNS server to a Windows DNS server.

This might be useful in branch office scenarios where a single Linux server in a field office runs the whole show. Clients in the field office may need to connect with hosts in other offices and that would require a DNS lookup. In this type of scenario, we would have our Linux server be a member of Active Directory (as we demonstrated in Chapter 3). Then that single Linux server in the branch office will be the "go to" server for DNS requests (and anything else you might want to throw at it).

Here, we'll leverage this idea to target three main goals, shown in Figure 9.7.

- Goal #1: Branch-office clients (Windows or Linux) send all DNS queries to a local DNS server

- Goal #2: The branch-office DNS servers gets updated from the home office

- Goal #3: Requests that cannot be answered by the branch-office DNS server gets forwarded up the food chain (to the branch office, and, if needed, to the Internet.)

FIGURE 9.7 We want to accomplish three goals when we put a Linux DNS server in the branch office.

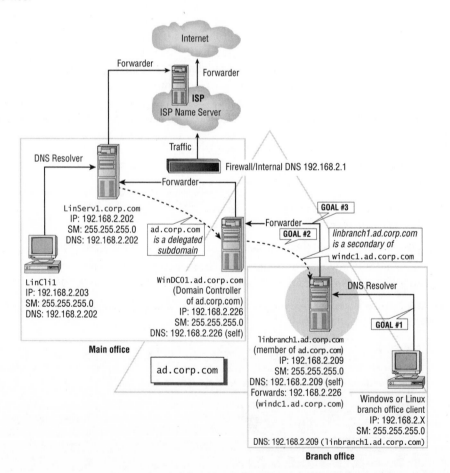

The secondary zone contains the same resource records as the primary zone in the home office, so by installing DNS on the Linux branch office server, clients in the branch office get replies to their DNS queries quickly with no need to traverse the WAN.

Queries for resource records outside the company's DNS zones are forwarded to DNS servers in the home office where you can take advantage of caching to improve lookup speeds.

In this example, we'll assume you're ready to install your new `linbranch1.ad.corp.com` Linux server. Let's talk about that configuration now.

If You're Using an Older DNS

Fedora Core 3 supports the DNS functions we need to make this happen. If you're not using Fedora Core 3, there are three main RFCs your Linux DNS should have compliance with in order to ideally interoperate with Windows DNS.

None of these first three are strictly required, but if your older DNS supports these three RFCs, things will be easier and faster all around.

Not required, but nice to have: RFC 1995—incremental zone transfers   Because this server is going to be the secondary server, it could download lots and lots of records from our main Active Directory DNS servers. To that end, RFC 1995 provides for incremental zone transfers that stipulate that only records that change will come across the WAN and onto this DNS server.

Not required, but nice to have: RFC 1996—DNS change notification   When your Linux server supports this RFC, changes from one DNS server are immediately transferred to other servers. In our case, we want all the central office's Active Directory DNS changes to immediately go to our branch office Linux server.

Not required, but nice to have: RFC 2308—negative caching   While not strictly required, negative caching improves performance in cases where clients look up a record that does not exist. This can be helpful in a scenario involving a slow link.

Absolutely required: RFC 2052   The last requirement is RFC 2052. Active Directory utilizes Service Location (SRV) resource records in a number of ways. In short, if your DNS doesn't support RFC 2052, it's simply not a good candidate to house Active Directory records.

Mostly, you'll need to ensure your DNS meets these minimum requirements if you're not using BIND 8.2 or BIND 9. Indeed, Bind 4 is still quite popular with some companies.

Installing Fedora on *linbranch1.ad.corp.com*

Setting up the branch office DNS server isn't difficult. To configure `linbranch1.ad.corp.com`, follow the procedure presented in Chapter 1 to install `linserv1.corp.com` in the "Installing Fedora Linux" section, with the following exceptions:

1. Set the IP address to 192.168.2.209.

2. Set the DNS server to `localhost`.

3. Set the hostname to `linbranch1.ad.corp.com`.

4. Add an "A" record for `linbranch1.ad.corp.com` to the Windows DNS server on `windc1.ad.corp.com`.

When you have completed the initial installation, make sure you also fetch security updates and other fixes by running up2date. BIND DNS is updated with some regularity to address security and other important issues, so it's a good idea to be current. Double-click the exclamation point icon in the upper-right corner and follow the steps given in Chapter 1 to update your system.

Now we're ready to set up DNS on `linbranch1.ad.corp.com`.

Setting up *linbranch1.ad.corp.com* as a Secondary DNS Server

Setting up zone transfers from a Windows primary DNS server to a Linux secondary DNS server involves three major steps:

-   Creating a "slave zone" for the `ad.corp.com` domain on `linbranch1.ad.corp.com`

-   Configuring the Linux DNS server to request zone transfers from the Windows DNS server

-   Configuring the Windows DNS server to accept zone transfer requests from the Linux DNS server and to notify the Linux DNS server when changes occur to the zone

So let's get to it.

Configuring Our Windows DNS Server to Transfer Our Zone to Linux

On the Windows DNS server, we need to specify the secondary servers from which zone transfer requests will be accepted. This is a security measure that prevents a bad guy from "dumping" the contents of a zone by pretending to be a DNS secondary server.

We also need to enable the "Notify" options so that zone changes are transferred immediately from the Windows primary to the Linux secondary DNS server. Otherwise, the secondary server will only ask for a zone transfer at specific refresh intervals, normally every 15 minutes.

To configure a Windows DNS server to allow zone transfers for the `ad.corp.com` zone to the Linux secondary DNS server and to notify the Linux secondary DNS server of changes, do the following:

1. On `windc1.ad.corp.com`, log in as Administrator.

2. Click Start ≻ All Programs ≻ Administrative Tools ≻ DNS.

3. We're only concerned with the `ad.corp.com` zone. Find it in `windc1` ≻ Forward Lookup Zones ≻ `ad.corp.com`, right-click `ad.corp.com` and select "Properties."

4. Click the "Zone Transfers" tab. Select "Allow zone transfers" and select "Only to the following servers." Enter the IP address of `linbranch1.ad.corp.com`, 192.168.2.209 as shown in Figure 9.8.

5. Click the "Notify" button (as shown at the bottom of Figure 9.6) to get to the "Notify" window.

6. Select "Automatically notify," select the "The following servers," and again, enter the address of `linbranch1.ad.corp.com`, 192.168.2.209 as shown in Figure 9.8.

7. Click "OK" to close the "Notify" tab, and click "OK" to close the "`ad.corp.com` Properties" window with the "Zone Transfers" tab.

F I G U R E 9 . 8   Configure Windows DNS so that it allows zone transfers and will also automatically notify secondaries when changes are available.

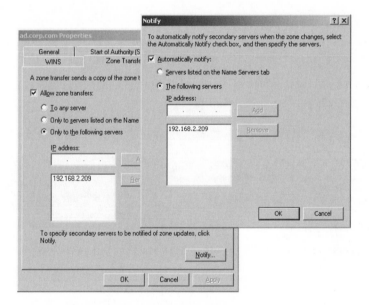

Configuring the BIND DNS Server with Webmin

By default, when we choose to install a DNS server, Fedora configures it as a simple caching proxy that is not the master for any domain but does save round trips over the WAN when several users look up the same host. That's 90 percent of the behavior we want. In addition, though, we want our server to act as a secondary or "slave" DNS server for the `ad.corp.com` domain, ensuring that all queries about that domain can be resolved more quickly with *no* round trips on the WAN for single queries from individuals. A true slave DNS server will fetch and update all of the information about the domain for which it acts as a slave in advance, which is known as a "zone transfer," rather than making queries of the primary server only when a user happens to need particular information.

As usual, we'll use Webmin to take care of the configuration settings we need. But first, we'll need to make sure the BIND DNS service, `named`, is up and running on the server. We'll do that using the familiar `chkconfig` and `service` commands.

Follow these steps on `linbranch1.ad.corp.com` to configure BIND as a secondary DNS server for the `ad.corp.com`:

1. Configure Fedora to start the `named` daemon on every reboot:

    ```
    chkconfig named on
    ```

2. Start the named daemon now:

    ```
    service named start
    ```

3. Log into Webmin in the usual way, at the URL `https://linbranch1.ad.corp.com:10000/`.
4. Click "Servers."
5. Click "Bind DNS Server."
6. Click "Create slave zone." This is found beneath the words "Existing DNS Zones." The "Create Slave Zone" page appears. We will configure this page as shown in Figure 9.9.

FIGURE 9.9   Use these settings to create a slave zone such that `linbranch1.ad.corp.com` is a secondary DNS server for the `ad.corp.com` domain.

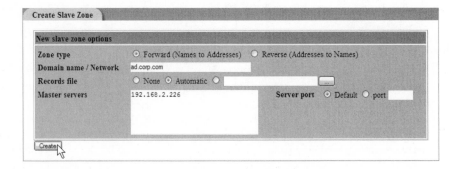

7. In the "Domain name/Network" field, enter **ad.corp.com**.
8. In the "Master servers" field, add this single entry:

    ```
    192.168.2.226
    ```

9. This of course is the IP address of `windc1.ad.corp.com`.
10. Leave the remaining fields set to their default values.
11. Click "Create" to create the slave zone. The "Edit Slave Zone" page appears.
12. Click "Return to zone list" to return to the "BIND DNS Server" page.

Now it's time to verify that the resource records have actually arrived in our slave DNS server's slave zone file. We'll do that in the same way we verified our success earlier when we configured `linserv1.corp.com` as the primary DNS server for `ad.corp.com`. As before, we'll need to restart the DNS server before checking the records, to make sure the records have actually been committed to the zone file where Webmin can find them.

Follow these steps to verify that the slave DNS zone actually contains the records for the `ad.corp.com` domain:

1. Log into Webmin as usual at the URL `https://linbranch1.ad.corp.com:10000/`.

2. Click "Servers."

3. Click "BIND DNS Server." The "BIND DNS Server" page appears.

4. Scroll to the bottom of the page and click "Apply Changes." This restarts the BIND DNS server. The "BIND DNS Server" page reappears.

5. Click "`ad.corp.com`" to access the "Edit Slave Zone" page.

6. Click "Address" (the "A" icon) to display a list of hosts in the `ad.corp.com` domain.

If the list of hosts is empty, make sure you have started the BIND DNS server and created the slave zone for `ad.corp.com`.

Verifying That Our Linux DNS Server Is Receiving Zone Transfers from Active Directory

Now that we've set up our Active Directory to send any changes to our Linux branch office server, we can test it out. The test takes two steps: first, we'll make an Active Directory change. Then, we'll verify that our Linux server got the change.

Making a Simple DNS Change in Active Directory

To make a simple DNS change in Active Directory, just create an A record. This is the same kind of record that is produced whenever a workstation joins the domain, but we'll pretend one is coming online by manually adding an A record.

To add an A record, in the DNS manager, right-click `ad.corp.com` and select "New Host (A)." You'll be presented with the "New Host" dialog. Enter the name of a new (fake) computer, such as **arecordtest1** (the `ad.corp.com` part will already be filled in the form for you), then add in an IP address that won't matter (we entered **192.168.2.222**). Once you have the A record in place, the previous steps should send the record over to our Linux secondary DNS server immediately.

Testing Linux for the Zone Transfer Record Change

As in the previous section, it's a little bit of a pain to make sure the secondary DNS server has really accepted the change. Again, the changes are written to a journal file that is not plaintext. We can ask the server to look up the new host, but that only proves that the server is smart enough to consult `ad.corp.com` if it doesn't contain the record itself.

So how do we tease out the truth? The same way as before: we'll restart the DNS server to force the contents of the journal file to be committed to the "official" `ad.corp.com.hosts` file so that BIND can start up again cleanly, and then we'll use Webmin to inspect the results.

Follow these steps to verify the successful arrival of `arecordtest1` in the slave DNS server's zone file:

1. Log into Webmin as usual at the URL `https://linbranch1.ad.corp.com:10000/`.

2. Click "Servers."

3. Click "BIND DNS Server." The "BIND DNS Server" page appears.

4. Scroll to the bottom of the page and click "Apply Changes." This restarts the BIND DNS server. The "BIND DNS Server" page reappears.

5. Click "`ad.corp.com`" to access the "Edit Slave Zone" page.

6. Click "Address" (the "A" icon) to display a list of hosts in the `ad.corp.com` domain.

If the list of hosts does not contain `arecordtest1`, make sure you enabled notification of `linbranch1.ad.corp.com` when configuring `peerad.corp.com`.

Forwarding Unknown Queries to Windows DNS

The final goal for our Linux branch office DNS server is to forward queries it cannot resolve up to our Active Directory `windc1.ad.corp.com`. Then, if `windc1.ad.corp.com` doesn't know the answer, it's already set up to forward to `linserv1.corp.com`. And if `linserv1.corp.com` doesn't know the answer, it asks the Internet.

In Chapter 1, we set up our `windc1.ad.corp.com` Windows DNS server to forward queries it didn't know about to our main DNS servers on `corp.com`.

Here, we'll set up `linbranch1.ad.corp.com` to forward queries it can't resolve over to `windc1.ad.corp.com`. Again, since we already set up `windc1.ad.corp.com` to forward to `corp.com`, and `corp.com` is forwarding to the Internet, we should complete the chain of command right here.

Setting up Our Linux Branch Office DNS Server to Forward to Our Active Directory DNS Servers

Webmin fully supports configuration of forwarding for DNS queries, so we can easily set up the DNS server to forward queries to `windc1.ad.corp.com` (192.168.2.226), which will forward them in turn to `linserv1.corp.com` (192.168.2.202) if needed. `linserv1.corp.com`, in turn, forwards them to the Internet at large when they are not locally resolvable.

To configure BIND on `linbranch1.ad.corp.com` to forward queries to `windc1.ad.corp.com`, follow these steps:

1. Log into Webmin in the usual way, at the URL `https://linbranch1.ad.corp.com:10000/`.

2. Click "Servers."

3. Click "Bind DNS Server."

4. Click "Forwarding and Transfers." We'll configure the "Forwarding and Transfers" page as shown in Figure 9.10.

FIGURE 9.10 Forward queries not resolved directly by this server to the next in line: windc1.ad.corp.com (192.168.2.226).

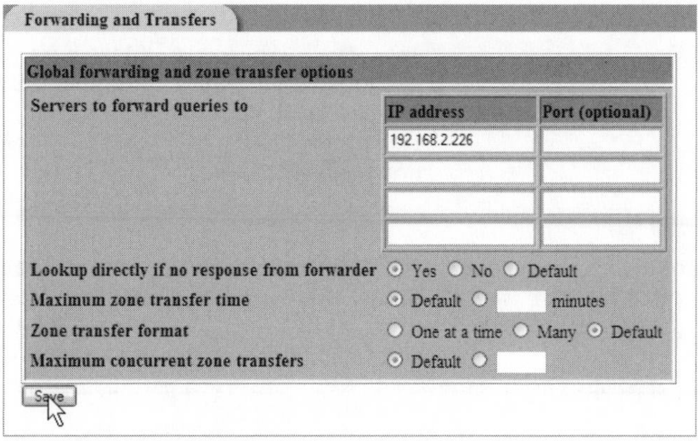

5. Clear any entries found in the "IP address" and "Port (optional)" columns of the "Servers to forward queries to" table. Add this single entry in the first row of the "IP address" column, leaving the "Port (optional)" column blank:

   192.168.2.226

6. The remaining options should already be set as shown.

7. Click "Save" to return to the "BIND DNS Server" page.

8. Click "Apply Changes."

Testing DNS Forwarding

How can we verify that DNS queries sent to linbranch1.ad.corp.com are really being forwarded first to windc1.ad.corp.com, then to linserv1.corp.com, and finally to the Internet?

We thought of elaborate ways to do this. Then we caught on: it's very simple to do! With one exception that is easy enough to avoid in the first place, there are obvious ways to detect each possible error. The following table presents the possible DNS misconfigurations, the telltale symptoms, why those symptoms occur, and how to correct the problem.

TABLE 9.1 Possible DNS misconfigurations.

Problem	Symptom	Why	Solution
linbranch1.ad.corp.com is making its own queries without consulting any "upstream" DNS server.	host linserv1.corp.com will not report 192.168.2.202.	The outside Internet can't "see" our internal DNS servers.	Verify that you have set up the "Forwarding and Transfers" page correctly and used the "Apply Changes" button.

TABLE 9.1   Possible DNS misconfigurations. *(continued)*

Problem	Symptom	Why	Solution
`linbranch1.ad.corp` `.com` is sending requests directly to `linserv1.corp.com` rather than `windc1` `.ad.corp.com`.	None.	`linserv1.corp.com` is capable of delegating queries to `windc1.ad` `.corp.com`, so this is not easily detected.	Make sure you entered 192.168.2.226 and not 192.168.2.202 on the "Forwarding and Transfers" page.
`linbranch1.ad.corp.` `com` is not resolving DNS queries at all.	`host linserv1.corp` `.com` and `host www` `.google.com` *both* fail.	BIND did not start up successfully.	Consult /var/log/ messages for errors during BIND startup and address them.

We've succeeded in doing some remarkable cross-platform networking tricks with DNS. But that's just for starters. We're going to have a lot more fun.

Creating Trusts between Samba and Active Directory Domains

As we stated in the goals for this chapter, the "big deal" we want to make happen is that anyone, from any client type should be able to log in via the VPN. The simplest way to that goal is to create a trust relationship between the Active Directory domain (ad) and the Samba domain (corp).

As everyone knows, it takes two to trust: one to trust and one to lie. No, no... that's not it. It takes one to trust and one to be trusted. The Samba domain is one-half of that relationship. It's going to be trusted. That is, user accounts that live in the Samba (corp) domain will be able to access resources that live on servers in the Active Directory (ad) domain.

It turns out that there's an incompatibility between Samba and Windows that we need to fix for VPN access to work properly, and the fix involves upgrading Samba. Let's do the fix before setting up the trust.

Upgrading Samba, If Needed

Domain trusts are well supported in Samba. They are a fundamental part of NT 4–style Windows authentication, which Active Directory continues to support. By configuring a trust, users in the corp domain can log in at workstations in the ad domain or access resources on servers in the ad domain. All we need to do is create a cross-domain trust. Samba is a team player here.

The Point to Point Tunneling Protocol (PPTP) used in VPNs *also* uses Windows authentication, so allowing users to log in over the Windows-hosted PPTP VPN shouldn't be hard either…right?

Well, almost. To utilize a Windows VPN server, users must have a special flag set before logging into the VPN. Under the hood, it's called "Grant dial-in permission to user."

Unfortunately, an incompatibility exists between the version of Samba (3.0.10-1-FC3) in Fedora Core 3 as of this writing and Microsoft's RAS (Remote Access Service). This incompatibility prevents RAS from "seeing" that a user in the Samba domain *does* have the dial-in permission flag set.

Are we stuck? Fortunately, no. This incompatibility was fixed in Samba 3.0.11. There's a good chance that by the time you read this, a fully updated installation of Fedora Core 3 already includes Samba 3.0.11 or better. So we'll first show how to verify that. And if you *do* have the older version of Samba, we'll also show how to upgrade relatively painlessly using Fedora Core 3–specific RPMs made available by the official Samba development team.

Verifying Your Samba Version

If your Samba is version 3.0.11 or better, you don't need to upgrade. How can you verify this? Like most well-written Unix tools, Samba's `smbd` daemon accepts a `--version` option on the command line. We'll use this option to find out what version we've got.

Use the following command on `linserv1.corp.com` to check your Samba version:

```
/usr/sbin/smbd --version
```

If you receive the following output:

```
Version 3.0.10-1.fc3
```

Or any output indicating a version *older than* 3.0.11, you'll need to upgrade. If not, you can skip the next section and move on to "Samba Side Trust Creation."

Upgrading Samba with Official Samba rpms

In the previous section we verified that Samba is older than version 3.0.11, and when we want RAS to be able to check the dial-up flag, that won't cut it. So how do we upgrade as painlessly as possible?

Very easily, as it turns out! The Samba project, as we've mentioned, offers rpms to upgrade Samba on Fedora Core 3 systems. These rpms are correctly preconfigured to find the right database and configuration files in the right places for Fedora Core 3. We strongly recommend them over attempting to build from source code.

We'll obtain the rpms by browsing through the binary download directories of the Samba website. Installing them is as simple as installing any other rpm. However, we will need to use the `--force` option of the `rpm` command to replace the official Fedora Samba rpms, which would otherwise produce an error message.

To download the rpms, follow these steps:

1. Access the page `www.samba.org/`.
2. Click "Binaries" in the navigation area at the left. A directory listing appears.

3. Click the "Fedora" folder. A new directory listing appears, offering "RPMS" and "SRPMS."

4. Click "RPMS" to obtain precompiled binaries. A directory listing of supported binary platforms appears.

5. Click "i386." A list of Fedora distribution types appears, with the sole option currently being "core."

6. Click "core." A list of Fedora Core versions for which rpms are currently available appears. Click "3." A list of current Samba binary rpms for Fedora Core 3 appears.

7. We need all of the rpms except for the SWAT interface, which we don't use in this book. Download each of the following files and move them to /tmp on linserv1.corp.com (version numbers will vary; use the currently available versions):

    ```
    samba-3.0.14a-1.i386.rpm
    samba-client-3.0.14a-1.i386.rpm
    samba-common-3.0.14a-1.i386.rpm
    ```

8. Shut down the running Samba server with this command:

    ```
    service smb stop
    ```

9. Install the rpms with the following command:

    ```
    rpm -i --force samba*.rpm
    ```

10. Verify that version 3.0.14a (or better) is now installed with this command:

    ```
    /usr/sbin/smbd --version
    ```

    This should produce

    ```
    Version 3.0.14a
    ```

    or a later version. If not, make sure the rpm command did not produce errors and that you remembered to specify the --force option.

11. Restart the Samba daemons, running the new versions:

    ```
    service smb start
    ```

Now that Samba has been upgraded to a sufficiently modern version, we'll move on to the creation of a domain trust.

Samba-Side Trust Creation

We're ready to create a domain trust. Our domain trust will allow users of any workstation that supports logons in the ad domain to also accept logons in the corp domain.

Users of Windows clients, such as xppro1.ad.corp.com, will now see corp as a drop-down possibility when choosing a logon domain. Later, when we use Windows XP's VPN client, we can specify credentials, which live either in corp or ad. We'll arrange the same access for Linux VPN clients.

So, who should trust whom? The goal is for the ad domain to trust the corp domain. That way, services like the Windows VPN server that rely on Active Directory for authentication will automatically gain the ability to accept corp domain logons as well.

This is established between the two domains by something called a "trust account." Strangely enough, though, the *domain to be trusted* is the one that must get the ball rolling to create a domain trust.

That means our Samba PDC on linserv1.corp.com has to make the first move in this dance. How do we set up the Samba side of the domain trust? By creating a domain trust account using the smbldap-useradd tool we first encountered in Chapter 2. We'll use options similar to those used to create a machine trust account, but we'll also add the -i option, which sets the "inter-domain trust" flag for that particular account. This distinguishes it from a machine trust account.

The following steps require that you have previously configured an LDAP-based Samba PDC for the corp domain, running on linserv1.corp.com, as described in Chapter 2.

To create the domain trust account, follow these steps:

1. In a production environment, choose a secure password for the domain trust. You'll need this password again when you configure the Windows side of the trust. For test purposes only, we used p@ssw0rd.

2. Execute this command on linserv1.corp.com to create the account:

   ```
   /usr/local/sbin/smbldap-useradd -w -i ad
   ```

3. You may see the following warnings, which may be safely ignored:

   ```
   Use of uninitialized value in string at /usr/lib/perl5/site_perl/smbldap_
   tools.pm line 169.
   Use of uninitialized value in string at /usr/lib/perl5/site_perl/smbldap_
   tools.pm line 169.
   ```

4. Enter and confirm the domain trust account password when prompted.

The Linux side of the domain trust is ready! Now we're ready to configure the Windows side and begin reaping the benefits.

Active Directory–Side Trust Creation

To create the actual trust, we need to fire up the Active Directory Domains and Trusts tool on windc1.ad.corp.com. To create the trust between ad and corp:

1. Select Start ➤ Administrative Tools ➤ Active Directory Domains and Trusts.

2. If you followed the instructions earlier in the chapter, you should have two domains listed, ad.corp.com and peerad.corp.com. We're interested in creating a trust between ad.corp.com and Samba's corp. Right-click over ad.corp.com and select "Properties."

3. In the "ad.corp.com Properties" page, click "Trusts." Then click "New Trust."

4. At the first page of the wizard, click "Next." In the "Trust Name" screen, in the "Name" field, enter corp and click "Next."

5. In the "Direction of Trust" page, select "One-way: outgoing" and select "Next."

6. In the "Outgoing Trust Authentication Level" page select "Domain-Wide authentication" and select "Next."

7. In the "Trust Password" page enter and re-enter the password we're using for the trust: **p@ssw0rd** and click "Next."

8. You'll find a "Trust Creation Complete" page. Your only option is to click "Next."

9. At the "Confirm Outgoing Trust" page, select "Yes, confirm the outgoing trust" and click "Next."

10. At the final page of the wizard, you should get a message that the trust relationship was successfully created. Click "Finish."

> Upon closing the wizard, you may get a notice about SID filtering. For the examples in this book, this can be safely ignored. Just click "OK" if prompted.

Ensuring *corp* Users Can Log on to a Windows XP Computer (joined to the *ad.corp.com* domain)

To verify the trust is active and in place, use xppro1.ad.corp.com (or any other computer joined to the ad.corp.com domain). Log off and then note if the corp domain is available from the "Log on to" drop-down as shown in Figure 9.11.

FIGURE 9.11   Once the trust to corp is established, it should be available within the "Log on to" drop-down

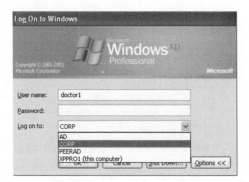

Go ahead and try to log on using the `corp` domain with the `doctor1` account. Use the password of **p@ssw0rd** and see if you can successfully log in. If not, check the following:

- Examine the event logs on `windc1.ad.corp.com`, the `ad` Domain Controller.
- Use the `tail` command to check the file `/var/log/samba/windc1.log` on `linserv1.corp.com`, which contains information about cross-domain authentication attempts.

A Cross-Platform VPN with PPTP

Users with laptops on the road and computers in their home offices need remote network access. By remote network access, we mean the ability to interact with other machines on your network as if the remote computer were physically attached to the same LAN. Although this is sometimes achieved via dial-up over dedicated phone lines, we'll be looking exclusively at *virtual* private networking connections (VPNs).

VPNs are popular because they allow users to create a secure, private connection to the company network over inexpensive broadband Internet services or dial-up connections to a local ISP's network access point rather than a long distance connection to a modem rack in the server room.

Linux and Windows Road Warriors: Connecting via PPTP

Any combination of Linux and Windows "road warrior" users might be out there needing access to the company network. We'll show you how to create a unified virtual private network (VPN) that serves all your users on whatever operating system they might be using.

Recall our earlier story:

`doctors` and `nurses` accounts live in `corp.com` on server `linserv1.corp.com` in an OpenLDAP directory service. Linux clients authenticate via LDAP. Windows clients see `linserv1` as a Samba-based PDC.

Sales, Marketing, and Human Resources accounts live in `ad.corp.com` on server `windc1.ad.corp.com` in an Active Directory service.

The goal is to ensure that all users, wherever their accounts "live," can get connected and authenticated to our corporate network; It shouldn't matter if they decide to use a Linux laptop or a Windows laptop. Take a look at Figure 9.12, which demonstrates our goals for this section.

We can permit users using both Linux and Windows clients to log on to the VPN with either `corp` (Linux) or `ad` (Windows) credentials.

In the bottom of the figure, you can see that users whose accounts live in Active Directory or OpenLDAP (our Samba PDC) can use whichever client computer they want and get access to our network.

Yes, you're reading that right. Both client types will be connecting to a Windows 2003 PPTP server and running a Microsoft protocol, PPTP (Point to Point Tunneling Protocol).

While PPTP has not been accepted as an Internet standard, it *is* a published and open protocol that is included with every Windows client. PPTP was built on top of PPP (Point to Point Protocol), a widely accepted Internet standard.

FIGURE 9.12   Using a Windows 2003 PPTP server, both Windows and Linux clients can log on with either corp domain or ad domain credentials. Now that the trust is in place.

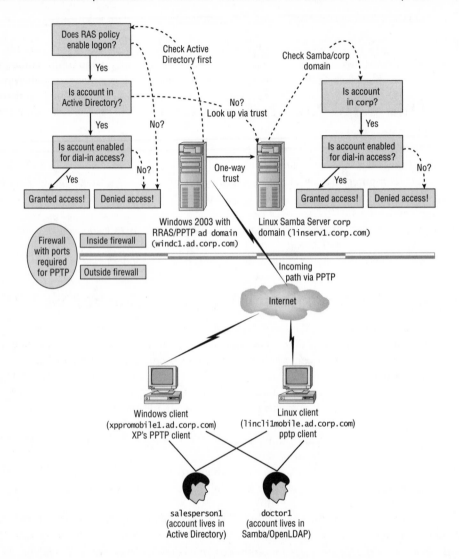

A PPTP client is *not* included in Fedora Core 3, but it is readily available. Since it's likely that you're already using Microsoft's PPTP as a VPN in production, we're going to stick with that here.

Linux PPTP clients support MSCHAP2, the authentication protocol Windows servers prefer to speak to, and that means that we can enable users to log on with either Windows Active Directory credentials (from the ad domain) or Linux domain credentials (from the corp domain), without reconfiguring the Windows server to accept a less secure method of authentication.

Alternatives to PPTP

There are alternatives to PPTP. These include the following.

OpenVPN   OpenVPN is an up-and-comer based on the same SSL protocol that underlies `ssh` connections and secure websites. OpenVPN is supported on both Windows and Linux, although Windows support is still lacking in user-friendliness. Since OpenVPN is not standard with Windows, users must install a client program to support it. We also found it quite difficult to authenticate OpenVPN users against both the ad and the corp domains simultaneously. Still, OpenVPN is a straightforward and flexible system that's well worth a look. See `http://www.openvpn.org/` for more information about OpenVPN.

IPSEC   IPSEC is an open standard that is supported on Windows and Linux. Unfortunately, however, a fully Windows-compatible installation of IPSEC on Linux is currently quite difficult to configure. While there is some support in the Fedora GUI for configuring IPSEC connections, don't get your hopes up too high—as of this writing, that GUI is only suitable for creating simple VPN tunnels between Fedora Linux and other Unix systems and is not suitable for use with Windows clients. See the Linux IPSEC HOWTO at `http://www.ipsec-howto.org/` for more information about IPSEC.

PPTP: Security Issues and Best Practices

PPTP is widely deployed. It comes in the box with Windows, and open source implementations exist. Why doesn't everybody use it? Well, security issues have been raised regarding Microsoft's PPTP in the past. A well-known article by Bruce Schneier of Counterpane Systems caused quite a stir in 1998 by pointing out serious cryptographic flaws in the *original* PPTP implementation. You can read that article at `http://www.schneier.com/pptp-faq.html`.

However, in the years since, Microsoft has standardized on the much-improved MSCHAP2 authentication protocol and improved other cryptographic aspects of its PPTP implementation. A more recent article by Mr. Schneier acknowledges that this addresses most of the technical flaws:

`http://www.schneier.com/pptp.html`

One lingering concern is the backward compatibility that, by default, Microsoft's PPTP server tries to provide with MSCHAP, thus allowing less secure authentication to be used on the network. However, this is no longer the case in Windows 2003, where MSCHAP is disabled by default.

However, there is still a concern regarding password attacks. Since password hashes do travel "over the wire" in PPTP, there are opportunities for malicious clients to capture the hashes and attack these passwords with fast offline password cracking programs.

Therefore, make it your practice to teach your users to choose passwords that are *not vulnerable to dictionary attacks*.

A password hacking program, such as the LC5 program found at http://www.atstake.com/products/lc/, can help you track down weak passwords so you can force your users to change them.

Old and Crusty Protocols that You Shouldn't Use

There are some older authentication protocols that shouldn't be used if at all possible. Just for reference, here's a quick rundown of those protocols and why you should avoid using them.

PAP (Password Authentication Protocol)   PAP authentication passes the password as cleartext. Obviously, this is not a secure solution, at least by itself. This is the only common method of dial-up authentication in which the password is available to the authentication server in cleartext form. PAP is still somewhat common for PPP (Point-to-Point Protocol) dial-up connections, such as those used to connect to popular ISPs. Here, you need to be worried that the bad guy is tapping the phone line, which is pretty unlikely. But for VPN authentication over the public Internet it's a really bad choice.

CHAP (Challenge Handshake Authentication Protocol)   CHAP passes only a hash of the password, based on a unique one-time challenge received from the server. If the hash is intercepted in transit, the party snooping on the connection still doesn't have the means to gain access to the user's account, because a hash mathematically matching that particular challenge will only be valid once.

Unfortunately, CHAP has a serious security flaw. For mathematical reasons beyond the scope of this book, the server can only verify the hash received from the client by keeping a cleartext copy of the password *on the server*. This is widely agreed to be a bad idea. Databases containing thousands of cleartext passwords have a history of becoming compromised at some point, and then, instead of one user's PAP password being cracked by a patient network sniffer, you have thousands of CHAP passwords cracked wide open. Thus begat MSCHAP.

MSCHAP (Microsoft Challenge Handshake Authentication Protocol)   MSCHAP authentication was Microsoft's first effort to fix CHAP's cleartext password storage problem. While similar to CHAP, MSCHAP does not require a cleartext password to be kept on the server. Instead, password hashes are kept as, not coincidentally, the very same password hashes that are used to authenticate users logging into domain member workstations. Alas, MSCHAP had security holes, thus leading to the birth of MSCHAP2.

Setting up Windows 2003 PPTP Server

It's quite likely that you've already set up a Windows 2003 PPTP server in the real world. However, for testing here in the test lab, let's go through the motions. Then, in the next two sections, we'll make our Windows XP clients connect to it, as well as our Linux clients.

In our example, we're going to set up `windc1` as the PPTP server. However, in real life you likely wouldn't do this. Instead, you'd likely set up a dedicated server for this, but in our test cases it'll be okay. Additionally, in real life you would need to forward TCP traffic on port 1723 through the firewall to `windc1` and all GRE (Generic Routing Encapsulation or "type 47") traffic as well.

Not all hardware based (or software based for that matter) are created equal. Many will let you pass TCP port 1723, which sounds like it *should* allow you to get PPTP through the firewall. Except that PPTP also uses a special IP payload called GRE (Generic Routing Encapsulation) or "Type 47" traffic. This is a distinct payload type, different from UDP or TCP, used to encrypt other payloads. In short, be sure the documentation of your firewall specifically states that it can allow "Type 47/GRE" traffic. If it doesn't, opening up TCP port 1723 won't matter.

Configuring PPTP for Windows 2003 Server

Setting up Windows PPTP happens within Windows 2003's Routing and Remote Access (RRAS) console. Contrary to popular belief, you can have incoming PPTP even if your server has only one network card. To configure Windows 2003 PPTP (with only one network card):

1. Click Start ➢ All Programs ➢ Administrative Tools ➢ Routing and Remote Access. The Routing and Remote Access console appears as shown in Figure 9.13.

FIGURE 9.13   PPTP is configured once the configuration of RRAS starts.

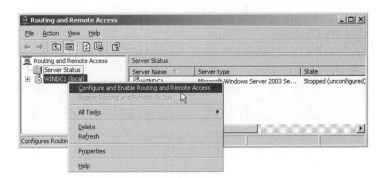

2. Right-click over the server name, and select "Configure and Enable Routing and Remote Access."

3. The Routing and Remote Access Wizard appears. Click Next at the introduction screen for the wizard.

4. At the "Configuration" screen, select "Custom configuration" and select "Next."

5. At the "Custom Configuration" screen, select "VPN access" (and nothing else) and click "Next." At the final page of the wizard, click "Finish." You'll be asked to start the RRAS service. Select "Yes."

6. Once back at the Routing and Remote Access console, right-click over the server name and select "Properties." On the "General" tab, click "Local area network (LAN) routing only" and ensure "Remote access server" is also checked. Click "OK" to return to the Routing and Remote Access console. You may be prompted to restart the RRAS services. Select "Yes" to restart them.

7. Back at the Routing and Remote Access console, right-click the icon labeled "Ports" and select "Properties." Select the line labeled "WAN Miniport (PPTP)" and select "Configure." Ensure "Remote access connections (inbound only)" is checked, as shown in Figure 9.14. While you're here, you can also change the maximum number of inbound connections by entering in a number in the "Maximum ports" spinner if you like. Click "OK" to close the "Configure Device—WAN Miniport (PPTP)" page. Click "OK" to close the "Ports Properties" page.

8. Back at the Routing and Remote Access console, click the icon labeled "Remote Access Policies." Right-click over the "Connections to Microsoft Routing and Remote access server" policy as shown in Figure 9.15 and select "Properties." On the properties page of the policy, select "Grant remote access permission" as shown in Figure 9.15.

FIGURE 9.14   Ensure "Remote access connections (inbound only)" is selected.

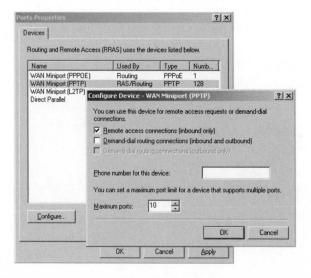

FIGURE 9.15   Be sure to select the policy and allow people access. By default RRAS denies everyone access.

Enabling Individual Users to Use the PPTP VPN

Now you need to specify each user who has access via VPN. You only need to do this step if your Active Directory domain is in the Mixed functional level. In the course of this book, we never changed it, so Mixed functional level is likely what you still have if you've been working through our exercises. To that end, use Active Directory Users and Computers and select the properties of any user you want to allow via VPN. In Figure 9.16, you can see we've selected `salesperson1`'s properties then clicked the "Dial-in" tab. Be sure to select "Allow access" or `salesperson1` won't be able to log on via the VPN.

Testing Your Microsoft PPTP VPN with a Microsoft XP Client (for Users in *ad.corp.com*)

In our examples, we'll assume you've got a machine named xpmobile1. This should *not* be a domain member workstation living "inside" the 192.168.2.x LAN. Instead, use an external PC that has no physical access to your internal network. A workstation at home connected via a public broadband ISP is a good example.

FIGURE 9.16   Ensure that the user you want to allow to dial in has been expressly assigned "Allow access" on the "Dial-in" tab.

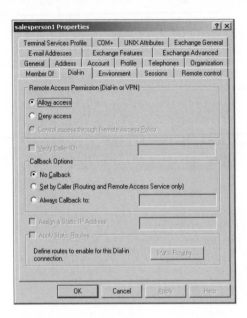

Such a workstation can only "see" the firewall, nothing else in the test lab. It's up to your firewall to forward PPTP traffic from its public interface back to the private interface where it can find `windc1`. This way, when we're able to ping machines inside the firewall, we'll know for certain that the PPTP connection has succeeded because otherwise we wouldn't see them at all! If we used a workstation inside the firewall, we would already be able to ping the systems behind it, and indeed in most cases this would happen without the benefit of the VPN over the existing unencrypted route to the local area network.

To create a VPN connection from `xpmobile1` to the PPTP server:

1. Log on to the machine. If the machine isn't joined to the domain, the only account is the local Administrator account.

2. Click Start ➢ My Network Places. Then in the left hand under "Network Tasks," select "View network connections."

3. Still under "Network Tasks," select "Create a new connection" to start the "New Connection Wizard." At the first screen of the wizard, select "Next."

4. At the "Network Connection Type" screen, select "Connection to the network at my workplace" and click "Next."

5. At the "Network Connection" screen, select "Virtual Private Network connection" and click "Next."

6. At the "Connection Name" screen, enter the company name, say, **corp.com**.

7. At the "Public Network" screen, select "Do not dial the initial connection."

8. At the "VPN Server Selection" screen, enter the publicly visible Internet IP address of the firewall box, which must be configured to forward TCP port 1723 and all GRE traffic to `windc1.ad.corp.com`, as we've mentioned earlier.

9. At the final screen of the wizard, click the "Add a shortcut to this connection to my desktop" check box (we'll reuse this dial-up tool many times) then click "Finish."

From your Windows XP client, you'll be able to enter credentials for any user in Active Directory. For now, enter **salesperson1** as shown in Figure 9.17. You can use the password of **p@ssw0rd**.

Once connected, you should get a pop-up balloon, as shown in Figure 9.18.

Now we can verify our success by using the `ping` command to access a system behind the firewall, which we normally wouldn't be able to find over the Internet:

1. Click Start ➢ Run. In the "Open" field enter **cmd** and press Enter. The command prompt appears.

2. Use the `ping` command to verify that you can communicate with `linserv1.corp.com`:

   `ping 192.168.2.202`

FIGURE 9.17 You can enter credentials as anyone in Active Directory who has been granted the specific right to log on via dial-in.

FIGURE 9.18 A pop-up balloon for Windows XP shows that you're connected to the VPN.

3. You should see lines similar to the following:

```
Reply from 192.168.2.202: bytes=32 time=100ms TTL=41
```

Since you are connecting over the Internet, it is possible that *some* packets will not come back. That's okay as long as most of them do come through.

Great! We've verified several things:

- PPTP is working.

- RRAS policies are allowing clients in.

- salesperson1 has been granted access to dial-in/VPN in.

- The firewall is correctly configured to forward PPTP traffic.

- If your connection is *not* successful, check the following:

- If you receive an error message stating that "the VPN server may be unreachable," double-check the Internet (not internal) IP address of your firewall. Then double-check the TCP port 1723 and GRE traffic forwarding rules you have configured on the firewall to forward traffic to windc1.ad.corp.com.

- Try establishing the connection from a workstation *inside* the local network, such as xppro1.ad.corp.com. This isn't particularly useful, because traffic will still travel unencrypted on the local network via the default route, but success here means that the firewall is not the problem.

- Make sure you have specifically enabled dial-in access for the user salesperson1.

- Check the event logs on windc1.ad.corp.com.

Okay, so we've logged into a Windows VPN with Windows domain credentials. That's nice, but not very cross-platform—not yet. Now we'll log in using corp domain credentials, demonstrating that users who "live" on our Samba PDC can also access the VPN thanks to our domain trust.

Initially Testing Your Microsoft PPTP VPN with a Microsoft XP Client (for Samba Users in the *corp* domain)

We've succeeded in logging in with ad domain credentials. Now let's try it as a user from the corp domain.

Right now, this is a test that *should* fail. That's because we haven't specifically allowed dial-in access for our individual corp domain users yet. We'll try the test now to see the symptom, then repeat the test after we administer the cure.

Go ahead and double-click the icon on the desktop you created for the dial-up tool. Now enter the credentials of doctor1, who resides in the corp domain as shown in Figure 9.19. Be sure to specify the corp domain in the "Domain" field. Also enter the password of p@ssw0rd.

When you try this, you will not successfully make a connection, as shown in Figure 9.20.

FIGURE 9.19   Enter credentials for `doctor1`, who lives in corp.

FIGURE 9.20   Your Samba accounts need to be specifically granted dial-in access.

Why? Because `doctor1` hasn't yet been granted access to "dial-in." The only way we've successfully found to enable this is to use the old-school NT 4 tools we saw previously in Chapter 2. This appears to be an unfortunate gap in the currently available Samba tools: Samba and its LDAP back end will cheerfully store the dial-in "flag," but there is currently no interface—command line or otherwise—to set it. There's no documentation about it either. Ouch. This is clearly another opportunity for Enterprising Linux Gurus to improve their karma by adding a rather straightforward new feature.

In the meantime, we'll dive in and solve the problem using the NT 4 tools. As discussed in Chapter 2, these run on a Windows domain member workstation and edit user accounts remotely. As far as they are concerned, Samba *is* an NT 4 server, which is a neat trick. But before we can set that up, we have to clean up our act a little by creating NT-style "domain groups" corresponding to our Unix `doctors` and `nurses` groups.

Creating Samba Domain Groups

Our Samba PDC already has two groups of users, `doctors` and `nurses`. That's worked fine for us so far, so you may be scratching your head at this point when we tell you that *our* groups aren't quite good enough.

What's the trouble? The Webmin LDAP Users and Groups module that we've relied upon in this book does a great job of creating users in such a way that they are valid both as Linux users and as NT-style domain users. However, it doesn't do such a great job with groups. Specifically, it doesn't automatically create a "group mapping" so that each new group is specifically advertised to NT domain members. For most applications, this doesn't matter, but the NT user administration tools do care. We need those tools in this chapter to grant "dial-in" (VPN) privileges to users in the corp domain, since Samba is currently missing native tools (and documentation!) for that purpose. The NT tools will complain with nasty message boxes unless we ensure that the group each user belongs to is advertised as a domain group.

So how do we take care of it? Using Webmin's Samba module, which we've seen many times before. This module allows us to easily create a Samba "group mapping" for any existing Unix group. Follow these steps to create Samba group mappings for the existing doctors and nurses groups:

1. Log into Webmin at http://linserv1.corp.com:10000/ with the username root and the password p@ssw0rd.

2. Click "Servers." The "Servers" page appears.

3. Click "Samba Windows File Sharing." The "Samba Windows File Sharing" page appears.

4. Click "Add and edit Samba groups." The "Samba Groups" page appears.

5. Click "Add a new Samba group." The "Create Samba Group" page appears.

6. In the "Group name" field, enter **doctors**.

7. From the "Group type" menu, select "Domain Group."

8. In the "Unix group" field, also enter **doctors**.

9. Click "Create." The "Samba Groups" page reappears.

10. Repeat steps 5–9 for nurses.

The doctors and nurses groups are now correctly advertised as domain groups in a way that is fully compatible with the NT user administration tools. As we've mentioned, this means we'll be able to grant "dial-in" (VPN) privileges to these users using the NT tools without frustrating error messages.

Leveraging the Old-School NT 4 Tools to Allow Dial-up Access

In Chapter 2, we used the old usermgr.exe and srvmgr.exe tools to manage Samba because Samba really pretends to be an NT 4 domain. In Chapter 2 we explained that the best course of action is to find an old NT 4 server CD-ROM and rip out the tools by hand. The files will be in the i386 directory in compressed format. All you need to do is use the expand command on two files: usrmgr.ex_ and svrmgr. For example, you'll type:

```
expand usrmgr.ex_ c:\usrmgr.exe
expand srvmgr.exe c:\srvmgr.exe
```

When you do this, you'll have two uncompressed and ready-to-run files in your c:\ directory. Once you run them on any Windows machine (say, xppro1.ad.corp.com), you'll be able to manage your Samba domain and provide the appropriate dial-in permission.

> The executables that worked for us were usrmgr.exe of size 299,280 bytes (date 7/26/1996) and svrmgr.exe of size 211,216 bytes (date 7/26/1996).

Now, log on to xppro1.ad.corp.com as the administrator of the corp domain. (If you're logged in as anyone else, this won't work, so be sure you're logged in as the administrator of the corp domain.) Then, run usrmgr.exe from wherever you unpacked it.

You'll be able to select the doctor1 "User Properties"; then select "Dial-in" and check the "Grant dial-in permission to user" check box as shown in Figure 9.21.

Click "OK" to close the "Dial-in Information" window, then click "OK" to close the "User Properties" window.

Retrying Your Microsoft PPTP VPN with a Microsoft XP Client (for Samba Users in *corp*)

Now that we have granted dial-in access, the Windows VPN should be happy with the response it gets from the Samba PDC. Go ahead and double-click the icon on the desktop you created for the dial-up tool. Now enter the credentials of doctor1, who resides in the corp domain as shown in Figure 9.19. Also enter the password of **p@ssw0rd**.

Now it should connect you successfully because that user has been granted the right to log on!

At this point, we have access to both domains from Windows. and that's impressive. However, the picture is incomplete without VPN access from a Linux workstation. That's where we're going next.

FIGURE 9.21   Samba users need the "Grant dial-in permission to user" set within the NT 4 User Manager tool.

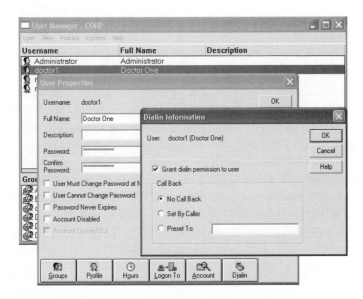

Connecting to the VPN with a Linux Client

We've made a VPN connection from a Windows client to our Windows PPTP server, using both ad domain and corp domain credentials. This is a great thing, and it is cross-platform in the sense that credentials from both Linux-hosted and Windows-hosted servers are honored. But we need to provide access for our Linux-based clients as well. We can do that using the Linux PPTP client software, which goes by the unsurprising name pptpclient.

We'll begin by installing pptpclient and the software it depends upon. We'll install them on a mobile Linux workstation *outside* the company network and call that workstation linmobile1.

Then we'll establish a VPN connection using the friendly GUI provided by pptpclient. We'll do that using both ad and corp domain accounts, showing that accounts from either the Active Directory domain or the Linux-hosted corp domain are accepted for VPN connections from Linux clients.

Installing the PPTP Client Software for Linux

Where does the PPTP client for Linux come from? The Linux PPTP client project has its home page at http://pptpclient.sourceforge.net. A Fedora Core 3 HOWTO is available on that site as well:

http://pptpclient.sourceforge.net/howto-fedora-core-3.phtml

 We'll show the steps needed to install pptpclient in detail, but be sure to consult the official HOWTO for up-to-date links and possible changes to the installation process. The URLs that follow are presented for illustrative purposes, as version numbers will almost certainly have changed. Be sure to bookmark that HOWTO document!

Installing pptpclient isn't too difficult, but there are a few requirements that must be taken care of first. Specifically, before installing pptpclient, we need to:

1. Install Fedora Linux on a "road warrior" PC, linmobile1. This will be our Linux-based VPN client.

2. Add support for MPPE (Microsoft Point-to-Point Encryption) to the kernel. MPPE provides encryption for our PPTP connections. Fortunately, installing this kernel module is not difficult thanks to good packaging.

3. Upgrade pppd (the Point-to-Point Protocol daemon) to version 2.4.3 or better, if necessary. PPTP is built upon PPP, and the implementation of PPP included with Fedora Core 3 has difficulties negotiating with Microsoft's VPN server as of this writing.

4. Install a few system libraries and tools that are required by the pptpclient graphical user interface pptpconfig.

We'll begin by installing Linux on linmobile1.

Installing Fedora Core 3 on *linmobile1*

linmobile1, the client machine we'll use in this section, is an Internet-connected PC *not* located inside the company LAN. For space reasons, we can't go into fanatical detail about the configuration of linmobile1, but we'll briefly discuss the key differences and the basics of hooking up to a typical home office broadband connection with Linux.

We recommend that you follow the instructions in Chapter 1 for configuring lincli1 .corp.com, except that:

1. You should enable DHCP (Dynamic Host Configuration Protocol) rather than specifying an IP address. DHCP is the default choice, so this is not difficult. This permits your cable/ DSL modem or home router to assign an IP address to your Linux system.

2. You should also allow DHCP to assign a DNS server address. Again, this is the default choice.

Also, although this is already included in our instructions for configuring linclil.corp.com, we'll mention that you *must* select the development packages. Otherwise, you'll have trouble installing the kernel modules needed to provide encryption for our VPN connection.

Once you have successfully installed Fedora Linux on linmobile1 and established a broadband Internet connection, you're ready to install the MPPE kernel module, upgrade pppd, and install other prerequisites that pptpclient depends upon.

Installing the Required Kernel Modules for PPTP on *linmobile1*

Installing pptpclient used to be difficult. That's because it requires a custom kernel module that adds support for MPPE (Microsoft Point-to-Point Encryption). Without MPPE, PPTP doesn't encrypt, it simply encapsulates.

Installing kernel modules doesn't sound easy, but fortunately, we can take advantage of DKMS (Dynamic Kernel Module Support). DKMS is a framework for easy management of Linux kernel modules that makes installing them a relatively painless operation. DKMS was created and is actively maintained by Dell's Linux support team.

 As of this writing, MPPE has been accepted into the mainstream Linux kernel. This will eventually remove the need for DKMS when installing pptpclient. However, this latest-and-greatest Linux kernel is not included in Fedora Core 3 as of this writing.

How do we install DKMS, and where do we get the MPPE module that takes advantage of it? Both are available from the poptop project. poptop is a PPTP server that is closely related to pptpclient. Both require the same MPPE support in the kernel, so the pptpclient site refers visitors to the poptop site to download Fedora Core 3–compatible rpms of DKMS itself and the MPPE module that takes advantage of it. You can find the latest links by visiting this page:

http://poptop.sourceforge.net/dox/

Click "Downloads." The DKMS and MPPE rpms appear first in the list of files available to download.

poptop is a Linux-based PPTP server project, closely associated with pptpclient. Space prevents us from discussing poptop fully. However, you can download a complete write-up on the subject from this chapter's section of our website, www.winlinanswers.com. There you'll learn how to configure a completely Linux-based PPTP server that authenticates against our Samba PDC. You'll also learn how to provide cross-domain authentication against our Active Directory domain when the PPTP server runs on Linux.

As of this writing, the correct URLs to download these two rpms are as listed here.
For DKMS

```
http://prdownloads.sourceforge.net/poptop/dkms-2.0.5-1.noarch.rpm
```

For MPPE

```
http://prdownloads.sourceforge.net/poptop/kernel_ppp_mppe-0.0.5-2dkms.noarch.rpm
```

You will definitely want to consult the **poptop** website for links to the very latest versions. We'll assume these versions in filenames shown in the steps that follow.

In previous chapters, we showed you how to use the wget command to download rpm packages, and you may be tempted to use wget to fetch these two files directly to linclimobile1.ad.corp.com from the command line. Alas, downloads from sourceforge.net via wget don't always work well. That's because sourceforge.net always interposes a "choose your preferred mirror site" page and displays an ad or two. Simply using wget will fetch the "choose your mirror" page, not the file you really want. You can work around this by accessing the "choose your mirror" page with your regular browser, clicking the link to download the file from your preferred mirror, and finally copying the URL that appears following the words "your download should begin shortly. If it does not..." This link *will* work with wget.

Follow these steps to install the MPPE kernel module on linmobile1:

1. Download dkms-2.0.5-1.noarch.rpm and kernel_ppp_mppe-0.0.5-2dkms.noarch.rpm from the locations listed previously.

2. Move these files to /tmp on linclimobile1.ad.corp.com.

3. Use the following rpm commands to install them:

```
rpm -i dkms-2.0.5-1.noarch.rpm
rpm -i kernel_ppp_mppe-0.0.5-2dkms.noarch.rpm
```

The preceding steps will produce warnings as follows:

```
warning: dkms-2.0.5-1.noarch.rpm: V3 DSA signature: NOKEY, key ID 23b66a9d
```

That's because we don't have a cryptographic key installed to verify the identity of these particular rpms. If this is a major concern for you in a production environment, see Chapter 6 for a discussion of how to install rpm keys.

The second rpm command will produce more extensive output, as various patches are automatically applied and the kernel module is compiled and installed. The final message will be:

```
DKMS: install Completed.
```

Now we need to load the module into the running Linux kernel, partly to verify our success and partly so that pptpclient can use it without rebooting. We can do this using a command called modprobe.

modprobe is the standard Linux utility to load a kernel module and all of the modules it depends on "on the fly." We'll ask modprobe to load a special module name, "ppp-compress-18," which automatically loads both MPPE and the PPP modules on which it depends. When this command succeeds, we know that we've installed the MPPE module properly.

To verify the successful installation of the MPPE kernel module, execute this command as root on linmobile1:

```
modprobe ppp-compress-18 && echo MPPE kernel module loaded
```

This command will print:

```
MPPE kernel module loaded
```

If it does not, consult the output of the rpm commands to determine the cause of the error, make sure you installed both rpms, and check the poptop and pptpclient websites for any changes to the installation process that have been made since this writing.

We're nearly finished with MPPE. The last step is to make sure that MPPE is available again when the server reboots. We'll do that by adding a modprobe command to /etc/rc.d/rc.local, which we've seen before. Commands in /etc/rc.d/rc.local are automatically executed after the rest of the boot process is complete.

To ensure that MPPE support loads every time the server is rebooted, add this line at the end of /etc/rc.d/rc.local:

```
modprobe ppp-compress-18 && echo MPPE kernel module loaded
```

We've taken care of the MPPE encryption issue. Are we done? Not quite. PPTP is built upon PPP (Point-to-Point Protocol), and Fedora Core 3 and virtually all other distributions include pppd, an application that is part of the standard implementation of PPP for Linux systems. However, pptpclient requires that we have a more up-to-date version of pppd than Fedora Core 3 currently provides, so we have a little bit of upgrading to do.

Upgrading *pppd* for Use with PPTP on *linmobile1*

In Linux, the PPP protocol on which PPTP is based is implemented partly by a program called pppd. (The rest of the implementation is inside the Linux kernel.) pptpclient requires version 2.4.3 or better for best results. Unfortunately, as of this writing, Fedora Core 3 provides only version 2.4.2, but this may have changed by the time you read this. If not, you can work around it by installing an rpm of version 2.4.3 from the poptop site.

Since Fedora Core 3 is constantly updated, we recommend that you first try the following command to check whether you already have version 2.4.3 or better:

```
pppd --version
```

As of this writing, this reports:

```
pppd version 2.4.2
```

If you also get this result (or an older version), you'll need to visit the pppd rpms page on the poptop website. You can find a current link to this and other related files by visiting `http://poptop.sourceforge.net/dox/`

Click "Download."

Locate the latest release. As of this writing, this is version 2.4.3-5. You'll want the version for the i386 architecture on Fedora Core 3 (fc3).

Follow these steps to install an updated version of the `pppd` software on `linclimobile1.ad.corp.com`:

1. Download `ppp-2.4.3-5.fc3.i386.rpm` (or the current version) and from the URL just given.

2. Move this file to `/tmp` on `linmobile1`.

3. Use the `rpm` command to install it. We add the `--force` option to avoid warnings about conflicts with the version of `pppd` that ships with Fedora Core 3:

    ```
    rpm -i --force ppp-2.4.3-5.fc3.i386.rpm
    ```

This command should produce no output other than a NOKEY warning.

Installing *pptpclient*

Now that we have the requirements installed, we'll fetch the actual pptpclient software. We will also need several libraries and utilities that provide a friendly user interface for creating PPTP connections as well as system services needed by that user interface. You can find the current links to these in the pptpclient Fedora Core 3 HOWTO. As of this writing, the required items and their download URLs (where needed) are:

pptpclient   The actual PPTP client software. Available here (but see the HOWTO for the most up-to-date URL):

```
http://prdownloads.sourceforge.net/pptpclient/pptp-1.6.0-1.i386.rpm
```

pptpconfig   A user-friendly interface to `pptpclient`. Available here (but see the `pptpclient` Fedora Core 3 HOWTO for an updated URL):

```
http://prdownloads.sourceforge.net/pptpclient/pptpconfig-20040722-6.noarch.rpm
```

php-pcntl   An interpreter for simple user-friendly configuration utilities needed by `pptpconfig`. Available here (but see the `pptpclient` Fedora Core 3 HOWTO for an updated URL):

```
http://prdownloads.sourceforge.net/pptpclient/php-pcntl-4.3.10-1.i386.rpm
```

php-gtk-pcntl   The graphical user interface component for `php-pcntl`. Available here (but see the `pptpclient` Fedora Core 3 HOWTO for an updated URL):

```
http://prdownloads.sourceforge.net/pptpclient/php-gtk-pcntl-1.0.1-2.i386.rpm
```

libglade   A system library required by `php-pcntl`. This library displays the actual user interface components via the `gtk+` library. `libglade` is standard in Fedora Linux. We'll install and upgrade it using the `up2date` command.

libxml   A system library required by `php-pcntl`. This library provides the ability to read and write files written in XML (eXtensible Markup Language). `libxml` is standard in Fedora Linux. We'll install and upgrade it using the `up2date` command.

Follow these steps to install pptpclient and its user interface on linmobile1. Execute all commands shown as the root user:

1. Download `pptp-1.6.0-1.i386.rpm` from the location just shown.

2. Move this file to `/tmp` on `linmobile1`.

3. Use the `rpm` command to install it:
   ```
   rpm -i pptp-1.6.0-1.i386.rpm
   ```
   This command produces no output on success, except for the NOKEY warning we've seen before.

4. Make sure that certain components of Fedora Linux required by pptpconfig are installed, using the up2date utility:
   ```
   up2date libglade libxml
   ```

5. Download `php-pcntl-4.3.10-1.i386.rpm` from the location just shown.

6. Move this file to `/tmp` on `linmobile1.ad.corp.com`.

7. Use the `rpm` command to install it:
   ```
   rpm -i php-pcntl-4.3.10-1.i386.rpm
   ```
   This command produces no output on success, other than the usual NOKEY warning.

8. Download `php-gtk-pcntl-1.0.1-2.i386.rpm` from the location just given.

9. Move this file to `/tmp` on `linmobile1.ad.corp.com`.

10. Use the `rpm` command to install it:
    ```
    rpm -i php-gtk-pcntl-1.0.1-2.i386.rpm
    ```
    This command produces no output on success, other than the NOKEY warning.

11. Download `pptpconfig-20040722-6.noarch.rpm` from the location just shown.

12. Move this file to /tmp on linmobile1.

13. Use the rpm command to install it:

```
rpm -i pptpconfig-20040722-6.noarch.rpm
```

This command produces no output on success, beyond the usual NOKEY warning.

We've installed the PPTP client software! Now we're ready to configure it and begin making VPN connections to the Windows VPN server.

Testing *pptpclient* by Logging In as an Active Directory *(ad)* User

Configuring pptpclient is made much easier by the user-friendly pptpconfig utility. This utility allows us to create and manage as many VPN connections as we find useful. It is, dare we say it, a darn nice GUI for a Linux application. Now that the utility is installed, we can access it using the standard Fedora menus and use it to connect to the RAS PPTP server on windc1.ad.corp.com. Follow these steps to create a linmobile1 to the VPN:

1. Log into linmobile1.

2. Select the "Applications" menu.

3. Select the "Internet" submenu.

4. Select the "PPTP Client" item.

 If you are not logged in as root, you will be asked to provide the root password. This is because establishing new network routes is a privilege reserved for root in Linux.

5. The pptpconfig tool then appears. In the next few steps we will configure the fields shown beneath the "Server" tab, as shown in Figure 9.22.

FIGURE 9.22 You can use pptpconfig to create a new PPTP VPN connection.

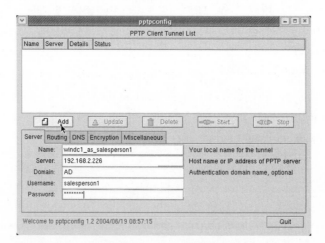

6. In the "Name" field, enter **windc1_as_salesperson1**.

7. In the "Server" field, enter the Internet-visible IP address of your router. Although you see 192.168.2.226 in the screen shot, this is only a placeholder. You should use the externally visible address of your router, which must be configured to forward PPTP traffic to 192.168.2.226 as described earlier in this chapter.

8. In the "Domain" field, enter **ad**.

9. In the "Username:" field, enter **salesperson1**.

10. In the "Password:" field, enter **p@ssw0rd**.

11. Click "Add." An entry for the windc1_as_salesperson1 connection now appears in the "PPTP Client Tunnel List" area.

12. Click the "windc1_as_salesperson1" entry in the "PPTP Client Tunnel List" area.

13. Click "Start." The "pptpconfig tunnel windc1_as_salesperson1" window appears, displaying the status of the connection. After a few moments, the display should resemble Figure 9.23. "Connected" should appear in the lower-left corner of the window.

FIGURE 9.23   You'll see "connected" in the pptpconfig status window up successfully connecting from linmobile1

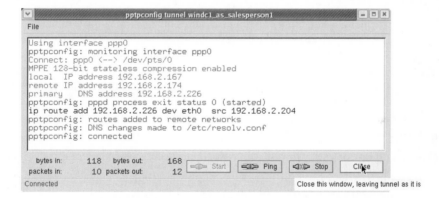

14. Click "Close" to dismiss the status window.

15. Click "Quit" to close the "pptpconfig tunnel windc1_as_salesperson1" window. This does *not* break the VPN connection.

What about the other tabs of the "pptpconfig" window? The most interesting tab is "Encryption," which can be used to specifically refuse to connect with various types of authorization and encryption. In our tests, this was not necessary when communicating with a Windows 2003 RAS server. 128-bit MPPE encryption and MSCHAP2 authorization were negotiated by default.

If the "pptpconfig tunnel `windc1_as_salesperson1`" status window does *not* display "Connected," examine the messages in the window and check the following:

- Make sure you specified the domain `ad` (not `corp`, since we used an `ad` username) in the "Domain" field.

- Make sure you loaded the MPPE kernel module and upgraded pppd to version 2.4.3 or better.

- Check the event logs on `windc1.ad.corp.com`.

Once you are connected, you can communicate with all hosts on the company network as if your machine were directly connected to it. You can verify this by pinging hosts such as 192.168.2.202, which would otherwise not be accessible from `linmobile1` because they are part of the nonpublic network behind the company firewall. Use the `ping` command from the Linux command line on `linmobile1` exactly as you used it in Windows on `xpmobile1`.

Great! We've logged into the company VPN using `ad` domain credentials from a Linux client. Just one more thing left to do: log into the VPN using `corp` domain credentials from that very same client.

Testing *pptpclient* by Logging In as Samba *(corp)* Users

Logging in to the VPN using `corp` credentials is an important scenario because users hosted on the Linux-based PDC are probably more likely to be logging in from Linux workstations in the first place.

To log into the VPN using `corp` domain credentials on a Linux workstation, follow the steps in the previous section, substituting the `corp` domain and the username `doctor1`. You'll be adding a second connection description in `pptpconfig`. The simplest way is to select the `windc1_as_salesperson1` connection description by clicking it. Then change the "Name," "Domain," and "Username" fields appropriately and click "Add" to add another connection description. Now you can right-click the new connection description and click "Start" to make a connection.

This connection should work just as smoothly as `salesperson1` and the `ad` domain. If you do have difficulties though, check the following:

- You must first complete the domain trust creation steps presented in this chapter.

- As described earlier, you must use the Windows NT tools to enable dial-in access to the `doctor1` account in the `corp` domain.

We're up and running! Both Windows and Linux clients can log into the VPN with either `ad` or `corp` domain credentials.

Final Thoughts

Network integration is straightforward at the most basic level. Windows and Linux boxes certainly have no trouble pinging each other or sending each other simple DNS queries. But when we want to go deeper, things get more challenging.

In this chapter we tackled four major network integration tasks. First, we convinced Windows Active Directory to use a Linux-based DNS server as its primary DNS server. Second, we configured a Linux-based DNS server as a "slave" DNS server for a branch office, preventing unnecessary round trips over a slow WAN link. Third, we convinced Active Directory to trust a Samba domain, allowing users to log into Windows workstations with either set of credentials. Finally, we built a Windows-hosted VPN with support for both Windows and Linux clients using either Active Directory or Samba credentials to log on. In addition, although space does not allow us to include it in this book, on our website, we also present a solution based on OpenVPN, a Linux VPN package. Again, check out `www.winlinanswers.com`.

When we go the extra mile, we can achieve great things with our cross-platform networks.

10

Web Interoperability

Nearly all organizations today operate an internal intranet, and many also maintain a presence on external Internet websites. Websites can be hosted on both Linux and Windows servers. And web browsers can be found on both Linux and Windows clients. Well-designed websites should work with any web browser software. And ideally, we should be able to host our websites on servers running the operating system of our choice. For simple sites, that's easy enough to do. But in the real world, certain popular technologies for creating *web applications* on the server are considered standard in the Linux server world. And certain other technologies are popular in the Windows world.

Depending on what your needs are at any given time, you might be challenged with trying to make "the other guy's" web application work. That is, you may have a Linux-based web server, but that doesn't mean you won't find yourself with web developers who have Windows skills. Or you may have a Windows-based web server and encounter a great piece of free web application software that would be perfect for your needs…but it's designed for Linux.

In this chapter, we'll show you how to keep your websites friendly to both Linux and Windows clients. That's web browser interoperability. And we'll also show you how to run Windows web applications on Linux and Linux web applications on Windows. That's web server interoperability. Let's look at each of these a little more closely. Then we'll dig in and achieve both goals.

Web browser interoperability   This is always an issue in any environment containing both Windows and Linux clients. Today, fortunately, incompatibilities between the major browsers are few. Most such problems are caused by the use of proprietary file formats, such as Macromedia's Flash (.swf) files, that are not open standards. (In some cases, limited access to the format specification is available, but usually under terms that prevent those who read it from writing compatible open-source players.) We'll provide pointers to resources that cover how best to cope with these nonstandard but popular file formats in detail.

Web server interoperability   This becomes an issue when trying to host on one server operating system web content originally intended for the other. Simple web pages, images, and so on are easy to migrate from one platform to the other, although there *are* issues here that we'll explore in the section titled "Static Website Interoperability."

But things get truly interesting when we want to run Web applications intended for one operating system on the other. Windows web developers, broadly speaking, are used to writing Active Server Pages (ASP) scripts (in some cases, in the newer ASP.NET style). And Linux web developers, though they also have other choices, are most often experienced with PHP Hypertext Preprocessor (PHP) scripts. This can cause a problem when developers with expertise on one platform are asked to present their content on another.

The good news is that it's possible to host many, though not all, Active Server Pages and ASP.NET applications on Linux. And PHP scripts can certainly be hosted on Windows. Though this is not a programming book, as the system administrator you will likely be asked to solve this problem by creating an environment that allows developers in your organization to work in their preferred scripting language on management's preferred server operating system. And in this chapter, we'll show you how to configure web servers to host web content originally written for the other operating system.

We'll begin with a quick review of the Web's workings. Even though this might be familiar ground, it's good to ensure we're all on the same page. Next we'll move into web browser interoperability concerns and then spend most of the chapter discussing the meatier subject of web server interoperability.

Before we get too far along in this chapter, let's put up a red-flag warning. That is, dealing with web pages is often pretty geeky, specialized, web-propeller-head stuff. We've done our level best to try to de-geekify this chapter and remove as many of the "programming" aspects as possible and try to get to the heart of the administrative issues. However, if possible, try to keep your head above water when the programming acronyms fly. These are important to understand—as you'll likely be the person taking the stuff the web programmer gives you and trying to make it happen. Again, this chapter isn't exactly like all the others. You'll see we've got lots of buzzwords, acronyms, and incantations like CLI, C#, ASP.NET, Mono, .NET, Java, VB.NET, PHP, ASP, IIS, MySQL, and more and more and more. But at the end, you'll be glad you tackled this chapter and mastered them.

Client and Server Choices and Assumptions for Windows and Linux

There are lots of web server and web browser programs in the world. For this chapter, we're going to make a handful of basic assumptions to keep things simple. Let's start with web servers.

The typical Linux web server runs the Apache web server software. Apache is currently home to more websites than any other software in the world. IIS is the second most popular web server in the world overall. These statistics are according to the Netcraft Server Survey found at http://news.netcraft.com/archives/web_server_survey.html.

A typical Windows web server could also run Apache, but most Windows administrators choose to run what's in the box—Microsoft's Internet Information Server (IIS), which we first saw in Chapter 6.

As for Web browsers, we'll be using Microsoft's Internet Explorer, on the Windows side, and Firefox, on the Linux side. Firefox, of course, can also be run on Windows, and Internet Explorer can run on Linux with some help from Crossover Office, as we described in Chapter 6. And there are, to be sure, other web browser options. For purposes of this chapter, though, we'll assume that Windows clients are running the built-in Internet Explorer and Linux clients are running the built-in Firefox.

Apache, IIS, Internet Explorer, and Firefox are all excellent applications. And the Web is an environment with many published standards and a high degree of interoperability. On a basic level, compatibility between, say, Firefox and IIS or Internet Explorer and Apache is excellent. So we don't need to ask questions like "How do I allow Internet Explorer users to connect to my Apache web server?" That just works, and it always has…at a basic level.

The hard part is making sure *all* of the features of our sites work on both browsers and making web applications designed for one server work when installed on the other. And that's what we'll tackle in this chapter.

Web Server and Browser Basics

Just how does the Web work, anyway? We'll take a whirlwind tour of the basics, introduce the major players and review the major standards that make web interoperability possible. These aren't any less important just because they are basics.

Everyone knows what a web browser is, but not everyone is so clear on what it does! The same is true for web servers. So what do they actually do?

A web browser downloads web pages and other content from web servers. Usually this is done via Hypertext Transfer Protocol (HTTP), a mature standard maintained by the World Wide Web Consortium (W3C, www.w3c.org). HTTP is a very simple, well-documented protocol spoken by literally thousands of applications as well as by the mainstream web browsers and servers. Typically the web browser downloads web pages written in HTML (or the newer XHTML) from the web server via HTTP. These pages contain text and hyperlinks and references to images in various formats. When the web browser encounters a reference to an image, it then downloads the image file, again via HTTP.

Rendering Web Pages to the Screen

Once the web browser has downloaded the content, the web browser *renders* HTML and XHTML web pages in a user-readable form—hopefully, with the appearance the web designer intended! The appearance of the page can be improved using configuration settings in *style sheets* written to follow the Cascading Style Sheets (CSS) standard. Style sheets are typically kept in separate files from the web pages they format. An entire website can use a single style sheet for consistency and ease of updates.

Handling Form Submissions

Some web pages include forms that allow users to send information back to a website application for additional processing. The web browser renders the form, gathers up the user entries, and submits the data back to the web server. Google's search page (www.google.com) is the best-known example, but forms are found in nearly all web applications.

Interactivity on the Browser Side

Not all pages consist of simple, static HTML content. Some contain code, written in the JavaScript language, intended to be interpreted by the web browser. Internet Explorer also supports VBScript, but since other web browsers do not, its use is discouraged and largely avoided. If the web browser includes support for the embedded script language, the script will generate output that does chores such as generating part of the page, verifying the accuracy of form submissions without waiting for a round-trip to the web server, and so on.

Other pages contain references to files that can be downloaded and processed by embedded *plug-ins*. These plug-ins typically offer interactivity that is more sophisticated than simple HTML text and images, such as Flash animations and Java applets. We'll talk about these more later in this section.

Open Standards for Web Content

The best way to keep your web pages compatible with major browsers on both operating systems is to require your company's pages to be standards compliant and forbid the use of plug-ins and add-ons that are not supported on all platforms. Although this isn't a web development book, the more "buzzword compliant" you are when these discussions take place, the more influence you'll have. So it pays to know what you're talking about. The following list includes some of the more important standards you'll encounter regarding web content development today:

HTML 3.2   The HTML 3.2 standard lacks support for style sheets and incorporates control of fonts and other layout issues directly into HTML. For those still concerned with Netscape 4.0 compatibility, HTML 3.2 remains an important fallback point. Fortunately, we can expect better from both Internet Explorer and Firefox. The Netscape 4.0 population has dwindled to less than 1 percent of the Internet community.

HTML 4.01   This is the last official version of the HTML standard. HTML 4.01-compliant web browsers are expected to work with CSS level 1 and 2 style sheets as well. Both of the major browsers implement all elements in HTML 4.01 rather well. HTML 4.01 is a reasonable choice of standard for intranet use; however, we recommend XHTML 1.0.

XHTML 1.0   XHTML has the same feature set as HTML 4.01, but documents must obey the more strict syntax of Extensible Markup Language (XML), a more general markup language of which XHTML is just one instance. XHTML is also a reasonable choice for intranets, since both major browsers implement the features of HTML 4.01 and accept the strict syntax required by XHTML. We recommend that you validate your intranet web pages for compliance with XHTML 1.0. Despite the change of name, XHTML is usually found in files with a `.html` extension.

ECMAScript-262   The web browser programming language referred to as both JavaScript and JScript has been standardized under the lesser-known name ECMAScript. Both browsers offer reasonably faithful implementations of this standard. In this chapter we'll refer to the language by the better-known name JavaScript. JavaScript can be embedded directly into web pages. JavaScript is typically used for tasks such as validating the user's data entry to "save a round-trip" to the web server. The user can wait for the browser to talk to the server, submit their phone number, and get back a complaint explaining that they left out a digit many tedious seconds later…or JavaScript code in the browser can detect that missing digit right away, pop up a warning, and save the user some trouble. Today, thanks to the Document Object Model (DOM) that we'll discuss next, JavaScript can also be used to create full-fledged interactive user interfaces like Google's gmail service that allow the user to do quite a bit of work without waiting to talk to the web server.

Document Object Model (DOM), Levels 1 and 2   The ECMAScript-262 standard covers the JavaScript language itself. But ECMAScript-262 says nothing about how JavaScript code should interact with the web browser. The Document Object Model fills this gap by specifying exactly how code written in a browser scripting language (practically speaking, JavaScript or, on Internet Explorer only, VBScript) can carry out tasks such as inserting new XHTML elements into the page or checking the user's entries in a form. Both browsers support all of DOM level 1 and most of the newer DOM level 2 specification.

Graphics Interchange Format (GIF)   GIF is a long-established image format universally supported by web browsers. It's limited to 256 colors and appropriate for line art and other *non-photographic, non-photorealistic* images only. GIF also supports simple animation. GIF images are usually kept in files with a `.gif` extension. At one time the free availability of GIF was threatened by patent issues, but the relevant patents have now expired.

Portable Network Graphics (PNG)   Intended as a replacement for GIF, PNG was originally intended to avoid an intellectual property problem with GIF. The relevant patents have since expired, but PNG also supports "true color." That means there is no 256-color limitation on PNG images. However, PNG does not support animation. PNG files normally have a `.png` extension.

Joint Photographic Experts Group (JPEG)   JPEG is another long-established, widely supported format. It is a *lossy* format intended for photographs and other photorealistic images. By discarding less important information about the picture, JPEG is able to reproduce a photograph with a drastically smaller file size than PNG or GIF. However, this means that JPEG files should never be saved, reopened, and saved again during image editing. JPEG is only intended for final publication. That makes it ideal for websites. JPEG files are often found with both `.jpg` and `.jpeg` extensions.

In 2002, a company called Forgent announced its acquisition of a patent relating to the JPEG format. Forgent has since levied license fees from or brought claims against a number of larger technology firms. This has led the ISO standardization committee to threaten to withdraw the JPEG standard because ISO standards must be royalty free. The JPEG Committee has called for submissions of "prior art" that may or may not invalidate this patent. To date, Forgent has not expressed interest in pursuing claims against individual websites that use JPEG-format files. The good news for the rest of us is that the patent expires in two years.

Standard Vector Graphics (SVG)   A newly emerging web standard, SVG offers an open alternative to Macromedia's Flash animation format. Unlike GIF, JPEG, and PNG, SVG describes graphics as a collection of geometric shapes. That means the graphics continue to look smooth even as you zoom in closer to them. Combined with JavaScript, SVG should one day be a full-fledged open replacement for Flash. SVG uses an open, XML-based file format and relies on JavaScript to add Flash-like interactivity. For now, though, SVG is one to watch, not one to rely upon. SVG support is not yet standard in either major web browser.

Ideally, web pages and other web content should comply fully with these standards. When they do, both browsers can support them without the hassles of reverse engineering.

Plug-Ins and Helper Applications for Special Content

The web browser also allows *plug-ins* and *helper applications* to handle file types it does not support directly. Examples of such file types include Macromedia's Flash and Shockwave animations, Sun's Java applets, and Adobe's Portable Document Format (PDF) printable documents and forms. Embedded audio and video file types are often handled by Microsoft's Windows Media Player or by RealNetworks's RealPlayer.

The distinction between plug-ins and helper applications is simple enough: If the content is embedded directly into the body of a web page, it's displayed by a plug-in. If the content is downloaded by the web browser but presented separately by an independent application with its own user interface, it's a helper application.

And plug-ins and helper applications are exactly where we are most likely to run into trouble on the browser side of the interoperability equation.

Web Browser Interoperability

If you plan to make extensive use of Linux clients, chances are you'll be using the Firefox web browser (`www.mozilla.org/firefox`) or a relative such as Mozilla that relies on the same core code. The Firefox browser is also available for Windows and, as of this writing, has achieved greater market share than any other alternative to Microsoft Internet Explorer (though still less than 10 percent of the public at large).

A second sometimes significant player is Apple's Safari browser, now the default web browser presented to new users of computers running Apple's MacOS X operating system. The Safari project shares much of its development with Konqueror, the second most common Linux browser. And Microsoft Internet Explorer, of course, is still used by the vast majority of the public as of this writing. Meanwhile, slightly less than 1 percent of users still use the severely outdated Netscape 4.*x* browser.

So what does this mean for the interoperability of our websites? For publicly accessible websites, there are three major players to concern ourselves with: Mozilla/Firefox, Konqueror/ Safari, and Microsoft Internet Explorer. That means we have at least *three* major browsers to thoroughly test our publicly accessible web pages with.

 There are exceptions. Other independent browsers, like Opera (www.opera.com), should also be tested if you know you'll be using them.

But advanced browser compatibility issues for publicly accessible websites are a bit beyond the scope of this book. We're primarily concerned here with issues that arise when an organization chooses to use Linux and Windows clients together *internally*.

Firefox is freely available for all Linux distributions, highly compatible with Internet Explorer, and standard in Fedora. So we'll simplify things by eliminating Konqueror/Safari from consideration. For the purposes of this book, Firefox is the standard Linux browser and Internet Explorer is the standard Windows browser. When we refer to "both browsers," we are referring to Firefox and Internet Explorer. Of course, Firefox for Windows behaves almost identically to Firefox for Linux, so most comments regarding Firefox apply equally on Windows. Indeed, standardizing on Firefox on both platforms may be an attractive option for some organizations.

For the most part, the two major web browsers are now highly compatible with one another. Internet Explorer and Firefox both implement open standards, and Firefox strives to implement lesser-known and unofficial features of Internet Explorer as well, with a great deal of success. Today, Web pages that adhere to the HTML 4.01 standard will typically render well on both browsers. Therefore we recommend validating your pages for compliance with HTML 4.01 or XHTML 1.0.

But there's one big catch: the use of plug-ins and helper applications that are not typically installed on Linux or, worse, not available at all.

Plug-ins are not the best way to develop content for the Web, unless the content you are creating simply cannot be expressed using the open standards mentioned earlier in this chapter. When you do have to use plug-ins, *never use obscure or platform-specific plug-ins*. For most applications, nonstandard formats simply are not necessary to implement the design you want. However, if you must use nonstandard formats, restrict yourself to those that are widely used and for which plug-ins or helper applications exist on many operating systems.

These "friendly" formats include Adobe's Portable Document Format (PDF) for printable forms and other printer-friendly documents, Macromedia's Flash (but not Shockwave!) format for interactive animations and games, Sun's Java plug-in for interactive miniature applications or *applets*, and RealNetworks's RealAudio and RealVideo for web-optimized audio and video. Plug-ins for these are available free of charge for both Windows and Linux, as well as MacOS. Alternatively,

MPEG Level 2 video and MP3 audio make good "common denominator" choices because they are supported by *all* of the major audio and video plug-ins and helper applications.

However, the plug-ins for most of these formats are not included directly with Fedora Core 3, although they are included with some non-free Linux distributions. In most cases, this is because the license terms attached to the plug-ins allow free distribution only from the website of the company that produces the plug-in. An exception is PDF: Fedora Linux includes an open-source PDF viewer as standard equipment. Even here, though, the official Adobe version does have worthwhile extra features like support for the "fill-in form" feature.

How can we install support for the plug-ins we need on the Linux platform to bring it closer to par with Internet Explorer's support for these file formats? Space prevents us from presenting every plug-in and helper application in detail. However, the Mozilla/Firefox project maintains an excellent page that provides pointers and instructions on installing each of the important plug-ins available for Linux. You can find that page here:

`http://plugindoc.mozdev.org/linux.html`

Another fine resource for this is Stanton Finley's excellent and frequently updated "Fedora Core 3 Installation Notes," which you can find here:

`http://stanton-finley.net/fedora_core_3_installation_notes.html`

Finley's page includes information about the use of alternative Fedora package repositories to make the process somewhat more automatic for some plug-ins. Unfortunately, in some cases, license terms rule out installing the plug-in automatically and the manufacturer's installation scripts must be used.

We recommend installing plug-ins and helper applications on every Linux client for Flash and Java. We also recommend installing RealPlayer to provide support for the major open audio and video formats as well as its own proprietary audio and video formats.

Static Website Interoperability

We'll begin our discussion of web server interoperability issues by examining those that come up with *static* websites. Static websites are those made up entirely of files that the web server delivers to the web browser without interpretation. This would include a site made up entirely of HTML pages, GIF images, and even Java applets, because the server treats them all much the same.

We'll then move on to the issues surrounding more complex dynamic websites. These would include sites using server-side programming languages such as PHP and ASP. The key difference is that some of the content on the website is generated on-the-fly when a web browser makes a request.

But first, we'll need web servers to work with! Let's take care of that chore, then move on to what we can do to make moving static web content between Windows and Linux a little easier.

Setting Up Our Web Servers: IIS and Apache

On the Windows side, we already have an IIS web server: exchange2003.ad.corp.com. We installed IIS on this server in Chapter 6 in order to check out Exchange 2003's web-based e-mail access. If you didn't do so then, you'll need to refer back to Chapter 6 now and configure IIS on exchange2003.ad.corp.com or another Windows server.

In a production environment, we'd likely never use an Exchange server as a general-purpose web server. That's because every new application introduces new security risks and our Exchange server is not a great choice of machine to expose to such risks. But for test lab purposes, there's no need to establish an entirely separate web server machine.

On the Linux side, though, we haven't had a need for a standard Apache web server until this point. We did select the Apache web server package when installing Fedora on linserv1.corp.com, but we never started it up or signaled the operating system to start it up on each reboot. Again, in a production environment it would be more secure to move the web server to a separate host. This is recommended because security holes are routinely found (and fixed) in popular third-party web applications that appear on many sites. But for test lab purposes, there's no harm in using a single server for many purposes. Let's take a moment now to take care of starting up Apache on linserv1.corp.com.

Follow these steps to start the Apache server and ensure that it starts every time the system is booted:

1. Use the chkconfig command to make sure the Apache server process, httpd, runs at boot time:

    ```
    chkconfig httpd on
    ```

2. Use the service command to start up Apache now:

    ```
    service httpd start
    ```

If either command produces an error message, you may not have installed Apache when you installed Fedora Linux on linserv1.corp.com. You can fix that quickly with the up2date command:

```
up2date httpd
```

Then repeat the two earlier steps.

Now let's verify that the Apache web server is actually working properly by creating a simple test HTML page. By default, Apache expects to find web pages in and beneath the directory /var/www/html. This behavior can be changed by editing the DocumentRoot setting in Apache's main configuration file, /etc/httpd/conf/httpd.conf.

Follow these steps to test the delivery of a simple web page by the Apache web server on linserv1.corp.com:

1. Using your preferred text editor, create the file /var/www/html/test.html.

2. Insert the following HTML code:

```
<html>
<head>
<title>Test HTML Page</title>
</head>
<body>
<h1>Test HTML Page</h1>
</body>
</html>
```

3. Access the web page with a web browser at `http://linserv1.corp.com/test.html`

In your browser window, you should see the text "Test HTML Page" in a large font. If you receive an error message instead, make sure you successfully followed the steps to start up the Apache web server.

Now that we have working web server environments for both Windows and Linux, we can look at how each server can be convinced to deliver web applications normally compatible with only one or the other.

Static Website Interoperability: "Gotchas" When Moving Content between Servers

A static website is the simplest type of website. Static websites can contain HTML pages, images, audio, video, and more. The key observation is that *all of the content comes from existing files,* with *no* database lookups or other forms of dynamically generated content. Sometimes a static website may utilize third-party providers to provide some dynamic features. For instance, Google Adsense (`www.google.com/adsense`) dynamically inserts advertising content using JavaScript code embedded in web pages. But JavaScript is a browser-side technology; nothing "interesting" is happening on the server side here. Similarly, many companies offer access counters that can be embedded in a web page. But these counters are implemented as references to images that reside on the web server of the company providing the counter service. From the standpoint of the web server that hosts the site, there's *nothing to do but deliver existing files directly to the web browser.*

Moving an existing static website from Linux to Windows or vice versa is a piece of cake…most of the time. There just a few interoperability issues on the server side. Indeed, since both the Apache web server found on Linux systems and the Microsoft Internet Information Server most commonly found on Windows systems have virtually no trouble delivering simple static files, one might think there would be no issues at all!

Can't one just copy the content from the IIS `inetpub` folder right on over to the `html` directory on the Apache server? Usually, yes. But there are three common problems to be dealt with: case-sensitive filenames, inconsistent file extensions, and differing directory index filenames. Be sure to consider these issues carefully before you move your files over.

Case Sensitivity

On Windows, filenames are not case sensitive. If you have an image file named `logo.png` and you copy another file named `Logo.png` into the same folder, the first file is replaced. Also, if a web page embeds that image with an HTML element like the following one, the image will be displayed because Windows always ignores case when considering filenames:

```
<IMG SRC="LoGo.png">
```

On Linux, filenames are case sensitive. An image file named `logo.png` and an image file named `Logo.png` can coexist in the same directory at the same time. The preceding HTML element will display nothing but a "broken image" icon in the web browser unless the actual image filename is *exactly* `LoGo.png`. And since Linux file extensions are also case sensitive and, by convention, always lowercase, a file named `logo.PNG` will *never* be correctly recognized as an image file. (Well, almost never. You *could* reconfigure Apache to recognize uppercase variations of each and every file extension it recognizes. But that's not a very practical way to do things.)

Unfortunately, case discrepancies like this tend to accumulate over time. And when it comes time to move the content to a Linux server running Apache...some of your links and images and so forth are mysteriously broken.

The correct solution to this problem is to fix your filenames and references to those filenames to be completely consistent with regard to case. You can do this by working methodically through your files, correcting case to be consistent. Doing so is far easier if you simply decide on a standard, such as all lowercase for all filenames. Since lowercase is much more common for files on Linux, with uppercase used only rarely for emphasis (as in filenames such as `README`), we suggest correcting all filenames to lowercase. Keep in mind that you must both rename the files *and* correct the case of every link to those files that appears in an HTML document. For those who know a little bit of HTML, that includes every `<IMG SRC="filename.gif">` that embeds an image and every `<A HREF="filename.html">` that links to a page.

OK, we all agree that's the right way. Now, what happens if you've been tasked to move a website to a Linux server in a hurry? Maybe you've had time to fix case issues, but you have a nagging suspicion that you missed a few. And you need that site to work properly on Linux *now*. So promise us you'll fix the problem the right way just as soon as you can and we'll let you in on a secret.

Apache is the most popular web server in the world for a reason. Well, for more than one reason. Apache is free, for one thing. But another major reason is its sheer flexibility. Apache can be extended to do new things by any programmer who wishes to do so by writing a new Apache *module*. And if you want to do something, chances are there's already an Apache module that allows you to do it. In many cases, the module you want is already part of Fedora's standard build of Apache, which means you won't have to compile anything from source code. That's the case for the `mod_speling` module (yes, that misspelling is intentional; those Apache developers have a cute sense of humor), which provides a quick and dirty solution to our case-sensitivity transition problem.

The `mod_speling` module is called into action every time a request for a file on the website is about to fail! Instead of rejecting the request, `mod_speling` checks for files with any number of case differences from the original. As an added bonus, mod_speling also tolerates one spelling error, such as an incorrect letter. This usually comes into play, of course, only if your web pages contain links or image references that were already broken on Windows. It does, however, come in handy when users manually mistype URLs on your website.

So how do we set it up? Like most generally useful modules, mod_speling is already loaded by Fedora's standard Apache configuration file, /etc/httpd/conf/httpd.conf, which we'll refer to as httpd.conf for brevity's sake. That means the feature is available to be turned on. But the switch hasn't actually been set yet. To do that, we must set the CheckSpelling option to on by adding one line to httpd.conf:

```
CheckSpelling on
```

And then we signal the web server to reload its configuration files using the service command:

```
service httpd reload
```

Yes, that's right: The module's name (mod_speling) contains a "cute" intentional spelling error, but the option that turns on the feature does not. Maybe it's not so cute after all.

You can also place this line within the <VirtualHost> ... </VirtualHost> container in httpd.conf for a single virtual website rather than applying it to all websites hosted by your web server.

The spelling correction feature of mod_speling is convenient, but there are pitfalls to consider. Case errors are detected first, so you needn't worry that a file with a different spelling will be delivered instead of one with a simple capitalization error. However, you should be concerned about leaving this feature in place for the long term. You don't want your designers to get sloppy and stop fixing their typos. And while it is never adequate security to "hide" a file by "just not linking to it," mod_speling increases the chances of a user accessing the wrong file by accident when filenames are similar enough. This is only an issue if that "private" file is sitting right in your public web folder, of course, which you would *never* allow. Right?

But how did we find the right Apache module to use? And how did we learn the right way to enable the feature we want in the Apache server configuration file? The Apache web server community maintains a website (http://httpd.apache.org) that always provides access to the latest and greatest Apache web server version and documentation for the current version as well as some older releases. Browsing there, especially on the Apache Frequently Asked Questions page (http://httpd.apache.org/docs/misc/FAQ.html), will usually reveal the information you need.

OK, so we've learned how to deal with non-case-sensitivity issues when moving content from Windows to Linux. But how does case non-case-sensitivity affect us when moving from Linux to Windows? You're in luck here: it usually doesn't. Completely case-consistent links and filenames won't do any harm when you copy them to an operating system that is not case sensitive. Migrating your static content from Linux to Windows is simpler in this regard.

But there's one catch! Even though most designers would never create separate files named `logo.png` and `LOGO.png`, under Linux—well, they could. And those files would be unique. And a page that embedded both images with `<IMG SRC="`*`filename`*`">` elements would display two different images.

If, by some chance, your web designers have chosen to do this, you'll need to rename those files so that their names are different even without regard to case. That is, `logo.png` and `LOGO.png` are *not* distinct on Windows, but `logo.png` and `logo2.png` are distinct.

Fortunately, this issue is rare. After all, designers who originally create their content on a case-insensitive Windows system would never develop the habit of expecting two filenames differing only in capitalization to refer to two distinct files in the same directory. And developers who work with Linux typically avoid putting files in the same directory if the names only differ in their case. If you do encounter this problem, though, take care to rename one of the conflicting files and change all links and references to it in HTML documents accordingly.

File Extensions and Mime Types

When it comes to file extensions, we often casually refer to, say, a GIF graphics file as a "dot-gif" or an HTML document as a "dot-html." Windows users, especially those who go back to the Windows 3.1 days, will sometimes refer to "dot-htm" as well. By popular convention, a file with a `.gif` extension is understood to be a Graphics Interchange Format (GIF) image file, and a file with a `.htm` or `.html` extension is understood to be an HTML document. But these file extensions are *not* universal standards. Indeed, at one point, the MacOS operating system did not use file extensions *at all,* relying on alternative methods to identify file types. While in the past few years file extensions have become more universally accepted across platforms, there is much less consistency in the naming of some newer file types, notably those used for video. That means the web browser can't rely solely on the file extension to tell it what sort of data the file contains. On the Web, this problem is solved by using *MIME types.*

Multipurpose Internet Mail Extensions (MIME) types avoid the problems of associating files with applications based on the file extension. MIME definitions are standardized to refer to specific file types regardless of the extension.

For instance, the MIME type for a GIF image is `image/gif`, and the MIME type for an HTML document is `text/html`. It does not matter whether the file was named `welcome.html` or `welcome.htm` or even `welcome.mytzylpk` on the web server's hard drive, *so long as the web server specifies the right MIME type when it sends the file to the web browser.*

For the most part, this technique works very well. It doesn't matter what the file is called on the server, so long as the server tells the browser what MIME type the file really contains. This is a sensible way of doing things: The web server, which is under the web designer's control, presumably knows what the files contain. The web browser shouldn't have to guess!

But what happens when we migrate files from a Windows web server to a Linux web server or from Linux to Windows? There's a possibility that a file extension recognized by one web server will be unknown to the other.

The good news is that most of the common file extensions, and quite a few of the less common ones, are recognized by both Apache and IIS "right out of the box." For instance, that includes both `.htm` and `.html`, even on Linux, where long filenames have always been available. But if you do encounter a file extension that your web server doesn't know about, the result is rarely desirable.

Apache will deliver the file using a default MIME type. This is often set to text/plain, which appears in the browser as plain text, or application/octet-stream, which most web browsers will offer to save to disk and not attempt to interpret further. Some web servers are configured to refuse to deliver a file at all if no MIME type is defined for the file extension. If the expected behavior is, say, MPEG video playback, then none of these behaviors are acceptable substitutes. So how do we solve this problem?

For the Apache server as found on Fedora systems, the standard file extensions are defined by the file /etc/mime.types. This file is used both by Apache and by other applications. But we don't recommend that you modify this file because you would lose the ability to update it automatically via the Red Hat Update Agent (that blinking exclamation point on your server's desktop).

Instead, edit your httpd.conf file and take advantage of the AddType option. For instance, to "teach" Apache to recognize the up-and-coming Scalable Vector Graphics (SVG) file format, an open alternative to Flash, and send the browser the correct MIME type when it sees a .svg file, we do the following:

1. Add this line to httpd.conf:

    ```
    AddType image/svg+xml .svg
    ```

2. Signal the web server to reload httpd.conf:

    ```
    service httpd reload
    ```

That's how we do it on Linux. What about Windows? IIS keeps its master list of MIME type assignments in the IIS *metabase*, a database of configuration information similar to but separate from the Windows Registry...because one Registry just isn't enough. Adding additional MIME type assignments is straightforward via the IIS snap-in, introduced in Chapter 3. In this example, we'll add support for serving files in the SVG file format as shown in Figure 10.1.

Following these steps will allow IIS to deliver .svg files with the right MIME type, image/svg+xml, for all websites hosted on WINDC1:

1. Click "Start."

2. Click "Administrative Tools."

3. Click "Internet Information Services (IIS) Manager."

4. Right-click "WINDC1 (local computer)" to display a pop-up menu.

5. Choose "Properties" from this menu.

6. In the "WINDC1 (local computer) Properties" dialog box, click "MIME Types."

7. Click "New" to add a new type.

8. In the "Extension" field, enter **svg** (note: no period).

9. In the MIME type field, enter **image/svg+xml** (note: no period).

10. Click "OK" to close each dialog box until you return to the IIS snap-in. Close the IIS snap-in by clicking the "X" in the upper-right corner.

FIGURE 10.1   Adding a new MIME type to file extension mapping in IIS

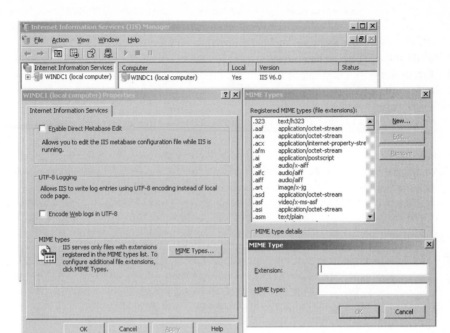

Running Windows Web Applications on Linux...and Linux Web Applications on Windows

So far we've examined issues that apply to static content, such as web pages, images, and other content *not* generated on-the-fly in response to particular conditions or user-submitted forms. Web servers can also generate web pages and other media types dynamically. For instance, a web page can be generated by fetching information from a database in response to search terms entered by a user.

Both operating systems have "native" ways to do this. Microsoft Windows users running Internet Information Server (IIS) can use Active Server Pages (ASP), a reasonably beginner-friendly system built on Microsoft's Visual Basic language. Microsoft's newest version of ASP, ASP.NET, allows many programming languages to be used, notably Microsoft's C# language. That's possible because ASP.NET leverages .NET's Common Language Interface (CLI), which we'll discuss in a bit more detail later. Of course, programmers can still use VB.NET, the latest version of the Visual Basic language that ASP programmers have traditionally used most often.

Although a wide range of programming languages can be used to extend Apache-based websites, including Perl, Python and Ruby, most Apache webmasters use PHP. PHP is quite friendly to beginning web developers. While past versions of PHP were lax about security issues, modern versions are as safe to use as other web programming languages.

Both PHP and ASP were originally intended for those who have mastered static web pages and need to sprinkle in a little bit of server-side programming rather than use scripts that run at the client. Both languages have a syntax that makes it convenient to include short snippets of code in a web page.

Today, however, both ASP.NET and PHP have evolved into mature systems that can be used to develop large web applications any webmaster might want to reuse…applications that, quite often, are open source. And that's great. But what if you're an IIS webmaster and the web application you want to use runs on PHP? For that matter, what if you're running Apache and you want to run an ASP application? We'll address both of these scenarios in the remainder of this chapter.

There is an important "third way" here: Sun's Java 2 Enterprise Edition (J2EE). J2EE offers the ability to create Java-language web applications called "servlets" that can accomplish goals similar to those of PHP and ASP.NET. We don't go into depth about J2EE in this chapter precisely because it is already well supported on both Windows and Linux. As a result, there aren't a lot of interoperability concerns there, and you won't need a lot of help from us to get started. We've chosen to focus on the more challenging tasks of making .NET work with Linux and making PHP work with Windows. But J2EE is certainly a viable option you should check out if you have the luxury of choosing your own web development environment. You can learn more about J2EE on Sun's website, at `http://java.sun.com/j2ee/index.jsp`.

Running Linux PHP Applications on Windows IIS Servers

For Windows webmasters who want to run PHP applications, there's great news: full-blown PHP *can* be used with IIS…for free! And so can the MySQL database engine that many worthwhile PHP applications depend upon. In fact, using the database instead of files to store information tends to make web applications *more* portable between Linux and Windows because Structured Query Language (SQL) is an open standard and MySQL behaves the same on both operating systems. In this chapter, we'll examine how to integrate PHP and MySQL with IIS and show how to run the popular PHP-based phpBB web-based bulletin board application on an IIS server.

Windows users can also choose to run the Apache web server on Windows in place of IIS. Apache for Windows has matured considerably in recent years, but the Apache website specifically warns that Apache for Windows has not yet been optimized for performance. By contrast, IIS 6.0 is tightly integrated with the Windows operating system kernel. You can learn more about Apache for Windows at the Apache Foundation website: www.apache.org.

So, PHP applications can run on IIS? Great! How do we get started? Actually, before we get started, it might be good for us to determine which PHP application we ultimately want to run on Windows IIS. If you check out www.winlinanswers.com and click on the Community Forum, you'll see that we're running a forum called phpBB—a simple bulletin board with a lot of power. Yes, on our particular real-world website, we're running it on a Linux server. But the point is that this is a cool piece of free software that we love and use for production work. And you might fall in love with it too. To that end, we'll show you how to set it up to run on a Windows IIS server if you so choose.

One word of warning about open-source web applications: keep them up-to-date or you risk security breaches! The good thing about open source is that security holes are quickly found and quickly fixed. But if you don't install the fixes, this doesn't help you. If you choose to install phpBB or a similar program, particularly in an Internet environment, you'll need to watch the home page of the software closely for announced updates and be sure to install any security fixes.

Installing the MySQL Database Engine and Creating a Database for phpBB

We'll begin by installing the free, open-source MySQL database engine on exchange2003.ad.corp .com, a server on which we already installed IIS in Chapter 6 in order to provide a web browser interface to the Exchange mail server. If you didn't install IIS on exchange2003.ad.corp.com in Chapter 6, you'll need to do so before proceeding.

Once we've installed MySQL, we'll use the MySQL command line client to create a database where phpBB can store forum posts, forum users, and the rest of its data.

For test lab purposes, there's no harm in running other web applications on our Exchange 2003 server. But in a production environment, this is not a good choice. All web applications such as phpBB expose the system to some risk because new security flaws are occasionally discovered and exploited in such applications. Responsible webmasters should minimize that risk by separating the general-purpose web server from the Exchange 2003 server.

Downloading and Installing MySQL

We'll start by downloading the latest stable version of MySQL for Windows, currently MySQL 4.1.12a. Follow these steps on exchange2003.ad.corp.com to download the latest stable version of MySQL for Windows:

1. Visit the MySQL home page, at: http://dev.mysql.com

2. Click "Downloads" to reach the "MySQL Downloads" page.

3. Scroll down to "MySQL 4.1" or whichever release is currently labeled as the "Generally Available (GA) Release (recommended)" and click the "MySQL 4.1" link. The "MySQL 4.1 Downloads" page will appear.

4. Scroll down to "Windows downloads" and locate the "Windows (x86)" package. Click "Pick a mirror" to begin the download process. A user information form appears.

5. Complete the user information form or, alternatively, click "No thanks, just take me to the downloads!"

6. Pick the mirror site closest to you. A ZIP file will begin to download. When prompted, save the ZIP file to the desktop.

We've downloaded the setup program, in the form of a ZIP archive. Now we're ready to unzip and install MySQL. The installation program has many screens, but we'll accept the defaults for most of these. For space reasons we won't mention defaults that are not relevant for our purposes.

The installation program is actually two programs: a setup wizard and a configuration wizard. The configuration wizard prompts for one noteworthy piece of information, a *root password*. The MySQL root password is *not* intended to be the same thing as your Windows administrator password. In a production environment, you should never use the Administrator password for the MySQL root password.

The MySQL root password is used only by programs and scripts that need permission to create and delete databases. Such programs can also create less privileged MySQL accounts that have access only to certain databases and cannot create new databases. For test lab purposes, we'll use the password p@ssw0rd, but you should choose a secure password in a production environment.

Follow these steps on exchange2003.ad.corp.com to unpack, install, and configure MySQL for Windows:

1. On the desktop, double-click the ZIP file we downloaded in the previous set of steps. The Setup.exe program will appear as the sole file inside the ZIP archive.

2. Double-click Setup.exe to launch the installer.

3. The "Welcome to the Setup Wizard for MySQL Server 4.1" screen appears. Click "Next" to proceed.

4. The "Setup Type" screen appears. Choose "Complete" for a complete installation and click "Next" to continue.

5. The "Ready to Install the Program" screen appears with a brief review of what will be done. Click "Install" to begin the actual installation.

6. The "MySQL.com Sign-Up" screen appears. Sign up for an account, or just select "Skip Sign-Up." Then click "Next."

7. The "Wizard Completed" screen appears, with a check box labeled "Configure the MySQL Server Now." Be sure this box is checked and click "Finish."

8. The "Welcome to the MySQL Server Instance Configuration Wizard" screen appears. Click "Next."

9. The "MySQL Server Instance Configuration" screen is displayed. Select "Standard Configuration" and click "Next."

10. The "Please set the Windows options" screen is shown. Make sure "Install As Windows Service" is checked, and click "Next."

11. The "Modify Security Settings" screen appears. The "Modify Security Settings" box should be checked. Enter **p@ssw0rd** in the root password field and click "Next."

12. The "Ready to Execute" screen is shown. Click "Execute" to complete the configuration of the MySQL server.

13. Click "Finish" to close the wizard.

MySQL is successfully installed on exchange2003.ad.corp.com. But we need to take care of a little snag. MySQL offers a Dynamic Link Library (DLL) that other applications, like PHP, can use to communicate with it. But this DLL is not automatically installed where PHP expects to find it. We will correct this by copying this DLL, `libmysql.dll`, from MySQL's library directory to `C:\WINDOWS\SYSTEM32` where all applications can find it.

To install `libmysql.dll` for PHP's benefit, follow these steps:

1. Using the Windows file manager, locate the file `libmysql.dll` in the folder `C:\Program Files\MySQL\MySQL Server 4.1\lib\opt`.

2. Copy this file to the folder `C:\WINDOWS\SYSTEM32`.

Initial MySQL Setup

Now we'll verify that MySQL is working properly. And we'll also take care of a necessary step toward running phpBB. We'll accomplish both by creating a database in which phpBB will be able to store information. We can accomplish these things using the simple command line client provided with MySQL.

A command-line utility is friendlier to typical MySQL users than it may sound because MySQL's administrative commands are just an extension of the familiar Structured Query Language (SQL) with which database-savvy web developers are often familiar. But don't worry, we don't need to master SQL to execute a few simple commands that create a database, create a new MySQL user called phpbb with the usual test lab password (p@ssw0rd), and grant that user the privilege of working with the database we've created.

To do these things, we'll use the `create database` command to make a database and use the `grant all privileges` command to offer control of that database to a specific user. The `grant all privileges` command creates the user for us along the way.

In addition, we'll use the `set password` command to adjust the password for compatibility with PHP. MySQL 4.1, by default, uses a new password authentication protocol that requires changes to client applications. PHP's standard MySQL support functions, even in the most current 5.x versions (we'll stick with the 4.3.x series in this book because it installs much more smoothly on Windows as of this writing), do not understand this protocol. An alternative MySQL extension for PHP 5.x does exist, but existing PHP applications may not know how to use it...and it isn't currently included in Windows distributions of PHP. Ugh! Fortunately, we can work around this by telling MySQL to use an "old-style" password for the phpbb account. Since the only database connections we allow are from `localhost` (the web and database server itself), there is no possibility that these passwords will be "sniffed" on the wire.

To create a database and a MySQL user account for phpBB on exchange2003.ad.corp.com, follow these steps:

1. Launch the command line client with this sequence of menu choices:

Start ➢ All Programs ➢ MySQL ➢ MySQL Server 4.1 ➢ MySQL Command Line Client

2. An "Enter password:" prompt appears. Enter the MySQL root password, which we have set to p@ssw0rd in our test lab. The mysql> prompt appears.

3. At the mysql> prompt, key in the following MySQL command to create a database for phpBB's benefit:

    ```
    create database PHPBB;
    ```

    You will receive a response similar to the following:

    ```
    Query OK, 1 row affected (0.02 sec)
    ```

4. Key in the following MySQL command to grant control of the new database to the user phpbb:

    ```
    grant all privileges on PHPBB.* to phpbb@localhost identified by 'p@ssw0rd';
    ```

    This will produce a response similar to the following:

    ```
    Query OK, 0 rows affected (0.02 sec)
    ```

    "0 rows affected" is not an error. Privileges have been set correctly.

5. Adjust the password for compatibility with the older MySQL client libraries used by PHP:

    ```
    set password for phpbb@localhost = OLD_PASSWORD('p@ssw0rd');
    ```

    This should produce a response similar to the following:

    ```
    Query OK, 0 rows affected (0.02 sec)
    ```

    "0 rows affected" is not an error. The password has been adjusted correctly.

6. Exit the client by typing the quit command and pressing Enter.

Installing and Testing PHP for Windows

We've verified that the MySQL database engine works properly. And we've created the database we'll use for phpBB. Now we're ready to install PHP for Windows itself, bringing PHP programming capabilities to our IIS web server. We'll install PHP and perform a simple test of its integration with IIS before demonstrating the big payoff by installing the phpBB forum software.

For the most part, installation is straightforward. Again, there are many prompts but for the most part we can accept the defaults. There *is* one catch. The PHP installation program uses scripts written in Microsoft's VBScript language to accomplish some of its tasks. And on our Windows 2003 / SP 1 server, we found that these scripts generated warning dialogs indicating that they could not be run by wscript, one of Microsoft's script interpreters. Fortunately, Windows offers up the alternative of running the scripts under Microsoft's cscript interpreter instead. The prompts are a bit cryptic, so we've spelled out the right steps for you.

One more issue: the current "stable" version of PHP is the 5.0 series. But we've found that integrating this version with MySQL on the Windows platform is quite difficult. So, like quite a few PHP users at this point, we're sticking with the PHP 4.3 series until things are a little more settled.

Installation of PHP 4.3 for Windows

Follow these steps to install PHP support on exchange2003.ad.corp.com:

1. Visit the PHP home page at www.php.net.

2. Click "downloads" to reach the "PHP: Downloads" page.

3. Scroll down to "Windows Binaries."

4. Scroll down farther and click "PHP 4.3.11 installer" (the version number you see may be newer).

5. A list of mirror sites appears. Select the mirror site closest to you.

6. Save the php-4.3.11-installer.exe file to the desktop.

7. Double-click the installation program on the desktop.

8. The "Welcome to PHP 4.3.11 Setup program" screen appears. Click "Next."

9. The PHP license terms appear. Review them before clicking "I Agree." The PHP license permits you to take full advantage of PHP in a for-profit fashion.

10. The "Installation Type" screen appears. Make sure "Standard" is selected and click "Next."

11. The "Choose Destination Location" screen appears. We recommend accepting the default location by clicking "Next."

12. The "Mail Configuration" screen appears. This screen only affects PHP scripts that send e-mail. In the "SMTP server" field, localhost is the default, which is correct because exchange2003.ad.corp.com is a mail server. In the "'from' address" field, enter root@corp.com. Then click "Next" to continue.

13. The "Server Type" screen appears. Here we indicate what type of web server we want to install PHP support for. By default, "Microsoft IIS 4 or higher" is selected. Change this to "Microsoft IIS 6 or higher" and click "Next."

14. The "Start Installation" screen appears. Click "Next" to perform the actual installation.

15. An "IIS has been configured" message box will appear, informing you that IIS has been configured to recognize PHP scripts. Actually, this is not quite true yet, as we'll see in a moment. Click the "OK" button to continue.

16. A "Windows Script Host" message box appears with the message "This script does not work with WScript." Click "OK" to continue.

17. A "Register CScript" message box appears with the message "Would you like to register CScript as your default host for VBScript?" Click "Yes." Otherwise PHP will *not* be correctly integrated with IIS.

18. A confirmation prompt appears indicating that CScript has been successfully registered. Just click "OK."

19. The "Installation complete" message box appears with additional information about user permissions that did not require modification in our tests. Click "OK."

PHP is installed and configured, with all the little details right for our needs. But how can we be sure it's working?

Testing PHP for Windows

We'll find out by creating a trivial PHP page, in the home directory of our IIS server. We'll spice up that page by including a simple command that prints out a fancy and highly readable listing of the PHP features that are enabled so that we can verify that MySQL support is available. Then we'll access that page with a web browser. If we see the output correctly, PHP is working. If we see an empty page, it's not.

Although this is not a programming book, it's handy to have some understanding of what we're looking at. PHP code, like that of other embedded web development languages, is typically inserted into HTML pages. PHP has a standard syntax for this, using `<?php` to begin a block of PHP code and `?>` to end it. Anything between those markers is interpreted by the PHP engine. The rest of the page is sent unmodified to the web browser as one would normally expect.

In our test PHP code, we'll use PHP's `echo` command, which outputs a quoted string of text to the web browser. By placing the actual body of the page here, we'll find out whether PHP is working. If PHP isn't working, we'll see an error message, or an empty page. If PHP *is* working, we'll see "PHP Test Page" in a large font, as shown in Figure 10.2.

We'll also use a second `echo` command, which will display the output of PHP's `phpinfo()` function. `phpinfo()` returns a rather nice HTML table that shows which PHP features are installed and available. We should see MySQL support listed in this table.

The home directory of our IIS server, if you didn't choose to change the default when configuring IIS, is `C:\inetpub\wwwroot`. This is the folder IIS looks in to find content when a web browser makes a request to access a file.

Follow these steps to create and test a simple PHP page on `exchange2003.ad.corp.com`:

1. Using Notepad, create the file `C:\inetpub\wwwroot\test.php`

2. Insert the following HTML with embedded PHP code:

```
<html>
<head>
<title>PHP Test Page</title>
</head>
<body>
<?php
  echo '<h1>PHP Test Page</h1>';
  echo phpinfo();
?>
</body>
</html>
```

3. Pull down the File menu and choose "Save As."

4. On the "Save as type:" pull-down menu, be sure to select "All Files." Otherwise an unwanted `.txt` extension will be attached onto the end of the filename.

5. In the "File name:" field, enter **test.php**.

6. Click the "Save" button.

7. With your web browser, access the URL

    `http://exchange2003.ad.corp.com/test.php`

When you complete these steps, you should see "PHP Test Page" in a large font followed by a listing of PHP features. Scroll down or search the page for "mysql" and you'll find the information shown in Figure 10.2. If instead you see "File not found" or a similar error, or you see a blank page, double-check that you created the `test.php` file and placed it in the proper directory. If so, we recommend running the PHP installation program again. Most likely the VBScript code used by the PHP installer did not work on the first try, probably because you did not answer "Yes" to registering CScript as the default VBScript interpreter. (Yes, this is a pain, and hopefully the next update of the Windows PHP installer will make this annoyance go away!)

If the page does appear otherwise correct but doesn't mention MySQL support, make sure that you have installed the PECL extension DLLs, enabled them in `php.ini`, and copied `libmysql.dll` to `C:\Windows\System` as described earlier.

Installing and Testing the phpBB Forum Software on Windows

Now that we've created a complete, database-capable PHP environment for our IIS server and created a database for phpBB specifically, we're ready to install phpBB. phpBB provides *bulletin boards*, or forums, with an impressive set of features for users and administrators alike. PHP's ease of use has led to an explosion of such simple and popular open-source software. Now you can leverage these tools under Windows.

Unlike some popular PHP applications, phpBB is actually rather Windows friendly and can be used with Microsoft SQL Server or even Microsoft Access ODBC instead of MySQL. However, we're using MySQL because it is a popular component of *many* open-source PHP web applications you may wish to run on your Windows server, not all of which can be used without modification with other database software—and, of course, because it's free and works really well.

FIGURE 10.2   The MySQL-related portion of the output shown in our PHP test page when PHP and MySQL support are correctly configured on `exchange2003.ad.corp.com`

PDO

PDO support	enabled
PDO drivers	mysql

pdo_mysql

PDO Driver for MySQL 3.x Client Libraries	enabled

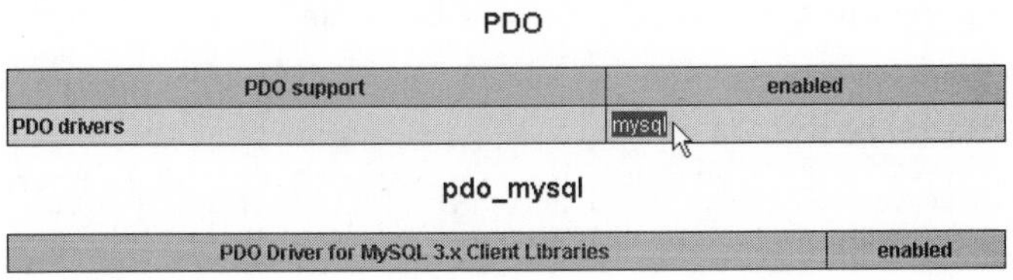

Downloading and Unpacking phpBB

Before we can install the software, we need to get hold of it! Follow these steps to download and unpack the phpBB software on exchange2003.ad.corp.com:

1. Visit the phpBB home page at www.phpbb.com.

2. Click the "Downloads" button to access the downloads page.

3. Locate the current full package download, currently labeled "phpBB 2.0.16 [Full Package]." Click on the ZIP icon to the right.

4. Save the ZIP file to the desktop.

5. Right-click the ZIP file on the desktop and select "Extract All."

6. The "Welcome to the Compressed (zipped) Folders Extraction Wizard" screen appears. Click "Next" to continue.

7. The "Select Destination" screen appears. Change the "Files will be extracted to this Directory:" field to C:\Inetpub\wwwroot. Click "Next" to continue.

8. The "Extraction Complete" screen appears. Leave the "Show extracted files" box checked, and click "Finish."

The contents of the C:\Inetpub\wwwroot\phpBB2 folder are now displayed in a Windows Explorer window. This folder is within the home directory of our web server, so it can be accessed with a web browser. Notice the install subfolder. This folder contains scripts that should be used only once to install phpBB. Once we're done with them, we'll remove this subfolder entirely.

Configuring phpBB

To begin configuring phpBB, we'll access the built-in, PHP-based installation scripts using a web browser. We need to do this promptly because until we do so, the newly installed software is exposed to the possibility that someone else will configure it first.

On phpBB's built-in configuration page, we'll make choices in three categories: general settings, database-related settings, and information about the phpBB administrative user. For space reasons, we won't mention options for which the defaults are acceptable and whose significance is outside the scope of this chapter.

To configure phpBB, follow these steps on exchange2003.ad.corp.com:

1. Access the following URL using Internet Explorer running *on exchange2003.ad.corp.com itself*. This will simplify later tasks:

   http://exchange2003.ad.corp.com/phpBB/install/install.php

2. The "Welcome to phpBB 2 Installation" page will appear.

3. Set "Database type:" to MySQL 4.x.

4. Leave "Choose your installation method:" set to "Install."

5. In the "Database server hostname:" field, accept the default setting of localhost. (This is correct because the MySQL server is running on the same computer as phpBB.)

6. Set the "Your Database Name:" field to PHPBB.

7. Set the "Database Username:" field to phpbb.

8. Set the "Database Password:" field to p@ssw0rd.

9. Set the "Admin Email Address:" field to root@corp.com or the address where you would prefer to have administrative notices from the software delivered.

10. The automatically detected setting for "Domain Name," exchange2003.ad.corp.com, is correct. What is meant here is the full hostname of the website. "Fully Qualified Domain Name" would have been less confusing.

11. Set the "Administrator Username:" field to admin.

12. Set both "Administrator Password:" fields to p@ssw0rd.

13. Click "Start Install" to carry out the configuration of phpBB.

Some time should pass before you see the page shown in Figure 10.3.

FIGURE 10.3　　Because IIS has tight security policies, phpBB can't write to its configuration file directly.

This page indicates that installation is going well but phpBB can't write directly to its configuration file. This is normal under IIS, which has tight security policies by default. Since, with the exception of a few global configuration settings, phpBB keeps all of its data in a MYSQL database, we won't tell IIS to lower the protections. Instead, we'll take advantage of the second option shown in Figure 10.3, downloading the configuration file and then copying it into place ourselves. (We won't actually use FTP. If you are running your browser on the server itself, you can simply copy the file to its final destination.)

Follow these steps to install the configuration file for phpBB:

1. Select the "Just send the file to me and I'll FTP it manually" option.

2. Click "Download Config."

3. Click "Save."

4. Save the file to the following folder:

   C:\inetpub\wwwroot\phpBB2

This overwrites the existing (but empty) file `config.php`.

Basic installation is almost complete! However, if you try to access phpBB2 now at the following URL, you'll receive the error "You are not authorized to view this page":

`http://exchange2003.ad.corp.com/phpBB2/`

That's because IIS is not configured to recognize `index.php` as a valid name for a directory home page, but most PHP applications assume that it will be treated as such. And IIS *is* configured to refuse to display a list of files present in a folder as an alternative when no directory home page exists. So we're out of luck unless we add `index.php` to the end of the URL...or are we?

As it turns out, we can fix the problem using the "Internet Information Services (IIS) Manager" application of Windows. Follow these steps to make `index.php` a valid name for a folder home page, or "default content page" in IIS terminology:

1. Choose Start ➤ Administrative Tools ➤ Internet Information Services (IIS) Manager.

2. The "Internet Information Services (IIS) Manager" window appears. In the left-hand pane, click "Exchange 2003 (local computer)." The right-hand pane will update to reflect aspects of this computer's web servers.

3. In the right-hand frame, double-click "Web Sites." A list of websites appears, containing only "Default Web Site."

4. Right-click "Default Web Site" and select "Properties." The "Default Web Site Properties" window appears.

5. Click the "Documents" tab.

6. Beneath "Enable default content page," which should be checked, click the "Add" button. The "Add Content Page" dialog appears.

7. Enter **index.php** and click "OK." `index.php` is added to the list of content page filenames.

Now we can access phpBB2 at the following URL:

`http://exchange2003.ad.corp.com/phpBB2/`

When we do, though, we'll see one last issue: a message reminding us to delete the `install` and `contrib` folders from the phpBB2 folder. These folders contain the installation pages we just used and contributed code that we don't need. Both are dangerous to leave lying around because a rogue user could use these pages to reconfigure phpBB2.

Fix the problem by following these steps on exchange2003.ad.corp.com:

1. Delete the folder `C:\inetpub\wwwroot\phpBB2\install`.

2. Delete the folder `C:\inetpub\wwwroot\phpBB2\contrib`.

We're finally ready to go! Access phpBB one last time:

`http://exchange2003.ad.corp.com/phpBB2/`

You'll see the phpBB welcome page as shown in Figure 10.4. Log on as the phpBB administrative user (username `admin`, password `p@ssw0rd`) to explore the capabilities of phpBB.

FIGURE 10.4   The welcome page of phpBB, open-source PHP-based forum software running successfully under PHP for Windows on Internet Information Server

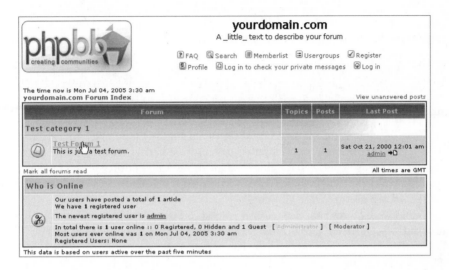

At this point, we'll stop and let you explore your phpBB universe if you like. We've achieved our goal. Again, if you're interested in actually configuring phpBB for your use in-house (or to put on the Web), be sure to check out www.phpbb.com.

Running Windows ASP and ASP.NET Web Applications on Linux Servers

PHP and its relatives are compelling choices for web design because of their simplicity, friendliness, and low cost. But the modern Windows platform has its own impressive option to offer: the .NET architecture. .NET (which is not an acronym) allows programmers and web designers to create code in a variety of modern programming languages and run that code in an environment in which many important tasks are taken care of automatically for the programmer.

In the past, web applications on IIS servers were often based on an older Microsoft technology, Active Server Pages (ASP). At first, these applications were nearly always written in Visual Basic, a language with its own following but not popular among those more accustomed to C, Java, Perl or C++. But today ASP.NET, the modern successor to ASP, allows any programming language supported by .NET to be used. This has far-reaching implications.

For instance, ASP.NET provides a good implementation of "user sessions," keeping track of individual users as they move through the website and providing the ability to easily program an ongoing interaction with each individual user. Visual Basic programmers always had access to this through ASP. Today, however, programmers can also use Microsoft's C# language, along with a *very* large number of other languages. The list includes Java (Microsoft's J#, which is compatible), JavaScript (Microsoft's JScript.NET, which is compatible), and C++ (when used with Microsoft's Extensions for C++, commonly referred to as Managed C++), along with many lesser-known languages. Even Python and Perl can be used, although the .NET versions of Python and Perl available at this time from `www.activestate.com` are still experimental. This is possible thanks to .NET's Common Language Interface (CLI), a published standard that allows anyone to add .NET support for an additional programming language.

But this isn't a programming book, so why are we talking about these issues here? Since ASP.NET and legacy ASP offer strong features for web development, many companies use them as part of their intranet and Internet websites. Web designers in an otherwise Linux-friendly company might not be familiar with PHP and other typically Linux-hosted options for server-side web programming. And existing third-party .NET and ASP applications may also be in use or of potential interest. As with the Samba-based Active Directory domain member file server we built in Chapter 4, the ability to do these things on the Linux platform can save wear and tear on a more expensive Windows server or remove a barrier to using Linux for a particular department's needs. Your web developers may know ASP, but they probably don't know system administration. That's where you can help them by providing an ASP environment on a Linux-based server.

But can Linux do it? That depends on your specific needs. The good news is that an open-source implementation of .NET called Mono (also not an acronym) has emerged for Linux and other non-Windows operating systems. The bad news is that, as of this writing, Mono doesn't implement *everything* that Microsoft's .NET environment provides. But if your needs are a good fit for what Mono does provide, you're in good shape. And important new features of Mono are close to release. Those features fill significant gaps in what Mono can do for us today. We'll highlight these features when we examine Mono more closely in this chapter.

Mono has one major weakness, as of this writing, from the perspective of Windows web developers. That weakness is the lack of a complete VB.NET compiler. That means that Mono is not currently a complete solution for those who want to write or maintain Active Server Pages containing code written in the Visual Basic language. Although C# is widely considered to be the best language choice for stand-alone .NET applications, Visual Basic skills are not uncommon among web developers who are used to a Windows environment. And since it was once the only serious option for ASP, Visual Basic is still particularly popular for web development. So this may be an issue for you if you attempt to move content to a Linux-based server using Mono.

You might ask why this matters if VB.NET code can be compiled on a Windows workstation and then run on the Mono platform. The answer is that ASP.NET pages can and do regularly contain VB.NET source code right in the web page, not unlike the way PHP is embedded in web pages. This is a common way to build simple intranet web applications. And it only works when a compiler for VB.NET is available *on the web server,* where those web pages are. That's why a complete VB.NET compiler for Mono is an important missing feature.

So what can we do if we need support for Active Server Pages written in Visual Basic today? The Mono VB.NET compiler is making rapid progress and should be available as a "technology preview" by the time this book hits the shelves. But there is also an alternative solution, one that is more appropriate for those who must have "traditional" ASP support and the Visual Basic language in its pre-.NET dialect. That solution is Sun's Sun Java System Active Server Pages 4.0. That's quite a mouthful, and a tough acronym to pronounce as well. So we'll refer to it simply as JASP for short.

The good news is that JASP is available now, and it works. The bad news is that JASP is not free. JASP licenses for single websites currently sell for prices in the neighborhood of $495 per server. And that can cast doubt on the business case for hosting ASP content on Linux, although it may be acceptable for web hosting companies who expect to host thousands of websites on a single server. We'll look more closely at JASP later in this chapter.

Running Windows ASP.NET on Linux with Mono

Mono is an open-source implementation of Microsoft's .NET architecture. That's an impressive achievement. How can such a thing exist? Is it a product of reverse engineering like Samba? For the most part, no. Important parts of .NET are published standards that anyone can potentially implement.

To be precise, parts of .NET are covered by Ecma standards #335 and #334. (Ecma International is an association that publishes industry standards.) Of course, Microsoft had sound business reasons for making this decision. Microsoft wants the world to use .NET and C#, as well as other .NET-friendly languages. And Sun's earlier attempt to achieve universal popularity for its Java architecture ran into trouble in part because of Sun's unwillingness to make Java an open standard. However, see the sidebar ".NET, Mono, and Intellectual Property Rights" for patent-related concerns about .NET and Mono.

.NET, Mono, and Intellectual Property Rights

Microsoft has made aspects of .NET an open standard and given some indication that it will be allowing these aspects to be used by anyone under royalty-free terms. Microsoft deserves credit for that. Before we take the love fest too far, though, it's worth pointing out that Microsoft has been aggressive in filing patents on many aspects of the .NET system. Microsoft has done nothing to suggest that it will aggressively enforce these software patents in the way that Unisys did with the infamous "GIF patent," which actually covered the encryption algorithm used in GIF-format images. But it certainly could, and some feel that is cause for concern. After all, Unisys did not take action until GIF had been in wide use for many years. If Mono "triumphs" and becomes the most popular way of developing software for Linux, Microsoft could choose to exact patent license fees on those who use certain aspects of it.

To be fair, IBM and other companies are also very aggressive in filing patents on their technology, and not all companies choose to enforce their patents on software development ideas. Since the patent office has had difficulties in recent years recognizing what is "prior art" (something that someone else has already done) and what is a new idea, patents are sometimes used defensively to ensure that other parties cannot enforce patents on the same concept. Still, at least one Microsoft patent on .NET does cite specific features by name that are not included in the open standard but *are* important parts of support for web applications. This could be used to shut down projects that provide free reimplementations of those features. For more information, see Derek Ferguson's March 27, 2003 article in .NET Developer's Journal:

http://dotnet.sys-con.com/read/38836.htm (shortened to http://tinyurl.com/bmson)

To Mono or Not to Mono

The fact that the CLI and C# are open standards greatly simplifies the process of creating an alternative implementation like Mono for the Linux platform. And not surprisingly, CLI and C# are the most mature components of Mono. In addition, Mono contains a fairly mature implementation of ASP.NET, the Active Server Pages engine that allows code to be embedded in web pages Microsoft style. Even better, Mono offers an Apache web server module that allows ASP.NET to be used in web pages served by Apache. As long as those pages contain code written in a language for which Mono offers a reasonably mature and complete compiler—and as of this writing, that pretty much means C#—you're in good shape.

MainSoft's Visual MainWin: Leveraging and Giving Back to Mono

MainSoft (www.mainsoft.com) is a software company focused on cross-platform software development. It has created a product called Visual MainWin, which heavily leverages the Mono project. And though its end product is not open source, it has contributed a significant amount of code back to the Mono project.

MainSoft's principal offering is Visual MainWin for J2EE, a plug-in for Microsoft's Visual Studio development tool. Wait a minute! What does Java 2.0 Enterprise Edition (J2EE) have to do with .NET? Well, Visual MainWin for J2EE allows .NET applications to be run on the J2EE platform, which is one valid way of achieving cross-platform portability for .NET applications.

How does Mono tie in? MainSoft has its own translator to "recompile" .NET binaries into Java binaries. But since those .NET programs will be expecting the entire .NET library to be out there, ready to use, translating the binaries doesn't solve the whole problem. Running existing .NET applications on J2EE requires that MainSoft essentially implement .NET on top of Java. And starting *that* project from scratch, when there's a promising open-source implementation of .NET kicking around, would be foolhardy. So Visual MainWin for J2EE relies heavily on Mono to implement the "middle layer" between .NET applications and MainSoft's Java-based "back end." And that provides MainSoft with a king-sized motivation to contribute fixes and improvements back to the Mono project, early and often.

Although the use of Java by Visual MainWin for J2EE does introduce one more layer between Linux itself and .NET, it also opens up options. Because they are actually running on top of Sun's J2EE environment, .NET applications built with Visual MainWin for J2EE can take advantage of existing third-party Java objects, better known as Enterprise JavaBeans (EJBs). Those interested in giving MainSoft's offering a whirl will want to check out Grasshopper, a freely distributed Visual Studio plug-in that demonstrates MainSoft's technology. Grasshopper is MainSoft's friendlier nickname for Visual MainWin for J2EE Developer Edition. Grasshopper provides all the pieces needed to build and run .NET applications on the Linux platform using J2EE and the Apache Tomcat server. See dev.mainsoft.com for more information about the free Grasshopper package. Be aware, however, that the free product's output is only licensed for use in the same small-workgroup environment where the developer is employed. Full commercial licensing of the Visual MainWin for J2EE product currently starts at $5,000 per developer.

It's worth mentioning that, while Mono only provides a mature compiler for one programming language, Mono's .NET environment *can* run already-compiled .NET code (DLLs and executables) created in other languages. However, most in-house web developers prefer to sprinkle source code into web pages using ASP. And coping with that source code requires a compiler. If the source code isn't in C#, you have a problem.

However, help is on the way. In addition to the forthcoming VB.NET compiler mentioned earlier, the Mono community is also in the process of creating a JScript (JavaScript) compiler. But this project is not mature as of this writing. More information is available at `www.mono-project.com/FAQ:_Technical`.

So Mono is a potential choice for your company's in-house ASP.NET pages that use the C# language. Great. But what about third-party .NET web applications? ASP.NET web applications don't *have* to place all of their source code inside web pages. They can, instead, refer to precompiled .NET DLLs. That protects the source code from prying eyes, so many third-party applications are distributed this way. An added bonus: since the code is already compiled into a binary format, it doesn't matter whether the code was written in a language for which Mono offers a compiler.

But can Mono run these applications? Yes...and no. Yes, Mono is compatible with existing .NET binaries. But no, they often cannot be used in practice because assumptions made by Windows programmers are not always valid when their application runs in a Linux environment. .NET applications can contain "hard-coded" assumptions that don't hold true on Linux. And that means these applications don't quite work under Mono on Linux...yet. But since Mono represents a potentially large market of Linux-based web servers that could run .NET software, and because the changes needed to accommodate Mono just as well as .NET are very minor, it is likely that more and more .NET applications will run well under Mono in the near future. See the sidebar "Why Some .NET Web Applications Have Trouble Running under Mono" for details on the compatibility issues and how they can be addressed when source code is available.

Why Some .NET Web Applications Have Trouble Running under Mono

There are just a few major "gotchas" that prevent .NET web applications from running under Linux with Mono. Here is a list of the most common:

- .NET applications may rely on the assumption that directories are separated by the \ character, while on Linux they are separated by /. .NET provides a portable way to construct filenames, but many programmers ignore it.

- Programmers may rely on the fact that Windows filenames are case-insensitive, resulting in "file not found" errors on a case-sensitive file system like those found in Linux.

- .NET Dynamic Link Libraries (DLLs) are currently compatible with Mono only if they are not compiled with what Microsoft calls "incremental compilation." And there's no way for us, as the customers, to control what options the third-party software vendor may have chosen to use when compiling software. The good news is that vendors can easily fix this by not using incremental compilation for their final release. Incremental compilation is just a convenience for faster development and doesn't improve the final product in any way.

> - Occasionally, web applications will rely on .NET libraries that are not fully imple-
>   mented by Mono. In most cases, however, the simpler issues listed previously are
>   all that require attention.
>
> Is there hope that third-party .NET applications will run smoothly on Mono? Yes! Jason Alex-
> ander, one the authors of nGallery, a well-regarded .NET application for managing photo-
> graphs, has offered tips for .NET programmers who wish to create applications that work
> smoothly with both Mono and Microsoft's .NET implementation:
>
> ```
> http://blogs.ngallery.org/jasona/archive/2004/04/27/200.aspx
> ```
>
> Although programming itself is beyond the scope of this book, those with a little bit of .NET
> programming expertise may find these tips useful for adapting third-party .NET applications
> for which source code is available.
>
> You may ask why we didn't demonstrate nGallery in this book if nGallery was written by a .NET
> programmer who cares about Mono compatibility. The answer is that nGallery has become
> part of the larger CommunityServer project, which is unfortunately not yet Mono compatible.

Installing Mono on Linux

But enough limitations, provisos, and quid pro quos! Let's stop talking and start doing. It's time
to install Mono on our Fedora Core 3 web server, `linserv1.corp.com`. And once we've done
that, we'll demonstrate how to activate support for Mono in the Apache web server and demonstrate that the Mono project's C# ASP examples work. The resulting environment is a potential place to host your company's own C#-based ASP.NET pages, which could formerly live
only in the IIS environment. And in the near future, the availability of a complete VB.NET compiler will make Mono a potential host for Visual Basic ASP.NET pages as well.

RPMs providing Mono for Fedora Core 3 are available from the Mono project. Although
there are many RPM files involved, they are conveniently packaged in two ZIP archives, one for
Mono in general and the other specifically for web application support. Web application support for Mono comes in the form of a specialized web server, called XSP, and a "shim" that
allows Apache to talk to it, known as mod_mono.

Follow these steps to download Mono and the supporting files for web application support
to linserv1.corp.com:

1. Visit the Mono project home page, at `www.mono-project.com`.

2. Click "Downloads." The Mono download page appears.

3. Scroll down to "Linux/x86," look right to locate "Red Hat," and click on "Fedora Core
   3 x86." The Mono Fedora Core 3 download page appears.

4. Beneath "Mono 1.1," click "All of these files in a ZIP file." This will download the file
   `mono-1.1.zip`.

5. Scroll farther down the page to "XSP/mod_mono" and click "All of these files in a ZIP
   file." This will download the file `webserver.zip`.

6. Create the directory /tmp/mono with this command:

```
mkdir /tmp/mono
```

7. Change directories there with this command:

```
cd /tmp/mono
```

8. Move the files mono-1.1.zip and webserver.zip to /tmp/mono. If you downloaded them to the desktop, drag them to /tmp/mono using the Fedora file manager.

9. Unpack the RPM files with the following two commands:

```
unzip mono-1.1.zip
unzip webserver.zip
```

We're almost ready to install the RPMs. But there's one catch: The latest versions of mono require a lightweight database engine called sqlite. And sqlite isn't standard in Red Hat's Fedora Core 3 repositories. Fortunately, it *is* available in the Dag Wieers repository, which we first explored in Chapter 9.

Since we've chosen not to directly integrate the Dag Wieers repository into the up2date package management system, we'll fetch the specific RPM we need from the repository. Follow these steps to download the latest version of sqlite for Fedora Core 3:

1. Visit the page http://dag.wieers.com/packages/sqlite/.

2. Locate and click the download link for Fedora Core 3 (fc3) on the Intel platform (i386).

3. Move the RPM file you have just downloaded to /tmp/mono where you unzipped the other RPMs.

We've obtained all the RPMs we need! All we have to do now is install them. Use the following command to install the RPMs:

```
rpm -i *.rpm
```

Mono is now installed on linserv1.corp.com! But we still need to configure the Apache web server (also known as httpd, for Hypertext Transfer Protocol Daemon) to support the use of ASP.NET code in web pages. We'll do that by configuring Apache to load the mod_mono module.

Apache can be configured using Webmin, but Webmin doesn't offer a facility for deciding which modules to load. Webmin *does* offer a way to edit httpd.conf directly as a text file, but this offers no advantages over a text editor...and a real text editor is superior to a web browser. So for this particular task, we'll edit Apache's main configuration file directly.

Apache is controlled by the file /etc/httpd/conf/httpd.conf, or httpd.conf for short. This file contains simple options to control the web browser's behavior in a variety of ways. Sometimes these options are grouped together in containers using an HTML-like syntax, like this:

```
<container-name value>
   sub-option value
</container-name>
```

Fortunately we don't need to understand all of the options already present in `httpd.conf` in order to get the job done. There are just a few that matter for our purposes:

LoadModule   The `LoadModule` option is used to load an external module providing support for a feature not already built into Apache. We'll use this option to load `mod_mono`. This option takes two parameters, the module name (in our case, `mono_module`) and the filename in which the module is found (`modules/mod_mono.so`). The module name option is there to distinguish between multiple modules released in a single file, although in practice this is rarely done.

Alias   By default, Apache serves up only the files beneath a single `DocumentRoot` folder. The `Alias` option, similar to virtual directories in IIS, allows web paths beginning with a particular folder name to be mapped to any desired directory on the web server. In this case, we'll map the name `/test` to the directory `/usr/share/doc/xsp/test`, which is where the ASP.NET samples for the Mono project are installed.

AddMonoApplications   As mentioned earlier, Mono web applications actually run in a separate server called XSP. The `mod_mono` module automatically starts up this server when needed. But since XSP is a separate program, it doesn't automatically know about the alias we just created between `/test` and `/usr/share/doc/xsp/test`. So we provide that information again for XSP's benefit using the `AddMonoApplications` option, which is provided by the `mod_mono` module and used to pass the information to XSP. In our example, `AddMonoApplications` takes only two arguments. The first argument is beyond the scope of this discussion and should be set to `default`. The second should be set to `"/test:usr/share/doc/xsp/test"` in order to tell XSP that requests for anything in the /test folder actually refer to content in `/usr/share/doc/xsp/test`.

Location   The `Location` option is a container that will hold additional options referring to a specific subdirectory, `/test`. The `Location` option begins with `<Location` followed by the subdirectory name `/test` followed by a closing `>`. This is followed by options that will apply specifically to `/test` and ended with `</Location>`.

SetHandler   By default, Apache would deliver the content in the `/test` virtual directory according to its usual rules. The ASP.NET pages would be downloaded as ordinary HTML without executing the ASP.NET code. The `SetHandler` option, which appears here enclosed in the `<Location /test>` container, specifies the "content handler" that will be responsible for delivering content in `/test`. In this case, we want to use the `mono` handler so that the `mod_mono` module can take over and deliver ASP.NET pages correctly via XSP.

Follow these steps to configure linserv1.corp.com's Apache web server to support ASP.NET pages in a `/test` virtual directory:

1.   Add the following lines to the end of your `/etc/httpd/conf/httpd.conf` file:

```
LoadModule mono_module modules/mod_mono.so
Alias /test "/usr/share/doc/xsp/test"
AddMonoApplications default "/test:/usr/share/doc/xsp/test"
<Location /test>
  SetHandler mono
</Location>
```

2. Restart the web server with mono support:

```
service httpd restart
```

If you receive error messages, make sure you actually installed the Mono RPMs following the steps presented earlier.

Access `http://linserv1.corp.com/test/` to see the results. Feel free to click on any of the examples, as shown in Figure 10.5.

FIGURE 10.5   Sample C# ASP.NET pages, working successfully under Linux via the Mono project

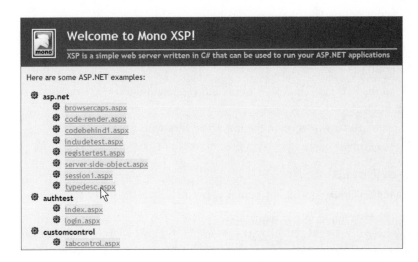

As we've discussed, `mod_mono` is a good solution for C#-based ASP.NET pages and .NET web applications for which you have the source code, which is typically the case when you are providing an environment for your own company's web developers. But as we've mentioned, support for commercial, closed-source .NET applications is not as thorough, and applications themselves often contain unportable assumptions that can't be fixed in a precompiled program. Since Mono represents a new market for the vendors of such applications, support is likely to improve.

Right now, Mono isn't a mature solution for Active Server Pages written in Visual Basic or JScript. And older ASP applications predating the ASP.NET era may never run unmodified on Mono.

Running Visual Basic Active Server Pages and Applications on Linux with JASP

There *is* a way to run older ASP applications on Linux. Sun Microsystems's Sun Java System Active Server Pages 4.0, which we refer to in this chapter as JASP for brevity's sake, allows many ASP applications to run unmodified on Linux...provided that they don't rely on external components that are not included with JASP.

The bad news is that JASP carries a hefty $495 price tag, and Fedora Core 3 is not a supported platform. However, the closely related Red Hat Enterprise Linux distribution *is* supported.

Of course, that doesn't mean we can't make it *run* on Fedora Core 3!

Installing JASP for Fedora Core 3

We've found that JASP does run under Fedora Core 3 with a little bit of effort. And we'll demonstrate that here. However, since using an unsupported operating system could limit your access to the support you deserve on this $495 product, you might consider adding the cost of Red Hat Enterprise 3.0 to that price tag when you do your calculations.

Follow these steps to download and unpack a free evaluation copy of JASP on the linserv1.corp.com web server:

1. Access the JASP home page at www.sun.com/software/chilisoft/index.xml.

2. Follow the download link for the latest version currently available, which as of this writing is version 4.02.

3. Download the Red Hat Enterprise Linux 3.0 version and move the resulting TAR file to /tmp on linserv1.corp.com.

4. Create a subdirectory to contain the unpacked files with this command:

   ```
   mkdir sjsasp402-linux
   ```

5. Change to that directory:

   ```
   cd sjsasp402-linux
   ```

6. Unpack the TAR file in the parent directory:

   ```
   tar -xf ../sjsasp402-linux.tar
   ```

7. Use the ls command to display a list of the files in the package, including install.sh, the installation script:

   ```
   ls
   ```

You could attempt to run install.sh now. If you did, though, you'd receive an error indicating that JASP requires the libstdc++-libc6.1-1.so.2 library, which is not installed. In fact, Fedora Core 3 includes a newer version of this package that is not backward compatible with applications already precompiled for older versions. And most packages in Red Hat Enterprise Linux 3.0 are older than the cutting-edge software included in Fedora Core 3.

So what to do? Is there an easy way to find the right command to install this missing file? We've already met the up2date package manager. But while up2date is useful, it doesn't provide an easy way to answer the question, If I need this specific version of a library, what command will install it for me?

We'll take advantage of an alternative Fedora package manager, yum, to answer that question. The yum package manager offers a provides option that can be used to locate the name of the package that contains a needed file.

yum provides will output the name of the package, separated by a space from additional information about the package that is beyond the scope of this discussion.

Follow these steps to identify and install the package we need:

1. Use the `yum provides` command to identify the package we want. `yum provides` will take a long time to complete:

    ```
    yum provides libstdc++-libc6.1-1.so.2
    ```

2. Examine the output to determine the package required. The output should resemble this:

    ```
    compat-libstdc++.i386 8-3.3.4.2 base
    ```

3. Use the `up2date` command to install that package. We can leave off the .i386 part, which is assumed since this is an Intel-based system:

    ```
    up2date compat-libstdc++
    ```

Once the `compat-libstdc++` package has been successfully installed, we're ready to run the JASP installer. This is a text-based but reasonably friendly installation program.

Follow these steps to install JASP:

1. Start the installation script:

    ```
    ./install.sh
    ```

2. Page through the license agreement with the spacebar.

3. Type **yes** to accept the agreement and press Enter.

4. You'll be asked where you wish to install the software. The default suggestion, `/opt/casp`, is a reasonable place. Press Enter to accept it.

5. The locale menu appears next, asking which national language and character set should be default. Select your preference and press Enter. We chose `English (United States)` by entering the number 1 and pressing Enter.

6. You'll be asked how JASP should go about locating Apache's configuration files in order to configure them. JASP can search your hard drive exhaustively for all possible Apache installation locations, but the default "moderate" option (option 2) works just fine for a standard installation of the Apache `httpd` package on Fedora Core 3. Type **2** and press Enter.

7. The "Web Server Configuration" prompt follows. Select option 1 and press Enter to install JASP on the detected Apache server. If you see no such option, make sure you installed the `httpd` package and install it if necessary with the `up2date httpd` command; then run `install.sh` again.

8. Next is the "Web Server Verification" prompt. Enter **y** and press Enter to accept the detected information.

9. An additional "Server Configuration" prompt appears. Select 1 and press Enter to perform a standard installation of JASP. There will be a delay while the installation takes place.

10. The "Administration Console Installation" prompt follows. The default option, option 1, will install a built-in administration console with a default administrative username and password. For test lab purposes, that's just fine. Enter **1** and press Enter.

11. The "Administrative Console Information" prompt appears. This prompt presents information about how to log into the administrative console of JASP, which you'll want to write down. During our installation, the reported information was as follows:

```
To connect from a browser, use this URL: http://linserv1.corp.com:5100
To start, stop and add users, use this script: /opt/casp/admtool
The console's username is: admin
The console's password is: root
```

12. Press Enter to move on to the "Product Verification" display, where the installation's success is verified. This takes a few minutes, after which the installation is complete.

JASP has been installed and is now integrated into Apache. From now on, all Active Server Pages found on the website will be recognized by their `.asp` extension and processed by the JASP engine.

Testing a Sample ASP Application with JASP

But does it work? Let's find out by creating a simple "Hello World" ASP page. Although this is not a programming book, a quick explanation of what we're looking at will still be helpful.

JASP, like Microsoft's pre-.NET ASP system, recognizes ASP code in an HTML page by looking for it between the markers <% and %>. One of ASP's most important capabilities is the ability to generate parts of the HTML page currently being sent to the user. This is what allows parts of the page to contain dynamically retrieved information, such as the results of a database query.

When we place the code

```
response.write("<h1>JASP Test Page</h1>")
```

between <% and %> and give the page a filename ending in `.asp`, the JASP engine will recognize that code and execute it every time a web browser accesses the page, and the HTML between the quotes will be sent to the browser as part of the page. The web browser never sees the code. The browser sees only the HTML that the code generates.

Since part of the HTML code for the page is generated by ASP code, the page will appear empty in a web browser unless the JASP engine is working. Follow these steps to create and view a test ASP page:

1. With your preferred text editor, create the file `/var/www/html/test.asp` on linserv1.corp.com.

2. Place the following content in the file:

```
<html>
<head>
<title>JASP Test Page</title>
</head>
<body>
<% response.write("<h1>JASP Test Page</h1>") %>
</body>
</html>
```

3. Access the following URL in your web browser:

`http://linserv1.corp.com/test.asp`

You should now see the text "JASP Test Page" in a large font in your browser window, as shown in Figure 10.6. If the browser window is empty (except for a title in the title bar), make sure you have completed the JASP install procedure successfully.

Apache::ASP: ASP-style programming in Perl on Apache without Mono

There's one other interesting ASP-on-Linux solution: an open-source Perl module called Apache::ASP. This sounds promising: it provides ASP's "object model" and embedding syntax for Apache. But there's a catch: it only supports one programming language for the code you embed in your web pages with it. And that language isn't Visual Basic, JScript or C#. It's Perl.

As you know from earlier chapters, we think Perl is a fine thing. But there are other solutions for embedding Perl in web pages. And folks looking for a Linux-hosted ASP solution are typically seeking to run existing ASP code written in Visual Basic. So Apache::ASP doesn't really meet our needs in this chapter…except, perhaps, in the unlikely case that you already have developers who are using the .NET CLI version of Perl to create ASP.NET pages on a Windows server. Still, it is an interesting project, and you can find out more about it at www.apache-asp.org.

FIGURE 10.6 When the JASP engine is correctly installed, ASP code found in a file with the `.asp` extension is correctly executed to generate the text of the page

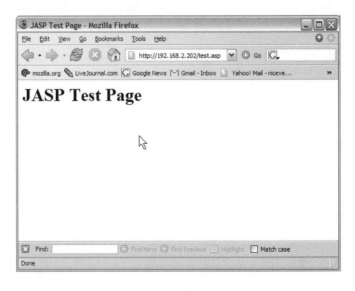

Final Thoughts

Web development is an exciting way to painlessly deliver information to users of many operating systems. Historically, browser compatibility was a major headache. But today the major web browsers interoperate very well when designers avoid the use of proprietary plug-ins. The real challenges come on the server side. While static web content is relatively easy to move from Windows to Linux or vice versa, dynamic web content is another story.

PHP pages and Active Server Pages are typically written with a particular operating system in mind. But in this chapter, we've shown how to get PHP working on Windows. And we've also shown how to get ASP working on Linux, both with the cutting-edge Mono ASP.NET environment and with Sun's JASP environment.

PHP running on Windows is a reasonable alternative to PHP running on Linux. Mono's ASP.NET environment is an increasingly viable alternative to ASP.NET running on Windows, though third-party ASP.NET applications are unlikely to work without some cooperation on the part of the vendor. And Sun's JASP provides an immediately practical alternative for those who need to host traditional Active Server Pages and applications on Linux today.

Index

Note to the reader: Throughout this index boldfaced page numbers indicate primary discussions of a topic. Italicized page numbers indicate illustrations.

F

G

T

U

Colophon

We thought you might find it interesting to understand how this book "got done."

The goal was for Jeremy and Tom to write both together and separately. We needed a way to enable this.

First, Jeremy granted Tom VPN access to Jeremy's internal network.

Then, we used virtual machine technology to craft the various machines mentioned in this book on one physical machine. We started with a Dual-Processor AMD 1Ghz machine with 1.5GB of RAM, running Windows Server 2003. We then installed VMware GSX server. This enabled us to create many, many guest virtual machines—both Windows and Linux. By the time the book was completed, we had a grand total of 16 test virtual machines. We worked primarily with Fedora Core 3, Windows 2003 and Windows XP but also tested Knoppix and Red Hat Enterprise Server. It was not uncommon to have 5–7 active virtual machines at any given point.

VMWare's Virtual Machine Console / remote-access software was indispensable for creating new virtual machines. Once a machine was up and running, though, Tom found that remote access via VPN was more responsive with VNC (for accessing Linux machines) or Remote Desktop (for accessing Windows machines).

Microsoft's Sharepoint Portal Server served as our document management system, allowing easy collaboration. Thanks to Sharepoint, "Who owns this Word document right now?" was not a question we had to worry about.

About twice a month, Tom joined Jeremy in his office to work together in person and hammer out the thorniest issues facing us in any particular chapter.

Our snacks of choice were takeout Chinese food (Stir Fried Tofu for Tom, General Tso's Chicken for Jeremy) and approximately two boxes of Wheat Thins (original) per visit. Roughly fifteen boxes were devoured during the nine-month writing process. We're hoping to get back to our pre-pregnancy weights any day now.